# Python Programming
# with the Java™
# Class Libraries

# Python Programming with the Java™ Class Libraries

## A Tutorial for Building Web and Enterprise Applications with Jython

*Richard Hightower*

✦✦ Addison-Wesley

Boston • San Francisco • New York • Toronto • Montreal
London • Munich • Paris • Madrid
Capetown • Sydney • Tokyo • Singapore • Mexico City

The publisher offers discounts on this book when ordered in quantity for bulk purchases and special sales. For more information, please contact:

U.S. Corporate and Government Sales
(800) 382-3419
corpsales@pearsontechgroup.com

For sales outside of the U.S., please contact:

International Sales
(317) 581-3793
international@pearsontechgroup.com

Visit Addison-Wesley on the Web: *www.awprofessional.com*

*Library of Congress Cataloging-in-Publication Data*

Hightower, Richard.
    Python programming with the Java class libraries : a tutorial for building Web and Enterprise applications with Jython / Richard Hightower.
        p. cm.
    ISBN 0-201-61616-5 (alk. paper)
    1. Python (Computer program language) 2. Java (Computer program language)
    3. Application software—Development.  I. Title.

    QA76.73.P98 H54 2002
    005.2'762—dc21

                                                                        2002066565

ISBN 0-201-61616-5

Text printed on recycled paper
1 2 3 4 5 6 7 8 9 10—CRS—0605040302
*First printing, July 2002*

# Contents

# *Preface*

Python is a dynamic programming language with the power of well-known languages such as Java, C++, and Smalltalk. In fact, Python is leaner and meaner than any of these languages and yet very expressive; it doesn't talk much, but it has a lot to say.

Python has another plus: the simplicity of languages such as VB Script and JavaScript, which makes it easy for beginning programmers to learn. Novices who know their way around a computer can pick it up quickly, particularly if they have ever created a spreadsheet that graphs and organizes data, written spreadsheet formulas, or created a Web page. For those who have, say, written macros and batch files or programmed in any language, Python will be a breeze.

## A Very Short History

Python was derived from a language called ABC created by Guido van Rossum and others in the early 1980s. The hope was that ABC's designed-in ease of use would become popular with novices as a way to get up to programming speed quickly and painlessly. This hope didn't pan out, so van Rossum began a new project, Python, which was released in 1990. He didn't forget ABC; in fact, there's a lot of ABC in Python's concise syntax and elegant expression, as well as in its ease of use. The formula worked this time; Python succeeded where ABC failed, and it has stood the test of time.

## What You Will Learn

Put simply, my goal with this book is to teach programming using Python. You'll learn the workings of Python and how to apply them, particularly for the following:

- Abstract Windows Toolkit (AWT) and Swing application development
- Java applet development
- Internet programming
- Regular expressions and pattern matching

You may not understand these concepts now, but you will by the end of the book.

If you're looking for a full language reference, you won't get it here. What you will get is a deep enough understanding of Python to get started on your own programming. I'm going to remind you often of my belief that the best way to learn programming is by doing it. That's why I've provided lots of hands-on exercises in the form of interactive programming sessions, which I hope you'll follow along with at the keyboard as you read.

## The Audience

As a reader of this book, you may be one of the following:

- A nonprogrammer who wants to learn a programming language
- A novice programmer who wants to learn Python

For simplicity, I'll call you both novices. You know your computer and how to use it to get the job done.

If you're not a novice and you're reading this book, then you're an experienced programmer who wants to learn a higher-level language that's quicker and more powerful than the one you're using now. For simplicity, I'll call you programmers.

### For Novices

You'll be introduced to Python in conversational English, with many step-by-step examples. Chapters 2 through 9 build progressively on the chapters preceding them, so you should be able to learn enough to begin writing useful Python programs. The goal is to give you as much of a headstart as possible. From Chapter 10 on you'll learn more about Python and about supporting Java and Python libraries on your own, as well as about Internet programming with Python.

### For Programmers

Most likely you're an experienced Java programmer who's aware of the close relationship between Java and Python and how it can lead to better application development (we'll get into this more in Chapter 1). You can skip over or skim the basic material and concentrate on the Advanced Topic sections and the various sidebars that are geared to your level of understanding.

Now let's get into our tour of Python—the destination is worth the trip.

## Acknowledgments

The author and publisher are grateful for the efforts of this book's developmental editor, Dianne Cannon Wood, and reviewer, Barry Busler. Countless hours and suggestions were extremely helpful during the book's production stages. Thanks.

**CHAPTER 1**     *Jython Overview*

———————————— *Terms in This Chapter* ————————————

- Applet
- Boolean value
- Bytecode
- Class
- Compiler
- Concatenation
- Control flow
- Expression
- Floating-point number
- for loop
- Function

- Immutability
- Index/Indexing
- Interactive mode
- Interpreter
- Iteration
- Macro
- Main method
- Method
- Module
- Object
- Programming

- Pseudocode
- Script
- Sequence
- Servlet
- Slice notation
- Statement
- String
- Syntax
- Type
- Value
- Variable

In this chapter you will learn just what Python programming is and how to save and run Python scripts.

## Programming, Briefly

You may have programmed a computer without even knowing it. For example, have you ever written or recorded a spreadsheet macro (or any other macro for any type of application)? If you have, you've programmed. Of course, programming

is a lot more complicated than writing macros; still, many people are overly appre-
hensive when it comes to learning this skill.

You're going to find out that there's often not much difference between a macro
or a scripting language and "real" programming. However, macro and script
don't intimidate novice users, whereas programming does. The point is that
learning programming doesn't have to be hard. In fact, the hardest part about it
is having the right attitude. If you believe you can't learn to program, you probably won't.

At its most basic level, programming is instructing the computer, in a language
that it understands, so that it can perform tasks. Like any language you learned in
high school, a programming language has a vocabulary, grammar, syntax, punctu-
ation, and parts of speech. The trick is knowing how to use these components correctly so that you get your point across and the job gets done.

Consider this very simple instruction:

```
write("Hello World")
```

Called a statement, it's the primary building block of programming. It "invokes,"
or "calls," the write function.

A function is a grouped set of statements. Within a program, one function can
perform a task in its entirety, but more likely it will call another function, which
in turn can call other functions, and so on, all of which together organize the program's statements. Remember being told in English class to organize your thoughts
into a cohesive whole to get your point across? This is what statements and functions do in computer languages.

Languages like Python need an interpreter to translate a human-generated program into a "machine-readable" form that the computer can understand. Other
languages, such as C and C++, use a compiler. The difference between the two is
that the compiler saves the translated code on the machine, allowing it to be run
independently on another occasion, whereas the interpreter holds it in memory
only for the duration of the program running when the translation was made. The
upshot is that compiled programs are faster than interpreted programs.

## Learning Python First

Learning any one programming language makes it much easier to understand
not only computers but other programming languages as well. As you'll see,
Python is perhaps the easiest language to learn and use. This makes it the logical
one to get under your belt as a first step on the way to Visual Basic, Java, and so
forth.

It's important to understand that not all languages are alike. For example, some,
such as C++, Java, and Python, are *terse*. That is, they get a lot done without a lot

of code. Others, like Assembly, are *verbose*. They need many lines of code to perform a simple task. To illustrate, let's pretend we're asking a computer to tell us how to get to downtown Phoenix, Arizona. Python would tell us to take Speedway Boulevard to I-10 and head west. Here's what Assembly would say:

1. Walk to your garage.
2. Open the garage door.
3. Walk to the driver's side of the car.
4. Put the key in the door.
5. Unlock the door.
6. Sit in the driver's seat . . .

You get the picture.

Assembly language needs to be verbose because it does its heavy lifting in building core operating system parts and high-speed optimized programs. Most programs don't require a low-level draft horse like Assembly, however, but a high-level language that offers greater productivity.

A higher-level language abstracts (i.e., hides) the complexity of a lower-level language. It looks at the bigger picture and omits the details, as we saw in how Python and Assembly tell us how to get to Phoenix. The tradeoff is that a lower-level language is friendlier to the computer—it can run faster—whereas a higher-level language is friendlier to the programmer—she can program faster. There's a hierarchy of complexity with programming languages: C and C++ are higher level than Assembly; Java is higher level than C++; and Python is higher level than Java. The higher the level, the greater the ease of use. The goal is making a language easy to use without draining its power.

## Python the Language

Python is a dynamic object-oriented language (i.e., flexible) for writing applications, Java applets and servlets, and the like. (We'll learn more about applets in Chapter 18.) It has a close relationship with Java. In fact, it can do pretty much anything Java can because it compiles to Java and uses the Java class libraries. With Python, you can create animated Web pages, automate monotonous jobs, and write Internet-interactive programs.

### Java and Python

No doubt you've heard of Java, even the novices among you. Over a thousand books on it are on bookstore and library shelves, so it's hard to miss.

Remember our discussion of compilers and interpreters? Like Python, Java is an interpreted language, but, like C++, it's also a compiled language. In other words, it compiles into an intermediate language called bytecode, which is then interpreted into machine code at runtime (that is, when the program is put to use by the user). This makes Java a hybrid; its ability to be both interepreted and compiled gives it flexibility as well as speed.

Java is popular among programmers because of its versatility and because it's a much easier language than C++. Still, it's a far cry from Visual Basic in the simplicity department. In fact, its complexity, along with its client-side speed and graphics problems, has allowed other languages, such as DHTML (that is, HTML combined with VBScript and/or JavaScript), to lure a substantial number of developers away from the Java camp.

None of this means that Java doesn't have the potential to become an excellent client-side development tool. I believe it does, and I program in it professionally. However, it doesn't fill the need for a higher-level scripting language that's easy on the programmer, and this is where Python comes in. Unlike Java, Python is easy enough for beginning programmers to master quickly and yet powerful enough to keep experienced programmers interested.

## Jython

Because of the success of Java, it made sense to make Java and Python compatible. Thus, one version of Python, called Jython, has been ported to Java and so can compile to bytecode. This move will likely make Python the next Internet development phenomenon, like Java or XML. At the least, it will make it available to a much broader audience and make it applicable in more environments. Consider, for example, that Jython makes it much easier to add user-defined types in Java. (Don't worry, *types* will be explained in due time.)

The Object Management Group (OMG) has adopted Python as one of the scripting component languages of CORBA, a standard distributed object model. In fact, CorbaScript, which is also a standard script, is one of Python's close cousins. Python also works with ActiveX (also known as COM+), a nonstandard distributed component model that ships with Windows operating systems, and with JavaBeans and RMI, which is a distributed object model for Java applications. With the addition of the OMG's CORBABean specification, which effectively gives CORBA a client-side tool-able component model, Python can be used to script CORBA objects as well.

The reason Python works so well with JavaBeans, ActiveX, and CORBA is that these products are all component models, that is, ways to manufacture components. Python serves as a means to wire together, or "glue," purchased or built components into an application. At the moment, Visual Basic is the de facto standard for scripting together ActiveX components into applications, but it's limited to Windows platforms. Python is becoming the standard for scripting together components from CORBA, JavaBeans, Enterprise JavaBeans, and ActiveX.

> **For Programmers and Novices: Jython Focus**
>
> Our focus will be primarily on Jython, rather than on CPython (the non-Java version). Either Jython or CPython can be used for an understanding of the core aspects of Python, but you'll definitely need the Java version when we get to JFC/Swing, applets, and the like.

You know the old saying "Every journey begins with the first step." Let's take that first step now.

## Starting with Python

To install Python you must have a recent version of the Java Development Kit (JDK). For installation details, refer to Appendix A.

Now you're up and running. I'm going to assume that you're sitting at the keyboard with this book situated so that you can follow along with the interactive sessions. This is critical even if you don't understand the topic under discussion. Once again, the only way to learn programming is to program, even if you're not sure what you're doing. Don't worry; you soon will.

### Python Interactive Mode

This section explains how to use Python in interactive mode, that is, the user and Python interacting one instruction at a time. It's a great way to learn the language. Also explained are the essential features of Python, including simple statements, expressions, and data types.

To get Python going, at the DOS prompt (or the equivalent for your operating system) type Python (for CPython) or Jython (for the Java-enabled version). You should see a welcome message showing the Python version number and a copyright notice.

```
C:\Jython>jython
Jython 1.1 on jdk1.3
Copyright 1997-1998 Corporation for National Research Initiatives
>>>
```

This is followed by a prompt for your first command, known as the *primary prompt* and denoted by >>>. If you enter print "Hello World" here and then hit the Enter key, Python will obey your command and print "Hello World" to the monitor.

```
>>> print "Hello World"
Hello World
>>>
```

If that's all you want Python to do at this point, you can exit the system with another command.

```
>>>raise SystemExit
```

This creates what's known as an "exception" (we'll go into exceptions in Chapter 7), which gets you out of Python. Another way to exit is to hit the Ctrl key in combination with whichever key your system designates for leaving a session. On Windows this is usually Ctrl-z; on UNIX it's usually Ctrl-d.

## Basic Functions with Python

The following sections cover how Python deals with the raw material of programming: numbers and text.

### Numbers

Python can serve as a simple calculator. The syntax it uses is nearly identical to that used for writing spreadsheet formulas. For novices who've created spreadsheets, all of this will seem familiar. The same is true for programmers who've worked with any language that uses an algebraic syntax, such as Pascal, Fortran, Basic, C, or Java.

In Python, you enter a mathematical formula (called an expression) just as you do with spreadsheets, and you're given a resulting value. In programming terms, an expression is a Python statement that returns a value. That value is printed to the console.

Python's *expression* syntax is straightforward. The addition (+), subtraction (-), multiplication (*), and division (/) operators work just like they do in spreadsheets and other programming languages. Parentheses work similarly as well, for grouping.

```
>>> (2*2)/4
1
```

The equal sign (=) assigns a value to a variable. In the first line of the following example, the variable is annual_salary, to which we assign a value of 20000. (My convention is to join two-word variable names with an underscore.)

```
>>> annual_salary = 20000
>>> monthly_salary = annual_salary/12
>>> monthly_salary
1666
>>> bosses_salary = annual_salary * 3
>>> bosses_salary
60000
```

In the second line, we divide annual_salary by 12 to arrive at a value for the variable monthly_salary. Then, in the third line, we enter monthly_salary at the prompt, which tells Python to print the value of that variable to the console. We can use `annual_salary` again in assigning a value to `bosses_salary`.

> **For Programmers: Implicit Variable Declaration**
>
> In Python variables are *implicitly declared.* That is, the first time a variable is used it is assigned a value. This assigned value determines its type. In the salary example, all variables are assigned values of type `Integer`.
>
> Novices, if you're reading this note and are confused by the concept of *type*, don't worry; we'll get to it. For understanding the ideas presented in the rest of the chapter, you just need to know that numbers can be of type `Integer`; text can be of types `String`, `List`, etc. Basically, the type assigned to a variable tells Python what values it can have and what operations can be performed on it.

The values assigned to the variables we've seen so far have been whole numbers. Python can also work with decimals, known in programming as floating-point numbers (of type `Float`).

```
>>> sum=1.3 + 1.4 + 1.56 + 1.7 + 1.2 + 1.9
>>> mean = sum /6
>>> mean
1.51
>>>
```

In the first line, we create a variable called `sum` and assign as its value the result of adding six floating-point numbers. In the second line, we create a new variable called `mean`, to which we assign as its value the value of `sum` divided by 6. In the third line, we enter the variable `mean`, and Python displays its value to the console.

## Text

Python, like all programming languages, works with text as strings of characters; individual strings are delimited by quotes. Take a look at the following code example:

```
>>> Name = "James Agular"
>>> HelloGreeting = "Hello " + Name + ", how are you?"
>>> print HelloGreeting
Hello James Agular, how are you?
>>>
```

In the first line, we create a variable called `Name` and assign as its value the string `"James Agular"`. In the second line, we create a variable called `HelloGreeting` and assign as its value the string `"Hello"` plus the value of `Name` plus `"how are you?"`. Note that this value is made up of three strings joined by two plus (+) signs. This is known as concatenation, which is a fancy term for the simple act of "stringing" strings together. In the third line, we ask Python to print `HelloGreeting`, which it does in the fourth line.

### Indexing

As in Java and C, we can work with individual characters in a string. To access them we use indexing, in which the string characters, starting with the first one, are assigned consecutive numbers, or indexes. Thus, the first character is assigned the index 0; the second character, the index 1; and so forth. We can refer to these as "0 index" and "1 index." The numbers assigned to characters in a string are referred to as the string's indexes.

The following example should give you a clear picture of indexing.

```
>>> sample = "abcdefghijklmnopqrstuvwxyz"
>>> sample
'abcdefghijklmnopqrstuvwxyz'
>>> sample[1]
'b'
>>> sample[0]
'a'
```

Here we first want the letter b, so we enter `sample[1]`. Next we want the letter a, so we enter `sample[0]`. Notice that the indexes are indicated by square brackets.

Just remember, novices, the index of the first character in a string is 0, not 1, which is why the index of z in the example above is 25, not 26.

### Slice Notation

Another way to access parts of a string is with slice notation, which, simply put, allows you to enter a string (or a list or a tuple, which we'll get to shortly) and extract the "slice" you want to work with.

Let's look at an example:

```
>>> alphabet = "abcdefghijklmnopqrstuvwxyz"
>>> AthruD = alphabet[0:4]
>>> AthruD
'abcd'
```

The first line assigns the letters of the alphabet to the variable `alphabet`; the second line assigns the value of indexes 0 through 3 to the variable `AthruD`; the third line instructs Python to output `AthruD`; the fourth line is the result: `'abcd'`.

Another way to write the slice `[0:4]` is as `[:4]`. An omitted first index tells Python to start at zero. In the same way, `[1:]` tells Python to start at index 1 and make the rest of the string the slice. The following example uses the slice notation in all three ways: without a first index in the first line; with both indexes in the fourth line; and without the second index in seventh line. Table 1–1 describes each of these slices in English.

```
>>> AthruD= alphabet[:4]
>>> AthruD
'abcd'
```

**Table 1–1**   *Slice Notation*

| Slice | Meaning |
| --- | --- |
| AthruD=alphabet[:4] | Assign the variable AthruD from the first character up to but not including the 4 index, i.e., index 0 through index 3. |
| EthruM=alphabet[4:13] | Assign the variable EthruM from the 4 index up to but not including the 13 index. |
| NthruZ=alphabet[13:] | Assign the variable NthruZ from the 13 index up to and including the last character in this string. |

```
>>> EthruM = alphabet[4:13]
>>> EthruM
'efghijklm'
>>> NthruZ = alphabet[13:]
>>> NthruZ
'nopqrstuvwxyz'
>>> alphabet2 = AthruD + EthruM + NthruZ
>>> alphabet2
'abcdefghijklmnopqrstuvwxyz'
>>> alphabet
'abcdefghijklmnopqrstuvwxyz'
```

**The Slice**

In a slice notation, the range of the slice is up to *but not including* the second index. Thus, a slice of [2:5] actually means the second through the fourth characters in a string.

**Lists**

A list is a built-in Python type (remember, we'll get to types in Chapter 2). It's in the same type family as a string and can contain either strings or numbers. Lists are somewhat like arrays in Java or C, except that they can contain values of different types.

The following example shows how a list uses slice notation:

```
>>> letters = "abcdefghijklmnop"
>>> numbers = "123456789"
>>> list = [letters, numbers, 1, 2, 3, 4, 5, 1.0, 2.0, 3.0, 4.0]
>>> list[0]
'abcdefghijklmnop'
>>> list[1]
'123456789'
>>> list[2]
1
>>> list[7]
1.0
>>> list[:]
```

```
['abcdefghijklmnop', '123456789', 1, 2, 3, 4, 5, 1.0, 2.0, 3.0, 4.0]
>>> len(list)
11
>>> list = ["hello", "goodbye"]
>>> list[0:2]
['hello', 'goodbye']
>>>len (list)
2
```

## Python as a Main Program

In interactive mode, you work with Python one instruction at a time. When it's set up as a standalone program (i.e., not needing user interaction), Python performs any number of consecutive tasks. Just turn it on, and it does all the rest. To use Python this way, you first have to write a program and then save it as a text file.

Enter the following at your console and save it as *campPython.py*.

```
print "hello mother"
print "hello father"
print "greetings from camp Python"
```

Go to the command prompt and enter Jython campPython.py.

```
C:\book\chap1>jython campPython.py
```

The output is

```
hello mother
hello father
greetings from camp Python
```

Essentially, you've created a module called *campPython.py*, and the text you typed in is the module's main method—the code that's executed first.

Now take a look at the next code example. It represents a module containing a class called Camp, a method called SayHello(), and a function called sayCampHello().

```
class Camp:
    def sayHello(self):
        return "\n Hello Mom \n Hello Dad"

def sayCampHello():
    camp = Camp()
    print ("Hello: " + camp.sayHello())

if __name__ == "__main__":
    sayCampHello()
```

If you're feeling adventurous, enter this module and run it, making sure to indent each line exactly as shown. Don't waste too much time trying to figure out what's going on, however. For that you have to know about functions, which are covered in Chapter 3, and classes, which are covered in Chapter 5 (along with methods). By the way, the line `if __name__=="__main__":` indicates that this part of the module should be executed if this script is run as the main program (from the command prompt example).

## For Programmers Only

Novices, go ahead and read the following two subsections if you like, but they're way over your head right now.

### Code Blocks

In the `Camp` example, notice that the class and function definitions don't have block delimiters but are delimited by whitespace only. In Python, indentation defines code blocks, so all Python programs look pretty much the same. This is in real contrast with other languages, such as C++ or Visual Basic, in which three different programmers can come up with three different styles for the same program. You should understand the issue if you've ever written a language style guide. In a Python style guide, defining the best style for delimiting code blocks is something you won't have to worry about.

### Passing Arguments to a Program

If you're writing a utility application, you might want to be able to pass command-line arguments to the program. In Python, we do this by putting the arguments on the command line after the script.

```
C:\book\chap1>jython args.py hello how are you
```

Here we enter four command-line arguments in the *args* module. These arguments are stored in a list called `argv` in the *sys* module (*sys* must be imported before it can be used by *args*). The *args.py* module is an example of using the `sys.argv` variable.

```
import sys
print(sys.argv[0])
print(sys.argv[1])
print(sys.argv[2])
print(sys.argv[3])
print(sys.argv[4])
```

The first line of *args* imports the *sys* module. The second through sixth lines place each command-line argument in the `sys.argv` list. This produces the following output:

```
args.py
hello
how
are
you
```

As you can see, `sys.argv[0]` equals `args.py`, which is the name of the script. `argv[1:]` equals the remaining command-line arguments—`hello`, `how`, `are`, `you`. Remember, the slice notation `argv[1:]` indicates the 1 index through the end of the `argv` list.

### Back to Basics

If you're working in a Python program, you can switch to interactive mode with the `-i` command-line argument, which allows the script to be interpreted and then inspected by the interactive interpreter. You'll be glad to have this feature if there's a bug in your code that you need to find and fix.

The following code is our *campPython.py* module, this time with the `-i` inserted before the module name in the first line.

```
C:\book\chap1>jython -i campHello2.py
Hello:
 Hello Mom
 Hello Dad
>>> camp = Camp()
>>> print camp.sayHello()

 Hello Mom
 Hello Dad
>>>
```

---

## *The Fast Track*

Python supports control flow, functions, exception handling, object-oriented programming, and more, much like Java, Visual Basic, Perl, Delphi, and C++, among others. In syntax, Python is a lot like C, whose syntax is the basis of that used in Java, JavaScript, and C++.

### Types

Python is a dynamically typed language, similar to Smalltalk. When you assign a variable a value, that value specifies the type. There are many built-in types in Python, but, unlike in Java, no primitive types. Functions, methods, classes, code blocks, namespaces, numbers, strings, and so forth, are all treated as objects that can be manipulated.

If you're a Smalltalk fan, you'll like Python. Of all of the mainstream programming languages, Python has the closest thing to Smalltalk's object model (it even has multiple inheritance).

#### *Numeric Types*

Numeric types are objects in Python. The built-in function `type()` indicates the type, as the following code snippet illustrates:

```
>>> myInt = 1
>>> type(myInt)
<jclass org.python.core.PyInteger>

>>> myFloat = 1.1
>>> type(myFloat)
<jclass org.python.core.PyFloat>

>>> myLong = 1l
>>> type(myLong)
<jclass org.python.core.PyLong>
```

You can add, subtract, divide, and multiply numeric types.

```
>>> num = 1 + 1
>>> print num
2
>>> average = (1+2+3)/3
>>> print average
2
```

Chapter 2 will tell you more about Python built-in types. Chapter 3 will tell you about Python-supported operators.

### Collection Types

Python supports four main built-in collection types: strings, dictionaries, lists, and tuples. Strings, lists, and tuples are called sequences, for which Python provides many built-in operations. If you know Java, think of a list as a vector and a dictionary as a hashtable. If you know Visual Basic, think of a dictionary as a collection object or, if you know Perl, as an associative array. Like Perl and Visual Basic, Python has a built-in syntax for dealing with collections, which makes the code that works with them easier to write and understand. Java has no such syntax.

The example that follows shows how to declare an instance of each collection type.

```
>>> list = [1,2,3,4,5,6]
>>> tuple = (1,2,3,4,5,6)
>>> string = "123456"
>>> dict = {"one":1, "two":2, "three":3, "four":4, "five":5, "six":6}
```

Here are the corresponding type names for each collection variable:

```
>>> type(list)
<jclass org.python.core.PyList>

>>> type (tuple)
<jclass org.python.core.PyTuple>

>>> type(string)
<jclass org.python.core.PyString>

>>> type(dict)
<jclass org.python.core.PyDictionary>
```

Also like Perl and Visual Basic, Python allows effortless iteration through collections. Here's an example of iterating through each item in a list, and printing it to the console, using a `for` loop:

```
>>> for item in list:
...     print item
...
1
2
3
4
5
6
```

Here's the same `for` loop for a string and a tuple, respectively:

```
>>> for item in string:
...     print item
...
1
2
3
4
5
6

>>> for item in tuple:
...     print item
...
1
2
3
4
5
6
```

Note the indentation that marks the body of the `for` statement in all three examples. (Chapter 4 deals with `for` loops and `for` statements.)

All of the Python collection types can be indexed using the [ ] notation—just like an array in Java or C. The following example shows how for lists, tuples, and strings:

```
>>> list[1]
2
>>> tuple[1]
2
>>> string[1]
'2'
```

With dictionaries you use a key to index a value.

```
>>> dict["one"]
1
```

For any collection type, if you try to index a value that's not available (out of range, a nonexistent key, etc.), the collection object will throw an exception.

You can use the index to change the value held by a list or a dictionary at that index.

```
>>> list [0]=0
>>> print list
[0, 2, 3, 4, 5, 6]

>>> dict["one"]=0
>>> print dict
{'one': 0, 'six': 6, 'two': 2, 'five': 5, 'three': 3, 'four': 4}
```

You can't do this with a string or tuple because these collection types are immutable.

Strings can be added and multiplied. Here's an example of addition:

```
>>> string2 = string + "789"
>>> print string2
123456789
```

Here's an example of multiplication:

```
>>> string2 = string * 2
>>> print string2
123456123456

>>> print string
123456
```

Addition and multiplication also work for lists and tuples.

```
>>> list = list + [7, 8, 9]
>>> list
[0, 2, 3, 4, 5, 6, 7, 8, 9]

>>> tuple = tuple + (7,8,9)
>>> tuple
(1, 2, 3, 4, 5, 6, 7, 8, 9)
```

There are many built-in operations for dealing with collections. One example finds the minimum and maximum item; another determines the collection length. See Chapter 2 for more on built-in types and Chapter 9 for more on built-in functions and operations.

## Control Flow

Python provides all of the **control flow** constructs (discussed in Chapter 4) that an experienced programmer is used to: if, while, and for. The only difference between these constructs in Python and their counterparts in other languages is their use of indentation to define code blocks.

Here's a simple `if` statement. Note that, unlike Java, Python uses numerics as Boolean values; thus, any nonzero value is considered true.

```
>>> var1=1
>>> if var1:
...     print "hello"
...
hello
```

Here's a more complex `if` statement that uses `elif` ("else if") and `else` blocks:

```
>>> var1 = 1
>>> if var1==1:
...     print "Hello"
... elif var1==2:
...     print "Goodbye"
... else:
...     print "Later on"
...
Hello
```

You see that, if the first test passes (var1 == 1:), the second (var1 == 2:) doesn't execute, even though both may be true.

`while` statements work as expected. The back quotes get a string representation of `var1`.

```
>>> while var1 > 10:
...     print "var1 = " + `var1`
...     var1 = var1 - 10
...
var1 = 100
var1 = 90
var1 = 80
var1 = 70
var1 = 60
var1 = 50
var1 = 40
var1 = 30
var1 = 20
```

Earlier we used a `for` loop to iterate through a collection. The use of `for` in a more traditional fashion requires the `xrange()` built-in function. The following Python example is equivalent to the one that follows it, which uses a basic C-like syntax.

```
>>> for index in xrange(0, 100, 10):
...     print `index`
...

        for(int index = 0; index < 100; index += 10){

             System.out.println(index)
        }
```

If you leave out the 10 in the call to xrange(), it defaults to incrementing by 1. Thus, the following example iterates 100 times (0–100).

```
>>> for index in xrange(0, 100):
```

Chapter 3 deals with comparison operators; Chapter 4, with control flow.

## Exception Handling

Like so much of Python, exception handling is a lot like its counterparts in other languages. For example, Python's try clause is like Java's try, and its except clause is like Java's catch. Consider an exception thrown by a dictionary object if we try a nonexistent key. In this case, the interpreter simply prints the exception out to the screen.

```
>>> dict = {"Green Eggs":"Ham"}
>>> dict["Blue Eggs"]
Traceback (innermost last):
  File "<console>", line 1, in ?
KeyError: Blue Eggs
```

To handle this exception we can do this:

```
>>> try:
...     dict["Blue Eggs"]
... except KeyError, error:
...     print "Sam, Blue Eggs do not go with Ham " + 'error'
...

Sam, Blue Eggs do not go with Ham <exceptions.KeyError instance at
-864407725>
```

KeyError refers to the class of the exception that we want to catch, and error refers to the instance of KeyError. Here's the equivalent Java pseudocode:

```
try{
            dict.index("Blue Eggs");
}
catch(KeyError error){

    System.out.println("Sam, Blue Eggs do not go with Ham"
                            + error);
}
```

C++'s pseudocode is similar.

In addition to try...except, Python has a try...finally block. Its finally clause works much like Java's finally block, but it can't be mixed with except, as Java's can be mixed with its catch. Instead, you have to nest Python's try...catch blocks inside its try...finally blocks.

Chapter 7 deals with Python exception handling.

## Functions

As usual, Python's functions are similar to other languages' functions. That is, they perform one action and return a value. However, unlike Visual Basic and Pascal, Python uses the same syntax to define both functions and procedures, which perform multiple actions.

Here's a function that sums two numbers and returns their value:

```
>>> def sum(num1, num2):
...     return num1 + num2
...
>>> sum(5,5)
10
```

It shows how Python, like Visual Basic, uses named arguments and default values, which allow customization of function calls.

```
>>> def sum(var1=0, var2=0, var3=0):
...     return var1 + var2 + var3
...
>>> sum()
0
>>> sum(1,1)
2
>>> sum(var1=5, var3=5)
10
```

Because Python is dynamically typed, the sum function works with numeric types as well as strings.

```
>>> sum("Hello, ", "Mom, ", "how are you?")
'Hello, Mom, how are you?'
```

A function that doesn't return a type automatically returns the value None. Python's None is like Java's null, Visual Basic's Nothing, and Delphi's Nil. It means nothing or no value, not the integer value zero.

Chapter 5 covers functions in detail.

## Modules and Packages

If you're from a Java or C++ background, a Python module will seem like a cross between a package and a class with static methods. Modules can contain classes, functions, and data objects. Essentially they're files that contain Python definitions—classes and functions—and Python statements; they can be imported into other modules or into the main module. Module file names are appended with the suffix *.py*.

Python modules are similar to *.java* files and look and act very much like Visual Basic modules. See Chapter 5 to learn more about them. This chapter also discusses Python packages, which help group and organize a set of related modules.

## Classes and OOP

Like their counterparts in other languages, classes in Python are collections of variables and the methods that operate on them. To illustrate, here's an example class, Car, that inherits from the two other classes, Automobile and Transportation:

```
>>> class Automobile:
...     pass
...
>>> class Transportation:
...     pass
...
>>> class Car(Automobile, Transportation):
...     make="Ford"
...     model="Taurus"
...     def __init__(self, make, model):
...             self.make=make
...             self.model=model
...     def __del__(self):
...             print "similar to a destructor"
...     def __str__(self):
...             str = "Make " + self.make
...             str = str + ", Model " + self.model
...             return str
...
```

We can create an instance of Car and call it car.

```
>>> car = Car("Chevy", "Nova") #Create an instance of car
>>> print car
Make Chevy, Model Nova
```

And we can show that car is also an instance of classes Car and Automobile.

```
>>> print isinstance(car, Car)
1
>>> print isinstance(car, Automobile)
1
```

Note that Car defines two methods: __init__, which acts as a constructor; and __del__, which acts as a destructor. __str__ returns a string representation of the class.

Unlike Java classes, Python classes can have multiple inheritance, which we saw above with Car inheriting functionality from both Automobile and Transportation. In this regard, Python is more like C++ and Smalltalk.

Chapters 5 and 6 cover Python classes. Chapter 9 covers built-in operations and functions that pertain to classes.

## Working with Java from Python

The following interactive session shows how to import and use Java classes from Python:

Import the `Frame` class from the *java.awt* package.

```
>>> from java.awt import Frame
```

Create an instance of `Frame`, named `frame`.

```
>>> frame = Frame("My first frame created in Jython")
```

Call `frame`'s `setVisible()` method

```
>>> frame.setVisible(1)
```

Import the `Button` class from *java.awt.*

```
>>>from java.awt import Button
```

Create an instance of `Button`, called `hit_me`.

```
>>>hit_me = Button ("Hit me!")
```

Create a handler for `Button` (the event handler is just a function).

```
>>>def hit_me_event_handler(event):
...      print "Ouch!"
...
```

Register the handler with the function.

```
>>>hit_me.actionPerformed = hit_me_event_handler
```

Add `button` to `frame` by calling `frame`'s `add()` method.

```
>>> frame.add(hit_me)
java.awt.Button[button0,0,0,0x0,invalid,label=Hit me!]
```

Call `frame`'s `pack()` method so that the button will be visible.

```
>>>frame.pack()
```

Click the button with the mouse and watch the output in the interactive interpreter. Chapter 11 covers working with Java APIs from Python.

## *The Power of Python*

Python can make tough tasks trivial. Let's prove this by an example. How many lines of code will it take you in your favorite language to parse the following string and put each value in a variable?

```
>>> str = "Rick Hightower, 555-1212,rick_m_hightower@emailcompany.com
```

Can you parse it in ten lines? Maybe five? Python can do it in one (not including the `import` statement).

```
>>>from string import split
>>>name, phone, email = split(str, ",")
```

This is what we get:

```
>>> print name
Rick Hightower
>>> print phone
 555-1212
>>> print email
 rick_m_hightower@emailcompany.com
>>>
```

Simple parsing using the `split()` function is covered in Chapter 10; more advanced parsing using regular expressions is covered in Appendix E.

Here's an easy way to print the variables `name`, `phone number`, and `email` from the above session. It shows how, in Python, every namespace equates to a dictionary.

```
>>> v = "%(name)s's phone number and email is %(phone)s and %(email)s" %
locals() #one line
>>> print v
Rick Hightower's phone number and email is 555-1212 and
rick_m_hightower@emailcompany.com
```

Chapter 3 covers Python string formatting. It's a lot like string formatting in C, with its `sprintf()` and `printf()` functions, so you should pick it up quickly if you have any C background.

## Where Do You Go from Here?

If you're an experienced C++ programmer you can skip to Chapter 8, although you might want to skim Chapters 2 through 7 and use them as a reference. Visual Basic programmers can skip to Chapter 8 as well, with detours to Chapter 6 (on object-oriented programming) and 7 (on exception handling) and a skim of Chapters 2 though 5.

Novice Java programmers with no C experience should concentrate on the last half of Chapter 3 (on string formatting) and the last half of Chapter 6 (on dynamic polymorphism and operator overloading) and skim Chapters 2 through 5. If you're comfortable with Java, see Appendix C, which creates equivalent Java and Python programs for comparison.

## Summary

This chapter introduced some basic programming concepts. Having downloaded and installed the Java Development Kit (JDK), Jython, and the Jython libraries, and having dipped your toe in the Python interactive interpreter, you should have a pretty good feel for what programming is. Don't worry if you still feel confused. Your confusion will go away after the next few chapters. Once you've read up through Chapter 8, you'll feel confident using Python—you'll feel like a programmer. After that, we'll get into the really fun stuff: graphical user interfaces and applets.

If you want to learn more about Python on your own, go to *www.python.org, www.sourceforge.net* and *www.jython.org*, or go to *www.sourceforge.net* and look for Jython. (That's not a typo. JPython now goes by the name Jython.) At any of these sites, you can sign up for the email list, view the documentation, visit some of the contributor sites, and join a newsgroup.

# CHAPTER 2   *Statements and Expressions*

In this chapter, we continue our tour of Python with perhaps the most basic feature: statements. We'll also look at data types, comments, variables, and literals.

Novices, you should know the drill by now: You learn to program by programming, so try to follow along with the interactive sessions in this chapter. If you get stuck on something, just enter in a few of the examples in Jython and skip the rest. Most of the ideas here will be used through the rest of the book, so what you don't understand here you may later on in a different context. Go ahead and read the Advanced Topic sections, but again, don't worry if they confuse you at this point.

You programmers can skim or skip this chapter. The material here—literals, variables, and the like—is common to almost all languages. If you do read the chapter through, focus on the parts that are unique to Python, particularly the section "Python Collection Types" and the Advanced Topic section "Determining Types at Runtime." Also read the "For Programmers" sidebars.

## Comments and Document Strings

Python has two ways to document, or explain, what your code is doing. One way uses code comments; the other uses document strings.

### Comments

Comments, unlike the code itself, don't tell Python what to do. They're more like notes to yourself, and to other programmers who may want to modify or edit your code later, that say, "This is why I wrote it this way." In Python, a comment starts with the pound (#) character, which tells the interpreter to ignore the text after it until the end of the line. Each line of a comment must start with this character.

As the following example shows, you can put comments on their own line or you can add them after a statement.

```
#The following example demonstrates
#printing hello world to the console
print ("hello world") #this prints hello world
```

> **For Programmers: Comments in Other Languages**
>
> Visual Basic uses two double quotes (" ") to indicate a comment, but otherwise it uses comments like Python does; so does UNIX. Java, C, and C++ have two types of comments. One is similar to Python's but uses two forward slashes (//). The other is a multiline comment starting with /* and ending with */. Python doesn't have a multiline comment style.

### Document Strings

Document strings are literals that you put at the beginning of modules, functions, classes, and methods. Unlike comments, they're not thrown away but can be displayed from the interactive interpreter. The following example (*comments.py*) shows a document string for a module, a class, and a function, respectively. (We'll get to these in Chapter 5.)

```
"""Example showing a module document string for the comments module. This
module document string is multi-line.
"""
```

```
class Camp:
    """Example showing a class document string"""
    def sayHello(self):
        return "\n Hello Mom \n Hello Dad"
def sayCampHello():
    """Example showing a function document string"""

    camp = Camp()
    print ("Hello: " + camp.sayHello())
if __name__ == "__main__":
    sayCampHello()
```

Here's another example. The `__doc__` attribute of the `Camp` class and the `sayCampHello()` function hold the document strings.

```
C:\book\chap2>jython -i comments.py
Hello:
 Hello Mom
 Hello Dad
>>> Camp.__doc__
'Example showing a class document string'
>>> sayCampHello.__doc__
'Example showing a function document string'
```

Let's say we want to learn something about a module named *comments* and we don't have the source code. So, we start a new Jython session, import *comments* to it, and view its document string.

```
>>> import comments
>>> print comments.__doc__
Example showing a module document string for the comments module. This module
document string is multi-line.
```

In the example below, notice the `dir` command. Python's `dir` is like the `dir` command at a DOS prompt, but, unlike the DOS `dir`, which lists files and directories, it shows members of a module, class, or instance. This means that you can use it to list a comment's attributes.

```
>>> dir (comments)
['Camp', '__doc__', '__file__', '__name__', 'sayCampHello']
```

Here we see the `__file__` and `__name__` attributes, which provide the file path and name of this module. We also see `Camp` and `sayCampHello`, so we can check if they have the `__doc__` attribute. (Follow along.)

```
>>> from comments import Camp, sayCampHello
>>> dir (Camp) # List the attributes for Camp class
['__doc__', '__module__', 'sayHello']
>>> dir (sayCampHello) # List attributes for sayCampHello
[]
>>> Camp.__doc__
```

```
'Example showing a class document string'
>>> sayCampHello.__doc__
'Example showing a function document string'
```

The Camp class does have a __doc__ attribute listing, but, strangely, the sayCampHello() function doesn't. Still, we can print out its document string. That's because, although functions don't show attributes, they do have the __doc__ attribute built in.

## Statements

A statement is simply an instruction to Python to perform a task. Through the interpreter, Python reads the statement and does as instructed. In other words, it executes the statement. In this example, each line is a statement.

```
Hello = "Hello %s how are you doing"
from java import awt
print ("Hello World")
```

By default, a statement is contained on a single line. A multiline statement is indicated by a backslash at the end of each of its lines and an indentation at the beginning of the next. Here's one complete statement spanning two lines:

```
>>> reallyLongLine = 5 + 5 - 5 * 5 /5 * 100 - 1000 \
 + 200 - 300 + 60 / 5
```

Two statements can fit on one line if they're separated by a semicolon.

```
>>> print("Hello"); print("Goodbye")
Hello
Goodbye
```

You can also end a statement with a semicolon.

```
>>> print ("This statement has a semicolon at the end");
This statement has a semicolon at the end
>>> print ("This one does not")
This one does not
>>>
```

Stylewise, an ending semicolon isn't the best idea, but if you're switching between Jython and Java or CPython and C or C++, it's a nice feature because in these languages using semicolons to terminate a line is standard. You can't do this when switching between C++ and Visual Basic. If you try, you'll probably get a few frustrating syntax errors.

> **For Programmers: Multiline Statements and Visual Basic**
>
> If you come from a Visual Basic background, Python's style of line continuation should be familiar. The only real difference between the two is Python's use of a backslash (\\) and Visual Basic's use of an underscore(_) and an End statement (Function End, Sub End, etc.) to mark the end of a statement instead of indentation.
>
> If you come from a Java background, Python's line continuation and code block indentation may seem a little weird. Java explicitly ends statements with a semicolon, so there's no need for a line continuation indicator. It uses the backslash for string continuation. Indenting in Java is strictly up to the taste and style of the individual programmer.

Statements use whitespace—tabs and spaces—to denote an associated block of code. It can also denote a suite associated with a clause in a compound statement. (Compound statements and suites will be covered in Chapter 3.) The amount of whitespace within a statement doesn't matter. All of the following examples do the same thing even though the whitespace in each is different.

```
x=1
x = 1
x =  1
x =     1
```

## Expressions

Expressions are also instructions to Python to perform a task. That task is to return a value, such as the result of a mathematical operation or the truth or falsity of a statement. Expressions can be assigned variables. Also, many of them use operators, which can be words like and, or, and not, or symbols such as + (plus), – (minus), * (multiplication), and = (equals). We'll cover operators in detail in Chapter 3. For now, just remember that expressions return a value and usually use operators.

> **For Novices: Expressions in Spreadsheets**
>
> If you've ever used spreadsheets, you've used expressions and operators. An expression is equivalent to a spreadsheet formula.
>
> Let's say that, in cell D1 of a spreadsheet, you have the formula =(A1*B1)/C1, which multiplies cell A1 by cell B1 and then divides their product by C1. The equivalent in Python is D1 = (A1*B1)/C1, where D1, A1, and C1 are variables. The right side of this equation—(A1*B1)/C1—is the actual expression.

To illustrate how expressions work, we'll first create three variables, x, y, and z.

```
>>> x,y,z = 1, 2, 3 # This is *not* an expression
```

(Notice the comment in the above example. See the box titled "Assignment" for an explanation.)

The following examples are pretty self-explanatory. They illustrate, in turn, the use of the multiplication operator, the division operator, and the logical operator and (all of which will be covered in Chapter 3). What they all demonstrate is this simple point: *Expressions are statements that return values.*

```
>>> y * 2
4

>>> 10 / z
3

>>> x and y
2

>>> x and 0
0
```

### Assignment

In the example that creates the variables we used in our expression, the comment stated `This is *not* an expression`. In fact, it may look like an expression, but in Python it's actually an assignment. Take a look at the following code, in which it appears that a value is returned:

```
x = y = z = 3
```

We might think that z = 3 returns 3, and y = z returns the value of z, which is 3, but this isn't the case. We know this because in interactive interpreter mode an expression is printed out to the screen.

```
>>> x = y = z = 3
>>> x = z
>>> x==z
1
```

As you can see, x = z and x = y = z = 3 aren't printed to the screen, which means that they don't return a value and so are not expressions. In Python, the use of the comparison operator (==), not the assignment operator, is what makes a statement an expression. This is because the == returns a value, usually 1 or 0, whereas = doesn't.

In Java, C, and C++, an assignment *is* an expression, which is why confusing the assignment and comparison operators is a common programmer error (mostly in C and C++; Java has its own way of dealing with this problem).

Consider these two examples:

```
if(x=z): pass
while(x=z): pass
```

Here the if and while statements expect an expression, that is, a value to be returned, but the assignment operator can't do this, and syntax errors are the result.

## Variables

Think of variables as individual storage containers that hold different kinds of data in memory. Each variable has a name and a value, and each variable value has a type.

### Declaring Variables

In most languages, before you can use a variable you have to declare it; that is, you must assign it a name and a type. Python is different; unlike in other languages, you declare a variable *implicitly* by assigning a value to it. Here's an example:

```
# declare age to be of type integer and of value 28.
age = 28

# declare name to be of type string
# and of value "rick"
name = "rick"
```

Variable declarations can go anywhere in a module. You can declare more than one variable at once by stringing them together. (Follow along).

```
>>> x,y,z = 1,2,3
>>> print ("x=" + `x` + " y=" + `y` + " z=" +`z`)
x=1 y=2 z=3
```

The first statement defines three variables as of type `Integer` (that is, whole numbers) and assigns them the values 1, 2, and 3, such that x = 1, y = 2, and z = 3. Notice that in the second statement the variable names are enclosed in back quotes. That tells Python to convert the variable to a string.

Here's an interactive example of Python stringing together several variable definitions with different types:

```
>>> name, age, sex = "Kiley", 22, "female"
>>> print (name + " is " + `age` + " and " + sex)
Kiley is 22 and female
```

### For Programmers: Variable Declarations in Python as Compared to Visual Basic and Java

In Python, you can't access a variable that you haven't declared, but remember: The first time you assign a value to a variable, you declare that variable. That means that you can't make the mistake of trying to use an unassigned variable, as you can in Visual Basic. Only if you don't use Visual's `Explicit` option can you use a variable that has no value assigned.

Visual Basic has a `Variant` type, which can be anything. Python variables don't have a type unto themselves but are whatever type is assigned to them—`String`, `List`, and so forth—so they support dynamic polymorphism with their late-binding features. Visual Basic also supports dynamic polymorphism as well. (Polymorphism is discussed in Chapter 6.)

In Java, variable declaration is very strict. You have to explicitly declare the variables themselves and their types. Even so, you can do dynamic polymorphic programming if you declare a variable a superclass of the instance you're working with.

Obviously, Python is more flexible and dynamic than Java, but not as type safe. If you come from a Smalltalk background, this is probably a boon, but probably not if you come from C++. Read Appendix C on the advantages of scripting languages, and then decide for yourself.

## Valid Variable Names

Variable names in Python can start with a letter or an underscore (_). After the first character, they can also contain numbers, and they can be as long as you want them to be. Keep in mind that variable names are case sensitive. That is, age, AGE, and Age mean different things to the interpreter. Here are a few valid variable names:

```
_name = "John Souza"
favorite_sport = "Baseball"
SF49ers = "San Francisco 49ers"
```

Here are some invalid ones:

```
$name = "John Souza"
favorite sport = "Baseball"
49ers = "San Francisco 49ers"
```

# Data Types

Each variable has a type, which can be the following:

- One of the six basic data types (see the next section)
- One of the five standard container types
- One of the standard callable types
- One of the two object-oriented types
- Any Java class or standard object

In this chapter we'll cover the basic types.

## The Basic Data Types

Most of the six basic data types in Python are analogous to the basic types in Visual Basic and Java. Here they are:

- String—sequences of characters
- Integer—integers (whole numbers)

- `Float`—floating-point numbers
- `Long`—large integers
- `None`—no value
- `Type`—type

All of them are built into the system. Unlike in Java, everything in Python is an object, including functions, modules, and types. (We'll get to objects in Chapter 6, which is on object-oriented programming.)

`Float`, `Integer`, and `Long` are numeric types. The table below shows their individual ranges—that is, the size of the values they can hold.

| Type | From | To |
|---|---|---|
| Integer | –2,147,483,648 | 2,147,483,647 |
| Float | 4.9e–324 | 1.7976931348623157e308 |
| Long | As small as you want | As big as you want |

### For Programmers: Numeric Type Ranges

The range of the numeric types depends on the system running them, unless, of course, they're running under Java. This means that, in Jython, `Integer` is implemented with Java `Int`, and `Float` is implemented with Java `Double`. The reverse is true in CPython: `Integer` is implemented with C `Long`, and `Float` with C `Double`. `Long` has an unlimited range in both CPython and Jython. Unlike in C, in Java `Integer` always holds the same range of values.

You often need to know the biggest or smallest `Integer` or `Float` type, but trying to remember this information is difficult. I'm going to show you an interactive session that will give you this information when you need it. Remember that `Float` in Python equates to Java `Double`, so the first thing to do is import class `Double` from the *java.lang* package.

```
>>> from java.lang import Double
```

We could instead do a `dir` on `Double` to see its MAX_VALUE and MIN_VALUE attributes.

```
>>> dir (Double)
['MAX_VALUE', 'MIN_VALUE', 'NEGATIVE_INFINITY', 'NaN',
'POSITIVE_INFINITY', 'TYPE', '__doc__', '__init__', '__module__',
'compareTo', 'doubleToLongBits', 'infinite', 'isInfinite', 'isNaN',
'longBitsToDouble', 'naN', 'parseDouble', 'toString', 'valueOf']
```

Here's how to access the largest and smallest `Float`, respectively:

```
>>> Double.MAX_VALUE
1.7976931348623157E308

>>> Double.MIN_VALUE
4.9E-324
```

Now we'll do the same thing for the biggest and smallest `Integer`.

```
>>> from java.lang import Integer
>>> max = Integer.MAX_VALUE
>>> min = Integer.MIN_VALUE
>>> max, min
(2147483647, -2147483648)
```

## TypeType

As I said before, everything in Python is an object, that is, a "container" for properties and methods. This means that all of the basic types are of type `Type`—that is,
a variable type that holds another variable type. Here's the proof:

```
>>> if type(FloatType) == TypeType:
...       print("FloatType is of TypeType")
...
FloatType is of TypeType
```

### For Programmers: Jython versus Python

In Jython, the built-in `type()` function returns the class name of the Java implementation for that type for Jython. For example:

```
>>> int = 1 #holds a integer
>>> float = 1.0 #holds a float
>>> long = 1L #holds a long
>>> string = "string" #holds a string
>>> type (int)
<jclass org.python.core.PyInteger at -712990957>
>>> type (long)
<jclass org.python.core.PyLong at 46702445>
>>> type (string)
<jclass org.python.core.PyString at -710631661>
>>> type (float)
<jclass org.python.core.PyFloat at -1307009172>
>>> type (FloatType)
<jclass org.python.core.PyJavaClass at -693854445>
>>> type (TypeType)
<jclass org.python.core.PyJavaClass at -693854445>
>>> type (None)
<jclass org.python.core.PyNone at -693592301>
```

In Python, the `type()` function returns `Int`, `Long`, `String`, and `Float` instead of the Java
class name.

## None

Variables that reference nothing are of type `None`, meaning that they have no
value. If you work with databases, think of `None` as similar to `NULL`. Don't think of

it as zero, which *is* a value. Programmers, you may know that in Java and Visual Basic the counterparts to Python's None are, respectively, null and Nothing. In Delphi, this same concept is called Nil.

## Python Collection Types

One thing that sets Python apart from most other languages is its built-in collection types. As in the real world, in programming a collection represents more than one item. By "built-in" I mean that Python uses a special syntax for its collections, which it calls sequences. Strings are also considered sequences in Python, so all of the rules that apply to strings also apply to collections—slice notation, indexes, and so forth.

### For Programmers: Hashtables, Vectors, and Collection Objects

If you use Java, you probably use hashtables and vectors in about 85 percent of the programs you write. Hashtables are similar to Python dictionaries, and vectors are similar to Python lists. The key difference is that Python's lists, dictionaries, and tuples have built-in syntax support for addition, multiplication, member referencing, literals, for loop iteration, and so forth. This makes things easier on the programmer. It also means that you can define objects to act like collections so that other programmers can use the syntax when working with them.

The Visual Basic collection object is like Python's list and dictionary rolled into one. Visual Basic supports for loop iteration, as Python does, but otherwise it offers no collection support. Perl's collection support is the only one that comes close to Python's.

## Lists

Whereas a string holds a sequence of characters, a list holds a sequence of objects of various types, which you access as you do characters in strings. You can even use slice notation, which we learned about in Chapter 1.

```
>>>     #Define a list with 5 values in it
>>> mylist = ["hello","goodbye", 1, 1.0, 50000000000000000L]
>>>     #print the first object in the list
>>> print (mylist[0])
hello
>>>     #print the first two objects in the list
>>> print (mylist[0:2])
['hello', 'goodbye']
>>>     #print the whole list
>>> print (mylist[0:])
['hello', 'goodbye', 1, 1.0, 50000000000000000L]
>>>
```

You can tell a list by the square brackets ([ ]) that surround it. Empty brackets mean that there are no items in the list.

Lists can be added and multiplied.

```
>>> list1 = [] #create an empty list
>>> list2 = ["a", "b", 10, 11, 12, 13]
>>> list1 # show the empty lists contents
[]

>>> list2 #show the contents of the list with items
['a', 'b', 10, 11, 12, 13]

>>> list1 = list2 + list2 #add the lists together
>>> list1
['a', 'b', 10, 11, 12, 13, 'a', 'b', 10, 11, 12, 13]

>>> list1 = list2 * 2 #multiply a list
>>> list1
['a', 'b', 10, 11, 12, 13, 'a', 'b', 10, 11, 12, 13]
```

You can also append and remove list items, with the list object's append() and remove() methods. Chapter 5 is where we'll cover methods and functions; for now all you need to know to use append() and remove() is the form variable_name.methodname(arguments). (You'll learn about arguments in Chapter 5 as well.) Here's an example that continues the previous interactive session:

```
>>> # remove 'a' from the list
>>> list1.remove('a')
>>> # display the contents of list1
>>> list1
['b', 10, 11, 12, 13, 'a', 'b', 10, 11, 12, 13]

>>> # remove 'a' from the list again
>>> list1.remove('a')
>>> #display the contents of the list
>>> list1
['b', 10, 11, 12, 13, 'b', 10, 11, 12, 13]

>>> #put the 'a' back in the list
>>> list1.append('a')
>>> list1
['b', 10, 11, 12, 13, 'b', 10, 11, 12, 13, 'a']

>>> len (list1)
11
```

Note that remove() gets rid of only the first occurrence of an item, so to remove both instances of 'a', we have to invoke list1.remove('a') twice. By the way, you can determine how many items are in a list with the len() (length) function.

Another interesting thing you can do with lists is sort them, with sort(), and reverse their order, with reverse(). For instance, you might want your list in alphabetical or reverse alphabetical order.

```
>>> names = []
>>> #append a bunch of names to the names list
>>> names.append("Kiley")
>>> names.append("Rick")
>>> names.append("Mary")
>>> names.append("Adam")
>>> names.append("Missy")
>>> names.append("Martha")
>>> #display names before the sort
>>> names
['Kiley', 'Rick', 'Mary', 'Adam', 'Missy', 'Martha']

>>> #sort the names alphabetically
>>> names.sort()
>>> #display names after sort
>>> names
['Adam', 'Kiley', 'Martha', 'Mary', 'Missy', 'Rick']

>>> #reverse the order of the list
>>> names.reverse()
>>> names
['Rick', 'Missy', 'Mary', 'Martha', 'Kiley', 'Adam']
```

With insert() you can insert items into the middle of a list. With index(), you determine where an item is numerically.

```
>>> #display the contents of the names list
>>> names
['Rick', 'Missy', 'Mary', 'Martha', 'Kiley', 'Adam']

>>> #determine the index of the "Rick" string
>>> names.index("Rick")
0

>>> #insert "Kiley" string next to "Rick"
>>> names.insert(1, "Kiley")
>>> names
['Rick', 'Kiley', 'Missy', 'Mary', 'Martha', 'Kiley', 'Adam']

>>> #find the index of the "Martha" string
>>> names.index("Martha")
4

>>> #insert the "Miguel" string next to Martha
>>> names.insert(5, "Miguel")
>>> #display the name list
>>> names
['Rick', 'Kiley', 'Missy', 'Mary', 'Martha', 'Miguel', 'Kiley', 'Adam']
```

count() determines the number of times an item occurs in a list.

```
>>> # Initialize the names list
>>> names = ["James", "James", "James", "Bob", "Joe", "Sam"]
>>> # Count number of "James" strings in names
>>> names.count("James")
3
```

## Tuples

Tuples are collection types similar to lists in that they contain items. However, they're immutable, which means that you can't change them once defined—you can't append or remove items or add two tuples together. All you can do is multiply them.

```
>>> # create an empty tuple
>>> tuple1 = ()
>>> # create a tuple with three greetings
>>> tuple2 = ("Hi", "Bye", "Salutations")
>>> # multiply this tuple2 and assign to tuple
>>> tuple1 = tuple2 * 2
>>> # display the contents of tuple
>>> tuple1
('Hi', 'Bye', 'Salutations', 'Hi', 'Bye', 'Salutations')
```

This example shows tuples being declared in parentheses, but this isn't mandatory. Furthermore, you can use a tuple to initialize more than one variable and use more than one variable to initialize a tuple. To see this, follow along with this interactive session.

```
>>> #initialize a tuple without parentheses
>>> tuple3 = 3,2,1
>>> tuple3
(3, 2, 1)
```

Here we initialized tuple3 with three numbers without parentheses. To be explicit, we defined a variable of type Tuple that contains three numeric items with values of 3, 2, and 1.

In the following example, we initialize three numbers with a tuple. In other words, we declare three variables named x, y, and z; then we assign 3 to x, 2 to y, and 1 to z.

```
>>> x,y,z = 3,2,1
>>> x
3
>>> y
2
>>> z
1
```

Now we can use these three variables to create a tuple. That is, we use them to declare a tuple, tuple4, that contains the three variables' values.

```
>>> tuple4 = x,y,z
>>> tuple4
(3, 2, 1)
```

The opposite of this is to use a tuple to declare three new variables by defining them and using tuple4 to initialize them.

```
>>> q,r,s = tuple4
>>> q
3
>>> r
2
>>> s
1
```

**For Novices: Lists and Tuples Are Both Sequences**

Lists work as tuples do for declaring multiple variables and for using variables to assign values to lists. The only difference is that they require brackets. The following example is similar to the examples we saw for tuples, but it uses lists instead.

```
>>> x,y,z = [5,6,7]
>>> x
5
>>> y
6
>>> z
7
>>> list1 = [x,y,z]
>>> list1
[5, 6, 7]
>>> q,r,s = list1
>>> q
5
>>> r
6
>>> s
7
```

## Dictionaries

A dictionary, another Python collection type, stores keys and values. It uses key/value pairs to locate a value, which can be any object of any type. The dictionary declares a series of key/value pairs using the notation key:value and separates the individual pairs with commas.

```
>>> namesToAges = {"joe":30, "kelly":32, "john":28}
>>> joesAge = namesToAges["joe"]
>>> print ("Joe is " + `joesAge` + " years old")
Joe is 30 years old
>>>
```

namesToAges is the dictionary, "joe" is the key, and 30 is the value.

Remember that a dictionary is a sequence, and like a sequence you access it by its name and by the index of the value in it that you're looking for. What's different is that the location is a key into the dictionary. In the last example, we wanted to find Joe's age. To do that we had to use the key, "joe", in square brackets like a list, in the namesToAges dictionary. Keys can be any object of any immutable type, such as strings, tuples, or numeric values. However, you can use tuples for dictionary keys only if they contain only immutable items.

A dictionary can be searched by its keys, its values, or its key/value pairs. To get all of a dictionary's keys, values, or pairs, you use keys(), values(), or items(), respectively. We'll continue the previous example to illustrate how.

```
>>>           #display namesToAges dictionary
>>> namesToAges
{'john': 28, 'joe': 30, 'kelly': 32}

>>>           #display keys in dictionary
>>> namesToAges.keys()
['john', 'joe', 'kelly']

>>>           #display values in dictionary
>>> namesToAges.values()
[28, 30, 32]

>>>           #display items in dictionary
>>> namesToAges.items()
[('john', 28), ('joe', 30), ('kelly', 32)]
```

To see if a particular key, such as "joe" or "james" is in a dictionary, we can do this:

```
>>> namesToAges.has_key("joe")
1
>>> namesToAges.has_key("james")
0
```

## Advanced Topic: Determining Types at Runtime

You can determine a type at runtime with the built-in type() function along with the Python *types* module, which defines all of the basic types.

First, we import the *types* module and create some variables from all of the basic types.

```
>>> from types import *
>>> int = 1 #holds a integer
>>> float = 1.0 #holds a float
>>> long = 1L #holds a long
>>> string = "string" #holds a string
```

Now we test to see if the variable string is of type String. Here we'll be using the if statement, which works like if in other languages. Just remember that if's subordinate statements must be indented. (We'll be covering this in Chapter 4.)

The . . . prompt tells you to enter the subordinate statement, print. Make sure to indent print, and then hit Enter to indicate that the if statement is finished.

Here is your first if statement, step by step.

1.  At the >>>, type
    ```
    >>> if type(string) == StringType: [hit Return]
    ```
2.  At the . . . prompt,
    ```
    [hit Tab] print ("string is a StringType") [hit Return]
    ```
3.  At the . . . prompt,
    [hit Return]

The next three interactive sessions test whether the variable int is of type Integer, the variable float is of type Float, and the variable long is of type Long.

```
>>> if type(int) == IntType:
...     print("int is a IntType")
...
int is a IntType

>>> if type(float) == FloatType:
...     print("float is a FloatType")
...
float is a FloatType

>>> if type(long) == LongType:
...     print("long is a Long")
...
long is a Long
```

Just for a sanity check, let's see if the string variable is a Float type.

```
>>> if type(string) == FloatType:
...     print("string is a float")
... else:
...     print("Don't be a GOOF!")
...
Don't be a GOOF!
```

## Literals

We've been using literals since Chapter 1, but we didn't call them that. The term is computerspeak for a constant value; that is, what you type is *literally* what you get. In the following interactive session, for example, the literals are "Hello World", 100, 3200000000000L, and 3.5.

```
>>> a_literal_string = "Hello World"
>>> a_literal_integer = 100
>>> a_literal_long = 3200000000000L
>>> a_float_literal = 3.5
```

Literals can be contained in statements.

```
print ("Hello I am a literal string")
```

**Table 2–1** *Escape Sequence Characters*

| Character | Meaning |
|-----------|---------|
| \\ | Backslash |
| \' | Single quote |
| \" | Double quote |
| \a | ASCII Bell (BEL) |
| \b | ASCII Backspace (BS) |
| \f | ASCII Formfeed (FF) |
| \n | ASCII Linefeed (LF) |
| \r | ASCII Carriage return (CR) |
| \t | ASCII Horizontal tab (TAB) |
| \v | ASCII Vertical tab (VT) |
| \\*ooo* | ASCII character with octal value *ooo* |
| \\*xhh* . . . | ASCII character with hex value *hh* . . . |

String literals are identified by the quotes that enclose them. The quotes can be single (' '), double (" "), triple single (' ' '), or triple double ( " " " ). Here are the four styles illustrated:

```
>>> string1 = "Hello World"
>>> print (string1) #print the string1 to the output
Hello World

>>> string2 = 'Hello World'
>>> print (string2) #compare this output to the first form
Hello World

>>> string3 = """Hello World"""
>>> print (string3) #compare this output to the 1st and 2nd form
Hello World
>>> string4 = '''Hello World'''
>>> print (string4) #compare this output to the first three forms of Strings
Hello World
```

If you're wondering why there are four ways to identify literals, I intend to tell you, but first I have to explain escape sequences.

An escape sequence is a way to add special ASCII characters to a new line or a formfeed. As in Java and C, it's identified in Python by the backslash (\)—for example \n (newline). Table 2–1 lists the escape sequence characters.

In the following example, we see that \n places the phrase Goodbye Earth on a new line.

```
>>> string = "Hello Mars \n Goodbye Earth \n"
>>> print (string)
Hello Mars
```

```
Goodbye Earth
>>>
```

Here we see that \t inserts tabs between `Hello Mars` and `Goodbye Earth` and between `Goodbye Earth` and `Goodbye Moon`.

```
>>> string = "Hello Mars \t Goodbye Earth \t Goodbye Moon"
>>> print (string)
Hello Mars     Goodbye Earth     Goodbye Moon
>>>
```

Escape sequences can get a little messy, especially when you add quotes or newlines to your string. Consider the following interactive session:

```
>>> print ("She said, \"I love you \" and I said \n \"remember Paris in the
spring") #one line
She said, "I love you " and I said
"remember Paris in the spring
>>>
```

Python has another way, and this is where the different quoting styles come in handy. Strings that use triple-double or triple-single quotes can span multiple lines and include actual quoted lines within them. That means that the previous example can be rewritten as

```
>>> print ("""She said, "I love you", and I said,
... "remember Paris in the spring" """) #two lines
She said, "I love you", and I said,
"remember Paris in the spring"
>>>
```

### Fun with Escape Characters

Redo the tabs (\t) interactive session with vertical tabs (\v). You should get something weird that looks like the universal symbol for male. Now cut and paste the output line from the DOS box into Microsoft Word. (Use Edit->Mark from the Windows menu from the DOS box. Once the text is selected, choose Edit->Copy Enter from the Windows menu of the DOS box, which will put the text on the clipboard. Then return to Word and paste the text.) What happens?

## Numeric Literals

We define integer literals in three ways: regular (base 10), hexadecimal (base 16), and octal (base 8). This code shows three literals that equate to the same integer value, 255.

```
>>> base10 = 255
>>> base16 = 0xff
>>> base8 = 0377
```

```
>>> base10,base16,base8
(255, 255, 255)
>>>
```

An octal starts with 0; a hexadecimal, with 0x. If you're not familiar with octal and hexadecimal numbers, don't worry; you don't need them to program in Python.

Exponential notation defines floating-point literals like this:

```
>>> million = 1e6
>>> million
1000000.0

>>> billion = 1e+9
>>> billion
1.0E9

>>> gates_net = 36.7e+9
>>> gates_net
3.67E10

>>> average_income = 30e3
>>> average_income
30000.0

>>> volts = 3e-3
>>> volts
0.003
```

We define arbitrarily long integers by appending an L to them.

```
>>> bignum = 9999999999999999999999999999999999999L
>>> bignum
9999999999999999999999999999999999999L
```

## Summary

In this chapter, we covered comments and document strings, which can be used to document Python code. Unlike comments, document strings can be accessed with the interactive interpreter.

We looked at Python easy-to-use built-in container types (dictionaries, tuples, and lists), the values of which are defined by literals. Literals indicate simple values of types Integer, Float, String, and Long.

Statements are instructions to Python to perform tasks. Expressions are simple statements that return a value and usually involve the use of operators. Function and class methods are made up of statements and expressions.

# CHAPTER 3    *Operators and String Formatting*

---

### *Terms in This Chapter*

---

- ◊ *Boolean value*
- ◊ *Class*
- ◊ *Concatenation*
- ◊ *Conversion*
- ◊ *Dictionary*
- ◊ *Directive*
- ◊ *Field*
- ◊ *Flag*

- ◊ *Format directives*
- ◊ *Hexdump*
- ◊ *Key*
- ◊ *Keyword*
- ◊ *Literal*
- ◊ *Modulus*
- ◊ *Operator precedence*

- ◊ *Operator (%, Arithmetic, Bitwise, Comparison, Conditional, Logical, Sequence, Shift)*
- ◊ *String*
- ◊ *Tuple*
- ◊ *Variable*

In this chapter, we'll cover operators and string formatting. Python string formatting controls the creation of strings. Done correctly, it makes the production of these strings simple and straightforward.

I've said it before, and I'll say it again: If you're a beginning programmer, remember that the only way to learn programming is by programming, so try to follow along with the interactive sessions throughout the chapter. The interactive interpreter mode will give you a hands-on understanding of Python operators and string formatting. If you have trouble with an Advanced Topic section, just skim over it; don't let it slow you down.

As in Chapter 2, most of the concepts in this chapter act as building blocks for more complex ideas. Don't worry if something seems unclear to you at this point; you might understand it later, in a different context. For example, logical and comparison operators may not be easily grasped here, but wait until Chapter 4, where we deal with the if statement, which makes frequent use of these operators and so should clear things up.

If you've programmed before, most of this chapter will be familiar. For example, operators and string formatting in Python and C are very similar. If you have in-depth programming experience, you can probably just skim this material, especially if you're comfortable with C, Java, and/or Visual Basic. Do, however, pay attention to the following sections:

- "Arithmetic with Strings, Lists, and Tuples"
- "% Tuple String Formatting"
- "Advanced Topic: Using the %d, %i, %f, and %e Directives for Formatting Numbers"

Also read the "For Programmers" sidebar (see pages 50–51).

## Operators

Recall from Chapter 2 our definition of expressions as simple statements that return a value. In Python, many expressions use operators, such as +, −, *, and =. The following subsections describe each operator type, and each section contains a table of the type's operators along with sample interactive sessions illustrating their use. If you feel as if you've been this way before, you have—we've been using operators since Chapter 1.

### Arithmetic Operators

Arithmetic operators work with the numeric types Float, Int, and Long. Table 3–1 describes them, including three we have yet to encounter: modulus (%), which gives the remainder; exponential (**), which raises one number to the power of another number; and abs, which gives a number's absolute value.

One example of modulus is 3/2, which gives the remainder of 1 ($\frac{3}{2} = 1\frac{1}{2}$). Another is 10/7, which gives a remainder of 3 ($\frac{10}{7} = 1\frac{3}{7}$). In Python, we express the previous sentence as

```
>>> 10 % 7
3
>>> 3 % 2
1
>>>
```

Once you understand modulus, the divmod() function, which we'll discuss in a later chapter, should come easily to you.

**Table 3–1**   *Arithmetic Operators*

| Operator | Description | Interactive Session |
|---|---|---|
| + | Addition | ```>>> x = 1 + 2```<br>```>>> print (x)```<br>```3``` |
| – | Subtraction | ```>>> x = 2 – 1```<br>```>>> print (x)```<br>```1``` |
| * | Multiplication | ```>>> x = 2 * 2```<br>```>>> print (x)```<br>```4``` |
| / | Integer division returns an Integer type; float division returns a float type | Integer division:<br>```>>> x = 10 / 3```<br>```>>> print (x)```<br>```3```<br><br>Float division:<br>```>>> x = 10.0 / 3.3333```<br>```>>> print (x)```<br>```3.000030000300003``` |
| % | Modulus—gives the remainder; typically used for integers | ```>>> x = 10 % 3```<br>```>>> print (x)```<br>```1``` |
| ** | Exponential | ```>>> x = 10**2```<br>```>>> print(x)```<br>```100``` |
| divmod | Does both of the division operators at once and returns a tuple; the second item in the tuple contains the remainder. divmod(x,y) is equivalent to x/y,x%y | This:<br>```>>> divmod (10,3)```<br>```(3, 1)```<br>Is the same as this:<br>```>>> 10/3,10%3```<br>```(3, 1)```<br>This:<br>```>>> divmod (5,2)```<br>```(2, 1)```<br>Is the same as this:<br>```>>> 5/2, 5%2```<br>```(2, 1)``` |
| abs | Finds the absolute value of a number | ```>>> abs(100)```<br>```100```<br>```>>> abs(-100)```<br>```100``` |
| -, + | Sign | ```>>> 1, -1, +1, +-1```<br>```(1, -1, 1, -1)``` |

### Numeric Conversion Operators

Many times we need to convert from one numeric type to another. The three operators that perform this conversion are Int(x), Long(x), and Float(x), where x is any numeric value. To illustrate, in the example that follows we create three numeric types: 1 (Long), f (Float), and i (Integer).

```
>>> l,f,i=1L, 1.0, 1
```

The output is

```
>>> l,f,i
(1L, 1.0, 1)
```

   The next three examples in turn convert i to Float, f and i to Long, and 1 and f to Integer.

```
>>> float (i)
1.0
>>> float(l)
1.0
>>> long(f), long(i)
(1L, 1L)

>>> int(l), int(f)
(1, 1)
>>>
```

### Logical Operators, Comparison Operators, and Boolean Values

Logical operators are a way to express choices, such as "This one *and* that one *or* that one but *not* this one." Comparison operators are a way to express questions, such as "Is this one *greater than* that one?" Both work with Boolean values, which express the answer as either true or false. Unlike Java, Python has no true Boolean type. Instead, as in C, its Booleans can be numeric values, where any nonzero value must be true and any zero value must be false. Thus, Python interprets as false the following values:

- None
- Empty strings
- Empty tuples
- Empty lists
- Empty dictionaries
- Zero

and as true all other values, including

- Nonempty strings
- Nonempty tuples
- Nonempty lists

- Nonempty dictionaries
- Not zero

Table 3–2 describes the logical operators. They return 1 for a true expression and 0 for a false expression. Table 3–3 describes the comparison operators. They return some form of true for a true expression and some form of false for a false expression.

Logical and comparison operators often work together to define application logic (in English, application logic simply means decision making).When they do, they're often used with `if` and `while` statements. Don't worry about `if` and `while` just yet; we'll get into them in detail in Chapter 4. For now, a simple way to visualize them is to imagine that you like vanilla and chocolate ice cream but hate nuts, and you want to express your preference in a way that Python will understand, like this:

```
if (flavor == chocolate or flavor == vanilla and \
    not nuts and mycash > 5):
        print("yummy ice cream give me some")

while(no_vanilla_left and no_chocolate_left ):
        print ("no more ice cream for me")
```

**Table 3–2**  *Logical Operators*

| Operator | Description | Interactive Session |
|----------|-------------|---------------------|
| and | And two values or comparisons together | `>>> x,y = 1,0`<br>`>>> x and y`<br>`0`<br>`>>> x,y = 1,1`<br>`>>> x and y`<br>`1` |
| or | Or two values together | `>>> x,y = 1,0`<br>`>>> x or y`<br>`1`<br>`>>> x,y = 0,0`<br>`>>> x or y`<br>`0` |
| not | Inverse a value | `>>> x,y = 0,0`<br>`>>> not x`<br>`1`<br>`>>> not y`<br>`1`<br>`>>> x = 1`<br>`>>> not x`<br>`0` |

**Table 3–3**  *Comparison Operators*

| Operator | Description | Interactive Session |
|---|---|---|
| == | Equal to | ```>>> x,y,z=1,1,2```<br>```>>> x==y```<br>```1```<br>```>>> x==z```<br>```0``` |
| >= | Greater than or equal to | ```>>> z>=x```<br>```1```<br>```>>> x>=z```<br>```0``` |
| <= | Less than or equal to | ```>>> z<=x```<br>```0```<br>```>>> x<=z```<br>```1``` |
| > | Greater than | ```>>> x>z```<br>```0```<br>```>>> z>x```<br>```1``` |
| < | Less than | ```>>> x<z```<br>```1```<br>```>>> z<x```<br>```0``` |
| != | Not equal to | ```>>> x!=y```<br>```0```<br>```>>> x!=z```<br>```1``` |
| <> | Not equal to | ```>>> x<>y```<br>```0```<br>```>>> x<>z```<br>```1``` |
| is | Object identity | ```>>> str = str2 = "hello"```<br>```>>> str is str2```<br>```1```<br>```>>> str = "hi"```<br>```>>> str is str2```<br>```0``` |
| is not | Negated object identity | ```>>> s1 = s2 = "hello"```<br>```>>> s1 is not s2```<br>```0```<br>```>>> s1 = s2 + " Bob"```<br>```>>> s1 is not s2```<br>```1``` |

**Table 3–3**  *Continued*

| Operator | Description | Interactive Session |
|----------|-------------|---------------------|
| in | Checks to see if an item is in a sequence | `>>> list = [1,2,3]`<br><br>`>>> 1 in list`<br>`1`<br><br>`>>> 4 in list`<br>`0` |
| not in | Checks to see if an item is NOT in a sequence | `>>> list = [1,2,3]`<br><br>`>>> 1 not in list`<br>`0`<br><br>`>>> 4 not in list`<br>`1` |

## Advanced Topic: Logical Operators and Boolean Returns

Comparison operators always return either 1 or 0 of type `Integer`.

```
>>> 1 > 2
0
>>> 1 < 2
1
```

Logical operators can return more than the `Integer` types 1 or 0, as we see in the following expression, which determines if 0 or (1,2,3) is true.

```
>>> 0 or (1,2,3)
(1, 2, 3)
```

Python equates 0 to false and a nonempty tuple (1, 2, 3) to true, so the logical operator returns the true statement, that is, the (1,2,3) tuple literal.

The following expression determines if 1 < 2 or the integer 5 is true:

```
>>> 1 < 2 or 5
1
```

Because 1 < 2 is true, the expression returns 1, which equates to true, but it equates 5 to true as well; however, only the first true statement in an or statement (1 above) is returned.

The next expression also determines if 1 < 2 or the integer 5 is true, but this time we swap the operands.

```
>>> 5 or 1 < 2
5
```

Once again, only the first true statement is returned, which is now 5.

Like or, and returns the first true operand. However, and is unlike or in that only the last operand can make it true.

```
>>> (1,1) and [2,2]
[2, 2]
>>> [2,2] and (1,1)
(1, 1)
>>> [2,2] and (3,3) and {"four":4}
{'four': 4}
```

Conversely, the first occurrences of a false are returned by and.

```
>>> [1,1] and {} and ()
{}
>>> (1,1) and [] and {}
[]
```

---

### For Programmers: Conditional Operators in Other Languages

C, C++, and Java have a conditional operator that works conveniently as shorthand for and and or. In Java, for example, the following two if statements are equivalent:

```
val = boolean_test ?      true_return : false_return;

if (boolean_test)
      val = true_return;
else
      val = false_return;
```

Python has no conditional operator, but you can simulate one with the form

```
val = (boolean_test and true_return) \
   or false_return
```

This works because or always returns the first true statement and and always returns the last one, so these two statements are equivalent:

```
>>> if ( 3 > 5):
...       num = 1
... else:
...       num = 2
...
>>>num
2

>>> num = (3>5 and 1) or 2
>>> num
2
```

The following two expressions are also equivalent:

```
>>> if ( 5 > 3):
...       num = 1
```

```
... else:
...      num = 2
...
>>>num
1

>>> num = (5>3 and 1) or 2
>>> num
1
```

Be warned: This simulation works only if the expressions `true_return` and `false_return` are *not* equivalent to false. If we need them to be false, we can do something like this:

```
>>> true_return = 0
>>> false_return = 2
>>> num = (5 > 3 and [true_return]) \
    or [false_return]
>>> num
[0]
```

Now the `num` variable is equivalent to a list containing one element, but this isn't exactly what we want. However, since this code is returning a list, we can put the entire expression to the left of the assignment operator in parentheses, which will achieve our desired result.

```
>>> num = ((5 > 3 and [true_return]) or [false_return])[0]
>>> num
0
```

   To sum up, Python's bulletproof equivalent of the conditional operator is

```
val = ((boolean_test and [true_return]) \
        or [false_return])[0]
```

which is no more verbose than another Python expression:

```
if (boolean_test): val = true_return
else: val = false_return
```

   Python's version of the conditional operator is hard to understand and use, so go easy with it. Perhaps one day Python will have a conditional operator of its own (and, I might add, its own += operator).

## Advanced Topic: Bitwise and Shift Operators

If you lack experience with any programming language or with Boolean algebra, you should ignore bitwise operators. Another reason to ignore them is that they're usually associated with low-level programming, and you're learning Python, which is much higher level than C, C++, or even Java. If for some reason you're curious about bitwise operators, any introductory C text will tell you all you need to know. The same goes for shift operators.

Just for the sake of completeness, Table 3–4 describes both operator types. To understand it, you need to know something of hexadecimal and Boolean algebra. (See Chapter 10 for an example of a hexdump file viewer, which uses the shift operators.)

## Operator Precedence

Operator precedence determines the order in which Python evaluates the parts of a statement. It generally follows the operator precedence you learned in high school algebra and is nearly identical to that used in any other common programming language. Here's an example in which y/z is processed before 2 + y, rendering x equal to 4 and not 6.

```
>>> x,y,z=1,4,2
>>> x = 2 + y / z
>>> x
4
```

When in doubt as to which operator will be evaluated first, use parentheses. They prevent many a mistake if you use them to force precedence, and they enhance code readability.

You may occasionally want to force a precedence other than the algebraic default to make it more explicit. The following example shows how to do this:

```
>>> x,y,z = 1,4,2
>>> x = 2 + (y/z)
>>> x
4

>>> x = (2+y) /z
>>> x
3
```

The choice of precedence here depends on which expression—2 + y or y/z—is to be evaluated first. Note, though, that the value of x changes according to the grouping and ends up as either 4 or 3. The first expression, 2 + y/z, is unnecessary except to adorn the code with parentheses for clarity, which is important for code maintainability.

Visit *www.python.org* for a detailed description of operator precedence. For now, the following list shows all operators in their precedence order:

- `[], (), {}, ''`      Parentheses, string conversion
- `seq[index]`      Indexing sequences or dictionaries
- `integer.MAX_INT`      Attribute reference
- `~I`      Bit inversion
- `-i, +i`      Unary minus, unary plus
- `*, /, %`      Multiplication, division, modulus
- `+, -`      Addition, subtraction

**Table 3–4**    *Bitwise and Shift Operators*

| Operator | Description | Interactive Session |
|---|---|---|
| << | Shift left | ```>>> # binary 1111 1111```<br>```>>> x = 0xff```<br><br>```>>> # z = 0011 1111 1100```<br>```>>> z = x << 2```<br>```>>> print (x)```<br>```255```<br><br>```>>> print (z)```<br>```1020``` |
| >> | Shift right | ```>>> # z = 1020```<br>```>>> #z = 1111 1111```<br><br>```>>> z = z >> 2```<br>```>>> z```<br>```255``` |
| & | Bitwise **and** | ```>>> # y = binary 0000 1010```<br>```>>> y = 0x0A```<br>```>>> print (y)```<br>```10```<br><br>```>>> print (x)```<br>```255```<br><br>```>>> z = y & z```<br>```>>> print (z)```<br>```10``` |
| \| | Bitwise **or** | ```>>> #continued example```<br>```>>> z = y | x```<br>```>>> print (z)```<br>```255``` |
| ^ | Bitwise **XOR** | ```>>> z = y ^ x```<br>```>>> z```<br>```245``` |
| ~ | Bitwise **not** | ```>>> y = 0xffffffff```<br>```>>> y```<br>```-1```<br><br>```>>> z = ~y```<br>```>>> z```<br>```0``` |

- `<<,>>`                          Bit shifting, left and right
- [bar], &, ^                     Bitwise operator or, and, XOR
- `<, >, >=, <=, ==, is not,`     Comparison operators
  `is, !=, <>, in, not in`
- `not`                           Logical not
- `and`                           Logical and
- `or`                            Logical or

### Arithmetic with Strings, Lists, and Tuples

As in Java, the addition operator (+) in Python works with string types to concatenate, that is, link strings. (Recall that we used + on strings in Chapter 1.) Unlike in Java, the multiplication operator (*) in Python is used to repeat string values. Consider the following interactive session:

```
>>> love = "I love my family" + (" very " * 4) + "much!"
>>> love
'I love my family very very very very much!'

>>> hugs_and_kisses = "XO" * 20
>>> hugs_and_kisses
'XOXOXOXOXOXOXOXOXOXOXOXOXOXOXOXOXOXOXOXO'
```

In the first line, we concatenate the string "I love my family" with the string "very" multiplied by 4, which gives "very very very very". If we want to sign our letter with hugs and kisses (Xs and Os), we can multiply to save time in a similar way.

Addition and multiplication also work for lists.

```
>>> friends = ["Joey", "Monica", "Ross", "Chandler"]
>>> old_friends = ["Fonz", "Ritchie", "Potsy"]
>>> strange_cast = friends + old_friends
>>> strange_cast
['Joey', 'Monica', 'Ross', 'Chandler', 'Fonz', 'Ritchie', 'Potsy']
```

They work for tuples as well.

```
>>> tuple1 = (1,2,3,4)
>>> tuple2 = ("5", 6L, 7.0, 0x8)
>>> tuple3 = tuple1 + tuple2
>>> tuple3
(1, 2, 3, 4, '5', 6L, 7.0, 8)

>>> tuple4 = tuple1 * 2
>>> tuple4
(1, 2, 3, 4, 1, 2, 3, 4)
```

### Sequence Operators

We've been using sequence operators since Chapter 1, so you've seen most of them. However, some of the operators in Table 3–5 will be new to you.

**Table 3–5**  *Sequence Operators*

| Operator | Description | Interactive Session |
|---|---|---|
| [index] | Get the indexed item | ```>>> nums = (0,1,2,3,4,5,6,7,8,9)```<br>```>>> nums[0]```<br>```0```<br><br>```>>> nums[1]```<br>```1``` |
| [:] | Slice notation | ```>>> nums = (0,1,2,3,4,5,6,7,8,9)```<br><br>```>>> nums [:]```<br>```(0, 1, 2, 3, 4, 5, 6, 7, 8, 9)```<br><br>```>>> nums [5:]```<br>```(5, 6, 7, 8, 9)```<br><br>```>>> nums [:5]```<br>```(0, 1, 2, 3, 4)``` |
| len() | Length | ```>>> nums = (0,1,2,3,4,5,6,7,8,9)```<br><br>```>>> len (nums)```<br>```10``` |
| max() | Get the largest item in the sequence | ```>>> nums = (0,1,2,3,4,5,6,7,8,9)```<br><br>```>>> max(nums)```<br>```9```<br><br>```>>> letters = "abcdefg"```<br>```>>> max (letters)```<br>```'g'``` |
| min() | Get the smallest item in the sequence | ```>>> nums = (0,1,2,3,4,5,6,7,8,9)```<br><br>```>>> min(nums)```<br>```0```<br>```>>> letters = "abcdefg"```<br><br>```>>> min (letters)```<br>```'a'``` |

## Formatting Strings—Modulus

Although not actually modulus, the Python % operator works similarly in string formatting to interpolate variables into a formatting string. If you've programmed in C, you'll notice that % is much like C's printf(), sprintf(), and fprintf() functions.

There are two forms of %, one of which works with strings and tuples, the other with dictionaries.

```
StringOperand % TupleOperand
```

```
StringOperand % DictionaryOperand
```

Both return a new formatted string quickly and easily.

### % Tuple String Formatting

In the `StringOperand % TupleOperand` form, `StringOperand` represents special directives within the string that help format the tuple. One such directive is `%s`, which sets up the format string

```
>>> format = "%s is my friend and %s is %s years old"
```

and creates two tuples, `Ross_Info` and `Rachael_Info`.

```
>>> Ross_Info = ("Ross", "he", 28)
>>> Rachael_Info = ("Rachael", "she", 28)
```

The format string operator (%) can be used within a `print` statement, where you can see that every occurrence of `%s` is respectively replaced by the items in the tuple.

```
>>> print (format % Ross_Info)
Ross is my friend and he is 28 years old
```

```
>>> print (format % Rachael_Info)
Rachael is my friend and she is 28 years old
```

Also note that `%s` automatically converts the last item in the tuple to a reasonable string representation. Here's an example of how it does this using a list:

```
>>> bowling_scores = [190, 135, 110, 95, 195]
```

```
>>> name = "Ross"
```

```
>>> strScores = "%s's bowling scores were %s" \
...                         % (name, bowling_scores)
>>> print strScores
Ross's bowling scores were [190, 135, 110, 95, 195]
```

First, we create a list variable called `bowling_scores` and then a string variable called `name`. We then use a string literal for a format string (`StringOperand`) and use a tuple containing `name` and `bowling_scores`.

### Format Directives

Table 3–6 covers all of the format directives and provides a short example of usage for each. Note that the tuple argument containing a single item can be denoted with the % operator as `item`, or `(item)`.

**Table 3–6**   *Format Directives*

| Directive | Description | Interactive Session |
|-----------|-------------|---------------------|
| %s | Represents a value as a string | ```>>> list = ["hi", 1, 1.0, 1L]```<br>```>>> "%s" % list```<br>```"['hi', 1, 1.0, 1L]"``` |
| | | ```>>> "list equals %s" % list```<br>```"list equals ['hi', 1, 1.0, 1L]"``` |
| %i | Integer | ```>>> "i = %i" % (5)```<br>```'i = 5'``` |
| | | ```>>> "i = %3i" % (5)```<br>```'i = 5'``` |
| %d | Decimal integer | ```>>> "d = %d" % 5```<br>```'d = 5'``` |
| | | ```>>> "%3d" % (3)```<br>```' 3'``` |
| %x | Hexadecimal integer | ```>>> "%x" % (0xff)```<br>```'ff'``` |
| | | ```>>> "%x" % (255)```<br>```'ff'``` |
| %x | Hexadecimal integer | ```>>> "%x" % (0xff)```<br>```'ff'``` |
| | | ```>>> "%x" % (255)```<br>```'ff'``` |
| %o | Octal integer | ```>>> "%o" % (255)```<br>```377``` |
| | | ```>>> "%o" % (0377)```<br>```377``` |
| %u | Unsigned integer | ```>>> print "%u" % -2000```<br>```2147481648``` |
| | | ```>>> print "%u" % 2000```<br>```2000``` |
| %e | Float exponent | ```>>> print "%e" % (30000000L)```<br>```3.000000e+007``` |
| | | ```>>> "%5.2e" % (300000000L)```<br>```'3.00e+008'``` |

*(continued)*

**Table 3–6**    *Format Directives (continued)*

| Directive | Description | Interactive Session |
|---|---|---|
| %f | Float | ```>>> "check = %1.2f" % (3000)```<br>```'check = 3000.00'```<br><br>```>>> "payment = $%1.2f" % 3000```<br>```'payment = $3000.00'``` |
| %g | Float exponent | ```>>> "%3.3g" % 100```<br>```'100.'```<br><br>```>>> "%3.3g" % 1000000000000L```<br>```'10.e11'```<br><br>```>>> "%g" % 100```<br>```'100.'``` |
| %c | ASCII character | ```>>> "%c" % (97)```<br>```'a'```<br><br>```>>> "%c" % 97```<br>```'a'```<br><br>```>>> "%c" % (97)```<br>```'a'``` |

Table 3–7 shows how flags can be used with the format directives to add leading zeroes or spaces to a formatted number. They should be inserted immediately after the %.

**Table 3–7**    *Format Directive Flags*

| Flag | Description | Interactive Session |
|---|---|---|
| # | Forces octal to have a 0 prefix; forces hex to have a 0x prefix | ```>>> "%#x" % 0xff```<br>```'0xff'```<br><br>```>>> "%#o" % 0377```<br>```'0ff'``` |
| + | Forces a positive number to have a sign | ```>>> "%+d" % 100```<br>```'+100'``` |
| – | Left justification (default is right) | ```>>> "%-5d, %-5d" % (10,10)```<br>```'10   , 10 '``` |
| " " | Precedes a positive number with a blank space | ```>>> "% d,% d" % (-10, 10)```<br>```'-100,10'``` |
| 0 | 0 padding instead of spaces | ```>>> "%05d" % (100,)```<br>```'00100'``` |

### Advanced Topic: Using the %d, %i, %f, and %e Directives for Formatting Numbers

The % directives format numeric types: %i works with Integer; %f and %e work with Float with and without scientific notation, respectively.

```
>>> "%i, %f, %e" % (1000, 1000, 1000)
'1000, 1000.000000, 10.000000e+002'
```

Notice how awkward all of those zeroes look. You can limit the length of precision and neaten up your code like this:

```
>>> "%i, %2.2f, %2.2e" % (1000, 1000, 1000)
'1000, 1000.00, 10.00e+002'
```

The %2.2f directive tells Python to format the number as at least two characters and to cut the precision to two characters after the decimal point. This is useful for printing floating-point numbers that represent currency.

```
>>> "Your monthly payments are $%1.2f" % (payment)
'Your monthly payments are $444.43'
```

All % directives have the form %min.precision(type), where min is the minimum length of the field, precision is the length of the mantissa (the numbers on the right side of the decimal point), and type is the type of directive (e, f, i, or d). If the precision field is missing, the directive can take the form %min(type), so, for example, %5d ensures that a decimal number has at least 5 fields and %20f ensures that a floating-point number has at least 20.

Let's look at the use of these directives in an interactive session.

```
>>> "%5d" % (100,)
'  100'
>>> "%20f" % (100,)
'          100.000000'
```

Here's how to truncate the float's mantissa to 2 with %20.2f.

```
>>> "%20.2f" % (100,)
'              100.00'
```

The padding that precedes the directive is useful for printing rows and columns of data for reporting because it makes the printed output easy to read. This can be seen in the following example (from *format.py*):

```
    # Create two rows
row1 = (100, 10000, 20000, 50000, 6000, 6, 5)
row2 = (1.0, 2L, 5, 2000, 56, 6.0, 7)

    #
    # Print out the rows without formatting
print "here is an example of the columns not lining up"
print `row1` + "\n" + `row2`
print
```

```
#
# Create a format string that forces the number
# to be at least 3 characters long to the left
# and 2 characters to the right of the decimal point
format = "(%3.2e, %3.2e, %3.2e, %3.2e, " + \
         "%3.2e, %3.2e, %3.2e)"

#
# Create a string for both rows
# using the format operator
strRow1 = format % row1
strRow2 = format % row2
print "here is an example of the columns" + \
      " lining up using \%e"

print strRow1 + "\n" + strRow2
print

    # Do it again this time with the %i and %d directive
format1 = "(%6i, %6i, %6i, %6i, %6i, %6i, %6i)"
format2 = "(%6d, %6d, %6d, %6d, %6d, %6d, %6d)"
strRow1 = format1 % row1
strRow2 = format2 % row2
print "here is an example of the columns" + \
      " lining up using \%i and \%d"

print strRow1 + "\n" + strRow2
print

here is an example of the columns not lining up
(100, 10000, 20000, 50000, 6000, 6, 5)
(1.0, 2L, 5, 2000, 56, 6.0, 7)

here is an example of the columns lining up using \%e
(1.00e+002, 1.00e+004, 2.00e+004, 5.00e+004, 6.00e+003, 6.00e+000, 5.00e+000)
(1.00e+000, 2.00e+000, 5.00e+000, 2.00e+003, 5.60e+001, 6.00e+000, 7.00e+000)

here is an example of the columns lining up using \%i and \%d
( 100,    10000,    20000,    50000,    6000,    6,    5)
(   1,        2,        5,     2000,      56,    6,    7)
```

You can see that the %3.2e directive permits a number to take up only three spaces plus the exponential whereas %6d and %6i permit at least six spaces. Note that %i and %d do the same thing that %e does. Most C programmers are familiar with %d but may not be familiar with %i, which is a recent addition to that language.

## String % Dictionary

Another useful Python feature for formatting strings is StringOperand % DictionaryOperand. This form allows you to customize and print named fields in the string. %(Income)d formats the value referenced by the Income key. Say, for example, that you have a dictionary like the one here:

```
Monica =    {
            "Occupation": "Chef",
            "Name" : "Monica",
            "Dating" : "Chandler",
            "Income" : 40000
            }
```

With `%(Income)d`, this is expressed as

```
>>> "%(Income)d" % Monica
'40000'
```

Now let's say you have three best friends, whom you define as dictionaries named Monica, Chandler, and Ross.

```
Monica =        {
                "Occupation": "Chef",
                "Name" : "Monica",
                "Dating" : "Chandler",
                "Income" : 40000
                }
Ross =              {
                "Occupation": "Scientist Museum Dude",
                "Name" : "Ross",
                "Dating" : "Rachael",
                "Income" : 70000
                }
Chandler =      {
                "Occupation": "Buyer",
                "Name" : "Chandler",
                "Dating" : "Monica",
                "Income" : 65000
                }
```

To write them a form letter, you can create a format string called message that uses all of the above dictionaries' keywords.

```
message = "%(Name)s, %(Occupation)s, %(Dating)s," \
          "    %(Income)2.2f"
```

Notice that `%(Income)2.2f` formats this with a floating-point precision of 2, which is good for currency. The output is

```
Chandler, Buyer, Monica, 65000.00
Ross, Scientist Museum Dude, Rachael, 70000.00
Monica, Chef, Chandler, 40000.00
```

You can then print each dictionary using the format string operator.

```
print message % Chandler
print message % Ross
print message % Monica
```

To generate your form letter and print it out to the screen, you first create a format string called `dialog`.

```
dialog = """
Hi %(Name)s,

How are you doing? How is %(Dating)s?
Are you still seeing %(Dating)s?

How is work at the office?
I bet it is hard being a %(Occupation)s.
I know I could not do it.
"""
```

Then you print out each dictionary using the `dialog` format string with the `%` format string operator.

```
print dialog % Ross
print dialog % Chandler
print dialog % Monica
```

The output is

```
Hi Ross,

How are you doing? How is Rachael?
Are you still seeing Rachael?

How is work at the office?
I bet it is hard being a Scientist Museum Dude.
I know I could not do it.

Hi Chandler,
How are you doing? How is Monica?
Are you still seeing Monica?

How is work at the office?
I bet it is hard being a Buyer.
I know I could not do it.

Hi Monica,
How are you doing? How is Chandler?
Are you still seeing Chandler?

How is work at the office?
I bet it is hard being a Chef.
I know I could not do it.
```

`%(Income)d` is a useful, flexible feature. You just saw how much time it can save you in writing form letters. Imagine what it can do for writing reports.

## *Summary*

String formatting is the way we organize instructions so that Python can understand how to incorporate data in the creation of strings. How strings are formatted determines the presentation of this data. The basis of string formatting is its use of the formatting directives.

Logical operators (and, or, not) return true or false values. Comparison operators (in, not in, is, is not, ==, !=, <>, >, >=, <, <=) compare two values—is one value greater than another, or is one value not equal to another? Comparisons always return 1 for true and 0 for false.

Any value in Python equates to a Boolean true or false. A false can be equal to none, a zero of numeric type (0, 01, 0.0), an empty sequence ('', (), []), or an empty dictionary ({}). All other values are considered true.

Sequences, tuples, lists, and strings can be added or multiplied by a numeric type with the addition and multiplication operators (+, *), respectively. Strings can be formatted with tuples and dictionaries using the format directives %i, %d, %f, and %e. Formatting flags can be used with these directives.

# CHAPTER 4 · *Control Flow*

---

————————————————— *Terms in This Chapter* —————————————————

- ◊ *Argument*
- ◊ *break and continue statements*
- ◊ *Built-in (intrinsic) functions*
- ◊ *Compound statement*
- ◊ *else/elif clause*
- ◊ *for loop*

- ◊ *Function*
- ◊ *if, for, and while statements*
- ◊ *Iteration*
- ◊ *Key/value pair*
- ◊ *Looping*
- ◊ *Method*
- ◊ *Modulus operator*

- ◊ *Nested dictionary*
- ◊ *Sequence*
- ◊ *String format operator*
- ◊ *Subordinate statement*
- ◊ *Suite*

Control flow instructs Python, on the basis of certain conditions, to execute particular statements and not others. It also allows repeated execution of statements until some conditions are met and permits branching of conditional execution. In this chapter, we'll cover the `if`, `while`, and `for` compound statements, all of which control statement execution in Python.

---

## The if Statement

The `if` statement conditionally executes a statement's suite. One form is shown here:

```
if(expression):
    suite
```

Python has to determine whether if's expression is true or false. If the expression is true, Python executes the suite; if not, it doesn't. As we discussed in Chapter 3, Python doesn't have a `Boolean` (true/false) type. Instead, it uses any numeric value other than zero to indicate true and uses zero, any empty sequence, and the value `None` to indicate false. For example, the following will print `"hello"` because the expression contains a value of 1.

```
>>> # 1 is true
>>> if(1):
...     print("hello")
...
hello
```

Notice that the subordinate statement, `print`, is indented, which shows that it's part of the suite associated with `if`. In interactive mode, you indent an `if` suite with the Tab key. The . . . prompt indicates a subordinate statement.

The next four statements further illustrate how Python determines whether or not to execute an `if` statement based on the value in the expression.

```
>>> #0 is an integer and 0 means false
>>> if (0):
...     print("goodbye")
...
>>> #3.3 is a float and not equal to 0 so it is true
>>> if (3.3):
...     print("hello")
...
hello
>>> #0.00 is equal to 0, which means false
>>> if (0.000):
...     print("goodbye")
...
>>> if(0.000000000000000000001):
...     print("hello")
...
hello
```

`if` can determine if a list is empty, as seen in the `checkSeq()` function shown in the first example below. The result is shown in the second example. Remember, an empty list indicates false.

```
>>> def checkSeq(seq):
...     if (seq):
...             print "has item"
...     else :
...             print "empty"
...
>>> non_empty_list = [1,2,3]
>>> empty_list = []
```

```
>>> checkSeq(empty_list)
empty
>>> checkSeq(non_empty_list)
has item
```

Typically, if statements contain expressions that use comparison and logical operators. To illustrate, let's say that a woman is looking for her perfect man—tall, dark, and handsome; the strong, quiet type between the ages of 27 and 35. In Python, she can express her preferences like this:

```
if (tall and dark and handsome and not talksAlot and (age>27) and (age<35)):
#(same line)
print ("Hi handsome")
```

Here's an interactive session that uses the above information to help our female friend meet the man of her dreams:

```
>>> tall = 1
>>> dark = 1
>>> handsome = 1
>>> talksAlot = 0
>>> age = 32
>>> if (tall and dark and handsome and not talksAlot and (age>27) and
(age<35)):
...     print("Hi handsome")
...
Hi handsome
```

At the beginning of the chapter, we saw the basic form of if. We will look at two other forms, containing else and elif clauses, respectively, in the two sections that follow.

## else

The else form appears as

```
if(expression):
        suite 1
else:
        suite 2
```

Before it can execute this expression, Python must determine, as usual, whether it's true. If so, Python executes the first suite; if not ("else"), it executes the second suite. The following simple greet() function illustrates the if:else form:

```
>>> def greet(name, sex):
...             #if female print Ms.
...     if(sex == "female"):
...             print ("Hello Ms. " + name)
...             #if male print Mr.
...     else:
...             print("Hello Mr. " + name)
...
```

```
>>>     # greet James who is a male
>>> greet("James Agular", "male")
Hello Mr. James Agular

>>>     # greet Jane who is a female
>>> greet("Jane Doe", "female")
Hello Ms. Jane Doe
```

We can see that the expression sex == "female" is false, which means that the first time we invoke greet() Python will execute the second suite and print ("Hello Mr. " + name"). However, the second time we invoke greet(), the expression sex = = "female" is true, so Python executes the first suite.

## Separating Suites

These two if statements illustrate the two styles of separating suites—semicolons and indenting:

```
>>> sex = "female"
>>> name = "Fran Dresser"

>>> #First if statement
>>> if (sex == "female"):print("Hello,"); print("It's good to see you Ms." + name)
...
Hello,
It's good to see you Ms.Fran Dresser

>>> #second if statement
>>> if (sex == "female"):
...     print("Hello,")
...     print ("It's good to see you Ms. " + name)
...
Hello,
It's good to see you Ms. Fran Dresser
```

## elif

The elif ("else-if") clause appears as

```
if(expression 1):
        suite 1
elif(expression 2):
        suite 2
else:
        suite 3
```

which Python translates as "If the expression is true, execute the corresponding suite; else, if the next expression is true, execute the corresponding suite," and so on. The else clause here is actually optional.

Here's an example of `elif` based on the previous interactive `greet()` session:

```
>>> def greet(name, sex):
...     if( sex == "female"):
...             print("Hello Ms. " + name)
...     elif( sex == "male"):
...             print ("Hello Mr. " + name)
...     elif( sex == "undeclared"):
...             print("Hello " + name)
...     else:
...             print("Hello " + name)
...
```

As you can see from the added clauses, there can be multiple `elif`s in an `if` statement. However, the `if` clause stays the same and uses the same expression. The second clause, `...elif (sex = = "male"):`, checks to see if the sex is male and, if so, prints out `"Hello Mr"`. The third clause, `...elif(sex == "undeclared"):`, checks to see if the sex has even been declared; if not, it prints a simple `"Hello"`.

So, if we invoke the `greet()` function like this, the second suite, associated with the first `elif` clause, is executed:

```
>>> greet("Bob Dole", "male")
Hello Mr. Bob Dole
```

But if we invoke it like this, the first suite, associated with the `if` clause, is executed:

```
>>> greet("Jane Smith", "female")
Hello Ms. Jane Smith
```

Similarly, if we invoke the `greet()` function like this, the third suite, associated with the second `elif` clause, is executed:

```
>>> greet("Jean Costello", "undeclared")
Hello Jean Costello
```

However, if we invoke it like this, the `else` clause's suite is executed:

```
>>> greet("Jean Smith", "")
Hello Jean Smith
```

Notice that `else` is the default, which means that its suite is executed if none of the other clauses' expressions turn out to be true.

To sum up, the `if` statement is used for conditional execution of suites. As a compound statement, it consists of the `if`, `elif`, and `else` clauses, each of which has an associated suite. By evaluating the expression in each clause until one is found to be true, Python determines which clause's suite to execute. As soon as it finds the right one, it stops evaluating. If all of the expressions are found to be false, Python executes the `else` clause's suite. If `else` isn't there and all other clause's expressions are false, no suite is executed.

## *The while Statement*

The `while` statement repetitively executes a suite until a condition is met. Its basic form is

```
while( expression ):
    suite
```

which you can think of in English as "While the expression remains true, execute the suite repeatedly." Python carries out this instruction by returning to the top of the statement to check if the expression is still true; if so, it executes the suite a second time and once again returns to the top (this is referred to as looping), repeating this process until the expression becomes false. Once that happens, Python stops executing, and the `while` statement's execution comes to a halt.

One use of the `while` statement is to remove items from a list—for example, every occurrence of the string `cat` from the list `pets`.

```
>>> pets = ["cat", "dog", "bird", "fish", "cat", "cat", "cat"] #same line
```

We know from Chapter 2 that a list has a `count()` method that returns the count of an item in the list and a `remove()` method that removes the first occurrence of an item. Our goal is to remove the `cat` string from the `pet` list while its count is greater than zero. We express this in Python as

```
>>> pets = ["cat","dog", "bird", "fish", "cat", "cat", "cat"] #same line
>>> while(pets.count("cat") > 0):
...     pets.remove("cat")
...     print (pets)
...
```

To demonstrate what happens at each iteration of the loop, we print each iteration's resulting `pets` list to get the following output:

```
['dog', 'bird', 'fish', 'cat', 'cat', 'cat']
['dog', 'bird', 'fish', 'cat', 'cat']
['dog', 'bird', 'fish', 'cat']
```

The first `cat` was removed on the first execution of the `while` statement, but there are still three occurrences of `cat` remaining, so the `while` loop's suite is executed three more times.

### break

The `break` statement allows you to break out of a `while` statement before it loops back to the top. This is useful, for example, when inputting several name/phone-number pairs in an address book application. The following statement uses the `raw_input()` built-in function (which reads a line from the console). An empty string indicates that inputting is complete:

```
>>> while(1):
...         name = raw_input("Enter in the name: ")
...         if(name == ""):
...                 break
...         phone_number = raw_input("Enter in the phone number: ")
...         #Do something useful with the name and phone_number
```

Notice the while(1): expression, which in effect tells Python to loop the suite forever. However, the break statement stops this "infinite looping" by instructing Python to break out of the loop if it hits an empty name string. Here's the interactive session, followed by its output:

```
...         if(name == ""):
...                 break
Enter in the name: Rick Hightower
Enter in the phone number: 555-5555
Enter in the name: Adam Carr
Enter in the phone number: 555-6666
Enter in the name:
>>>
```

As you can see, the last time we're asked to enter a name, we hit Enter so that the string returned from raw_input is empty.

### continue

The continue statement is similar to the break statement. However, instead of instructing Python to break out, it tells it to return to the top of the while statement, that is, where the expression is evaluated. We'll stick with the address book example to illustrate continue, adding the ability to enter an address. If the first line of the address is empty, we can assume that the user doesn't want to exercise this option, and we go back to the top of the loop.

```
>>> while (1):
...         name = raw_input("Enter in the name: ")
...         if (name == ""):
...                 break
...         phone_number = raw_input("Enter in the phone number: ")
...         address_line1 = raw_input("Enter address line one: ")
...         if (address_line1 == ""):
...                 continue
...         address_line2 = raw_input("Enter address line two: ")
...         address_line3 = raw_input("Enter address line three: ")
...         #Do something useful with the data we just collected
...
```

As with break, while(1) triggers an infinite loop of the associated suite. Again, the only way to end the loop is via the break statement.

Since we've added the address option, we test to see if address_line1 is empty. If so, we continue with the next entry, that is, the next iteration of the loop, by adding the following statement:

```
...         address_line1 = raw_input("Enter address line one: ")
...         if (address_line1 == ""):
...                 continue
```

In English, this says, "Get the first line of a person's address from the user and test to see if it's an empty string. If so, continue executing at the top of the while statement; in other words, get the next person's information."

Below are samples of the output, in order, from the four iterations of the preceding name/phone-number program.

```
Enter in the name: Rick Hightower
Enter in the phone number: 555-5555
Enter address line one: 123 Main St.
Enter address line two: Tucson, AZ
Enter address line three: 85226

Enter in the name: Adam Carr
Enter in the phone number: 555-6666
Enter address line one:

Enter in the name: Bob Ninny
Enter in the phone number: 555-7777
Enter address line one: 1234 South Dobson
Enter address line two: Mesa, AZ
Enter address line three: 85228

Enter in the name:
```

In the first iteration, we fill in all fields for Rick Hightower, including the optional address fields. In the second, we fill in only Adam Carr's name and phone number, and at the first address field, hit Enter. The statement below instructs Python to return to the top of the while statement to begin executing again, thus skipping the rest of the statements in while's suite:

```
...         if (address_line1 == ""):
...                 continue
```

In the third iteration, all of Bob Ninny's fields are filled in. In the fourth iteration, when the program asks us to enter a name, we hit Enter, causing raw_input() to return an empty string. This means that the following statement forces the while loop to terminate:

```
...         if(name == ""):
...                 break
```

## else

Like if, while can contain an else clause:

```
while (expression):
      suite 1
else:
      suite 2
```

Like if's else, while's else repeatedly tests the expression. If the expression is true, the first suite is executed. If the expression is false, or becomes false during the loop, else's suite is executed, and the while loop ends. If the executed suite contains a break statement, the loop terminates, and the else suite is *not* executed.

Continuing with our address book example, we'll use the else clause to add the option of quitting the program by sending an email of the address book to someone—say, me. Typing in quit when we get the name means that we want to break—not send—the email. Entering " " (empty string) means that we want to execute the statements in the else clause and send the email. Of course, we won't actually send any email, so the emailData() function is commented out.

```
name = " "
while (name != ""):
        name = raw_input("Enter in the name: ")
        if (name == ""):
                continue
        elif (name == "quit"):
                break
        phone_number = raw_input("Enter in the phone number: ")
        address_line1 = raw_input("Enter address line one: ")
        if (address_line1 == ""):
                continue
        address_line2 = raw_input("Enter address line two: ")
        address_line3 = raw_input("Enter address line three: ")
        #do something useful with the addresses
else:
        print("send the email to Rick")
        #emailAddresses("rick_m_hightower@emailcompany.com")
```

Let's break down the changes made to the program.

First, if the while clause encounters an empty string for the name variable, it exits the loop.

```
while (name != ""):
```

If we pass an empty string for name, the continue clause kicks in, returning execution to the beginning of the while statement. Then the expression in the while clause is evaluated. The empty string there allows the while loop to terminate gracefully, as opposed to breaking out, so the else clause is executed.

```
elif (name == "quit"):
                break
```

The elif clause in the if statement ensures that, if the name string equals quit, we break out of the loop (we terminate ungracefully). So the else clause *isn't* executed, allowing us to quit without sending the email, and I don't get my address list.

```
else:
        print("send the email to Rick")
        #emailAddresses("rick_m_hightower@emailcompany.com")
```

Here we've added the `else` clause to the `while` loop with the same indentation as that of the `while` clause of the `while` statement. Try executing this script.

## The for Statement

The `for` statement repeatedly executes a suite of statements as it iterates through the items in a sequence. It appears as

```
for item in sequence :
        suite
```

The expression should be a valid sequence (a tuple, string, or list). At the beginning of each iteration, the next item in the sequence is assigned to the `item` variable, and the suite is executed. This continues until all items have been dealt with.

To illustrate `for`, let's say that we have a list of email addresses for a monthly newsletter.

```
>>> email_list = ["rick_m_hightower@emailcompany.com",
"adam_s_carr@hottermail.com", "bill_g_smith@hottestmail.com"]
>>>
>>> for address in email_list:
...        print ("Sending email to " + address)
...        # sendEmail(address, "Nothing new here")
Sending email to rick_m_hightower@emailcompany.com
Sending email to adam_s_carr@hottermail.com
Sending email to bill_g_smith@hottestmail.com
>>>
```

Like the `while` loop, the `for` loop uses an `else` clause—when there are no more items in the list, `else` is executed. The `break` and `continue` statements work in `for` as they do in `while`.

### The range() Function and for Loops

The `for` loop in Python can be used similarly to the `for` loop in Java and C with the `range()` function, whose purpose is to return a list of numeric values. The simplest example is a list of 1 through 9 in increments of 1.

```
>>> range(1,10)
[1, 2, 3, 4, 5, 6, 7, 8, 9]
```

Other examples of `range()` follow. Respectively, they illustrate 1 through 20 by increments of 2; 0 through 100 by increments of 10; −100 through 200 by increments of 30; and 100 through −100 by increments of −20.

```
>>> range(1, 20, 2)
[1, 3, 5, 7, 9, 11, 13, 15, 17, 19]

>>> range (0, 100, 10)
[0, 10, 20, 30, 40, 50, 60, 70, 80, 90]
```

```
>>> range (-100, 200, 30)
[-100, -70, -40, -10, 20, 50, 80, 110, 140, 170]
>>> range (100, -100, -20)
[100, 80, 60, 40, 20, 0, -20, -40, -60, -80]
```

To create a loop that iterates from 0 through 100 by increments of 10, we enter

```
>>> for x in range(0, 100, 10):
...     print("x equals " + `x`)
...
```

which outputs

```
x equals 0
x equals 10
x equals 20
x equals 30
x equals 40
x equals 50
x equals 60
x equals 70
x equals 80
x equals 90
```

Or we can iterate backward from 100 to 0 by decrements of 10 by entering

```
>>> for x in range (100, 0, -10):
...     print("x equals " + `x`)
...
```

which outputs

```
x equals 100
x equals 90
x equals 80
x equals 70
x equals 60
x equals 50
x equals 40
x equals 30
x equals 20
x equals 10
```

### xrange()

xrange() is nearly identical to range(), except that it doesn't create individual items in a range until requested to do so, which makes it more efficient than range() for large ranges. Here's an example of xrange(), called *xrange.py*, followed by its output:

```
print ("This for loop uses xrange, which lazily creates members in the range")
for x in xrange (-1000000000, 1000000000):
```

```
     if( (x % 100000) == 0): print (`x`)
     if (x == -999900000): break
print ("Get ready to hit control C")
print ("This for loop uses range")

for x in range (-1000000000, 1000000000):
     if( (x % 100000) == 0): print (`x`)
     if (x == -999900000): break

>>> import xrange
This for loop uses xrange, which lazily creates members in the range
-1000000000
-999900000
Get ready to hit control C
This for loop uses range
Out of Memory
```

Notice that when we try to create the second range we run out of memory. In essence, the second range() tries to create a list containing 2 billion integers, each 32 bits wide (4 bytes). For this we need a computer with 8 billion bytes, or 8 gigabytes, of memory.

---

## Putting It All Together

Now it's time to create a program that uses everything we've learned so far. This program will generate a list of house prices and find their average (mean, mode, and median) and range. The following sections will describe each function in turn.

### getRange()

getRange() iterates through a set of numbers passed to it and calculates the minimum and maximum values. It then returns these values and their range in a tuple.

```
def getRange (nums):

     min = 300000000
     max = -300000000
for item in nums:
     if (item > max): max = item
     if (item < min): min = item

return (min, max, max-min)
```

First getRange() declares two variables, min and max. The min variable refers to a very large number, so the first item extracted from the list is less than that number and is assigned the min value. The max variable contains a negative number, so the first item extracted will be more than the large negative value and is assigned to the max variable.

> ### Making getRange() More Efficient
>
> The getRange() example will work only if the numbers passed to it are in the range of min and max. To make it more general purpose, we can use either of the following:
>
> ```
> from java.lang import Double
> ```
>
> ```
> from java.lang import Double
> ```
>
> and then either of these:
>
> ```
> min = Double.MAX_VALUE
> max = Double.MIN_VALUE
> min = Integer.MAX_VALUE
> max = Integer.MIN_VALUE
> ```
>
> This will make the function work well with Integer or Double types. The question is how well it will work with Long types. We'll have our answer shortly.

To figure min and max, getRange() iterates through the nums sequence.

```
for item in nums:
    if (item > max): max = item
    if (item < min): min = item
```

The expression item > max determines if the item's value is greater than max. If so, max is assigned to it, as expressed by this compound statement:

```
if (item > max): max = item
```

The following compound statement indicates that the item's value is less than min, so it's assigned to min:

```
if (item < min): min = item
```

When the loop stops iterating through the values, getRange() returns min, max, and max-min (range).

```
return (min, max, max-min)
```

The approach just described is a simple one, but it has a flaw. It works only if the numbers passed to xrange() are within max-min. The solution is the nums variable, which is a sequence with an intrinsic operation (otherwise known as a built-in function) for finding min and max in a list. nums is an improvement over getRange() because it's much shorter and can work with all numeric types as well as all Longs, Floats, and Doubles at their maximum range of precision. With nums there's no for loop and no figuring out what max and min should be initialized to (that is, given a default value).

Here's an example of nums:

```
def getRange2 (nums):
    return (min(nums), max(nums), max(nums)-min(nums))
```

### getMean()

The getMean() function figures out the mean of a number sequence. It iterates through the sequence, adding all of the values together and storing them in sum. It then figures out the mean by dividing sum by the sequence length.

In the following getMean() example, notice the use of the sample argument, the for loop, the if and else clauses, and the len() built-in function (which determines the length of a sequence).

```
def getMean (nums, sample):
    """
    Define mean that finds two types of mean,
    namely: population mean and sample mean
    """

            sum = 0.0        # holds the value of sum

                #
                # iterate through the sequence of
    # numbers and sum them
            for x in nums:
                sum = sum + x

                #
                # Check to see if this is a sample mean
            if(sample):
                average = sum / (len(nums)-1)

                #
                # Else it is a population mean
            else:
                average = sum / len(nums)
            return average
```

Here's the breakdown.

First we create a variable called sum that holds the sum.

```
sum = 0.0
```

Then we iterate through the nums sequence, accumulating the value of the item x.

```
for x in nums:
    sum = sum + x
```

Next, using the sample argument, we check to see if this is a sample mean. If so, we figure the average by dividing sum by the number of items in nums less 1, or we divide the sum by the number of items in the nums sequence.

```
if(sample):
        average = sum / (len(nums)-1)
        #
        # Else it is a population mean
else:
        average = sum / len(nums)
```

Finally we return the average.

```
return average
```

## getMode()

The getMode() function finds the value that repeats most often in a sequence. First it duplicates the sequence so it can modify it. Then it iterates through the items in the nums sequence, counting occurrences of the current items with the built-in count() method. Once getMode() counts an item, it removes it from the duplicated sequence.

In the getMode() example that follows, notice the use of the for and while loops, the if statement, the count() method, and the nested for loop.

```
def getMode (nums):
        """Find the number that repeats the most. """

            #
            # make a duplicate copy of the nums argument
        duplicate = nums[:]
        highest_count = -100
        mode = None

            #
            # calculate the highest_count and the mode
        for item in nums:

            count = duplicate.count(item)
            if (count == 0): continue

            if (count > highest_count):
                    highest_count = count
                    mode = item

            while(duplicate.count(item) > 0):
                    duplicate.remove(item)

        return mode
```

Let's break this down.

First we duplicate the nums sequence and create a variable to hold highest_count (and assign it a negative starting number) and a variable to hold the nums sequence mode.

```
duplicate = nums[:]
highest_count = -100
mode = None
```

Next we iterate through each item in nums and count duplicate nums occurrences.

```
for item in nums:

    count = duplicate.count(item)
    if (count == 0): continue
```

As we iterate through the list, we see if the current count is greater than highest_count. If it is, we assign it to highest_count and item to mode.

```
if (count > highest_count):
    highest_count = count
    mode = item
```

Continuing our iteration, we remove all occurrences of the item from the duplicate sequence with the following while statement:

```
while(duplicate.count(item) > 0):
    duplicate.remove(item)
```

Finally we return mode.

```
return mode
```

## getMedian()

The getMedian() function finds the middlemost value once the sequence is sorted. In the following getMedian() example, notice the use of the modulus operator (%), the if statement, the else clause, and the built-in sort() operation.

```
def getMedian (nums):

        "Find the Median number"

                # create a duplicate since
    # we are going to modify it
        seq = nums[:]

                #sort the list of numbers
        seq.sort()

        median = None # to hold the median value

        length = len(seq) # to hold the length of the seq

                # Check to see if the length is an even number
        if ( ( length % 2) == 0):
                    # since it is an even number
                    # add the two middle numbers together
            index = length / 2
            median = (seq[index-1] + seq[index]) /2.0
    else:
                    # since it is an odd number
                    # just grab the middle number
            index = (length / 2)
            median = seq[index]
        return median
```

Once again, let's break it down.

First we duplicate the nums sequence and sort the duplicate (seq).

```
seq.sort()
```

Then, with the expression length%2, we check if the length is an even number. (Remember that the modulus operator returns the remainder.) If the length is even, the expression length%2 returns zero, and we calculate the median by adding together the two most central numbers and figuring their average.

```
length = len(seq)

if ( ( length % 2) == 0):
    index = length / 2
    median = (seq[index-1] + seq[index]) /2.0
```

If the length is odd, we grab the middle value.

```
else:
    index = (length / 2)
    median = seq[index]
```

Finally we return the median.

```
return median
```

### reportStatistics()

reportStatistics() calls all of the functions implemented in our house prices example—getMean(), getMode(), getRange(), getMedian(), and nested dictionaries—and stores their return values in two dictionaries, averages and ranges. It puts these dictionaries in another dictionary called report, which it returns.

```
def reportStatistics (nums):
            # get central tendencies
    averages = {
            "mean":getMean(nums,0),
            "median":getMedian(nums),
            "mode":getMode(nums)
            }

            # get range
    range = getRange(nums)

            # put ranges in a dictionary
    ranges = {
            "min":range[0],
            "max":range[1],
            "range":range[2]
            }

    report = {
            "averages": averages,
            "ranges": ranges
            }

    return report
```

Breaking this down, we first get the averages—mean, median, and mode—using getMean(), getMedian(), and getMode(). Notice that "mean":getMedian defines a key/value pair.

```
averages = {
      "mean":getMean(nums,0),
      "median":getMedian(nums),
      "mode":getMode(nums)
      }
```

Then we get the range parameters—min, max, and max–min—from getRange(). We use range[0], range[1], and range[2] in the returned sequence. Notice that "min":range[0] defines a key/value pair in the ranges dictionary.

```
      # get range
range = getRange(nums)
      # put ranges in a dictionary
ranges = {
      "min":range[0],
      "max":range[1],
      "range":range[2]
      }
```

Now we define a dictionary called report that contains the averages and ranges dictionaries.

```
report = {
      "averages": averages,
      "ranges": ranges
      }
```

Lastly we return the report dictionary.

```
return report
```

### Using reportStatistics()

RunReport() uses reportStatistics() to get the report dictionary it needs to print out the report. In the following runReport() example, note the use of the string format operator (%), the %f format directive, nested dictionaries, and the use of the format operator with a dictionary.

```
from chap4 import reportStatistics
house_in_awahtukee = [100000, 120000, 150000, 200000, 65000, 100000]
report = reportStatistics(house_in_awahtukee)

range_format = """
Range:
The least expensive house is %(min)20.2f
The most expensive house is %(max)20.2f
The range of house price is %(range)20.2f
"""
average_format = """
Averages:
The mean house price is %(mean)20.2f
The mode for house price is %(mode)20.2f
The median house price is %(median)20.2f
"""

print range_format % report["ranges"]
print average_format % report["averages"]
```

Here's the output:

```
Range:
The least expensive house is 65000.00
The most expensive house is 200000.00
The range of house price is 135000.00

Averages:
The mean house price is 122500.00
The mode for house price is 100000.00
The median house price is 110000.00
```

## *Summary*

Control flow allows programs to execute nonsequentially using the if, while, and for compound statements. if conditionally executes a statement, while executes a statement while a condition is true, and for iterates through a sequence. All three can contain else clauses that execute when the if condition is false, when it becomes false, or when the items in a list are or become empty, respectively.

As compound statements, if, while, and for contain clauses. Clauses contain suites and control their execution. if contains if, elif, and else clauses; while contains while and else clauses; and for contains for and else clauses. Within the while and for statements, break and continue, as their names imply, break out of a loop and continue a loop from the top.

Specific to the for statement are the range() and xRange() functions. range() returns a list of numbers; xRange() returns a number in a range only when requested to do so.

We created a sample application to compute range, mean, mode, and median for a group of house prices. The application highlighted the following key concepts from Chapters 1 through 4:

- for loop
- while loop
- if statement
- if and else clauses
- Nested loops
- len(), count(), and sort()
- Modulus (%)
- %f format directive
- Nested dictionaries
- Use of a dictionary with the format operator

# CHAPTER 5

# *Organizing Your Code*

─────────────────── *Terms in This Chapter* ───────────────────

- ↻ *Attribute*
- ↻ *Class*
- ↻ *Code block*
- ↻ *Constructor*
- ↻ *Destructor*
- ↻ *Encapsulation*
- ↻ *First class object*
- ↻ *Flag*
- ↻ *Function*
- ↻ *global statement, variable, namespace*

- ↻ *Identity operator*
- ↻ *Immutability*
- ↻ *import statement*
- ↻ *Instance*
- ↻ *Interface*
- ↻ *Instantiation*
- ↻ *Introspection*
- ↻ *Keyword argument*
- ↻ *Main block*
- ↻ *Method*

- ↻ *Module*
- ↻ *Namespace*
- ↻ *Nesting*
- ↻ *Package*
- ↻ *Positional argument*
- ↻ *Script*
- ↻ *Search path*
- ↻ *self argument*

In this chapter, we'll cover how and why you should organize your code. You'll learn about namespaces and code blocks and about modules, functions, classes, and methods.

## *Evolution of a Programmer*

As your programs grow, or as you increase your understanding of Python, you'll use more of Python's organization features. For example:

- You want to learn how to do a task, so you use the interactive interpreter to learn Python.

- You want to automate a task, so you write a script. (See Appendix C on scripts.)
- You want to reuse script functionality, so you organize scripts into different modules.
- You want to use generalization and abstraction to reuse code common to many scripts, so you organize scripts into classes.
- You want to share modules with co-workers or a development team, so you organize your modules into packages.
- You want to use packages of modules from other sources and share your modules with others, so you organize your packages into other packages and into subpackages.

Even as your needs change, you'll still seek out the least sophisticated approach, even for more complicated tasks. For instance, you might write a script to do testing, or you might use interactive mode to learn a new module or to debug one you've already written.

## Organizing Your Code

No matter how far you progress as a programmer, you'll need to know how to organize your code. In Python, you can organize your statements into functions and methods; your methods and data into classes; your classes, functions, and statements into modules; your modules into packages; and, lastly, your packages into other packages. Figure 5–1 illustrates this organization. The following sections show you how to achieve it.

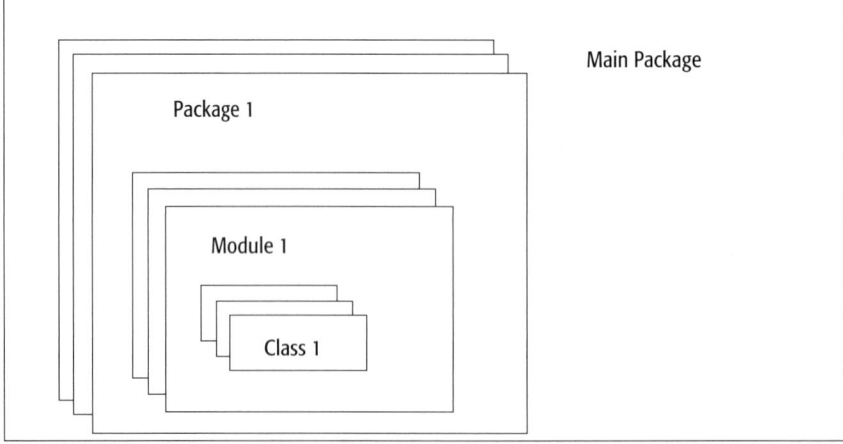

**Figure 5–1**    *Program Organization*

### Nesting

Classes can have other classes nested within them. Functions and methods can have nested classes as well as nested functions. Typically, the inner classes and functions in a method are small and serve a purpose only in the context of the class in which they nest.

For example, in the following class definition, the class `topclass` has a member method, `method()`, which has an inner function, `function()`, which has an inner class, `innerclass1`. Notice that `topclass` has a second inner class, `innerclass2`.

```
>>> class topclass:
...       def method():
...             def function():
...                   class innerclass1:
...                         pass
...       class innerclass2:
...             pass
...
```

# Code Blocks and Namespaces

Code blocks are pieces of executable Python code that you can think of as collections of statements. Modules, classes, and functions are all examples.

Modules may be scripts that execute only once. Since Python is unlike other languages in its lack of a main method, it starts executing code (program text) from the top of the module. To re-execute the module, you have to reload it.

Modules can contain classes and functions (both code blocks), which may be executed many times. Also, functions can contain classes as well as other functions, and classes can contain methods as well as other classes. Variables defined in a code block are associated with that code block's namespace.

### The Main Block

Python may not have a main method, but it does have something similar, the main block, which looks like this:

```
if __name__ == "__main__"
    #Put main code here
```

Modules have a `__name__` attribute, which contains the module name (e.g., *sys, string, mymodule*). The main block is called `__main__` and is executed from the command line. Since a module is a code block, anything in it will be executed when it is run from the command line or imported from another module. `__name__` thus limits execution to the main module.

A namespace is a way to organize variables in a large program. It provides separate contexts for individual variables so that two with the same name can be used without one adversely affecting the other. Think of namespaces as directories on your hard drive. If there are two directories, `user1` and `user2`, and both have a file named `readme.txt`, you can be sure that these are two different files—one you access as `\user1\readme` and the other as `\user2\readme`.

Packages provide namespaces for modules and other packages. Say you create a module called *sys* but *sys* is also the name of a standard module. This can cause problems. However, if you put your *sys* module in a package called *mycompany,* you can access it via *mycompany.sys* without interfering with the standard *sys* module. Packages also provide namespaces for other packages, just as file directories provide namespaces for each other.

Modules provide namespaces for variables, classes, and functions. You might have a class called `stats` and download a class from the Web also called `stats`. You can use both classes in the same program because they're in their own modules—*my_module.stats* and *their_module.stats.*

Similarly, classes provide namespaces for variables and methods. For example, a method called `getMean()` in a class called `stat` won't interfere with a function called `getMean()` in the same module.

We'll discuss namespaces and variable scope more later. The key point here is that Python allows you a lot of flexibility in program organization. It also gives you more control over how you manipulate and introspect your namespace.

## *Modules*

Without defining them, we've been using modules since Chapter 1. These are files that contain Python statements and definitions (classes and functions) and can be imported into other modules or into the main module. Module files are identified by the suffix *.py.*

If you're a programmer coming from a Java background, you may think that a module is similar to a package. Once you work with Python modules for a while, you may think of them more as a cross between a package and a final public class (with all static variables and a private constructor).

### Import

The `import` statement allows you to import classes, functions, and variables from one module into the current module's namespace. Table 5–1 describes its forms. Here is an example module, *module1.py*, which we'll use throughout this section to illustrate `import`.

```
def class1:
  def method1(self):
```

**Table 5–1** Import *Statement Forms*

| Form | Description |
|------|-------------|
| `import module_name`<br><br>Example: `import module1` | Imports the module into the current module. Items can be accessed as `module1.class1`, `module1.function1`, `module2.function2`. Imports a definition from the current module but not the module itself. |
| `from module_name import class_name, func_name`<br><br>Example: `from module1 import class1, function1` | Items can be accessed without the module name as `class1`, `function1`; but `module1.function2` needs the module name to be accessed. |
| `from module_name import *`<br><br>Example: `from module1 import *` | Imports all of the definitions in the module but not the module itself. All items can be accessed without the module name as `class1`, `function1`, `function2`. |

```
  def method2(self, arg1, arg2):
      self.attribute1 = arg1
      self.attribute2 = arg2
def function1():
  pass

def function2():
  pass
def class1:
  def method1(self):
      pass

  def method2(self, arg1, arg2):
      self.attribute1 = arg1
      self.attribute2 = arg2
def function1():
  pass

def function2():
  pass
```

Breaking things down, we first go to the directory that holds *module1.py*. Then we start up a new Jython session at the command line.

```
C:\Pythonbook\samples\chap5>jython
Jython 1.0.3 on java1.2fcs
Copyright 1997-1998 Corporation for National Research Initiatives
```

On our first attempt, we use `function1()`, but that results in a `NameError`, which means that Python didn't find that function in the current namespace.

Next we try `function1()` with the module name, but again that produces a name error because *module1* is not in the current namespace.

```
>>> module1.function1()
Traceback (innermost last):
  File "<stdin>", line 1, in ?
NameError: module1
```

So we import *module1* into the current namespace and use `function1()` as follows:

```
>>> import module1
>>> module1.function1()
```

After we import *module1*, we can call `function1()` using the `module1.function1()` form.

```
>>> function1
Traceback (innermost last):
  File "<stdin>", line 1, in ?
NameError: function1
```

Yet again, a name error. The problem is that to use `function1()` without the module name we have to import `function1()` from *module1*.

```
>>> from module1 import function1
>>> function1
<function function1 at -1811886282>
```

Finally, we use the `from module import*` form with *module1* and then `dir()` to see the contents of the current namespace. Notice that all of the items in the module have been imported, even the variables `string1` and `number1`.

```
>>> from module1 import *
>>> dir ()
['__name__', 'class1', 'function1', 'function2', 'module1', 'number1',
'string1']
```

---

### Immutability

Although `string1` and `number1` are in the current namespace, they're not the same as the variables in *module1*. At first, they refer to the same object.

```
>>> import module1
>>> module1.number1 is number1
1
```

returns 1 which means true

However, they no longer both refer to that object once their values change. That's because they are immutable. Here's an example of `number1`:

```
>>> module1.number1 = 600
>>> module1.number1
600
```

```
>>> number1
1

>>> module1.number1 is number1
0

>>> #returns 0 which means false
```

Here's the same example using `string1`:

```
>>> module1.string1 is string1
1

>>> string1 = "hi"
>>> module1.string1 is string1
0

>>> module1.string1 == string1
0

>>> module1.string1
'Hello, how are you?'
```

### Module Search Path

So far, we've been importing modules from one place to another within the same directory they were written in. However, as you write more and more modules, you'll want to organize them across directories. You can do this as long as the modules are in your module search path—the equivalent of the DOS PATH environment—which tells Python where to look for Python modules.

For CPython, you set the module search path by declaring the PYTHONPATH environment variable. You can't do this in Jython because you can't access environment variables in Java. Instead, you access the search path in the registry file, which is similar to *.ini* files in Windows or to the Windows registry.

You can edit the registry (*C:\Jython\Registry*) with your favorite text editor. The module search path is stored in a registry setting called `python.path`.

```
#Python Registry

python.path=.;

...

...
```

In the example above, the registry setting points to the current directory only. If we want Jython to always search a directory called *C:\Python\modules*, we set `python.path` as follows (note the semicolons to delimit directories, as for the DOS PATH environment variable):

```
python.path=.;c:\\python\\modules;
```

This means that the current directory is searched first, then the *C:\JythonLib* directory.

> **sys**
>
> The *sys* module holds the current value of the module search path in the path variable.
>
> ```
> >>> sys.path
> ['.', 'C:\\Jython\\Lib']
> ```

Let's edit the *python.path* module to include *C:\Python\modules*. Open the registry file in your favorite editor, and set *python.path* to *.;C:\\Python\\modules*. Then start up an interactive session, and query the value of python.path.

```
>>> import sys
>>> sys.path
['.', 'C:\\Python\\modules', 'C:\\Jython-1.0\\Lib']
```

To test if this is working, create the directory *C:\Python\modules,* and create a module called *path.py*.

```
def youfoundme():
  print "You found me"
```

Put *path.py* in *C:\Python\modules*. Now go anywhere else in the directory. Start up the Jython interpreter, and try to import *path.py*.

```
C:\>jython
Jython 1.0.3 on java1.2fcs
Copyright 1997-1998 Corporation for National Research Initiatives
>>> import path
>>> path.youFoundMe()
You found me
```

Because sys.path is a list, you can add paths at runtime.

> **Warning**
>
> When Python is trying to import a module, it loads the first one it finds on *python.path*. That means that, if you have a module called *path* in your current directory that has the following listing:
>
> ```
> path.py listing of path in current path:
> print "Wrong one dummy"
> ```
>
> and you try to import it from that directory, you will get the wrong one. This can be a difficult problem to debug, especially if the first module in the path is an older version of the one you're trying to load.
>
> ```
> >>> import path
> Wrong one dummy
> ```

## Functions and Methods

Remember that a function is a code block and that code blocks are collections of statements. Methods are similar to functions, and you define them the same way. The only difference is that, unlike functions, methods are associated with classes and are defined within them. Because of the similarities, the terms *function* and *method* will be used interchangeably in this section.

### Step by Step: Defining and Calling a Method

To define, or declare, a function or method, you enter the keyword def followed by the function name, a list of arguments enclosed in parentheses, and finally a colon. Next come the statements, which make up the body of the function. They start on a new line and, like all code blocks, are indented (if you don't indent, you'll get an error). The statements are where the action is.

Here's an example of a simple function, sayHello():

```
>>> def sayHello (strName):
...     strHello = "Hello " + strName
...     print (strHello)
...

>>> sayHello("Mom")
Hello Mom

>>> sayHello("Dad")
Hello Dad
```

Here's the breakdown.

First we define a method called sayHello() with the argument strName.

```
>>> def sayHello (strName):
```

Then we add two statements. The first takes the string literal "Hello" and the function argument strName and concatenates them. It then assigns their value to the strHello variable.

```
...     strHello = "Hello " + strName
```

The second statement prints out the value of strHello to the console.

```
...     print (strHello)
```

Next we invoke this function a couple of times, each time substituting a value for strHello. Notice that we invoke this function the same way we invoke the built-in functions.

```
>>> sayHello("Mom")
Hello Mom

>>> sayHello("Dad")
Hello Dad
```

The sayHello() function doesn't return a value. In fact, all functions return None by default.

Now we'll create a function, sumNumbers(), that does return a value; it sums two numbers and returns the total.

```
>>> def sumNumbers(x, y):
...     return x + y
...

>>> sumNumbers(5, 10)
15
```

Of course, most functions are more useful, and more complex, than these examples. They can have any number of arguments and can be stored for later use by more than one program.

## Calling Methods and Defining Arguments

There are three ways to call a method: by positional arguments, by keyword arguments, and by a combination of the two. There are three ways to define a method: with default values, with a variable number of positional arguments, and with a variable number of keyword arguments.

Consider the following method:

```
>>> def sayHello(name, title, message):
...     print ("Hello " + title + " " + name + " " + message)
...
```

It can be called using positional arguments:

```
>>> sayHello("Hightower", "Mr.", "How are you")
Hello Mr. Hightower How are you
```

or using keyword arguments (keyword=value):

```
>>> sayHello(name="Hightower", title="Mr.", message="How are you")
Hello Mr. Hightower How are you
```

Keywords equate to argument names. You can use them in any order, which means that in the last example we could have put the message keyword in the first position.

```
>>> sayHello(message="How are you?", name="Hightower", title="Mr.")
Hello Mr. Hightower How are you?
```

In the combined form, you can use one positional argument and two keywords.

```
>>> sayHello("Hightower", message="How are you?", title="Mr.")
Hello Mr. Hightower How are you?
```

Calling methods with keywords doesn't seem very useful; so far it just adds more typing. The payoff comes when you use keywords with default arguments.

Continuing the previous example, if we want default values for title and name, we first define our function with two default arguments.

```
>>> def sayHello(name, title="Mr.", message="Hello %s %s, how are you?"):
...     print message % (title, name)
...
```

Now we can use the function with only one positional argument.

```
>>> sayHello("James Estrada")
Hello Mr. James Estrada, how are you?
```

If we need to, we can override the default values.

```
>>> sayHello("Mark Green", "Dr.")
Hello Dr. Mark Green, how are you?
```

```
>>> sayHello("Ally McBeal", "Ms.")
Hello Ms. Ally McBeal, how are you?
```

Notice that both of these functions use positional arguments.

Another way to override default arguments is with keywords. Let's say that we want to override the last argument from above.

```
>>> sayHello("Al McMeal", message="Hello %s %s, are you hungry, would you
like to go to lunch?")
Hello Mr. Al McMeal, are you hungry, would you like to go to lunch?
```

This comes in handy when there are ten arguments with default arguments and you want to override only the tenth one.

This example won't work because name has no default value.

```
>>> sayHello(title="Mrs.", message="Hi %s %s, how are you doing? How is your
husband?")
Traceback (innermost last):
  File "<stdin>", line 1, in ?
TypeError: sayHello() not enough arguments; expected
```

## Putting Things Together

Recall from Chapter 4 that we wrote a function called getMean() that figured the average of a set of house prices. Well, we can change it to accept two default arguments. The first argument, sample, is a flag that tells getMean() if the set of numbers passed to it is from a sample of a population or the population as a whole. (The mean and the average of a sample are calculated differently.) The second argument, display, is a flag that tells getMean() to optionally display the results to the monitor.

### getMean()

Here's getMean()() defined:

```
def getMean (nums, sample=0, display=0):
  for x in nums:
      sum = sum + x
  if(sample):
      average = sum / (len(nums)-1)
  else:
      average = sum / len(nums)
  if(display):
      print ("mean = " + 'average')
  return average
```

Here are some examples:

```
#Define example sample and population numbers
sample =(1,2,3,3,2,1,1,1,2,2,3,3,2,2,2,2,2,2,2,2,2,2,2,2)
population=(1,2,3,3,2,1,1,1,2,2,3,3,2,2,2,2,2,2,2,2,2,2,2,2)
  #call with positional arguments
populationMean = getMean(population, 0)
  #call using default arguments
  #call using default arguments
sampleMean = getMean(sample)

print ("population mean " + 'populationMean')
print ("sample mean " + 'sampleMean')

  #call with positional arguments and print
populationMean = getMean(population, 0, 1)

  #call using keyword arguments
sampleMean = getMean(sample, display=1)
```

The script (in the *samples/chap5* directory) essentially demonstrates the use of keywords to include default and keyword arguments.

The following definition says in English, "Define a method called getMean() with three arguments":

```
def getMean (nums, sample=1, display=0):
```

The first argument, nums, holds the input numbers; the second, sample=1, tells getMean() whether or not this is a sample or a population; and the third, display=0, tells getMean() whether or not it should display the mean to the console. Remember that Python doesn't have a Boolean (true/false) type, so any nonzero value (1 above) equals true and a zero value (0 above) equals false.

```
if(sample):
     average = sum / (len(nums)-1)
else:
     average = sum / len(nums)
```

Once again, in English this says, "If sample is equal to true, do the first equation to figure the mean; else, do the second equation." When this method is invoked without `sample` specified, the default is true. In that case, average = sum/(len(nums)-1 is invoked. If `sample` is false, average = sum/len(nums) is invoked.

The `display` argument works like the `sample` argument.

```
if(display):
    print ("mean = " + 'average')
```

That is, "If `display` is true, print the mean to the console."

### *Variable Number of Arguments*

Here we use the asterisk symbol (*) to define a variable number of `nums` arguments:

```
>>> def sum(*nums):
...     total = 0
...     for num in nums:
...             total = total + num
...     return total
...
```

`nums` is a sequence, so it works with the `for` statement. The `sum()` function iterates through each `num` in the variable argument list.

At first it may look as though we could have used any sequence, but see how we call `sum()`.

```
>>> sum(19,20,21)
60
```

Note that the variable number of argument declarations is of type `Tuple`.

```
>>> def func(*args):
...     print type(args)
...
>>> func()
<jclass org.python.core.PyTuple at -801600693>
```

You can mix and match multiple arguments with the positional arguments, as in this nostalgic `printf()` example:

```
>>> def printf(format, *args):
...     print format % args
...
```

Here are some other examples:

```
>>> printf ("Hi %s, how is %s?", "Martha", "Miguel")
Hi Martha, how is Miguel?

>>> printf ("Martha is %i, Miguel is %i", 30, 29)
Martha is 30, Miguel is 29
```

Programmers, if you're familiar with C, you can see that C's `printf()` and Python's are similar. With the way we've defined `printf()`, you need at least one argument and can have as many as you like.

### Variable Number of Keyword Arguments (with Dictionary)

Another way to declare multiple keyword arguments is with the double asterisk symbol (**).

```
>>> def printKeywords(**keywords):
...     for item in keywords.items():
...             print item
...
```

You can use this function with any number of keyword arguments.

```
>>> printKeywords(name="Whit", eyes="blue", weight="28", age="2")
('age', '2')
('weight', '28')
('eyes', 'blue')
('name', 'Whit')
```

The variable (i.e., changeable) keyword argument is a dictionary, which we can prove.

```
>>> def func(**args):
...     print type (args)
...
>>> func (arg=1, arg2=2, arg3=3)
<jclass org.python.core.PyDictionary at -1146189863>
```

Variable keyword arguments (**) can be mixed and matched with variable positional arguments (*) and regular arguments to improve the workings of a function. Here's an example using `printf()`:

```
>>> def printf(format, *args, **kargs):
...     if(len(args)):
...             print (format % args)
...     elif(len(kargs)):
...             print (format % kargs)
...     else:
...             print format
...
```

Now `printf()` can accept any number of keyword or positional arguments.

```
>>> printf("Hi %s", "Missy")
Hi Missy

>>> printf("Hi %(name)s", name="Missy")
Hi Missy

>>> printf("Hi Missy")
Hi Missy
```

### Step by Step

Define a function, `printf()`, with one positional argument, `format`; one variable argument, `args`; and one variable keyword argument, `kargs`.

```
>>> def printf(format *args, **kargs):
```

Check if the args tuple has items in it.

```
...     if(len(args)):
```

If so, use it in the format % args expression as the tuple in a string format operation. Print the expression.

```
...             print (format % args)
```

If args is empty, check if the kargs dictionary has items in it. Print the resulting format % kargs expression.

```
...     elif(len(kargs)):
...             print (format % kargs)
```

If both args and kargs are empty, print the format string by itself.

```
...     else:
...             print format
...
```

### if(args)

In the printf() example, we used the statement if(len(args)): to determine whether the variable number of positional arguments was equal to zero. Instead, we could have used if(args) to see if the list has items in it, rewriting printf() as

```
def printf(format, *args, **kargs):
  if(args):
      print (format % args)
          elif(kargs):
      print (format % kargs)
  else:
      print format
```

Remember that an empty dictionary is equivalent to false in a Boolean test.
  Of course, you can also rewrite printf() to be very readable.

```
def printf(format, *args, **kargs):
  if(len(args) > 0):
      print (format % args)
  elif(len(kargs) > 0):
      print (format % kargs)
  else:
      print format
```

This approach makes the code a little verbose, but readability should win out. In six months when you need to read the code you wrote (to figure out what it's doing so you can change it), you'll be happy.

Remember, functions are code blocks and code blocks are collections of statements. Default function argument values save time.

## Classes

A class consists of data and the functions that act on that data. In classes, functions are referred to as methods. A way to understand classes is to think of them as functions with multiple entry points. In this way they provide data encapsulation.

You define a class with the `class` keyword.

```
class class_name:
  class_attributes
```

Classes can have many attributes. These attributes can be variables or definitions of either functions or other classes. For example, the definition of the class `chapter` has three variable attributes: `number_of_pages`, `title`, and `toc`.

```
class chapter:
        number_of_pages = 20
        title = "Organizing your program"
        toc = ["Introduction", "Modules", "Functions", "Packages", "Classes"]
```

Notice that the class attributes are indented, just as the subordinate statements in an `if` statement are indented.

Class attributes can be accessed with the form `class_name.attribute`.

```
chapter.number_of_pages = 30
print `chapter.number_of_pages`
toc.append("Scope and Namespaces")
```

Classes can also have function definitions (*book.py*).

```
class chapter:
  """ Document String for chapter class """
  number_of_pages = 20
  title = "Organizing your program"
  toc = ["Introduction", "Modules", \
      "Functions", "Packages", \
      "Classes"]
  def print_me(self):
      print chapter.title + " " +`chapter.number_of_pages`
      for section in chapter.toc:
          print " " + section
```

Note here that the function definitions are indented to show that they're members of the class and that their subordinate statements are further indented to show that they belong to the functions. The point to remember is that *indentation shows ownership or membership.*

> **For Programmers: self**
>
> The `self` argument to the `print-me()` method in the `chapter` class holds the reference to the class instance. It's similar to the `this` reference in Java or the `Me` reference in Visual Basic.

## Exploring a Defined Class

For this section, follow along in the interactive session by loading class `chapter` using the `-i` option in Jython. You'll find `chapter` in module *book.py* in directory *chap5*. Here's the prompt:

```
C:\python\book\chap5>jython -i book.py
```

Now enter

```
>>> dir()
['__name__', 'chapter']
```

The `dir()` built-in function with no arguments gives you the names in the current namespace. If we supply it with the argument `chapter`, it gives us `chapter`'s attributes.

```
>>> dir(chapter)
['__doc__', '__module__', 'number_of_pages', 'print_me', 'title', 'toc']
```

The `__doc__` attribute holds the class's document string; the `__module__` attribute holds its associated module. The rest of the attributes are ones we defined for `chapter`. Note that `print_me()` is listed as an attribute.

We call a method of a class with the form `class_name.method_name()`.

```
>>> chapter.print_me(None)
Organizing your program 20
    Introduction
    Modules
    Functions
    Packages
    Classes
```

This is similar to calling a regular function, the only difference being that the function name must be prepended with the class name. The syntax looks a lot like the syntax for calling a function in a module.

If we had imported the *book.py* module (instead of loading it at the command line with Jython), we would have had to use the module name to call `print_me()`.

```
module_name.class_name.function_name.
```

```
>>> import book
>>> book.chapter.print_me(None)
Organizing your program 20
```

```
Introduction
Modules
Functions
Packages
Classes
```

---

**First Class Object**

In the `print_me()` example, we passed the argument `None`. The first argument in a method usually refers to an instance of a class, but not here. Instead we're using the class itself because, in Python, the class is a first class object.

---

To access the member variables in `chapter` we use the form `class_name.variable_name`. Again, the syntax is like that for accessing variables in a module.

```
>>> chapter.number_of_pages, chapter.title
(20, 'Organizing your program')
>>> chapter.toc
['Introduction', 'Modules', 'Functions', 'Packages', 'Classes']
```

Here we accessed both `number_of_pages` and title (the tuple format). Python returned a tuple containing the values of `number_of_pages` and `title`, respectively. Then we accessed the values in the member list called `toc`.

We can also change the attributes of a class.

```
>>> chapter.toc.append("Scope and Namespaces")

>>> chapter.title="Organizing your code"

>>> chapter.number_of_pages = 30
```

To confirm the changes, we run the `print_me()` function.

```
>>> chapter.print_me(None)
Organizing your Python code into packages, modules, classes and functions 30
    Introduction
    Modules
    Functions
    Packages
    Classes
    Scope and Namespaces
```

## Class Instances

Say we want to create 20 `chapter` classes. To do this with what we've learned so far, we'd have to redefine `chapter` 20 times.

```
class chapter1:
  number_of_pages = 1
  ...
```

```
class chapter2:
  number_of_pages = 2
  ...

class chapter3:
  number_of_pages = 3
  ...
```

Time consuming, isn't it? With what we're about to learn, we can instead create an instance of chapter for each chapter in our book.

Think of a class as a cookie cutter and an instance as an actual cookie. You use the cookie cutter to stamp the cookie out. With classes, stamping out the class instances is called instantiation.

When a class is instantiated, the instance shares all of its attributes. The attributes of both initially refer to the same objects, but the instance can also define its own attributes (just as you can decorate each cookie a different way). You access the instance attributes with the form instance_name.attribute. This form refers to the class attributes if the instance hasn't defined its own, or to its own if it has.

This concept is easier to show than to explain, so we'll instantiate our chapter class to illustrate. For the next interactive session, load module *book.py* using the jython -i option.

First we assign chap1 to the results of the class constructor expression, which is an instance of class chapter.

```
>>> chap1 = chapter()
```

---

**For Programmers: No new Keyword**

There's no new keyword in Python as there is in Java, C++, and Visual Basic. Therefore, the example

```
>>> chap1 = chapter()
```

is equivalent to the following in Java, C++, and Visual Basic, respectively:

```
chapter chap1 = new chapter();
```

```
chapter *chap1 = new chapter();
```

```
Dim chap1 As New chapter
```
or
```
Dim chap1 As chapter
Set chap1 = New chapter
```

---

Here's how we access the members of chap1:

```
>>> chap1.title
'Organizing your program'
```

```
>>> chap1.toc
['Introduction', 'Modules', 'Functions', 'Packages', 'Classes']
>>> chap1.number_of_pages
20
```

Note that all of these attributes are the same as those of the `chapter` class. So, is the instance of `chapter` the same as `chapter` itself? Let's see using the `is` identity operator.

```
>>> chap1 is chapter
0
```

   Okay, `chap1` is *not* the same as `chapter`, even though it has the same attributes. Or does it? We know that `dir()` lists the attributes of a module and a class. It also lists the attributes of an instance, so let's use it to solve this mystery.

```
>>> dir (chap1)
[]
>>> dir (chapter)
['__doc__', '__module__', 'number_of_pages', 'print_me', 'title', 'toc']
```

It looks like `chap1` has no attributes at all, yet when we accessed its attributes we got back the values for `chapter`. What happens if we try to change a `chap1` attribute? Does the class attribute change?
   First let's change `chap1.title` and see what the title is.

```
>>> chap1.title = "Getting Started"
>>> chap1.title
'Getting Started'
```

Next let's check the value of the `chapter` class's title.

```
>>> chapter.title
'Organizing your program'
```

`chapter.title` and `chap1.title` are no longer the same value. Initially, Python uses the class attributes for `chap1`. However, if we change an instance attribute, Python creates an attribute only for the instance, so we should now have a new attribute in `chap1`'s namespace called `title`. Let's check this with the `dir()` function.

```
>>> dir (chap1)
['title']
```

As you can see, there's a new variable called `title` in `chap1`'s namespace. Just as we thought. However, this technique works only for assigning new values. For example, if we append a string to the `toc` list, the instance doesn't get a new attribute.

```
>>> chap1.toc.append("Welcome to Python")
>>> chap1.toc is chapter.toc
1
```

Notice that, even after we append a string to `toc`, `chap1.toc` and `chapter.toc` point to the same object. But what about this:

```
>>> chap1.toc = ["Do not fear", "What is Python", "Why Python"]
>>> chap1.toc is chapter.toc
0
```

It shows that assignments change what an instance's member variables refer to.
    Let's wrap up this interactive session.

```
>>> chapter.number_of_pages is chap1.number_of_pages
1
>>> dir (chap1)
['title', 'toc']
```

This shows that, since number_of_pages was never assigned a value in chap1, the
chapter and chap1 attributes for it point to the same object (they're actually the same
reference). It also shows that chap1 has the title and toc attributes in its namespace but not number_of_pages.

### Constructor (__init__)

The __init__ method, if present, is called when an instance is first created or constructed. It's the constructor, and its arguments are the same ones passed to the
class constructor expression. __init__ is usually used to define (i.e., initialize)
instance variables.
    For example, this class constructor expression passes the title argument to
__init__:

```
chap1 = chapter(title="Introduction")
```

    Let's define our chapter class with a constructor that takes three arguments for
each instance variable. Notice that we've removed the class variables and are using
only instance variables. (Compare this example, *book1.py*, to our earlier example,
*book.py*.)

```
class chapter:
      """ Document String for chapter class """

      def __init__(self, title="", numPages=0, toc=[]):
                  self.numPages = numPages
          self.title = title
          self.toc = toc
      def print_me(self):
          print self.title + " " + `self.numPages`
          for section in self.toc:
              print " " + section
```

Here we've defined a constructor that initializes all of an instance's attributes.
Note that chapter's constructor uses default arguments to initialize the member
variables. Remember that the self argument refers to the current instance.
    Below we create an instance of chapter and set its title to Getting started. When
calling a constructor, you don't pass a value for the positional self argument.

```
>>> chap1 = chapter("Getting started")
>>> chap1.print_me()
Getting started 0
```

Next we create an instance of chapter and set its title to Fundamentals, its number of pages to 20, and its table of contents to Literals, Types, and Lists.

```
>>> chap2 = chapter("Fundamentals", 20, ["Literals", "Types", "Lists"])
>>> chap2.print_me()
Fundamentals 20
    Literals
    Types
    Lists
```

Now we create an instance of chapter with the title Operators and set the table of contents to String operators and Arithmetic.

```
>>> chap3 = chapter(toc=["String operators", "Arithmetic"],title="Operators")
>>> chap3.print_me()
Operators 0
    String operators
    Arithmetic
```

### Destructor (__del__)

The __del__ method is the destructor, which is called when the class instance is about to be destroyed.

```
class chapter:
  """ Document String for chapter class """

  def __init__(self, title="", numPages=0, toc=[]):
      self.numPages = numPages
      self.title = title
      self.toc = toc

  def __del__(self):
      print "Leaving"

  def print_me(self):
      print self.title + " " + `self.numPages`
      for section in self.toc:
          print "    " + section

chap = chapter()
chap.print_me()
del chap
```

## Encapsulation with Private Variables

One of the things that separate classes from records or structures in other languages is the concept of encapsulation. Encapsulation hides the implementation details of your class and in doing so reduces code coupling. Coupling is bad.

Let's say, for example, that you create a simple address book class that downloads all of the addresses from a corporate database and stores them in a list called names. Other programmers who use your class simply access this names list.

Well, imagine that the company you work for has just landed some major accounts and is hiring more employees. Now you want to change your address book class to work with a middleware server that connects to the database and helps you cache addresses based on usage and changes. You also want to provide a dictionary-like object to work with the names list. You do all this, but when you change the names over to the dictionary object, all the other company programmers' code stops working. This is coupling, and you can see why it's bad.

To reduce coupling you want to hide the implementation details of your class and provide a well-defined interface to outside users. Private variables and private methods allow you to do this because they aren't visible outside the class in which they're defined.

A well-defined interface to your class is a collection of public methods for class access, but it prohibits access to the private variables to limit the number of things that can go wrong. Consider if everyone had access to every variable in your class—the number of potential problems would be staggering. By limiting variable access to well-defined methods, you better control the internal state of your class and minimize such problems. If something does go wrong, you're more likely to know which method to fix.

What all this comes down to is good code organization. Packages allow you to organize your modules, on the basis of functionality or services, so that you don't run into naming conflicts with other programmers.

There's no keyword to declare a variable or method as private. Rather, you prepend a double underscore to the variable or method name. Here's an example (module *book2.py*):

```
class chapter:
  """ Document String for chapter class """

  def __init__(self, title="", numPages=0, toc=[]):
  self.__numPages = numPages
      self.__title = title
      self.__toc = toc

  def print_me(self):
      print self.__title + " " + `self.__numPages`
      for section in self.__toc:
          print "      " + section
```

Below we define the three instance variables as private, which means that they can't be viewed with the dir() function.

```
>>> from book1 import chapter
>>> dir (chapter)
['__doc__', '__module__', 'print_me']
```

## *Packages*

Packages are a way of organizing Python modules and a way to prevent one programmer from stomping on the module of another. You assign a module to a package with the form `Package_Name.Module_Name`. Thus, the module name *mystuff.sys* indicates a module named *sys* in a package named *mystuff*.

Packages are essentially directories that contain a special *__init__.py* file to indicate to Python that the directory it's dealing with is a package. This file is used when the package is first loaded. Let's create our own package and call it *package1/__init__.py*.

First we create a directory called *package1*. Then we create a file named *__init__.py* with one Python statement that prints "`Hello from package1`", and save it to the *package1* directory. Next we create a module called *module1* in *package1* and put in it a Python statement that prints "`hello from module1 in package1`". In module1, we define one do-nothing function and one do-nothing class named `class1` that contains a do-nothing method named `method1`.

Here's *package1/__init__.py*.

```
print "Hello from package1"
```

Here's *package1/module1.py:*

```
print "hello from module1 in package1"

def function1():
  pass

class class1:

def method1():
  pass
```

Make sure that the *package1* directory is in the module search path. Then move out of *package1* and fire up the Jython interpreter.

```
>>> from package1.module1 import class1
Hello from package1
hello from module1 in package1

>>> dir()
['__name__', 'class1']
```

Here we see that the code in *__init__.py* and *module1* is executed when we load `class1`.

Now exit and restart the Jython interpreter and try this:

```
>>> import package1
Hello from package1

>>> dir()
['__name__', 'package1']
```

```
>>> dir(package1)
['__file__', '__name__', '__path__']

>>> vars(package1)
{'__file__': 'C:\\python\\book\\chap5\\.\\package1\\__init__.py'
, '__path__': ['.\\package1'], '__name__': 'package1'}
```

Notice that, when we import the package, its __init__.py module is executed. Look at the package's namespace. (Remember that the vars command is like the dir command except that it lists the namespace's names and values.)

Within __init__.py you can define a list called __all__, which is used with package import* to tell Python to import all modules in this package. Actually, Python imports all modules listed in the package's __all__ list, so if you want to import a module with the * command, you have to put it in __all__.

Packages can have subpackages. These are subdirectories under the package with __init__.py modules. Since __init__.py is part of the package, the package can contain anything that you find in a regular module, such as classes and functions.

## Globals and the Global Statement

The word "global" strikes fear in the hearts of object-oriented programmers (and structured programmers, for that matter). That's because global variables—variables that are in a global namespace (one that's available to all modules, functions, and classes)—are usually a bad thing and should be avoided.

In fact, there aren't any real global variables in Python. All variables have to be in the context of a module, class, or function. However, Python does have a global statement, which allows you to share variables between functions in the same module.

Here's an example that has two functions and a module-level variable:

```
var = "hi"  #module level variable

    def sayHi1():
        print var

    def sayHi2():
        print var

    def sayHiMom():
        var = var + " Mom"
        print var
```

Both sayHi1 and sayHi2 work, but sayHiMom doesn't. To make it work you have to import the var variable into the functions' local namespaces, using the global command like this:

```
var = "hi"  #module level variable
...
...
```

```
def sayHiMom():
global var
var = var + " Mom"
print var
```

There's nothing wrong with using the `global` statement to import module-level variables into a function's namespace.

---

## *Summary*

In this chapter, we learned about the benefits and methods of organizing your code. We explained namespaces, code blocks, and working with namespaces for modules, functions, classes, and methods. We also discussed the `import` statement, which allows you to import objects from one module to another, and the `global` statement, which allows you to import module-level variables into a local namespace.

**CHAPTER 6**

# *Object-Oriented Programming*

---
*Terms in This Chapter*
---

- ⌕ *Aggregation/ containment*
- ⌕ *Attribute*
- ⌕ *Cardinality*
- ⌕ *Class*
- ⌕ *Class hierarchy*
- ⌕ *Code reuse*
- ⌕ *Cohesion*
- ⌕ *Coupling*

- ⌕ *Encapsulation*
- ⌕ *First class object*
- ⌕ *Garbage collection*
- ⌕ *Getter/Setter methods*
- ⌕ *Inheritance (implementation/ interface)*
- ⌕ *Instance*
- ⌕ *Instantiation*

- ⌕ *Late-bound polymorphism*
- ⌕ *Multiple inheritance*
- ⌕ *Object*
- ⌕ *Replaceability*
- ⌕ *Specialization*
- ⌕ *Typed polymorphism*

This chapter explains the fundamentals of object-oriented programming, as well as why it's important and how to do it in Python.

---

## What Is OOP?

Object-oriented programming (OOP) is a tool for organizing your programs into reusable objects. It won't necessarily make you program better or faster, yet it's one of the best ideas in programming to come along so far. A common myth about object-oriented programming is that it's hard to learn and that you should learn a non-OOP language first, but you don't have to do this. In fact, OOP is easy to learn because it models the real world. Bottom line? Don't fear object-oriented programming.

Here are the triple pillars of OOP:

- Polymorphism
- Encapsulation
- Inheritance

Of the three, polymorphism is the most important because it supports the replaceable nature of objects.

### Objects as Black Boxes (Encapsulation)

Say you're driving along and a young child racing toward his fleeing ball runs right in front of your car. Do you pause and think about what to do? No. Instinctively, your foot reaches for the break pedal.

Think of the break pedal as the interface to your car's breaking system. You know how to use it because it's well defined, whether this is your car or one you've rented or borrowed, whether the breaks are drum or antilock. The details of the system's implementation are encapsulated—that is, hidden from you. All you need to know is how to use the interface to the break system—the break pedal.

What does all this have to do with OOP? A great deal. With OOP you define classes that support interfaces, and you use them to instantiate objects. Two classes with the same interface can be used interchangeably. You can organize your program into many objects, each of which has a specific role (this is called cohesion). The objects perform their roles in ways that are encapsulated from the rest of the program, which means that you change the way an object works and keep the rest of your program intact.

Here are some important object-oriented ideas:

- *Coupling* is when you change one module or class, and doing so adversely affects another module or class. (Some coupling may be necessary.)
- *Cohesion* is defining modules and classes that have specific roles. (Cohesion helps to reduce coupling.)
- *Encapsulation* is hiding the implementation details. In OOP, we hide them behind an interface.
- *Interface,* in OOP speak, is a collection of methods associated with a class or module.

## Objects and Classes

Objects in the real world are made up of many other objects (in OOP speak this is called aggregation or containment). For example, a car object contains tire objects, an engine object, a steering system object, a breaking system object, and so forth. Organizing a program into a hierarchy of objects helps us conceptualize it. Essentially, you break down the program into interrelated objects, which are in turn broken down into other objects. This is called inheritance.

A class is a template for creating objects by defining their behavior and attributes. Thus, a car class defines the behaviors of a car, such as

- Moving forward or backward
- Breaking
- Turning

It also defines the car's attributes, such as

- Make
- Model
- Color
- Year
- Two door or four door

The car class acts as a generic template for cars. Just as there are many cars in the world, so there can be many car objects in your program (this concept is known as object cardinality), but they share attributes and behavior. So, for example, you can stop and start both a Volvo and a Chevy. Think of the class as a cookie cutter and its objects as the cookies it stamps out. The cookies themselves are the instances of the class.

The great thing about programming in Python (and Java for that matter) is that you don't have to start from scratch. There are lots of general-purpose classes and modules for doing common things. For example, Python has a URL module that knows how to work with files from FTP and HTTP servers.

Let's review the key concepts so far:

- A class (Car) is a template for defining objects (Volvo).
- Attributes describe an object's appearance, state, or quality.
- Behavior defines how an object acts.
- Cardinality is the number of instances of an object in a system.

Define a Car class in Python as.

```
    jython -i car.py):

class Car:
        make = "?"
        model = "?"
        color = "?"
        running = 0 #1 is true, 0 is false
```

## Attributes

Here we see that the attributes of `Car` are defined by its variables, which are indented. We can use this class template to create `car` instances.

```
                # create an instance of my car
        # and display its attributes
myCar = Car()
print "After Create:", myCar.color, myCar.make, myCar.model

            # Set myCars attributes then display attributes
myCar.color, myCar.make, myCar.model = "Red", "Ford", "Taurus"
print "After set:", myCar.color, myCar.make, myCar.model
```

The output is

```
After Create: ? ? ?
After set: Red Ford Taurus
```

## Behavior

An object's behavior is determined by methods defined by its class. Let's return to the `Car` class example and add `start` and `stop` behavior.

```
class Car:
        make = "?"
        model = "?"
        color = "?"
        running = 0 #1 is true, 0 is false

        def start(self):
                if self.running == 1:
                        print "The car is already running"
                else:
                        self.running = 1

        def stop(self):
                if self.running ==0:
                        print "The car is already stopped"
                else:
                        self.running = 0
```

Here are some examples of the `Car` class methods followed by their output:

```
car = Car()
car.color = "Red"
car.make = "Ford"
car.model ="Taurus"

            # Start the car
car.start()
print "After Start:", car.color, car.make, car.model, car.running

            #Stop the car
car.stop()
print "After Stop:", car.color, car.make, car.model, car.running
```

```
After Start: Red Ford Taurus 1
After Stop: Red Ford Taurus 0
```

### The Python Objects Model

Unlike in Java, everything in Python is an object—functions, modules, classes, packages, numeric types—everything. Objects have an identity, a type, and a value. The type determines the methods and operations that an object supports. The value can be changeable (dictionaries, classes, lists) or immutable (strings, integers, tuples).

You know, for example, that you can create many instances of the same class. But did you know that a class is itself an object, a first class object, that can be dynamically modified? When you modify the template (class), you in effect modify the class instances not yet created.

To illustrate, we'll modify the attributes of the Car class for Fords.

```
>>> Car.make, Car.model, Car.color = "Ford", "Taurus", "Red"
```

Then we'll create a list of three Ford cars.

```
>>> ford_cars = [Car(), Car(), Car()]
```

Next we'll print out their make.

```
>>> ford_cars[0].make, ford_cars[1].make, ford_cars[2].make
('Ford', 'Ford', 'Ford')
```

Now we use the same technique to create three Hondas.

```
>>> Car.make, Car.model = "Honda", "Civic"
>>> honda_cars = [Car(), Car(), Car()]
>>> honda_cars[0].make, honda_cars[1].make, honda_cars[2].make
('Honda', 'Honda', 'Honda')
```

As you can see, when you can change the template, you essentially create objects with new attributes.

---

## Special Class Methods

In Python you can define special methods for classes that have special meaning. You can also define methods to make your class look like other objects such as lists, dictionaries, and tuples.

### Creating and Destroying Class Instances

Like other OOP languages, Python has a destructor and a constructor. A constructor is called when an instance is instantiated. A destructor is called when an instance is garbage-collected. The method __init__ denotes the constructor. The method __del__ denotes the destructor.

Here's the Car class (*Car2.py*) with its constructor and destructor:

```
class Car:
    make = "?"
    model = "?"
    color = "?"
    running = 0 #1 is true, 0 is false

    def __init__(self, make, model, color):
        self.make = make
        self.model = model
        self.color = color
        print "constructor called"

    def __del__(self):
        print "destructor called"
    ...
```

The __init__ method takes the form

```
__init__ (self[, args...]):
```

The __del__ method takes the form

```
__del__ (self):
```

First we create an instance of the Car class. Notice that constructor called is printed out, because the __init__ method is called when we instantiate Car.

```
>>> myCar = Car("Ford", "Taurus", "Red")
constructor called
```

Next we print out the attributes that were set when the constructor was called.

```
>>> myCar.make, myCar.model, myCar.color
('Ford', 'Taurus', 'Red')
```

Then we try to destroy this instance to see if the destructor is called.

```
>>> myCar = None
>>> myCar is None
1
>>> None
>>> None
destructor
```

The destructor isn't called when we assign myCar to None. That's because Car isn't destroyed until it's garbage-collected, which may never happen. For example, the garbage collector may be implemented to run only if there's no more memory left.

## Representing the Class Instance as a String

There are two methods for creating string representations of an object: __repr__ and __string__.

The \_\_repr\_\_ method represents your object in such a way that it can be recreated with the eval statement. eval evaluates a string as a Python expression and works much like the interactive interpreter. \_\_repr\_\_ is called when you use back quotes or call the repr command. Here's what it looks like:

```
__repr__ (self):
```

The \_\_str\_\_ method is a way to do a nice looking string for printing. It's called by the str() built-in function and by the print statement. Here's what it looks like:

```
__str__ (self):
```

We can add \_\_str\_\_ to our Car class like this:

```
class Car:
        ...

        ...
        def __str__(self):
                strRun = ""
                if self.running == 1:
                        strRun="\nThe car is running"
                else:
                        strRun="\nThe car is stopped"

                str = "make " + make + \
                        "\nmodel " + model + \
                        "\ncolor " + color + strRun

                return str
```

Here's the output (from the *Car2.py* module) in interactive mode:

```
C:\py\book\chap9>jython -i Car2.py
>>> car = Car("Ford", "Mustang", "Cherry Red")
constructor called

>>> print car
make Ford
model Mustang
color Cherry Red
The car is stopped
```

\_\_repr\_\_ can also be used for display. However, if at all possible, it should evaluate to an expression that returns the object. Thus, if you use the Python eval statement, which reads in text and parses it to an expression, you should be able to recreate the instance with the string that \_\_repr\_\_ returns.

Here's an example of \_\_repr\_\_:

```
def __repr__(self):
        format = """Car("%s","%s","%s")"""
        return format % (self.make, self.model, self.color)
```

Here's the output (from the *Car2.py* module) in interactive mode:

```
C:\py\book\chap9>jython -i Car2.py
```

```
>>> car = Car ("Ford", "Mustang", "Midnight Blue")
constructor

>>> print `car`
Car("Ford","Mustang","Midnight Blue")

>>> print car
make Ford
model Mustang
color Midnight Blue

The car is stopped
>>> car2 = eval(`car`)
constructor

>>> print car2
make Ford
model Mustang

color Midnight Blue
The car is stopped
```

In the above example, we used the return from `car.__repr__()` in conjunction with the `eval` statement to create `car2`. The `car2` instance has the same attributes as the original `car` instance.

### Comparing, Hashing, and Truth Testing

Three other methods, shown in Table 6–1, have special meaning in Python. We'll use module *Car3.py* to demonstrate them.

```
max_Price = 7000
running = 0

def __nonzero__(self):
        if (self.price > Car.max_Price):
                return 0
        else:
                return 1

def __cmp__(self, other):
        if (self.price > other.price): return 1
        if (self.price < other.price): return -1
        if (self.price == other.price): return 0

def __hash__(self):
        v= self.make + self.model + self.color + `self.price`
        return hash(v)

def __init__(self, make, model, color, price=5000):
        self.make = make
        self.model = model
        self.color = color
        self.price = price
        ...
        ...
```

**Table 6–1**  *Python Class Methods*

| Method | Description |
| --- | --- |
| `__cmp__ (self, other)` | Called by the comparison operators, ==,=>, >, <, =< |
| `__hash__ (self)` | Used in conjunction with the hash function to return a 32-bit integer used for hash values in dictionaries |
| `__nonzero__ (self)` | Used for Boolean truth testing; is the object in a true state or a false state |

Here we've added a class variable called `max_Price` and an instance variable called `price`. The __nonzero__ method uses `max_Price` to see if the price of the instance is under the maximum price. The __cmp__ method uses the price to compare another `Car` instance to the current one. The hash is calculated by creating a large string representation of all the hash values of the individual attributes of the `Car` instance.

The following code is also part of *Car3.py*.

```
if __name__ == "__main__":
      car1 = Car("Ford", "Mustang", "Midnight Blue", 5000)
      car2 = Car("Chevrolet", "Corvette", "Champagne gold", 9000)
            #To demonstrate compare __cmp__
      if (car1 > car2):
            print car1
      else:
            print car2

            #to demonstrate Boolean __nonzero__
      if(car1): print "Buy It"
      if(not car2): print "I can't afford it"

            #to demonstrate hash __hash__
      print `hash(car1)`
```

The output looks like this:

```
C:\py\book\chap9>jython car3.py
make Chevrolet
model Corvette
color Champagne gold
The car is stopped
Buy It
I can't afford it
-1273809553
```

## Getting, Setting, and Deleting Attributes

We can override the default behavior for how objects are displayed, printed, constructed, compared, truth-tested, and so forth. We can also override how member variables in our instance are accessed. The methods shown in Table 6–2 customize attribute access for class instances.

**Table 6–2**    *Instance Access Methods*

| Method | Definition |
|---|---|
| __getattr__ (self, name) | Gets the value of an attribute |
| __setattr__ (self, name, value) | Sets the value of an attribute |
| __delattr__ (self, name) | Deletes an attribute |

Essentially, you provide getter/setter methods to control access to your member variables. Let's create a version of the Car class that controls access to the price attribute so that users can't set the price under $1,000.

```
class Car:
    ...
    ...
    def __setattr__(self, name, value):
        if name == "price":
            if (value > 1000):
                self.__dict__["price"] = value
            else:
                self.__dict__["price"] = 1000
        else:
            self.__dict__[name] = value
    ...
    ...
```

Notice that we use the __dict__ method that contains all of the member variables of the class instance. If we had tried to use self.attribute_name, we would have thrown our program into an endless loop of recursive calls to __setattr__ (I know this from experience). The method checks to see if the name of the attribute is price. If so, we provide some special handling for setting price. Otherwise, we just set the value of all other attributes: self.__dict__[name] = value, which, by the way, is the behavior of the default implementation. A similar technique could be used for __getattr__ and __delattr__. The sample code here uses the above added logic in the __setattr__ method.

```
C:\py\book\chap9>jython -i car4.py
>>> car = Car("Ford", "Mustang", "Bright Orange", 5000)
>>> car.price = 2000
>>> car.price
2000

>>> car.price = 1001
>>> car.price
1001

>>> car.price = 900
>>> car.price
1000
```

## *Inheritance*

Inheritance allows you to reuse common code and so has a profound effect on the way you implement your Python classes. It also allows you to organize your classes into a hierarchical arrangement. Classes toward the bottom of the hierarchy inherit from classes higher up (like a family tree). Thus, if you create a class, classB, that inherits behavior and attributes from another class, ClassA, then classB becomes the subclass of classA, and classA becomes the superclass of classB.

A subclass can override or create new behavior and attributes specific to its role. This is called specialization.

### The Limits of Inheritance

It may look like one, but inheritance is no silver bullet. In fact, there are reasons to limit its use. Like all good things, inheritance should be used in moderation, primarily to avoid coupling between subclass and superclass.

There are two forms of inheritance: implementation and interface.

Remember that the implementation of a class is one of the things we try to hide with encapsulation. If you're going to do implementation inheritance from a weakly written base class (superclass), watch out—if a base class is buggy, so are all of its subclasses. And, if you introduce a bug into the base class, you introduce it into all of the subclasses.

I'm not saying organizing your classes into a hierarchy of classes is wrong; just proceed with caution because inheritance provides code reuse at the expense of encapsulation.

A good book on object-oriented design is *Design Patterns* (Gamma et al., Addison-Wesley, 1995). It describes some of the pitfalls of inheritance, including tight coupling of subclasses to superclasses, and provides blueprints for good designs. The book is indispensable to OOP programmers.

## Code Reuse and the Class Hierarchy

One of the major advantages of object-oriented programming is code reuse. We'll illustrate this with a real-world example of inheritance.

Cars and trucks are similar in that they both have certain physical characteristics like doors and windows and they both have a make, model, and vehicle identification number (VIN). Of course, they're also very different. One is for carrying loads; the other is for carrying passengers. Still, we can put the things common to trucks and cars in a base class, which we can then subclass into separate car and truck classes

Based on these principles we can create a base class called Automobile that consists of make, model, VIN, price, mpg, and so forth. The Truck subclass may specialize Automobile with towing capacity, bed size, and the like; the Car subclass may do so with trunk capacity and number of passengers.

The class hierarchy for cars and trucks might look like Figure 6–1.

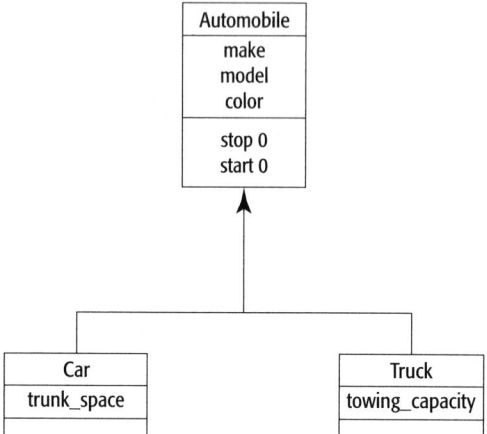

**Figure 6–1**    Automobile *Class Hierarchy*

Now we'll derive two classes from Automobile called Car  and Truck, as in the figure. Here is the base class (from *Automobile1.py)*:

```
class Automobile:
     max_Price = 7000
     running = 0

     def __setattr__(self, name, value):
         ...

     def __nonzero__(self):
         ...

     def __cmp__(self, other):
         ...
         ...

     def __hash__(self):
         ...

     def __init__(self, make, model, color, price=5000):
         ...

     def __del__(self):
         ...

     def start(self):
         ...

     def stop(self):
         ...

     def __str__(self):
         ...

     def __repr__(self):
         ...
```

Here are the Car and Truck subclasses (from *Automobile2.py*):

```
class Car (Automobile):
        def __init__(self, make, model, color, price, trunk_space= 5):
                Automobile.__init__(self, make, model, color, price)
                self.trunk_space = trunk_space

class Truck (Automobile):
        def __init__(self, make, model, color, price, tow_capacity = 2):
                Automobile.__init__(self, make, model, color, price)
                self.tow_capacity = tow_capacity
```

The statement class Car (Automobile) tells Python to subclass a Car class from Automobile. The statement Automobile.__init__(self, make, model, color, price) tells Python to call the base class constructor. The constructor isn't doing much right now, but when we build graphical user interfaces it will do a lot.

When you create a new instance of the Truck class, you get the attributes defined in it as well as all attributes defined in its base class, Automobile. Thus, the base classes and current classes mix to assemble a template for the class instance. Then each class instance is initialized with the attribute data that describes it.

Methods work similarly. An instance can access all of the methods of its class and its superclasses (base classes). If you call a method on an instance, Python checks its class for that method definition. If it finds it, it calls the method. If not, it checks the superclass (or superclasses). Python will look all the way up the class hierarchy for the method to call, so when you define a method with the same name as that of a base class method, you effectively override that method's functionality.

Python, unlike Java, provides multiple inheritance, which means that it can inherit functionality from more than one class. Java provides single inheritance, which means that a class can inherit only from one superclass.

There are problems with multiple inheritance. For example, two base classes can have a method with the same name. Python gets rid of these problems by having left-to-right multiple inheritance. That is, the base class to the left in the definition of the class overrides the base class to the right.

Let's say that our Car class inherits from two base classes, Automobile and Vehicle. Let's also say that both of these classes have a __start__ method. If we want Car to use Vehicle's __start__ method, we have to define it like this:

```
def Car (Vehicle, Automobile):
```

If we want Car to use Automobile's __start__ method, we have to define it like this:

```
def Car (Automobile, Vehicle):
```

## *Polymorphism*

Of the three pillars of OOP, inheritance and encapsulation are nice to have but polymorphism is the true key to OOP's success. Polymorphism gives objects the most important feature of all: replaceability.

There are two forms of polymorphism: late-bound and typed. Visual Basic uses late-bound, whereas Java uses typed. Python polymorphism is a hybrid of the two.

## Late-Bound Polymorphism

In Python, late-bound polymorphism means that class instances can appear to be other objects if their class implements special methods. Thus, because a function is an object, a class can act like a function just by implementing a special method. Numeric types are also objects, so with special methods a class can act like a numeric type.

For example, to make a class act like a function we can use the function notation with the class to make a call and pass instances of the class where we expect a function object. All we need to do is add a __call__ method to a class in the form __call__(self[, args...]. The following interactive session shows how:

```
>>> class hello:
...         def __call__(self):
...                 print "Hello World"
...
>>> hi = hello()    # define an instance of hello
>>> hi()            # use the hi instance as a function
Hello World
```

Also, we can use a variable number of arguments with the __call__ method as follows:

```
>>> class Add:
...         def __call__(self, num1, num2):
...                 return num1 + num2
...
>>> add = Add()     #define an instance of the Add class
>>> add(1,2)        # use the add instance as a function
3
```

We can define classes that act like numeric types with the __add__, __radd__, __sub__, and __rsub__ methods. The method used depends on the class, as shown in Table 6–3. To demonstrate how we use them, let's define a simple Car class that implements __add__. Follow along in interactive mode.

```
>>> class Car:
...         def __init__(self, inventory):
...                 self.inventory = inventory
...         def __add__(self, other):  #define an __add__ method
...                 return self.inventory + other
...
>>> #define a Car instance to hold the # of buicks
>>> buicks_in_lot = Car(5)

>>> #define a Car instance to hold the # of chevys
>>> chevys_in_lot = Car(20)
```

**Table 6–3**  *Methods That Define Classes to Act Like Numbers*

| Method | Behavior |
| --- | --- |
| __add__ (self, other), __radd__ (self, other) | >> num1 + num2 |
| __sub__ (self, other), __rsub__ (self, other) | >> num1 - num2 |
| __mul__ (self, other), __rmul__ (self, other) | >> num1 * num2 |
| __div__ (self, other), __rdiv__ (self, other) | >> num1 / num2 |
| __mod__ (self, other), __rmod__ (self, other) | >> num1 % num2 |
| __divmod__ (self, other), __rdivmod__ (self, other) | >> divmod(num1, num2) |
| __pow__ (self, other), __rpow__ (self, other) | >> num1 ** num2 |
| __lshift__ (self, other), __rlshift__ (self, other) | >> num1 << num2 |
| __rshift__ (self, other), __rrshift__ (self, other) | >> num1 >> num2 |
| __and__ (self, other), __rand__ (self, other) | >> num1 & num2 |
| __xor__ (self, other), __rxor__ (self, other) | >> num1 ^ num2 |
| __or__ (self, other), __ror__ (self, other) | >> num1 \| num2 |
| __neg__ (self) | >> num1 = 1<br>>> -num1<br>-1 |
| __pos__ (self) | >> num1 = 1<br>>> +num1<br>1 |
| __abs__ (self) | >> num1 = -1<br>>> abs(num1)<br>1 |

```
>>> buicks_in_lot + 5          # if we add 5 more…how many buicks?
     10
>>> chevys_in_lot + 5          # if we add 5 more; how many chevys?
     25
```

Now we can add numeric types to our instances.

What about adding other instances? For example, what happens if we add `chevys_in_lot + buicks_in_lot`?

```
>>> chevys_in_lot + buicks_in_lot
Traceback (innermost last):
  File "<interactive input>", line 0, in ?
  File "<interactive input>", line 5, in __add__
TypeError: __add__ nor __radd__ defined for these operands
```

Of course, this isn't what we want. To get the proper behavior we need to define a __radd__ method, which is necessary when the operand is on the right and the left operand doesn't support __add__. To add both instances together, we have to do this (follow along):

```
>>> class Car:
...          def __init__(self, inventory):
...              self.inventory = inventory
...          def __add__(self, other):
...              return self.inventory + other
...          def __radd__(self, other):
...              return self.inventory + other
...
>>> buicks_in_lot, chevys_in_lot = Car(5), Car(20)
>>> chevys_in_lot + buicks_in_lot
25
```

If you define the methods shown in Table 6–4, you can create a class whose instances act like a dictionary. Let's create such a class that implements all of the methods in the table and calls a real dictionary.

```
class MyDict:
      def __init__(self):
          self.dict = {}
      def __len__(self):
          return len(self.dict)
      def __getitem__(self, key):
          return self.dict[key]
      def __setitem__(self, key, value):
          self.dict[key]=value
      def __delitem__(self, key):
          del(self.dict[key])
      def keys(self)    :
          return self.dict.keys()
      def values(self):
          return self.dict.values()
      def items(self):
          return self.dict.items()
      def has_key(self, key):
          return self.dict.has_key(key)
      def get(self, key):
          return self.dict.get(key)
      def clear(self):
          self.dict.clear()
      def copy(self):
          return self.dict.copy()
      def __str__(self):
          return str(self.dict)
      def __repr__(self):
          return repr(dict)
      def update(self, dict):
          self.dict.update(dict)
```

**Table 6–4**   *Methods That Define Classes to Act like Dictionaries*

| Method | Behavior |
|---|---|
| __len__(self) | >> len(dict) 3 |
| __getitem__(self, key) | >> dict[key] 'Missy' |
| __setitem__(self, key, value) | >> dict[key] = value |
| __delitem__(self, key) | >> del dict[key] |
| keys(self) | >> dict.keys() ['Miguel', 'Adam', 'Rick'] |
| values(self) | >> dict.value() ['Martha', 'Missy', 'Kiley'] |
| items(self) | >> dict.items() [('Rick', 'Kiley'), ('Adam', 'Missy'), ('Miguel', 'Martha')] |
| has_key(self, key) | >> dict.has_key(key) 1 |
| get(self, key) | >>> dict.get('Rick') 'Kiley' |
| clear(self) | >>dict.clear() |
| copy(self) | >>cdict = dict.copy() |
| update(self, dict) | >>dict2.update(dict) |

To test the dictionary, we write the following code:

```
if __name__ == "__main__":
      main()

def main():
      dict = MyDict()
      print "test __setitem__"
      dict["Ham"] = "Eggs"
      dict["Tom"] = "Jerry"
      dict["Mike"] ="Ike"
      print "setitem ", dict

      print "test __getitem__ and get"
      print "getiem ", dict["Ham"], dict["Tom"], dict["Mike"]
      print "get ", dict.get("Ham"), dict.get("Tom"), dict.get("Mike")

      print "test del"
      del dict["Ham"]
      print dict

      print "test keys"
      for key in dict.keys():
            print " " + key

      print "test values"
      for value in dict.values():
            print " " + `value`
```

```
print "test items"
for item in dict.items():
        print " " + `item`

print "test has_keys"
print "true " + `dict.has_key("Tom")`
print "false " + `dict.has_key("Ham")`

print "test copy"
cdict = dict.copy()
print cdict

print "test clear"
dict.clear()
print dict

print "test update"
dict.update(cdict)
print cdict
```

We put the code we use to test the dictionary in the section of the module that runs only as a main module. That is,

```
>>> import dict
>>> dict.main()
test __setitem__
setitem {'Tom': 'Jerry', 'Mike': 'Ike', 'Ham': 'Eggs'}
test __getitem__ and get
getitem Eggs Jerry Ike
get Eggs Jerry Ike
test del
{'Tom': 'Jerry', 'Mike': 'Ike'}
test keys
  Tom
  Mike
test values
  'Jerry'
  'Ike'
test items
  ('Tom', 'Jerry')
  ('Mike', 'Ike')
test has_keys
true 1
false 0
test copy
{'Tom': 'Jerry', 'Mike': 'Ike'}
test clear
{}
test update
{'Tom': 'Jerry', 'Mike': 'Ike'}
```

As promised, our dictionary class acts just like a regular dictionary.

To find out more about how to simulate built-in objects, refer to the documentation that ships with Python. It's a wealth of well-written information.

> ### The Power of Polymorphism
>
> The dictionary we created is simple; it only delegates operations to a real dictionary object. Imagine building a dictionary-like class that accesses a file, a database, or a directory server. To the application developer, this class looks just like another dictionary but does far more. You can even use it like a class instance transparently, with code written to work with built-in dictionaries. This is truly a powerful concept.

To write a class whose instances behave like a list, you implement the methods __getslice__(), __setslice__(), __delslice__(), append(), count(), index(), insert(), pop(), remove(), reverse(), and sort(), just like you do with Python standard list objects. For concatenation you use __add__() and __radd__().

> ### Python's List and Dictionary Modules
>
> Python ships with two class modules, *userdict* and *userlist*, that implement a dictionary and a list, respectively. Both are well documented.

We won't implement a list in this section. As an exercise at the end of the chapter, you'll create a list using a technique similar to the one we used for a dictionary.

## Typed Polymorphism

With OOP you can build an entire framework of extensible reusable components. Python, unlike other languages, isn't strictly typed. In Java, Visual Basic, and C++, classes become types that the user can make into objects (i.e., instances), whereas in Python all instances of a class are of type Instance; also, classes aren't types unto themselves but are part of a type class. The following examples illustrate these ideas.

First we define a simple class, Myclass.

```
>>> class Myclass:
...     pass
...
```

Then we create an instance of Myclass and check its type.

```
>>> an_instance = Myclass()
>>> type(an_instance)
<jclass org.python.core.PyInstance at 5325988>
```

Next we check the type of Myclass.

```
>>> type(Myclass)
<jclass org.python.core.PyClass at 7914640>
```

Programmers, if you're used to other languages that use typed classes, you may think that Python is a little weird. Actually, the typed system of other languages is orthogonal to Python's. The only real difference is a little bit of syntax and the fact that in Python classes don't define types.

For example, in Java you do this to get the type of a class:

```
an_instance.getClass().getName()
```

whereas in Python you do this:

```
an_instance.__class__.__name__
```

Again, in Java you do this to see if an object is an instance of a class:

```
if(an_instance instanceof MyClass)System.out.println("true");
```

In Python you do this:

```
if(isinstance(an_instance, MyClass)): print("true")
```

In Python, classes and instances are objects that can be manipulated at runtime, which is a good thing. For instance, you can add a method to a class at runtime so that every instance of that class has that method available in its interface. Also, you can add members to an instance at runtime. Whether those members are methods or other objects doesn't matter, because everything is an object that can be manipulated. This makes Python very flexible.

So, why have a section on typed polymorphism if Python doesn't really support it? Actually, Python has something very close. For example, you can check to see if an instance is a class type like this:

```
if isinstance(an_instance, MyClass)
```

Let's go back to our earlier example of cars and trucks with a function that takes a list of automobiles and starts each one.

```
def startAuto(list):
        for auto in list:
                if isinstance(auto, Automobile):
                        auto.start()
```

The function invokes the __start__ method of each auto instance in the list. It doesn't care if the instance is a Car or a Truck because any instance of either is also an instance of Automobile and thus supports the __start__ method. This is the form of polymorphism most people with a Java background are used to.

The __start__ method works not only with the Car and Truck subclasses but also with any future subclass that inherits from Automobile, such as Motorcycle.

## Summary

In this chapter we covered the fundamentals of object-oriented programming: polymorphism, inheritance, and encapsulation. We also looked at typed and late-bound polymorphism.

# CHAPTER 7    *Errors and Exceptions*

Bad things happen to good programs: Disks crash, files are corrupted, and batteries fail. Such things are typically more the exception than the rule, and to plan for all of them would make for some very complicated code. That's why modern programming languages like Python have the ability to handle bad things, called exceptions in programming speak.

The old way of dealing with errors was to check the return types of functions, but this was very time consuming. Each function call would require an `if` statement with perhaps many `elif` clauses; code would have to be written to extract what had happened. The new way is exception handling, in which the exception has the information about what went wrong. Instead of checking after each of the method calls, you can set up one exception handler that works with many methods.

**129**

By the end of this chapter, you should understand `try`, `raise`, and `finally` statements. You should also have a firm grasp on the class-based exceptions that Python defines. A class-based exception allows you to create a hierarchy of exception classes.

## Syntax and Sequence Errors

If you followed along with the interactive sessions in previous chapters as recommended, you ran into errors, most of them involving syntax (I know I have). Here's an example:

```
>>> for x in xrange(0, 100)
... Traceback (innermost last):
  (no code object) at line 0
  File "<stdin>", line 1
        for x in xrange(0, 100)
                                    ^
SyntaxError: invalid syntax
```

Using `SyntaxError: invalid syntax` as a clue, we discover that we forgot to put the colon at the end of the `for` header. There's not much you can do about syntax errors except fix them. As you learn Python, you'll see such errors less and less.

Perhaps some readers have run into exceptions like this one:

```
>>> list = 1
>>> for x in list:
...     print(`x`)
...
Traceback (innermost last):
  File "<stdin>", line 1, in ?
AttributeError: __getitem__
```

Here we tried to use an integer like a sequence, and, by throwing an exception, Python is telling us we can't do that.

Before we go any further, I should clear up the difference between and error and an exception. An error usually involves syntax, such as a missing comma, whereas an exception usually involves an operation gone wrong, such as dividing by zero. Think of it this way: Exceptions can be correct syntax but wrong operations.

## The Danger of Exceptions

An unhandled exception can stop a program dead in its tracks. This may be okay if you're still developing it, but it's bad if the program has been delivered. Consider the following function (from *divby()-1.py*), which stops as soon as it runs into a 0 value as a denominator in the list.

```
def figurePercentage(figures):
    for tuple in figures:
        numerator = tuple[0]
        denominator = tuple[1]
        percent = numerator/denominator
        print ("The percentage is " + `percent`)
```

Here the function `figurePercentage()` expects to receive a sequence of sequences that each contain two numeric fields. So we create a list sequence that contains several tuples, each containing two numeric values, and we invoke `figurePercentage()` with the sequence as follows:

```
figures = [(10.0,20.0), (100.0, 200.0), (300.0, 400.0), (1.0, 0.0),
(11.0,20.0), (110.0, 200.0) ]
figurePercentage(figures)
```

The `figurePercentage()` function iterates through each tuple in the list, extracting its 0-indexed item as the numerator and its 1-indexed item as the denominator.

```
for tuple in figures:
    numerator = tuple[0]
    denominator = tuple[1]
    percent = numerator/denominator
    percent = percent * 100
    print ("The percentage is " + `percent` + "%")
```

One tuple has a `0.0` denominator, and we know that we can't divide any number by zero. Let's run this and see what happens.

```
>>> import divby0_1
The percentage is 50.0%
The percentage is 50.0%
The percentage is 75.0%
Traceback (innermost last):
  File "<stdin>", line 1, in ?
  File "C:\\.\divby0_1.py", line 10, in ?
  File "C:\\.\divby0_1.py", line 5, in figurePercentage
ZeroDivisionError: float division
>>>
```

The function stops as soon as it hits the zero denominator because a `ZeroDivision Error` exception has occurred.

One way to solve such a problem is to prevent it from happening. We can do this by checking for a zero denominator before we divide the numerator by the denominator. In a lot of C and older C++ programs that predate exception handling, this is exactly what you have to do. (We'll cover when to handle a problem as an exception and when to check beforehand for possible errors later in the chapter.)

But what if we don't expect to get a zero value in the denominator? What if this value is an exceptional occurrence? If we add tests for every possible thing that can go wrong, our code can become messy and hard to read. Conversely, if we don't handle this error, our program will just stop working when it receives a zero divisor. Mission-critical programs aren't supposed to stop working for minor problems like this. What if this is a function in a payroll program? Would you want to get paid late because someone forgot to check for a divide-by-zero exception?

## The try Statement

The `try` statement specifies a way to handle exceptions. One form is the following:

```
try:
      suite
except expression-target:
      suite
except:
      suite
```

which can have one or many `except` clauses—the exception handlers. If an exception occurs in the `try` clause's suite of statements, an exception handler that best fits it will be invoked. An `except` clause that doesn't have an expression target can act as a `catchall` bucket. If an exception doesn't have a specific exception handler and an `except` clause without an expression target is present, the exception will go to that clause.

---

**The Call Stack**

A call stack represents the order of called functions. For example, if a module calls function `A()` and function `A()` calls function `B()` and function `B()` calls function `C()`, the call stack is `A->B->C`. If an exception occurs in function `C()` and isn't handled, it propagates to function `B()`. If function `B()` doesn't handle it, the exception propagates to function `A()`. If function `A()` doesn't handle it, the program stops.

---

**Matching a Handler to an Exception**

Unlike in Java, in Python there is no common base class such as `Throwable`, `Runtime Exception`, or `Exception` for all exceptions. Even so, Python has generally adopted the Java approach to exception handling, as we'll see later.

Similar to Java's way, in Python an exception matches a handler if the handler is the object that identifies the exception or a base class of the exception, or if the object thrown exactly matches the handler's object identity.

Also, in Python the handler matches the exception if it has a tuple containing an item that matches the exception. This means that you can handle several exceptions in one `except` clause.

Here is figurePercentage() (from *divby0-2.py*) expanded with exception handling:

```
def figurePercentage(figures):
    for tuple in figures:
        try:
            numerator = tuple[0]
            denominator = tuple[1]
            percent = numerator/denominator
            percent = percent * 100
            print ("The percentage is " + `percent` + "%")
        except ZeroDivisionError:
            print ("percentage error")

figures = [(10.0,20.0), (100.0, 200.0), (300.0, 400.0), (1.0, 0.0),
(11.0,20.0), (110.0, 200.0)]
figurePercentage(figures)
```

The output looks like this:

```
>>> import divby0_2
The percentage is 50.0%
The percentage is 50.0%
The percentage is 75.0%
percentage error
The percentage is 55.0%
The percentage is 55.0%
>>>
```

## The except Clause

Notice that the program in the example above doesn't stop midway in its iteration through the list. Instead, it prints out that there was an error in one of the percentage calculations and continues on its way. The magic to this is the try statement with the except clause.

```
try:
    numerator = tuple[0]
    denominator = tuple[1]
    percent = numerator/denominator
    print ("The percentage is " + `percent`)
except ZeroDivisionError:
        print ("percentage error")
```

In English this says, "Try to execute these statements. If the ZeroDivisionError exception occurs, go to the except clause and execute its statement." This handling of the exception allows the program to continue.

What if someone passes a list that doesn't have just sequences? Follow along in interactive mode.

```
>>> from divby0_2 import figurePercentage
>>> nasty_list = [(1.0, 1.0), (2.0, 2.0), 2, (3.0, 3.0)]
>>> figurePercentage(nasty_list)
```

Here's the output:

```
The percentage is 1.0
The percentage is 1.0
Traceback (innermost last):
  File "<stdin>", line 1, in ?
  File "C:\\.\divby0_2.py", line 19, in ?
  File "C:\\.\divby0_2.py", line 4, in figurePercentage
AttributeError: __getitem__
```

Even though we handled the divide-by-zero problem, we didn't handle the
AttributeError exception. So we add an except clause with an empty target expression to catch this and any other possible exceptions.

### The Catchall Exception Handler

Let's continue figuring percentages and add the ability to handle a nonsequence
being passed to figurePercentage(). The following example is from *divby0_3.py*.

```
def figurePercentage(figures):
    for tuple in figures:
        try:
            numerator = tuple[0]
            denominator = tuple[1]
            percent = numerator/denominator
            percent = percent * 100
            print ("The percentage is " + `percent` + "%")
        except ZeroDivisionError:
            print ("divide by 0 percentage error")
        except:
            print ("percentage error")
print("The nice list")
figures = [(10.0,20.0), (100.0, 200.0), (300.0, 400.0), (1.0, 0.0),
(11.0,20.0), (110.0, 200.0)]
figurePercentage(figures)

print("------------------------------------------")
print("The nasty list")
nasty_list = [(1.0, 1.0), (2.0, 2.0), 2, (3.0, 3.0)]
figurePercentage(nasty_list)
```

This time when we run our program, the error is caught. Note that we changed
the exception handler of the ZeroDivisionError exception to print that there was a
divide-by-zero error. The catchall exception handler prints out that there was a
generic percentage error as before. Here's the output:

```
The nice list
The percentage is 50.0%
The percentage is 50.0%
The percentage is 75.0%
divide by 0 percentage error
The percentage is 55.0%
The percentage is 55.0%
------------------------------------
```

```
The nasty list
The percentage is 100.0%
The percentage is 100.0%
percentage error
The percentage is 100.0%
```

In essence, the catchall exception handler

```
except:
     print ("percentage error")
```

says, "If any exception is raised, catch it and print out "percentage error"." To highlight that this statement is a catchall exception, let's send figurePercentage() another list, this time with a sequence that contains only one item (this example is from *divby0_3.py*).

```
>>> from divby0_3 import figurePercentage
...
...
>>> list1 = [[0,0], [1,1], [2,2], [3], [4,4]]
>>> figurePercentage(list1)
divide by 0 percentage error
The percentage is 100%
The percentage is 100%
percentage error
The percentage is 100%
```

list[3] is a list with only one item in it, so we get an IndexError exception when we try to get the denominator.

Generally it's a bad idea to sprinkle catchall exception handlers throughout your code. However, instead of a hard and fast rule this is more an issue of style and application specifics. For instance, if you expect a zero in the denominator from time to time, you should test for this rather than rely on catching it as an exception. The same is true if you expect an occasional integer instead of a sequence in a list.

Because we added exception handling for zero denominators, we're saying that we don't expect them, but if we add the check

```
if(denominator == 0):
     print ("The percentage cannot be calculated")
elif:
percent = numerator/denominator
     percent = percent * 100
     print ("The percentage is " + `percent` + "%")
```

we're saying that we do expect them.

Using exception handling is a matter of program requirements; in other words, it's application specific. Exception handling is expensive and should be used only in exceptional cases, not in the normal execution of code. Remember, though, you should never put go code (for beginners, "go code" is code essential to running the program) in an exception handler.

*Exception Handling and Interfacing with Other Systems*

When you interface with other systems, such as components you didn't write, non-standard libraries, or, worse, end users, the chances of an exception happening that you can't plan for increase. As I said, one uncaught exception can bring down the whole program, so just before deployment put catchall exception handlers in your code where this interfacing will take place. (At a minimum, the catchall should be able to log the error or you should be able to enable logging with problematic code to catch exceptions.)

You don't want a catchall exception handler when you're developing a program. Rather, you want to identify and handle as many exceptional conditions as needed, especially for mission-critical systems. To avoid a harmless exception bringing down such a system, log all exceptions and evaluate them offline or try to recreate them in a controlled setting and develop a handler for them. You may be able to recover from some exceptions gracefully.

## The else Clause

Another feature of the first form of the `try` statement is the `else` clause. `else`'s suite is executed only if no exceptions occurred.

```
try:
        suite
except expression-target:
        suite
except:
        suite
else:
        suite

The percentage is 1.0
The percentage is 1.0
Traceback (innermost last):
  File "<stdin>", line 1, in ?
  File "C:\\.\divby0_2.py", line 19, in ?
  File "C:\\.\divby0_2.py", line 4, in figurePercentage
AttributeError: __getitem__
```

Using our denominator example (*divby0_4.py*), if we want to determine if any exceptions occurred, we can add an `else` clause to the end of our `try` statement as follows:

```
def figurePercentage(figures):
    for tuple in figures:
        try:
            numerator = tuple[0]
            denominator = tuple[1]
            percent = numerator/denominator
            percent = percent * 100
            print ("The percentage is " + `percent` + "%")
        except ZeroDivisionError:
            print ("divide by 0 percentage error")
```

```
        except:
                print ("percentage error")
        else:
                print ("No exceptions occurred")
```

If no exceptions occurred, the `figurePercentage()` function prints out "`No exceptions occurred`" during each iteration in which that statement remains true.

## The raise Statement

A `raise` statement forces an exception to be raised. One form is

```
raise exception-expression, description-expression
```

In our denominator example, it raises a specific exception.

```
>>> raise ZeroDivisionError, "Sequence has a Zero value in the denominator"
Traceback (innermost last):
  File "<stdin>", line 1, in ?
ZeroDivisionError: Sequence has a Zero value in the denominator
```

The `exception-expression` must be of type `String` or be an instance object. The `description-expression` is optional. If you use `raise` with no `exception-expression`, it reraises the last exception.

You can easily define your own exception using a string variable.

```
>>> badListForm = 'badListForm'
>>> try:
...     raise badListForm, "The list had a malformed tuple"
... except badListForm, msg:
...     print ("Exception occurred :" + badListForm + " " + msg)
...
Exception occurred :badListForm The list had a malformed tuple
>>> raise badListForm, "Hi Mom"
>>> badListForm = 'badListForm'
>>> try:
...     raise badListForm, "The list had a malformed tuple"
... except badListForm, msg:
...     print ("Exception occurred :" + badListForm + " " + msg)
...
Exception occurred :badListForm The list had a malformed tuple

>>> raise badListForm, "Hi Mom"
```

### Strings: Bad Style for Exceptions

The use of strings to raise exceptions has fallen out of favor and will likely be phased out of the language. The more "Pythonically" correct method is to use a class instance, which we'll cover a little later. I used the string example here because strings are easy to define and thus make it easy to illustrate exceptions.

Here's how we can modify our figurePercentage() example to handle and reraise (throw) an exception we've already defined:

```
badListForm = 'badListForm'

def figurePercentage(figures):
    for tuple in figures:
        try:
            numerator = tuple[0]
            denominator = tuple[1]
            percent = numerator/denominator
            percent = percent * 100
            print ("The percentage is " + `percent` + "%")
        except ZeroDivisionError:
            print ("divide by 0 percentage error")
            raise
        except AttributeError:
            raise badListForm, "An item in the list is not a sequence"
        except IndexError:
            raise badListForm, "A sequence in the list does" \
                        " not have two items"
        except:
            print ("percentage error")

        else:
            #print ("No exceptions occurred")
            pass
```

First, let's examine the ZeroDivisionError exception handler

```
except ZeroDivisionError:
    print ("divide by 0 percentage error")
    raise
```

which, as we see, prints out an error message and then uses the raise statement with no expressions. (Remember, raise with no expressions reraises the active exception.) The following code snippet passes a list containing a tuple with a zero for the denominator:

```
try:
    print("The nice list")
    figures = [(10.0,20.0), (100.0, 200.0), (300.0, 400.0), (1.0, 0.0),
(11.0,20.0), (110.0, 200.0)]
    figurePercentage(figures)
except ZeroDivisionError, msg:
    print("Exception:" + `ZeroDivisionError` + ": " + msg)
```

As soon as figurePercentage() hits the zero denominator tuple ((1,0,0,0)), it catches the exception, prints a message, and then reraises the exception, which in the above code will be caught by the exception handler at the top of the call stack. Here's the output:

```
The percentage is 50.0%
The percentage is 50.0%
The percentage is 75.0%
divide by 0 percentage error
Exception:'ZeroDivisionError': float division
```

In the following example, we define our own exception, badListForm, and raise it when we get an AttributeError or an IndexError. Notice that the raise statement is used to raise badListForm with two different messages.

```
badListForm = 'badListForm'
        ...
        ...
        except AttributeError:
                raise badListForm, "An item in the list is not a sequence"
        except IndexError:
                raise badListForm, "A sequence in the list does" \
                                " not have two items"
```

Therefore, if we execute the code snippet

```
try:
        print("---------------------------------------")
        print("The list with a non sequence")
        nasty_list = [(1.0, 1.0), (2.0, 2.0), 2, (3.0, 3.0)]
        figurePercentage(nasty_list)
except badListForm, msg:
        print ("Exception:" + `badListForm` + " : " + msg)

try:
        print("---------------------------------------")
        print("The list with a sequence that contains less items than 2")
        nasty_list = [(1.0, 1.0), (2.0, 2.0), [3], (4.0, 4.0)]
        figurePercentage(nasty_list)
except badListForm, msg:
        print ("Exception:" + `badListForm` + " : " + msg)
```

we get the following output:

```
---------------------------------------
The list with a non sequence
The percentage is 100.0%
The percentage is 100.0%
Exception:'badListForm' : An item in the list is not a sequence
---------------------------------------
The list with a sequence that contains less items than 2
The percentage is 100.0%
The percentage is 100.0%
Exception:'badListForm' : A sequence in the list does not have two items
```

> ### *Equality Is Not Enough*
>
> Having the same value string is not enough. The string exception in the `except` clause must be exactly the same as the object that was raised, which in Pythonese means
>
> `str1 == str2 being true is not enough`
>
> instead of
>
> `str1 is str2 has to be true.`

## The finally Clause

The second of the two forms of `try` cleans up an exception. It includes a `finally` clause, and looks like this:

```
try:
        suite
finally:
        suite
```

You can't use a `finally` clause and an `except` clause in the same `try` statement.

Here's a simple `try...finally` example:

```
>>> try:
...     raise "hello", "Hello Error"
...     print "Hello"
... finally:
...     print "Finally"
...
Finally
Traceback (innermost last):
  File "<stdin>", line 2, in ?
hello: Hello Error
```

The `try...finally` clause guarantees that the `finally` clause will be executed whether or not an exception occurs. You want cleanup code in a `finally` clause—it's like closing a database connection or a file. We'll use `finally` a lot when we deal with files in Chapter 8.

## *Classes and Instances as Exceptions*

Earlier we defined our own exception using a string object, making it user defined. The new Python way of defining exceptions is with classes and class instances, which means that the `raise` statement can take the following form:

```
raise class, class_instance
```

```
raise class_instance
```

In the except clause, you list the name of the class. If the exception instance raised is an instance of that class (a direct instance or an instance of a subclass), except will catch it. The exception class you define *should* be derived from the Exception class, which is defined in the exception module (*exception.py*). As of now, this isn't a requirement, but it likely will be in the future. If you use an instance of Exception in conjunction with the str() function, it will return all of the arguments passed to its constructor.

I know these concepts are hard to visualize, so let's do a few quick examples to make them easier to grasp.

## Type Exception

First we raise an error of type Exception as follows:

```
>>> try:
...       error = Exception("Not working", "Something Broke", "Better call for help")
...       raise error
... except Exception:
...       print "Got an error"
...
Got an error
>>>
```

We catch the raised exception with our except Exception: handler, which is useful but doesn't do anything with the arguments we passed as our exceptions instance.

The next listing (*chap7_1*) shows how to use the arguments we passed to the Exception constructor in conjunction with the str statement. (We're going to make things gradually more complex, so be sure to follow along.)

```
try:
     error = Exception("Not working", "Something Broke", "call for help")
     raise error
except Exception, instance:
     print "Got an error " + str( instance)
     print instance.__class__.__name__
```

As you can see, the second argument passed to the exception handler is the instance we raised. When you use the str statement with the instance of the Exception class, you get the argument passed to the constructor converted to a string. The output from the above code is

```
Got an error ('Not working', 'Something Broke', 'call for help')
Exception
```

Just so we leave no doubt that the second argument to the except clause is in fact the instance we threw (I meant to say "raised"—more on this later), we print out the name of the instance class, that is, Exception.

## User-Defined Class-Based Exceptions

To round out our examples of class-based exceptions, we'll create our own (that is, user-defined). Of course, we did this before using the old way with string objects, but now we'll do it using classes. Here is a listing (*chap7_2*) that defines three user-defined exceptions.

```
Listing chap7_2
class CarException(Exception):
        pass
class BrakeFailed(CarException):
        pass
class EngineFailed(CarException):
        pass

if __name__ == "__main__":
        main()

def main():
        try:
                        error = BrakeFailed("Not working", "Something Broke",
                                "Better call for help", "Get an Airbag")
                        raise error
        except BrakeFailed, instance:
                        print "Got a BrakeFailed exception " + str(instance) \
                        + " " + instance.__class__.__name__

        try:
                        error = BrakeFailed("Brakes Not working", "Something
                                Broke", "Better call for help", "Get an Airbag")
                        raise error
        except CarException, instance:
                        print "Got a Car Exception " + str(instance) + " " \
                        + instance.__class__.__name__
        except Exception, instance:
                        print "Got an exception " + str(instance) + " " \
                        + instance.__class__.__name__

        try:
                        error = BrakeFailed("Not working", "Something Broke",
                                "Better call for help", "Get an Airbag")
                        raise error
        except Exception, instance:
                        print "Got an exception " + str(instance) + " " \
                        + instance.__class__.__name__
```

Here's the output:

```
Got a BrakeFailed exception ('Not working', 'Something Broke', 'Better call
for help', 'Get an Airbag') BrakeFailed
Got an exception ('Not working', 'Something Broke', 'Better call for help',
'Get an Airbag')
BrakeFailed
Got a Car Exception ('Brakes Not working', 'Something Broke', 'Better call
for help', 'Get an Airbag') BrakeFailed
```

## Exception Hierarchy

Using the class approach, you can build a hierarchy of exceptions. This allows programmers who use the methods of one of your classes to decide the level of detail or granularity they care about. For example, you can define 30 CarException classes that can be thrown when the Car class starts—that is, when someone calls the class's __start__ method. One user of your Car class may care about all 30. Another may care only if any CarException is thrown and therefore write an except clause only to catch any exception derived from it.

The first try block in the main function of the *chap7_2* module raises an instance of BrakeFailed. Here we demonstrate an except clause that catches a BrakeFailed class. The second parameter should be the instance we raised.

```
try:
        error = BrakeFailed("Not working", "Something Broke", "Better call for
                help", "Get an Airbag")
        raise error
except BrakeFailed, instance:
        print "Got a BrakeFailed exception " + str(instance) + " " \
        + instance.__class__.__name__
```

To take our demonstration further, we show that not only can we catch a Brake Failed instance with an except clause that specifies a BrakeFailed class, but we can also catch the BrakeFailed instance with any base class of the BrakeFailed base class.

```
try:
        error = BrakeFailed("Brakes Not working", "Something Broke", "Better
                call for help", "Get an Airbag")
        raise error
except CarException, instance:
        print "Got a Car Exception " + str(instance) + " " \
        + instance.__class__.__name__
```

In the above code, we catch the BrakeFailed instance with an except block that specifies a CarException. We can do this because CarException is a base class of BrakeFailed. We can also catch a BrakeFailed class with any base class.

```
try:
        error = BrakeFailed("Not working", "Something Broke", "Better call for
                help", "Get an Airbag")
        raise error

except Exception, instance:
        print "Got an exception " + str(instance) + " " \
        + instance.__class__.__name__
```

Here we catch the BrakeFailed instance with the exception handler (the except clause) using the Exception class. With the above approach we can create hierarchies of exceptions that can all be caught by except clauses that specify the exceptions' base classes.

> ### Don't Give Up
>
> If you still don't understand these concepts, fire up the interactive interpreter and import the `BrakeFailed` class from module *chap7_2*, and try raising and catching the error inside a try block.
>
> Once again, the only way to learn programming is to program. I guarantee that the people having the hardest time understanding this chapter are probably the ones who aren't following along with the examples. Remember, if a picture is worth a thousand words, a working model is worth a thousand pictures.

### Most to Least Specific Order

What happens if you have two except clauses that both catch base classes of the instance you're throwing (raising)? Does the most specific class prevail? By most specific, I mean the class that's closest in the class hierarchy to the class of the instance being raised. Look at the listing for *chap7_2*, which shows the catch() method.

```
def catch():
        print "the most specific to the least specific"
        try:
                error = BrakeFailed()
                raise error
        except BrakeFailed, instance:
                print "I got it-1"
        except CarException, instance:
                print "Excuse me, but I've got it-2"
        except Exception, instance:
                print "No I beg your pardon, I've got it-3"

        print "Least specific to most specific"
        try:
                error = BrakeFailed()
                raise error
        except Exception, instance:
                print "Exception"
        except CarException, instance:
                print "CarException"
        except BrakeFailed, instance:
                print "BrakeFailed"
```

In the following excerpt from *chap7_2.catch()*, we see that the `BrakeFailed` exception is being raised and that there are three except clauses that can potentially catch it.

```
try:
        error = BrakeFailed()
        raise error
except BrakeFailed, instance:
        print "I got it-1"
except CarException, instance:
        print "Excuse me, but I've got it-2"
```

```
except Exception, instance:
        print "No I beg your pardon, I've got it-3"
```

The first except can catch BrakeFailed simply because it declares BrakeFailed in its clause. The next except also seems like a candidate because it declares a Car Exception in its clause and CarException is a base class of BrakeFailed. The third except seems to be a candidate as well because Exception is also a base class of BrakeFailed. (Exception is a direct base class of CarException, and CarException is a base class of BrakeFailed; thus, Exception is a base class of BrakeFailed, and an instance of BrakeFailed is also an instance of Exception.)

If we run the above code segment, we get

```
I got it-1
```

So in this case the most specific except caught the exception—that is, the first one, which has BrakeFailed in its clause. This being the case, what do you think the following code will do? Is it always the case that the most specific except clause will catch the exception?

```
try:
        error = BrakeFailed()
        raise error
except Exception, instance:
        print "Exception"
except CarException, instance:
        print "CarException"
except BrakeFailed, instance:
        print "BrakeFailed"
```

Unlike the last example, here we organized the order of except clauses from least to most specific. When we run this code, we get the following output:

```
Exception
```

### Java versus Python versus Delphi versus Visual Basic Exception Handling

Java's handling of exceptions is very similar to Python's. The following table shows the equivalent exception statements in the two languages as well as in Delphi and Visual Basic.

| Python | Java | Delphi (Object Pascal) | Visual Basic |
|--------|------|------------------------|--------------|
| try | try | try | on error goto label |
| except | catch | except | label |
| raise | throw | raise | raise |
| finally | finally | finally | on error resume next |

Exception handling in Java and Python isn't completely the same. One key difference is that Java allows you to declare the type of exception that a method will throw (that is, "raise" in Python). The method code must catch that exception or its base class.

Another key difference is that it's a syntax error in Java to list `catch` statements (`except` clauses in Python) as anything but most to least specific. This feature won't allow you to write code that will never be reached. In my opinion, Python should do something like this or, better yet, should always send the raised exception to the most specific handler (`except` clause).

Python and Delphi share similar keywords, but Python's syntax for handling errors seems a little closer to Java's than to Delphi's. Regardless, exception handling in the three languages is close. Visual Basic does its own type of error handling.

Thus, the first `except` that has a base class of the class of the instance we're raising catches that raised instance. The last two in the example are never reached. This proves that the most specific `except` does not always catch the exception, and it means that we have to be careful in how we organize our `except` clauses to make sure that they're in most to least specific order.

### Garden Variety Exceptions

The exceptions described in the subsections that follow are used as base classes.

#### *Exception*

`Exception` is the root class for all exceptions—all built-in exceptions are derived from it, and all user-defined exceptions *should* be derived from it. The following interactive session shows that `ZeroDivisionError` is derived from `Exception`.

```
>>> try:
...     1/0
... except Exception, instance:
...     print instance.__class__.__name__
...
ZeroDivisionError
```

#### *StandardError*

`StandardError`, derived from `Exception`, is the base class for all built-in exceptions. The following interactive session shows that `StandardError` is a base class of `Zero DivisionError`.

```
>>> try:
...     1/0
... except StandardError, error:
...     print error.__class__.__name__
...
ZeroDivisionError
```

The code uses the `StandardError` class in the `except` clause, which will catch all exceptions that are either instances of `StandardError` or instances of its subclasses. (Remember, all instances of subclasses of `StandardError` are considered instances of `StandardError`.)

As I said before, all user-defined exceptions should be subclasses of the `Exception` class, but don't subclass your exception from `StandardError`, which is reserved for the built-in variety. It's easy to tell the difference between a system (built-in) exception and an application (or library) exception. It's built in if it's an instance of a `StandardError` subclass.

### ArithmeticError

`ArithmeticError` is the base class for built-in exceptions representing arithmetic errors, such as `OverflowError`, `ZeroDivisionError`, and `FloatingPointError`.

```
>>> try:
...    1/0
... except ArithmeticError, aerror:
...    print aerror
...    print aerror.__class__.__name__
integer division or modulo
ZeroDivisionError
```

### LookupError

`LookupError` is a base class for the exceptions associated with items not in a collection object (mapping or sequence)—for example, `IndexError` and `KeyError`. The following example shows how to catch a `LookupError`:

```
>>> dictionary = {"Hello":"Hi", "Goodbye":"Bye", "See ya Later":"Later"}
>>> print dictionary["Hello"]
Hi
>>> try:
...    print dictionary["Ciao"]
... except LookupError, error:
...    print error.__class__.__name__
...
KeyError
```

We can see that `KeyError` is a subclass of `LookupError`, from which it derives.

### AttributeError

`AttributeError` is used in conjunction with classes and instances. It signifies an attribute reference or a failed assignment.

```
>>> class clazz:
...    a = 1
...    b = "hi"
...    c = None
...
>>> clazz.b
'hi'
```

```
>>> try:
...    clazz.a = clazz.e
... except AttributeError, error:
...    print "Class does not support attribute e"
...
Class does not support attribute e
```

### EOFError
EOFError signifies that a built-in function has hit the end of the file—possibly unexpectedly. We'll leave this example to Chapters 8 and 9.

### FloatingPointError
FloatingPointError signifies the failure of a floating-point operation.

### IOError
IOError signifies failure of an I/O operation. We'll discuss this more in Chapter 9.

### IndexError
IndexError signifies that a subscript is out of range. The following example shows how you might get such an exception:

```
>>> seq = (1,2,3,4,5)
>>> seq[1]
2
>>> seq[5]
Traceback (innermost last):
  File "<stdin>", line 1, in ?
IndexError: tuple index out of range
```

### KeyError
KeyError signifies a key not found in a dictionary, which the following example demonstrates:

```
>>> dictionary = {"Hello":"Hi", "Goodbye":"Bye", "See ya Later":"Later"}
>>> print dictionary["Hello"]
Hi
>>> try:
...    print dictionary["Ciao"]
... except KeyError, error:
...    print "Ciao not in dictionary"
...
Ciao not in dictionary
>>>
```

Does this example look familiar? As an exercise, compare it to the one for LookupError.

### NameError

NameError signifies that a name isn't found in the current namespace.

```
>>> name1 = None
>>> name2 = None
>>> name1
>>> name2
>>> name3
Traceback (innermost last):
  File "<stdin>", line 1, in ?
NameError: name3
```

Here two variables, name1 and name2, are defined. After the interactive session accesses their values, it tries to access a variable that it didn't define. Thus, an exception is uncaught and displayed in the interactive interpreter.

To catch the exception, we do this:

```
>>> try:
...     print name3
... except NameError, error:
...     print "name3 is not present"
...
name3 is not present
>>>
```

### OverflowError

OverflowError signifies that a number is too big to fit in a number variable.

### TypeError

TypeError signifies that the code is trying to use a built-in object with a function or operation that doesn't support it. In this example, we try to multiply a list by another list, which can't be done. We'll try to get a TypeError.

```
>>> list = [1,2,3]
>>> list2 = [1,2,3]
>>> list = list * list2
Traceback (innermost last):
  File "<console>", line 1, in ?
TypeError: can't multiply sequence with non-int
```

Do you remember that a dictionary key has to be immutable? If you use a mutable object as a key, what happens? Fire up the interactive interpreter, and try the following example:

```
>>> dict = {}
>>> list = [1,2,3]
>>> dict[list]="item"
Traceback (innermost last):
  File "<console>", line 1, in ?
TypeError: unhashable type
```

### *ValueError*

`ValueError` signifies the wrong type for the current operation or function. In this example, the string module uses it to indicate that a string can't be evaluated to a number when the `atoi` (ASCII-to-Integer) function is called (see Chapter 10).

```
>>> import string
>>> string.atoi("123")
123
>>> string.atoi("YOU")
Traceback (innermost last):
  File "<interactive input>", line 0, in ?
ValueError: invalid literal for atoi(): YOU
```

First the code imports the string module and then invokes the module's `atoi` function to convert the string "123" to an integer. Next it uses `atoi` to convert the string "YOU" to an integer, which raises a `ValueError` exception because that string has no integer equivalent.

`ValueError` is used in all kinds of modules. It's a nice way of saying that the value is out of the range a particular function was expecting.

### *ZeroDivisionError*

We used `ZeroDivisionError` a lot in the examples earlier in the chapter. Remember that it occurs when you have a zero in the denominator.

```
>>> 1/0
Traceback (innermost last):
  File "<stdin>", line 1, in ?
  ZeroDivisionError: integer division or modulo
```

## *Getting the Most Out of Your Exceptions*

Exception class instances have the attributes `filename`, `lineno`, `offset`, and `text`. You can access these details to locate where your code failed. The next example (*chap7_3.py*) shows how:

```
class MyException(Exception):
      pass
def raiseMyException():
      raise Exception()
def catchMyException():
      try:
            raiseMyException()
      except MyException, err:
            print "line number " +err.lineno
            print "file name " + err.filename
            print "offset " + err.offset
            print " text " + err.text
```

## *Summary*

Exception handling is easier than the traditional approach of always checking the return type from functions. Exceptions can be class objects or string objects, although string object exceptions are no longer in favor. The newer, more correct way is to use class instances. In fact, as of Python version 1.5, all of the standard exceptions are class instances.

The `try` statement tries a block of code; if that block raises an exception, `try` either handles that exception or performs some type of cleanup. There are two forms of `try`. One has `try`, `except`, and `else` clauses. The `except` clause handles all exception classes derived from the class it mentions. The `else` clause is the default handler for code that must be executed if no exceptions are raised.

The other form of `try` has a `finally` clause. `finally` guarantees that some form of cleanup code (like file closing) is performed. The `raise` statement allows programmers to raise an exception in their code.

# CHAPTER 8    *Working with Files*

---

*Terms in This Chapter*

- ⏷ *Class instance*
- ⏷ *Comment*
- ⏷ *Data persistence*
- ⏷ *Data structure*
- ⏷ *Document string*
- ⏷ *Dump*
- ⏷ *File*
- ⏷ *File object*

- ⏷ *File pointer*
- ⏷ *for, if, and while statements*
- ⏷ *for loop*
- ⏷ *Java Virtual Machine*
- ⏷ *Method*
- ⏷ *Mode*
- ⏷ *newline*

- ⏷ *Object instance*
- ⏷ *pickle module*
- ⏷ *Scaffolding*
- ⏷ *try . . . except*
- ⏷ *try . . . finally*
- ⏷ *while loop*

I've written programs that read and write data from files in Java, Delphi, Visual Basic, C++, and C. None have such a straightforward and easy approach to dealing with files as Python's. In this chapter we'll be covering file input and output, which is important for saving data. First we'll cover simple I/O; later we'll deal with persisting class instances.

Writing a program that resides only in memory is good for illustration, but eventually you'll need to write that program to a file. Do you remember our address book example in Chapter 4? What happened to the addresses when the program ended? Gone, and that isn't good. We need a way to save addresses so that we can use them again. Files fit the bill.

## *Simple File Operations*

Before we begin our tour of files, we'll create a directory, *c:\dat*, where we'll put the data file we'll be working with throughout the chapter.

In Python, file I/O is built into the language, so working with files doesn't require an API or library. You just make a call to the intrinsic (built-in) `open()` function, which returns a file object. The typical form of `open()` is `open(filename, mode)`.

Say, for example, that you want to open a file in *c:\dat* and write `"Hello World"` to it. Here's how to do that. (Start up the interactive interpreter and follow along.)

```
>>> file = open("c:\\dat\\hello.txt", "w")
>>> file.write("Hello World ")
>>> file.write("Hello Mars ")
>>> file.write("Hello Jupiter ")
>>> file.close()
```

Now, using your favorite editor, open up *c:\dat\hello.txt*. You should see this:

```
Hello World Hello Mars Hello Jupiter
```

### Determining the File Object Type

To see the type of a file object, enter

```
>>> file = open("\\dat\\test.dat","w")
>>> type(file)
```

Under Jython and Jython you get

```
<jclass org.python.core.PyFile at 2054104961>
```

Under Python (a.k.a CPython) you get

```
<type 'file'>
```

### File Modes

The Python file object supports the following modes:

- Write—`"w"`, `"wb"`
- Read—`"r"`, `"rb"`
- Read and write—`"r+"`, `"r+b"`
- Append—`"a"`, `"ab"`

The `"b"` appended to the mode signifies binary, which is necessary under Windows and Macintosh operating systems to work with binary files. You don't need binary mode with Jython because its code executes in the context of the Java Virtual Machine (JVM), which in this case is like a virtual operating system sitting atop the base operating systems, making them behave alike. You don't need binary mode, either, if you're running CPython under UNIX

### Persisted Data

Writing to files without reading them doesn't do you much good unless you're creating a report of some kind. If you want to persist data so you can use it later, you have to be able to read it back into the program. Here's how we read the data that we wrote in the first example (please follow along):

```
>>> file = open("\\dat\\hello.txt", "r")
>>> file.read()
'Hello Mars Hello Jupiter'
>>> file.close()
```

The `read()` method returns a string representing the contents of the file.

## Common File Methods

The Python file object supports the methods shown in the following list:

- `read()`—read in data from the file
- `readline()`—read a line of data from a file
- `readlines()`—read all the lines in the file and return them as a tuple of strings
- `write()`—write data to a file
- `writelines()`—write a tuple of lines to a file
- `seek()`—move to a certain point in a file
- `tell()`—determine the current location in the file

This is only a partial list. You can read about other file object methods in the Python documentation.

---

*A Little Review*

You can get a list of methods that a file object supports by using the `dir()` command like this:

```
>>> file = open("\\dat\\hello.txt")
>>> dir (file)
['close', 'closed', 'fileno', 'flush', 'isatty', 'mode', 'name', 'read',
'readinto', 'readline', 'readlines', 'seek', 'softspace', 'tell',
'truncate', 'write', 'writelines']
dir() lists all public members of a class.
```

## write() and readline()

In our *c:\dat\hello.txt* example, we wrote three strings. Then we used a text editor to read that file and saw that all three strings were on the same line. Of course, this is a very short file, but if all of the items we wrote to a standard-size file were written on the same line, the file would be hard to read and parse. To avoid this, we can write a newline character (\n) at the end of each line to denote that the text that follows begins a new line.

Let's continue with some examples that demonstrate writing data on separate lines. Follow along in the interactive interpreter.

First we write three lines to a file like this:

```
>>> fname = "c:\\dat\\data.txt"
>>> f = open (fname, "w")   #open the file in write mode
>>> f.write("line1 \n")             #write out a line of text.
>>>                                 # the \n signifies newline
>>> f.write("line2 ")               #write out some text.
>>> f.write(" still line2")         #write out some more text
>>> f.write(" \n")           #write out a newline character
>>> f.write("line3 \n")             #write out a line of text
>>> f.close()            #close the file
>>> f = None             #set the ref to none
```

Without the newline character, all of the text is on the same line, which you can see by opening the file (*c:\dat\data.txt*) and comparing each line of text with the code that created it.

```
f.write("line2 ")       #write out some text.
f.write(" still line2") #write out some more text
f.write(" \n")                  #write out a newline character
```

Now let's reopen our file in read mode and read each line individually with the readline() method.

```
>>> f = open (fname, "r")   # open the file in read mode
>>> line = f.readline()             # read one line in and store it in line
>>> line                            # line one contains the first line we
>>>                                 # wrote. Note "\n" = "\12"
'line1 \ 12'
>>> print line                      # print the line. note that the newline
>>>                                 # is still attatched to the line
line1

>>> f.readline()            #read the second line.
'line2    still line2 \ 12'
>>> f.readline()            #read the third line
'line3 \ 12'
>>> f.close()           #close the file
>>>
```

Notice that we have a lot fewer `readline()` calls than we had `write()` calls. This is because `readline()` reads a line of text until it hits the newline character, which it interprets as the last character in the input string.

## readlines()

The `readlines()` method (note plural) reads all of the lines in the file and puts them in a list of strings. To illustrate, we'll read all of the lines in the file at once with the following interactive session:

```
>>> f = open(fname, "r")    #reopen the file in read mode
>>> list = f.readlines()    #read in all the lines at once
>>> list                              #display the list
['line1 \ 12', 'line2   still line2 \ 12', 'line3 \ 12']
>>> for line in list:                  #print out each line
...          print line
...
line1

line2 still line2

line3
>>>
```

### Getting Rid of \n

You may want to dispose of the newline character when you read in a line. Here's the not very Python way of doing this:

```
>>> f = open("\\dat\\data.txt")  #reopen the file again
>>> line = f.readline()     #read in the line
>>> line                        #before removing the newline character
'line1 \ 12'

>>> line = line[0:len(line)-1] #chop of the newline character
>>> line                        #After the newline character is gone.
'line1 '
>>> f.close()        #close the file
```

Here's the more Python way:

```
>>> f = open("\\dat\\data.txt")   # reopen the file
>>> line = (f.readline())[:-1]    # read the line and chop
>>>                               # the newline character off.
>>> line
'line1 '
```

We're doing two things at once with this call. We're putting `readline()` in parentheses and then using the [] operator with slice notation on the list it returns.

```
line = (f.readline())[:-1]                # read the line and chop
                              # the newline character off.
```

In case you didn't catch what we just did, here's the same thing in slow motion, reading the second line, with a few more code steps for clarity.

```
>>> line2 = f.readline()    # Read in line2.
>>> line2 = line2[:-1]           # Using slice notation assign
>>>                               # line2 to line2 from the first
>>>                               # character up to but not including
>>>                    # the last character.
>>> line2                  # Display line2
'line2 still line2 '
```

For a review of slice notation, go back to Chapters 1, 2, and 3.

### read()

Let's start a new example to show how to use read(). First we'll create a file and write the hex digits 1 through F to it. Then we'll open the file (*c:\\dat\\read.txt*) in write mode. (Don't worry about hex for now; just follow along.)

```
>>> f = open("\\dat\\read.txt", "w")
>>> f.write("0123456789ABCDEF")
>>> f.close()
```

That's the setup. Now we'll demonstrate the different ways to use read().

```
>>> f = open("\\dat\\read.txt", "r")
>>> f.read(3)        # Read the first three characters.
'012'

>>> f.read(3)        # Read the next three characters in the file.
'345'

>>> f.read(4)        # Read the next four characters in the file.
'6789'

>>> f.read()         # Read the rest of the file.
'ABCDEF'
```

We can see that read(size) reads a specified number of characters from the file. Note that calling read() with no arguments reads the rest of the file and that the second read() starts reading where the first one left off.

### tell() and seek()

We just saw that the file object keeps track of where we left off reading in a file. What if we want to move to a previous location? For that we need the tell() and seek() methods. Here's an example that continues our read() example:

```
>>> f.seek(0)          #reset the file pointer to 0
>>> f.read()  #read in the whole file
'0123456789ABCDEF'
```

```
>>> f.tell()  #see where the file pointer is
16

>>> f.seek(8) #move to the middle of the file
>>> f.tell()    #see where the file pointer is
8

>>> f.read()    #read from the middle of the file to the end
'89ABCDEF'
```

The second line reads in the whole file, which means that the file pointer was at the end. The third line uses `tell()` to report where the file pointer was, and then `seek()` positions the pointer to the middle of the file. Again, `tell()` reports that location. To demonstrate that `read()` picks up from the file pointer's location, we'll read the rest of the file and display it.

---

### For Beginners: Try It Out

If you're sitting there staring at the book and wondering what I'm talking about, you need to do three things:

1. Enter in the last example in the interactive interpreter, and experiment with `tell()`, `seek()`, and `read()`.
2. Open the file with your favorite text editor, and count the characters in it.
3. Move around the file, and read various characters. To read a single character, call the `read()` method with `1` as its argument.

If you still don't get it, don't worry; we'll cover this more in the next section.

---

## Putting It All Together: The Address Book Example

In Chapter 4, we used an address book application to demonstrate the `if`, `for`, and `while` statements. We're bringing it back to review the concepts we've learned so far.

```
name = "    "
while (name != ""):
        name = raw_input("Enter in the name: ")
        if (name == ""):
                continue
        elif (name == "quit"):
                break
        phone_number = raw_input("Enter in the phone number: ")
        address_line1 = raw_input("Enter address line one: ")
        if (address_line1 == ""):
                continue
        address_line2 = raw_input("Enter address line two: ")
```

```
        address_line3 = raw_input("Enter address line three: ")
        #do something useful with the addresses
else:
        print("send the email to Rick")
        #emailAddresses("rick_m_hightower@emailcompany.com")
```

## Organization

The first thing we want to do is organize our program to store the data structures, so we'll create a class (the code is from *address1.py*).

```
class Address:
        def __init__(self, name="", phone_number="", address_lines=[]):
                self.__name=name
                self.__phone_number=phone_number
                self.__lines=address_lines
```

The Address class represents an entry in our address book. Later we'll add a __save__ method so we can write Address's contents out to a file. Before we do that, though, we need to change the address program to store the addresses in instances of Address, and we need to store the instances in some collection object—I picked a dictionary. (I also added comments to make the flow of the program clear for those of you who forgot Chapter 4.) Here's the amended code (from *address1.py*):

```
dict = {}       # to hold the addresses, i.e., to hold
        # instances of the Address class
name = "    "
while (name != ""):
        # Get the name of the person
name = raw_input("Enter in the name: ")

        # if the name is empty then continue at the top of the loop
        # else if the name equal quit then break out of the loop
if (name == ""):
        continue
elif (name == "quit"):
        break

        # Get the phone number for the person
phone_number = raw_input("Enter in the phone number: ")

        # Get the address of the person
        # If the first address line is blank then continue
# with entering in the next address
        # Otherwise gather the other two address lines
address_line1 = raw_input("Enter address line one: ")
if (address_line1 == ""):
                #Create an address object and store
        # it in the dictionary
        address = Address(name, phone_number, [])
        dict[name]=address
        continue
```

```
address_line2 = raw_input("Enter address line two: ")
address_line3 = raw_input("Enter address line three: ")
        #Create an address object and store it in the dictionary
address = Address(name, phone_number, [address_line1, address_line2,
address_line3])
        dict[name]=address

        #do something useful with the addresses
else:
        print("send the email to Rick")
```

The code consists of a `while` loop that gathers addresses from the user. If the user enters a blank string for the name, the loop starts at the top. If the user returns a blank for the first address line, that line is left off. Once all fields have been gathered, we construct an instance of the `Address` class and store it in the dictionary. As an exercise, try running the program from *address1.py*.

## File Support

The next thing we do is provide file support for our program by adding the `__save__` method in the `Address` class. Taking a file object as an argument, `__save__` saves members of the class instance to a file. The following, from *address2.py*, shows `Address.save`:

```
class Address:
        ...
        ...
        def save(self, file):
                file.write(self.__name + "\n")
                file.write(self.__phone_number + "\n")
                        # if there are address lines then write them out
                # to the file
                if(len(self.__lines)>0):
                        file.write("true" + "\n")
                        file.write(`self.__lines` + "\n")
```

As you can see, `save` writes all of the members of the class. The code checks for any address lines; if there aren't any, it just skips writing them. If there are, it writes out "true" to the file and then writes out the address lines using the string representation `self.__lines`.

---

### *For Beginners: repr()*

Remember the `repr()` built-in function from Chapter 6? It prints the string representation of an object so that it can be rebuilt with a call to the `eval` statement. Thus, when we do this:

```
file.write(`self.__lines` + "\n")
```

we get a string representation of the built-in list object. Note that `repr()` is called when you use back quotes, so `self__lines` is equivalent to `repr(self.__lines)`.

repr() is essential for reading the list back in from the file. We'll review it with this interactive session:

```
>>> list = ["item1", "item2", "item3"] # create list
>>> list                  # show the contents of the list
['item1', 'item2', 'item3']

>>> string = `list`          # return string representation of the list
>>> type(string)           # show that this is a string
<type 'string'>

>>> string              #print the string to the console
"['item1', 'item2', 'item3']"

>>> list2=eval(string)          # use the eval statement to create
>>>                            # the object from the string

>>> list2                   # show that the newly created object
>>>                        # is a list like the other list
['item1', 'item2', 'item3']

>>> list ==list2
1

>>> type(list2)
<jclass org.python.core.PyList at 161274>
```

## Writing to the File

The next thing we add is the ability to write each address out to the file (this example is from *address2.py*).

```
dict = {} #to hold the addresses
name = "    "
while (name != ""):
        ...
        ...
else:
            #Open up the file for writing
        file = open ("\\dat\\address2.txt", "w")
            #write each address in the dictionary to the file
        for address in dict.values():
            address.save(file)
```

In the else clause of the while loop, we write out the addresses that we collected in the dictionary. First we open up *c:\dat\address2.txt* for reading. Then we create a for loop to iterate through the address objects in dict (the dictionary object). We write out each address instance by calling __save__ and pass it the file object we opened.

Let's run our program (*address2.py*), enter a few addresses, and look at the output from the file; we can compare it to the source code that generated it.

Wait a minute. There's no use writing items to a file unless we're going to read them back, so let's first add another method, read(), to our class. Here's the code (*address3.py Address.read*) for showing how to read an address instance:

```
def read(self, file):
    """
    The read method reads fields of the instance from a file.
    The read method has one argument. The file argument holds
the reference to the output file object.
    """

        # Read in the name field.
    self.__name = (file.readline())[:-1]

        # Read in the phone number field.
    self.__phone_number = (file.readline())[:-1]

        # Check to see if the address lines are present.
        # If the lines are present, read in the address
    # lines string. Use the eval statement to recreate
    # the address lines.
    if(file.readline()[:-1]) == "true":
            string = (file.readline()[:-1])
            self.__lines=eval(string)
```

### Scaffolding Code

It's often useful to develop what's known as scaffolding code to test the code we're writing. One good reason to do so is that testing code in an interactive session can be cumbersome. The `while` loop we used above to gather address information isn't a good place for code testing, so we'll add methods that do nothing but test if a piece of functionality is working. Any method that starts with the word `test` is a scaffolding method.

Here we're reading back the fields one by one. We read in the list that contains the three lines in one call to readline(). Then we use eval to recreate the object. (If this idea seems weird, take another look at the repr() notebook.)

Now that we have both the read() and write() methods for Address, let's create some functions to test them. The following code writes addresses and then reads them back and prints them for display:

```
def test():
    test_write()
    test_read()

def test_write():
    file = open("\\dat\\testaddr.txt", "w")
    address = Address("Rick Hightower", "920-555-1212", ["123 Main St",
            "Antioch Ca, 95432", "Line 3"])
    address.save(file)
    address = Address("Missy Hightower", "920-555-1212", ["123 Main St",
            "Denver Co, 80202", "Line 3"])
```

```
        address.save(file)
        address = Address("Martha Hightower", "602-555-1212", ["123 Main St",
                "Denver Co, 80202", "Line 3"])
        address.save(file)
        address = Address("Mary Hightower", "520-555-1212", [])
        address.save(file)

def test_read():
        file = open("\\dat\\testaddr", "r")
        for index in range(0,3):
                address = Address()
                address.read(file)
                print address
```

If you try to run this code without adding a __str__ method to the Address class, you'll get some very uninteresting and somewhat useless output. Therefore, we'll add __str__ to Address to display a pretty print string representation of the address object.

```
class Address:
        ...
        ...
        def __str__(self):
                str = self.__name + "\n"
                str = str + self.__phone_number + "\n"
                for line in self.__lines:
                        str = str + line + "\n"
                return str
```

Having a meaningful string representation of a class instance can make debugging very easy.

When we run our test, we get the following output. Eyeball it for correctness.

```
>>> from address3 import *
>>> test()
Rick Hightower
920-555-1212
123 Main St
Antioch Ca, 95432

Line 3
Missy Hightower
920-555-1212
123 Main St
Denver Co, 80202
Line 3

Martha Hightower
602-555-1212
123 Main St
Denver Co, 80202
Line 3
```

This is what the `testaddr.txt` file looks like:

```
Rick Hightower
920-555-1212
true
['123 Main St', 'Antioch Ca, 95432', 'Line 3']
Missy Hightower
920-555-1212
true
['123 Main St', 'Denver Co, 80202', 'Line 3']
Martha Hightower
602-555-1212
true
['123 Main St', 'Denver Co, 80202', 'Line 3']
Mary Hightower
520-555-1212
false
```

## Writing Out and Reading the File

Of course, now that we've added and tested our reading and writing, we need to put this functionality in `getAddresses`. Actually, we've already added writing, but we need to be able to write out a dictionary of addresses; our writing code does not do any error checking; and the file is getting pretty long. For these reasons, we have to add reading to `getAddresses`. What we'll do is create two functions that read and write out a dictionary of address instances, and we'll add the necessary `try. . .except` and `try. . .finally` blocks to the code.

```
def readAddresses(filename, dict):
    """

    Read in a dictionary of addresses.
    This method takes two arguments as follows:

       filename    holds the filename of the file to read in address
                     instances from

       dict        holds reference to the dictionary object that
                     this function adds addresses to

    """
    file = None #to hold reference to the input file object

        # Use try..finally block to work with the file
        # If you can't work with the file for any reason close it
    try:
            #    try to read in the addresses from the file
            #    if you can't read the addresses then print an
#      error message
        try:
            file = open(filename,"r")          #open the file in read mode
            strLength=(file.readline())[:-1] # read in the length
            length = int(strLength)            # convert length to an int
```

```
                        #read in the addresses from 0 to length
                for index in range(0, length):
                    address=Address()
                    address.read(file)
                    dict[address.name()]=address

        except Exception, error:
            print error.__class__.__name__
            print error
    finally:
            if not (file is None): file.close()

def writeAddresses(filename, dict):
    """

            Write the addresses instances in a dictionary to a file.
            writeAddresses has two arguments as follows:

            filename        holds the name of the output file
            dict            holds the dictionary of address instances

    """

    file=None  #to hold the output file object

        #try..finally: try to write the instances to a file.
        #if all else fails then close the file object
    try:
            #       Write the address instances in dict to a file
            #       specified by filename.
            #       If there are any errors then print an error message
        try:
            file = open (filename, "w")
            length = str(len(dict))         # determine the number of
                                            # address instances in dict

            file.write(length + "\n")       # write the length of dict to a
                                            # file.

                        # for each address in dict.values write out the
                        # address instance to the file object
            for address in dict.values():
                    address.save(file)

        except Exception,error:
            print error.__class__.__name__
            print error
    finally:
            if(file):file.close()
```

To make the read() and write() functions workable, we'll add the following
method to the Address class:

```
def name(self):
        return self.__name
```

name is used as the key into the dictionary.

I added many comments to the previous methods. Make it a habit to read them and any document strings in the code listings. Consider document strings and comments as part of the text of this book. Also, be sure to amply comment your own code.

## Testing

So far we've added read and write functionality to the Address class and added functionality for reading in an entire dictionary of addresses and for writing an entire dictionary of address instances. Now we need to update getAddresses() to use all of these functions. Before we do that, though, we need to test read Addresses() and writeAddresses(), which means more scaffolding code.

```
def test_read_write():
    """
        Scaffolding code to test reading and writing dictionaries
    of addresses.
    """
        # populate a dictionary object with some sample data
    dict={}
    address = Address("Rick Hightower", "920-555-1212", ["123 Main St",
            "Antioch Ca, 95432", "Line 3"])
    dict["Rick Hightower"] = address
    address = Address("Missy Hightower", "920-555-1212", ["123 Main St",
            "Denver Co, 80202", "Line 3"])
    dict["Missy Hightower"]=address
    address = Address("Martha Hightower", "602-555-1212", ["123 Main St",
            "Phoenix, AZ, 85226", "Line 3"])
    dict["Martha Hightower"]=address
    address = Address("Mary Hightower", "520-555-1212", [])
    dict["Mary Hightower"]=address

    fname="\\dat\\testaddr.txt" #to hold output filename

        # write the dictionary full of addresses out to the file
    print "calling writeAddresses"
    writeAddresses(fname, dict)

        # read in the dictionary full of addresses back from
    # the file we just wrote it to
    dict_in = {}                            #to hold input addresses
    print "calling readAddresses"
    readAddresses(fname, dict_in)

        #show that the input matches the output
    print "Input"
    print dict_in
    print "Output"
    print dict

        #return whether these equal each other
    return dict==dict_in
```

Essentially, our scaffolding code populates a Python dictionary with address instances. Then it writes the dictionary to a file and reads it back. Next it displays the input and output dictionaries so that you can test them visually. Finally it tells us whether the input dictionary is equal to the output dictionary. With the way the code is written, it should work until we hit the last line.

For the last line to work, we need to add a \_\_cmp\_\_ method to our Address class that iterates through all items in the dictionary and compares them. If all of the items are equal, \_\_cmp\_\_ returns that the dictionaries themselves are equal. Here's how we add \_\_cmp\_\_ to the Address class:

```
def __cmp__(self,other):
    """
    Compares one address instance to another.
    If the address instances are equal the __cmp__ returns 0.
    If the address instances are not equal then we return a
        non-zero value.
    """
        # To implement this all we do is compare the
    # dictionaries of the class
        # The __dict__ member of the instance holds all
    # of the instance fields in a dictionary
    return cmp(self.__dict__ ,other.__dict__)
```

### \_\_cmp\_\_ and Equality versus Default Object Identity

If we don't define \_\_cmp\_\_, the comparison of objects won't work. To prove this, let's do a small interactive session.

First we define a simple class.

```
>>> class class1:
...     var="hi"
...
```

Then we create two instances.

```
>>> instance = class1()
>>> instance2 = class1()
```

The instances have the same values, yet when we compare them they aren't equal (a 0 value equals false).

```
>>> instance == instance2
0
```

The default operation for \_\_cmp\_\_ is to check for object identity. Thus, if we set another instance to equal the first and then test for equality, we get a true (1 value).

```
>>> instance3 = instance
>>> instance3 == instance
1
```

However, if we don't define \_\_cmp\_\_, testing for equality is the same as testing for identity. That means that the following is equivalent to the above code:

```
>>> instance3 is instance
1
```

We can use scaffolding to retest the code whenever we add fields to the Address class or whenever we change our reading and writing. The following interactive session demonstrates the use of scaffolding code to test the reading and writing of dictionaries of addresses:

```
>>> from address3 import *
>>> test_read_write()
calling writeAddresses
calling readAddresses
Input
{'Rick Hightower': <address3.Address instance at 60188>, 'Martha Hightower':
<address3.Address instance at 5fe4c>, 'Missy Hightower': <address3.Address
instance at 5ffec>, 'Mary Hightower': <address3.Address instance at 5fc7c>}
Output
{'Mary Hightower': <address3.Address instance at 5ea58>, 'Martha Hightower':
<address3.Address instance at 5e9dc>, 'Missy Hightower': <address3.Address
instance at 5e950>, 'Rick Hightower': <address3.Address instance at 5e890>}
1
```

As you can see, our code passed because the function returned true. This means that every address in the output dictionary is equal to every address in the input dictionary.

## The Full address3.py Code

Now it seems that we have everything we need to run our program, but first let's see all of *address3.py*, including the scaffolding code.

```
class Address:
        """This class represents an entry in an address book"""

        #Constructor
    def __init__(self, name="", phone_number="", address_lines=[]):
        """
The constructor takes three arguments:
                name to hold the persons name              (string)

                phone_number to hold the persons phone number  (string)

                address_lines to hold the address of the person (list)
        """
                # assign the name, phone_number and address_lines to the
                # instance variables
                # __name, __phone_number, and __lines
```

```
            self.__name=name
            self.__phone_number=phone_number
            self.__lines=address_lines

            #Methods
        def save(self, file):
            """
            The save method saves the instance out to a file.
            The save method has one argument.
                file        holds the reference to a file object.

            """
                # write the __name and __phone_number instance variables
                # to the file. each variable is on its own line.
            file.write(self.__name + "\n")
            file.write(self.__phone_number + "\n")
                # if there are address lines then write them out to the file
                # Since these lines are optional, write "true" if they are
                # present and "false" if they are not present.
            if(len(self.__lines)>0):
                file.write("true" + "\n")
                file.write(`self.__lines` + "\n")
            else :
                file.write("false\n")

        def read(self, file):
            """
            The read method reads fields of the instance from a file.
            The read method has one argument.

                file        holds the reference to the output file object.
            """
                # Read in the name field.
            self.__name = (file.readline())[:-1]

                # Read in the phone number field.
            self.__phone_number = (file.readline())[:-1]

                # Check to see if the address lines are present.
                # If lines are present, read in the address lines string.
                # Use the eval statement to recreate the address lines.
            if(file.readline()[:-1]) == "true":
                string = (file.readline()[:-1])
                self.__lines=eval(string)

        def name(self): return self.__name

        def __cmp__(self, other):
            """
            Compares one address instance to another.
            If the address instances are equal the __cmp__ returns 0.
            If the address instances are not equal then we return a non-zero
value.
            """
# to implement this, __cmp__ compares the dictionaries of
# two instances. The __dict__ holds all of the members.
```

```
                return cmp(self.__dict__ ,other.__dict__)

        def __hash__(self): return hash(self.__name)

        def __str__(self):
            str = self.__name + "\n"
            str = str + self.__phone_number + "\n"
            for line in self.__lines:
                str = str + line + "\n"
            return str

def getAddresses():
    dict = {} #to hold the addresses

            # Call read addresses to get the dictionary of addresses
# from the file
    readAddresses("c:\\dat\\addressbook.txt", dict)

    name = " "
    while (name != ""):
                # Get the name of the person
        name = raw_input("Enter in the name: ")
                # if the name is empty then continue at the top of the loop
                # if the name equals quit then break out of the loop
        if (name == ""):
            continue
        elif (name == "quit"):
            break

            #Get the phone number for the person
        phone_number = raw_input("Enter in the phone number: ")

            # Get the address of the person
        address_line1 = raw_input("Enter address line one: ")

            # If the first address line is blank then continue with
            # entering in the next address
            # Otherwise gather the other two address lines
        if (address_line1 == ""):

                    # Create an address object and store it in the
                    # dictionary
            address = Address(name, phone_number, [])
            dict[name]=address
            continue

        address_line2 = raw_input("Enter address line two: ")
        address_line3 = raw_input("Enter address line three: ")

            # Create an address object and store it in the dictionary
                lines = [address_line1, address_line2, address_line3]
        address = Address(name, phone_number, lines)
        dict[name]=address
        # Write the addresses we created and the ones that
        # we read back to the file
    writeAddresses("c:\\dat\\addressbook.txt",dict)

    test_read()
```

```
def test_write():
        file = open("\\dat\\testaddr.txt", "w")
        address = Address("Rick Hightower", "920-555-1212", ["123 Main St",
                  "Antioch Ca, 95432", "Line 3"])
        address.save(file)
        address = Address("Missy Hightower", "920-555-1212", ["123 Main St",
                  "Denver Co, 80202", "Line 3"])
        address.save(file)
        address = Address("Martha Hightower", "602-555-1212", ["123 Main St",
                  "Denver Co, 80202", "Line 3"])
        address.save(file)
        address = Address("Mary Hightower", "520-555-1212", [])
        address.save(file)

def test_read():
        file = open("\\dat\\testaddr.txt", "r")
        for index in range(0,3):
                address = Address()
                address.read(file)
                print address

def test_equal():
        address1 = Address("Missy Hightower", "920-555-1212", ["123 Main St",
                   "Denver Co, 80202", "Line 3"])
        address2 = Address("Missy Hightower", "920-555-1212", ["123 Main St",
                   "Denver Co, 80202", "Line 3"])
        return address1==address2
```

## Using getAddresses()

We'll fire up an interactive session as an exercise, and enter three addresses using the getAddresses() function.

```
>>> from address3 import getAddresses
>>> getAddresses()
Enter in the name: Rick Hightower
Enter in the phone number: 925-555-1212
Enter address line one:
Enter in the name: Kiley Hightower
Enter in the phone number: 925-555-1212
Enter address line one:
Enter in the name: Whitney Hightower
Enter in the phone number: 925-555-1212
Enter address line one: 123 Main St.
Enter address line two: Antioch, CA
Enter address line three: line 3
Enter in the name:
>>> getAddresses()
Enter in the name: Jenna Paul
Enter in the phone number: 925-555-1255
Enter address line one: 125 Main St.
Enter address line two: Antioch, CA
Enter address line three: line 3
Enter in the name: quit
```

Here's the listing for our session:

```
4
Whitney Hightower
925-555-1212
true
['123 Main St.', 'Antioch, CA', 'line 3']
Jenna Paul
925-555-1255
true
['125 Main St.', 'Antioch, CA', 'line 3']
Rick Hightower
925-555-1212
false
Kiley Hightower
925-555-1212
false
```

## *Persisting Objects with pickle*

I've got good news for you. There's a way to write Python programs that persist Python objects that's much easier than the way we've just done it. It's called the pickle module.

Let's redefine our Address class and take away its ability to write itself to a file. Then we'll use it to demonstrate *pickle*. This example is from *address4.Address.*

```
class Address:
    """This class represents an entry in an address book"""

        #Constructor
    def __init__(self, name="", phone_number="", address_lines=[]):
        """The constructor takes three arguments:
            name to hold the persons name                  (string)
            phone_number to hold the persons phone number (string)
            address_lines to hold the address of the person     (list)
            """

        # Assign the name, phone_number and address_lines to

        # the instance variables
        # __name, __phone_number, and __lines.
        self.__name=name
        self.__phone_number=phone_number
        self.__lines=address_lines

        #Methods
    def name(self): return self.__name

    def __cmp__(self,other):
        """
        Compares one address instance to another.
        If the address instances are equal the __cmp__ returns 0.
        If the address instances are not equal then we return
        a non-zero value.
```

```
        """
                # To implement this, all we do is compare the
                # dictionaries of the class
                # the __dict__ member of the instance holds
                # all of the instance fields in a dictionary
            return cmp(self.__dict__ ,other.__dict__)

    def __hash__(self): return hash(self.__name)
    def __str__(self):
            str = self.__name + "\n"
            str = str + self.__phone_number + "\n"
            for line in self.__lines:
                    str = str + line + "\n"
            return str
```

We haven't added anything new to the class. Essentially we've just removed the read() and write() methods, and we've taken out the read() and save() methods of the Address class. Now let's show reading and writing this class to a file with the *pickle* module.

Import the *address4* and *pickle* modules.

```
>>> import address4
>>> import pickle
```

Create an instance of Address, and print it to the screen.

```
>>> address = address4.Address("Tony Scalise", "555-555-3699")
>>> print address
Tony Scalise
555-555-3699
```

Open a file for outputting the address.

```
>>> dump_file = open("c:\\dat\\pickle.txt","w")
```

Call the pickle.dump() method, and close the file object.

```
>>> pickle.dump(address,dump_file)
>>> dump_file.close()
```

Read the file back in and print it out to the screen to show that it's the same.

```
>>>            #open the file for reading
>>> address_file = open ("c:\\dat\pickle.txt", "r")

>>>            #load the address instance from the file
>>> address2 = pickle.load(address_file)

>>>     #print the address instance to the screen
>>> print address2
Tony Scalise
555-555-3699
```

Test to make sure that the values are equal but that this isn't the same object.

```
>>> address == address2    # the objects are equal
1

>>> address is address2            # the objects are not the same object
0
```

### Editing a *pickle* File

At this point you may be wondering what the file created with the *pickle* module looks like. It's just a text file. In fact, we can edit it to change its values. Here's the original file:

```
(iaddress4
Address
p0
(dp1
S'_Address__name'
p2
S'Tony Scalise'
p3
sS'_Address__lines'
p4
(lp5
sS'_Address__phone_number'
p6
S'555-555-3699'
p7
sb.
```

With your favorite text editor, change `'Tony Scalise'` to `'Kelly Pagleochini'` (or any name you like), and change the phone number from `'555-555-3699'` to `'555-555-2577'`.

```
(iaddress4
Address
p0
(dp1
S'_Address__name'
p2
S'Kelly Pagleochini'
p3
sS'_Address__lines'
p4
(lp5
sS'_Address__phone_number'
p6
S'555-555-2577'
p7
sb.
```

Now, in an interactive session, we'll show how this changes the object instance.

First close the file and reopen it.

```
>>> address_file.close()              # close the file
>>> address_file = open("c:\\dat\\pickle.txt", "r")   # reopen it
```

Then read in the instance using the `pickle.load()` function.

```
>>>     #load the new instance from the file
>>> address3 = pickle.load(address_file)
>>> print address3  # print the new instance out.
Kelly Pagleochini
555-555-2577

    >>> address_file.close()
```

I don't recommend that you edit the file that *pickle* dumps, but it's nice to know that you can. It comes in handy when you're debugging an application, and it's especially useful for viewing dumped files. Are you wondering what S, sS, p0, p1, and the like, mean? They denote the type and placement of the attributes of an object in a file. To learn more about their exact meanings, refer to the *pickle* Python Library reference.

## Writing Out Objects with *pickle*

With the *pickle* module you can do more than just write out class instances to a file; you can write out any Python object as well.

Open a new file for writing.

```
>>> file = open("c:\\dat\\pickle2.txt", "w")
```

Create a dictionary, populating it with a string, an integer, a float, a list, and another dictionary, and write it to a file.

```
>>> dict = {}
>>> dict["string"] = "string"             #add a string to the dictionary
>>> dict["int"]= 1                    #add an int to the dictionary
>>> dict["float"]=1.11                    #add a float to the dictionary
>>> dict["list"]=[1,2,3]              #add a list to the dictionary
>>> dict["dict"]={"martha":"miguel"} #add a dictionary to the dictionary
>>> pickle.dump(dict,file)           #write the dictionary to the file
>>> file.close()
```

The output looks like this:

```
(dp0
S'int'  <----- here is the int item's key
p1
I1              <----- here is the int item's value
sS'string'    <----- here is the string item's key
p2
g2
sS'dict'      <---- here is the dictionary item's key
p3
```

```
(dp4
S'martha'
p5
S'miguel'
p6
ssS'float'      <--- here is the float item's key
p7
F1.11           <--- here is the float item's value
sS'list'        <--- here is the list item's key
p8
(lp9
I1
aI2
aI3
as.
```

Of course, we can read back the dictionary object.

Open the file for reading, and read in the pickled dictionary.

```
>>>             #open the file for reading
>>> file = open("c:\\dat\\pickle2.txt","r")
>>>             #load the dictionary object from the file
>>> dict2 = pickle.load(file)
```

We can see that the dictionary read in from the file is equal to the dictionary written to it, but the two are not the same object.

```
>>> dict2 == dict         # test for equality
1

>>> dict2 is dict    # test: see if the dictionaries are the same object.
0

>>> file.close()
```

For efficiency, you can write a pickled object as a binary instead of a text image:

```
>>> file = open("c:\\dat\\pickle3.bin","w")
>>> pickle.dump(dict,file,1)
>>> file.close()
>>> file = open("c:\\dat\\pickle3.bin","r")
>>> dict3 = pickle.load(file)
>>> file.close()
>>> dict==dict3, dict is dict3
(1, 0)
```

The above session is a lot like the one before it. The main difference is the third argument to the `pickle.dump()` function. We passed it a true (nonzero) value to denote that we wanted this written in binary mode. Of course, looking at this file with a text editor won't do you any good because you need a utility to view binary files. Here's what it would look like. (You may not know how to read it, but at the least you can see that it's much harder to read and edit than the text mode.)

```
0FBD:0100 7D 71 00 28 55 03 69 6E-74 71 01 4B 01 55 06 73 }q.(U.intq.K.U.s
0FBD:0110 74 72 69 6E 67 71 02 68-02 55 04 64 69 63 74 71 tringq.h.U.dictq
0FBD:0120 03 7D 71 04 55 06 6D 61-72 74 68 61 71 05 55 06 .}q.U.marthaq.U.
0FBD:0130 6D 69 67 75 65 6C 71 06-73 55 05 66 6C 6F 61 74 miguelq.sU.float
0FBD:0140 71 07 46 31 2E 31 31 0D-0A 55 04 6C 69 73 74 71 q.F1.11..U.listq
0FBD:0150 08 5D 71 09 28 4B 01 4B-02 4B 03 65 75 2E 00 02 .]q.(K.K.K.eu...
0FBD:0160 75 08 F7 06 23 D3 00 04-74 04 81 CD 00 40 C6 06 u...#...t....@..
```

### pickling an Object to a String

In addition to reading and writing to files, you can read and write to strings. Instead of the dump() function, you use the dumps() function (note plural), as follows.

Dump the dictionary into a text string.

```
>>> string = pickle.dumps(dict)
```

Dump the dictionary into a binary string.

```
>>> bin_string = pickle.dumps(dict,1)
```

Load the dictionary from the text string.

```
>>> dict4 = pickle.loads(string)
```

Load the dictionary from the binary string.

```
>>> dict5 = pickle.loads(bin_string)
```

Check to see if the loaded dictionaries are equal to the dumped dictionary.

```
>>> dict == dict4, dict == dict5
(1, 1)
```

Check to see if the loaded dictionaries have the same identity as the dumped dictionary.

```
>>> dict is dict4, dict is dict5
(0, 0)
```

Earlier we said that binary mode is more efficient than text mode. The question is how much. We can find out by comparing the size of the binary string to the size of the text string from the last example.

```
>>> len(string), len(bin_string)
(129, 93)
```

In this example, binary mode is 40 percent more efficient than text mode. But of course more than just size efficiency is involved. When you use text mode, the *pickle* module has to convert text strings into their binary equivalents; if you use binary mode, less conversion is necessary.

## *pickle and the Address Book Application*

Now that we have a handle on the *pickle* module, we can change our address book program to use it. Here's the listing for *address4* (areas of interest are highlighted in bold):

```
class Address:
      """This class represents an entry in an address book"""
            #Constructor
      def __init__(self, name="", phone_number="", address_lines=[]):
            """
The constructor takes three arguments:
                  name to hold the persons' name                    (string)
                  phone_number to hold the persons' phone number (string)
                  address_lines to hold the address of the person  (list)
            """

                  # assign the name, phone_number and address_lines to the
                  # instance variables
                  # __name, __phone_number, and __lines
            self.__name=name
            self.__phone_number=phone_number
            self.__lines=address_lines

            #Methods

      def name(self): return self.__name

      def __cmp__(self,other):
            """
            Compares one address instance to another.
            If the address instances are equal the __cmp__ returns 0.
            If the address instances are not equal then we return a non-zero
               value.
            """
                  # to implement this all we do is compare the dictionaries of
                  # the class. the __dict__ member of the instance holds all
                  # of the instance fields in a dictionary.
            return cmp(self.__dict__ ,other.__dict__)
      def __hash__(self): return hash(self.__name)
      def __str__(self):
            str = self.__name + "\n"
            str = str + self.__phone_number + "\n"
            for line in self.__lines:
                  str = str + line + "\n"
            return str

def readAddresses(filename):
      import pickle
      """
      Read in a dictionary of addresses.
      This method takes two arguments as follows:
            filename                  holds the filename of the file to read in
                                      address instances from
      """
```

```
        file = None    #to hold reference to the input file object

            # try..finally to work with the file
            # if you can't work with the file for any reason close it
        try:
                # try to read in the addresses from the file
                # if you can't read addresses then print an error message
            try:
                file = open(filename,"r") #open the file in read mode
                dict = pickle.load(file)
                return dict
            except Exception, error:
                print error.__class__.__name__
                print error
                return {}
        finally:
            if not (file is None): file.close()

def writeAddresses(filename, dict, bin=0):
    import pickle
    """
        Write the addresses instances in a dictionary to a file.
        writeAddresses has two arguments as follows:
                filename    holds the name of the output file
                dict        holds the dictionary of address instances
                bin         whether to use binary mode or not for the
                            pickler

    """

    file=None    #to hold the output file object

        # try..finally: try to write the instances to a file.
        # if all else fails then close the file object
    try:
            # Write the address instances in dict to a file
            # specified by filename.
            # If there are any errors then print an error message
        try:
            file = open (filename, "w")
            pickle.dump(dict, file, bin)
        except Exception,error:
            print error.__class__.__name__
            print error
    finally:
        if(file):file.close()

def test_read_write():
    """
        Scaffolding code to test reading and writing dictionaries of
        addresses.
    """
        # populate a dictionary object with some sample data
    dict={}
    address = Address("Rick Hightower", "920-555-1212", ["123 Main St",
        "Antioch Ca, 95432", "Line 3"])
```

```
        dict["Rick Hightower"] = address
        address = Address("Missy Hightower", "920-555-1212", ["123 Main St",
                "Denver Co, 80202", "Line 3"])
        dict["Missy Hightower"]=address
        address = Address("Martha Hightower", "602-555-1212", ["123 Main St",
                "Phoenix, AZ, 85226", "Line 3"])
        dict["Martha Hightower"]=address
        address = Address("Mary Hightower", "520-555-1212", [])
        dict["Mary Hightower"]=address

        fname="c:\\dat\\testaddr.dat" #to hold output filename

            #write the dictionary full of addresses out to the file
        print "calling writeAddresses"
        writeAddresses(fname, dict)

            #read in the dictionary full of addresses back from the
            # file we just wrote it to
        print "calling readAddresses"
        dict_in = readAddresses(fname) #to hold input addresses

            #show that the input matches the output
        print "Input"
        print dict_in
        print "Output"
        print dict
            #return whether these equal each other
        return dict==dict_in

def test_equal():
        address1 = Address("Missy Hightower", "920-555-1212", ["123 Main St",
                "Denver Co, 80202", "Line 3"])
        address2 = Address("Missy Hightower", "920-555-1212", ["123 Main St",
                "Denver Co, 80202", "Line 3"])
        return address1==address2
```

You have to notice that the *pickle* version is much shorter than the original (*address3.py*). Shorter is better because less code to write means less code to maintain.

## Summary

Python allows you to read and write to files. The Python file object, which is built into the language, supports the following methods:

- read()—read in data from a file
- readline()—read a line of data from a file
- readlines()—read all the lines in the file and return the lines as a list of strings
- write()—write data to a file
- writelines()—write a sequence of lines to a file

- seek()—move to a certain point in a file
- tell()—determine the current location in the file

Python makes working with files straightforward. In addition, its *pickle* and *cPickle* modules allow the persisting of objects to a file or string and make for speedy development of persisted class data.

In this chapter, we expanded on the address book example from Chapter 4. We also covered such issues as using __str__ and __repr__ with class instances. If you followed along with our expansion of the address book program to read and write files, you reviewed a lot of the first seven chapters of the book.

# CHAPTER 9   *Built-In Functions*

---
*Terms in This Chapter*
---

- Built-in (intrinsic) function
- Bytecode
- Collection
- eval statement
- exec statement
- Functional programming
- Hashtable
- Hash value
- Hierarchy
- Identity operator
- is operator
- Keyword
- Lambda function
- Mutable/Immutable
- Namespace
- Name/value pair
- Octal
- Parameter
- Sequence

A good part of the simplicity and elegance of Python comes from its built-in (or instrinsic) functions. Many of these are longhand for other operators—for example, the `cmp()` function, which performs the `==`, `=>`, `=<`, `<`, `>` operations, and the `repr()` function, which back-quotes an object. When there's no equivalent operator, the built-in function is often referred to simply as an "operator."

Generally, Python built-in functions are equivalent to keywords in other languages. One example is C++'s keyword `sizeof()`, which determines the size of an array or other structure; its Python counterpart is `len()`, which determines the length of a sequence. Similarly, Java's `instanceof()` is equivalent to Python's `isinstance()`.

## *Conversion*

Sooner or later you're going to need to convert from one type to another. You may be reading in strings from files and want to convert them to text, or, before writing numbers to a text file, you may want to convert them to strings. Python has several built-in functions to do this.

### Converting Numbers to Strings: chr(), str(), hex(), oct()

The chr() function converts a number to a character. Remember that there are no characters in Python, so chr() returns a single character in a string.

```
>>> chr(97)
'a'
>>> chr(122)
'z'
```

It may seem that you would rarely use chr(), but wait until Chapter 12, when it will come in handy for converting a Java binary array into a Python string.

The str() function converts any object, including numeric types, into a string. (Remember, unlike other languages Python treats all types as objects.)

```
>>> str(1)
'1'
```

The hex() function converts a number into its hexadecimal equivalent.

```
>>> hex(255)
'0xff'
>>> hex(11)
'0x1L'
```

Hexadecimal is a base 16 numbering system used in many computers that allows you to display a byte with two digits. We'll see it again when we cover the Java InputStream in Chapter 12.

The oct() function converts a number into its octal equivalent. Octal is a base 8 numbering system.

```
>>> oct(1)
'01'
>>> oct(9)
'011'
```

oct() and hex() work only with integers and longs. They don't work with floats.

You probably won't use chr(), oct(), or hex() very much, if at all, but str() you'll use a great deal.

### Converting Strings to Numbers: float(), int(), long(), ord()

The float() function converts a string to a float.

```
>>> f = float("1.1")
>>> type(f)
<jclass org.python.core.PyFloat at 1662336>
>>>
```

The int() function converts strings to integers.

```
>>> str = "1"
>>> num = int(str)
>>> type(num)
<jclass org.python.core.PyInteger at 3414368>
>>>
```

The long() function converts a string into a long.

```
>>> long("12345678901234567890")
12345678901234567890L
```

The ord() function converts a character (that is, a string with one element) into its ASCII value.

```
>>> ord("A"), ord("Z")
(65, 90)
>>>
```

## Converting Numbers to Different Numeric Types: coerce()

The coerce() function converts one numeric type into another, or rather it changes the type of one value to another type. Actually, coerce() doesn't change the value but returns it in a tuple.

Declare some variables to convert.

```
>>> myinteger = 1        # an int
>>> mylong = 1l          # a long
>>> myfloat = 1.0        # a float
>>> mystring = "1"  # a non-numeric object
```

Coerce an integer into a long.

```
>>> coerce(mylong, myinteger)
(1L, 1L)
```

Do the same as above, but swap the position of the integer and the long.

```
>>> coerce(myint, mylong)
(1L, 1L)
```

Coerce an integer into a float.

```
>>> coerce(myint, myfloat)
(1.0, 1.0)
```

Coerce a long into a float. (The long has to be in the range of allowable values for the Float type.)

```
>>> coerce(mylong, myfloat)
(1.0, 1.0)
```

coerce() works only with numeric types. It won't work with strings, as you can see here:

```
>>> coerce(mystring, myint)
Traceback (innermost last):
  File "<interactive input>", line 0, in ?
TypeError: number coercion failed
>>>
```

To convert an integer or a long into a float, do this:

```
>>> myint = 10
>>> myint = coerce(1.0, 10)[1]
>>> print myint
10.0
```

### Converting Sequences: list(), tuple()

Remember that tuples are immutable, which means that you can't add items to them. If you need to add items to a sequence, you have to use a list. Conversely, you can't use a list as a key into a dictionary. Since dictionaries store items based on a hashtable that uses the hash value of the key, they need types that won't change—that is, immutable tuples. Python has two built in functions to deal with these problems.

The list() function converts an immutable sequence (such as a tuple) into a mutable one (such as a list). Here's an example.

Create a tuple.

```
>>> tup = (1,2,3,4,5,6,7,8,9)
```

Try to add something to it (you'll fail).

```
>>> tup.append(1)
Traceback (innermost last):
  File "<stdin>", line 1, in ?
AttributeError: 'tuple' object has no attribute 'append'
```

Convert the tuple, tup, into a list, ls.

```
>>> ls =list(tup)
>>> ls.append(10)
```

The tuple() function converts a mutable sequence into a tuple. We'll continue our last example to demonstrate how it works.

Convert ls to a tuple, tup, and display it.

```
>>> tup=tuple(ls)
>>> tup
(1, 2, 3, 4, 5, 6, 7, 8, 9, 10)
>>>
```

### *tuple() and list()*

The `tuple()` and `list()` functions take any kind of sequence. Here's what happens if you pass `tuple()` a tuple:

```
>>> tup = (1,2,3)
>>> id(tup), id(tuple(tup))
(201160, 201160)

>>> tup is tuple(tup)
1
```

As you can see, the `id` of `tup` and the `id` of the tuple returned from `tuple()` are the same. We can demonstrate this with the identity operator, which returns as a true statement that `tup is tuple(tup)`.

If you pass a list to `tuple()`, you get a new tuple.

```
>>> lst = [1,2,3]
>>> id(lst), tuple(lst)
(332828, (1, 2, 3))

>>> id(lst), id(tuple(lst))
(332828, 321564)

>>> lst is tuple(lst)
0
```

Notice that, every time you call `list(ls)`, you get a new copy of `ls`.

## Converting Objects to Strings: str(), repr()

The `str()` function converts all object types to strings. The `repr()` function converts all object types to strings that might be able to reconstruct the object with a call to `eval`. Here's an example of both.

Create a list, a tuple, a string, and an integer object.

```
>>> list, tuple, string, int = [1,2],(1,2),"12",12
```

Create a dictionary object that contains the list, tuple, string and integer objects just created.

```
>>> dict ={"list":list, "tuple":tuple, "string":string, "int":12}
```

Show the string representation of the dictionary object.

```
>>> str(dict)
"{'tuple': (1, 2), 'string': '12', 'list': [1, 2], 'int': 12}"
```

Show the `repr()` string representation of the dictionary object.

```
>>> repr(dict)
"{'tuple': (1, 2), 'string': '12', 'list': [1, 2], 'int': 12}"
```

## Namespace: dir(), globals(), locals(), vars()

In most languages, the namespace is decided at compile time, and there is no way to determine which variables are in it unless you try to use them and the program doesn't compile. With Python, you can see the variables in the namespace, and you can see what variables a given object exposes.

### dir()

dir([object]) returns a list of namespace variables. If no arguments are passed, it returns a list of names in the current namespace; otherwise, it returns a list of an object's attribute names.

Here are two examples of dir() showing what's in the current namespace in a function and in a module, respectively:

```
>>> var1, var2, var3, var4 = 1,2,3,4
>>> dir()
['__builtins__', 'var1', 'var2', 'var3', 'var4']
>>> def func(lvar1, lvar2,lvar3,lvar4):
...     return dir()
...

>>> func(var1,var2,var3,var4)
['lvar1', 'lvar2', 'lvar3', 'lvar4']
>>>
```

Here's an example showing dir() inspecting a module and a class.
Inspect the attributes of the *sys* module.

```
>>> import sys
>>> dir(sys)
['__doc__', '__name__', '__stderr__', '__stdin__', '__stdout__', 'argv',
'builtin_module_names', 'copyright', 'dllhandle', 'exc_info', 'exc_type',
'exec_prefix', 'executable', 'exit', 'getrefcount', 'maxint', 'modules',
'path', 'platform', 'prefix', 'ps1', 'ps2', 'setcheckinterval', 'setprofile',
'settrace', 'stderr', 'stdin', 'stdout', 'version', 'winver']
```

Inspect the Exception class.

```
>>> dir(Exception)
['__doc__', '__getitem__', '__init__', '__module__', '__str__']

>>> type (Exception) #just to show that it is a class
<jclass org.python.core.PyClass at 4958626>
```

Inspect an instance of the Exception class.

```
>>> e = Exception()
>>> dir (e)
['args']
```

## globals()

With a few exceptions, the `globals()` function is similar to `dir()`. It always returns the variable names defined in the current module, and it returns a dictionary where the name in the name/value pairs is the name of the object (the variable name) and the value is the object itself (the value). Even if you call `globals()` in a function call, it returns the global variables for that module.

```
>>> gvar1,gvar2,gvar3=1,"two",[3,3,3]
>>> def func():
...     return globals()
...
>>> func()
{'func': <function func at 428fc>, 'gvar3': [3, 3, 3], 'gvar1': 1, 'gvar2':
'two', '__builtins__': {'cmp': <built-in function cmp>, 'dir': <built-in
function dir>, 'round': <built-in function round>, 'AttributeError': <class
exceptions.AttributeError at 280e8>, 'SystemExit': <class
exceptions.SystemExit at 28bd0>, 'str': <built-in function str>,
'ArithmeticError':
...
```

## locals()

The `locals()` function is like `globals()` except that it returns the variables in the innermost namespace.

```
>>> def func2(var1, var2, var3):
...     return locals()
...
>>> func2(1,2,3)
{'var2': 2, 'var3': 3, 'var1': 1}
```

This shows the use of `locals()` in the body of `func2` to print out the variables in func2's namespace.

`locals()` also returns any variables defined inside the function.

```
...     var4 = "more"
...     var5 = "five"
...     return locals()
...
>>> func3(1,2,3)
{'var2': 2, 'var3': 3, 'var1': 1, 'var4': 'more', 'var5': 'five'}
```

Here var4 and var5 are returned as well as the arguments passed to func3.

## vars()

The `vars()` function is like `locals()` except that you can use it for any object type to list the object's public attributes. Here we use `vars()` to list the attributes in the Exception class. (Exception is always—well, almost always—in the namespace.)

```
>>> vars(Exception)
{'__module__': 'exceptions', '__init__': <function __init__ at 27b8c>,
'__doc__': None, '__str__': <function __str__ at 27be0>, '__getitem__':
<function __getitem__ at 24d58>}
```

---

## Type Checking: callable(), type()

The `callable(object)` function returns true if the object can be called like a function. Since more than object types can be callable (lambdas, functions, methods, class instances, etc.), this feature is very useful. Here's an example:

```
>>> callable(dir)
1
```

This is nice, but how do you use it? Let's say that you want to find out which objects in the current module are callable.

Define a class whose instances are callable.

```
>>> class myclass:
...    def __call__(self):
...            return "hello"
...
```

Define an instance of the callable class.

```
>>> hello = myclass()
```

Define some not so useful functions.

```
>>> def func():pass
...
>>> def func1():pass
...
>>> def func2():pass
...
>>> def func3():pass
```

Iterate through the list of variables in the module namespace, and see which objects are callable.

```
>>> for (name,value) in vars().items():
...    if (callable(value)):
...            print name + " is callable"
...
hello is callable
myclass is callable
func is callable
func1 is callable
func2 is callable
func3 is callable
```

The `type()` function returns the type of the object.

```
>>> type(myclass)
<jclass org.python.core.PyClass . . .>

>>> type (func)
<jclass org.python.core.PyFunction . . .>

>>> type (dir())
<jclass org.python.core.PyList . . . >

>>> type(hello)
<jclass org.python.core.PyInstance . . .>
```

## *Operations*

This section deals mostly with functions that are longhand for operators.

### Numeric Operations: cmp(), divmod(), pow(), abs(), round()

cmp(x,y) compares two numeric types. It also works for sequences, dictionaries, and other numeric objects. cmp() returns a positive number if the $x$ argument is greater than the $y$ argument, a negative number if the $y$ argument is greater than the $x$ argument, and 0 if $x$ and $y$ are equal.

```
>>> cmp(1,0)
1

>>> cmp(0,1)
-1

>>> cmp(0,0)
0
```

cmp() is related to the equality operators (==, >=, <=, etc.). If you want these operators to work with class instances, you need to implement cmp() for the class by executing cmp(instance1, instance2), instance1 == instance2, or instance1 > instance2).

The divmod() function divides $a$ by $b$ and returns a tuple containing the divider and the remainder. With divmod(), these two examples are equivalent:

```
>>> 100 / 10, 100 % 10
(10, 0)

>>> divmod(100,10)
(10, 0)
```

The pow() function raises $x$ to the power of $y$, so these two examples are the same:

```
>>> 5**3
125

>>> pow(5,3)
125
```

The abs() function returns the absolute value of a number.

```
>>> abs(1), abs(-1)
(1, 1)
```

The round(x, [n]) function rounds a number with a fraction to the nearest whole integer (or, if you specify the n argument, to the nearest position in the mantissa). Here's an example.

Declare a variable containing a float with a long mantissa.

```
>>> myfloat = 1.1111111111111111
```

Round to the nearest whole integer.

```
>>> round(myfloat)
1.0
```

Round to the second decimal place in the mantissa.

```
>>> round(myfloat, 2)
1.11
```

Round to the third decimal place in the mantissa.

```
>>> round(myfloat, 3)
1.111
```

## Identity: hash(), id()

The hash() function returns a number that represents the data of an object, called the hash value. Hash values are integers that can be used to efficiently compare dictionary keys.

```
>>> myint= 1
>>> myfloat = 1.0
>>> hash(myint)
1

>>> hash(myfloat)
1
```

The id(object) function assigns objects in the system a unique ID. It implements the is operator. In the following statements, id and is are functionally equivalent:

```
>>> dict = {}
>>> id(dict)==id(dict), dict is dict
(1, 1)
```

## Class, Instance, and Modules: delattr(), getattr(), hasattr(), setattr()

The delattr(object,name) function removes attributes from a class or instance or removes variables from a module namespace. It works similarly to del(). Consider the following example, which defines an empty class, myclass, creates an instance of it, and adds attributes to the instance.

Define myclass.

```
>>> class myclass:pass
...
```

Create an instance of myclass, ci ("class instance"), and add to it the attributes "hello" and "goodbye".

```
>>> ci = myclass()
>>> ci.hello = "hello"
>>> ci.goodbye = "goodbye"
```

Display the attributes.

```
>>> vars(ci)
{'goodbye': 'goodbye', 'hello': 'hello'}
```

Use the del keyword to delete the "hello" attribute: then display the attributes that remain.

```
>>> del ci.hello
>>> vars(ci)
{'goodbye': 'goodbye'}
```

Use delattr()to delete "goodbye" from the class instance, and use vars() to show that the instance has no more attributes.

```
>>> delattr(ci,"goodbye")
>>> vars(ci)
{}
```

> ### Del
> You can't use delattr() to remove items (key/value pairs) from a dictionary; only the del keyword can do that. del and delattr() are equivalent only for classes, instances, and modules.

Here's an example that works with a module, *mymodule.py*. It just defines two variables, attr1 and attr2.

```
attr1=1
attr2=2
```

Import *mymodule.py* into the interactive interpreter.

```
>>> import mymodule
```

Show *mymodule*'s namespace with the dir() function.

```
>>> dir (mymodule)
['__builtins__', '__doc__', '__file__', '__name__', 'attr1', 'attr2']
```

Use delattr() to remove attr1 from the namespace.

```
>>> delattr(mymodule, "attr1")
```

Verify the removal.

```
>>> dir(mymodule)
['__builtins__', '__doc__', '__file__', '__name__', 'attr2']
```

Use del() to do the same thing with attr2.

```
>>> del mymodule.attr2
>>> dir(mymodule)
['__builtins__', '__doc__', '__file__', '__name__']
```

The getattr() function, strange as it may seem, "gets" an attribute from a class, instance, or module. Here's an example using a class, myclass2, whose instances have the attributes name and height.

Define myclass2.

```
>>> class myclass2:
...    def __init__(self):
...            self.name = "Bob"
...            self.height = "5'11"
...
>>> ci = myclass2()
```

Display the attributes of the class instance.

```
>>> vars(ci)
{'height': "5'11", 'name': 'Bob'}
```

Get the height attribute.

```
>>> getattr(ci, "height")
"5'11"
```

There's an easier way to do this.

```
>>> ci.height
"5'11"
```

But with getattr() we can get attributes dynamically at runtime.

The getattr() function also works with modules:

```
>>> getattr(mymodule, "attr1")
1
```

which is equivalent to

```
>>>mymodule.attr1
1
```

The hasattr() function checks to see if a class, instance, or module has an attribute. It returns true if so, false if not. Continuing our *mymodule.py* example, we have the following:

```
>>> hasattr(ci,"height")
1

>>> hasattr(ci,"weight")
0
```

hasattr() also works with modules.

```
>>> hasattr(mymodule, "attr1")
1
```

The setattr() function sets an attribute for a class, instance, or module. Still with the same example, we'll add the weight attribute to the class instance.

Determine if the ci class instance already has weight.

```
>>> hasattr(ci,"weight")
0
```

The 0 (false) value indicates no, so add it.

```
>>> setattr(ci,"weight", 220)
```

Now does it have it?

```
>>> hasattr(ci,"weight")
```

The 1 (true) value indicates yes.

We know the other way to add the weight attribute, but first we need to remove it.

```
>>> delattr(ci, "weight")    #remove it
>>> hasattr(ci, "weight")    # make sure it is gone
0
```

Now we set it and check to see if it's there.

```
>>> ci.weight = 220
>>> hasattr(ci,"weight")
1
```

### Working with Modules
Here's an example of how setattr(), hasattr(), and delattr() work with modules.

Import the *sys* module.

```
>>> import sys
```

Get the exit and version objects.

```
>>> getattr(sys, "exit")
<built-in function exit>

>>> getattr(sys, "version")
'1.5.1 (#0, 07/16/98 22:30:00) [MSC SH3]'
```

Remove the `exit()` function and make sure it's gone.

```
>>> delattr(sys, "exit")
>>> hasattr(sys, "exit")
0
```

Redefine the exit object in the context of the *sys* module.

```
>>> setattr(sys,"exit","exit has left the building")
```

Display the new `exit()` function.

```
>>> getattr(sys, "exit")
'exit has left the building'
```

## cmp() and Classes and Dictionaries

`cmp()` works with many object types. For example, if left undefined, it works with class instances just as `id` or `is` does. As with numeric objects, `cmp()` returns 0 if the objects are equal. Here's an illustration.

Create two class instances.

```
>>> ci1,ci2 = myclass2(),myclass2()
```

Compare them.

```
>>> cmp(ci1,ci2)
-1
```

Even though the values are the same, the instances are unequal because the default is to check object identity (to make sure that the variable references the same object).

Compare one instance to itself.

```
>>> cmp(ci1,ci1)
0
```

Since `cmp()` checks identity for equality, comparing an object to itself returns 0, which means equality.

The `cmp()` method defines the behavior of the equality operators. That means that the following is like using the identity operator:

```
>>> ci1 == ci2
0

>>> ci1 == ci1
1

>>> ci1 is ci2, ci1 is ci1
(0, 1)
```

Chapter 8 has an example of \_\_cmp\_\_ defined for the Address class. Here's an excerpt:

```
def __cmp__(self,other):
    """
    Compares one address instance to another.
    If the address instances are equal the __cmp__ returns 0.
If the address instances are not equal then we return a non-zero
value.
    """
                        # To implement this all we do is compare
    # the dictionaries of the class
                        # The __dict__ member of the instance holds
    # all of the instance fields
    # in a dictionary
        return cmp(self.__dict__ ,other.__dict__)
```

This compares all attribute values of one instance of Address with those of another instance. Remember, the default is just to compare identity.

## Sequence and Collection: len(), max(), min(), cmp()

We covered sequences and collections in Chapter 1, so we'll just review them here.

The len(s) method returns the length of a sequence or dictionary. It works with tuples, lists, and dictionaries, as shown in the following three examples:

```
>>> len((1,2,3))
3
```

```
>>> len([1,2,3])
3
```

```
>>> len({1:1,2:2,3:3})
3
```

The max(s) function returns the max value in a sequence. It uses cmp() to determine which item in the list is the greatest.

```
>>> max((1,2,3))
3
```

The min(s) function returns the min value in the list.

```
>>> min((1,2,3))
1
```

The cmp(x,y) method compares sequences (list and tuple) to sequences and dictionaries to dictionaries. Here's how.

Create three tuples, the first and second having equal values.

```
>>> list1,list2,list3=(1,2,3),(1,2,3),(1,2,4)
```

Compare the first and the second tuples.

```
>>> cmp (list1, list2) #cmp returns 0 if they are equal
0
>>> list1==list2
1
```

Compare the second and third tuples.

```
>>> cmp(list2, list3)
-1
>>> cmp(list3, list2)
1
>>> list2==list3
0
```

Create two dictionaries.

```
>>> dict1,dict2 = {1:1,2:2,3:3}, {1:1,2:2,3:3}
```

Compare them.

```
1
>>> cmp (dict1, dict2) #cmp returns 0 if they are equal
0
```

Add an item to the first dictionary.

```
>>> dict1["cow"]="moo"
```

Compare the first and second dictionaries again.

```
>>> dict1==dict2
0
>>> cmp(dict1,dict2)
1
```

## Modules: reload()

The reload() function allows you to dynamically reload a module. It comes in very handy when you're debugging code. Here's an example with the *string* module:

```
>>> import string
>>> reload(string)
<module 'string'>
```

During development of a module, it's often necessary to make minor changes. Instead of exiting the interactive interpreter, you can make your changes and then reload.

reload()needs a reference to the module. Let's say you're using the from <module> import <object> form of the import statement. In that case, you don't have a reference to the module, even though the module is loaded. (You need to exit and restart the interactive interpreter for this example.)

```
>>> from string import find
>>> print find
<built-in function find>
>>> print string
Traceback (innermost last):
  File "<interactive input>", line 1, in ?
NameError: string
```

Although we have access to the `find()` function, we don't have access to the *string* module, so when we try to print it out we get a `NameError`. To reload `find()` we have to first import and reload *string* (which puts it in the current namespace). We'll continue with our example.

Explicitly import *string*.

```
>>> import string
```

Reload it.

```
>>> reload (string)
<module 'string'>
```

Access `find()`as before.

```
>>> del string #optionally remove string from your namespace
>>> print find
<built-in function find>
```

Reloading the *string* module will reload all of its code; any changes will be reflected at that time. This is a great tool for debugging your Python modules.

The `__import__()` function (`__import__(name, [globals], [locals], [fromlist])`) works like the `import` statement, except that it allows you to pass the name of the module as a string. Imagine a program that, given a command-line argument, loads a module and executes its `test()` function. You can use this test harness with many different modules with many different names. Now imagine another program that detects how it connects to the home office and, based on that information, loads the correct module to talk to the boss.

Here's an example of `__import__()`:

```
>>> __import__("string")
<module 'string'>
```

## Class Operations: isinstance(), issubclass()

We covered the built-in `isinstance()` and `issubclass()` functions in Chapter 6, but let's briefly review them. We're going to use the following code, which defines a class hierarchy:

```
>>> class animal:
...     pass
...
```

```
>>> class mammal(animal):
...     pass
...
>>> class human(mammal):
...     pass
...
>>> class geek:
...     pass
...
>>> class programmer(geek, human):
...     pass
...
```

The isinstance(object,class) function determines if the instance is of a particular class. It works with the instance's base class; that is, if the human class is a subclass of the mammal class, any instance of human is also an instance of mammal. For example:

```
>>> Rick = programmer()
```

Is the Rick class instance an instance of programmer?

```
>>> isinstance(Rick,programmer)
1
```

Is Rick a geek?

```
>>> isinstance(Rick,geek)
1
```

Are programmers human?

```
>>> isinstance(Rick,human)
1
```

Since Rick is an instance of programmer and programmer is a subclass of human, Rick is an instance of human.

Of course, it doesn't stop with the immediate base classes. Rick is an instance of mammal and animal because these are in the base class hierarchy of programmer.

Is Rick a mammal?

```
>>> isinstance(Rick, mammal)
1
```

Is Rick an animal?

```
>>> isinstance(Rick, animal)
1
```

Since Rick is a human and humans are subclasses of mammals, Rick is a mammal. Since Rick is a mammal and mammals are subclasses of animals, Rick is an animal.

`issubclass(class1, class2)` returns whether one class is a subclass of another. Our illustration of `issubclass()` will continue our class hierarchy.

Is human a subclass of `animal`?

```
>>> issubclass(human, animal)
1
```

Is human a subclass of `mammal`?

```
>>> issubclass(human, mammal)
1
```

Is geek a subclass of `animal`?

```
>>> issubclass(geek,animal)
0
```

`issubclass()` doesn't work just for immediate subclasses but for subclasses anywhere in the hierarchy that have a class as a base class anywhere in their own hierarchy.

### I/O: open(), raw_input()

The `open(filename, [mode], [bufsize])` function returns a file object. Again, this is just a brief review since we covered I/O in Chapter 7.

Open a file for reading.

```
>>> file = open("\\dat\\exp.txt", "w")
>>> file.write("Hello")
>>> file.close()
```

Open a file for writing.

```
>>> file = open("\\dat\\exp.txt")
>>> file.read()
'Hello'
```

The `mode` argument specifies read ("r"), write ("w"), read/write ("r+"), and append ("a") mode. `bufsize` sets the size of the buffer. Setting the buffer to zero means no buffering. (For more on buffering see Chapter 12.)

The `raw_input([prompt])` function reads input from the user. The prompt tells the user what that input should be and returns it when the user hits Enter. Try following this:

```
>>> raw_input("Enter your age: ")
Enter your age: 31
'31'
```

## *Advanced Topic: Functional Programming*

You don't need to know functional programming to develop Python code, but learning it can reduce the amount of code you write.

## apply(), filter(), map(), reduce

The apply(function, args, [keywords]) function needs a callable object as the function argument, which it calls with args as the argument list (and keywords as the named argument list). args is a sequence, keywords a dictionary.

The function

```
>>> def hello(str):
...     print "hello " + str
...
```

can be called with apply() like this:

```
>>> apply(hello,("Bobby",))
hello Bobby
```

Without apply() it's called like this.

```
>>> hello("Bobby")
hello Bobby
```

You can use apply() to call several functions. Or you can have several functions operating on the same data.

The filter(function, list) function filters out items in a list. Its argument is a callable object that takes an item out of the list and returns true or false. Let's say the only list items we want are those that begin with *R*.

Create a list containing names.

```
>>> list = ["Mary", "Adam", "Bob", "Rick", "Robert"]
```

Define a function that returns true if the name starts with *R*.

```
>>> def Rfilter(name):
...     if name[0]=="R": return 1
...     else:            return 0
...
```

Invoke filter(), passing it the Rfilter and list arguments.

```
>>> filter(Rfilter,list)
['Rick', 'Robert']
```

This example is, admittedly, contrived. In a real situation, the items in the sequence can be much more complex than just strings; they can be class instances or dictionaries with 100 items, or tuples with dictionaries, class instances, and lists. Also, the function passed can be just short of rocket science. The point is that filter() returns every item in the list where the item applied to it returns a true value.

As an exercise, rewrite the above functionality with for loops instead of filter(). Which code is more concise? Which code is easier to understand? Once you answer these questions, I think you'll find that filter() is very useful.

The map(`function, list`) function is similar to `filter()`. It applies functions to every item in a list and returns the results for each function (item) call. `map()`'s first argument is a callable type; its second argument is a list.

As an example, let's say you have the following sequence that you want to convert into a string:

```
>>> seq = (72, 105, 32, 77, 111, 109)
```

which you can do with a for loop.

```
>>> list = []
>>> for item in seq:
...     list.append(chr(item))
...
>>> from string import join
>>> str = join(list,"")
```

After this code executes, str will contain a string version of the sequence, and it will take only four lines (we won't count `from string import join`). With the map() function, you can do all four lines of code in one method call.

```
>>> str = join(map(chr,seq),"")
```

Note that the call to map() is inside the join() function call.

You may be wondering what str contains. To unravel this mystery, enter in the code example.

```
>>> str
```

The reduce(`function, list, [initializer]`) function is very similar to `filter()` and map() in that a function parameter is applied to each item in a sequence. However, instead of returning a list it returns one value.

Let's say that you want to sum up the following list (the list variable is really a tuple):

```
>>> list = (1,2,3,4,5,6,7,8,9,10)
```

To do so with a for loop, you need to do something like this:

```
>>> sum=0
>>> for num in list:
...     sum = sum + num
>>> sum
55
```

With reduce(), you do something like this:

```
>>> def add(a,b): return a + b
...
>>> reduce (add,list)
55
```

which cuts out two lines of code.

If you want to cut out a third line, you can rewrite the above with a lambda function, which turns four lines into one (how very Pythonesque).

```
>>> reduce(lambda a,b: a+b,list)
55
```

Lambdas are a new concept. Think of them as anonymous functions but without names or parentheses. If you want to know more about lambda functions, consult the Python documentation.

Although powerful and elegant, `reduce()`, `apply()`, `map()`, and `filter()` (and, for that matter, lambdas) can be confusing. Don't let them trip you up, though—you don't need to master them to program in Python.

## Advanced exec and eval

Imagine easily sending code to update changes to a program or easily moving code around the network to update remote clients. How about adding scriptability so that end users can write scripts to automate common tasks? In other languages, these things are hard to accomplish. In Python they're built into the language.

### compile()

The `compile(string, filename, kind)` function converts a string into a code object that represents Python bytecode. The `filename` argument states the origin of the code, that is, the file name; the `kind` argument specifies how the code should be compiled based on the contents of the `string` argument. There are three choices for `kind`:

- `exec`—a group of statements
- `eval`—a single expression
- `single`—a single statement

`compile()` works in conjunction with the `eval` statement, which you use to execute the code object. More than likely you'll use it to execute a string representing code over and over again so that `eval` won't have to execute the string by recompiling the code object each time.

Here's an example of `compile()` with the `exec` kind argument. It pretends that it has read the string from a file called *friends.py*.

```
>>> string = """
... friends = ['Ross','Rachel','Chandler','Joey','Tom','Jerry','Monica']
... for myfriend in friends:
...    print "Hello " + myfriend
... """
>>> code = compile(string,"Friends.py","exec")
```

```
>>> eval(code)
Hello Ross
Hello Rachel
Hello Chandler
Hello Joey
Hello Tom
Hello Jerry
Hello Monica
>>>
```

Here's an example compiling an expression that returns a dictionary:

```
>>> str = "{1:1,2:2,3:3,4:4}"
>>> cd = compile (str,"string","eval")
>>> eval(cd)
{4: 4, 3: 3, 2: 2, 1: 1}

>>> dict = eval(cd)
>>> type (dict)
<jclass org.python.core.PyDictionary at 6190231>
```

which compiles a single statement:

```
>>> cd2 = compile("""print "Hello World" """, "string", "single")
>>> eval (cd2)
Hello World
```

Of course, we've covered eval(expressions, [globals], [locals]) quite a few times. Here we'll drill down to the details that can make you stumble.

## globals and locals

eval's globals and locals arguments are dictionaries that contain the global variables, where the keys are the variable names and the values are the objects to which the variables refer. Not specifying globals or locals is the same as doing this:

```
eval(str, globals(), locals())
```

which passes the variables from the current namespace.

Here's an example of calling an eval statement:

```
>>> a = 1
>>> eval("a")
1
```

Since the a variable is in the global namespace, and we're not passing a dictionary for the global variables, it's the one used.

In this next call to eval, we pass a dictionary for the globals argument. You can see that the value of a in the dictionary overrides the value of a in the global area of the module.

```
>>> eval("a", {"a":2})
2
```

Here we pass a variable named a in the `locals` dictionary. The inner namespace—`locals`—overrides the value of the a global dictionary.

```
>>> eval("a",{"a":2}, {"a":3})
3
```

Continuing this example, here we use a local a (that is, local to the `func()` function). You can see that the a in the local area takes precedence over the a in the global area (where we set a to 1).

```
>>> def func():
...     a=4
...     print eval("a")
...
>>> func()
4
```

### execfile()

The `execfile(file, [globals], [locals])` function acts just like the `exec` statement, except that it reads the contents of a file and executes it. As with `eval`, you can specify `globals` and `locals` arguments. `Execfile()` may seem a lot like `import()`, but the code executed with it acts as if it were executed in the current namespace. There is no namespace management with `execfile` as when a module is imported.

Here's an example of `exec` printing `'hello world'` from a string.

```
>>> exec "print 'hello world'"
hello world
```

As an exercise, create a text file containing Python code that prints `'hello world'` to the console. Then, in the interactive interpreter, read and execute the file with `execfile()`.

---

## Summary

Of all of the chapters so far, this one was the most fun to write, simply because Python's numerous built-in functions make simple things even simpler and impossible things possible. We reviewed a lot from other chapters, but we also covered many new items, such as functional programming and executing scripts.

# CHAPTER 10

# *Working with Strings*

---

## Terms in This Chapter

- ♭ Argument
- ♭ Decimal 10
- ♭ Exception
- ♭ Field
- ♭ Function

- ♭ Hexadecimal 16
- ♭ Namespace
- ♭ Octal 8
- ♭ Parsing
- ♭ Separator

- ♭ Sequence
- ♭ string module
- ♭ Substring
- ♭ Whitespace

---

Sooner or later, you'll need to format, parse, or manipulate strings. For these tasks, you'll likely use the functions in the Python *string* module. Spend some time familiarizing yourself with this module by following along with the examples in this chapter.

---

## Conversion: atoi(), atof(), atol()

atoi(s[,base]) converts a string into an integer. The default is decimal, but you can specify octal 8, hexadecimal 16, or decimal 10. If 0 is the base, the string will be parsed as a hexadecimal if it has a leading 0x and as an octal if it has a leading 0. Otherwise, it will be treated as a decimal.

Let's do an example. In this and all other examples in this chapter, you have to first import the *string* module: from string import *.

Convert "1" to an integer.

```
>>> atoi("1")
1
```

Convert "255" to a base 10 integer.

```
>>> atoi("255",10)
255
```

Convert "FF" to a base 16 integer.

```
>>> atoi("FF",16)
255
```

The atof(s) function converts a string to a float.

```
>>> atof("1.1")
1.1
```

The atol(s[, base]) converts a string to a long.

```
>>> atol("1")
1L
```

```
>>> atol("255", 16)
0xFFL
```

## Case Change: *capitalize(), capwords(), swapcases(), lower(), upper()*

The capitalize(word) function capitalizes a given word in a string.

```
>>> capitalize("bill")
'Bill'
```

The capwords(s) function capitalizes all words in a string.

```
>>> str = "bill joy"
>>> str = capwords(str)
>>> print str
Bill Joy
```

The swapcases(s) function converts uppercase letters to lowercase letters and vice versa.

```
>>> swapcase("ABC abc 123")
'abc ABC 123'
```

(Frankly, I don't see the value of this one.)

The lower(s) function converts uppercase letters to lowercase letters.

```
>>> lower("ABC abc 123")
'abc abc 123'
```

The upper(s) function converts lowercase letters to uppercase letters.

```
>>> upper("ABC abc 123")
'ABC ABC 123'
```

---

## Finding: find(), rfind(), index(), rindex(), count(), replace()

The finding functions in the *string* module locate a substring within a string. For example, substrings of "Python is fun" are "Pyt", "is", "fun", "n is f", and so forth. Using a substring helps in parsing string data.

The find(s, sub, [start],[end]) function finds the first position of a substring in a given string. You can set the start and stop position arguments, which determine where in the string the search will begin and end. Here's an example:

```
>>> str = "apple peach pear grapes apple lime lemon"
>>> position = find(str, "pear")
```

Here's a real-world use of find(): extracting text out of a tag when reading in an HTML file from a server.

Create some sample text embedded in HTML tags.

```
>>>     #simulated input string from some file
>>> str = "<h1> text we want to extract </h1>"
```

Set the start and stop strings (the HTML tags).

```
>>> start = "<h1>"              #html tag
>>> stop = "</h1>"             #html tag
```

Find the position of the first and second strings.

```
>>> begin = find(str,start)        #find the location of the 1st tag
>>> end = find(str,stop)    #find the location of the 2nd tag
```

Locate the text to be extracted.

```
>>>    #compute where the start of the string we want is:
>>> begin = begin + len(start)
```

Extract the text embedded in the HTML tags, and display it.

```
>>>     #using slice notation extract the text from the string
>>> text = str[begin:end]
>>> print text
text we want to extract
```

The HTML tags supply the boundaries of the desired text.

rfind(s, sub, [start],[end]) is similar to find(), but it searches the substring from right to left. Here it finds the last occurrence of "apple" in the str string.

```
>>> str = "apple orange tangerine apple pear grapes"
>>> rfind(str,"apple")
23
```

```
>>> find(str, "apple") #find finds the first occurrence
0
```

index(s, sub, [start],[end]) works like find() with one difference. When find() can't locate a substring, it returns a –1; when index() can't, it throws an exception.

```
>>> find(str, "commodore")
-1
```

```
>>> index(str, "commodore")
Traceback (innermost last):
  File "<stdin>", line 1, in ?
  File "D:\Apps\Python\Lib\string.py", line 226, in index
ValueError: substring not found in string.index
```

rindex(s, sub, [start],[end]) searches from the back of the string for a substring. It's like rfind(), but throws an exception if it fails.

Find "green" in the str string.

```
>>> str = "blue blue blue green red red red"
>>> rindex(str,"green")
15
```

Find "purple".

```
>>> rindex(str, "purple")
Traceback (innermost last):
  File "<stdin>", line 1, in ?
  File "D:\Apps\Python\Lib\string.py", line 243, in rindex
ValueError: substring not found in string.index
```

count(s, sub, [start],[end]) finds the number of occurrences of a substring in a string.

Count "blue" in the str string.

```
>>> str = "blue blue blue green red red red"
>>> count(str, "blue")
3
```

Count "red".

```
>>> count(str, "red")
3
```

replace(str, old, new, [max]) replaces one substring with a new one. The max argument specifies the number of occurrences you want replaced. The default is all occurrences.

Create a string with four "apple" substrings.

```
>>> str = "apple, apple, apple, apple"
```

Replace the first "apple" with "pear".

```
>>> replace(str, "apple", "pear", 1)
'pear, apple, apple, apple'
```

Replace every occurrence of "apple" with "orange".

```
>>> replace(str, "apple", "orange")
'orange, orange, orange, orange'
```

## *Splitting and Joining: split(), splitfields(), join(), joinfields()*

`split(s, [sep], [maxsplit])` and `splitfields(s, [sep], [maxsplit])` both split a string into a sequence. With the `sep` argument you can specify what you want to use for the separator—the default is `whitespace` (spaces or tabs). The `maxsplit` optional argument allows you to specify how many items you want to break up; the default is all.

Here, with one line of code, we parse an address containing five fields. (Try to do this with Java, C, Delphi, or Visual Basic—you can't.)

```
>>> input_string = "Bill,Gates,123 Main St., WA, 65743"
>>> fname, lname, street, state, zip = split(input_string,",")
>>> print """
... Name: %(fname)s %(lname)s
... Street: %(street)s
... %(state)s, %(zip)s""" % locals()

Name: Bill Gates
Street: 123 Main St.
WA, 65743
```

### A Few Things to Note

- You can assign multiple variables to a sequence (Chapter 12).
- The `locals()` built-in function (Chapter 9) returns a dictionary that contains the variables in a local namespace, so the statement

  ```
  >>> locals()["lname"]
  ```
  returns

  ```
  'Gates'
  ```

- The `%` format string operator works with dictionaries or sequences (Chapter 3).

Here we demonstrate that `split()` and `splitfields()` do the same thing:

```
>>> split (input_string)
['Bill,Gates,123', 'Main', 'St.,', 'WA,', '65743']

>>> splitfields(input_string)
['Bill,Gates,123', 'Main', 'St.,', 'WA,', '65743']
```

Here's an example demonstrating the default operation for `split()`:

```
>>> split("tab\tspace word1 word2        word3\t\t\tword4")
['tab', 'space', 'word1', 'word2', 'word3', 'word4']
```

`join(words, [sep])` and `joinfields(words, [sep])` also do the same thing. Here's our last example showing how to build an address string from a sequence of fields:

```
>>> seq = (fname, lname, street, state, zip)
>>> input_string = join(seq, ",")
>>> print input_string
Bill,Gates,123 Main St., WA, 65743
```

The next two examples demonstrate the similarities of `join()` and `joinfields()`:

```
>>> seq = ("1","2","3","4","5")
>>> join(seq, "#")
'1#2#3#4#5'

>>> joinfields(seq,"#")
'1#2#3#4#5'
```

## Stripping and Parsing: lstrip(), rstrip(), strip()

When you parse strings, you often need to get rid of whitespace. This is what the stripping functions do. They're handy and convenient; I think you'll use them quite a bit.

### Whitespace Variables

Whitespace is defined by the public variable `whitespace` in the *string* module. This code contains a tab and spaces:

```
>>> whitespace
'\ 11 '
```

The `lstrip(s)` (left strip) function removes leading whitespace (on the left) in the string. The `rstrip(s)` (right strip) function removes the trailing whitespace (on the right). The `strip(s)` function removes both leading and trailing whitespace. Here's an example of all three:

```
>>> str = "    String    String "

>>> lstrip(str)
'String    String          '

>>> rstrip(str)
'      String    String'

>>> strip(str)
'String    String'
```

## Adjusting Text: ljust(), rjust(), center(), zfill(), expandtabs()

The functions for adjusting text are as handy and convenient as the parsing functions. You'll use them a lot, particularly for attractive report printing.

The ljust(s, width) function left-justifies a string to a given width. The rjust(s, width) function right-justifies it. The center(s, width) function centers a string to a given width. Here are examples of all three:

```
>>> rjust("String",20)
'              String'
>>> rjust ("str",20)
'                 str'
>>> ljust("String",20)
'String              '
>>> ljust("str",20)
'str                 '
>>> center("str",20)
'        str         '
>>> center("String",20)
'       String       '
```

zfill(snum,width) pads a numeric string with leading zeros.

```
>>> zfill("0.1", 10)
'00000000.1'
```

expandtabs(s,tabsize) converts tabs into spaces that equal the width of the tabsize argument.

Create a string with tabs denoted by \t.

```
>>> str = "tab\ttab\ttab\t"
```

Expand the tabs to five spaces.

```
>>> expandtabs(str, 5)
'tab  tab  tab '
```

Expand the tabs to ten spaces.

```
>>> expandtabs(str,10)
'tab       tab       tab       '
```

Expand the tabs to twenty spaces.

```
>>> expandtabs(str, 20)
'tab                 tab                 tab                 '
```

## Summary

In its standard distribution, Python provides a rich set of functions to manipulate and parse strings not found in other programming languages. My guess is that you'll use these functions a lot.

# CHAPTER 11    *Interfacing with Java*

---— *Terms in This Chapter* ——

- ◊ *Applet*
- ◊ *AWT*
- ◊ *Base class*
- ◊ *Bean*
- ◊ *Built-in object*
- ◊ *Buffer*
- ◊ *Content pane*
- ◊ *Constructor*
- ◊ *Coupling*
- ◊ *Design pattern*
- ◊ *Event*

- ◊ *Event handler*
- ◊ *Event listener*
- ◊ *First class object*
- ◊ *Frame*
- ◊ *get() and set() methods*
- ◊ *-h option*
- ◊ *Interface*
- ◊ *Java API*
- ◊ *JFC*
- ◊ *Object wrapper*

- ◊ *Packing*
- ◊ *Primitive type*
- ◊ *Property*
- ◊ *Public function*
- ◊ *self*
- ◊ *Superclass*
- ◊ *Subclass*
- ◊ *Typecode*
- ◊ *Type signature*
- ◊ *Unicode*

Java's vast array of application programming interfaces (APIs) help you build GUIs, optimize network communications, create distributed objects, build components, work with databases, and design Web applications. This chapter is about how to use them with Jython.

**Downloading the Java Documentation**

To get the most out of this chapter, go to the JavaSoft site (*http://www.java.sun.com*) and download the Java API documentation.

## *Using the Java APIs*

To see how easy it is to use the Java APIs, follow along with this interactive session. Import two classes from the Java package *javax.swing*: JFrame and JButton. (We'll cover these classes in depth in Chapter 13.)

```
>>> from javax.swing import JFrame, JButton
```

Create an instance of each.

```
>>> frame = JFrame()
>>> button = JButton("Hello Java APIs")
```

(Note that you create Java instances and Python instances in the same way.) Add the button instance to the content pane.

```
>>> pane = frame.getContentPane() # get access to the content pane
>>> pane.add(button)              # add the button to the content pane
javax.swing.JButton ...
```

Pack the components in the frame.

```
>>> frame.pack()
```

Make the frame visible.

```
>>> frame.visible = 1             # make the frame visible
>>>     # define the function that does the event handling
>>> def button_clicked(event):
... print "Hello from Java APIs!!!!"
...
>>> button.actionPerformed = button_clicked    #set up the event handler
```

Figure 11–1 shows the output you get after clicking the button several times. Figure 11–2 shows the form we just created.

Java classes are pretty much like Python classes. Importing classes are the same in the two languages, except that Java classes come from packages whereas

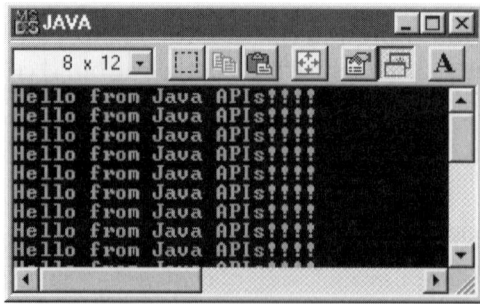

**Figure 11–1** *Output from the Button Event*

**Figure 11-2**    `JFrame` *Form*

Python classes come from modules. There are a few other slight differences, which we'll cover later, that don't change the basic similarities.

## Java Types

In this section we're going to cover how Python handles the conversion from Java types when you pass arguments to Java methods and when those methods return values. First, though, let's briefly cover the Java basic types:

- `boolean`—contains true or false
- `char`—contains Unicode characters
- `byte`—contains 8-bit signed integers
- `short`—contains 16-bit signed integers
- `int`—contains 32-bit signed integers
- `long`—contains 64-bit signed integers
- `float`—contains 32-bit floating-point numbers
- `double`—contains 64-bit floating-point numbers
- `String`—contains a string of Unicode characters
- `array`—contains arrays of objects or primitive types

> **Primitive versus Basic Types**
>
> I define as Java basic types all of the primitive types plus any classes that have special operators or literal notation. Thus, for example, you can add `String` instances together using the + operator, and you can create them using literals, so, by definition, strings are a basic Java type. I hope this terminology catches on.

### Passing Arguments to Java Methods

One of the key differences between calling methods in Java and calling them in Python is that Java expects Java types. At first, this may seem complex, but Jython takes care of all of the conversion transparently. All you need to know is how a Java type maps to the corresponding Python type so that, for example, when you read the Java API documentation you know which Python type to pass to a particular method.

Java has many more basic types than Python has. For example, the Python `Float` is like the Java `double`. Python has no `Double`, so you can use `Float` whenever you need a Java `double` or `float`.

Again, Java has three ways to describe an integer—`byte`, `short`, and `int`—which take up varying levels of space. Python has just one integer type, `Integer`, that can take the place of any Java integer type. Fewer types mean less to worry about and remember.

Table 11–1 shows the mapping from Java types to Python types for calling Java methods. Notice that eleven Java types map to only five Python types. The Python `Integer` alone corresponds to four Java types (`boolean`, `byte`, `short`, and `int`). The Python `String` type corresponds to three Java types.

## Getting Return Values from Java Methods

Jython converts the values returned from Java methods to Python types. Table 11–2 lists these mappings. The conversion also works with Java primitive-type object wrappers, as illustrated in Table 11–3.

## Putting Things Together

Let's use the Java class `Float` to demonstrate the Python conversion of basic Java data types. `Float`, from the *java.lang* package, converts various Java basic types to a Java `float`.

In particular, we'll look at the following `Float` methods:

- `static Float valueOf(String str)`—converts a `string` to a `float`
- `float floatValue()`—gets the primitive `float` wrapped in a `Float` instance
- `static boolean isInfinite(float v) Boolean`—checks to see if the `float` is infinite and returns a primitive

**Table 11–1**   *Java/Python Type Mapping*

| Java | Python |
| --- | --- |
| char | String (must have length 1) |
| boolean | Integer (false = zero, true = nonzero) |
| byte, short, int, | Integer |
| long | Long (in the range of Java long or integer) |
| float, double | Float |
| java.lang.String | String |
| byte[] | String |
| array[] | Jarray |

**Table 11–2**  *Java/Python Type Mappings for Return Values*

| Java Basic Type | Returned Python Type |
|---|---|
| char | One-character String—"a" or 'a' but not "ab" |
| boolean | Integer (true = 1, false = 0) |
| byte | Integer |
| short | Integer |
| int | Integer |
| long | Long |
| float, double | Float |
| java.lang.String | String |
| java.lang.Class | JavaClass (org.python.core.PyJavaClass) |
| Instance | PyInstance (org.python.core.PyInstance) |
| ClassInstance[] | Array (contains objects of class or subclass of ClassInstance) |

**Table 11–3**  *Java/Python Mappings for Object Wrappers*

| Java Object Wrapper | Python Type |
|---|---|
| java.lang.Char | String (with one character) |
| java.lang.Integer | Integer |
| java.lang.Boolean | Integer |
| java.lang.Byte | Integer |
| java.lang.Short | Integer |
| java.lang.Long | Long |
| java.lang.Double | Float |
| java.lang.Float | Float |

The static keyword specifies that a method isn't bound to a class instance; that is, it can be called without a class instance being created. Static methods in Java are thus like functions defined in Python modules. If you're confused, follow along with this quick example.

Import the Java class Float.

```
>>> from java.lang import Float
```

Demonstrate a function that returns a Float wrapper object.

```
>>>    #valueOf returns a java.lang.Float
>>> myFloatObject = Float.valueOf("1.1")
>>> type(myFloatObject)
<jclass org.python.core.PyFloat at -1329353172>
```

Notice that the value returned from `valueOf()` (stored in `myFloatObject`) is converted to a Python `Float`.

Now let's use the `isInfinite()` method to demonstrate the return of a primitive. In this case, `isInfinite()` returns a primitive `Boolean`.

```
>>> myBoolean = Float.isInfinite(myFloatObject)
>>> type(myBoolean)
<jclass org.python.core.PyInteger at -820007380>
```

Before I can show you an example of `floatValue()`, I need to explain Java constructors.

---

### *A Reminder about Returning Types in CPython and Jython*

In CPython, types are returned as follows.
Return an `Int`.

```
>>> myint = 1
>>> type(myint)
<type 'int'>
```

Return a `Float`.

```
>>> myfloat = 1.1
>>> type(myfloat)
<type 'float'>
```

Here's how types are returned in Jython.
Return an `Int`.

```
>>> myint = 1
>>> type(myint)
<jclass org.python.core.PyInteger at -820007380>
```

Return a `Float`.

```
>>> myfloat=1.1
>>> type(myfloat)
<jclass org.python.core.PyFloat at -1329353172>
```

The following will work the same in both Python and Jython. Import `IntType` and `FloatType` from the *types* module.

```
>>> from types import IntType, FloatType
```

Test to see if `myint` is `IntType`. If so, print "Integer type".

```
>>> if(type(myint)==IntType):print "Integer type"
Integer type
```

Test to see if `myfloat` is `FloatType`; if so, print "Float type".

```
>>> if(type(myfloat==FloatType)):print "Float type"
Float type
```

## Java Constructors

All instances of Java classes are of type `Instance` (`org.python.core.PyInstance`). Here I use a constructor to create a date. In Java, as in Python, a constructor is a method in a class, so this example demonstrates a method returning an instance of class `Date`.

```
>>> from java.util import Date
>>> date = Date()
>>> type(date)
<jclass org.python.core.PyInstance at -1204237921>
```

Constructors don't behave like regular Java methods in Jython, however. Instead, they convert `PyInstances` of the class even if the class is a Java primitive wrapper. (Remember, methods that return primitive wrappers are converted to the corresponding Python types.) In this context, the `Integer` and `Float` constructors return `PyInstances`.

Import the Java primitive wrappers `Integer` and `Float`.

```
>>> from java.lang import Integer, Float
```

Create the Java primitive wrapper `Integer` with the constructor, and view its type.

```
>>> i = Integer(1)
>>> type(i)
<jclass org.python.core.PyInstance at -1292653012>
```

Create the Java primitive wrapper `Float` with the constructor, and view its type.

```
>>> f = Float(1.1)
>>> type (f)
<jclass org.python.core.PyInstance at -1292653012>
```

As you can see, the primitive types don't come back as corresponding Python types but as `PyInstances`. Conversely, the `valueOf()` method of class `Integer` and class `Float` returns the Java primitive object wrappers `Integer` and `Float`, respectively, which are converted to corresponding Python types. In short, the rules that apply to Java methods don't apply to Java constructors.

Now back to `floatValue()`. Here's an example of Python converting the Java return values of `int` and `float` to Python `Integer` and `Float`:

```
>>> type(i.intValue())
<jclass org.python.core.PyInteger at -820007380>
```

```
>>> type(f.floatValue())
<jclass org.python.core.PyFloat at -1329353172>
```

Convert the object wrapper instance `java.lang.Float` to `PyFloat`.

```
>>> type(Float.valueOf("1.1"))
<jclass org.python.core.PyFloat at -1329353172>
```

Convert the object wrapper instance `java.lang.Float` to `PyInteger`.

```
>>> type(Integer.valueOf("1"))
<jclass org.python.core.PyInteger at -820007380>
```

By the way, instances of Java classes used to be of type `JavaInstance` (`org.python.core.PyJavaInstance`), but that changed with the release of Jython 1.1.

```
>>> from org.python.core import PyJavaInstance
>>> type(b)==PyJavaInstance
0
```

> ### For Beginners: Why the Minutiae
>
> You can program in Python without understanding how Python takes care of Java types. However, when you deal with the more advanced Java APIs, the minutiae we're dealing with here may become important. The good news is that Jython takes care of all Java type conversion transparently, so 95 percent of the time you don't need to worry. It's that other 5 percent that may get you.

## Java Arrays and jarray

The closest thing to a Java array in Python is a tuple. Remember that a tuple is immutable and a list is mutable. Like a list, a Java array is mutable but, like a tuple, it's of fixed length. You may think that a tuple or a list is a likely candidate for an array, but that's not exactly the case. You see, an array is like a homogeneous tuple or list—every item in it is of the same type; but a tuple is heterogeneous—items in it can be of different types. A lot of Java methods have Java arrays as arguments, so when you pass an array to a Java method, Python has to guarantee that it will be homogeneously typed.

Just a note: Because they're strongly typed, Java arrays can hold Java objects or primitive types.

Jython adds `PyArray` class support for Java arrays—`org.python.core.PyArray` to be exact. Instances of `PyArray` are returned from Java methods that return Java arrays. You need to create instances of `PyArray` to pass to Java methods that require arrays. Python makes creating a `PyArray` painless with the *jarray* module, which defines two public functions, described in Table 11–4.

> ### No Built-In Java Objects
>
> A Java object is only an instance of a class. There are no other object types, so there are no built-in Java objects as there are in Python. The closest things Java has to Python's built-in objects are strings and arrays, which require special syntax.

**Table 11–4**  *jarray Public Functions*

| Function | Description |
| --- | --- |
| `array(sequence, type)` | Creates an array of a specific type with values from the sequence; the array is the same size as the sequence |
| `zeros(length, type)` | Creates an empty array the length of the `length` parameter |

The `type` argument for both `zeros()` and `array()` can be either a string or a Java class object. You can use a single-character string typecode to specify that the array will hold primitive values. Table 11–5 shows the typecodes and their primitive types.

Here's an example of creating arrays with the `array()` and `zeros()` methods from the *jarray* module.

Create a Boolean array using the `array()` method.

```
>>> from jarray import array, zeros
>>> seq = (1,0,1,0,1,0)
>>> booleanArray = array(seq, 'z')
```

Inspect its contents.

```
>>> booleanArray
array([1, 0, 1, 0, 1, 0], boolean)

>>> print `booleanArray`
array([1, 1, 1, 1, 1, 0], boolean)
```

See what type it is.

```
>>> booleanArray
array([1, 0, 1, 0, 1, 0], boolean)

>>> print `booleanArray`
array([1, 1, 1, 1, 1, 0], boolean)
```

**Table 11–5**  *Typecodes and Primitive types*

| Typecode | Primitive Type |
| --- | --- |
| `'z'` | boolean |
| `'c'` | char |
| `'b'` | byte |
| `'h'` | short |
| `'i'` | int |
| `'l'` | long |
| `'f'` | float |
| `'d'` | double |

Change its values.

```
>>> booleanArray[1]=1
>>> booleanArray[3]=1
>>> booleanArray
array([1, 1, 1, 1, 1, 0], boolean)
```

You can use the same operations on an array that you use on a sequence (a tuple or a list). Here's an example:

```
>>> for boolean in booleanArray:
...     print `boolean`
...
1
1
1
1
1
0
>>> len(booleanArray)
6
```

Even though an array is mutable, it's still of fixed length; that means that you can't append to it as you can a Python list. If you try, you'll get an attribute error.

```
>>> booleanArray.append(1)
Traceback (innermost last):
  File "<console>", line 1, in ?
AttributeError: instance of 'org.python.core.PyArray' has no attribute
'append'
```

Let's create an array with the zeros() method.

```
>>> IntArray = zeros(10,'i')
>>> print IntArray
array([0, 0, 0, 0, 0, 0, 0, 0, 0, 0], int)
```

As the above example shows, you can think of PyArray essentially as a Python built-in type that's specific to Jython. Like other features Jython has for integrating with Java, PyArrays are transparent to the programmer (when returned from a Java method). Creating one is easy with Jython's *jarray* module.

## Java Arrays and Methods

Let's see some examples of using arrays to get values from and pass values to Java methods. We'll use three methods of the Java String class (from the *java.lang* package): valueOf(), getBytes(), and getChar(), which are described in Table 11–6.

Since the valueOf() method takes char[] as an argument, we need to create an array of primitive type char. In Java the [] notation denotes an array.

**Table 11–6**   *Example Java* `String` *Class Methods*

| Method | Description |
| --- | --- |
| `static String valueOf(char[] data)` | Converts an array of primitive type `char` into a string |
| `byte[] getBytes()` | Returns the byte data associated with a `string` |
| `void getChars(int srcBegin, int srcEnd, char [] dst, int dstBegin)` | Copies characters from the `string` into a `char` array |

Import `java.lang.String` and `jarray.array`.

```
>>> from java.lang import String
>>> from jarray import array
```

Create a sequence whose items can be converted into primitive Java type `char`.

```
>>> seq = ('H','e','l','l', 'o', ' ', 'W', 'o', 'r', 'l' , 'd')
>>> seq
('H', 'e', 'l', 'l', 'o', ' ', 'W', 'o', 'r', 'l', 'd')
```

Use the `array()` method to create a `PyArray` of primitive Java type `char`.

```
>>> data = array(seq, 'c')
>>> data  #Display just to show you what is in it.
array(['H', 'e', 'l', 'l', 'o', ' ', 'W', 'o', 'r', 'l', 'd'], char)
```

The `valueOf()` method, which takes a `char[]`argument (a `char` array), takes the array of Java primitive `chars` and turns it into a Java `string`.

```
>>> str = String.valueOf(data)
>>> print str
Hello World
```

Use `getBytes()` to demonstrate returning an array.

```
>>> hi = String("Hello Cruel World")
>>> bytes = hi.getBytes()
>>> bytes       #display what is in bytes
array([72, 101, 108, 108, 111, 32, 67, 114, 117, 101, 108, 32, 87, 111, 114,
    108, 100], byte)
>>> chr(bytes[0]) #The chr function converts an integer to a character
'H'
```

In Java, you often supply the buffer (Java array), which the method fills with the output results. The `getChars()` method expects a character buffer (char array), but it doesn't matter what's in it because it's only for output. Thus, we can use the `jarray.zeros()` method to create an empty, or zero-initialized, buffer.

Import `zeros()` and `String()`.

```
>>> from jarray import zeros
>>> from java.lang import String
```

Create an instance of `java.lang.String`.

```
>>> hi = String("Here we are now")
```

Use the `zeros()` method to create the `char` array, `dst`.

```
>>> dst = zeros(10, 'c')
```

Use the `getChars()` method to fill `dst`.

```
>>> hi.getChars(0,10, dst, 0)
>>> print dst
array(['H', 'e', 'r', 'e', ' ', 'w', 'e', ' ', 'a', 'r'...], char)
```

Dealing with Java arrays in Python demonstrates how the Python language keeps things simple.

## Bean Properties

With Jython, you can use JavaBeans properties like instance attributes, which makes it easy to interact with Java classes. You can also use them as keyword arguments to Java class constructors (like Tcl/Tk).

> ### About JavaBeans
> JavaBeans have properties and events, much like ActiveX controls, which are a lot like OLE controls (OCXs), which are like Visual Basic controls (VBX). To make a short story long, JavaBeans allow IDE (Integrated Development Environments) to do mundane things that you used to have to write code for.

In Java, you need the `set()` and `get()` methods to define a property. Let's say that you create a property called `name` that you want to be both read and write. You can define two methods for it.

```
public void setName(String name)
public String getName()
```

(By the way, `void` in Java means that the method doesn't return anything.) If you want `name` to be read-only, define only the `getName()` method.

In Python, you can access the `name` property as follows (assuming you defined the methods in a class called `myJavaClass`).

```
>>> instance = myJavaClass()
>>> instance.name = "Rick"
>>> print instance.name
Rick
```

You can also set name when you call the constructor.

```
>>> instance = myJavaClass(name= "Rick")
>>> print instance.name
Rick
```

We'll show some real examples of this later in the chapter.

## Properties

Sometimes properties are more complex than basic Java types—for example, a property can be a type of class. You can set properties that expect class instances with tuples that correspond to the constructor of the property type. (This only works for things like java.awt.Dimension.)

An example of this is the setSize() method of javax.swing.JFrame. The size property expects an instance of class Size, whose constructor expects width and height integer arguments.

The following code recaps what we've learned so far about using properties. We'll show how to create a frame and set its size property with a tuple, and we'll show the frame's visible property. Don't worry that you don't know JFC/Swing. I'll walk you through it.

Import the JFrame class.

```
>>> from javax.swing import JFrame
```

Create a JFrame instance.

```
>>> f = JFrame()
```

What happens? Nothing. That's because the default for creating a JFrame instance is that it be invisible. If we want it to be visible, we can pass it the visible property keyword argument as follows, or we can just set the property like any other instance attribute.

Set the visible property in the constructor.

```
>>> f = JFrame (visible=1)
```

Set the visible property as a property.

```
>>> f.visible = 0
>>> f.visible = 1
```

As you can see, even though visible, the frame isn't very big. We can set the frame size by passing it a size parameter.

```
>>> f = JFrame(size=(250,250), visible=1)
```

Now we have a big, blank frame, which we can make even bigger.

```
>>> f.size = 500,500
>>> f.background = 0,255,255
>>> f.background = 255,0,255
>>> f.background = 0,255,255
>>> f.background = 255,255,0
>>> f.background = 0,255,0
>>> f.background = 255,0,0
>>> f.background = 0,0,255
```

No, I didn't forget to tell you what the above code does. I didn't want to tell you. I want to shame those of you who aren't doing the examples into putting down the book and starting to program.

## Event Properties

You can think of event properties as properties that take methods as arguments. As a Java programmer, you can think of them as a way to implement Java events. In Python, you set an event property so you can be notified when an event happens. Notification comes when the class instance calls the method you passed to the property when the event occurred.

For example, JButton has an event property called actionPerformed, which represents the button being pressed. Whenever this happens, the method passed to actionPerformed is called. This is much easier to explain with code.

Import the JButton and JFrame classes from the *javax.swing* package, and create an instance of JFrame. Set its size at 200,200 pixels, and make it visible.

```
>>> from javax.swing import JButton, JFrame
>>> f = JFrame(visible=1, size=(200,200))
```

Define an event handler for JButton.

```
>>> def Hello(event):
...     print "Hello World"
...
```

Create an instance of JButton called button, and pass the event handler as the actionPerformed property.

```
>>> button = JButton("Hello World", actionPerformed=Hello)
```

Add the button to the frame, and pack the frame with the components.

```
>>> f.getContentPane().add(button)
javax.swing.JButton[,0,0,0x0,invalid,layout=javax.swing.OverlayLayout,
    alignmentX
...
>>> f.pack()
```

If you hit the "Hello World" button, you'll see "Hello World" print to the console. Note that the argument the event handler needs is the event object passed to it.

If you program in Java 1.1 or later, you know that AWT (and JFC) components are handled by passing an instance of a class that implements a specific event handler interface. In Jython, things are much easier because functions and methods are considered first class objects.

## Java Event Handling

Here's an example of Java event handling in Jython. It does the same thing the example in the previous section did but in the Java (Jython) way.

```
>>> from javax.swing import JFrame, JButton
>>> from java.awt.event import ActionListener
>>> class hello(ActionListener):
...     def actionPerformed(self, event):
...             print "Hello"
...
>>> f = JFrame()
>>> b = JButton("Hello from Java Events")
>>> hi = hello()
>>> b.addActionListener(hi)
>>> f.getContentPane().add(b)
>>> f.pack()
>>> f.visible = 1
```

I think you'll prefer the more Pythonesque way of doing things because it's brief and easy. Unfortunately, however, you need to know the Java way to understand the Jython way. For example, the only way to know that JButton supports an event property is to know that it supports the method addActionListener(), and that addActionListener() takes an instance of the ActionListener interface (an interface is a totally abstract class), and that ActionListener has a method called action Performed(). In other words, the inventors of Jython expect you to know the Java event model.

So then, Jython isn't really for beginners. To help in this regard, I've created a module to let you inspect the Java event model, and I've added a section explaining it in detail so that when you read the Java APIs you'll know how the events map.

### The *jinfo* Module

I've created a module called *jinfo* that allows you to inspect Java class event properties. Let's look at JButton (javax.swing.JButton).

Import the *jinfo* module and the JButton class.

```
>>> from jinfo import *
>>> from javax.swing import JButton
```

Use the getEventsInfo() method to view the events associated with JButton.

```
>>> getEventsInfo(JButton, 1)
>>>
```

Nothing happened here because the events associated with JButton are defined in JButton's superclass. Thus, we need to find out what that superclass is.

```
>>> JButton.superclass
<jclass javax.swing.AbstractButton at 1250890579>
```

Now we can query its events.

```
>>> from javax.swing import AbstractButton
>>> getEventsInfo(AbstractButton)
[<beanEventProperty itemStateChanged for event interface
java.awt.event.ItemListener at -1327819950>,
 <beanEventProperty actionPerformed for event interface jav
a.awt.event.ActionListener at -1284828334>,
<beanEventProperty stateChanged for event interface
javax.swing.event.ChangeListener at -1331489966>]
```

The code above is a little hard to read, so I'll show you another way to use the getEventsInfo() information.

```
>>> events = getEventsInfo(AbstractButton)
>>> len (events)
3
>>> printEventProperty(events[0])
```

```
Event Property:            itemListener
Defined in:                java.awt.event.ItemListener
Event:                     java.awt.event.ItemEvent

Event properties for java.awt.event.ItemEvent:
    itemSelectable        Type: org.python.core.PyBeanProperty
    stateChange           Type: org.python.core.PyBeanProperty
    item                  Type: org.python.core.PyBeanProperty
Public Event fields for java.awt.event.ItemEvent:
    static final ITEM_FIRST                    Type: int
    static final ITEM_LAST             Type: int
    static final ITEM_STATE_CHANGED    Type: int
    static final SELECTED              Type: int
    static final DESELECTED            Type: int
```

Now you can look up the event information in the class's java.awt.event.Item Listener interface and java.awt.event.ItemEvent class in the Java API documentation. The properties that the event passes to itemListener are also shown.

Let's do another example. We're familiar with this event because we've used it in many of the previous examples.

```
>>> printEventProperty(events[1])
```

```
Event Property:            actionListener
Defined in:                java.awt.event.ActionListener
Event:                     java.awt.event.ActionEvent
```

```
Event properties for java.awt.event.ActionEvent:
    modifiers               Type: org.python.core.PyBeanProperty
    actionCommand           Type: org.python.core.PyBeanProperty
Public Event fields for java.awt.event.ActionEvent:
    static final SHIFT_MASK          Type: int
    static final CTRL_MASK           Type: int
    static final META_MASK           Type: int
    static final ALT_MASK            Type: int
    static final ACTION_FIRST        Type: int
    static final ACTION_LAST         Type: int
    static final ACTION_PERFORMED    Type: int
```

We can use this information to determine which classes to look up in the documentation: `ActionListener` and `ActionEvent`. We can use the fields from `ActionEvent` in our event handler. The following code uses this information to display the `Modifiers` and `ActionCommand` of `ActionEvent`:

```
>>> from javax.swing import JButton, JFrame
>>> f = JFrame(visible=1)
>>> b = JButton("Hello")
>>> def hello(event):
...     print "Modifiers: " + `event.modifiers`
...     print "ActionCommand: " + `event.actionCommand`
...
>>> b.actionPerformed = hello
>>> f.contentPane.add(b)
javax.swing.JButton[,0,0,0x0,invalid,layout=javax.swing.OverlayLayout,`
    alignmentX
...
...
>>> f.pack()
```

Try hitting the button a few times. You'll see that you can print out the attributes of the event based on the information obtained using `getEventsInfo()` and `printEventProperty()`. If you want to know what the properties for the event were used for, look them up under `java.awt.event.ActionEvent` in the Java documentation.

## Advanced Topic: The JavaBeans Event Model in Detail

The Java 1.1 event model was introduced so that you would no longer have to subclass a GUI component in order to handle events, as you did with the Java 1.0 version. JFC, AWT, and JavaBeans use the version 1.1 event model, which defines the following:

- *Source*—the origin of the event
- *Listener*—a class that listens for an event, that is, the event handler
- *Event*—information about the event

In this model, to define an event you have to subclass a class from `EventObject`, which contains event information. One piece of information is the `source` property, which provides the event's origin. In our last example, we had a `JButton` instance called b, which was the source of the `ActionEvent` instance passed to the event method handler (in the last example this method was called `hello()`).

An event listener registers itself with the event source, which notifies the listener when the event happens by calling a method on it. All listeners must implement the method the event source needs to call. To do so they have to implement a listener interface.

An interface is like an abstract Java class, so it can't be instantiated. It defines a contract between the event source and the event listener. Classes that want to listen for `ActionEvents`, for example, must implement the `ActionListener` interface. All listener interfaces must extend the `java.util.EventListener` interface.

Classes that act as event sources must define methods that allow event listeners to register themselves. These methods typically take the form `addXXListener` `(XXListener listener)` and `removeXXListener(XXListener listener)`, where `XX` is the event name. The class maintains a list of listeners registered for that event. When the event occurs, the event source class has the code to notify them.

The individual methods in the listener interface need only one argument, of type `Event`. For example, `XXListener`'s methods take one argument of `XXEvent`. Let's say you've written a class that monitors stock prices (we'll call it `StockPriceChecker`), which acts as an event source for an event called `StockPrice`. As the stock price rises and falls above or below certain levels, the class sends out `StockPrice` events to all classes that are registered to receive them.

The `StockPriceChecker` class has the following methods for registering `StockPriceEvent` listener objects:

- `addStockPriceListener(StockPriceListener listener)`
- `removeStockPriceListener(StockPriceListener listener)`

The `StockPriceEvent` class might have the following methods that provide data on the `StockPrice` event:

- `getPrice()`—returns a `float`
- `getName()`—returns the name of the stock

Contained in `StockPriceEvent` is the data that `StockPriceChecker` sends out to the `StockPrice` event listeners.

The `StockPriceListener` interface can have the following methods, which define specific occurrences of events:

- `priceDropped(StockPriceEvent event)`
- `priceIncreased(StockPriceEvent event)`

Any class implementing the interface can register with the event source, Stock-PriceChecker, to receive StockPrice events.

---

**Design Patterns**

Java is chockful of design patterns. These are ways to organize classes and objects to solve recurring software engineering problems. The Java event model is an example of the Observer/Observable design pattern, also known as Publish and Subscribe. Its purpose is to reduce coupling of the source and the sink (the listener).

Once you've mastered Python programming and read *Object-Oriented Analysis and Design with Applications* (Booch, 1994), make sure to read *Design Patterns* (Gamma et al., 1995).

---

Now, if you use the StockPriceChecker class in Python, you don't have to implement the StockPriceListener interface and register an instance with StockPrice Checker. StockPriceChecker has two event properties corresponding to the methods in the interface of StockPriceListener—priceDropped and priceIncreased—so you can pass an event handler function that has one argument, which is passed as StockEvent.

If you're confused at this point, fear not. We'll do lots of examples using both Python and Java event handling when we cover GUI programming in Chapter 13.

---

**Technical Tip: Bean Introspection**

Jython uses the bean introspection features of Java, which provide the ability to inspect a bean's properties, events, and methods. Any Java class can be a bean if it follows certain design patterns in method, interface, and class-naming conventions. Also, instead of naming conventions, developers can define BeanInfo classes that describe the methods corresponding to actions such as event registration.

---

## Subclassing Java Classes

You can subclass Java classes like Python classes. Here's an example of subclassing the Java class java.util.Date (from *MyDate.py*):

```
from java.util import Date

class MyDate(Date):
        def __init__(self, num=None):
                if num is None:
                        Date.__init__(self)
                else:
                        Date.__init__(self, num)
```

```
def __str__(self):
    str = Date.toString(self)
    str = "MyDate: " + str
    return str
```

## Working with Java Constructors

When you subclass a Java class, you call its superclass's constructor, just as you do in regular Python. As we saw, the *MyDate.py* example subclassed the `Date` class from `java.lang` and defined two constructors that called `Date`'s base class constructors.

As an exercise, look up the constructors of `java.lang.Date` in the Java API documentation. You'll find them in a section called Constructor Summary.

The constructor of `Date` is defined in Java as

```
Date ()
```

You call it from Python like this:

```
Date.__init__(self)
```

The second constructor of `Date` is defined in Java as

```
Date (long date)
```

You call it from Python like this:

```
Date.__init__(self, num)
```

Here's how to call both `Date` constructors:

```
class MyDate(Date):
    def __init__(self, num=None):
        if num is None:
            Date.__init__(self)
        else:
            Date.__init__(self, num)
```

In Java, constructors are special language constructs that always have the same name as that of their class. In Python, the constructor is always a method called `__init__`. You call Java constructors in Python just as you do Python constructors; however, you can only do so in your subclass's constructor.

## Working with Java Methods

When subclassing a Java class, you can call all methods from a Java base class that you can from a Python base class. In our *MyDate.py* example, we subclass `Date` and add a `__str__` method.

```
def __str__(self):
    str = Date.toString(self)
    str = "MyDate: " + str
    return str
```

Unlike Python methods, Java methods can be overloaded, which essentially means that a Java class can have several methods with the same name. An example of this is java.io.OutputStream, which defines three write() methods:

- abstract void write(int b)
- void      write(byte[] b)
- void write (byte[] b, int off, int len)

As you can see, these methods can be called with different argument types.

To subclass OutputStream, we need a way to override any or all of the write() methods. The following example shows how to do this. (Before we get started, however, read up on the OutputStream class in the Java API documentation.)

```
from java.io import OutputStream
import types

class OutputScreen (OutputStream):
    def write (self, b=None, off=None, len=None):
        if (type(b) is types.IntType):
            print b
        elif (off is None):
            print b
        else:
            print b[off:off+len]
```

This code imports OutputStream, a Java class from the *java.io* package. OutputScreen subclasses OutputStream and overrides its write() methods (all three versions). Thus, each clause of the if statement in write() mimics a different overloaded signature of OutputStream's write()s.

---

### *Overloading*

Strongly typed languages like Java, C++, and Delphi allow method overloading. In other words, they allow more than one method with the same name but different signatures. The type of the method's arguments defines the signature. With overloaded methods, the signature determines which method is actually being invoked.

Python doesn't allow method overloading based on type signatures because it isn't a strongly typed language. (Some may say it's loosely typed; Pythonians prefer the term "dynamically typed.") To override a method from a subclass in Python, the class must define a method with the same name.

---

To illustrate, the following code mimics the functionality of void write(int b) by determining that the first argument, b, is of type Integer.

```
if (type(b) is types.IntType):
    print b
```

This code mimics the functionality of void write(byte[]b) by determining that off wasn't passed (and that the first type was not Integer).

```
elif (off is None):
     print b
```

This mimics the functionality of void write (byte[]b, int off, int len) by a process of elimination.

```
else:
     print b[off:off+len]
```

Let's test each of these scenarios. Start the *overload.py* module from Jython with the –i option and try the following statements in an interactive session.

```
from jarray import array

screenOut = OutputScreen()

screenOut.write(33)

seq = [0,1,2,3,4,5,6,7,8,9,0xA,0xB,0xC,0xD,0xE,0xF]
bytearray = array(seq, 'b')

screenOut.write(bytearray)
screenOut.write(bytearray, 5, 14)
```

Essentially, we're calling all three write() methods. Here's the code step by step.
Import the array() function from *jarray* to create Java byte arrays (byte[]).

```
from jarray import array
```

Create an OutputScreen instance called ScreenOut.

```
screenOut = OutputScreen()
```

Invoke the first form of the write() method, void write(int b).

```
screenOut.write(33)
```

Create a byte array for an argument for the second and third forms of write().

```
seq = [0,1,2,3,4,5,6,7,8,9,0xA,0xB,0xC,0xD,0xE,0xF]
bytearray = array(seq, 'b')
```

Invoke the second form of write(), void write(byte[] b).

```
screenOut.write(bytearray)
```

Invoke the last form of write(), void write (byte[]b, int off, int len).

```
screenOut.write(bytearray, 5, 14)
```

The output should be

```
33
array([0, 1, 2, 3, 4, 5, 6, 7, 8, 9, 10, 11, 12, 13, 14, 15], byte)
array([5, 6, 7, 8, 9, 10], byte)
```

## Advanced Topics

To understand what I'm going to talk about here, you should have some Java background and have read the API documentation for OutputStream.

### Overriding write()

Another way to override all of write()'s forms is to override only the abstract version and then just call the others. You can also use a variable number of arguments for write() and then just use the apply() method to execute the nonabstract forms. Let me show you what I mean. (The following code is from *Overload.py*.)

```
class OutputScreen2 (OutputStream):
    def write(self, *args):
                    # If the args length is greater than one or the first
                    # argument is not type IntType, use the apply method.
            if len(args) > 1 or not type(args[0]) is types.IntType:

                    # Use the apply method to call other forms:
                    #       void write(byte[] b)
                    #       void write(byte[] b, int off, int len)
                apply(OutputStream.write, (self,)+args)

                    # Otherwise just print the first argument
                    # , i.e., write(int b).
        else:
                print args[0]
```

To determine which form of write() is being invoked, OutputScreen2's write() method checks if the length of the args tuple is greater than 1 or if the first argument isn't an integer. If either is the case, void write(byte[] b) or void write(byte[] b int off, int len) is being called. Otherwise, write(int b) is being called.

The code to test this (*Overload.py*) looks like the code to test OutputScreen2, although the output is much different.

```
print "OutScreen2"
screenOut = OutputScreen2()

screenOut.write(33)

seq = [0,1,2,3,4,5,6,7,8,9,0xA,0xB,0xC,0xD,0xE,0xF]
bytearray = array(seq, 'b')

print "void write(byte[])"
screenOut.write(bytearray)

print "void write(byte[], int off, int len)"
screenOut.write(bytearray, 5, 5)
```

The Java API documentation states, "Applications that need to define a subclass of OutputStream must always provide at least a method that writes one byte of output." Basically this means that, if you define void write (int b), the default implementation of the other two `write()` forms calls `void write (int b)`, which is why the output is different. Essentially, `write()` is called for each item in the byte array passed to `void write(byte[])`, and for each byte in the range within the byte array for `void write(byte[], int off, int len)`.

## Compiling Java Classes

To build applets, JavaBeans, and servlets, or to subclass Python classes in Java, you need to compile the classes into *.class* files. The Jython distribution includes a utility called `jythonc` to do this.

If you execute `jythonc` from the command line with the `-h` option, it will describe the command-line options for the compiler. Go ahead and try it. (If you're a Jython user, you can type `jythonc` instead of `jpythonc`.)

The following options are used with `jythonc`:

- `-p`—the `package` option; puts the compiled classes in the specified package
- `-j`—the `jarfile` option; puts the compiled classes in a jar file
- `-d`—the `deep` option; compiles Python dependencies of the compiled classes (necessary for creating applets that will run on most browsers, including Internet Explorer)
- `-c`—the `core` option; compiles all dependencies and includes the core Jython libraries (necessary for creating applets that will run in Netscape Navigator)
- `-a`—the `all` option; everything in the core plus the compiler and parser
- `-b`—the `bean` option; puts classes in the jar file and adds a manifest file for the bean (necessary for creating JavaBeans)
- `-w`—the `workdir` option; specifies where to compile the code (the default puts the code in a directory under the current directory called *jpywork*)

We'll cover creating a JavaBean and an applet later. For now, using *Overload.py*, let's create a Python class that can be subclassed in Java. Before we can do this with `jythonc`, we have to put the class in a module with the same name, and the class has to subclass a Java class or interface. To compile the `OutputScreen` class, we need to put it in a file called *OutputScreen.py*. `OutputScreen` already subclasses a Java class called `OutputStream`.

Here's an exercise using the `OutputScreen` class:

```
from java.io import OutputStream
import types

        # Class OutputScreen is a subclass of Java class OutputStream.
class OutputScreen (OutputStream):

    def write(self, *args):

                # If the args length is greater than one or the first
                # argument is not type IntType, use the apply method.
        if len(args) > 1 or not type(args[0]) is types.IntType:
```

```
                    # Use the apply method to call other forms:
                    #          void write(byte[] b)
                    #          void write(byte[] b, int off, int len)
              apply(OutputStream.write, (self,)+args)
         else:
                    # Overide the write (int) method.
              print args[0]
```

Go to the DOS prompt where the source code is located, and then enter `pythonc` `-d OutputScreen` at the command line.

```
C:\jpybook\chap11>jythonc -d OutputScreen.py
```

jythonc creates a directory called *jpywork*, in which it places the Java source code and the compiled Java class.

```
C:\jpybook\chap11\jpywork>dir
Directory of C:\jpybook\chap11\jpywork

.               <DIR>         08-05-99 5:46p .
..              <DIR>         08-05-99 5:46p ..
OUTPUT~1 JAV     6,221  08-05-99 5:46p OutputScreen.java
OUTPUT~1 CLA     3,305  08-05-99 5:46p OutputScreen.class
OUTPUT~2 CLA     3,224  08-05-99 5:46p OutputScreen$_PyInner.class
         3 file(s)        12,750 bytes
         2 dir(s)      2,432.67 MB free
```

There should be one source file called *OutputScreen.java* and two class files. The following listing shows part of the `OutputScreen` class.

```
import org.python.core.*;

public class OutputScreen extends java.io.OutputStream implements
org.python.core.PyProxy {
...
...
            //The overloaded write method
public void write(int arg0) throws java.io.IOException {
       PyObject inst = Py.jgetattr(this, "write");
       try {
           inst._jcallexc(new Object[] {Py.newInteger(arg0)});
       }
       ...
       ...
}

     //The write method
public void write(byte[] arg0, int arg1, int arg2) throws java.io.IOException {
     PyObject inst = Py.jfindattr(this, "write");
     if (inst != null) try {
            inst._jcallexc(new Object[] {arg0, Py.newInteger(arg1),
            Py.newInteger(arg2)});
     }
     ...
...
```

```
        else super.write(arg0, arg1, arg2);
}

            //The write method
public void write(byte[] arg0) throws java.io.IOException {
      PyObject inst = Py.jfindattr(this, "write");
      if (inst != null) try {
          inst._jcallexc(new Object[] {arg0});
      }
...
...
      else super.write(arg0);
}
```

The code for the `write()` method that takes only one argument has the Python instance of `OutputScreen` and gets the `write` attribute from it. Then it executes the method.

First it defines `void write(int)`.

```
public void write(int arg0) throws java.io.IOException {
```

Next it gets the `write` attribute from the Python instance of `OutputScreen`, called `Py`. The attribute is stored in `inst`.

```
PyObject inst = Py.jgetattr(this, "write");
```

Then it executes the attribute.

```
inst._jcallexc(new Object[] {Py.newInteger(arg0)});
```

Now the code has multiple arguments. The forms that were not overridden check to see if the Python instance of `OutputScreen` has a `write()` method. If it doesn't, the superclass `OutputStream` is called; if it does, the `write()` method of the Python instance is invoked, and the arguments are passed to it.

Next the code defines `void write(byte[] arg0, int arg1, int arg2)`.

```
public void write(byte[] arg0, int arg1, int arg2) throws
java.io.IOException {
```

Then it attempts to get the `write()` method from the `Py` instance.

```
PyObject inst = Py.jfindattr(this, "write");
```

If successful, it invokes the method with the following arguments:

```
if (inst != null) try {
    inst._jcallexc(new Object[] {arg0, Py.newInteger(arg1),
                        Py.newInteger(arg2)});
}
```

If not successful, it invokes the superclass's (`OutputStream's`) `write()` method.

```
else super.write(arg0, arg1, arg2);
```

Now that we've explained a little bit of how compiled Python code works underneath, let's create some Java that uses it.

### Java Code That Uses a Jython Class

Here's testOutScreen.java, which treats OutputScreen like any other Java class:

```java
public class testOutScreen{
    public static void main(String[] args){
        OutputScreen os = new OutputScreen();

        byte [] bytes = {0,1,2,3,4,5,6,7,8,9,0xa,0xb,0xC};

        try{
            os.write(1);
            os.write(bytes, 5, 5);
            os.write(bytes);
        }
        catch(java.io.IOException e){
            // do something useful with this exception
        }
    }
}
```

The preceding code needs little explanation, as all it does is create an instance of OutputScreen and call all three forms of the overloaded write() method. To compile and run it, do this:

```
C:\jpybook\chap11\jpywork>javac testOutScreen.java
```

```
C:\jpybook\chap11\jpywork>java testOutScreen
```

> **The Java Default Package**
>
> Both OutputScreen and testOutScreen are in the Java default package, which is okay for illustration. However, any experienced Java programmer knows that leaving anything there is impolite. To put OutputScreen in its own package use the –p option.
>
> ```
> C:\jpybook\chap11>jythonc -d -p examples.chap11 OutputScreen.py
> ```

## Summary

In this chapter, we covered how to integrate Java and Python. Essentially, Jython makes this integration easy and, most of the time, transparent. The mappings from Java types to Python types for passing arguments and returning values from Java methods are straightforward.

Jython has added the *jarray* module, which allows the creation of the built-in array type that maps to Java arrays. *jarray* allows you to create both empty arrays and arrays initialized with the contents of a sequence. A Java array is like a homogeneously typed Python sequence with a fixed length, so you can use a Python sequence operation on it.

# CHAPTER 12

# *Working with Java Streams*

Streams are the Java programming language's way to support I/O. A stream can represent a file, a network connection, or the access of a Web site. Learning to deal with Java streams is essential for understanding Java's networking APIs.

Most of the time conversion to and from the Java type system is transparent. When it isn't, this chapter will demonstrate how to do low-level type conversion straightforwardly.

> ### *As If One Way Weren't Bad Enough*
> The joke is that there are always two ways of doing things in Jython: the Python way and the Java way. For example, if you use Python to prototype for Java applications, you need to know how Java does it. You also need Java streams to do various forms of Java I/O, such as networking APIs.

## *The Java Way of File Operations*

Interfaces and classes for dealing with files and other I/O types are in the *java.io* package. An interface is a class that contains abstract methods. Classes in *java.io* form a class hierarchy.

The two main class types in *java.io* are text oriented (character streams) and binary oriented (byte streams). Subclasses of the Reader and Writer classes are text oriented; those of the InputStream and OutputStream classes are binary oriented.

InputStream and OutputStream are abstract; that is, they can't be instantiated directly. To use an abstract class you must subclass it and instantiate the subclass. The subclasses of InputStream and OutputStream allow the reading of binary data to and from various types of input and output such as byte arrays (memory), files, and even network sockets.

Streams can be chained to provide extra functionality. For example, you can buffer a FileInputStream by chaining it to a BufferedInputStream Then you can chain the BufferedInputStream to an ObjectInputStream to read in whole objects at one time. (This is similar to the *pickle* functionality in Python.)

Java 1.1's binary data input streams are complemented by somewhat equivalent text input streams. The parents of these classes are the abstract classes Reader and Writer. Having an equivalent set of text-oriented character stream classes allows the conversion of Unicode text. Readers and Writers, like streams, can be chained together. For example, you can buffer a FileReader by chaining it to a BufferedReader. (Buffering will be explained shortly.)

### I/O Classes to Be Covered

There are more than thirty I/O classes, not including interfaces and abstract classes. This seems like a lot, but if you understand how Reader, Writer, InputStream, and OutputStream work, you can easily understand the rest.

Reader and Writer subclasses deal with character streams, that is, text. InputStream and OutputStream subclasses deal with binary streams. An easy way to remember this is, if you can read it, use Reader and Writer; if you can't, use InputStream and OutputStream.

> ### For Beginners: Understanding Streams
> Think of a stream as an abstract file. Just as you can read and write to a file, you can read and write to a stream. You might use a stream for reading and writing with an RS-232 serial connection, a TCP/IP connection, or a memory location (like a sequence). A stream is abstract, so if you know how to read and write to a file, you basically already know how to read and write to a memory location or an RS-232 serial connection or, for that matter, a Web site. This is the art and magic of polymorphism.

## Text Streams

All of the text-oriented classes are derived from `Reader` and `Writer`. By understanding them, you'll have a handle on dealing with their descendents.

### Writer

The `Writer` class writes character data to a stream. It has the following methods:

- `write(c)`—writes a single character to the text stream
- `write(cbuf)`—writes a sequence of characters to the text stream
- `write(cbuf, off, len)`—writes a sequence of characters to the text stream starting at the offset into the stream and copying to `len` in the buffer
- `write(str)`—writes out a string to the text stream
- `write(str, off, len)`—writes out a string from the given offset to the given length
- `close()`—closes the text stream
- `flush()`—flushes the content of the text stream; used if the stream supports `BufferedOutput`

`Writer` is the superclass of all character output streams, for example, `FileWriter`, `BufferedWriter`, `CharArrayWriter`, `OutputStreamWriter`, and `PrintWriter`.

### Reader

The `Reader` class reads data from a stream. `Reader` is the superclass of all character input streams. It has the following methods:

- `read()`—reads in a single character
- `read(cbuf)`—reads in a sequence of characters
- `read(cbuf, iOff, iLen)`—reads from the current position in the file into the sequence at the given offset
- `ready()`—determines if the buffer has input data ready
- `mark(int readAheadLimit)`—sets the read-ahead buffer size
- `markSupported()`—returns true if the `mark()` method is supported

- `skip()`—skips a certain number of characters ahead in the text input stream
- `reset()`—moves the file pointer to the marked position
- `close()`—closes the file

I can't show you any examples of using `Reader` or `Writer` because they're abstract and can't be instantiated on their own. However, I can show examples of their subclasses, `FileReader` and `FileWriter`, which are concrete.

As an exercise, look up `Reader` and `Writer` in the Java API documentation, and compare their Python-friendly method definitions to the official Java versions. Notice the conversion from one type to another.

## FileReader and FileWriter

`FileReader` and `FileWriter` read and write text files. They have the same methods their base classes have as well as the following constructor methods.

*FileReader:*

- `__init__(strFilename)`—opens the file specified by the string (`strFilename`)
- `__init__(File)`—opens the file specified by the file object
- `__init__(fd)`—opens the file specified by the file descriptor

*FileWriter:*

- `__init__(strFilename)`—opens the file specified by the string (`strFilename`)
- `__init__(strFilename, bAppend)`—same as above, but optionally opens the file in append mode
- `__init__(File)`—opens the file specified by the file object
- `__init__(fd)`—opens the file specified by the file descriptor

As an exercise, look up `FileReader` and `FileWriter` in the Java API documentation. Then modify the address book application from Chapter 8 to use these classes.

### Creating a File with FileWriter

The following interactive session creates a file with `FileWriter` and writes some text to it. (Follow along.)

Import the `FileWriter` class from the *java.io* package.

```
>>> from java.io import FileWriter
```

Create an instance of it.

```
>>> fw = FileWriter("c:\\dat\\File.txt")
```

Write a single character to the output character stream.

```
>>> fw.write('w')
```

Write out a string.

```
>>> fw.write("\r\nthis is a string")
```

Write out a sequence of characters.

```
>>> characters = ('\r','\n','a','b','c')
>>> fw.write(characters)
```

Close the file.

```
>>> fw.close()
```

Here's what the file we just created, called *c:\dat\file.txt,* looks like. You can open it with Notepad or any other text editor.

```
w
this is a string
abc
```

### Finding the File Length

You can use a *java.io* file to see the length of *c:\dat\file.txt*. It should be 22 bytes.

```
>>> from java.io import File
    >>> f = File("c:\\dat\\File.txt")
    >>> file.length()
    22L f
```

Don't worry too much about what the `File` class does; we'll cover it later. For now, just think of it as a way to specify a file and get its properties.

Reopen *c:\dat\file.txt* in append mode.

```
>>> fw = FileWriter('c:\\dat\\File.txt', 1)
```

Append some text.

```
>>> fw.write("\r\nAnother String appended to the File")
>>> fw.close()
```

We open the file in append mode by passing a `true` (1) to the second parameter of the `FileWriter` constructor. This means that we want to append text. You can see from the following example (*c:\dat\file.txt*) that the text has been added.

```
w
this is a string
abc
Another String appended to the File
```

If we now write to the file and don't open it in append mode, all of the old text will be deleted.

```
>>> fw = FileWriter(File)
>>> fw.write("Oops where is all the other text")
>>> fw.close()
>>> f.length()
32L
```

Look at the file with a text editor. It should have text only in the last `write` statement.

By the way, the concepts just covered for working with `FileWriter` aren't much different from those for working with the Python file object.

### *Reading a File with FileReader*

Now it's `FileReader`'s turn with an interactive session. We'll open *c:\dat\file\txt* and read the text we wrote to it with `FileWriter`.

Import the `FileReader` class from the *java.io* package.

```
>>> from java.io import FileReader
>>> File_Reader = FileReader("C:\\dat\\File.txt")
```

The tricky part is that the `read()` method expects you to pass it a `chars` array that it can fill in, but the closest thing in Python to a Java array is a sequence or list, and neither is close enough. So Jython has added a helper class, called `PyArray`, that passes primitive arrays to Java methods (see Chapter 11).

Import the `zeros()` function from the *jarray* module.

```
>>> from jarray import zeros
```

Use `zeros()` to create a `PyArray`.

```
>>> chars = zeros(4, 'c')
```

Print the `chars` array to the screen.

```
>>> chars
array(['\x0', '\x0', '\x0', '\x0'], char)
```

The first argument to `zeros()` tells it how big we want our array. The second argument tells `zeros()` that we want our array to be of type `char`. Now `zeros()` creates an array in which all of the values are zeros. When we call `File_Reader.read`, the `read()` method fills in the empty slots with characters from the file.

Here's our call to the `read()` method, which should read the first four letters of the file.

```
>>> File_Reader.read(chars)
4
```

As you can see, `chars` contains the first four letters in our file, `'O'`, `'o'`, `'p'`, and `'s'`.

```
>>> chars
array(['O', 'o', 'p', 's'], char)
```

This is nice but what we really want is a string object, `'Oops'`. For this we need `PyArray`, which we can use anywhere a sequence is suitable, such as the Python class library.

The Python *string* module has methods for doing special things with strings. One method, `joinfields()`, combines strings in a sequence to form a string object. Let's use `joinfields()` to convert `chars` to a string.

Import the *string* module.

```
>>> import string
```

Use `joinfields()` to turn the `chars` array into a Python string.

```
>>> first_word = string.joinfields(chars, "")
```

Print the value of `first_word` to the screen.

```
>>> first_word
'Oops'
```

Notice that the second argument to `joinfields()` specifies the separator we want for the fields. Since we don't want any separator, we pass an empty string.

Let's recap what we've learned to read in the whole *c:\dat\file.txt* file at once.

```
>>> from jarray import zeros         # import the zeros to create an array of
    primitives
>>> from java.io import FileReader, File # import the File to get the length
    of the file
>>> from string import joinfields   # import the joinfields to convert arrays
    to strings
>>> file = File("c:\\dat\\file.txt")       # create a java.io.File instance
>>> chars = zeros(file.length(), 'c')      # create an array to hold the
    contents of file.txt
>>> file_Reader = FileReader(file) # create a FileReader instance to read the
    file >>> >>> file_Reader.read(chars)   # Read in the whole file
    32
```

That took only eight steps. Let's see the same thing with the Python file object.

```
>>> python_file = open("c:\\dat\\file.txt","r")   # open the file
>>> str = python_file.read()                # read the contents of the file
>>> print str
Oops where is all the other text
```

What took eight steps with the `java.io.FileWriter` instance now takes two steps. Which one would you rather work with?

## BufferedReader and BufferedWriter

The `BufferedReader` class provides input buffering to the `Reader` stream. The `BufferedWriter` class provides output buffering to the `Writer` stream. Input buffering consists of prefetching data and caching it in a memory queue so that, for example, not every call to the `read()` method equates to a read operation on the physical I/O. Output buffering applies writes to a memory image that is periodically written out to a character stream. You want buffering support for input and output streams, especially large ones, to gain speed and efficiency.

BufferedReader and BufferedWriter have all of the methods that Reader and Writer have, as well as the following:

*BufferedWriter:*

- __init__ (Writer_in)—creates a BufferedWriter instance with the specified output stream
- __init__(Writer_in, iBufSize)—same as above but specifies the size of the buffer
- newLine()—writes a newline character to the output stream

*BufferedReader:*

- __init__ (Reader_in)—creates a BufferedReader instance with the specified input stream
- __init__(Reader_in, iBufSize)—same as above but specifies the size of the buffer
- readLine()—reads in a line of text from the input stream

### Using the Buffering Classes

Let's have a short interactive session showing how to use our buffering classes. We'll also cover the newLine() and readLine() methods.

Import the BufferedReader and BufferedWriter classes and the FileReader and FileWriter classes.

```
>>> from java.io import BufferedReader, BufferedWriter, FileReader, FileWriter
```

Create a FileWriter instance that creates a file called *c:\dat\buf_file.txt*.

```
>>> file_out = FileWriter("c:\\dat\\buf_file.txt")
```

Create a BufferedWriter instance, buffer_out, passing it as an argument to the BufferedWriter constructor.

```
>>> buffer_out = BufferedWriter(File_out)
```

Write three lines of text to the file using write() to write the characters and then newLine() to write the platform-specific newline characters.

```
>>> buffer_out.write("Line 1"); buffer_out.newLine()
>>> buffer_out.write("Line 2"); buffer_out.newLine()
>>> buffer_out.write("Line 3"); buffer_out.newLine()
```

Close the stream.

```
>>> buffer_out.close()
```

This code demonstrates chaining a `BufferedWriter` to a `FileWriter`, which adds buffering to file output.

The next session uses `FileReader` to open the file we created in the last example.

Create a `FileReader` instance, and pass it to the `BufferedReader` constructor to create a `BufferedReader` instance.

```
>>> file_in = BufferedReader(FileReader("c:\\dat\\buf_File.txt"))
```

Read in all three lines at once with three method calls to `readLine()`.

```
>>> line1, line2, line3 = file_in.readLine(), file_in.readLine(),
    file_in.readLine()
```

Print all three lines at once.

```
>>> print line1; print line2; print line3
Line 1
Line 2
Line 3
```

You may be wondering why there's a `newLine()` function in `BufferedWriter`. It's there because it knows how to represent a newline character on whatever operating system you happen to be writing your code for. (We used "\r\n" in our `FileWriter` example, which won't work on UNIX or Mac.)

## PrintWriter

`PrintWriter` provides a `print()` and a `println()` function for all primitive types. These functions convert primitive types to characters and then write them to the output stream. `PrintWriter` has all of `write()` methods, as well as these:

- `print()`—writes out primitive data types to an output stream (as readable text)
- `println()`—same as above, but adds a newline character to the ouput

In the next example, you'll see how to use `PrintWriter`, how to chain output streams together, and how to work with Java primitive types.

Import the classes needed.

```
>>> from java.io import PrintWriter, FileWriter, BufferedWriter
```

Create a `PrintWriter` by passing it a new instance of `BufferedWriter`, which is created from a new instance of `FileWriter`.

```
>>> out = PrintWriter(BufferedWriter(FileWriter("pr.txt")))
```

Write three strings to a file using `println()`.

```
>>> out.println("Line1")
>>> out.println("Line2")
>>> out.println("Line3")
```

Use `println()` to write a Python `Double` object and a Python `Integer` object to a file.

```
>>> out.println(4.4)
>>> out.println(5)
```

Write a Java `Boolean` to the file.

```
>>> from java.lang import Boolean
>>> out.println(Boolean(1))
>>> out.println(Boolean("true"))
```

Write a Java `Byte` to the file.

```
>>> from java.lang import Byte
>>> out.println(Byte(1))
```

Show how `print()` works.

```
>>> out.print("Line 9")
>>> out.print("still line 9")
>>> out.close()
```

(It also works with primitive types.)

Now you know how to chain stream classes to add the functionality you want. The `out` instance, for example, can write to files from `FileWriter`, work with output buffering from `BufferedWriter`, and work with primitive types from `PrintWriter`. By the way, the technique of chaining `Writer` stream classes is known as the Decorator design pattern. To learn more about if read *Design Patterns* (Gamma et al., [1995]).

## Binary Streams: InputStream and OutputStream

`InputStream` is the analog of `Reader`; `OutputStream` is the analog of `Writer`. Their methods are listed here.

*InputStream:*

- `read(byte_sequence)`—reads a sequence of bytes and returns the actual bytes read
- `read(byte_sequence, off, len)`—same as above but allows you to set the slice for the sequence; returns the number of actual bytes read
- `read()`—reads one byte of data from the input stream
- `skip(n)`—skips to a given offset in the file
- `close()`—closes the stream
- `reset()`—moves the file pointer to the marked position
- `mark(iReadlimit)`—marks the file pointer
- `available()`—returns the number of bytes available that can be read without blocking (similar to the `Reader` class's `ready()` method)

*OutputStream:*

- `close()`
- `flush()`—flushes the buffer, that is, forces the output buffer to be written to the output stream
- `write(b)`—writes a single byte to the output stream
- `write(byte_sequence)`—writes a sequence of bytes to the output stream
- `write(byte_sequence, off, len)`—same as above, but specifies the slice

## FileInputStream and FileOutputStream

`FileInputStream` and `FileOutputStream` extend `InputStream` and `OutputStream`, respectively. They are the analogs to `File Reader` and `FileWriter`. Here are their methods.

*FileInputStream:*

- `__init__(strFilename)`—opens the file specified by the string (`strFilename`)
- `__init__(File)`—opens the file specified by the file object
- `__init__(fd)`—opens the file specified by the file descriptor

*FileOutputStream:*

- `__init__(strFilename)`—opens the file specified by the string (`strFilename`)
- `__init__(strFilename, bAppend)`—same as above, but optionally opens the file in append mode
- `__init__(File)`—opens the file specified by the file object
- `__init__(fd)`—opens the file specified by the file descriptor

Reading and writing to a file with `FileInputStream` and `FileOutputStream` are a lot like reading and writing to a file with `FileReader` and `FileWriter`. That being the case, I'm omitting much of the detail in the following example (*Output Stream1.py*) to avoid repetition.

```
    # First we import the FileOutputStream class from the java.io package
from java.io import FileOutputStream
from jarray import array

    # Next create an instance of the FileOutputStream
out = FileOutputStream("c:\\dat\\file.bin")

    # Now write a byte to the output binary stream
out.write(1)

    # Now write some more bytes to the binary stream
out.write([2,3,4,5,6,7,8,9,10,11,12,13,14,15,16])

    # Next write out a string
#out.write("\r\nthis is a string") #Jython converts this automatically
```

```
# Here is the hard way
str = "\r\nthis is a string"

# First convert every character in the string into its ASCII equivalent
seq = map(ord, str)

# Now convert the sequence into a Java array of the primitive type byte
bytes = array(seq, 'b')

# Now write out this string to the file as follows
out.write(bytes)

out.close()
```

The code above may seem familiar at first, but as you examine it you'll notice a couple of strange things. First, since write() works only with bytes and byte arrays, we have to use the *jarray* module again. Second, Jython converts a string into a byte array automatically, but if the class has two write() methods—one that takes a string and one that takes a byte array—we have to do some extra work to make sure that the correct method is called. Thus, we have to convert the string to a byte array if we want the byte array method.

Using the intrinsic functions ord() and map(), we'll see how to manually convert the string into a byte array before passing it to the write() method.

### *ord()*

Remember from Chapter 9 that the ord() function takes a single character from a string and converts it to its ASCII equivalent (i.e., the number representation of the character stored in the file). Let's work with an interactive example.

Convert "A", "B", and "C" to ASCII.

```
>>> ord("A"), ord("B"), ord("C")
(65, 66, 67)
```

Convert "a", "b", and "c" to ASCII.

```
>>> ord("a"), ord("b"), ord("c")
(97, 98, 99)
```

Figure the distance from "a" to "z" and from "A" to "Z".

```
>>> ord("z") - ord("a")
25
>>> ord("Z") - ord("A")
25
```

### *map()*

The built-in map() function deals with sequences, as we also learned in Chapter 9. It takes two arguments: first, a callable object such as a function or a method; second, a type of sequence like a string, list, or tuple. map() executes the callable object against every item in the sequence and then returns a list of the results. Thus,

```
>>> [ord("a"), ord("b"), ord("c"), ord("d")]
[97, 98, 99, 100]
```

is the same as

```
>>> map(ord,"abcd")
[97, 98, 99, 100]
```

Once we have a sequence, we can convert it into a byte array using the array() function from *jarray* (see the section on FileReader). array() takes two arguments: the first is a sequence and the second is a character representing the Java primitive type you want the array to be. (This is an extra step; Jython automatically converts an integer sequence into a byte array.)

This code creates an array full of bytes:

```
>>> from jarray import array
>>> seq = map(ord, "abcd")
>>> array(seq, 'b')
array([97, 98, 99, 100], byte)
```

### The Debug Utility

Of course, having both binary data and text data makes the file difficult to read. We can at least read the text part with a text editor, but besides the text there's only a lot of black boxes where our binary data should be. To see the binary contents of the file, we need another program.

If you're running some variation of Windows or DOS, you can use the debug utility, *C:\dat.debug\file.bin*. As shown below, the -d command dumps some of the file to the screen, and the -q command quits the program. You have to enter the commands the way you enter statements in Jython.

```
C:\dat>debug File.bin
-d
0E7F:0100 01 02 03 04 05 06 07 08-09 0A 0B 0C 0D 0E 0F 10 ................
0E7F:0110 0D 0A 74 68 69 73 20 69-73 20 61 20 73 74 72 69 ..this is a stri
0E7F:0120 6E 67 2B DE 59 03 CB 8B-D6 C6 06 BB DB 00 E3 31 ng+.Y..........1
0E7F:0130 49 AC E8 D9 F6 74 08 49-46 FE 06 BB DB EB EF E8 I....t.IF.......
0E7F:0140 DB F9 75 04 FE 06 17 D9-3C 3F 75 05 80 0E 1B D9 ..u.....<?u.....
0E7F:0150 02 3C 2A 75 05 80 0E 1B-D9 02 3A 06 02 D3 75 C9 .<*u......:...u.
0E7F:0160 4E 32 C0 86 04 46 3C 0D-75 02 88 04 89 36 D9 D7 N2...F<.u....6..
0E7F:0170 89 0E D7 D7 C3 BE BC DB-8B 4C 05 8B 74 09 E8 08 .........L..t...
-q
```

What you have is three main columns of data. To the far left is the position of the file in hexadecimal notation. In the middle is the value of the binary data, also in hexadecimal notation, and to the far right is the data's ASCII equivalent.

*Hexadecimal*

Hexadecimal is a base 16 number system. This list shows some decimal numbers and their hexadecimal equivalents:

| Decimal | Hexadecimal |
|---------|-------------|
| 1 | 1 |
| 2 | 2 |
| 3 | 3 |
| 4 | 4 |
| 5 | 5 |
| 6 | 6 |
| 7 | 7 |
| 8 | 8 |
| 9 | 9 |
| 10 | A |
| 11 | B |
| 12 | C |
| 13 | D |
| 14 | E |
| 15 | F |

Here's the first line of binary data. Every two digits represent a single byte.

```
01 02 03 04 05 06 07 08-09 0A 0B 0C 0D 0E 0F 10
```

We wrote it the following calls:

```
out.write(1)

out.write([2,3,4,5,6,7,8,9,10,11,12,13,14,15,16])
```

You can see that the bytes in the file increase from 1 to 16 in hexadecimal.

Let's see how to read the file back in by reading in the string.

Import FileInputStream, and then create an instance that refers to *c:\dat\file.bin*.

```
>>> from java.io import FileInputStream
>>> file = FileInputStream("c:\\dat\\file.bin")
```

Import the jarray buffer to create binary input buffers. The 'b' flag, the second argument to the zeros() function call, signifies a byte array. We'll use input_buffer to read in the first 16 bytes of data.

Import the zeros() function from the *jarray* module.

```
>>> from jarray import zeros
```

Create a byte input buffer with zeros().

```
>>> input_buffer = zeros(16, 'b')
```

Read in the first 16 bytes to the buffer with the `read()` method, which returns the number of bytes read in.

```
>>> file.read(input_buffer)
16
```

Print the array of bytes buffered.

```
>>> input_buffer
array([1, 2, 3, 4, 5, 6, 7, 8, 9, 10, 11, 12, 13, 14, 15, 16], byte)
```

Create a small buffer to read "\r\n".

```
>>> input_buffer = zeros (2,'b')
>>> file.read(input_buffer)
2
```

Read in "this is a string" from the file.

```
>>> input_buffer = zeros(16,'b')        #read in the bytes for the string
>>> file.read(input_buffer)
  16
```

Since we read this in as bytes, the code shows the ASCII equivalents for the characters we want instead of the actual characters of the string. We need to convert this byte array into a string sequence.

```
>>> input_buffer
array([116, 104, 105, 115, 32, 105, 115, 32, 97, 32, 115, 116, 114,
    105, 110, 103], byte)
```

To do the conversion we create a sequence and iterate through the byte array. At the same time we append the results of executing the `chr()` built-in function against each byte array item. `chr()` is the reverse of `ord()`; it converts a number (ASCII code) into a character (i.e., a string with one item).

Lastly, we convert the sequence into a string with a call to `string.joinfields()`.

```
>>> seq = []                    # create an empty sequence
>>> for num in input_buffer:    # for every number in the input_buffer
...      seq.append(chr(num))   # append the results of chr(num) to the
                                # sequence

...
>>> seq                         # show what the sequence contains
    ['t', 'h', 'i', 's', ' ', 'i', 's', ' ', 'a', ' ', 's', 't', 'r', 'i',
    'n', 'g']

>>> import string               # import the string module
>>> str = string.joinfields(seq, "") # create the string from the sequence
>>> print str                   # print out the string
```

Of course, a more Pythonesque way to convert the byte array into a string is with the built-in `map()` function.

```
>>> str = string.joinfields(map(chr,input_buffer),"")
>>> print str
this is a string
```

map()can be very useful; it takes one line of code to accomplish what previously took four.

## BufferedInputStream and BufferedOutputStream

BufferedInputStream and BufferedOutputStream provide the same kind of support to InputStream and OutputStream that BufferedReader and BufferedWriter provide to Reader and Writer: input and output buffering to their respective derivations. As I said before, input buffering entails prefetching data and caching it in memory so that read operations don't have to fetch the data off a slow device. Output buffering applies write operations to a memory image that's periodically written out to a stream.

BufferedInputStream and BufferedOutputStream have all of the methods that InputStream and OutputStream have plus the following:

*BufferedInputStream:*

- __init__(InputStream)—creates an input buffer for the specified input stream
- __init__(InputStream, iBufSize)—same as above, but specifies the size of the input buffer

*BufferedOutputStream:*

- __init__(OutputStream)—creates an output buffer for the specified output stream
- __init__(OutputStream, iBufSize)—same as above, but specifies the size of the output buffer

The mark(), markSupported(), reset(), skip(), and flush() methods provide the buffering support.

BufferedOutput can be chained to an existing stream, as the following example shows. Import BufferedOutputStream and FileOutputStream.

```
>>> from java.io import BufferedOutputStream, FileOutputStream
```

Create a BufferedOutputStream instance chained to a new FileOutputStream instance.

```
>>> out = BufferedOutputStream(FileOutputStream("bufout.bin"))
```

Write a sequence of bytes from 0 to 16 (0x0 to 0xF in hexadecimal).

```
>>> out.write([ 0, 1, 2, 3, 4, 5, 6, 7, 8, 9, 10, 11, 12, 13, 14, 15, 16])
```

Write a sequence of bytes from 17 to 31 (0x10 to 0x1F in hexadecimal).

```
>>> out.write([17, 18, 19, 20, 21, 22, 23, 24, 25, 26, 27, 28, 29, 30, 31])
```

Write 255 (0xFF hexadecimal) a few times.

```
>>> for index in xrange(0,16):
...     out.write(255)
...
```

Here's another way of writing out a string:

```
>>> str = "Hello"
>>> for char in str:
...     out.write(ord(char))
>>> out.close()
```

The output for the file created looks like this (from *C:\dat>debug bufout.bin*):

```
-d
0E7F:0100 00 01 02 03 04 05 06 07-08 09 0A 0B 0C 0D 0E 0F ................
0E7F:0110 10 11 12 13 14 15 16 17-18 19 1A 1B 1C 1D 1E 1F ................
0E7F:0120 FF FF FF FF FF FF FF FF-FF FF FF FF FF FF FF FF ................
0E7F:0130 48 65 6C 6C 6F 00 00-00 00 00 00 00 00 00 00 00 .Hello..........
```

The first line has the hexadecimal numbers 0x0 to 0xF. The second line lists the numbers 0x10 to 0xlF. The third line contains the 255 (0xFF) we wrote out, and the fourth line contains the "Hello" string we wrote out.

### Using BufferedInputStream

Now it's time for a small example of BufferedInputStream. This one demonstrates the mark(), skip(), and reset() methods.

Import the classes needed, and create the BufferedInputStream instance, chaining it to a FileInputStream instance.

```
>>> from java.io import BufferedInputStream, FileInputStream
>>> input = BufferedInputStream(FileInputStream("bufout.bin"))
```

Mark the position in the file we want to return to.

```
>>> input.mark(100)
```

Read in first three bytes. (Remember, we set the first three bytes to 0x0, 0x1, and 0x2—1, 2, and 3 in decimal—in the last example.)

```
>>> input.read(), input.read(), input.read()
(0, 1, 2, 3)
```

Use the skip() method to skip ahead twenty bytes in the file.

```
>>> input.skip(20)
20L
```

The `reset()` method sets the file back to the position marked with the `mark()` method, which happens to be at the beginning. A reading of the first three bytes proves this.

```
>>> input.reset()
>>> input.read(), input.read(), input.read()
(0, 1, 2)
```

Reset the file at the beginning. Use the `zeros()` function to create byte arrays to read in the first three lines. (The lines aren't real, like lines of text, but refer to the way the hexdump program—that is, the debug program—displays the data.) Then read in the first three lines and display them.

```
>>> input.reset()            # reset to the beginning of the file.
>>> from jarray import zeros  # import the zeros function
>>> line1 = zeros(16, 'b')    # buffer to read in first 16 bytes
>>> line2 = zeros(16, 'b')    # buffer to read in next 16 bytes
>>> line3 = zeros(16, 'b')    # buffer to read in the third 16
>>> input.read(line1)         # read in line 1
16

>>> input.read(line2), input.read(line3)    #read in line 2 and 3
(16, 16)

>>> line1 #display line1
array([0, 1, 2, 3, 4, 5, 6, 7, 8, 9, 10, 11, 12, 13, 14, 15], byte)

>>> line2         #display line2
array([16, 17, 18, 19, 20, 21, 22, 23, 24, 25, 26, 27, 28, 29, 30, 31], byte)

>>> line3 #display line3
array([-1, -1, -1, -1, -1, -1, -1, -1, -1, -1, -1, -1, -1, -1, -1, -1], byte)
```

Compare the output to the hexdump we did with the debug program.

Now lets read in the "Hello" string. This repeats the `FileInputStream` exercise, so we won't cover it in the same detail as before.

Read in the bytes from the "Hello" string. (A better way would have been to create a Java array of bytes with `jarray`, but I wanted to show this way.)

```
>>> binstr=input.read(),input.read(),input.read(),input.read(),input.read()
>>> binstr         #display it
(72, 101, 108, 108, 111)
```

Convert the byte array to a sequence of characters.

```
>>> char_seq = []
>>> for num in binstr:
...     char_seq.append(chr(num))
...
```

Convert the sequence of characters to a string.

```
>>> char_seq
['H', 'e', 'l', 'l', 'o']
```

```
>>> import string
>>> str = string.joinfields(char_seq, "")
>>> print str
Hello
```

## DataInput and DataOutput

`DataInput` and `DataOutput` read and write primitive Java types from a stream. Since they're interfaces, all of their methods, which follow, are abstract and so do nothing until they're instantiated.

*DataInput:*

- `readBoolean()`
- `readByte()`
- `readFloat()`
- `readChar()`
- `readDouble()`
- `readInt()`
- `readShort()`
- `readLong()`
- `readLine()`
- `readUTF()`
- `readUnsignedByte()`
- `readUnsignedShort()`
- `readFully(byte_sequence)`
- `readFully(byte_sequence, off, len)`
- `skipBytes(n)`

*DataOutput:*

- `write (b)`
- `write(byte_sequence)`
- `writeBoolean(boolean)`
- `writeByte(byte)`
- `writeBytes(string)`
- `writeChar(char)`
- `writeChars(string)`
- `writeDouble(double)`
- `writeFloat(float)`
- `writeInt(int)`
- `writeLong(long)`
- `writeShort(short)`
- `writeUTF()`

## DataInputStream and DataOutput Stream

The data stream classes, `DataInputStream` and `DataOutputStream`, implement the `DataInput` and `DataOutput` interfaces, respectively, reading and writing Java primitive types to a stream. Here are their methods.

### *DataInputStream:*

- `__init__` (InputStream)—creates a buffered writer with the specified writer output stream

### *DataOutputStream:*

- `__init__` (InputStream)—creates a buffered reader with the specified reader input stream

### *Using DataInputStream*

To demonstrate `DataInputStream`, we'll read in the file we wrote with `DataOutput Stream` in the last interactive session.

Import the classes needed.

```
>>> from java.io import DataInputStream, FileInputStream
```

Create a `DataInputStream` instance that's chained to a new instance of `FileInput Stream`.

```
>>> data_in = DataInputStream(FileInputStream("data_out.bin"))
```

Read in a `Boolean` from the stream.

```
>>> data_in.readBoolean()
1
```

Read in a `Byte` from the stream.

```
>>> data_in.readByte()
1
```

Read in a `Char` from the stream.

```
>>> data_in.readChar()
'\x1'
```

Read in an `Int` from the stream.

```
>>> data_in.readInt()
1
```

Read in a `Long` and a `Short` from the stream.

```
>>> data_in.readLong(), data_in.readShort()
(1L, 1)
```

Close the stream.

```
>>>data_in.close()
```

### Using DataOutputStream

Though not very creative, the following example shows how to write the Java primitive types using DataOutputStream:

```
>>> from java.io import DataOutputStream, FileOutputStream
>>> data_out = DataOutputStream(FileOutputStream("data_out.bin"))
>>> data_out.writeBoolean(1)
>>> data_out.writeByte(1)
>>> data_out.writeChar(1)
>>> data_out.writeInt(1)
>>> data_out.writeLong(1)
>>> data_out.writeShort(1)
>>> data_out.close()
```

Here's a hexdump listing of data_out.bin:

```
0E7F:0100 01 01 00 01 00 00 00 01-00 00 00 00 00 00 00 01 ................
0E7F:0110 00 01 FF FF FF FF FF FF-FF FF FF FF FF FF FF FF ................
```

## readUTF() and writeUTF()

Two methods that make life easier are readUTF() and writeUTF(), which read and write strings in Unicode (UTF-8 transformation format).

Here's an example of writing two strings:

```
>>> from java.io import *
>>> out = DataOutputStream(FileOutputStream("strs.bin"))
>>> out.writeUTF("Hello world")
>>> out.writeUTF(" Hello earth")
>>> out.close()
```

Here's an example of reading two strings:

```
>>> input = DataInputStream(FileInputStream("strs.bin"))
>>> input.readUTF()
'Hello world'
>>> input.readUTF()
' Hello earth'
>>> input.close()
```

As you can see, it is a lot easier to write strings with this technique than with the others we had to use without DataInputStream and DataOutputStream.

## The File Class

The Java File class is nothing like the Python file object, in spite of the name. It allows you to check the following attributes of a file:

- Read
- Write
- Size
- Last modification date
- Directory or not a directory

It also provides the methods listed below to view a directory's contents, to create and delete directories, and to delete directory files:

- canRead()—determines permission and access to read the file
- canWrite()—determines read-only or read/write access
- delete()—deletes the current file referenced by this file object
- equals(File)—determines if the file referenced by this object is the same as the argument
- exists()—determines if the file exists
- getPath()—gets the file path (can be relative)
- getAbsolutePath()—same as above, but resolves relative to absolute paths
- getCanonicalPath()
- getName()—gets the file name
- getParent()—gets the parent directory
- isAbsolute()
- isDirectory()—determines if the file is a directory
- isFile()—determines if the file is a regular file
- lastModified()—gets the date the file was last modified
- length()—gets the length of the file
- list()—lists the files in the directory
- list(filter)—lists the files in the directory with a filter
- mkdir(dir)—creates a directory
- mkdirs()—creates several directories
- renameTo()—renames the file
- toString()—returns the string equivalent of the file (toString is inherited from Object)

## File Interactive Session

Let's look at an example of File. Import the File class from the *java.io* package.

```
>>> from java.io import File
```

Create an instance of the file object that refers to the properties of the file (*c:\\dat\\File.txt*).

```
>>> file = File("c:\\dat\\File.txt")
```

Determine if the file is read-only by calling `canWrite()`. If `canWrite()` returns 1 (true), the file is read/write. (If you change the properties of the file to read-only, `canWrite()` returns 0, that is, false.)

```
>>> file.canWrite()
1
```

Determine if the file exists. If not, the `exists()` function returns 0.

```
>>> file.exists()
1
```

Get just the file name without the path.

```
>>> file.getName()
'File.txt'
```

Get the file path.

```
>>> file.getPath()
'c:\\dat\\File.txt'
```

Get the path of the parent directory.

```
>>> file.getParent()
'c:\\dat'
```

In the following code, we'll see if the file is a directory. Then we'll create a `File` instance that refers to the file's parent directory and test if the directory is actually a directory.

Is the file a directory? (1 means yes; 0 means no)

```
>>> file.isDirectory()
0
```

Create a `File` instance that refers to the file's parent directory, and then see if the directory is a directory.

```
>>> directory = file(File.getParent())
>>> directory.isDirectory()
1
```

Is the file a file?

```
>>> file.isFile()
1
```

Is the directory a file?

```
>>> directory.isFile()
0
```

The `lastModified()` method returns the time, as a `Long`, which refers to the milliseconds elapsed since Jan. 1, 1970.

```
>>> file.lastModified()
934294386000L
```

You can convert the Long to a date using the following technique. Import the Date class, passing its last modified value to its constructor.

```
>>> from java.util import Date
>>> date = Date(File.lastModified())
>>> print date
Tue Aug 10 07:13:06 PDT 1999
```

Get the length of the file.

```
>>> file.length()
63L
```

Is the class an absolute path (*c:\dat\text.tx*) or a relative path (*..\..\text.txt*)?

```
>>> file.isAbsolute()
1
```

Delete the file and check to see if it exists; get its length.

```
>>> file.delete()
1
```

```
>>> file.exists()           # File no longer exist
0
```

```
>>> file.length()           # Thus its length is zero
0L
```

Create a new File instance that refers to the relative location of autoexec.bat.

```
>>> file = File ("..\\..\\..\\autoexec.bat")
```

Check to see if the file exists.

```
>>> file.exists()
1
```

Get the path (note that it's relative).

```
>>> file.getPath()
'..\\..\\..\\autoexec.bat'
```

Get the absolute path (this looks weird).

```
>>> file.getAbsolutePath()
'C:\\book\\..\\..\\..\\autoexec.bat'
```

Get the canonical path (this looks better).

```
>>> file.getCanonicalPath()
'C:\\AUTOEXEC.BAT'
```

***Path Separators: Sometimes \\, Sometimes /***

The path separator can vary depending on what operating system you're using, so it's not a good idea to hardcode it. On Windows machines, the path separator is \, but on Unix it's /.

Given this situation, the proper way to create the directory string is

```
>>> new_directory = directory.getCanonicalPath() + File.separator \
...                    + "MyNewDir"
```

not

```
>>> new_directory = directory.getCanonicalPath() \
                       + "\\MyNewDir"
```

File class instances can work with directories as well. Create a relative directory that points to the current directory.

```
>>> directory = File(".")
>>> directory.isAbsolute()
0
```

List the files in the current directory (an array of Java strings is returned).

```
>>> directory.list()
array(['TOC2.txt', 'readme.txt', 'Silver', 'status.xls', 'TOC.txt', 'chap9',
'chap5', 'chap3', 'chap2', 'chap10', 'chap1', '~WRL1019.tmp', '~WRL0244.tmp',
'~WRL2798.tmp', '~WRL2319.tmp', 'Code Samples', 'chap6', 'scripts', 'Gold'],
java.lang.String)
```

Let's create a new directory called *MyNewDir*. First create the directory string.

```
>>> new_directory = directory.getCanonicalPath() + "\\MyNewDir"
```

Show it.

```
>>> print new_directory
C:\book\MyNewDir
```

Create an instance of the directory that will be created.

```
>>> newDir = File(new_directory)
```

See if the directory to which the instance refers already exists.

```
>>> newDir.exists()
0
```

Create the directory with the mkdir() method.

```
>>> newDir.mkdir()
1
```

See if it exists (it should).

```
>>> newDir.exists()
1
```

## The RandomAccessFile Class

RandomAccessFile both reads and writes to binary output streams. It's most similar to the Python file object and has the following methods:

- __init__(strName, strMode)—opens the file in the specified mode
- __init__(File, strMode)—same as above, but passes a Java file object
- getFD()—gets the file descriptor
- getFilePointer()—similar to the tell() method for the Python file object
- length()—gets the length of the file
- seek()—similar to the seek() method for the Python file object
- read(byte_sequence)—similar to the read() method in InputStream
- read(byte_sequence, off, len)—similar to the read() method in InputStream

The following abstract methods are from DataInput:

- readBoolean()
- readByte()
- readFloat()
- readChar()
- readDouble()
- readInt()
- readShort()
- readLong()
- readLine()
- readUTF()
- readUnsignedByte()
- readUnsignedShort()
- readFully(byte_sequence)
- readFully(byte_sequence, off, len)
- skipBytes(n)
- write (b)

These abstract methods are from DataOutput:

- write(byte_sequence)
- writeBoolean(boolean)

- writeByte(byte)
- writeBytes(string)
- writeChar(char)
- writeChars(string)
- writeDouble(double)
- writeFloat(float)
- writeInt(int)
- writeLong(long)
- writeShort(short)
- writeUTF(string)

> **Advanced Note: The Shortcoming of Single Inheritance**
>
> Instead of RandomAccessFile inheriting from both InputStream and OutputStream, it inherits from DataInput and DataOuput (which are interfaces). Of course, it could have inherited from these stream classes if they were interfaces, but because Random AccessFile doesn't support them, it can't chain to them.
>
> A while back I wanted a random access file that worked with ObjectOutputStream and ObjectInputStream. To get it I had to write my own class that extended from ObjectOutput and ObjectInput, and re-implement object streaming. This is a situation where the single inheritance model of Java falls short.

## RandomAccessFile Modes

The RandomAccessFile modes are r for read only, which is similar to Python's r, and rw for read/write, which is similar to Python's r+. Working with RandomAccess File isn't much different from working with DataInputStream and DataOutputStream. It's also not much different from working with the Python file object, as I said before. Since there are no truly new concepts here, this next interactive session is a short one. (You still have to follow along, though.)

Import RandomAccessFile from *java.io*.

```
>>> from java.io import RandomAccessFile
```

Create an instance of it in read/write mode.

```
>>> file = RandomAccessFile("c:\\dat\\rFile.bin", "rw")
```

Create an array that can be written to the file; write it to the file.

```
>>> import jarray
>>> byte_array = jarray.array((0,1,2,3,4,5,6,7,8,9,10), 'b')
>>> print byte_array
array([0, 1, 2, 3, 4, 5, 6, 7, 8, 9, 10], byte)

>>> file.write(byte_array)
```

Write some strings to the file.

```
>>> file.writeUTF("Hello")
>>> file.writeChars(" how are you")
>>> file.writeBytes(" fine thanks")
```

Get the location in the file.

```
>>> file.getFilePointer()
54L
>>> location = file.getFilePointer()    # Save it for later
```

Move to the start of the file using the `seek()` method.

```
>>> file.seek(0)
```

Create an empty array ( `buffer`), and read in the values from `byte_array` (written a few steps back). Notice that `buffer`'s values are the same as `byte_array`'s values after the `file.read()` function call.

```
>>> buffer = jarray.zeros(11, 'b')
>>> file.read(buffer)
11
>>> print buffer
array([0, 1, 2, 3, 4, 5, 6, 7, 8, 9, 10], byte)
```

Move to the saved location; show that it's the same place in the file.

```
>>> file.seek(location)
>>> file.getFilePointer()
54L
```

Write the buffer to the file and show its current location.

```
>>> buffer[10] = 0xa
>>> file.write(buffer)
>>> file.getFilePointer()
65L

>>> file.close()
```

---

### *Unicode*

Unicode is a standard for working with character sets from all common languages. It's essential for internationalizing software.

   Are you the least bit curious about the differences between `writeUTF()`, `writeChars()`, and `writeBytes()`? Here they are:

```
>>> file.writeUTF("Hello")
>>> file.writeChars(" how are you")
>>> file.writeBytes(" fine thanks")
```

In essence, writeChars() writes the Unicode representation of the characters to the file; writeUTF() and writeBytes() write out the ASCII equivalents. (More precisely, writeUTF() writes in a Java-modified UTF-8 format, which you can read about in the Java API documentation under the DataInput interface. In the previous interactive example, UTF-8 equated to ASCII.)

The Unicode data in this example is represented by two bytes, whereas the write Bytes() and writeUTF() data is represented by one byte. Fire up a hexdump utility, and see for yourself (this is a hexdump of the *rfile.bin* file):

```
C:\dat>debug rFile.bin
-d
1876:0100 00 01 02 03 04 05 06 07-08 09 0A 00 05 48 65 6C  ............Hel
1876:0110 6C 6F 00 20 00 68 00 6F-00 77 00 20 00 61 00 72  lo. .h.o.w. .a.r
1876:0120 00 65 00 20 00 79 00 6F-00 75 20 66 69 6E 65 20  .e. .y.o.u fine
1876:0130 74 68 61 6E 6B 73 00 01-02 03 04 05 06 07 08 09  thanks..........
1876:0140 0A 02 D3 74 0A 41 3C 22-75 E6 80 F7 20 EB E1 5E  ...t.A<"u... ..^
1876:0150 58 C3 A1 D7 D7 8B 36 D9-D7 C6 06 1B D9 00 C6 06  X.....6.........
1876:0160 17 D9 00 8B 36 D9 D7 8B-0E D7 D7 8B D6 E3 42 51  ....6.........BQ
1876:0170 56 5B 2B DE 59 03 CB 8B-D6 C6 06 BB DB 00 E3 31  V[+.Y.........1
```

Notice that the how are you in the right column, which was written with writeChars(), has a period (".") between each character, while the Hello and the fine thanks don't. This shows that how are you is using 2-byte Unicode.

## *The StreamTokenizer Class*

StreamTokenizer breaks up an input stream into tokens and can be used to parse a simple file (excuse me, "input stream"). Read the Java API documentation on StreamTokenizer, and then compare what you read to the following methods

- __init__(Reader)
- __init__(InputStream)
- nextToken()—returns the next token in the stream
- lineno()—returns the current line number
- lowerCaseMode(flag)—returns all words to lowercase if passed a true value
- parseNumbers()—sets the parsing of floating-point numbers
- pushBack()—pushes the token back onto the stream, returning it to the next nextToken() method call
- quoteChar(char)—specifies the character string delimiter; the whole string is returned as a token in sval
- resetSyntax()—sets all characters to ordinary so that they aren't ignored as tokens

- commentChar(char)—specifies a character that begins a comment that lasts until the end of the line; characters in a comment are not returned
- slashSlashComments(flag)—allows recognition of // to denote a comment (this is a Java comment)
- slashStarComments(flag)—allows recognition of /* */ to denote a comment
- toString()
- whitespaceChars(low,hi)—specifies the range of characters that denote delimiters
- wordChars(low, hi)—specifies the range of characters that make up words
- ordinaryChar(char)—specifies a character that is never part of a token (the character should be returned as is)
- ordinaryChars(low, hi)—specifies a range of characters that are never part of a token (the character should be returned as is)
- eolSignificant(flag)—specifies if end-of-line (EOL) characters are significant (they're ignored if not, i.e., treated like whitespace)

StreamTokenizer's variables are ttype (one of the constant values TT_EOF, TT_EOL, TT_NUMBER, and TT_WORD); sval (contains the token of the last string read); and nval (contains the token of the last number read).

## Using StreamTokenizer

Reading the documentation probably isn't enough to get you started with Stream Tokenizer, so we're going to work with a simple application that produces a report on the number of classes and functions in a Python source file. Here's the source code:

```
class MyClass:        #This is my class
    def method1(self):
        pass
    def method2(self):
        pass

#Comment should be ignored
def AFunction():
    pass

class SecondClass:
    def m1(self):
        print "Hi Mom"         #Say hi to mom
    def m2(self):
        print "Hi Son"         #Say hi to Son

#Comment should be ignored
def BFunction():
    pass
```

Follow along with the next interactive session. Afterward we'll look at the code to count the classes and functions.

Import the `FileInputStream` class from *java.io*, and create an instance of it.

```
>>> from java.io import FileInputStream
>>> file = FileInputStream("C:\\dat\\ParseMe.py")
```

Import the `StreamTokenizer` class, and create an instance of it. Pass its constructor the `FileInputStream` instance.

```
>>> from java.io import StreamTokenizer
>>> token = StreamTokenizer(File)
```

Call `nextToken()` to get the first token in the file (that is, class).

```
>>> token.nextToken()
-3
```

As you can see, `nextToken()` returns a numeric value, although you may have been expecting a string value containing "class". In fact, `nextToken()` returns the type of token, that is, a word, a number, or an EOL or EOF (end-of-file) character, so -3 refers to TT-WORD.

The `ttype` variable holds the last type of token read.

```
>>> token.ttype
-3
```

The `sval` variable holds the actual last token read. If we want to check if the last token type was a word, we can write this, and, if it was a word, we can print it out.

```
>>> if token.ttype == token.TT_WORD:
...      print token.sval
...
class
>>>
```

Call `nextToken()` again to get the next token, which is `MyClass`.

```
>>> token.nextToken()
-3

>>> print token.sval
MyClass
```

Call `nextToken()` again; this time it should return the '#' token.

```
>>> token.nextToken()
58

>>> print token.sval
None
```

Since the token is a ':' `StreamTokenizer` doesn't recognize it as valid. The only valid types are NUMBER, EOL, EOF, and WORD. So for ':' to be recognized, it has to be registered with the `wordChars()` method.

```
>>> token.TT_NUMBER
-2

>>> token.TT_EOL
10

>>> token.TT_EOF
-1

>>> token.TT_WORD
-3
```

If the type isn't one of these, the number corresponding to the character encoding is returned. Let's see what `nextToken()` returns for the next character.

```
>>> token.nextToken()
35
```

The 35 refers to '#', which you can prove with the built-in `ord()` function.

```
>>> ord('#')
35
```

Get the next token.

```
>>> token.nextToken()
-3
```

The token is a word (-3 equates to TT_WORD). Print `sval` to find out what the word is.

```
>>> print token.sval
This
```

As you can see, the `StreamTokenizer` instance is reading text out of the comment from the first line. We want to ignore comments, so we need to return the tokens we took out back into the stream.

Push the token back into the stream.

```
>>> token.pushBack()
```

Attempt to push the token before the last one back into the stream.

```
>>> token.pushBack()
```

Set `commentChar()` to ignore '#'. (`commentChar()` takes an integer argument corresponding to the encoding of the character.)

```
>>> token.commentChar(ord('#'))
```

Get the next token, and print it out.

```
>>> token.nextToken()
-3

>>> print token.sval
This
```

Are you wondering why we still have the comment text? The `pushback()` method can only push back the last token, so calling it more than once won't do any good. Let's start from the beginning, creating a new `FileInputStream` instance and a new `StreamTokenizer` instance.

Create the `StreamTokenizer` instance by passing its constructor a new instance of `FileInputStream`.

```
>>> file = fileInputStream("c:\\dat\\parseMe.py")
>>> token = StreamTokenizer(File)
```

Iterate through the source code, printing out the words in the file. Quit the `while` loop when the token type is `EOF`.

```
>>> while token.ttype != token.TT_EOF:
...      token.nextToken()
...      if(token.ttype == token.TT_WORD):
...              print token.sval
```

Notice that the comment text isn't in the words printed out.

```
class
MyClass
def
method1
self
pass
def
method2
self
pass
def
AFunction
pass
...
...
```

## Parsing Python with StreamTokenizer

Okay, we've done our experimentation. Now it's time for the actual code for counting the classes and functions in our Python source code.

```
from java.io import FileInputStream, StreamTokenizer

        # Create a stream tokenizer by passing a new
        # instance of the FileInputStream
token = StreamTokenizer(FileInputStream("c:\\dat\\parseMe.py"))

        # Set the comment character.
token.commentChar(ord('#'))

classList = []
functionList = []
```

```python
            # Add an element to a list
def addToList(theList, token):
  token.nextToken()
  if (token.ttype == token.TT_WORD):
        theList.append (token.sval)

            # Adds a class to the class list
def parseClass(token):
  global classList
  addToList (classList, token)

            # Adds a function to the function list
def parseFunction(token):
  global functionList
  addToList (functionList, token)

            # Iterate through the list until the
            # token is of type TT_EOF, end of File
while token.ttype != token.TT_EOF:
  token.nextToken()
  if(token.ttype == token.TT_WORD):
        if (token.sval == "class"):
              parseClass(token)
        elif(token.sval == "def"):
              parseFunction(token)

            # Print out detail about a function or class list
def printList(theList, type):
  print "There are " + `len(theList)` + " " + type
  print theList

            # Print the results.
printList (classList, "classes")
printList (functionList, "functions and methods")
```

Here's the output:

```
There are 2 classes
['MyClass', 'SecondClass']
There are 6 functions and methods
['method1', 'method2', 'AFunction', 'm1', 'm2', 'BFunction']
```

The main part of the code (where all the action is happening) is

```python
            # Iterate through the list until the
            # token is of type TT_EOF, end of File
while token.ttype != token.TT_EOF:
  token.nextToken()
  if(token.ttype == token.TT_WORD):
        if (token.sval == "class"):
              parseClass(token)
        elif(token.sval == "def"):
              parseFunction(token)
```

Let's look at it step by step.

If the token type isn't equal to EOF, get the next token.

```
while token.ttype != token.TT_EOF:
    token.nextToken()
```

If the token type is WORD,

```
if(token.ttype == token.TT_WORD):
```

check to see if the token is a class modifier. If it is, call the parseClass() function, which uses the StreamTokenizer instance to extract the class name and put it on a list.

```
if (token.sval == "class"):
    parseClass(token)
```

If the token isn't a class modifier, check to see if it's a function modifier. If so, call parseFunction(), which uses StreamTokenizer to extract the function name and put it on a list.

```
elif(token.sval == "def"):
    parseFunction(token)
```

StreamTokenizer is a good way to parse an input stream. If you understand its runtime behavior (which you should from the preceding interactive session), you'll be more likely to use it.

The more astute among you probably noticed that functions and methods were counted together in the last example. As an exercise, change the code so that each class has an associated list of methods and so that these methods are counted separately.

*Hint*: You'll need to use the resetSyntax() method of StreamTokenizer to set all characters to ordinary. Then you'll need to count the spaces (ord(" ")) and tabs (ord("\t")) that occur before the first word on a line. For this you also need to track whether you hit an EOL token type. (If you can do this exercise, I do believe that you can do any exercise in the book.)

As another exercise, create a stream that can parse a file whose contents look like this:

```
[SectionType:SectionName]
value1=1
value2 = 3         #This is a comment that should be ignored
value4 = "Hello"
```

SectionType defines a class of section, and SectionName is like defining a class instance. value equates to a class attribute.

Here's an example.

```
[Communication:Host]
type = "TCP/IP" #Possible values are TCP/IP or RS-232
port = 978          #Sets the port of the TCP/IP
```

```
[Communication:Client]
type = "RS-232"
baudrate = 9600
baudrate = 2800
baudrate = 19200

[Greeting:Client]
sayHello = "Good morning Mr. Bond"

[Greeting:Host]
sayHello = "Good morning sir"
```

Create a dictionary of dictionaries of dictionaries. The name of the top-level dictionary should correspond to the section type (Communication, Greeting); its value should be a dictionary whose name corresponds to the section names (Client, Host) and whose values correspond to another dictionary. The names and values of the third-level dictionaries should correspond to the name values in the file (sayHello = "Good morning Mr. Bond", type = "RS-232"). If, like baudrate, the name repeats itself, you should create a list corresponding to the name baudrate and, instead of a single value inserted in the bottom-tier dictionaries, put the list as the value.

The structure will look like this:

```
{}-Communication----{}-- Client {}- type = "rs-232"
   |                    |         |
   |                    |          - baudrate = [9600, 2800, 19200]
   |                    |
   |                    |- Host {} - type = "TCP/IP"
   |                              |
   |                               - port = 978
   |
Greeting ----------{}- Client{}- sayHello = "Good morning Mr. Bond"
                      |
                      |- Host - sayHello = "Good morning sir"
```

## Persisting Objects with Java Streams

ObjectOutputStream writes out Java class instances (objects) to an output stream. It accomplishes for Java what the *pickle* module does for Python. Only Java instances that have the Serializable class (interface) as a base class (interface) can be serialized with ObjectOutputStream. All Jython objects (class instances, functions, dictionaries, lists) implement Serializable.

Here's a short example. Import ObjectOutputStream and FileOutputStream from the *java.io* package.

```
>>> from java.io import ObjectOutputStream, FileOutputStream
```

Create an instance of ObjectOutputStream, passing the constructor a new instance of FileOutputStream.

```
>>> oos = ObjectOutputStream(FileOutputStream("c:\\dat\\out.bin"))
```

Define a simple class.

```
>>> class MyClass:
...     def __init__(self):
...             self.a = "a"
...
```

Create an instance of the class.

```
>>> object = MyClass()
```

Write the instance to the output stream with the writeObject() method.

```
>>> oos.writeObject(object)
>>> oos.close()      #From here
```

Now we can use ObjectInputStream to read the object back. Import ObjectInput Stream and FileInputStream from package *java.io*.

```
>>> from java.io import ObjectInputStream, FileInputStream
```

Create an instance of ObjectInputStream.

```
>>> ois = ObjectInputStream(FileInputStream("c:\\dat\\out.bin"))
```

Read the object from the stream.

```
>>> object2 = ois.readObject()
```

Show that the attribute of object2 is the same as the attribute of object but that object and object2 aren't the same.

```
>>> print "The a attribute of object 2 is " + object2.a
>>> print "Are object and object2 the same? " + `(object is object2)`
```

As I said, object streams function a lot like the *pickle* module.

As an exercise, modify the address book application from Chapter 8 to use object streams instead of *pickle*.

## Using Java Streams to Work with Memory

We spoke earlier about streams being abstract metaphors for files or, more precisely, any type of input/output mechanism. With streams, for example, you can write data to a byte array, which is essentially a location in the computer's memory. ByteArrayInputStream and ByteArrayOutputStream allow reading and writing to and from memory. You might want to look them up in the Java API documentation.

Instead of passing a file stream to a stream derivation, you can pass a byte array stream. Here's the earlier example showing this (the differences are in bold).

```
from java.io import ObjectOutputStream, ByteArrayOutputStream
bytes = ByteArrayOutputStream()
oos = ObjectOutputStream(bytes)

class MyClass:
   def __init__(self):
         self.a = "a"

object = MyClass()
oos.writeObject(object)
oos.close()
print "Here is the binary image on a Jython class instance"
print bytes.toByteArray()

from java.io import ObjectInputStream, ByteArrayInputStream
ois = ObjectInputStream(ByteArrayInputStream(bytes.toByteArray()))
object2 = ois.readObject()

print "The a attribute of object 2 is " + object2.a
print "Are object and object2 the same? " + `(object is object2)`
```

Note that, to create the ByteArrayInputStream instance, I passed the byte array returned by the toByteArray() method of the ByteArrayOutputStream instance. In a later chapter, I'll show you how to work with network streams.

As an exercise, read the Java API documentation on CharArrayReader and CharArrayWriter, and write a simple program that reads and writes text strings to and from a memory location.

---

## Summary

Streams are Java's way to support I/O. They can represent a file, a network connection, or access to a Web site. In this chapter, we dealt mostly with file streams because they're easy to work with and demonstrate stream fundamentals. Learning to deal with Java streams is essential for learning to use the Java APIs.

We covered some nonstream classes—RandomAccessFile, File, and Stream Tokenizer. As we saw in the examples, RandomAccessFile works most like the Python file object. The Java File class allows access to a file's attributes: Is the file read-only? Is it a directory? and so forth. It also allows the creation of directories. The StreamTokenizer class works with any text stream (a class derived from Reader) or binary stream (a class derived from InputStream).

Streams work with more than just files. We demonstrated the ByteArrayInput Stream and the ByteArrayOutputStream classes, which allow reading and writing to memory buffers.

# CHAPTER 13

# *JFC Fundamentals*

---

## *Terms in This Chapter*

---

- ⬦ *Abstract Window Toolkit*
- ⬦ *Checkbox*
- ⬦ *Container*
- ⬦ *Data model*
- ⬦ *Dropdown list*
- ⬦ *Event object*
- ⬦ *File path*
- ⬦ *Frame*
- ⬦ *gif/jpeg*

- ⬦ *Java APIs*
- ⬦ *Java Foundation Classes/Swing*
- ⬦ *Layout management*
- ⬦ *Listener*
- ⬦ *Menu (menubar/popup)*
- ⬦ *Mnemonics*
- ⬦ *Model View Controller*
- ⬦ *Packing*

- ⬦ *Panel*
- ⬦ *Polymorphism*
- ⬦ *Radio/Toggle button*
- ⬦ *Single inheritance*
- ⬦ *Superclass*
- ⬦ *Titlebar*
- ⬦ *Toolbar*
- ⬦ *Vector*

In this chapter, we're going to cover the construction of Java GUI applications, including listboxes, text fields, menus, buttons, windows, checkboxes, and panels. In previous chapters, we played with Java applications to work with events and Java classes. Events will be the focus here.

There are two ways to build GUIs in Java—Abstract Window Toolkit (AWT) and Java Foundation Classes (JFC)/Swing, which are conceptually similar although very different in execution. JFC is the newer of the two and is supported only by current browsers. AWT is supported by newer and older browsers, but our AWT tour will include only its post-Swing incarnation.

---

**AWT or JFC**

If you can't control the client—that is, what browser he's using—you may want to use AWT. You'll probably also use it when you're working with hand-held devices. Even so, JFC has many features that have no AWT equivalent, so it's a better general-purpose tool.

Actually, JFC encompasses both AWT and Swing, but Swing is the newer, so-called lightweight version of GUI widgets (components). Basically, Swing widgets have no operating system counterpart.

---

Learning GUI programming in Java is a fairly tall order, especially when you factor in all of the advanced JFC controls such as trees and tables. Covering this topic fully will take several chapters, and even then we can only cover the basics. If you want more, there are plenty of good books out there. One I recommend is *Graphic Java*, volumes 1 and 2 (Geary, 1998 and 1999), which provides exhaustive references and scores of code examples. Geary documents components by their properties, which makes them easy for Jython users to read and work with. Other good sources are the Java tutorial on JFC and the abundant, and free, Java API documentation.

Like most of the chapters in this book, this one is hands on. For example, we don't go into detail about the Model View Controller (MVC) architecture that JFC uses, but we show examples that use it. If you want to understand the dynamic behavior of MVC, you have to follow along. Repeat after me: *The only way to learn programming is to program.*

---

## Components and Containers

In Java, you organize components as nested elements. Typically you have a frame, which contains several panels and maybe a toolbar and a menubar. In fact, each panel can contain other components such as text fields and labels or even other panels, so a complete graphical user interface can consist of many nested elements. The JFC and AWT containers are components themselves and can be contained in other containers. You can see this in their class diagrams, which also show their points of similarity.

---

**Design Patterns**

AWT and JFC use the design patterns Publish and Subscribe, Observer/Observable, Decorator, and Strategy, among others. These are described in *Design Patterns* (Gamma et al., 1995)—a must read for a deep understanding of the Java APIs.

---

## *JFrame*

Frames are top-level interfaces that pop up as windows and can be resized and closed. As containers, they typically contain panels and other components, for which they initiate layout management. They can also have an associated menubar and icons.

Here's an example of how a simple frame works using JFrame.

Import JFrame from *javax.swing*. Create an instance of it, show it, size it, change its title.

```
>>> from javax.swing import JFrame
>>> frame = JFrame()
>>> frame.show()
>>> frame.size = 200,200
```

Set the title to "Hello JFC".

```
>>> frame.title = "Hello JFC"
```

### Setting the Frame's Mouse Cursor

With a frame, as with all components, you can set the mouse cursor. You'll probably want to make the cursor wait during a long operation so it shows a wristwatch or hourglass that lets the user know the application is busy. In the example that follows, we'll set the cursor to WAIT, TEXT, and HAND. After each command, position the mouse over the middle of the frame, and note the image the pointer becomes.

Import Cursor from *java.awt*, and change the cursor three times.

```
>>> from java.awt import Cursor
>>> frame.setCursor(Cursor.WAIT_CURSOR)
>>> frame.setCursor(Cursor.TEXT_CURSOR)
>>> frame.setCursor = Cursor.HAND_CURSOR
```

### Adding Components to the Frame

To illustrate adding components to the frame, we'll import some components from AWT. Then we'll create and add a button, a label, a checkbox, and a text field.

```
>>> from javax.swing import JButton,      JLabel
>>> from javax.swing import JCheckBox, JTextField
```

Add a button component.

```
>>> frame.contentPane.add(JButton("Button"))
```

Add a label component.

```
>>> frame.contentPane.add(JLabel("Label"))
```

Add a checkbox component.

```
>>> frame.contentPane.add(JCheckBox("Checkbox"))
```

Add a text field component.

```
>>> frame.contentPane.add(TextField("TextField"))
```

You may think that our frame should be showing some components at this point, but it won't until we tell it to by calling the pack() method.

```
>>> frame.pack()
```

> **A Reminder**
> Doing this:
> ```
> >>> frame.contentPane.add(Button("Button"))
> ```
> is equivalent to doing this:
> ```
> >>> button = Button("Button")
> >>> frame.contentPane.add(button)
> ```
> The first way creates an anonymous instance of Button and adds it to the frame, which is okay since we don't need access to the button component for this example.

### BorderLayout versus FrameLayout

Only the last component added to the frame shows up. Why? The answer lies in the default layout manager for Frame—BorderLayout—which lays out components along the borders. I won't go into detail about BorderLayout here (see Chapter 14 for that). Suffice it to say that we need to change to another manager, FlowLayout, which arranges the components from left to right as long as there's room.

I'll tell you more about FlowLayout later. For now, we'll import the FlowLayout class from the *java.awt* package and set the frame's layout property to a FlowLayout instance. Then we'll pack the frame, that is, invoke the layout manager.

```
>>> from java.awt import FlowLayout
>>> frame.contentPane.layout = FlowLayout()
>>> frame.pack()
```

Now all of the added components are visible.

### JFrame's Lineage

JFC frames work much like AWT frames because they're both cut from the same cloth. Let's examine JFrame's lineage, which is easy to do from the interactive interpreter.

Import JFrame from *javax.swing*.

```
>>> from javax.swing import JFrame
```

Print out JFrame's superclass, which is *java.awt.Frame*.

```
>>> print `JFrame.superclass`
<jclass java.awt.Frame at 227114466>
```

This tells us that Frame is an AWT frame. (Follow along.)

```
>>> import java.awt.Frame
>>> JFrame.superclass is java.awt.Frame
1
```

There are some differences between Frame and JFrame. For example, if you try to add a component to JFrame you get an exception. That's because components can be added only to JFrame's content pane.

---

**JFrame's Design Flaw**

One of the key benefits of inheritance is polymorphism, so you might think we could replace Frame with JFrame whenever possible. That's not the case, however. According to the Java API Documentation, JFrame and java.awt.Frame are not fully compatible.

In my opinion, making JFrame's add() method throw an exception is a design flaw. Its correct behavior should be to add the component to the content pane and then have separate methods for adding it directly to JFrame. Instead, by redefining the semantics and function of add(), the developers broke the contract of Frame's interface.

The key to working with JFrame is not to do this:

```
jframe.add(component)
```

but to do this:

```
frame.contentPane.add(child);
```

---

## Handling Events with JFrame

Since Frame is a subclass of java.awt.Frame, which is a subclass of java.awt.Window, you can listen for window events with its event mechanism. Import the jinfo class to inspect the event properties of Frame (JFrame's superclass).

```
>>> import jinfo
>>> from java.awt import Frame
>>> jinfo.getEventsInfo(Frame)
[]
```

As you can see, Frame has no event properties, because its events are defined from its base class, java.awt.Window.

```
>>> Frame.superclass
<jclass java.awt.Window at 228949474>
```

Therefore, we need to inspect `Window`'s event properties.

```
>>> jinfo.getEventsInfo(Window)
[<beanEventProperty windowIconified for event interface
java.awt.event.WindowListener at 861240813>, <beanEventProperty
WindowActivated for event interface java.awt.event.WindowListener at
863600109>, <beanEventProperty windowClosing for event interface
java.awt.event.WindowListener at 862551533>, <beanEventProperty windowClosed
for event interface java.awt.event.WindowListener at 862813677>,
<beanEventProperty windowDeiconified for event interface
java.awt.event.WindowListener
at 861502957>, <beanEventProperty windowOpened for event interface
java.awt.event.WindowListener at 860978669>, <beanEventProperty
windowDeactivated for event interface java.awt.event.WindowListener at
862289389>]
```

There's a lot of them. I've done a little formatting to make them more readable.

```
[<... windowIconified for event interface java.awt.event.WindowListener ...>,
 <... WindowActivated for event interface java.awt.event.WindowListener ...>,
 <... windowClosing for event interface java.awt.event.WindowListener ...>,
 <... windowClosed for event interface java.awt.event.WindowListener ...>,
 <... windowDeiconified for event interface java.awt.event.WindowListener ...>,
 <... windowOpened for event interface java.awt.event.WindowListener ...>,
 <... windowDeactivated for event interface java.awt.event.WindowListener
 ...>]
```

Notice that the `getEventsInfo()` function extracts all of the information needed to work with event properties, but it's a little hard to read. Here's an easier way.

Import all of `jinfo` and import `java.awt.Window`.

```
>>> from jinfo import *
>>> from java.awt import Window
```

Use `getEventsInfo()` to get the sequence of event properties from `Window`.

```
>>> eProps = getEventsInfo(Window)
```

Use `len()` to determine how many properties there are.

```
>>> print `len(eProps)`
7
```

Once you know how many properties there are, invoke `printEventProperty()` to print out details about the event.

```
>>> printEventProperty(eProps[0])
Event Property:           windowOpened
Defined in:               java.awt.event.WindowListener
Event:                    java.awt.event.WindowEvent
Event properties for java.awt.event.WindowEvent:
    window              Type: org.python.core.PyBeanProperty
Public Event fields for java.awt.event.WindowEvent:
    static final WINDOW_FIRST        Type: int
    static final WINDOW_LAST         Type: int
```

```
    static final WINDOW_OPENED           Type: int
    static final WINDOW_CLOSING          Type: int
    static final WINDOW_CLOSED           Type: int
    static final WINDOW_ICONIFIED        Type: int
    static final WINDOW_DEICONIFIED      Type: int
    static final WINDOW_ACTIVATED        Type: int
```

printEventProperty() tells you three important things:

- The name of the interface that defines the listener—java.awt.event. WindowListener
- The name of the class that defines the event object passed to the listener— java.awt.event.WindowEvent
- The properties and fields associated with the event object

Let's look at windowDeactivated:

```
>>> printEventProperty(eProps[6])
Event Property:           windowDeactivated
Defined in:               java.awt.event.WindowListener
Event:                    java.awt.event.WindowEvent
Event properties for java.awt.event.WindowEvent:
    window              Type: org.python.core.PyBeanProperty
Public Event fields for java.awt.event.WindowEvent:
    static final WINDOW_FIRST            Type: int
    static final WINDOW_LAST             Type: int
    static final WINDOW_OPENED           Type: int
    static final WINDOW_CLOSING          Type: int
    static final WINDOW_CLOSED           Type: int
    static final WINDOW_ICONIFIED        Type: int
    static final WINDOW_DEICONIFIED      Type: int
    static final WINDOW_ACTIVATED        Type: int
    static final WINDOW_DEACTIVATED      Type: int
```

You might want to look up the rest of the event properties and traverse Frame's lineage until you reach a superclass called Object.

---

### Two Ways to Look Up Events with One Method

This one works best on Windows 98 because it pauses after each event:

```
>>> import jinfo
>>> from java.awt import Window
>>> jinfo.getEventsInfo(Window, 1, 1)
```

This one works best on Windows NT because you can scroll the DOS box to see the results:

```
>>> import jinfo
>>> from java.awt import Window
>>> jinfo.getEventsInfo(Window, 1)
```

**Table 13–1**   *Frame, JFrame, and Window Events*

| | |
|---|---|
| `windowOpened(WindowEvent e)` | The window is first opened. |
| `windowClosed(WindowEvent e)` | The Window is closed. |
| `windowClosing(WindowEvent e)` | The user is requesting to close the window— a good time to see if the user wants to save any unsaved data. |
| `windowActivated(WindowEvent e)` | The window is the active window; the window or one of its contained components have the keyboard focus. |
| `windowDeactivated(WindowEvent e)` | The window doesn't have keyboard focus. |
| `windowIconified(WindowEvent e)` | Invoked when the window is minimized. |
| `windowDeiconified(WindowEvent e)` | The window has been restored to its size before it was iconified. |

Table 13–1 lists and describes the events supported by `Frame`, `JFrame`, and `Window`. All of the event properties have a one-to-one correspondence to a method in their listener interface.

## Event Handling for Frame and JFrame

The following example demonstrates Java event handling for both `JFrame` and `Frame`. It also shows how to treat the two classes polymorphically.

Create a `Listener` class by extending the `java.awt.event.WindowListener` interface.

```
from java.awt.event import WindowListener

class Listener (WindowListener):
    def windowOpened(self, windowEvent):
        self.handleEvent("windowOpened",windowEvent)
    def windowClosed(self, windowEvent):
        self.handleEvent("windowClosed", windowEvent)
    def windowClosing(self, windowEvent):
        self.handleEvent("windowClosing",windowEvent)
    def WindowActivated(self, windowEvent):
        self.handleEvent("WindowActivated", windowEvent)
    def windowDeactivated(self, windowEvent):
        self.handleEvent("windowDeactivated", windowEvent)
    def windowIconified(self, windowEvent):
        self.handleEvent("windowIconified", windowEvent)
    def windowDeiconified(self, windowEvent):
        self.handleEvent("windowDeiconified", windowEvent)
    def handleEvent(self, event_name, event):
        print "Event: " + event_name
        print "Event info: " + `event.class`
        print "Source: " + `event.source.title`
        print "----------------"
```

> **Adapters**
>
> In the `Listener` code example, we were interested in all methods, so we used `Window Listener`. To save time you can derive the listener from `WindowAdapter` and only override the events that interest you.
>
> All listener classes have corresponding adapter classes. The best way to know if a particular event listener interface has a corresponding event listener class is to check the Java API documentation.

Essentially we've created a class that implements `java.awt.event.WindowListener`. We handle every event by calling the `handleEvent()` method, which prints out the event name, a string denoting which event occurred, the name of the event class that contains information regarding the event, and the source's title property.

Now we'll create two frames, `javax.swing.JFrame` and `java.awt.Frame`. Then we'll pass an instance of the listener class (`listener`) with `addWindowListener` to register the event listener with the event source. To create and set up the frames, I've created a function called `createFrame()`, which takes a class and a title as arguments. `CreateFrame()` uses the class to create an instance of `Frame` and then sets its size, title, and visibility. The reason we can use `createFrame()` is that, `JFrame` being derived from `Frame`, both implement the same interface.

Here's the `createFrame()` method (from *WindowEventListener.py*).

```
def createFrame(clazz, title, listener):
    frame = clazz()
    frame.addWindowListener(listener)
    frame.setSize(200, 200)
    frame.setTitle(title)
    frame.setVisible(1)
    return frame
```

Note that the call to `addWindowListener` registers an instance of the `Listener` class with a frame.

Now we'll use the `createFrame()` function to create both a `Frame` and a `JFrame`.

```
from java.awt import Frame
from javax.swing import JFrame
...
...
    listener = Listener()

    raw_input ("Press Enter to create a JFC Frame")
    jfc_frame = createFrame(JFrame, "JFC Frame", listener)

    raw_input ("Press Enter to create an AWT Frame")
    awt_frame = createFrame(Frame, "AWT Frame", listener)
```

Since the same `listener` instance is registered with both `Frame` and `JFrame`, it will get events from both.

Run the `WindowEventListener` class and, when it asks you to "Press Enter to create a JFC Frame," do so. You should see the following in the DOS box:

```
Event: WindowActivated
Event info: <jclass java.awt.event.WindowEvent at 1384027101>
Source: 'JFC Frame'
----------------
Event: windowOpened
Event info: <jclass java.awt.event.WindowEvent at 1384027101>
Source: 'JFC Frame'
----------------
```

When the window is first created, it sends the `WindowActivated` and `windowOpened` events.

Now return to where you ran the script; you should get the following message:

```
Event info: <jclass java.awt.event.WindowEvent at 1384027101>
Source: 'JFC Frame'
----------------
```

As you can see, the JFC frame is no longer active, so it sends out a `window Deactivated` event.

Now that the DOS box is the active window, hit Return. You should get the following messages:

```
Event: WindowActivated
Event info: <jclass java.awt.event.WindowEvent at 1408756942>
Source: 'AWT Frame'
----------------
Event: windowOpened
Event info: <jclass java.awt.event.WindowEvent at 1408756942>
Source: 'AWT Frame'
----------------
```

Move the AWT frame so that you can see the JFC frame as well. Select each a few times (by clicking once on their individual captions). As you go from one to the other, you should get the following messages:

```
Event: windowDeactivated
Event info: <jclass java.awt.event.WindowEvent
Source: 'JFC Frame'
----------------
Event: WindowActivated
Event info: <jclass java.awt.event.WindowEvent
Source: 'AWT Frame'
----------------
Event: windowDeactivated
Event info: <jclass java.awt.event.WindowEvent
Source: 'AWT Frame'
----------------
Event: WindowActivated
Event info: <jclass java.awt.event.WindowEvent
Source: 'JFC Frame'
----------------
```

If you minimize the JFC frame, you should get these messages in the DOS box:

```
Event: windowIconified
Event info: <jclass java.awt.event.WindowEvent
Source: 'JFC Frame'
----------------
Event: windowDeactivated
Event info: <jclass java.awt.event.WindowEvent
Source: 'JFC Frame'
----------------
Event: WindowActivated
Event info: <jclass java.awt.event.WindowEvent
Source: 'AWT Frame'
----------------
```

When the JFC frame is minimized, it sends out a `windowIconified` event followed by a `windowDeactivated` event. Since the AWT frame was the last active window, it becomes the active window again and sends out a `WindowActivated` event. If you can maximize the JFC frame, you'll get the following messages:

```
Event: windowDeactivated
Event info: <jclass java.awt.event.WindowEvent
Source: 'AWT Frame'
----------------
Event: WindowActivated
Event info: <jclass java.awt.event.WindowEvent
Source: 'JFC Frame'
----------------
Event: windowDeiconified
Event info: <jclass java.awt.event.WindowEvent
Source: 'JFC Frame'
----------------
```

First the AWT frame and then the JFC frame are deactivated; then the JFC frame sends a `windowDeactivated` event. Close the JFC frame by clicking on its close control (on Windows 95/98/NT, it's an X in the top right corner next to the caption). You should get the following messages:

```
Event: windowClosing
Event info: <jclass java.awt.event.WindowEvent
Source: 'JFC Frame'
----------------
Event: windowDeactivated
Event info: <jclass java.awt.event.WindowEvent
Source: 'JFC Frame'
----------------
Event: WindowActivated
Event info: <jclass java.awt.event.WindowEvent
Source: 'AWT Frame'
----------------
```

Now try to close the AWT frame using the same technique. What happens? Why?

The JFC frame's default method of closing a window is hiding the frame. Since the AWT frame doesn't handle the `windowClosing` event, you have to add a handler and do it yourself.

Unlike `java.awt.Frame`, `javax.swing.JFrame` responds when a user attempts to close a window. You can change the default behavior (hiding the frame) by invoking the `setDefaultCloseOperation()` method to make the frame exit the application. Look this up, as well as other default operation-closing methods, in the Java API documentation.

### The Complete Java Event-Handling Code

Here's the complete listing (*WindowEventListener.py*) for the Java way of handling events:

```python
from java.awt import Frame
from javax.swing import JFrame
from java.awt.event import WindowListener
class Listener (WindowListener):
    def windowOpened(self, windowEvent):
        self.handleEvent("windowOpened",windowEvent)
    def windowClosed(self, windowEvent):
        self.handleEvent("windowClosed", windowEvent)
    def windowClosing(self, windowEvent):
        self.handleEvent("windowClosing",windowEvent)
    def WindowActivated(self, windowEvent):
        self.handleEvent("WindowActivated", windowEvent)
    def windowDeactivated(self, windowEvent):
        self.handleEvent("windowDeactivated", windowEvent)
    def windowIconified(self, windowEvent):
        self.handleEvent("windowIconified", windowEvent)
    def windowDeiconified(self, windowEvent):
        self.handleEvent("windowDeiconified", windowEvent)
    def handleEvent(self, event_name, event):
        print "Event: " + event_name
        print "Event info: " + `event.class`
        print "Source: " + `event.source.title`
        #print "Event Properties: " + `dir(event)`
        print "-----------------"

    def createFrame(clazz, title, listener):
        frame = clazz()
        frame.addWindowListener(listener)
        frame.setSize(200, 200)
        frame.setTitle(title)
        frame.setVisible(1)
        return frame

    def main():
        listener = Listener()

        raw_input ("Press Enter to create a JFC Frame")
        jfc_frame = createFrame(JFrame, "JFC Frame", listener)
```

```
            raw_input ("Press Enter to create an AWT Frame")
            awt_frame = createFrame(Frame, "AWT Frame", listener)

    if __name__ == "__main__":
        main()
```

## The Python Way of Handling Events

The following brief interactive session highlights the Python way of handling events:

```
>>> def closing(event):
...      print "windowClosing"
...
>>> def closed(event):
...      print "windowClosed"
...
>>> def open(event):
...      print "windowOpened"
...
```

Import a JFrame, create an instance of it, and configure the instance.

```
>>> from javax.swing import JFrame
>>> frame = JFrame()
>>> frame.title = "JFrame frame"
>>> frame.size = 200,200
```

Set the event properties of the frame to the functions created.

```
>>> frame.windowClosing = closing
>>> frame.windowClosed = closed
>>> frame.windowOpened = open
```

Notice that the event properties windowClosing, windowClosed, and windowOpened correspond to the methods in the java.awt.WindowListener interface. Show the window for the first time to get the windowOpened event.

```
>>> frame.visible = 1
windowOpened
```

Close the frame using the Close button in the upper right corner to get the DOS box message.

```
windowClosing
```

Make the frame visible again. (You don't get another windowOpened event; that happens only when the frame becomes visible for the first time.)

```
>>> frame.visible = 1
```

Call the frame's dispose() method to actually close the window. You'll get a windowClosed event.

```
>>> frame.dispose()
windowClosed
```

As you can see, for just a few events you can define just a few event handlers and assign them to the event property of the `frame` instance. The event properties always correspond to the event listener's methods.

## Python's WindowEventListener

The following example illustrates the same functionality as in the *WindowEvent Listener.py* module, except that everything is written using Python event properties and handlers instead of the more Java-centric way of doing things. Read the code, and see if you can pick out the differences.

```python
from java.awt import Frame
from javax.swing import JFrame

def windowOpened(windowEvent):
    handleEvent("windowOpened",windowEvent)
def windowClosed(windowEvent):
    handleEvent("windowClosed", windowEvent)
def windowClosing(windowEvent):
    handleEvent("windowClosing",windowEvent)
def WindowActivated(windowEvent):
    handleEvent("WindowActivated", windowEvent)
def windowDeactivated(windowEvent):
    handleEvent("windowDeactivated", windowEvent)
def windowIconified(windowEvent):
    handleEvent("windowIconified", windowEvent)
def windowDeiconified(windowEvent):
    handleEvent("windowDeiconified", windowEvent)
def handleEvent(event_name, event):
    print "Event: " + event_name
    print "Event info: " + `event.class`
    print "Source: " + `event.source.title`
    #print "Event Properties: " + `dir(event)`
    print "-----------------"

def createFrame(clazz, title):
    frame = clazz()

    frame.windowClosing = windowClosing
    frame.windowOpened = windowOpened
    frame.windowClosed = windowClosed
    frame.windowIconified =    windowIconified
    frame.windowDeiconified = windowDeiconified
    frame.WindowActivated = WindowActivated
    frame.windowDeactivated = windowDeactivated

    frame.size = 200, 200
    frame.title = title
    frame.visible = 1
    return frame
```

```
def main():
    raw_input ("Press Enter to create a JFC Frame")
    jfc_frame = createFrame(JFrame, "JFC Frame")

    raw_input ("Press Enter to create an AWT Frame")
    awt_frame = createFrame(Frame, "AWT Frame")
if __name__ == "__main__":
    main()
```

I find myself using the Python way more often than the Java way, mainly because I have to import fewer classes and have to remember only the name of the event handler, not every method in the listener.

## The Class Hierarchy for JFrame and Frame

For review, let's cover the class hierarchy of JFrame and then Frame. Start up the interactive interpreter and follow along. To get the superclass of JFrame, import JFrame, and then inspect its superclass property.

```
>>> from javax.swing import JFrame
>>> JFrame.superclass
<jclass java.awt.Frame at 214168159>
```

To find out Frame's superclass, append another superclass to it. Since superclass is an instance of jclass and jclass has the property superclass, we can get the superclass of JFrame's superclass like this:

```
>>> JFrame.superclass.superclass
<jclass java.awt.Window at 217313887>
```

We can continue to do this until we hit Object.

```
>>> JFrame.superclass.superclass.superclass
<jclass java.awt.Container at 219411039>
```

```
>>> JFrame.superclass.superclass.superclass.superclass
<jclass java.awt.Component at 221770335>
```

```
>>> JFrame.superclass.superclass.superclass.superclass.superclass
<jclass java.lang.Object at -1247546800>
```

Unlike Python classes, Java programming language classes can only singly inherit from a superclass, so they have a narrow chain of superclasses. JFrame's class hierarchy looks like this:

```
Object → Component → Container → Window → Frame → JFrame
```

Frame's class hierarchy looks like this:

```
Object → Component → Container → Window → Frame
```

What's revealed is that JFrame and Frame inherit functionality from Container, Component, and Window. To find out more about these base classes and how they relate to JFrame and Frame, look them up in the Java API documentation.

### Component Functionality Inherited from JFrame and Frame

Now let's look at some of the functionality that JFrame and Frame get from Component. As always, follow along. Create a frame.

```
>>> from javax.swing import JFrame
>>> frame = JFrame()
>>> frame = JFrame(visible=1, size=(200,200))
```

From Component comes the ability to move the frame around the screen.

```
>>> from javax.swing import JFrame
>>> frame = JFrame()
>>> frame = JFrame(visible=1, size=(200,200))
```

The bounds() method takes four arguments: the x and y positions of the upper left corner of the frame and the frame's width and height. If you want to change the location of a frame without changing its width and height, use setLocation().

```
>>> frame.setLocation(50,50)
>>> frame.setLocation(0,0)
```

The background property from Component allows you to change the RGB (red-green-blue) value of the frame's background.

```
>>> frame.background = (255, 0 , 0)
```

```
>>> frame.background = (0, 255, 0)
```

```
>>> frame.background = (0, 0, 255)
```

```
>>> frame.background = (255, 255, 0)
```

Here are some other familiar properties that come from Component:

```
>>> frame.size = 150, 150
>>> frame.visible = 1
>>> frame.visible
1
```

## JPanel

Panels allow you to organize portions of a larger user interface within a frame, a dialog, or a window. Like frames (java.awt.Frame and javax.swing.JFrame), panels extend the java.awt.Container class, which means that they can contain other components. However, they can't exist on their own but must be in the context of a window, dialog, or frame, or in the context of another panel contained in a top-level window (like Dialog, Frame, or Window).

Here's a JFC/Swing example of adding components with JPanel, in which every time the Add button is pressed another button is added to a panel. Import JPanel and JFrame from the *javax.swing* package.

```
>>> from javax.swing import JPanel, JFrame, JButton
```

Create a frame variable in the global space of the main module. Also, create an instance of JPanel called pane, and initialize the count to 0.

```
>>> frame = None
>>> pane = JPanel()
>>> count = 0
```

Define an add() function that takes the global variables pane, count, and frame into its local namespace and adds a button to the panel called Pane. add() also increments the count variable, which keeps track of how many buttons are added.

```
>>> def add(event):
...     global pane
...     global count
...     global frame
...     count = count + 1
...     pane.add(JButton('Button' + `count`))
...     frame.pack()
...
```

Define a remove() function that removes the last button. This method uses the count variable (which is in the module namespace) to determine the last button removed.

```
>>> def remove(event):
...     global pane
...     global count
...     global frame
...     pane.remove(count-1)
...     count = count -1
...     frame.pack()
```

Supply an Add button (addB) to add a button to the pane and a Remove button (removeB) to remove a button. The event handler for the Add button is set to the add() function.

```
>>> addB = JButton ("Add", actionPerformed = add)
>>> removeB = JButton("Remove", actionPerformed = remove)
>>> pane.add(addB); pane.add(removeB)
>>> count = 2
```

Create a frame, and set its title to "Panel Demo." Set the content pane to the pane instance defined earlier, and make the frame visible.

```
>>> frame=JFrame(title="Panel Demo", contentPane=pane, visible=1)
>>> frame.pack()
```

Hit the Add button twice to add a third and a fourth button to the panel. Hit it two more times to add a fifth and a sixth button. Hit the Remove button twice to remove the fifth and sixth buttons. Hit the Add button a good 10 to 20 times, and then you can resize the frame with the mouse.

## JLabel

Labels are components for placing text in a container. From a user perspective, they're read-only, although their text can be changed programmatically. Let's have a short interactive session that demonstrates using javax.swing.JLabel.

Import the classes needed.

```
>>> from javax.swing import JLabel, JFrame
```

Create a frame to hold the label.

```
>>> frame = JFrame(visible=1, title="Label Demo")
```

Create the label, and add it to the frame; then pack the frame to make the label visible.

```
>>> label = JLabel("Hello World")#Create a label
>>> frame.contentPane.add(label) #add the label to the frame
>>> frame.pack()
```

For this next exercise we need to resize the window with the mouse so we can read all of the text in the frame caption (sometimes referred to as the titlebar). You can set the alignment of the label text for center, right, or left.

```
>>> label.horizontalAlignment = JLabel.CENTER
>>> label.horizontalAlignment = JLabel.RIGHT
>>> label.horizontalAlignment = JLabel.LEFT
```

## JComponent

JLabel is derived from JComponent, which is full of functionality such as the ability to set an icon or tooltip to a label. The following example illustrates some of the things you can do. Import the JLabel and JFrame classes.

```
>>> from javax.swing import JLabel, JFrame
```

Create a frame and a label; put the label in the frame's content pane.

```
>>> frame = JFrame(visible=1, title="JComponent/JLabel Demo")
>>> label = JLabel("JComponent/JLabel demo")
>>> frame.contentPane.add(label); frame.pack()
```

We'll use the label just created for the following exercises and examples.

## Working with Tooltips

The first `JLabel` we'll look at is `toolTip`, which provides help text about what a component does.

```
>>> label.toolTipText = "Tooltips are cool"
```

If you go to the frame and hover the mouse over the `JLabel` for a few seconds, a little window pops up with the message "Tooltips are cool."

## Color and the Opaque Property

The opaque property allows a component to set its own background color rather than use the color of the container's background (the default).

```
>>> label.opaque
0
```

The 0 (false) value tells us that the default is set, so the code above will change if we change the background.

```
>>> frame.contentPane.background = (255,0,0)
```

However, just changing the label background won't do anything. When we execute the following code setting the panel to green, the label stays the same:

```
>>> label.background = (0, 255, 0)
```

Instead, we have to set the opaque property to `true` (1). Once we do that, we'll get the right label color when the label background changes.

```
>>> label.opaque = 1
```

You can also set the foreground of a component.

```
>>> label.foreground = (255,255,255)
```

> ### *An Easier Way to Work with Colors*
>
> You don't have to remember the RGB values for your common colors. The `java.awt.Color` class makes working with colors pretty simple by defining the following constants:
>
> ```
> Color.black
> Color.blue
> Color.cyan
> Color.darkGray
> Color.gray
> Color.green
> Color.lightGray
> Color.magenta
> Color.orange
> ```

```
Color.pink
Color.red
Color.white
Color.yellow
```

Try this short exercise:

```
>>> from java.awt import Color      #import the color class
>>> label.background = Color.black    #set the background black
>>> label.foreground = Color.white    #set the foreground white
```

Now take a look at the frame that contains your label.

```
>>> label.foreground = Color.black    #set the foreground black
>>> label.background = Color.white    #set the background white
```

Unlike `javax.swing.JLabel`, `java.awt.Label` is pretty much always opaque and so has no opaque property. However, the foreground and background properties work the same for both.

## Fonts

`JComponent` has a font property that allows you to see what font the label is using. It works essentially the same in both `java.awt.Label` and `javax.swing.JLabel`.

```
>>> label.font
javax.swing.plaf.FontUIResource[family=dialog.bold,name=Dialog,style=bold,
    size=12]
```

`label.font` also allows you to set the label font.

```
>>> font = Font("Times New Roman", Font.BOLD, 12)
>>> label.font = font
```

### *Finding Fonts*

Import `GraphicsEnvironment`.

```
>>> from java.awt import GraphicsEnvironment
>>> ge = GraphicsEnvironment.getLocalGraphicsEnvironment()
```

Invoke `len()`.

```
>>> fontlist = ge.getAllFonts()
>>> len(fontlist)
98
>>> for x in range (0, 10):
...     print fontlist[x].name
...
```

Print the output.

```
Abadi MT Condensed Light
Arial
Arial Black
Arial Cursiva
Arial Narrow
Arial Narrow fed
Arial Narrow fed kursiv
Arial Narrow kursiv
Arial Negreta
Arial Negreta cursiva
```

To save space only the first ten fonts appear. To deal with large font lists we can start with the font families, which group fonts that have similar characteristics.

```
>>> families = ge.getAvailableFontFamilyNames()
>>> len(families)
62

>>> for x in range (0, 10):
...     print families[x]
...
Abadi MT Condensed Light
Arial
Arial Black
Arial Narrow
Book Antiqua
Bookman Old Style
Calisto MT
Century Gothic
Comic Sans MS
Copperplate Gothic Bold
```

To find out more about fonts, look up `java.awt.Font`; then try to create an italicized font.

## Icons

`JLabel` has an icon property that you can use to set an image in the label component.
Import `ImageIcon` from *javax.swing*.

```
>>> from javax.swing import ImageIcon
```

Create the image icon, and assign it to the icon property. (In this example, I used one of the images that ships with the JDK. You may have to adjust the file path if you installed the JDK somewhere else or if you're using a different JDK version.)

```
>>> label.icon = ImageIcon("c:\\jdk1.2.1\\demo\\jfc\\java2d\\images\\duke.gif")
>>> frame.pack()
```

Note that the `ImageIcon` constructor we're using takes a file path to an image. You can use any gif or jpeg image. You also can change the position of the text relative to the icon.

```
>>> label.horizontalTextPosition = JLabel.RIGHT
>>> label.verticalTextPosition = JLabel.TOP
```

Look up `setVerticalTextPosition` and `setHorizontalTextPosition` for `JLabel` in the Java API documentation; then move the label text to the bottom, to the right of the Duke icon.

Images make graphical user interfaces graphical. `JLabel` can easily display images as icons, but for `java.awt.Label` image display is not so simple.

## Mnemonics

Mnemonics allow users to select a component for input with the keyboard and can be displayed with labels. However, since labels can't do anything other than display text and images, they need the help of another component to receive the input, such as a container or text field. Here's how to set a mnemonic:

```
>>> label.setDisplayedMnemonic('J')
```

The first *J* is underlined, which signifies it as the mnemonic. `JLabel`'s `labelFor` property allows you to set the component that will receive the input focus when the mnemonic is pressed. On Windows, you activate the mnemonic by pressing Alt-J; on most UNIX boxes, you press meta-J.

Using `labelFor`, let's set up a few components and associate one of them with the label's mnemonic. Add two buttons to the frame, and set the layout so that the frame displays all of the components, that is, the two buttons and the label.

```
>>> from javax.swing import JButton      #import the JButton class
>>> j = JButton ("J button")             #create two buttons
>>> b2 = JButton ("button 2")
>>> frame.contentPane.add(j)             #add the buttons to the frame
>>> frame.contentPane.add(b2)
>>> from java.awt import FlowLayout      #import the FlowLayout class
>>> frame.contentPane.layout = FlowLayout() #set the layout
>>> frame.pack()                         #layout the components
```

Associate the label with the `J` button.

```
>>> label.labelFor = j
```

When you press Alt-J, the `J` button will receive the input focus. You can tell because its text becomes outlined in light gray. Now use the Tab key to put the focus on the `b2` button (the one with "button 2"). Most often, `labelFor` is assigned a text field or some other component that is incapable of displaying a mnemonic.

## *JButton*

We touched on buttons in Chapter 11. They're pretty simple, so we'll cover them here. Import the JFrame, JButton, Frame, and Button classes.

```
>>> from javax.swing import JFrame, JButton
>>> button = JButton("J Button")
>>> frame = JFrame(visible=1)
>>> frame.title = "JFC"
>>> frame.contentPane.add(button)
>>> frame.pack()
```

### Java Event Handling and JButton

To demonstrate Java event handling we'll create a class that implements Action Listener. Then, using addActionListener, we'll register an instance of the Listener class to the button.

Define the Listener class.

```
>>> from java.awt.event import ActionListener
>>> class ButtonListener(ActionListener):
...     def actionPerformed(self, e):
...             print e.getSource().getText() + " was clicked"
...
```

Create an instance of Listener, and register it with the button.

```
>>> listen = ButtonListener()
>>> button.addActionListener(listen)
```

Click the J button a few times to see the following message in the DOS box:

```
J button was clicked
J button was clicked
J button was clicked
```

### Python Event Handling and JButton

Again, since we covered Java event handling in Chapter 11, we'll just quickly review it here, continuing with the Java example. Define the event handler, which is just a function with an argument.

```
>>> def actionPerformed(e):
>>>    print "The Python event handler"
>>>    source = e.source
>>>    if source.class is JButton:
>>>            print source.text + " was clicked"
```

Assign the handler by setting the button's actionPerformed event property to the actionPerformed event.

```
>>> button.actionPerformed = actionPerformed
>>> def actionPerformed(e):
```

```
>>>    print "The Python event handler"
>>>    source = e.source
>>>    if source.class is JButton:
>>>            print source.text + " was clicked"
>>> button.actionPerformed = actionPerformed
```

Try the event handler by pressing the button with the mouse pointer. If you haven't been following along—as you should have been—read and run *buttons.py* in Chapter 12.

## Button and JButton Shared Properties

Using the enabled(Boolean b) property, disable the AWT and JFC buttons.

```
>>> button.enabled = 0
```

You'll notice that the buttons' text is grayed out. If you click on them, you won't get any action event. To enable the buttons again use:

```
>>> button.enabled = 1
```

There are some things you can do with java.swing.JButton that you can't do with java.awt.Button. For one, with the mnemonic (char mnemonic) property you can set the button so that it receives input focus when you press a shortcut key.

You can set up the frame to show more than one component and then add an extra component to it. Import FlowLayout (we'll get into layout managers in Chapter 14).

```
>>> from java.awt import FlowLayout
```

Add a second button to each of the frames.

```
>>> frame.contentPane.add(JButton("second button"))
```

Set the layout to FlowLayout so that the extra components are visible.

```
>>> frame.contentPane.layout = FlowLayout
```

Pack the frames so that the layout takes effect.

```
>>> frame.pack()
```

To see how the mnemonic property works, set it with JButton.

```
>>> button.setMnemonic('J')
>>> button.mnemonic = ord('J')    #Does the same as above
```

Go to the JFC frame, and use the Tab key to select the second button. Now type in Alt-J (meta-J on UNIX or apple-J on Mac). The result is that JButton will have input focus.

Want to try this with java.awt.Button? You can't. Mnemonics are a JFC-only feature. Another JFC exclusive is associating an image icon with a button. The icon property works just like its Jlabel counterpart.

```
icon (Icon defaultIcon)
```

Here's how you set an image in a button:

```
>>> from javax.swing import ImageIcon
>>> button.icon =
ImageIcon("c:\\jdk1.2.1\\demo\\jfc\\java2d\\images\\duke.gif")
>>> frame.pack()
```

You can also move the button's text in relation to its icon. Again, this works just like it does in JLabel, as we saw in an earlier example.

As an exercise, look up the properties for the JButton class; then create a button whose image changes when the mouse rolls over it. *Hint*: Check out javax.swing. AbstractButton, the superclass of JButton, particularly its setRolloverEnabled() and setRolloverIcon() methods. AbstractButton contains much of the functionality for JButton. It's also a base class for JCheckBox, JRadioButton, JMenuItem, and JToggle Button, which means that all of those classes can be used interchangeably (that is, polymorphically). Many of the methods and properties we use with JButton we can also use with any of AbstractButton's subclasses.

## JTextField

JTextField allows you to edit text in text fields. It's pretty basic and can be explained with a simple example. Import JTextField and JFrame from the *javax.swing* package.

```
>>> from javax.swing import JTextField
```

Create a frame and a text field, and add it to the frame. We'll use this text field to demonstrate how to set and read text. Create the frame.

```
>>> frame = JFrame()
```

Create the TextField instance.

```
>>> textField = JTextField(20)
```

Add the instance to the center of the frame.

```
>>> from java.awt import BorderLayout
>>> frame.add(textField, BorderLayout.CENTER)
```

> ### Default Layout Manager
> The default layout manager for the frame is BorderLayout, which essentially allows you to add components to a frame's north, south, east, and west borders and its center region. We'll cover it and the other layout managers in Chapter 14.

Now we'll create a toolbar, using a panel and two buttons, that will allow us to work with the text field's properties. Import Panel, and create a panel for a toolbar.

```
>>> from java.awt import Panel
>>> toolbar = Panel()
```

Create two buttons for setting and reading text field text.

```
>>> readText = JButton("Read Text")
>>> setText = JButton("Set Text")
```

Add the buttons to the toolbar.

```
>>> toolbar.add(readText)
>>> toolbar.add(setText)
```

Add the buttons to the north border of the frame.

```
>>> frame.add(toolbar, BorderLayout.NORTH)
```

Pack the frame to make the component layout visible.

```
>>> frame.pack()
>>> frame.visible = 1
```

Set up the button event handlers to manipulate the text field. This one reads the text and prints it out to the console window:

```
>>> def readTextClicked(e):
...     print textField.text
...
```

This one sets the text field text:

```
>>> def setTextClicked(e):
...     textField.text = "I really like Java and Python"
...
```

Associate the handlers with the `actionPerformed` event by assigning them to the button's `actionPerformed` property.

```
>>> readText.actionPerformed = readTextClicked
>>> setText.actionPerformed = setTextClicked
```

Enter in some text in the text field, and hit the Read Text button a few times

```
Hello how are you
Hello how are you
Hello how are you
```

Hit the Set Text, and then the Read Text button.

```
I really like Java and Python
I really like Java and Python
I really like Java and Python
```

Work with the buttons and the text field to verify that the field is working like `java.awt.TextField`.

Most of the functionality for JTextField is in JTextComponent. This is an abstract class and the superclass of JTextField and JTextArea (the latter represents a multi-line text field). JEditorPane and JTextPane are subclasses of JTextComponent; they add the ability to view HTML and RTF (Rich Text Format) text and to display in-text components and icons.

As an exercise, look up JTextField and JTextComponent in the Java API documentation. Try creating an application that uses JEditorPane to view an HTML page.

## JCheckBox

Checkboxes represent a true or false condition. Let's illustrate them with an example application for choosing pizza toppings (*jfc_checkbox.py*). Import java.awt. Checkbox, and create checkboxes that represent pizza toppings.

```
>>> from javax.swing import JCheckBox
>>> pepperoni = JCheckBox("pepperoni")
>>> peppers = JCheckBox("peppers")
>>> olives = JCheckBox("olives")
>>> anchovies = JCheckBox("anchovies")
>>> onions = JCheckBox ("onions")
>>> sausage = JCheckBox ("sausage")
```

Create a frame to put the checkboxes in.

```
>>> from java.swing import JFrame
>>> frame = JFrame(title="Pick your topping", visible = 1)
```

Add the checkboxes to the frame.

```
>>> frame.contentPane.add(pepperoni)
>>> frame.contentPane.add(peppers)
>>> frame.contentPane.add(olives)
>>> frame.contentPane.add(anchovies)
>>> frame.contentPane.add(onions)
>>> frame.contentPane.add(sausage)
```

Set pepperoni as the default.

```
>>> pepperoni.selected = 1
```

Remember that the default layout for a frame is BorderLayout. If we want to show all of the checkboxes created, we need to reset the layout manager to FlowLayout.

```
>>> from java.awt import FlowLayout
>>> frame.contentPane.layout = FlowLayout()
>>> frame.pack()
```

Set the event handler for closing the frame to inspect the checkboxes' state.

```
>>> def frameClosing(event):
...      for checkbox in frame.components:
...              if(checkbox.selected == 1): print checkbox.label
...
>>> frame.windowClosing = frameClosing
```

Work with the checkboxes to select toppings; then press the Close button on the frame's top left border (for Windows NT/9X).

```
pepperoni
onions
sausage
```

## Putting Things Together with JCheck Box

Here's the pizza topping application we just wrote. Follow along, and make sure to read the comments.

```
    # Import JCheckBox and create checkboxes that represent pizza toppings.
from javax.swing import JCheckBox
cb = JCheckBox

#cb is the JCheckBox class. Remember classes are first class objects in Python.
pepperoni = cb("pepperoni")
checkboxes=(pepperoni,cb("peppers"),cb("olives"),cb("anchovies"),cb("onions")
        ,cb("sausage"))

    # Import JFrame and create a frame to hold our checkboxes.
from javax.swing import JFrame
frame = JFrame(title="Pick your topping", visible = 1)

    # Import JPanel and set the frame's contentPane to a JPanel.
from javax.swing import JPanel
panel = JPanel()
frame.contentPane = panel

    # Now add the checkboxes to the Panel
for a_checkbox in checkboxes:
    panel.add(a_checkbox)

    # Set the pepperoni's state to selected.
pepperoni.selected = 1

    # Pack the frame
frame.pack()
def frameClosing(event):
    for checkbox in checkboxes:
        if(checkbox.selected == 1): print checkbox.text

frame.windowClosing = frameClosing
```

Now we want to offer a one-topping special, which means that we have to change the program so that the customer can select only one checkbox. (The changes are highlighted in bold.) Add each checkbox to a button group.

```
frame.title = "Choose your one Topping"

    #Import the ButtonGroup
from javax.swing import ButtonGroup
group = ButtonGroup()

    #Add each check box to the group.
for a_checkbox in checkboxes:
group.add(a_checkbox)

    # Now let's assume that most people want pepperoni.
pepperoni.selected = 1
```

It doesn't work, does it? Read on.

## JRadioButton

With JFC, to make the buttons look and behave like radio buttons, you have to
use JRadioButton. Let's continue our one-topping example, using JRadioButton in
a button group to allow only one checkbox to be selected.

```
for a_checkbox in checkboxes:
    panel.remove(a_checkbox)

group = ButtonGroup()

from javax.swing import JRadioButton
rb = JRadioButton    #rb is JRadioButton class.
    #Remember classes are first class objects in Python.
pepperoni = rb("pepperoni")

radiobuttons=(pepperoni,rb("peppers"),rb("olives"),rb("anchovies"),
            rb("onions"),rb("sausage"))

for a_radiobutton in radiobuttons:
    group.add(a_radiobutton)
    panel.add(a_radiobutton)

pepperoni.selected = 1
frame.pack()
```

Try these exercises:

- Change the event handler to work with JRadioButton, and then look up
  AbstractButton, the superclass of JButton, JCheckBox, and JRadioButton. You
  might also try adding picture icons to represent the different toppings.
- With the technique we used to replace checkboxes with radio buttons, replace
  radio buttons with toggle buttons (javax.swing.JToggleButton). Can you
  think of ways to switch between all three? *Hint*: JToggleButton has the same
  properties that JCheckBox and JRadioButton have. Remember that JButton gets
  much of its functionality from AbstractButton, so all of its properties—icon,

text, mnemonics, and so forth—work for these classes as well. If you want to add icons or change text, you do it in the same way.

## List and JList

List components represent choices. They can be in single-selection mode (one item) or multi-selection mode (more than one item). Let's create an example list in the interactive interpreter.

```
>>> from javax.swing import JList
>>> list_items = ["Bruce", "Darrell", "Tony", "Debbie", "Karen"]
>>> list = JList(list_items)
```

Here's the interactive session to create a frame:

```
>>> from javax.swing import JFrame
>>> frame = JFrame("JList example")
>>> frame.contentPane.add(list)
>>> frame.pack()
>>> frame.visible=1
```

### List Events

Now we want to do something with our list—that is, handle the list events—so we need to inspect JList's event properties (or look them up in the Java API documentation).

Here's the interactive session to inspect the list properties, with the output formatted to make it a little more readable.

```
>>> getEventsInfo(JList)
[<beanEventProperty valueChanged for event interface
javax.swing.event.ListSelectionListener>]
```

We can inspect the events more closely using getEventsInfo to print and pause.

```
>>> getEventsInfo(JList, 1, 1)
Event Property:         valueChanged
Defined in:             javax.swing.event.ListSelectionListener
Event:                  javax.swing.event.ListSelectionEvent

Event properties for javax.swing.event.ListSelectionEvent:
    lastIndex           Type: org.python.core.PyBeanProperty
    valueIsAdjusting    Type: org.python.core.PyBeanProperty
    firstIndex          Type: org.python.core.PyBeanProperty
```

If you look up the list properties in the Java API documentation, these are the ones you'll find:

- LastIndex—last row that may have changed
- ValueIsAdjusting—true if this is multiple change events
- FirstIndex—first row that may have changed

ListSelectionEvent allows handling of an item selection event, either the Java way or the Python way. Here's the Python way:

```
>>> def eventListener(event):
...     list = event.source # get a reference to the list,
...                         # the event's source
...     index = event.firstIndex
...     print list.model.getElementAt(index)
...
```

Now try selecting some list items.

I'm going to leave the Java way as an exercise. I'll give you two hints to help you, but don't read them unless you get stuck. *Hint 1*: Create a class that subclasses java.awt.event.ItemListener; then create an instance of that class, and pass it to the list.addItemListener() method. *Hint 2*: The subclass should override the itemStateChanged() method with the arguments self and event.

## JComboBox

JComboBox is a combination dropdown list and text field that comes in handy when you have limited real estate on a panel. It's something of a cross between java.swing.JList and javax.swing.JTextField. In fact, JComboBox looks a lot like javax.swing.JList, its only real difference being that it uses the addItem() method to add items to the list.

Here's the JComboBox code:

```
# Import List, create a list instance and populate the list instance.
from javax.swing import JComboBox
list = JComboBox()
list_items = ("Bruce", "Darrell", "Tony", "Satesh", "Debbie", "Karen")

for item in list_items:
    list.addItem()()(item)

    # Create a frame and add the list to the frame.
from javax.swing import JFrame
frame = JFrame("Combobox Example")
frame.contentPane.add(list); frame.visible=1; frame.pack()

    # Handle item event.
from java.awt.event import ItemEvent
def eventListener(event):
    list = event.itemSelectable
    item = event.item
    print "Current item :" + `item`
    if (event.stateChange == ItemEvent.SELECTED):
        print " --selected items--"
        for item in list.selectedObjects:
            print " " + `item`
list.itemStateChanged = eventListener
```

It's a little different from the JList version, but close enough.

As an exercise, try changing the previous example to make the combo box editable. *Hint*: Look up the JComboBox properties and methods, particularly setEditable.

## Working with JList

The Model View Controller (MVC) architecture splits the logic for the model, view, and controller into different class sets. For example, the JList component constructor takes a reference to ListModel. Here's an example of JList (*JList.py*) that's similar to our JComboBox example:

```
    # Import List, create a list instance and populate the list instance.
from javax.swing import JList

list_items = ("Bruce", "Darrell", "Tony", "Debbie", "Karen")

    # Create a list with a default model that uses the above list items
list = JList(list_items)

    # Create a frame and add the list to the frame.
from javax.swing import JFrame
frame = JFrame("JList Example")
frame.contentPane.add(list); frame.visible=1; frame.pack()

    # Import this for selection constants
from javax.swing import ListSelectionModel
list.selectionMode = ListSelectionModel.MULTIPLE_INTERVAL_SELECTION

    # Handle item event.
from java.awt.event import ItemEvent
def eventListener(event):
    list = event.source
    print "Current item :" + list.selectedValue
    if (list.selectionMode ==
ListSelectionModel.MULTIPLE_INTERVAL_SELECTION):
        print " --selected items--"
        for item in list.selectedValues:
            print " " + `item`

list.valueChanged = eventListener
```

I said that JList was similar to JComboBox, but there are differences (highlighted in bold). First, JList has no addItem() (or equivalent) method to add items to the list, so we have to pass list_item to the constructor (we could have passed it to the java.awt.List constructor). Second, we have to import javax.swing.ListSelection Model to get access to the constants to set selectionMode. selectionMode allows three types of selection: single (one item), single contiguous range (a set of items next to each other), and multiple interval (multiple items). Third, the Jlist and JComboBox event properties are different.

As an exercise, look up javax.swing.ListSelectionModel in the Java API documentation, and inspect the event properties of JList with jinfo. Then look up the listener and event classes associated with them. Change the last example to use Java event handling.

The output for our `JList` example is as expected.

```
Current item :Karen
  ----selected items----
    'Karen'
Current item :Tony
  ----selected items----
    'Tony'
    'Karen'
Current item :Bruce
  ----selected items----
    'Bruce'
    'Tony'
    'Karen'
```

Try to map the output to the code.

Don't you think it's a little strange not to have an `addItem()`method? I do. Remember that `JList` uses the MVC architecture, which keeps the data from view by putting it in the model (the M in MVC). The view (the V in MVC) is the `JList` itself. If you pass a vector (a sequence in Python) or an array, `JList` will create a model based on `AbstractListModel`.

If you want to create an easy-to-use list similar to `java.awt.List` (which is much easier than `JList`), you can pass `JList` an instance of `DefaultListModel`. `Default ListModel` is mutable, so you can add items to it that will show up in the list.

Here's an example (`JList_Model`) of creating a mutable list based on our `java.swing.JComboBox` example. I've highlighted the differences in bold and omitted the last part, which doesn't change.

```
    # Import List, create a list instance and populate the list instance.
from javax.swing import JList, DefaultListModel

list_items = ("Bruce", "Darrell", "Tony", "Satesh", "Debbie", "Karen")

    # Create a list with an empty default model
list = JList(DefaultListModel)
model = list.getModel()

for item in list_items:
    model.addElement(item)
...
...
```

### An Easier Way with DefaultListModel

Since `model` is a property of `Jlist`, an easier way to write the above would have been

```
list = JList(DefaultListModel())

for item in list_items:
    list.model.addElement(item)
```

I wrote it the way I did to highlight where the model was coming from.

As an exercise try the `JList_Model` example again, without an instance of `DefaultListModel`, and pass it to the `JList` constructor. What happens? Why? *Hint*: Look up `AbstractDefaultListModel`, and inspect the class hierarchy returned from the `getModel()` method.

## Advanced MVC and JList

The real advantage to using MVC is that you can have multiple views of the same data model. When the data changes, the model notifies all of the views so that they're updated.

Remember our address book application? We can create a list data model that uses it, so that when an address changes in the list we can automatically display the change in all open views. To create a data model that's compatible with `JList`, we need to implement the `ListModel` interface.

For brevity, we're going to create a very small subset of the `Address` and `Address Book` classes that highlights the MVC list.

What we'll do is define an address class that implements the `toString()` method from `java.lang.Object` so that it can be displayed in the listbox. Next we'll define an `AddressBook` class that contains instances of `Address` and acts as a data model. It will have to extend `ListModel` to work with `javax.swing.JList`. Finally, we'll populate an address book—the data model—with sample addresses.

> ### *MVC in JTree and JTable*
>
> The techniques I'm showing you in the MVC example are the same ones you use with `JTree` and `JTable`. You have to master them if you want to use advanced Swing components.
>
> MVC, along with the related design patterns (e.g., Observer/Observable), is explained in *Design Patterns* (Gamma et al., 1995). Reading this book will make you appreciate why MVC was picked for `JList`, `JTable`, and `JTree`.

## JList_AddressModel.py

Here's the complete code for *JList_AddressModel.py*.

```python
from string import *
from javax.swing import JList, ListModel
from javax.swing.event import ListDataEvent
from java.lang import Object

    # Define an address class to hold an address
class Address(Object):
    def __init__(self, name, phone):
        self.name = name
        self.phone = phone
    def __str__(self):
        return ljust(self.name,35) + ": " + self.phone
```

```
    def toString(self):
        return self.__str__()
    def __repr__(self):
        return self.__str__()

    # Define an address book to hold addresses
class AddressBook(ListModel):
    def __init__(self):

            # Fill in some initial data
        self.list_items = [Address("Darrell", "555-1212")]
        self.list_items.append(Address("Bruce", "555-1212"))
        self.list_items.append(Address("Karen", "555-1212"))
        self.list_items.append(Address("Tony", "555-1212"))
        self.list_items.append(Address("Chris", "555-1212"))

        self.listeners = []      # To hold listeners

        # public int getSize()
        # Returns the length of the list.
    def getSize(self):
        return len(self.list_items)
        #      public Object getElementAt(int index)
        # Returns the value at the specified index.
    def getElementAt(self, index):
        return self.list_items[index]

        # public void addListDataListener(ListDataListener l)
        # Add a listener that gets notified when the list data
        # model gets changed
        # Parameters:
        # l - the ListDataListener
    def addListDataListener(self, listener):
        print "somebody is listening: " + `listener.class`
        self.listeners.append(listener)

        # public void RemoveListDataListener(ListDataListener l)
        # Removes a listener
        # Parameters:
        # l - the ListDataListener
    def RemoveListDataListener(listener):
        print "somebody is ignoring: " + `listener.class`
        self.listeners.remove(listener)

        # AddAddress()
        # Adds an address to the address book
    def AddAddress (self, name, number):
        self.list_items.append(Address(name, number))

            # Notify each listener that our data has changed.
            # Being aware that our data changed, they can
            # update their view to reflect the changes
        for each_listener in self.listeners:
            start = len(self.list_items)
            end = len(self.list_items)
            type = ListDataEvent.INTERVAL_ADDED
```

```
                event = ListDataEvent(self, type, start, end)
                each_listener.intervalAdded(event)

AddressBook = AddressBook()

     # Create 2 lists using our address book list model
list = JList(AddressBook)
list2 = JList(AddressBook)

     # Create a frame and add the lists to the frame.
from javax.swing import JFrame
from java.awt import FlowLayout
frame = JFrame("JList Custom Data Model Example")
frame.contentPane.layout = FlowLayout() #Added to show both lists
frame.contentPane.add(list); frame.contentPane.add(list2)
frame.visible=1; frame.pack()

     #Import this for selection constants
from javax.swing import ListSelectionModel
list.selectionMode = ListSelectionModel.MULTIPLE_INTERVAL_SELECTION

     #Handle item event.
from java.awt.event import ItemEvent
def eventListener(event):
    list = event.source
    print "Current item :" + `list.selectedValue`
    if (list.selectionMode ==
ListSelectionModel.MULTIPLE_INTERVAL_SELECTION):
        print " --selected items--"
        for item in list.selectedValues:
            print " " + `item`

list.valueChanged = eventListener

def addNames():
    AddressBook.AddAddress("Geoff", "555-1234")
    AddressBook.AddAddress("Bill", "555-1235")
    AddressBook.AddAddress("Robert", "555-1257")
```

Run the following in the interactive interpreter:

```
>>> addNames()
>>> frame.pack()
```

First, we define the Address class.

```
     # Define an address class to hold an address
class Address(Object):
    def __init__(self, name, phone):
        self.name = name
        self.phone = phone
    def __str__(self):
        return ljust(self.name,35) + ": " + self.phone
    def toString()(self):
        return self.__str__()
    def __repr__(self):
        return self.__str__()
```

Address defines three methods: __str__, __repr__, and toString(). __str__creates the string representation of Address for Python; toString() is its Java equivalent. We need to make Address a string because the listbox uses toString() to display the method. __repr__displays the string in Python when the object is referenced with back quotes. To override toString(), Address uses java.lang.Object as its base class.

Next we define the custom list model, which presents an interesting opportunity to demonstrate events. In previous event examples, our code was geared to listening for (handling) events. In this example, it publishes events (AddressBook is an event source). To turn things inside out, JList will be registering a listener with AddressBook to listen for events that tell it that data has changed.

AddressBook implements ListMode; AddressBook is thus a subclass (in Python speak) of ListModel.

```
    # Define an address book to hold addresses
class AddressBook(ListModel):
```

AddressBook has to override all of ListModel's methods, which are

- int    getSize()
- Object getElementAt(int index)
- void   addListDataListener(ListDataListener l)
- void   RemoveListDataListener(ListDataListener l)

In the code that follows, be sure to read all of the comments before each AddressBook method, since they show which ListModel method is being overridden and what it does.

```
    # public int getSize()
    # Returns the length of the list.
def getSize(self):
    return len(self.list_items)

    # public Object getElementAt(int index)
    # Returns the value at the specified index.
def getElementAt(self, index):
    return self.list_items[index]

    # public void addListDataListener(ListDataListener l)
    # Add a listener that gets notified when the list
    # data model gets changed
    # Parameters:
    # l - the ListDataListener
def addListDataListener(self, listener):
    print "somebody is listening: " + `listener.class`
    self.listeners.append(listener)

    # public void RemoveListDataListener(ListDataListener l)
    # Removes a listener
    # Parameters:
    # l - the ListDataListener
```

```
def removeListDataListener(listener):
    print "somebody is ignoring: " + `listener.class`
    self.listeners.remove(listener)
```

addListDataListener and removeListDataListener register and unregister listeners for ListDataEvents from AddressBook (which, you'll remember, is an event source, which means that it publishes events when they occur). addListDataListener prints out a listener's registration. When you set a model, JList registers listeners to it; when you remove a model, JList unregisters those listeners.

The AddressBook class has the AddAddress()method, which adds a new address to list_items and then notifies each listener by calling its intervalAdded() method. AddAddress() first creates a ListDataEvent instance to pass to the listener's interval Added() method.

```
    Rest of 85, 86, top 87# AddAddress()
    # Adds an address to the address book
def AddAddress(self, name, number):
    self.list_items.append(Address(name, number))

    # Notify each listener that our data has changed.
    # Being aware that our data changed, they can
    # update their view to reflect the changes
for each_listener in self.listeners:
    start = len(self.list_items)
    end = len(self.list_items)
    type = ListDataEvent.INTERVAL_ADDED
    event = ListDataEvent(self, type, start, end)
    each_listener.intervalAdded()(event)
```

Now we'll create an instance of AddressBook. Then we'll create two JFC lists, passing the instance to them. At this point, the JList instance will call addData Listener to register listeners with the model. You can verify this with the console output.

```
AddressBook = AddressBook()
    #Create 2 lists using our address book list model
list = JList(AddressBook)
list2 = JList(AddressBook)
```

The rest of the code for this example is pretty much the same as that for the earlier ones. As a final step, we'll define a function called addNames() that adds three addresses to the AddressBook list model.

```
def addNames():
    AddressBook.AddAddress("Geoff", "555-1234")
    AddressBook.AddAddress("Bill", "555-1235")
    AddressBook.AddAddress("Robert", "555-1257")
```

AddAddress()notifies all the listeners that an address has been added. (The listeners are the two JList components.)

To run this example from the interactive interpreter, start *JList_AddressModel.py* with the –i option. Then call `AddAddress()` from the interactive interpreter.

```
>>> addNames()
>>> frame.pack()
```

Both of the lists are updated because they use the same example. (You have to call the `frame.pack()` method to resize `JList` so that all of the items appear. We'll fix this in the next example).

As an exercise, look up `javax.swing.ListModel`, `javax.ListDataEvent`, and `javax.ListDataListener`.

Essentially, `JList` registers for (that is, subscribes to) events in `ListModel`. When the model data changes (that is, when addresses are added to the address book), all registered views are notified and thus updated.

In the previous example, both views are `JList` components; however, in a real MVC application the same model may have more than one view type. For example, a spreadsheet application may have data mapped to a spreadsheet view and a graph view, both of which change when the model for the spreadsheet view changes.

### An Easier Way to Create the Address Book

An easier way to create the address book is to use the `AbstractListModel` class, which implements all of the methods for registering event listeners and notifying them of changes. Here's the changed `JList_AddressModel` (*JList_AddressModel2.py*), which uses `AbstractListModel` for the superclass of `AddressBook`.

```python
class AddressBook(AbstractListModel):
    def __init__(self):

            # Fill in some sample data
        self.list_items = [Address("Darrell", "555-1212")]
        ...

        ...
        self.list_items.append(Address("Chris", "555-1212"))

        # public int getSize()
        # Returns the length of the list.
    def getSize(self):
        return len(self.list_items)

        # public Object getElementAt(int index)
        # Returns the value at the specified index.
    def getElementAt(self, index):
        return self.list_items[index]

    def AddAddress(self, name, number):
        self.list_items.append(Address(name, number))
        start = len(self.list_items)
```

```
        end = len(self.list_items)
        fireIntervalAdded(self, type, start, end)
```

Notice that the code to implement AddressBook (ListModel) is now significantly shorter. I recommend using the AbstractListModel class instead of the ListModel interface, which I used simply to explain MVC.

### Working with JScrollPane and the Decorator Design Pattern

The JList class uses Gamma's Decorator design pattern to add scrolling, which essentially adds a JFC frame to a scroll pane by passing a JList instance to JScroll Pane's constructor. Thus, the code changes from this:

```
list = JList(AddressBook)
list2 = JList(AddressBook)
```

to this:

```
list = JScrollPane(JList(AddressBook))
list2 = JScrollPane(JList(AddressBook)
```

That's all. The same technique works for adding scrolling to JTree and JTable. When you run this in the interactive interpreter, you don't have to call frame.pack() after you call addNames(). The names show up automatically, and so do the scroll-bars.

Now start *JList_AddressModel2.py* with the -i option. Then call the AddAddress() method from the interactive interpreter.

```
>>> addNames()
>>> frame.pack()
```

## *Summary*

In this chapter, we covered the basics of AWT and JFC components, some of which are polymorphically related. We also covered MVC, which, although advanced, is essential for working with some of the more interesting components of JFC. Learning MVC is good for learning about events, since the architecture publishes events to views.

There's a lot more to cover on JFC and AWT, but we've gleaned enough information to get started. We'll learn more in coming chapters.

# First Swing Application, Layout, and Menus

In the last chapter, we covered Swing with short code snippets; in this chapter, we'll build an example Swing application. Snippets are great for learning how to use an API, but to see how things really come together you need a more involved example.

We'll continue with the address book application, but we'll start off with minimal features and add more as we put the application together, gradually showing more of Java GUI programming like menus and layout managers. Before we add any features, though, we'll do a prototype in an interactive session to give you hands-on, instant gratification.

## Putting Things Together with Basic Java GUIs

As promised, we're going to extend the address book application with a GUI front end. For this extension we'll use *Address5.py* ,which is based on *Address4.py* from Chapter 8 with a few changes, all within the readAddresses() and writeAddresses() functions. One change is the use of ObjectOutputStream instead of the Python *pickle* module; another is the introduction of the __repr__ method for the Address class, which allows us to create address objects with `eval` and makes the printing of dictionaries more meaningful.

As an exercise, run the `text_read_write()` function in `readAddresses()` and `writeAddresses()` in both files. What differences do you notice in the output? How are these differences related to `__repr__`? Also try creating one instance of `Address` using the `eval` function and the return value from `__repr__` of another instance.

## Adding an Input Form for an Address Entry: The Prototype

In an interactive session, let's create a GUI form that can edit an address entry. We want a frame that holds text field components, which will be used to gather the address information. We also want an OK button, which signifies that the user is done entering the current address.

To get the layout for the frame components, we'll use a technique that layers components in a container. For this we'll put the text fields in one panel and the OK button in another. The panels themselves are components that we'll put in the frame.

The first thing we need to do is import the `JFrame`, `JButton`, and `JTextField` classes from *javax.swing*.

```
>>> from javax.swing import JFrame
>>> from javax.swing import JButton, JTextField
```

Next we create a frame with the titlebar set to "Address Entry," create an OK button and a panel to hold it, set the frame's layout to `BorderLayout`, and add the panel to the south region of the frame. Then we pack the frame and look at the results.

```
>>> frame = JFrame("Address Entry", visible=1)
>>> okay = JButton("OK")
>>> from javax.swing import JPanel
>>> buttonbar = JPanel()
>>> buttonbar.add(okay)
>>> from java.awt import BorderLayout
>>> frame.contentPane.add(buttonbar, BorderLayout.SOUTH)
>>> frame.pack()
```

### Adding Text Fields

Now we want to add text fields to the frame. There may be many of them, and the frame is using `BorderLayout`, which can hold only five components (EAST, WEST, NORTH, SOUTH, and CENTER). Therefore, we add the fields to another panel, which we place in the CENTER region of the frame. We'll use `GridLayout` for the layout manager of the panel, which will lay the components out in a grid. As we add fields, we'll label them so that the user knows what each one represents. We'll do this by adding instances of the `Label` class near the corresponding text field.

Import `GridLayout`, and create an instance of it that lays out components in a 2-by-2 grid. Create a panel to hold the text fields called `contentPane`. Set the layout of `contentPane` to the `GridLayout` instance.

```
>>> from java.awt import GridLayout
>>> grid = GridLayout(2,2)
>>> contentPane = JPanel()
>>> contentPane.setLayout(grid)
```

Create a `JTextField` instance called `name`. Import the `Label` class, create an instance of it, and add it to `contentPane`. Add the name `JTextField` to the panel. Then pack the frame, and look at the results.

```
>>> name = JTextField()
>>> from java.swing import JLabel
>>> contentPane.add(JLabel("Name"))
>>> contentPane.add(name)
>>> frame.pack()
>>> frame.contentPane.add(contentPane, BorderLayout.CENTER)
>>> frame.pack()
```

Now use the same technique to add phone number and email text fields.

Add the phone number field.

```
>>> phoneNumber = JTextField()
>>> contentPane.add(JLabel("Phone Number"))
>>> contentPane.add(phoneNumber)
```

Add the email field.

```
>>> email = JTextField()
    >>> contentPane.add(JLabel("eMail"))
    >>> contentPane.add(email)
    >>> frame.pack()
```

## Adding Event Handlers

We could improve our form by setting the labels' alignment to the right, but pretty interfaces are only the start. For the form to be useful, we need to set up the event handlers. This is just the prototype, so the event handlers will access the text field component data but only print it to the console.

To set up the event handler for the OK button, we need to define an event handler that takes one argument to hold the event.

Create a function that acts as an event handler for the OK button.

```
>>> def okayHandler(event):
...     global name, email, phoneNumber
...     print (name.text, email.text, phoneNumber.text)
...
```

Register the `okayHandler()` function with the OK button's `actionPerformed` event property.

```
>>> okay.actionPerformed = okayHandler
```

Now we have a working prototype. Try it out by entering a name, a phone number, and an email address, and then hit the OK button.

## *Adding an Input Form for an Address Entry: First Cut*

At this point, you probably feel comfortable with the concepts the prototype introduces. To incorporate these concepts into the address book program, let's organize our code into a class called AddressForm. This class extends the javax.swing.JFrame class, which makes it a JFrame.

AddressForm is passed an instance of the Address class in its constructor. okay-Handler() populates the fields of the instance with values extracted from Address-Form's text fields. Look at *Address6.py* below and make sure to read all of the comments.

```
from javax.swing import JFrame, JButton, JTextField, JLabel, JPanel
from java.awt import BorderLayout, GridLayout
        # AddressForm Class.

        # This class is used to edit an instance of the Address class
class AddressForm(JFrame):
        def __init__(self, address):
            """Constructor for the AddressForm class \n """
                # Call constuctor
            JFrame.__init__(self, "Address Entry", visible=1)

                # Declare private variables
            self.__address = address #hold address to be edited
            self.__name = NONE    #hold the private name textfield
            self.__email = NONE    #hold the private email textfield
            self.__phoneNumber = NONE #hold the private phone# field

            self.__init__CreateButtonBar()
            self.__init__CreateTextFieldPanel()

        def __init__CreateButtonBar(self):
            """ Create okay button, a panel for the button. \n """
            """    Add the button panel to this frame.           """
            okay = JButton("OK")
            buttonbar = JPanel()
            buttonbar.add(okay)
            self.contentPane.add(buttonbar, BorderLayout.SOUTH)

                # Set the event handler for the okay button.
            okay.actionPerformed = self.__okayHandler

        def __init__CreateTextFieldPanel(self):
            """ Set up the email, phoneNumber and name text fields """

                # Create the panel and set the grid layout.
                # The grid has a layout of a
```

```
                      # 3 row by 2 column grid.
            editPane = JPanel()
            editPane.setLayout(GridLayout(3,2))
            self.contentPane.add(editPane, BorderLayout.CENTER)

                      # Create the name textfield and add it and its
                      # associated label to the contentPane.
                      # Note that name is a member of AddressForm
            self.__name = JTextField()
            editPane.add(JLabel("Name"))
            editPane.add(self.__name)

                      # Create the phoneNumber textfield and add it and its
                      # associated label to the contentPane.
                      # Note that phoneNumber is a member of AddressForm.
            self.__phoneNumber = JTextField()
            editPane.add(JLabel("Phone Number"))
            editPane.add(self.__phoneNumber)

                      # Create the email textfield and add it and its
                      # associated label to the contentPane.
                      # Note that email is a member of AddressForm.
            self.__email = JTextField()
            editPane.add(JLabel("eMail"))
            editPane.add(self.__email)
            self.pack()

            #Defines the event handler for the okay button
        def __okayHandler(self, event):
            """Event handler for the okay button"""
            print (self.__name.text, self.__email.text,
                   self.__phoneNumber.text)
            Address.__init__(self.__address, self.__name.text,
                             self.__phoneNumber.text, self.__email.text)
            print self.__address
```

Try adding the ability to edit the address lines of the Address class and to right-align the labels that describe the text fields.

---

## Adding a Main Window for the Address Book Application: Prototype

The main window will have a list of names from the address book. As you select a name from the list, an AddressForm instance pops up in which you edit the Address instance corresponding to that name.

As a rule, code written to access data shouldn't be in the same module with code written to build GUIs, so first we have to break our code into separate modules:

- *AddressForm.py*—holds the AWT version of AddressForm
- *Address7.py*—holds the address data code

- *AddressMain.py*—holds the main window of the code
- *AddressFormPane.py*—holds the AWT panel version of `AddressForm`

The first step is creating a frame that acts as the main window and then adding a list to it. Then we pack the frame and make it visible.

Import `JFrame` and `JList` from *javax.swing*.

```
>>> from javax.swing import JFrame, JList
```

Create instances of `JFrame`. Import `DefaultListModel`, and create a JFC list using an instance of it. Add the instance to the frame container.

```
>>> frame = JFrame("Main Frame")
>>> from javax.swing import DefaultListModel
>>> addresses = JList(DefaultListModel())
>>> frame.contentPane.add(addresses)
```

Pack the frame, and make it visible.

```
>>> frame.pack()
>>> frame.visible=1
```

## Adding Names

A list with no items is like a pizza with no toppings. For this next part, we're going to add names to our list from the dictionary that holds a collection of address entries.

Import everything from *address7.py*. (Run it as a main module to create a clean set of data files.)

```
>>> from address7 import *
```

Use the `readAddresses()` function to open the *testaddr.dat* file, which is full of address entries.

```
>>> fname="c:\\dat\\testaddr.dat"
>>> dict = readAddresses(fname)
```

Iterate through the keys of the dictionary of address entries returned by read Addresses(), and add the keys as names in the list.

```
>>> for name in dict.keys():
...   addresses.model.addElement(name)
...
>>> frame.pack()
```

Now our list has the names from our address application. The frame should look like Figure 14–1.

## Adding Event Handlers

Next we need to add some functionality to our list. First we'll make the `Address Form` instance pop up when we select an item, so we need to define a list event han-

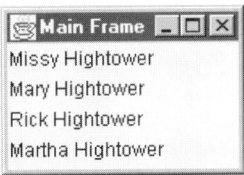

**Figure 14–1**
*Address Book Names List*

dler. How do we know which one? Remember that you can use the *jinfo* module to inspect a component's event properties. Or, if you remember which event listener a component handles, you can inspect it.

For example, you may remember that JList handles ListSelectionListener, or you may haved looked up JList in the Java API documentation and seen the addListSelectionListener() method, which is a dead giveaway. Let's say that we remembered, so we can do the following:

Import ListSelectionListener from the *javax.swing.event* package.

```
>>> from javax.swing.event import ListSelectionListener
```

Use the dir() function to list ListSelectionListener's methods.

```
>>> dir(ListSelectionListener)
['valueChanged']
```

Let's also say that we remember that all methods of a given XListener interface take an XEvent argument, so we can inspect the interface of the event object that will be passed to our event handler.

As an exercise look up the ListSelectionListener interface and the ListSelection Event class in the Java API documentation.

Import ListSelectionEvent from *javax.swing.event*, and inspect its attributes with the dir() function.

```
>>> from javax.swing.event import ListSelectionEvent
>>> dir(ListSelectionEvent)
['firstIndex', 'getFirstIndex', 'getLastIndex', getValueIsAdjusting',
    'valueIsAdjusting']
```

Now that we understand the event properties for List, we can set up our event handler to pop up an AddressForm instance when an item in the list is clicked.

Import AddressForm from the AddressForm module.

```
>>> from AddressForm import AddressForm
```

Create an event handler that gets the selected item from the list, looks up the corresponding Address instance in the dictionary, and passes it to the AddressForm instance, where it can be edited.

```
>>> def itemSelected(event):
...      list = event.source
...      name = list.selectedValue
...      address = dict[name]
...      form = AddressForm(address)
...
```

Register the event handler with the event property of the list.

```
>>> addresses.valueChanged = itemSelected
```

Now, every time you click on the listbox, a new window pops up that lets you edit the address. So far, so good, but we've left out a few things, like reading and writing files and closing the main window.

---

## Adding a Main Window: First Cut

We're going to create the main window for the address book application, which will have the list on the left side of the frame—when the user selects an item, it appears in the AddressForm instance on the right side. To do this we'll convert AddressForm so that it extends java.awt.Panel instead of java.awt.Frame. We'll also need to add some code to initialize the text fields in the AddressForm class (in *AddressForm.py*) so that every time an address is passed to AddressForm (that is, when the user selects a name in the list), AddressForm shows that Address instance.

Here is a listing of AddressForm in *AddressFormPane.py*:

```
from Address7 import Address
...

      # AddressForm Class.
      # This class is used to edit an instance of the Address class
class AddressForm(JPanel):
      ...
      ...
      def set(self, address):
            """Used to put a new address in this form
                 Initializes all of the text fields with
                 the attributes from self.__address.
            """
            self.__address = address
            self.__name.text = address.name()
            self.__email.text = address.email()
            self.__phoneNumber.text = address.phoneNumber()
      ...
      ...

def __init__CreateTextFieldPanel(self):
            """ Set up the email, phoneNumber and name text fields """
...
...
```

```
            # Create the name textfield and add it and its
            # associated label to the contentPane.
            # Note that name is a member of AddressForm
        self.__name = JTextField(self.__address.name())
        editPane.add(JLabel("Name"))
        editPane.add(self.__name)
            # Create the phoneNumber textfield and add it and its
            # associated label to the contentPane.
            # Note that phoneNumber is a member of AddressForm.
        self.__phoneNumber=JTextField(self.__address.phoneNumber())
        editPane.add(JLabel("Phone Number"))
        editPane.add(self.__phoneNumber)
            # Create the email textfield and add it and its
            # associated label to the contentPane.
            # Note that email is a member of AddressForm.
        print self.__address.email()
        self.__email = JTextField(self.__address.email())
        editPane.add(JLabel("eMail"))
        editPane.add(self.__email)
```

Notice that I've added extra functions to the Address class—email(), name(), and phoneNumber()—to allow access to the private variables of the Address instance.

## Moving Things Around

Now let's change the application so that the list shows up on the left side of the screen and the information shows up on the right side. The next example, from *AddressMain.py*, shows the AddressMain class. Much of its code was covered in the prototype from the last section.

> ### Don't Overdo the Comments
> I don't recommend using comments as I have here when you're writing real code. For more on writing comments and maintainable code, read *Enough Rope to Shoot Yourself in the Foot* (Holub, 1995).

```
from javax.swing import JFrame, JList, DefaultListModel
from java.awt import BorderLayout
from address7 import *
from AddressFormPane import AddressForm

class AddressMain(JFrame):
    def __init__(self):
            # Call the base class constructor
        JFrame.__init__(self, "Main Frame")

            # Create a list.
        self.addresses = JList(DefaultListModel())
```

```
                    # Add the addresses list to the
                    # container, on the left side
        self.contentPane.add(self.addresses, BorderLayout.WEST)

                    # Open up the file.
        self.fname="c:\\dat\\testaddr.dat"
        self.dict = readAddresses(self.fname)
                    # Populate the address list.
        for name in self.dict.keys():
                self.addresses.model.addElement(name)

                    # Set the event handler for the addresses.
        self.addresses.valueChanged = self.__itemSelected

                    # Create the AddressForm and add it to the EAST.
        self.form = AddressForm()
        self.contentPane.add(self.form, BorderLayout.EAST)

                    # Pack the frame and make it visible.
        self.pack()
        self.visible=1

        self.windowClosing = self.__windowClosing

    def __itemSelected(self, event):
        name = event.source.selectedValue
        address = self.dict[name]
                #Notify the panel that the address has changed
        self.form.set(address)

    def __windowClosing(self,event):
        writeAddresses(self.fname, self.dict)
        from java.lang import System
        System.exit(0)
if __name__ == "__main__":
    mainWindow = AddressMain()
```

If you run *AddressMain.py*, you should get a frame that looks like Figure 14–2. Notice that, when you click on a name in the list, its fields are displayed in the form. You can edit the fields and then hit the Apply button. Also notice that, when you change the names and then reload the application, the changed values are displayed.

## Changes in AddressMain.py

As for what's different in *AddressMain.py*, the most obvious thing is that all of the code is contained in a class. We created an instance of AddressForm and added it to the main frame.

```
    # Create the AddressForm and add it to the EAST.
self.form = AddressForm()
self.container.add(self.form, BorderLayout.EAST)
```

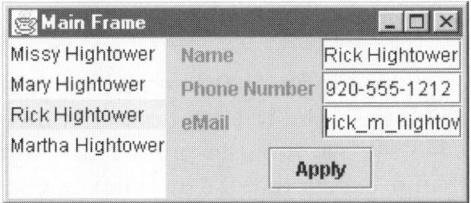

**Figure 14–2**  *Address Main Frame*

Another difference appears in the list event handler. In the prototype, we created a new instance of `AddressForm` and passed its constructor an `address` instance from the dictionary. Here we passed the `address` instance from the dictionary to `AddressForm`'s `set()` function. The `set()` function changes the `address` attribute of the `AddressForm` instance and initializes the text fields.

```
class AddressMain(Frame):
...
    def __itemSelected(self, event):
        if (event.stateChange == event.SELECTED):
            name = event.itemSelectable.getItem(event.item)
            address = self.dict[name]
                    # Notify the panel that the address has changed
            self.form.set(address)

class AddressForm(Panel):
    ...
    ...
    def set(self, address):
        """Used to put a new address in this form
        Initializes all of the text fields with
        the attributes from self.__address.
        """
        self.__address = address
        self.__name.text = address.name()
        self.__email.text = address.email()
        self.__phoneNumber.text = address.phoneNumber()
```

### Where to Find the Example

Throughout this chapter and into the next, we'll return to this *AddressMain.py* and make improvements to it. We'll put each improvement in a new directory within the current chapter directory, so the next improvement will be in the *One* directory within the *Chap14* directory of the Web site's *Examples* directory (i.e., *C\JYTHONBook\ Examples\Chap14\One*).

We've created a GUI application that wins no prizes for beauty and grace but gets the job done. Now, as all good programmers do, let's muck with it.

## *Adding a Toolbar and a Dialog for the Address Book Application*

We want to be able to add new addresses to the address list. Essentially, that means two new buttons, Add and Remove, which we'll put in a new panel in the north region of the main frame. (See Figure 14–3.) When the user presses the Add button a dialog pops up. A dialog is like a frame, except that it's modal (i.e., you have to close it before you can continue using your application).

### The Dialog Class

The dialog class, `AddAddressDialog`, is in the same module as `AddressMain` and contains an instance of the `AddressForm` panel. It extends `java.awt.Dialog`.

```
from java.awt import Dialog
class AddAddressDialog(Dialog):
    ...
    ...
```

`AddAddressDialog` gets most of its functionality from `AddressFormPane`, which it contains, and adds two buttons, OK and Cancel, which appear on a panel that acts as a toolbar. (See Figure 14–4.) The toolbar is placed in the south region of the panel. The `AddressFormPane` instance is placed in the center region.

```
class AddAddressDialog(JDialog):
    ...
    ...
    def __init__(self, frame):
        ...
        ...

            # Create a dialog box and add the AddressForm to it.
        self.contentPane.add(self.__form, BorderLayout.CENTER)

            # Create a toolbar with two buttons and
            # add it to the south part of the dialog
        toolbar = Panel()
        ok = Button("OK")
        cancel = Button("Cancel")
```

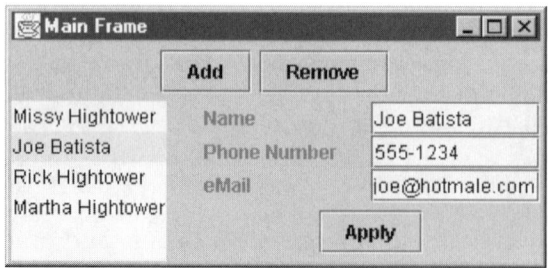

**Figure 14–3**  *The Add and Remove Buttons*

**Figure 14–4**  *The Okay and Cancel Buttons*

```
toolbar.add(ok)
toolbar.add(cancel)
ok.actionPerformed = self.__okEventHandler
cancel.actionPerformed = self.__cancelEventHandler
self.contentPane.add(toolbar, BorderLayout.SOUTH)
```

Pressing the OK button hides the dialog, saves its state, and invokes a `commit()` method that commits the changes to the `AddressForm` instance.

```
class AddAddressDialog(JDialog):
    OK = 0
    CANCEL = 1
        ...
        ...
    def __okEventHandler(self,event):
        self.visible = 0
        self.__state = AddAddressDialog.OK
        self.__form.commit()
class AddressForm(Panel):
    ...
    ...
    def commit(self):
        self.__address.__init__(self.__name.text,
        self.__phoneNumber.text, self.__email.text, [])
```

Pressing the Cancel button hides the dialog and saves its state.

```
class AddAddressDialog(JDialog):
    OK = 0
    CANCEL = 1
        ...
        ...
    def __cancelEventHandler(self,event):
        self.visible = 0
        self.__state = AddAddressDialog.CANCEL
```

`AddAddressDialog` has a method called `GetState()`, which returns whether the dialog was closed with OK or Cancel, and a method called `getAddress()`, which returns the new `address` instance.

```
class AddAddressDialog(JDialog):
      OK = 0
      CANCEL = 1
           ...
      def GetState()(self):
           return self.__state

      def getAddress()(self):
           return self.__address
```

Here is the complete listing for AddAddressDialog (from *One\AddressMain.py*):

```
from java.awt import BorderLayout
from javax.swing import JFrame, JList, DefaultListModel, JPanel, JDialog,
JButton
from address import *
from AddressFormPane import AddressForm
class AddAddressDialog(JDialog):
      OK = 0
      CANCEL = 1

      def __init__(self, frame):
            JDialog.__init__(self, frame, "Add a new address")

            self.__address = Address() #hold the address to be added.
            self.__form = AddressForm(self.__address)

                  # Create a dialog box and add the AddressForm to it.
            self.contentPane.add(self.__form, BorderLayout.CENTER)

                  # Create a toolbar with two buttons and
                  # add it to the south part of the dialog
            toolbar = JPanel()
            ok = JButton("OK")
            cancel = JButton("Cancel")
            toolbar.add(ok)
            toolbar.add(cancel)
            ok.actionPerformed = self.__okEventHandler
            cancel.actionPerformed = self.__cancelEventHandler
            self.contentPane.add(toolbar, BorderLayout.SOUTH)

                  # Pack it, make it modal, and show it
            self.setModal(1)
            self.pack()
            self.show()

      def __okEventHandler(self,event):
            self.__state = AddAddressDialog.OK
            self.__form.commit()

      def __cancelEventHandler(self,event):
            self.visible = 0
            self.__state = AddAddressDialog.CANCEL

      def GetState(self):
            return self.__state
```

```
def getAddress()(self):
    return self.__address
```

## Adding the Toolbar

Remember that the dialog is opened in response to a click of the Add button. Let's take a look at Add in a partial listing of AddressMain with the toolbar added.

```
class AddressMain(JFrame):
    def __init__(self):
            # Call the base class constructor
        JFrame.__init__(self, "Main Frame")

        ...

        self.__init__toolbar()

        ...
        ...

    def __init__toolbar(self):
            # Create the toolbar panel and
            # add it to the NORTH border of the container.
        toolbar = JPanel()
        self.contentPane.add(toolbar, BorderLayout.NORTH)

            # Create two buttons
        addAddress = JButton("Add")
        removeAddress = JButton ("Remove")

            # Add the buttons to the toolbar
        toolbar.add(addAddress)
        toolbar.add(removeAddress)

            # Registers the buttons event handler
        addAddress.actionPerformed=self.__addAddress_Clicked
        removeAddress.actionPerformed=self.__RemoveAddress_Clicked

    def __addAddress_Clicked(self,event):
        dialog = AddAddressDialog(self)
        if dialog.GetState() == AddAddressDialog.OK:
            addr = dialog.getAddress()
            self.dict[addr.name()] = addr
            self.addresses.add(addr.name())
        else:
            print "Cancel Add: " + `dialog.getAddress()`

    def __RemoveAddress_Clicked(self,event):
        index = self.addresses.selectedIndex
        key = self.addresses.selectedItem
        del self.dict[key]
        self.addresses.remove(key)

            # Get the index of the item before this one.
            # Unless the index of the item we removed is 0.
```

```
if index-1 < 0: index = 0
else: index = index -1

        # Select the index of the adjacent item.
if len(self.dict.keys()) > index:
    print self.dict.keys()[index]
    self.addresses.select(index)
        # set the form to the index
        # that we selected in the list
    address = self.dict[self.dict.keys()[index]]
    self.form.set(address)
```

The __init__toolbar method creates a toolbar and adds it to the north region of the main frame. Then it instantiates two buttons and adds them to the toolbar. The Add and Remove buttons are registered with the event handler methods. __addAddress_Clicked and __RemoveAddress_Clicked.

```
def __init__toolbar(self):

        # Create the toolbar panel and
        # add it to the NORTH border of the container.
    toolbar = Panel()
    self.container.add(toolbar, BorderLayout.NORTH)

        # Create two buttons
    addAddress = Button("Add")
    removeAddress = Button ("Remove")

        # Add the buttons to the toolbar
    toolbar.add(addAddress)
    toolbar.add(removeAddress)

        # Registers the buttons event handler
    addAddress.actionPerformed=self.__addAddress_Clicked
    removeAddress.actionPerformed=self.__RemoveAddress_Clicked
```

## Adding and Removing Addresses

The __addAddress_Clicked event handler is where the AddAddressDialog class is used. It creates an instance of AddAddressDialog called dialog. After the user opens the dialog to enter an address (or not), the method checks to see if the OK button was pressed by calling dialog's GetState() method. If the OK state is set, the address is added to the address dictionary (dict) and the address list (addresses).

```
def __addAddress_Clicked(self,event):
    dialog = AddAddressDialog(self)
    if dialog.GetState() == AddAddressDialog.OK:
        addr = dialog.getAddress()
        self.dict[addr.name()] = addr
        self.addresses.add(addr.name())
    else:
        print "Cancel Add: " + `dialog.getAddress()`
```

Clicking the Remove button calls __RemoveAddress_Clicked(). This method is a little long, so we'll go through it step by step.

First, we get the index of the selected item in the address list (addresses). Then we get the value of the string at that index, which is the name of the person in the address entry.

```
index = self.addresses.selectedIndex
key = self.addresses.selectedItem
```

Now we can remove the person from the address dictionary (dict) and from the address list.

```
del self.dict[key]
self.addresses.remove(key)
```

Next we need to select another person in the list and reinitialize the address form so that both are synchronized. This means that we have to get the index of the item before this one, unless the index of the item we removed is 0.

```
if index-1 < 0: index = 0
else: index = index -1
```

Then we select the index of the adjacent item in the list and the form. We also do some sanity checking to see if the dictionary has enough items in it—that is, that the index value is no greater than the number of items in the dictionary.

```
if len(self.dict.keys()) > index:
```

Select the address in the list.

```
self.addresses.select(index)
```

Get the address instance from the dictionary; then select the address in the form.

```
address = self.dict[self.dict.keys()[index]]
self.form.set(address)
```

The following line of code does a lot and may be hard to understand:

```
address = self.dict[self.dict.keys()[index]]
```

Essentially, it's equivalent to writing these three lines of code:

```
listAddressNames = self.dict.keys()
currentAddressKey = listAddressNames[index]
address = self.dict[currentAddressKey]
```

Here's what it means step by step:

Get the dictionary keys, which act as a list of names from address instances.

```
listAddressNames = self.dict.keys()
```

Get the name corresponding to the value of the index, which is the address closest to the address just removed.

```
currentAddressKey = listAddressNames[index]
```

Use that name as a key into the dictionary to get the address instances corresponding to the address that was next to the address just removed.

```
address = self.dict[currentAddressKey]
```

Set the AddressForm instance, form, to the new address.

```
self.form.set(address)
```

Now that you have a good understanding of how to add and remove addresses, run *AddressMain.py*, and try these exercises:

- Add and remove a couple of address entries. Get the feel for how the program works because you'll need it for the rest of the exercises.
- Add a company field and a title field to the Address class. You'll need an extra text field in the AddressForm class for this.
- Add a flag argument called isDialog in the constructor of AddressForm that allows you to forgo adding the Apply button to the form. This flag will be used when the form acts as a dialog. Also, change the background color of the dialog to match the background color of the address form.
- Add two buttons to the toolbar of MainAddressForm. The Copy button (copy Address) should copy the current selected address. The Insert button (insert Address) should insert the address into the list.

## Menus

In Java there are two types of menus: menubar and popup. The following section shows how to add a menubar to a frame.

### JMenu Bar

Import the JMenuBar class from *java.swing*.

```
>>> from javax.swing import JJMenuBar
```

Create an instance of it.

```
>>> bar = JJMenuBar()
```

Import and create an instance of JFrame.

```
>>> from javax.swing import JFrame
>>> frame = JFrame()
```

Set the JMenuBar property of the frame to the JMenuBar instance.

```
>>> frame.JJMenuBar = bar
>>> frame.visible=1
```

Now that we have a menubar added in the frame, we need to add a menu to it. Create a menu (JMenu), and add it to the menubar.

```
>>> from javax.swing import JMenu
>>> fruitMenu = JMenu("Fruit")
>>> bar.add(fruitMenu)
>>> frame.pack()
```

Add menu items to the menu.

```
>>> from javax.swing import JMenuItem
>>> fruitMenu.add(MenuItem("Apple"))
>>> fruitMenu.add(JMenuItem("Pear"))
>>> fruitMenu.add(JMenuItem("Peaches"))
```

### Menus Event Handling

The menu just created should look like the one in Figure 14–5 (if not, try manually resizing the frame). It's pretty, but it doesn't do anything. We need to handle events from the menu or menu items.

Define an event handler.

```
>>> def actionPerformed(event):
...      print event.source
...      print event.paramString()
...      print event.actionCommand
...
```

Get the Apple menu from the Fruit menu. It's the first one, so it's at index 0.

```
>>> appleMenu = fruitMenu.getMenuComponent(0)
```

Set the actionPerformed event property to actionPerformed.

```
>>> appleMenu.actionPerformed = actionPerformed
```

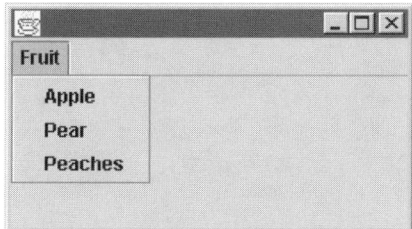

**Figure 14–5**  *The Fruit Menu*

Try selecting the Apple menu item in the Fruit menu again. You should get the following output from the event handler we just defined:

```
javax.swing.JMenuItem[...]
ACTION_PERFORMED,cmd=Apple
Apple
```

Notice that `actionCommand` is a string set to `Apple`. Now try selecting `Pear` and `Peaches`. Nothing happens because we didn't register event handlers for them.
   Set the event handlers for all menu items.

```
>>> for menuItem in fruitMenu.menuComponents:
...     menuItem.actionPerformed = actionPerformed
...
```

Select `Pear` and `Peaches` again.
   In this next example we'll add another menu to `JMenuBar` called Veggies. Then we'll add menu items to it and handle events from specific items instead of from the menu as a whole.
   Create the Veggies menu.

```
>>> veggiesMenu = JMenu("Veggies")
```

Create three menu items.

```
>>> spinach = JMenuItem("Spinach")
>>> carrots = JMenuItem("Carrots")
>>> peas = JMenuItem("Peas")
```

Define event handlers for each menu item and register them.

```
>>> def spinachEvent(event):
...     print "You Picked Spinach"

>>> spinach.actionPerformed = spinachEvent
>>> def carrotEvent(event):
...     print "What's up DOC?"
>>> carrots.actionPerformed = carrotEvent


>>> def peaEvent(event):
...     print "Yuck!"
>>> peas.actionPerformed = peaEvent
```

Add the menu items to the Veggies menu.

```
>>> veggiesMenu.add(spinach)
>>> veggiesMenu.add(carrots)
>>> veggiesMenu.add(peas)
```

Add the Veggies menu to the menubar.

```
>>> bar.add(veggiesMenu)
>>> frame.pack()
```

Select each menu item; notice that its handler is called.

```
You Picked Spinach
What's up DOC?
Yuck!
```

Now we'll add cooking options to the Veggies menu so that, once the user selects an option (Fry, Broil, Boil, Roast), he can select the Cook menu item to prepare the veggies accordingly. The exercise that follows will use separators and checkboxes.

Add a separator to the end of the Veggies menu using the `addSeparator()` method.

```
>>> veggiesMenu.addSeparator()
```

Add a submenu to Veggies by creating `cookMenu` and adding it to `veggiesMenu`.

```
>>> cookMenu = JMenu("Cooking")
>>> veggiesMenu.add(cookMenu)
```

Add a menu item to `cookMenu` called `Cook`.

```
>>> cookMenuItem = JMenuItem("Cook")
>>> cookMenu.add(cookMenuItem)
>>> cookMenu.insertSeparator(cookMenu.itemCount)
```

Now we'll demonstrate creating and using checkboxes.

Import `JCheckboxMenuItem` from *javax.swing*.

```
>>> from javax.swing import JCheckBoxMenuItem
```

Create a list of item names, and create a dictionary to hold mappings from the items to the names.

```
>>> cookItems = ('Fry', 'Broil', 'Boil', 'Roast')
>>> dict ={}
```

Add each item in the above list to the Cook menu (`cookMenu`). In addition, add the item to the dictionary so it can be found easily.

```
>>> for item in cookItems:
...     cb = JCheckBoxMenuItem(item)
...     dict[item]=cb
...     cookMenu.add(cb)
```

Now let's set up the event handler, `cookOptionEvent`, to handle these checkbox menu items. For clarity, let's go through it step by step. The currently selected menu item's caption is equal to `event.item`. If it's Broil, `event.item` is `Broil`.

```
...     if event.item in cookItems:
```

Iterate through each item in `cookItems`, which you'll recall holds all of the possible cooking options.

```
...         for item in cookItems:
```

If the item in `cookItems` *isn't* the current item, make sure its checkbox isn't selected.

```
...       if (item != event.item):
...            cb = dict[item]
...            cb.state = 0
```

The statement `cb = dict[item]` looks up the `JCheckboxMenuItem` instance in the dictionary that contains mappings of strings to menu items. The statement `cb.state = 0` sets the state of the `JCheckBoxMenuItem` instance (`cb`) to false, which removes its check.

Now we need to set up the event handler for `cookMenuItem`.

```
>>> def cookEvent(event):
...     for item in cookItems:
...          if dict[item].state:
...               print "I will " + item + " your veggies"

>>> cookMenuItem.actionPerformed = cookEvent
```

At this point, the menu in your frame should look like the one in Figure 14–6. If it doesn't, try resizing it.

Now try selecting Fry and then Cook. You should get the following output:

```
I will Fry your veggies
```

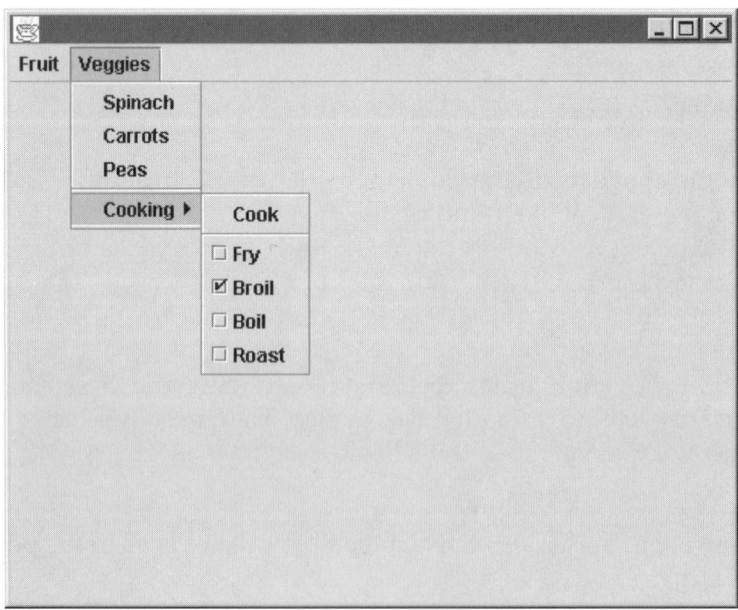

**Figure 14–6** *The Veggies Menu with the Cooking Submenu*

Then try Broil and Boil.

```
I will Broil your veggies
I will Boil your veggies
```

Here are some more things to try:

- Convert the previous interactive session into a class that contains all of the functionality derived from Frame. Remember how we converted an earlier interactive session that worked with Frame into a class.
- Change the code to use JRadioButtonMenuItem. Remember from Chapter 13 that JMenuItem and JRadioButtonMenuItem inherit functionality from Abstract Button. *Hint*: Add all of the JRadioButtonMenuItems to ButtonGroup.
- Add icons to the various menu items.
- Set the mnemonics of the JFC menu items.

## JPopupMenus

Popup menus are context-sensitive. Typically, they appear when you right-click an icon or component. The following example demonstrates popup menus. Using JFC creates a frame with two buttons: Switch and Pop.

Import JPopupMenu and all of its support classes from *javax.swing*.

```
>>> from javax.swing import JPopupMenu
>>> from javax.swing import JFrame, JButton, JPanel, JLabel
```

Create instances of the popup menu.

```
>>> popup = JPopupMenu("JFC Popup")
```

Put some menu items in it.

```
>>> fruits = ("Apple", "Oranges", "GrapeFruit", "Grapes")
>>> for fruit in fruits:
...     popup.add(fruit)
```

Create a frame, a pane, and a label. The label holds a string, which shows the state of the current popup menu—JFC.

```
>>> frame = JFrame(size=(200,200))
>>> pane = JPanel()
>>> label = JLabel("JFC Popup Menu")
>>> pop = JButton("Pop")
```

Add the popup menu to the pane.

```
>>> pane.add(popup)
```

Add the label and pop components to the pane. Add the pane to the frame.

```
>>> pane.add(pop)
>>> pane.add(label)
>>> frame.contentPane.add(pane)
```

Create an event handler for `pop` that pops up the current menu at the x, y location—20,10 in the pane.

```
>>> def popEvent(event):
...     global popup, pane
...     popup.show(pane, 20, 10)
```

Register the event handlers with the corresponding buttons.

```
>>> pop.actionPerformed = popEvent
```

Pack the frame, and show it off.

```
>>> frame.pack()
>>> frame.visible=1
Putting Things Together with Menubar Menus and Popup Menus
```

## Adding Menus to the Address Application

Let's add a menubar menu and a popup menu to our address application. Essentially, we'll set the menubar property of `AddressMain` to a `JMenuBar` instance. Then we'll add the Address menu to the menubar and give it two items, Add and Remove. The `actionPerformed` event properties of these items are set to the same handler as for the Add and Remove buttons.

All of this is done from the constructor of `AddressMain`. It's rather long, so we'll break out the functionality of adding the menu to a method called `__init__menu()`. Here's the code (from class `AddressMain` in *Two\AddressMain.py*):

```
def __init__(self)
    ...
self.__init__menu()
    ...
def __init__menu(self):

                # Create the JMenuBar and
                # add it to the addressMenu.
            jmb = JMenuBar()
            self.JMenuBar = JMenuBar
            addressMenu = JMenu("Address")

                # Create two menu items.
            addAddress = JMenuItem("Add")
            removeAddress = JMenuItem("Remove")

                # Add the menu items to the menu.
                # then add the menu to the menu bar
            addressMenu.add(addAddress)
            addressMenu.add(removeAddress)
            JMenuBar.add(addressMenu)

                # Register the menu items event handler
            addAddress.actionPerformed = self.__addAddress_Clicked
            removeAddress.actionPerformed= self.__RemoveAddress_Clicked
```

We also want to add a popup menu to our application that appears when the user clicks the address list. The `__init__popup` method is similar to `__init__menu`, the only difference being that the `mousePressed` event is handled for addresses. Notice that, if `event.metaDown` (in the event handler for `mousePressed`) is true (1), the right mouse button was clicked.

```
def __init__(self)
        ...
self.popup = NONE      #to hold the popup menu
self.__init__popup()
self.addresses.mousePressed = self.__popupEvent
...

def __popupEvent(self, event):
            if event.metaDown == 1:
                    self.popup.show(self.addresses, event.x, event.y)

def __init__popup(self):
            self.popup = JPopupMenu("Address")
            self.addresses.add(self.popup)
                # Create two menu items.
            addAddress = JMenuItem("Add")
            removeAddress = JMenuItem("Remove")

                # Add the menu items to the menu.
            self.popup.add(addAddress)
            self.popup.add(removeAddress)

                # Register the menu item's event handler
            addAddress.actionPerformed = self.__addAddress_Clicked
            removeAddress.actionPerformed= self.__RemoveAddress_Clicked
```

As an exercise, add and then remove an address entry with the Add and Remove menu items on `JMenuBar`. Do it again with `JPopupMenu`. Also create a duplicate menu item for both the menubar menu and the popup menu that allows an address to be duplicated, that is, copied and pasted into the list.

## Layout Managers

If you've worked with Visual Basic or any other tools that support GUI code generation, you may be accustomed to laying out components on a form and specifying their size and position in pixels. (A pixel is ½₀ inch.) The problem is, of course, that you may develop your application on a 25-inch monitor, and then someone will try to use it on a 12-inch monitor, leaving half the GUI off the screen. This problem becomes even more pronounced if you have no control over the type of display your GUI will be used on. For these reasons, Java needs a flexible way to display user interfaces on a variety of platforms.

Layout managers provide a way to lay out components in a container with great flexibility, but with flexibility comes greater complexity, and sometimes there's just no substitute for absolute positioning. Even so, in most cases you should use layout managers, and if you do use absolute positioning, make sure it's in a container whose container is a layout manager.

The positioning of components on the screen is decided by the order in which they're added to the container, the constraints passed to the container's add() method, and the layout manager properties the container is using.

Each type of container has its own default layout manager. For example, java.awt.Frame and javax.swing.JFrame use BorderLayout whereas Panel and JPanel use FlowLayout. However, you can change the default so that a frame can use FlowLayout and a panel can use BorderLayout.

In one GUI, you'll usually have many layout managers. Nested containers with different layout managers will give you the desired result, as we saw with the address book application. There AddressMain used BorderLayout; ToolBar, which contains the Add and Remove buttons, used FlowLayout; and editPane used Grid Layout (to arrange the labels and text fields used to edit the addresses).

The key to understanding layout managers is using them, so we'll be doing plenty of interactive examples and exercises. I've also provided a tutor application (*Layout3.py*) that works with FlowLayout, BorderLayout, GridLayout, and GridBag Layout. Feel free to fire up *Layout3.py* and experiment with layout managers at any time.

### Strategy Design Pattern

The layout manager approach uses the Strategy design pattern developed by Gamma and his colleagues (*Design Patterns*, 1995). This is another reminder to read Gamma, but first read *Object-Oriented Analysis and Design with Applications* (Booch, 1994).

## FlowLayout

The FlowLayout class is the simplest of the layout managers. (Actually, it's the second simplest; I'll explain later.) As components are added one at a time to the container, they're positioned from left to right and from top to bottom. When one row fills up, the components begin filling up the next row. You can set the alignment of each row so that the components can be centered or left- or right-aligned.

Here's an interactive FlowLayout example. Import the FlowLayout class and some container and component support classes.

```
>>> from java.awt import FlowLayout
>>> from javax.swing import JFrame, JButton, JTextField, JLabel
```

Create an instance of Frame, and set its layout to FlowLayout, that is, an instance of the FlowLayout class. Remember that the frame is a container.

```
>>> frame = JFrame("FlowLayout", size = (200, 200), visible=1)
>>> frame.contentPane.layout = FlowLayout()
```

Add a label to the frame, and validate the frame. (`validate()` forces the frame to redraw itself, which makes the label just added visible.)

```
>>> frame.contentPane.add(JLabel("Name"))
javax.swing.JLabel[...text=Name,...verticalTextPosition=CENTER]
>>> frame.validate()
```

Add a text field to the frame, and validate the frame.

```
>>> frame.contentPane.add(JTextField(20))
>>> frame.validate()
```

Remember, if the component doesn't fit on the current row, it's added to the next row. If we eyeball the components, they look like they almost fit. To be sure, we have to check their width.

```
>>> frame.contentPane.components[0].width +
frame.contentPane.components[1].width
253
```

The first component's width (`frame.contentPane.components[0]`) plus the second's width (`frame.contentPane.components[1]`) is 253. Take a look at the call to the constructor to see what the frame width is.

```
>>> frame.width
200
```

Clearly both components can't fit on the same row. (We'll make them fit later.)

Let's make this example more interesting and add eight more components to the container (frame). Create a tuple of strings and iterate through it, creating buttons with the strings and adding them to the frame.

```
>>> blist = ("one", "two", "three", "four", "five", "six", "seven", "eight")
>>> for label in blist:
...     frame.contentPane.add(Button(label))
...
>>> frame.validate()
```

The frame should now look like Figure 14–7. Notice that the components in each row are centered, which is the default row alignment with FlowLayout (FlowLayout.CENTER). We'll change the alignment to the left and then to the right. Then we'll change the vertical and horizontal spacing between the components.

Set the layout of the frame to the left.

```
>>> frame.contentPane.layout.alignment = FlowLayout.LEFT
>>> frame.contentPane.doLayout()
```

It should look like Figure 14–8. Notice that the components are aligned along the left border. If we change the layout to right alignment, the frame should look like Figure 14–9.

```
>>> frame.contentPane.layout.alignment = FlowLayout.RIGHT
>>> frame.contentPane.doLayout()
```

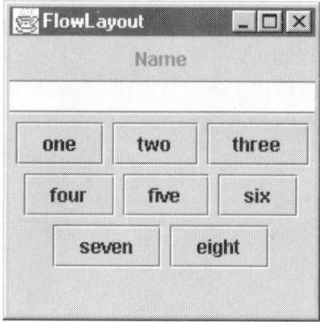

**Figure 14–7** *Center Alignment of Components (*FlowLayout*'s Default)*

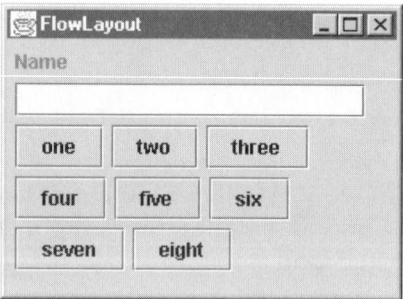

**Figure 14–8** *Left Alignment of Components with* FlowLayout

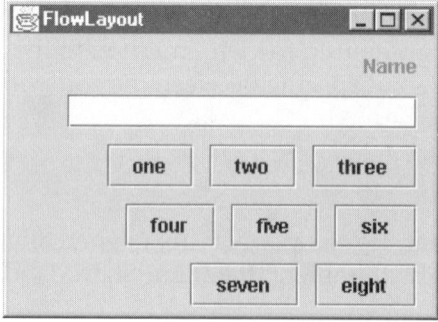

**Figure 14–9** *Right Alignment of Components with* FlowLayout

Recall that the first two components didn't fit on the first row. What would happen if we made the frame bigger than the 253 pixels that make up the width of the label plus the width of the text field? Change the width of the frame to 275 pixels.

```
>>> frame.size = 275, 200
>>> frame.contentPane.doLayout()
>>> frame.validate()
```

The frame should now look like Figure 14–10.

Let's set the spacing between the components with the vgap property, which controls vertical spacing, and the hgap property, which controls horizontal spacing. Set vgap and hgap to 0 so that your frame will look like the one in Figure 14–11.

```
>>> frame.contentPane.layout.vgap=0
>>> frame.contentPane.layout.hgap=0
>>> frame.contentPane.doLayout()
```

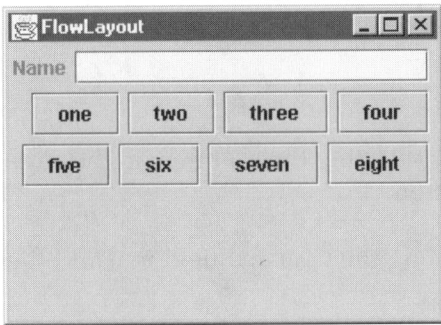

**Figure 14–10**   *Effect of Resizing on Component Layout*

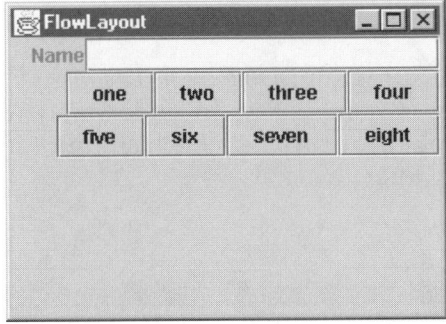

**Figure 14–11**   *Vertical and Horizontal Gap Set to 0*

Now set vgap and hgap to 10 pixels.

```
>>> frame.contentPane.layout.vgap=10
>>> frame.contentPane.layout.hgap=10
>>> frame.contentPane.doLayout()
```

Finally, we want to pack the frame with FlowLayout if the container is an instance of JFrame, JDialog, or Window. FlowLayout lays out the components' preferred Size property (if you try to resize a component yourself, FlowLayout will change it back) and adjusts the width of the frame to the cumulative width of all of its components. If you pack the frame (frame.pack()), FlowLayout will try to fit all of the components on the top row, as in Figure 14–2.

### *Surprise*

All of you who weren't following along (and you know who you are), fire up *layout4.py*, which lets you adjust properties for all of the layout managers that we discuss in this chapter. It looks like Figure 14–13. Notice, in the frame at the left, that you can adjust the properties of the current layout and those of the components (or those of the constraint objects associated with a component). Play around with it:

1. Set the layout manager to FlowLayout.
2. Align the components on the left by selecting the LEFT item in the alignment list and then clicking the Apply button.
3. Align the components on the right.
4. Change the vertical gap to 0 by editing the vgap text field to 0 and then hitting the Apply button.
5. Change the horizontal gap to 0.
6. Change the vertical and horizontal gaps to 20.
7. Size the frame with the mouse so that it's half its original size.
8. Hit the Resize button on the control frame.
9. Hit the Pack button to resize the frame.
10. Try all of the available layout managers.

There are four versions of the layout program, *Layout.py*, *Layout2.py*, *Layout3.py*, and *Layout4.py*, which increase in complexity. To understand what's going on, examine *Layout.py* without looking at *Layout4.py*, which, since it supports all of the layout managers, is pretty long.

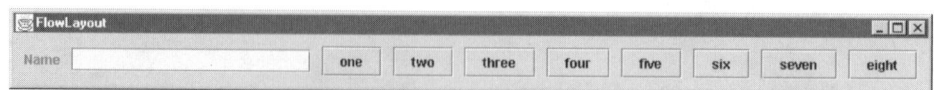

**Figure 14–12**    *Result of Packing the Frame*

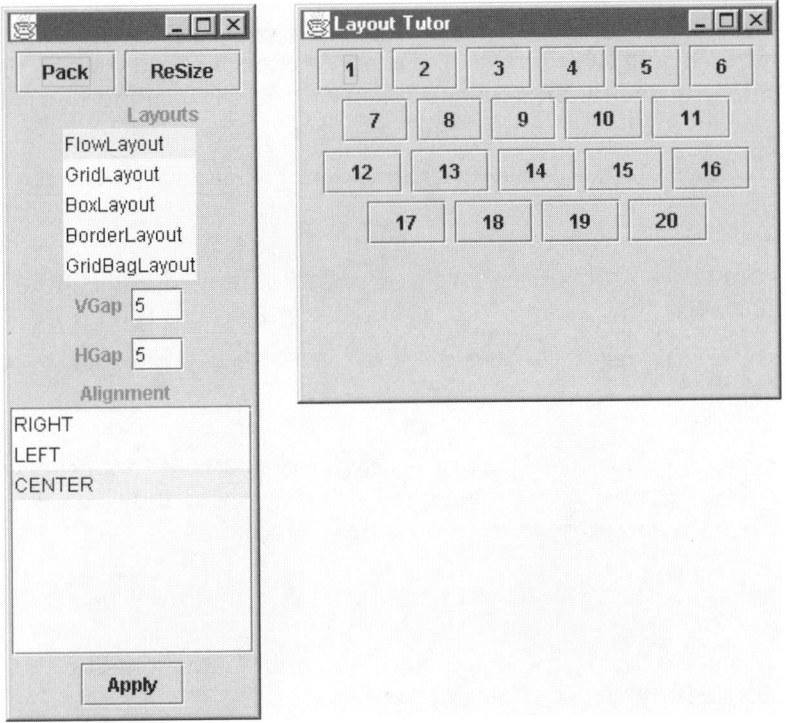

**Figure 14–13**    Layout4.py *after Playing with It*

## BoxLayout

You may remember that I referred to FlowLayout as the second simplest layout manager. It used to be the easiest, but that was before BoxLayout, which was added as part of JFC/Swing. BoxLayout can be used with AWT components, but it works better with the JFC variety.

BoxLayout has only one parameter, AXIS, and there are only two choices: X and Y. Here's a short interactive example.

Import BoxLayout, JFrame, and JButton from *javax.swing*.

```
>>> from javax.swing import BoxLayout, JFrame, JButton
```

Create a frame, and add some buttons to it.

```
>>> frame = JFrame("BoxLayout Example", size = (300,200), visible=1)
>>> list = ["one","two","three", "four"]
>>> for button in list:
...     frame.contentPane.add(JButton(button))
...
```

Change the layout of the frame to BoxLayout, which uses X_AXIS. (invalidate() tells the frame that something has changed and that the window needs to be redrawn; validate() tells the frame that it's time to fix any problems. Calling invalidate() and then validate() forces the frame to call doLayout.)

```
>>> frame.contentPane.layout=BoxLayout(frame.contentPane, BoxLayout.X_AXIS)
>>> frame.invalidate()
>>> frame.validate()
```

Look at Figure 14–14, and notice that BoxLayout has arranged things from left to right along the *x* axis. Now arrange the layout along the *y* axis (Figure 14–15).

```
>>> frame.contentPane.layout=BoxLayout(frame.contentPane, BoxLayout.Y_AXIS)
>>> frame.invalidate()
>>> frame.validate()
```

Like FlowLayout, BoxLayout uses the preferredSize property. It simply spaces the components evenly against a given axis. Try this exercise using BoxLayout from *Layout4.py*. Explain what happens in each step.

1. Set the axis to X_AXIS. (Remember to hit the Apply button on the control frame.)
2. Reduce the size of the frame to half and then half again along the *x* axis.
3. Hit the Resize button on the control frame.
4. Hit the Pack button on the control frame. (This is the same as calling frame.pack().)
5. Set the axis to Y_AXIS.
6. Hit the Resize button again to set the frame to the default starting size.
7. Reduce the size of the layout frame by half and then by half again along the *y* axis.
8. Hit the Pack button again.

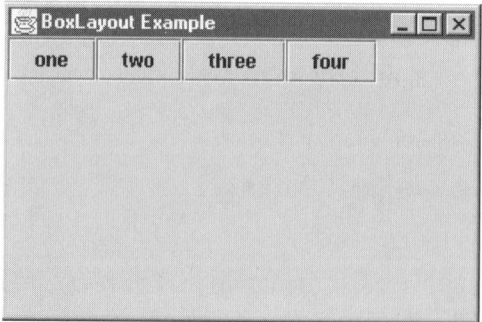

**Figure 14–14** *Components Laid Out Left to Right on the* x *Axis*

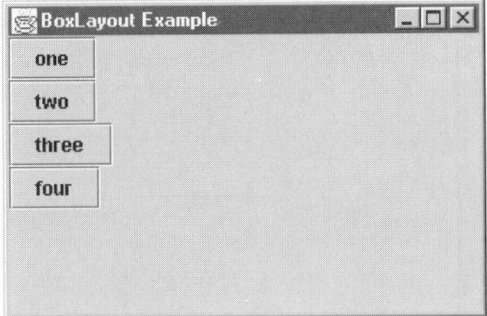

**Figure 14–15**   *Components Laid Out Vertically on the* y *Axis*

## GridLayout

The GridLayout manager lays out components in a grid. We used it in the address application for editPane. Like FlowLayout, GridLayout has the vgap and hgap properties that set the vertical and horizontal spacing between components.

GridLayout also has properties that specify the rows and columns of the grid. The row property is dominant. The only component property that GridLayout pays any attention to is minimumSize. If you pack the container (frame.pack()), it uses minimumSize to create the smallest components that are all the same size. It ignores preferredSize and stretches the width and height of the components so that they all have the same area and fill the container (if possible). Here's an example.

Import the classes needed.

```
>>> from java.awt import GridLayout
>>> from javax.swing import JFrame, JButton
```

Create a frame and add some components to it.

```
>>> frame = JFrame("GridLayout Example", size=(300,300), visible=1)
>>> blist = ("One", "Two", "Three", "Four", "Five", "Six", "Seven", "Eight")
>>> for label in blist:
...     frame.contentPane.add(JButton(label))
...
```

Create a grid layout that lays out components in a 2-by-4 grid.

```
>>> frame.contentPane.layout = GridLayout(2,4)
>>> frame.contentPane.doLayout()
```

Your frame should look like Figure 14–16. Notice that neither the width nor the height is observed from preferredSize. With the mouse, drag the right corner of the frame so that it's twice its original size, which doubles the width and height of the components as well. Now return the frame to its original size.

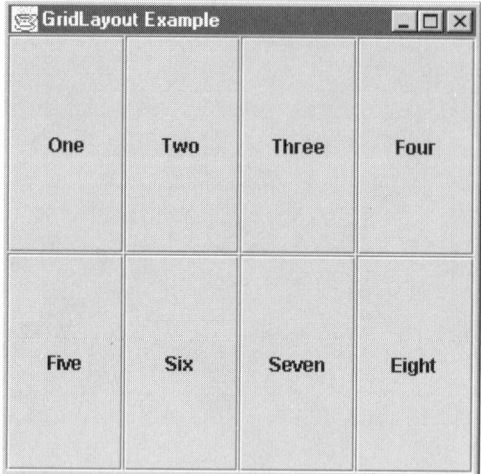

**Figure 14–16**    *A 2-by-4 Component Layout with* GridLayout

Set the row property of the GridLayout instance to 3.

```
>>> frame.contentPane.layout.rows=3
```

Your frame should now look like Figure 14–17. Although we didn't change the columns to 3, only three columns show up. That's because GridLayout adjusts the number of columns to fit the desired number of rows. Also, the grid is 3 by 3 and, since we only have eight components, the last cell is left blank.

Now set the rows to four. Then print out the row and column properties (layout.rows and layout.columns).

```
>>> frame.contentPane.layout.rows=4
>>> frame.contentPane.doLayout()
>>> layout=frame.contentPane.layout
>>> print layout.rows, layout.columns
4 4
```

Your frame should look like Figure 14–18. Again, the number of columns has changed to accommodate the number of rows; however, the column property is still set to 4 because, as I said earlier, the row property is dominant.

Set vgap and hgap of frame.layout to 3. Look at the frame, and then set these properties to 7.

```
>>> layout.vgap, layout.hgap = 3,3
>>> frame.contentPane.doLayout()
```

Look at the frame.

```
>>> layout.vgap, layout.hgap = 7,7
>>> frame.invalidate();frame.validate()
```

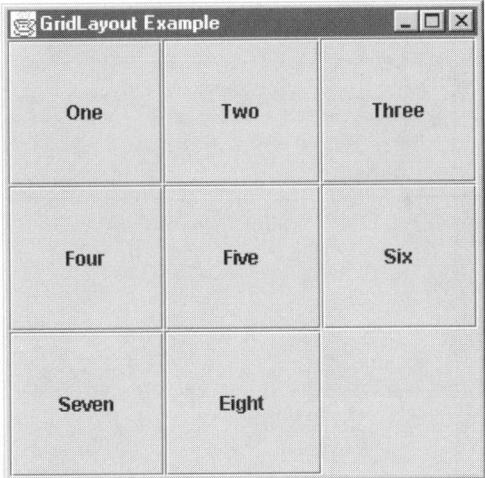

**Figure 14–17**    *A 3-by-3 Layout (with the Last Cell Blank)*

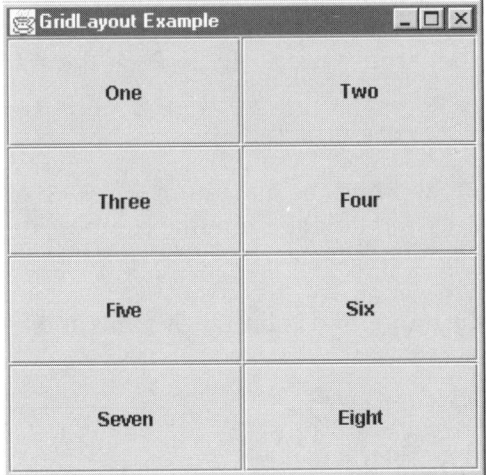

**Figure 14–18**    *A 4-Row Layout*

It should look like Figure 14–19. Notice that the spacing is between the components and not between the components and the edges. (If you want to set the area between the components and the edges, you need to set the `insets` of the frame.)

Set the layout back to the way it was.

```
>>> layout.vgap, layout.hgap = 0,0
>>> frame.contentPane.layout = GridLayout(2,4)
```

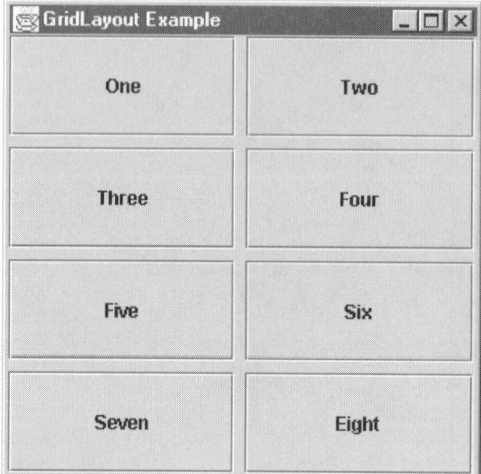

**Figure 14–19**    *Horizontal and Vertical Gap Set to 3*

As we discussed, GridLayout uses minimumSize when you pack the frame. It lays out all components with the same size by checking the minimum size for each one and then setting all of them to the largest size it finds. Pack the frame. It should look like Figure 14–20.

```
>>> frame.pack()
```

Now let's go through the components and find the maximum minimumSize. First we'll create two lists to collect the widths and heights from the components.

```
>>> widths, heights = [], []
```

Iterate through the components in the frame, and collect the widths and heights in the widths and heights lists.

```
>>> for component in frame.contentPane.components
...     widths.append(component.minimumSize.width)
...     heights.append(component.minimumSize.height)
```

Print the maximum minimumSize width.

```
>>> print "Minimum width " + `max(widths)`
Minimum width 48
```

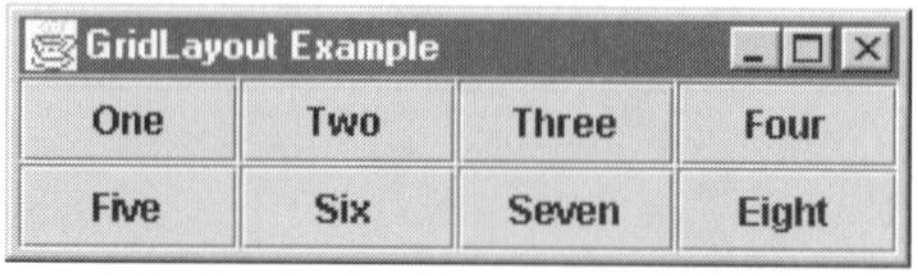

**Figure 14–20**    *Packed Frame*

Print the maximum `minimumSize` height.

```
>>> print "Minimum height " + `max(heights)`
Minimum height 23
```

Print the actual size of the components. (Remember that with `GridLayout` all components are the same size.) Notice that the width and height match the maximum `minimumSize`.

```
>>> print "Size of all of the components " + `frame.components[0].size`
Size of all of the components java.awt.Dimension[width=48,height=23]
```

Try this exercise with *layout4.py*:

1. Select `GridLayout` from the layouts list in the control pane.
2. Hit the Pack button. You should have a frame that looks like Figure 14–21.
3. Change `hgap` and `vgap` to 5 pixels. Then hit the Apply button. The frame should look like Figure 14–22.
4. Hit the Pack button again.
5. Change the number of columns to 100. What happens?
6. Set the number of columns to 0. What happens?
7. Set the number of columns back to 5. What happens?
8. Set the rows from 4 to 6. Then hit Pack. Notice that the last two rows are empty (Figure 14–23).
9. Increment the rows by 1 until you reach 10. Be sure to hit Apply each time, and then repack the frame with Pack.

## BorderLayout

`BorderLayout` works well with top-level containers. It can have at most five components, so the components added to it are usually containers themselves—that is, panels.

The five regions of `BorderLayout` are north, south, east, west, and center. What you put in them is up to you and is application-specific. North is used mainly for toolbars (panels with buttons or similar components); south, usually for status windows (panels with labels that show the status of an application). West can be used for tree views, lists, and the like; east, for toolboxes (panels with buttons and property text fields). Center is usually the main view of the application, perhaps where the text fields for editing an object are located.

The north and south regions span the full width of the parent container. Their height is the preferred height of the component. The east and west regions span the full height of the container minus the height of the north and/or south regions (if any). Their width is the preferred width of the component. The center region gets whatever is left over, usually the largest portion of the frame. Now for our `BorderLayout` example.

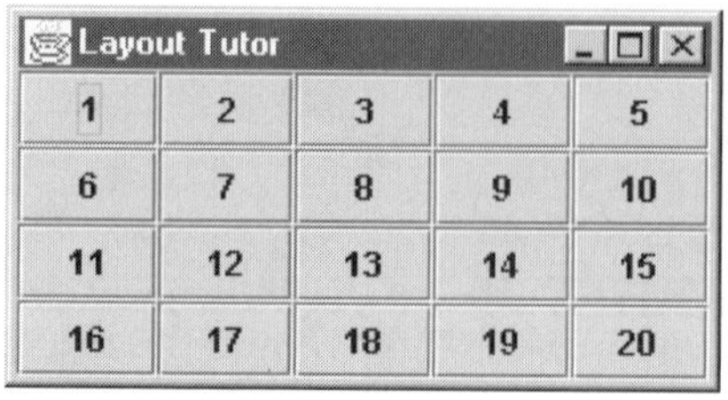

**Figure 14–21**    *Packed* GridLayout *Frame*

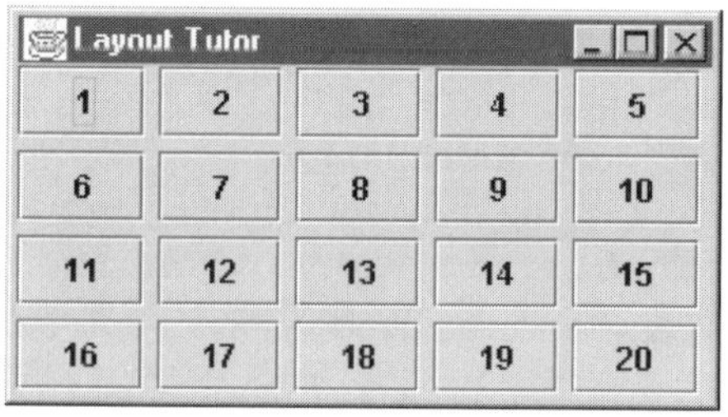

**Figure 14–22**    *Frame with Horizontal and Vertical Gaps of 5*

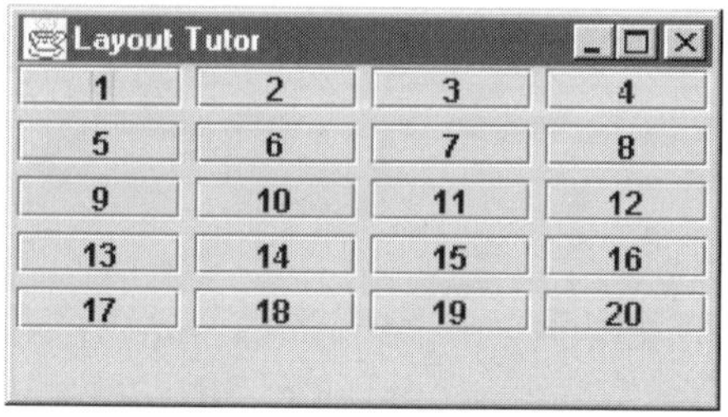

**Figure 14–23**    *Six-Row Packed Frame with Last Two Rows Empty*

Set up a frame.

```
>>> from java.awt import BorderLayout
>>> from javax.swing import JFrame, JButton
>>> f = JFrame("BorderLayout", size = (300,300), visible=1)
>>> f.contentPane.layout = BorderLayout()
```

Add a button to the north region, and force the frame to lay out the components (Figure 14–24).

```
>>> f.contentPane.add(JButton("NORTH"),BorderLayout.NORTH)
>>> f.contentPane.doLayout()
```

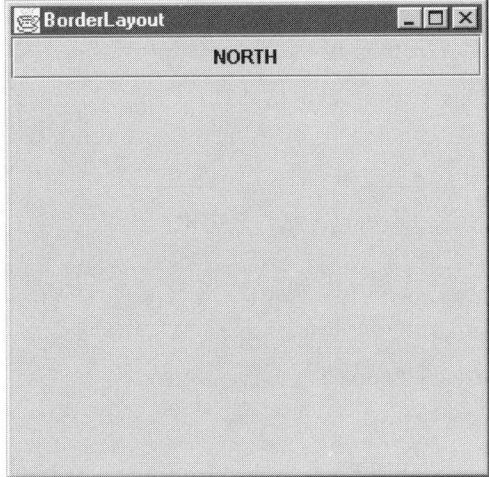

**Figure 14–24**    BorderLayout *Frame with a Button in the North Region*

**Figure 14–25**    BorderLayout *Frame with a Button Added in the East Region*

Notice that the button's width is stretched to the full width of the container. Add a button to the east region (Figure 14–25).

```
>>> f.contentPane.add(JButton("EAST"), BorderLayout.EAST)
>>> f.contentPane.doLayout()
```

Notice that its height is the full height of the container minus the height of the button added to the north region. Add a button to the west region (Figure 14–26).

```
>>> f.contentPane.add(JButton("WEST"), BorderLayout.WEST)
>>> f.contentPane.doLayout()
```

Add a button to the south region (Figure 14–27).

```
>>> f.contentPane.add(JButton("SOUTH"), BorderLayout.SOUTH)
>>> f.contentPane.doLayout()
```

Notice that the height of the west and south buttons decreases by the height of the south button. Add a button to the center region (Figure 14–28).

```
>>> f.contentPane.add(JButton("CENTER"), BorderLayout.CENTER)
>>> f.contentPane.doLayout()
```

Notice that it gets all the leftovers.

Let's verify that the width of the east and west regions is equal to the preferred size of the components added to them. Set up some constants to extract the components from the container.

```
>>> NORTH,EAST,WEST,south=0,1,2,3
```

Get the preferred size and the actual size of the component added to the east region.

```
>>> f.contentPane.components[EAST].preferredSize
java.awt.Dimension[width=65,height=27]
>>> f.contentPane.components[EAST].size
java.awt.Dimension[width=65,height=219]
```

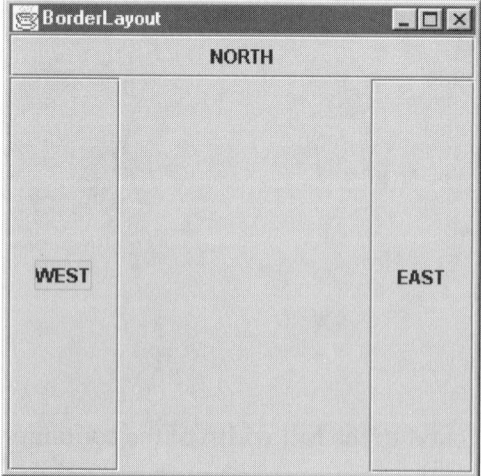

**Figure 14–26** BorderLayout *Frame with a Button Added in the West Region*

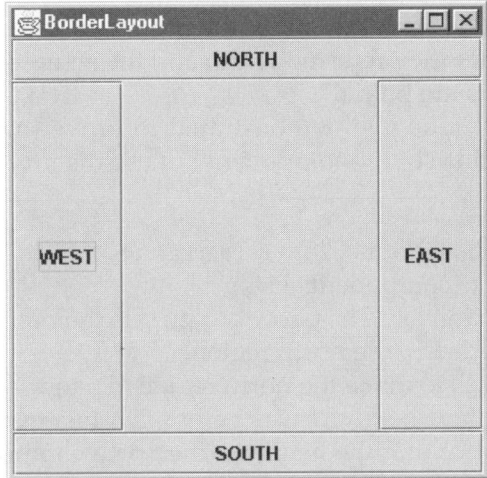

**Figure 14–27**    BorderLayout *Frame with a Button Added in the South Region*

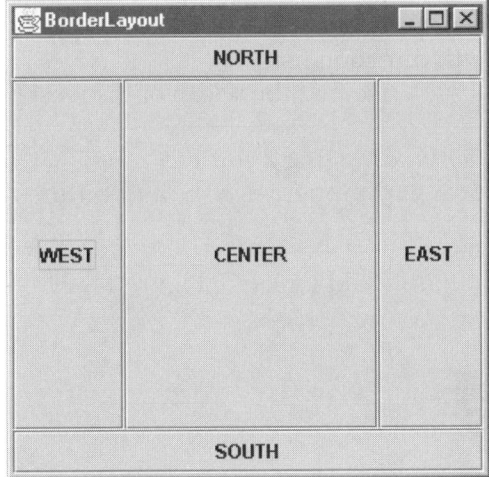

**Figure 14–28**    BorderLayout *Frame with a Button Added in the Center Region*

Get the preferred size and the actual size of the component added to the west region.

```
>>> f.contentPane.components[WEST].preferredSize
java.awt.Dimension[width=69,height=27]
>>> f.contentPane.components[WEST].size
java.awt.Dimension[width=69,height=219]
```

Notice that the preferred width and the actual width of the button added to the east region are both 65. Also notice that the preferred width and the actual width of the button added to the west region are both 69.

As an exercise, use the same technique just demonstrated to prove that the north and south regions stretch the width of the component but use the preferred height. Then, using *Layout4.py*, try this:

1. Change the layout manager in the layouts list to BorderLayout.
2. Select the north component in the components list.
3. Select height in the growth direction list. The Grow button sets the preferred height of the button that was added to the north region.
4. Hit the Grow button several times to make the north region expand.
5. Make the frame half the width and height it was before. Do this in small increments with the mouse. Notice that the height of the north component doesn't change.
6. Hit the Resize button to set the size back to normal.
7. Make the frame twice as big (use the mouse to drag the corner of the frame). Notice that the north component doesn't change.
8. Hit the Resize button.
9. Select the west component in the components list.
10. Select the width item in the growth direction list.
11. Hit the Grow button several times. Notice that the width of the west button grows.
12. Make the frame larger and smaller by dragging a corner.
13. Change the horizontal and vertical gap properties to 5, and hit the Apply button.

If you've followed along the layout frame should look like Figure 14–29.

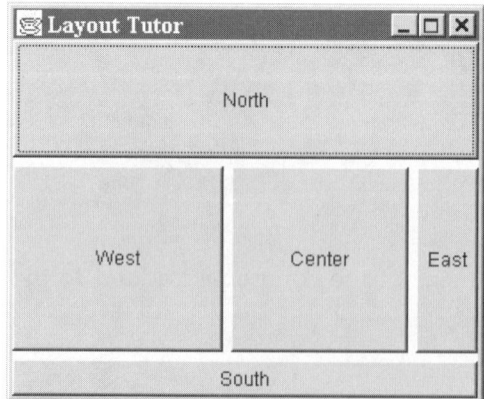

**Figure 14–29**   Layout4.py *Result*

## GridBagLayout

`GridBagLayout` is the most complex and most feared layout manager. It's also the most hated and yet the most loved. Most important, it's the most powerful and, in my opinion, the most useful.

This layout manager is somewhat like `GridLayout` in that you lay out components in cells in a grid. However, its components can span multiple cells, and the cells aren't always the same size. Instead, you set the ratio of container space the cells will use. For example, one column of cells can span half the width of the container; the other two columns can span a quarter of the width.

Unlike in `GridLayout`, in `GridBagLayout` components don't have to span the width and height of the cells, so their preferred size can be maintained. You can specify that the component width and/or height span the cell width or height. You can also specify that the component be anchored in the center, north, south, east, or west region of a cell.

### *GridBagConstraints*

To create a `GridBagLayout` component, you need to master the `GridBagConstraints` class, which specifies all constraints for a given cell. The instances of this class are associated with components added to the container that has `GridBagLayout` as its layout manager. `GridBagConstraints` determines the placement, cell dimensions, alignment, ratio, and so forth. The association among the `GridBagLayout` instance, `GridBagConstraints`, and each component defines the overall layout of components in the container.

Here are `GridBagConstraint`'s properties:

- `gridx`, `gridy`—defines the cell location of the constraint
- `gridheight`, `gridwidth`—defines the cell width and cell height
- `weightx`, `weighty`—defines the ratio between the cells
- `anchor`—defines the justification of a component within the cell (CENTER, NORTH, WEST, etc.)
- `fill`—holds the fill type, i.e., whether or not the component spans the width or height of the cell (possible values are BOTH, VERTICAL, NONE, HORIZONTAL)
- `insets`—sets the insets
- `ipadx`, `ipady`—sets additional padding needed for a cell (width or height in addition to the ratio defined by `weightx` or `weighty` for a particular cell)

The number of rows and columns in the container is a function of the largest `gridx` and `gridy` specified in a constraint if no rows or columns are blank. Say you specify a particular cell location as `gridx=5`, `gridy=5`. If there are no cells in the fourth row or column but there are cells in the third row or column, cell 5,5 actually equates to cell 4,4.

GridBagLayout lays out cells left to right and then top to bottom, so `gridx=0` and `gridy=0`, respectively, indicate the first row and first column at the top left corner of the component.

`gridheight` and `gridwidth` specify the cell width. If we have a constraint that has a `gridx` and a `gridy` of 1 and a `gridheight` and a `gridwidth` of 2, that region spans multiple cells (1,1 to 3,3).

`weightx` and `weighty` specify the ratio given to a certain cell. If the `weightx` is 0, there's another cell in the same column setting the ratio of width space for it. If `weighty` is 0, there's another cell in that row setting the ratio of height space for the column. If three cells in the row have `weightx` of 33, each cell gets a horizontal width equal to 33 percent of the width of the container, in other words, each cell width = 33/(33+33+33) = 33%.

If three cells in the same column have a weight of 33, each cell gets a vertical height equal to 33 percent of the height of the container, in other words, each cell height = 33/(33+33+33) = 33%.

`fill` holds the fill type. The possible values in this situation are BOTH, VERTICAL, NONE, and HORIZONTAL. BOTH specifies that the component span both the vertical and horizontal space of the cell (this is similar to the `GridLayout` cells). VERTICAL specifies that the component stretch across the vertical area of the cell. HORIZONTAL specifies that the component stretch across the horizontal area of the cell. NONE specifies that the component not stretch in either direction, so that it remains its preferred size in the cell.

---

## A GridBagLayout Example

Theory is good, but we need to put some code behind these abstract concepts. The following example, from *GridBag.py*, takes us step by step through the layout of components with `GridBagLayout`. At first we'll use only buttons; then we'll graduate to other components such as text fields and labels. To start, import the classes needed.

```
>>> from javax.swing import JButton, JTextField, JFrame, JButton, JPanel, JLabel
>>> from java.awt import GridBagLayout, GridBagConstraints
```

### Constraints

Define a helper function for creating `GridBagConstraints`. If you're following along in the interactive interpreter, enter `from GridBag import makeConstraint`.

```
def makeConstraint()
gridx=0, gridy=0,        # Holds the x, y cell location in the grid
gridheight=1, gridwidth=1, # Holds the cell width and cell height
weightx=0,weighty=0,     # Determines ratio relative to another.
anchor= GridBagConstraints.CENTER,  # Holds the justification
fill=GridBagConstraints.NONE,       # Holds the fill type BOTH, NONE,...
```

```
insets=Insets(0,0,0,0),
ipadx=0, ipady=0          ):
return
GridBagConstraints(gridx,gridy,gridwidth,gridheight,weightx,weighty,anchor,
fill,insets, ipadx, ipady)
```

Import the helper method to create `GridBagConstraints` without specifying all of its parameters.

```
>>> from GridBag import makeConstraint
```

Create a `GridBagLayout` instance. Then create a panel that has its layout manager property set to the `GridBagLayout` instance.

```
>>> gbag = GridBagLayout()
>>> contentPane = JPanel(layout=gbag)
>>> frame = JFrame(contentPane=contentPane)
```

Create a 2-row–by–2-column layout, first defining the top left region.

```
>>> top_left = makeConstraint(0,0,1,1, weightx=20, weighty=50,
fill=GridBagConstraints.BOTH)
```

Notice that `gridx` and `gridy` are both set to 0, so this component will be in the top left, or the first row, first column of the grid.

Define the top right region.

```
>>> top_right = makeConstraint(1,0,1,1, weightx=80,
fill=GridBagConstraints.BOTH)
```

Notice that `gridx` is set to 1 and `gridy` is set to 0, which means that this region equates to the cell located at the first row, second column of the grid.

Define the bottom left region.

```
>>> bottom_left = makeConstraint(0,1,1,1, weighty=50,
fill=GridBagConstraints.BOTH)
```

`gridx` is set to 0, so this is the first column. `gridy` is set to 1, so this is the second row.

```
>>> bottom_right = makeConstraint(1,1,1,1,fill=GridBagConstraints.BOTH)
```

Notice that `weightx` of cell `top_left` (0,0) is set to 20 and `weightx` of cell `top_right` (1,0) is set to 80. This means that the top left cell will get 20/(20+80), or 20 percent, of the width of the container and that the top right cell will get 80/(20+80), or 80 percent, of the width. Also notice that both cells, `top_left` and `top_right`, have `weighty` of 50, so each gets 50/(50+50), or 50 percent, of the height of the container, The fill is set so that the components fill the full height and width of the cell.

## Components

Now that we've set the dimensions of the cells, let's create some components and add them to the containers.

Define some sample components—buttons whose labels correspond to where they'll be added in the grid layout.

```
>>> tl = JButton("Top Left")
>>> tr = JButton("Top Right")
>>> bl = JButton("Bottom Left")
>>> br = JButton("Bottom Right")
```

Add the components to the contentPane using their corresponding GridBag Constraints.

```
>>> contentPane.add(tl, top_left)
>>> contentPane.add(tr, top_right)
>>> contentPane.add(bl, bottom_left)
>>> contentPane.add(br, bottom_right)
```

Size the frame and show it.

```
>>> frame.size=(400,200)
>>> frame.validate()
>>> frame.visible=1
```

If you've been following along, your frame should look like the one in Figure 14–30. Now change the size of the container to 600,100.

```
>>> frame.size=(600,100)
>>> frame.validate()
```

Notice that the 80:20 ratio between the top left and top right widths remains consistent. So does the 50:50 ratio between the top left and bottom left heights. Your frame should look like the one in Figure 14–31.

Let's change the size to 500,500 so you can get the true feel of things.

```
>>> frame.size=(500,500)
>>> frame.invalidate()
>>> frame.validate()
```

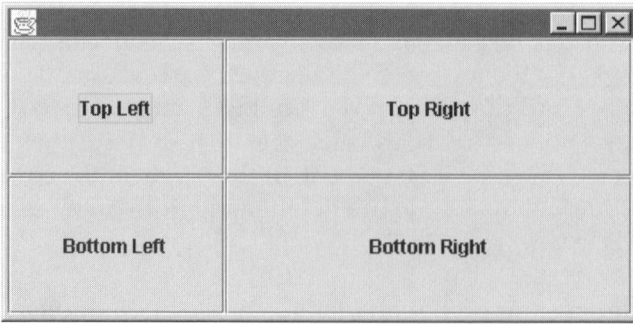

**Figure 14–30** GridBag.py *Example*

**Figure 14–31** GridBag.py *Example with a Container Size of 600,100*

Try packing the frame. What do you think will happen?

```
>>> frame.pack()
```

## Adding and Removing Components

For this next set of exercises, we're going to remove and add components after each step. We'll define a set of helper functions to do this. (Import them from *GridBag.py*.)

```
def addComponents(contentPane, comps):
    for (component, constraint) in comps:
        contentPane.add(component, constraint)

def removeComponents(contentPane):
        #Remove the components
    for x in range (0,contentPane.componentCount):
        contentPane.remove(0)
```

Import the addComponents() and removeComponents() functions.

```
>>> from GridBag import addComponents, removeComponents
```

Group component/constraint pairs into a list.

```
>>> comps = [(tl, top_left),(tr, top_right),(bl, bottom_left),(br,
            bottom_right)]
```

We've essentially defined a list of tuples, each of which contains a component and a constraint. We can use them to iterate through the component/constraint pairs and add them to the panel.

```
for (component, constraint) in comps:
    contentPane.add(component, constraint)
```

Set the ipadx and ipady properties for the top left and top right cells, and set the fill to NONE for both. Then resize the frame to 600,100, and add and remove the components from the container. (See Figure 14–32.)

```
>>> top_left.ipadx, top_left.ipady, top_left.fill = 10, 10,
GridBagConstraints.NONE
>>> top_right.ipadx, top_right.ipady, top_right.fill = 10, 10,
GridBagConstraints.NONE
>>> removeComponents(contentPane)
>>> addComponents(contentPane, comps)
>>> frame.size=(600,100); frame.validate()
```

**Figure 14–32**   *Modified* GridBag.py *Example*

**Figure 14–33**   *Modified* GridBag.py *Example with* anchor *Set to* EAST

Notice that the top left and top right components are centered in their cells. That's because the default anchor is CENTER. Remember that the anchor property moves the component to a particular anchor or justification within a cell.

Set the anchor to EAST for the top left and top right constraints.

```
>>> top_left.anchor = GridBagConstraints.EAST
>>> top_right.anchor = GridBagConstraints.EAST
>>> removeComponents();addComponents()
>>> frame.invalidate()
>>> frame.validate()
```

Notice that the top left and top right components are lined up along the east borders of their cells (Figure 14–33).

### The Prototype

Now let's prototype a real application that subsets to the components the address form needs. First, though, we need to clean house.

```
>>> frame.visible=0
>>> frame.dispose()
>>> frame = NONE
>>> contentPane = NONE
```

Define some convenience variables for CENTER, WEST, and EAST.

```
>>> CENTER=GridBagConstraints.CENTER
>>> WEST=GridBagConstraints.WEST
>>> EAST=GridBagConstraints.EAST
```

Create a 2-column–by–3-row grid that's almost identical to the one created before except for the addition of an extra row at the bottom called last (last goes underneath bottom).

```
>>>                              # x,y,w,h
>>> top_left      = makeConstraint(0,0,1,1, weightx=20,weighty=33, anchor=EAST)
>>> top_right     = makeConstraint(1,0,1,1, weightx=80,            anchor=WEST)
>>> bottom_left   = makeConstraint(0,1,1,1,            weighty=33, anchor=EAST)
>>> bottom_right  = makeConstraint(1,1,1,1,                        anchor=WEST)
>>> last          = makeConstraint(1,2,1,1,            weighty=33)
```

Define some sample components: labels, text fields, and a button.

```
>>> tl = JLabel("Name", JLabel.RIGHT)   #Top Left component
>>> tr = JTextField(20)                 #Top Right component
>>> bl = JLabel("eMail", JLabel.RIGHT)  #Bottom Left component
>>> br = JTextField(30)                 #Bottom Right component
>>> okay = JButton("Okay")
```

Notice that we're using the same nomenclature as in the last example. Only the components are different.

Set up the frame with a panel that uses GridBagLayout.

```
>>> gbag = GridBagLayout()
>>> contentPane = JPanel(layout=gbag)
>>> frame = JFrame(contentPane=contentPane)
```

Add the sample components to contentPane. They have the same name so we can use the addComponents() method. Group the components with the constraints (the OK button and the last constraint are now on the end).

```
>>> comps = [(tl, top_left),(tr, top_right),(bl, bottom_left),(br,
bottom_right),(okay,last)]
>>> addComponents(contentPane, comps)
```

Size the frame, and make it visible. Your frame should look like the one in Figure 14–34.

```
>>> frame.size=(400,200)
>>> frame.visible=1
```

Now let's try resizing the frame to see what happens to the components. Change the frame size to 500,500.

```
>>> frame.size=(500,500)
>>> frame.invalidate()
>>> frame.validate()
```

Change the size to 600,100.

```
>>> frame.size=(600,100)
>>> frame.invalidate()
>>> frame.validate()
```

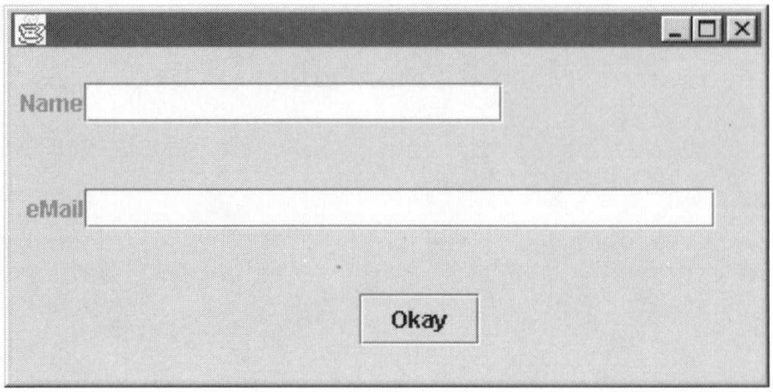

**Figure 14–34**    *Prototype of Name/Email Address Book Entry Form*

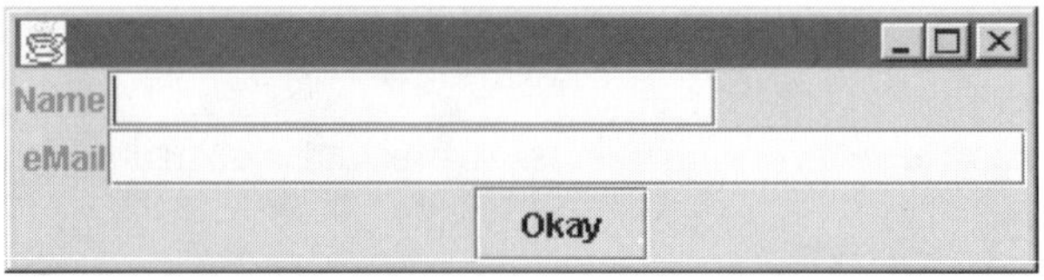

**Figure 14–35**    *A Better-Looking Version of the Name/Email Address Book Entry Form*

Now pack the frame, and see how good it looks. (It should look like Figure 14–35.)

```
>>> frame.pack()
```

Change `ipadx` and `ipady` for `top_left`. Space is added only to the first column, and there's more space between the components.

```
>>> top_left.ipadx, top_left.ipady = 20,20
>>> removeComponents()
>>> addComponents()
>>> contentPane.add(okay, last)
>>> frame.pack()
```

## Experimenting

`GridBagLayout` takes some up-front planning and a lot of messing around with constraints to get what you want, but the reward is a good-looking GUI that can be resized and still display a reasonable layout.

In *Layout4.py*, try this exercise:

1. From `layouts` select `GridBagLayout`. Notice that a 3-by-3 grid is defined. You should get two frames that look like Figure 14–36.
2. Select the top right component in the components list.

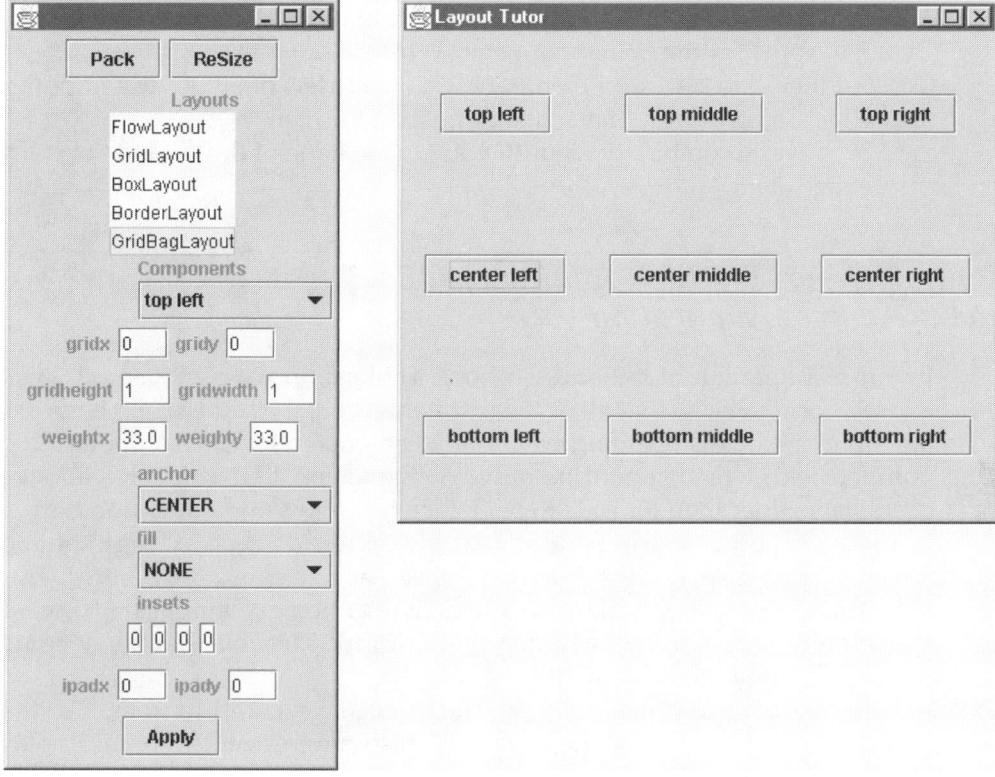

**Figure 14–36**   Layout4.py *after the Exercise*

3. Change the anchor to WEST from the anchor list. Then hit the Apply button. What happens?

4. Select the center right component from the components list. Then change the anchor to EAST, and hit the Apply button. What happens?

5. Try all possible combinations with anchor on several components. Then exit, and restart *Layout4.py*.

6. Hit the Pack button. Select All from the components list. Change the fill from NONE to BOTH, and hit the Apply button. Notice that the anchors for center right and top right no longer have any effect. What happens?

7. Hit Pack, and resize a few times.

8. Change the fill type to HORIZONTAL; then hit the Apply button. What happens?

9. Change the anchor to SOUTH; then hit the Apply button. What happens?

10. Select the top left component, and set its gridx to 3. What happens? Hit the Apply button. What happens? Why?

11. Select the top right component, and set its gridx to 4. What happens? Hit the Apply button. What happens? Why?

12. Select the top middle component, and set its `gridx` to 5. What happens? Hit the Apply button. What happens? Why?
13. Set the fill to `BOTH`, and then play with the insets of all of the components.
14. Create a constraint that spans more than one cell.
15. Try several combinations until you get the hang of things. Don't be afraid to experiment.

---

## Putting Things Together: Adding GridBagLayout to the Address Application

In our last iteration of the address book application we used `GridLayout` for the address form pane so that all of the text fields were the same size. That's okay for the name field, which should be about 20 characters, but what about the phone number field, which should be only 13 characters? Left alone, it's about seven characters wider than it needs to be, which is sloppy, not to mention ugly.

To fix the address form pane so that the text fields vary in length but are still flexible across displays, we'll use `GridBagLayout` to create a 3-by-3 grid. The code to do this is nearly identical to the interactive session explaining `GridBagLayout`, so you should be able to follow along without much trouble. In case of confusion, I've added numerous comments.

Review the code (from *three\AddressFormPane.py*), and then look at the new address book application in Figure 14–37. Also run this version of the application, and try resizing the frame to see what happens to the components.

```
def __init__CreateTextFieldPanel(self):

        """ Set up the email, phoneNumber and name text fields """
            # Create the panel and set the grid layout.
            # The grid has a layout of a 3 rows by 2 columns.
        editPane = JPanel()
        self.cadd(editPane, BorderLayout.CENTER)
        editPane.setLayout(GridBagLayout())

            # Set up some constants for the anchor.
        CENTER=GridBagConstraints.CENTER
        WEST=GridBagConstraints.WEST
        EAST=GridBagConstraints.EAST
            # Now let's create a 2 column by 3 row grid.
            # This will be almost identical to the one we created
            # before.
                        # x,y,w,h
        top_left=makeConstraint(0,0,1,1,weightx=20,weighty=33,anchor=EAST)
        top_right = makeConstraint(1,0,1,1,weightx=80,anchor=WEST)
        CENTER_left = makeConstraint(0,1,1,1,weighty=33,anchor=EAST)
        CENTER_right = makeConstraint(1,1,1,1,anchor=WEST)
        bottom_left = makeConstraint(0,2,1,1,weighty=33, anchor=EAST)
        bottom_right = makeConstraint(1,2,1,1,anchor=WEST)
            # Create the name textfield. Then add it and its
            # associated label to the contentPane.
```

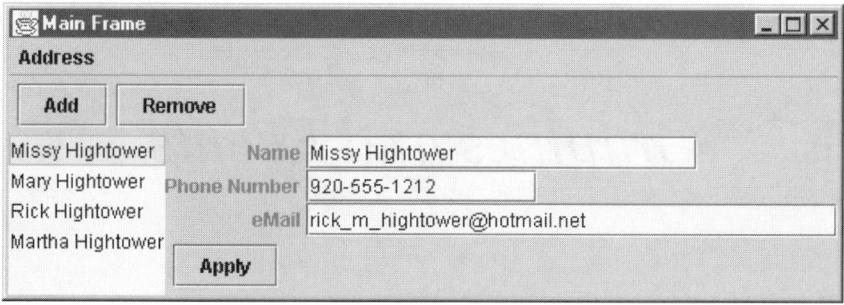

**Figure 14–37**   *Address Book Entry Form with Varying-length Fields*

```
        # Add the label to the top_left and the __name
        # textField to the top_right.
self.__name = JTextField(22, text=self.__address.name())
editPane.add(JLabel("Name ", JLabel.RIGHT), top_left)
editPane.add(self.__name, top_right)
        # Create the phoneNumber textfield. Then add it and
        # its corresponding label to the contentPane.
        # Add the label to the CENTER_left. Add the
        # __phoneNumber textfield to the CENTER_right.
self.__phoneNumber=
    JTextField(13,text=self.__address.phoneNumber())
editPane.add(JLabel("Phone Number ", JLabel.RIGHT), CENTER_left)
editPane.add(self.__phoneNumber, CENTER_right)
        # Create the email textfield. Then add it and its
        # associated label to the contentPane.
        # Add the label to the bottom_left. Add the __email
        # textfield to the bottom_right.
self.__email = JTextField(30, text=self.__address.email())
editPane.add(JLabel("eMail ", JLabel.RIGHT), bottom_left)
editPane.add(self.__email, bottom_right)
```

Compare Figure 14–37 to Figure 14–17, which uses GridLayout for the address form instead of GridBagLayout. Which do you think looks better?

## *Summary*

In this chapter, we used the things we've learned about Java GUIs to add a GUI to our address book application. Along the way, we added other things: a list to select address entries based on a person's name, a toolbar, menubar, and popup menus.

With the address book application, we worked with GridLayout, FlowLayout, GridBagLayout, and BorderLayout. We also covered the ins and outs of Java menuing systems and layout managers.

# CHAPTER 15

# Graphics and Events

- ⟡ Coupling
- ⟡ Encapsulation
- ⟡ Event-driven programming
- ⟡ Event model

- ⟡ Graphics object
- ⟡ Hit testing
- ⟡ Input focus
- ⟡ Modularity
- ⟡ Polyline

- ⟡ Scaffolding code
- ⟡ Static versus interactive mode
- ⟡ Unit level test

In this chapter, we'll learn the basics of events and graphics. These are the things you'll need to know when you write your own graphical components. In particular, you'll need to understand the event model and some rudimentary graphics programming. In a later chapter, we'll see how to package your component in a Java bean so you can distribute it to the unsuspecting world. We're just scratching the surface of graphics in this book.

## A Quick Graphics Tour

Every AWT component has a method called `getGraphics()`, which returns the instance of the graphics object associated with it. The graphics object allows you to draw on the component. With the `java.awt.Graphics` object you can draw arcs, images, lines, ovals, polylines, and such. We can't cover all of the possibilities, only enough to whet your appetite. Later we'll build a drawing package that works with text, rectangles, circles, and ovals. For now, let's do an interactive session that introduces drawing on a component.

Import a frame, and create an instance of it. We'll use it to do our drawing.

```
>>> from javax.swing import JFrame, JPanel
>>> frame = JFrame("Drawing", size=(400,400), visible=1)

>>> graphics = frame.contentPane.graphics
```

Get the graphics instance from the frame, and draw a line, but first make sure that no other window is obscuring the frame. You may have to reduce the size of the window that contains the Jython prompt for this.

Draw a line with starting coordinates of 50,50 and ending coordinates of 200,200 (in pixels).

```
>>> graphics = frame.getGraphics()()
>>> graphics.drawLine(50, 50, 200,200)
```

Draw a circle (actually an oval with equal width and height).

```
>>> graphics.drawOval(50,50,300,300)
```

To put text on the frame, pass the starting coordinates and the string you want to draw to the graphic's drawString() method. The string will be in the component's current font. Draw a string with starting coordinates of 50,50.

```
>>> graphics.drawString("Hello World", 50,50)
```

Draw a string with starting coordinates of 75,75.

```
>>> graphics.drawString("I am late again", 75,75)
```

Draw a string with starting coordinates of 200,200.

```
>>> graphics.drawString("Hello Cruel World", 200, 200)
```

We can draw filled shapes as well as outlines. We can also change color by setting the graphics color property. Draw an oval.

```
>>> graphics.fillOval(150,150, 50, 100)
```

Draw a blue oval.

```
>>> from java.awt import Color
>>> graphics.color = Color.blue
>>> graphics.fillOval(150,150, 100, 50)
```

Dispose of the graphics resource. You must always do this when you're done with your drawing.

```
>>> graphics.dispose()
```

Your frame should look like Figure 15–1. Notice that, if you resize or obscure the frame with another window, the image is erased. This simply won't do. We need something a little less transitive, which gets us back to event-driven programming. Enter the paint() method, which will tell us when the window needs to be redrawn so that we can take the necessary action.

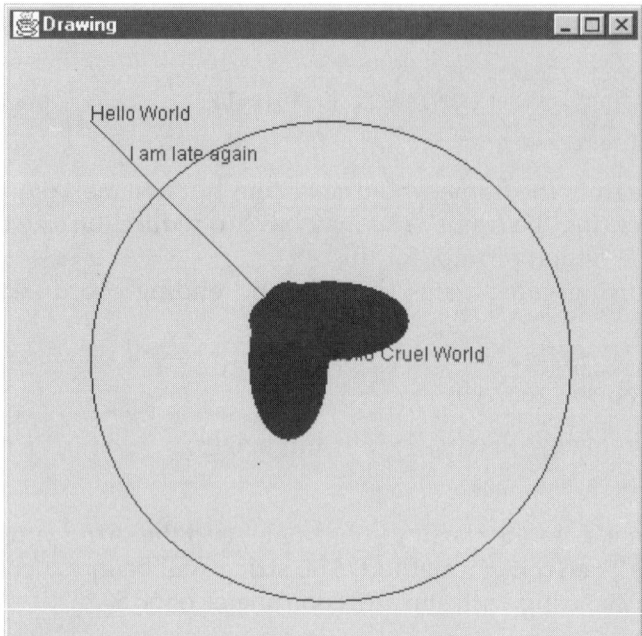

**Figure 15–1** *Outlined and Filled Shapes*

A component (window, frame, panel, etc.) is notified that its window needs to be redrawn via the paint() method. paint() is passed a Graphics class instance that refers to the current component. With paint(), you don't dispose of this instance when you're done.

Here's an example of the paint() method (class DrawPicture from *draw2.py*) showing how it redraws the image we created in our first session. This time we'll be able to resize and obscure the window, and it will always redraw the picture properly.

```
from javax.swing import JFrame
from java.awt import Color

class DrawPicture(JFrame):
    def __init__(self):
        JFrame.__init__(self,"Drawing", size=(400,400), visible=1)
        def closing(event):
            from java.lang import System
            System.exit(0)
        self.windowClosing = closing

    def paint(self,graphics):
            #Draw a line and a circle.
        graphics.drawLine(50, 50, 200,200)
        graphics.drawOval(50,50,300,300)
```

```
            #Draw some strings
        graphics.drawString("Hello World", 50,50)
        graphics.drawString("I am late again", 75,75)
        graphics.drawString("Hello Cruel World", 200, 200)

            #Draw an Oval
        graphics.fillOval(150,150, 50, 100)

            #Draw a Blue Oval
        graphics.color = Color.blue
        graphics.fillOval(150, 150, 100, 50)
if __name__ == '__main__':
        d = DrawPicture()
```

The frame should now look like Figure 15–2. Notice that you can resize it and obscure it with other windows. Every time you return to the picture, it will be just like it was when you left it.

That was a painless introduction to graphics programming. Look up `java.awt.` `Graphics` in the Java API documentation; you'll see that we've covered only a fraction of what you can do with it. You may also want to learn about the 2D and 3D APIs.

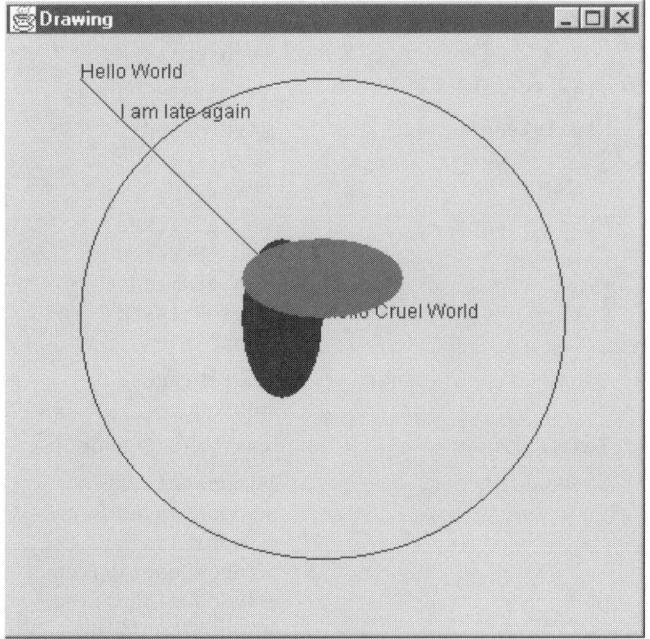

**Figure 15–2**   *Figure 15–1 Redrawn with the* `paint()` *Method*

## A Quick Tour of Common Events

Table 15–1 lists common events and their corresponding event properties. Table 15–2 lists common events and the first component in the class hierarchy to which each event maps. The first thing you may notice in Table 15–2 is that some components are missing, such as JFrame and, for that matter, Frame. Remember, though, that JFrame is a subclass of Frame, and that Frame is a subclass of Window. Thus, JFrame publishes window events through the Window's interface, Window Listener.

**Table 15–1** *Common Graphics Events and Their Event Properties*

| Event | Listener Interface | Property |
|---|---|---|
| ActionEvent | ActionListener | actionPerformed |
| AdjustmentEvent | AdjustmentListener | adjustmentValueChanged |
| ComponentEvent | ComponentListener | componentHidden<br>componentMoved<br>componentResized<br>componentShown |
| ContainerEvent | ContainerListener | componentAdded<br>componentRemoved |
| FocusEvent | FocusListener | focusGained<br>focusLost |
| ItemEvent | ItemListener | itemStateChanged |
| KeyEvent | KeyListener | keyPressed<br>keyReleased<br>keyTyped |
| MouseEvent | MouseListener | mouseClicked<br>mouseEntered<br>mouseExited<br>mousePressed<br>mouseReleased |
| MouseEvent | MouseMotionListener | mouseDragged<br>mouseMoved |
| TextEvent | TextListener | textValueChanged |
| WindowEvent | WindowListener | windowActivated<br>windowClosed<br>windowClosing<br>windowDeactivated<br>windowDeiconified<br>windowIconified<br>windowOpened |

**Table 15–2**   *Common Graphic Events and Their Class Hierarchy Mappings*

| Component | Event Published through Listener | Meaning |
|---|---|---|
| AbstractButton | ActionEvent, ActionListener | User clicked button |
| JButton | ActionEvent, ActionListener | User clicked button |
| JCheckBox | ItemEvent, ItemListener | User selected or unselected checkbox |
| JCheckBoxMenuItem | ItemEvent, ItemListener | User selected or unselected CheckboxMenuItem |
| Component | ComponentEvent, ComponentListener | Component moved, resized shown, or hidden |
| | FocusEvent, FocusListener | Component lost or got focus |
| | MouseEvent, MouseListener | User clicked, pressed, and released mouse, and mouse cursor entered or exited component |
| | MouseEvent, MouseMotionListener | User moved mouse in component, and dragged mouse, i.e., pressed button while moving mouse cursor |
| Container | ContainerEvent, ContainerListener | Component added or removed |
| JComboBox | ActionEvent, ActionListener | Item double-clicked |
| | ItemEvent, ItemListener | Item selected or unselected |
| JList | ListSelectionEvent, ListSelectionListener | Item double-clicked |
| | ItemEvent, ItemListener | Item selected or unselected |
| JMenuItem | ActionEvent, ActionListener | Menu item selected |
| JScrollBar | AdjustmentEvent, AdjustmentListener | User moved scrollbar |
| JTextField | ActionEvent, ActionListener | User pressed Enter in text box |
| Window | WindowEvent, WindowListener | Window was opened, closed, iconified, restored, or a close was requested |

It doesn't stop there. Window is a subclass of Container, so JFrame publishes container events through the ContainerListener interface as well. And, like other components, JFrame is a subclass of Component, so it publishes component events through the ComponentListener interface, focus events through the FocusListener interface, and mouse events through the MouseListener and MouseMotionListener interfaces (Container is a direct subclass of Component). The point is that a component doesn't just publish the events it defines; it publishes all events from its hierarchy of superclasses.

Another example of this is JButton, which is a subclass of AbstractButton, which is a subclass of JComponent, which is a subclass of Container, which is a subclass of Component. As such, it publishes all of the events that its superclasses define.

## An Event Frame

Let's create a frame that handles every possible event—that is, essentially, one frame that handles every event mentioned in the last section that Frame supports. We'll use the Frame class in *java.awt* (from which Swing gets much of its behavior and design). Examine the source code closely (it's from *FrameEvents.py*). Later we'll break it down.

```
from java.awt import Frame, List, Panel, Button, FlowLayout, BorderLayout

class EventFrame(Frame):
    def __init__(self, event_viewer):
        Frame.__init__(self, "Event Frame")

        self.event_viewer = event_viewer
        self.layout = FlowLayout()

            #ComponentEvent publishes to ComponentListener
        self.componentHidden = self.__handle_event
        self.componentMoved = self.__handle_event
        self.componentResized = self.__handle_event
        self.componentShown = self.__handle_event

            #ContainerEvent publishes to ContainerListener
        self.componentAdded = self.__handle_event
        self.componentRemoved = self.__handle_event

            #FocusEvent publishes to FocusListener
        self.focusGained = self.__handle_event
        self.focusLost = self.__handle_event

            #KeyEvent publishes to KeyListener
        self.keyPressed = self.__handle_event
        self.keyReleased = self.__handle_event
        self.keyTyped = self.__handle_event

            #MouseEvent publishes to MouseListener
        self.mouseClicked = self.__handle_event
        self.mouseEntered = self.__handle_event
        self.mouseExited = self.__handle_event
```

```
            self.mousePressed = self.__handle_event
            self.mouseReleased = self.__handle_event

                # MouseEvent publishes to MouseMotionListener
            self.mouseDragged = self.__handle_event
            self.mouseMoved = self.__handle_event

                # WindowEvent publishes to WindowListener
            self.windowActivated = self.__handle_event
            self.windowClosed = self.__handle_event
            self.windowClosing = self.__handle_event
            self.windowDeactivated = self.__handle_event
            self.windowDeiconified = self.__handle_event
            self.windowIconified = self.__handle_event
            self.windowOpened = self.__handle_event

               self.size=(100,100)
            self.visible=1

            #handles all of the events in this demo
        def __handle_event(self, event):
            self.event_viewer.addEvent(event)

 .  .  .
 .  .  .

class EventViewer(Frame):
        def __init__(self, close):
            Frame.__init__(self,"Event Viewer")

                 # Create a list to display events
            self.__list = List()
            self.add(self.__list, BorderLayout.CENTER)

                 # Set up toolbar to add and remove components from frame
            add = Button("Add")
            add.actionPerformed = self.__handle_add
            remove = Button("Remove")
            remove.actionPerformed = self.__handle_remove
            tool_pane = Panel()
            tool_pane.add(add)
            tool_pane.add(remove)
            self.add(tool_pane, BorderLayout.NORTH)
            self.size=(500,400)
            self.visible=1
            self.location=(300,300)
            .  .  .

        def addEvent(self, event):
            self.__list.add(`event`,0)

            #add a component to the frame
        def __handle_add(self, event):
            global frame
            frame.add(Button(`frame.componentCount`))
            frame.invalidate();frame.validate()
```

```
                    #removes a component from the frame
        def __handle_remove(self, event):
            if (frame.componentCount > 0):
                frame.remove(frame.componentCount-1)
                frame.invalidate();frame.validate()
if __name__ == '__main__':
    viewer = EventViewer(close)
    frame = EventFrame(viewer)
```

## Window Events with EventFrame

The code for our example is pretty simple. In the constructor of the EventFrame
class, we register for every event that Frame publishes. All of the events are registered to the same event handler method, __handle_event().

```
        #handles all of the events in this demo
def __handle_event(self, event):
        self.event_viewer.addEvent(event)
```

The event handler calls self.event_viewer.addEvent, which adds the event to a
listbox so we can view it. addEvent() forces the event to the top of the list, using
back quotes to get its string representation.

```
def addEvent(self, event):
        self.__list.add(`event`,0)
```

Now let's use EventFrame to examine all of the events that the frame handles:

- windowActivated
- windowClosed
- windowClosing
- windowDeactivated
- windowDeiconified
- windowIconified
- windowOpened

To use WindowActivated, all we need to do is start *EventFrames.py*. When the window comes up, we get the following events:

- java.awt.event.WindowEvent[**WINDOW_ACTIVATED**] on frame0
- java.awt.event.FocusEvent[**FOCUS_GAINED**,permanent] on frame0
- java.awt.event.ComponentEvent[**COMPONENT_SHOWN**] on frame0
- java.awt.event.WindowEvent[**WINDOW_OPENED**] on frame0

WindowEvent, with its ID set to WINDOW_ACTIVATED, corresponds to the window
Activated event property of the frame. This pattern repeats itself for all event
properties and event IDs. Notice that, in addition to windowOpened and window
Activated, Frame publishes focusGained and componentShown.

When the focus changes to another window, you get the following window Deactivated events. Click on the caption of the event viewer.

- `java.awt.event.WindowEvent[`**`WINDOW_DEACTIVATED`**`] on frame0`
- `java.awt.event.FocusEvent[`**`FOCUS_LOST`**`,temporary] on frame0`

To get a windowIconified event, we have to minimize the window by clicking the Minimize button on the right side of the window's caption. The following events result:

- `java.awt.event.FocusEvent[`**`FOCUS_LOST`**`,temporary] on frame0`
- `java.awt.event.WindowEvent[`**`WINDOW_ICONIFIED`**`] on frame0`
- `java.awt.event.WindowEvent[`**`WINDOW_DEACTIVATED`**`] on frame0`

Now we want to restore the frame, so we go to the taskbar and click the Frames icon. These are the events we get:

- `java.awt.event.WindowEvent[`**`WINDOW_ACTIVATED`**`] on frame0`
- `java.awt.event.WindowEvent[`**`WINDOW_DEICONIFIED`**`] on frame0`
- `java.awt.event.FocusEvent[`**`FOCUS_GAINED`**`,permanent] on frame0`

Then we click the window's Close button to get the windowClosing event:

- `java.awt.event.WindowEvent[`**`WINDOW_CLOSING`**`] on frame0`

The event is a request to close, not the actual closing. For that we have to restart the application in the interactive interpreter and type

```
>>> frame.visible = 0
java.awt.event.ComponentEvent[COMPONENT_HIDDEN] on frame0

>>> frame.dispose()
java.awt.event.WindowEvent[WINDOW_CLOSED] on frame0
```

Hiding the frame doesn't close it. The dispose() function does that.

## Container Events with EventFrame

On the event viewer window are the Add and Remove buttons, which add components to and remove them from the frame. If you hit Add twice and Remove twice, you'll get the following events:

- `java.awt.event.ContainerEvent[COMPONENT_ADDED,child=button0] on frame0`
- `java.awt.event.ContainerEvent[COMPONENT_ADDED,child=button1] on frame0`
- `java.awt.event.ContainerEvent[COMPONENT_REMOVED,child=button1] on frame0`
- `java.awt.event.ContainerEvent[COMPONENT_REMOVED,child=button0] on frame0`

## Key Events with EventFrame

If you make the frame the active window and press the A key, you should get the following events:

- `java.awt.event.KeyEvent[KEY_PRESSED,keyCode=65,keyChar='a'] on frame0`
- `java.awt.event.KeyEvent[KEY_TYPED,keyCode=0,keyChar='a'] on frame0`
- `java.awt.event.KeyEvent[KEY_RELEASED,keyCode=65,keyChar='a'] on frame0`

If you hold the key down, you'll get `keyPressed` and `keyTyped`, but you won't get `keyReleased`.

As an exercise, look up `KeyListener` in the Java API documentation. Note the difference between `keyPressed` and `keyTyped`. If you want to create a typing program, which event do you handle for capturing alphanumeric characters? Which one for handling special keys like Enter and Backspace? You'll need to know this later.

## Mouse Events from FrameEvent

If you click in the `FrameEvent` frame, you'll get the `mousePressed`, `mouseClicked`, and `mouseReleased` mouse events. If you hold the mouse button down and drag it, you'll get the `mouseDragged` event. If you move the mouse pointer anywhere in the work area of the frame (or any place but the caption [titlebar] and system menus), you'll get the `mouseMoved` event. Table 15–3 lists the mouse events.

Try these exercises:

- Click on the frame's work area with both the right and the left buttons. What's the difference in the output?
- This sample application was written in AWT components, which are similar to Swing components. Convert to JFC/Swing. (The component events must be set up with `JFrame`'s `contentPane`.)

**Table 15–3**   *Mouse Events and Event Properties*

| Event | Listener Interface | Property |
|---|---|---|
| MouseEvent | MouseListener | mouseClicked<br>mouseEntered<br>mouseExited<br>mousePressed<br>mouseReleased |
| MouseEvent | mouseMotionListener | mouseDragged<br>mouseMoved |

> **To AWT or Not to AWT**
>
> Many of the concepts in Swing and AWT are very similar. Most of the examples in this book are written in Swing because that's the dominant choice for the Java Standard Edition. However, for the Java Micro edition (Windows CE and handheld devices) AWT is still the best. That's why I used it for some of the examples.

## Putting Things Together: A Drawing Program

Although not as ubiquitous as the famous "Hello World", the sample application explained in the following sections is quite common. We want it to draw ovals, rectangles, circles, and so forth. I've opted for simplicity rather than perfection in my design. Later I'll point out what's wrong with it.

We'll incorporate ideas from many chapters in our program, which we'll develop in two modules and three phases. The first phase is a simple application that draws ovals and rectangles. The second phase will add circles, squares, rounded rectangles, and text. (I know text isn't a shape, but I don't like the correct terminology, "glyph.") The third phase will correct a serious design flaw introduced in the first and second phases.

The first module, *Shapes*, contains all of the graphics. The second module, *DrawShapes*, defines the user interface, that is, the event handling and the component container layout.

### Phase 1: Shapes

The *Shapes* module contains four main classes: Shape, Rectangle, Oval, and Shapes. Shape is the superclass of the others; it defines the interface that all shape classes use so they all can be treated polymorphically (one can be replaced with another). Rectangle inherits most of its functionality from Shape, as does Oval. Shapes represents a collection of shape objects and implements the Shape interface.

The Shape class defines three methods:

- The constructor—stores shape parameters like *x*, *y* position, dimensions (width, height), and color
- The paint() method—paints a shape using the given graphics context
- The draw_filled() method—draws a filled shape
- The draw_outline() method—draws the outline of a shape

The constructor stores five values: *x,y* position, width, height, color, and fill/nofill. Here's some of its code. (All of the following examples are from *One\Shape.py*.)

```
class Shape:
      def __init__(self, x, y, width=0, height=0, color=None, fill=0):
            self.x=x
            self.y=y
            self.width=width
            self.height=height
            self.color=color
            self.fill=fill
```

paint() paints on the given graphics context and so takes a graphics object as an argument. It also checks to see if a color was assigned; if so, it sets the graphics color property to the shape color property and saves the original color to be restored later. If the fill attribute is true, paint()calls the draw_filled() method; otherwise, it calls the draw_outline() method.

### paint() Code and Breakdown
Here's the code for paint():

```
def paint (self, graphics):

      if not self.color is None:
            oldcolor = graphics.color
            graphics.color = self.color

      if self.fill:
            self.draw_filled (graphics)
      else:
            self.draw_outline(graphics)

      if not self.color is None:
            graphics.color = oldcolor
```

draw_filled() and draw_outline()draw the shape as filled or outlined, respectively. They're abstract, meaning that they don't do anything until they're defined by subclasses of Shape. This makes sense when you think about it—for example, only the Rectangle class knows how to draw a rectangle.

Here are the two drawing methods as defined by Shape:

```
def draw_filled(self, graphics):
      pass

def draw_outline(self, graphics):
      pass
```

The draw_outline() method gets the bounds of the shape: position (x,y) and dimensions (width, height). We'll use these to calculate the area of the window that needs to be redrawn. First, we need the getRect() function.

```
def getRect(self):
      return self.x, self.y, self.width, self.height
```

Both Rectangle and Oval subclass Shape, and both implement the abstract methods draw_filled() and draw_outline(). To implement them, the Rectangle class uses the java.awt.Graphics methods fillRect() and drawRect(), respectively; the Oval class uses fillOval() and drawOval().

Here are the Rectangle and Oval classes:

```
class Rectangle(Shape):
    def __init__(self, x, y, width, height, color=None, fill=0):
        Shape.__init__(self, x, y, width, height, color, fill)

    def draw_filled(self,graphics):
        graphics.fillRect(self.x, self.y, self.width, self.height)

    def draw_outline(self,graphics):
        graphics.drawRect(self.x, self.y, self.width, self.height)

class Oval(Shape):
    def __init__(self, x, y, width, height, color=None, fill=0):
        Shape.__init__(self, x, y, width, height, color, fill)

    def draw_filled(self,graphics):
        graphics.fillOval(self.x, self.y, self.width, self.height)

    def draw_outline(self,graphics):
        graphics.drawOval(self.x, self.y, self.width, self.height)
```

### The Shapes Class

The Shapes class (note the plural) holds many shapes and, like Rectangle and Oval, subclasses Shape. Shapes overrides only the paint() method, which when overridden iterates through the list of shapes in the Shapes instance and calls each one of their paint() methods. Also, Shapes calls a getRect() method that calculates the union of all of the bounds of all of the shapes it contains.

Here's the Shapes class:

```
class Shapes (Shape):
    def __init__(self):
        self.__shapes=[]

    def addShape(self, shape):
        self.__shapes.append(shape)

    def paint(self, graphics):
        for shape in self.__shapes:
            shape.paint(graphics)

    def getRect(self):
            # Lists to hold x,y, height and width
            # from shape in shapes
        xl,yl,wl,hl = [],[],[],[]

            # Iterate through the list gathering each shapes
            # bounding rectangle
        for shape in shapes:
            x,y,width, height = shape.getRect()
            xl.append(x)
            yl.append(y)
            wl.append(width)
            hl.append(height)
```

```
                    # Calculate and return the bounding
                    # rectangle for all of the shapes.
                return min(xl), min(yl), max(wl), max(hl)
```

*Testing*

Before we start building the graphical interface, we need to create a unit level test for this module to test the classes defined in Shape. It's much easier to debug the classes in static than in interactive mode. We also need scaffolding code to test the module. (Our scaffolding code adds three shapes to the TestPanel class.)

```
        # This is for testing only
if __name__ == '__main__':
        from javax.swing import JFrame, JPanel
        from java.awt import Color, Font

        class TestPanel(JPanel):

        def __init__(self):
                self.background=Color.white

        def addShape(self,shape):
                self.shapes.addShape(shape)

        def __init__(self):
                self.shapes = Shapes()
                self.addShape(Rectangle(0,0,100,100,Color.blue, 1))
                self.addShape(Rectangle(100,0,100,100,Color.blue))
                self.addShape(Oval(0,100,100,100,Color.blue,1))
                self.addShape(Oval(100,100,100,100, Color.blue))

        def paint(self,graphics):
                self.shapes.paint()(graphics)
frame = JFrame("Test Shapes", size=(400,440), visible=1)
pane = TestPanel()
frame.contentPane = pane
frame.validate()
```

After every major change to the *Shapes* module, you'll want to update the scaffolding code, if necessary, and retest.

## Phase 1: DrawShapes

The *DrawShapes* module does the actual shape drawing. It defines classes to work with mouse and key events, shows the status of operations, sets a shape's fill attribute, and sets up components that allow the user to select rectangles or ovals.
    DrawShapes defines four classes:

- ShapeButton—draws a shape in a button
- ToolBox—holds components; has a preferred size
- StatusBox—displays the status of a drawing operation
- PaintBox—displays shapes the user has drawn
- DrawShapes—as the user interface frame, contains all of the above

### Shapes Button

ShapeButton represents a particular shape and extends javax.swing.JButton. It's passed a Shape instance and draws the shape in its overridden paint() method. It also defines the preferred width and height for the button.

```
class ShapeButton(JButton):
      def __init__(self, shape):
            self.shape = shape

      def paint(self, graphics):
            JButton.paint()(self, graphics)
            self.shape.paint()(graphics)

      def getPreferredSize(self):
            d = Dimension(30,30)
            return d
```

### ToolBox

ToolBox holds ShapeButton and extends javax.swing.Jpanel. It doesn't do much besides define a preferred size.

```
class ToolBox (JPanel):
      def __init__(self):
            JPanel.__init__(self)

      def getPreferredSize(self):
            d = Dimension(40, 0)
            return d
```

### StatusBox

StatusBox holds the current status of events and also extends javax.swing.JPanel. As a helper class, it displays the current status of the drawing options, such as the x,y position of the mouse pointer and the shape being drawn.

```
class StatusBox (JPanel):
      def __init__(self):
            JPanel.__init__(self)
            self.coordinates = JTextField(15, editable=0)
            self.format = 'x = %d, y = %d'
            self.add(self.coordinates)

            self.event_type = JLabel ('MOUSE STATUS ')
            self.add(self.event_type)
            self.shape_type = JLabel ('SHAPE STATUS ')
            self.add(self.shape_type)

      def setXY(self, x,y):
            self.coordinates.text = self.format % (x,y,)

      def setMouseDrag(self, x, y):
            self.event_type.text = 'MOUSE DRAG '
            self.setXY(x,y)

      def setMouseMove(self, x, y):
            self.event_type.text = 'MOUSE MOVE '
            self.setXY(x,y)
```

```
def setMousePress(self, x, y):
    self.event_type.text = 'MOUSE PRESS '
    self.setXY(x,y)

def setMouseRelease(self, x, y):
    self.event_type.text = 'MOUSE RELEASE '
    self.setXY(x,y)

def setShapeType(self, shape_type):

        # Set the label based on the shape type
    if shape_type == PaintBox.RECTANGLE:
        self.shape_type.text = 'RECTANGLE'

    elif shape_type == PaintBox.OVAL:
        self.shape_type.text = 'OVAL'
```

### PaintBox

PaintBox performs all of the graphics operations and handles the mouse events (later it will handle the key events). It's the bread and butter of this sample application, the center ring in this three-ring circus.

When the user hits the mouse button in the paint box, the shape drawing begins. As he drags the lower corner of the shape, an outline appears (this is called rubberbanding). When he lets go of the mouse, the shape is created, added to the other shapes, and redrawn when PaintBox's paint()method is called.

PaintBox extends JComponent. It can draw either rectangles or ovals and has four attributes that determine how the current shape will be drawn: color, fill, rectangle, and oval. The constructor defines these attributes and sets up the event handlers for the mouseDragged, mouseMoved, mousePressed, and mouseReleased events. It's passed an instance of StatusBox (status), which it uses to show the status of the drawing operations.

Here's the PaintBox constructor:

```
class PaintBox (JComponent):
    RECTANGLE=1
    OVAL=2

    def __init__(self, status):
        JComponent.__init__(self)
            self.opaque=1
            self.background=Color.white
        self.status = status
        self.shapes = Shapes()
        self.shape_type = PaintBox.RECTANGLE

        self.mouseDragged = self.handle_mouseDragged
        self.mouseMoved = self.handle_mouseMoved
        self.mousePressed = self.handle_mousePress
        self.mouseReleased = self.handle_mouseRelease

        self.fill=0
        self.color=Color.red
```

The drawing mechanism starts off when the user clicks the mouse button, which fires the `handle_mousePress` method. The event handler sets the shape's starting point (`start`) and initializes its ending point (`last`) to that value.

```
def handle_mousePress(self, event):

        # Print the status
    self.status.setMousePress(event.x, event.y)

        # Save the initial location.
        # In addition save the initial
        # location as the last.
    self.last = self.start = event.point
```

As the user drags the mouse, she gets visual feedback via rubberbanding. When called, the event handler for `mouseDragged` draws an outline of the shape and sets the last point to the current point. Then it calls `drawRubberShape()` twice, once with the last point and once with the current point.

```
def handle_mouseDragged(self,event):

        # Print the status.
    self.status.setMouseDrag(event.x, event.y)

        # Erase the old rubberband shape at the
        # old location. Create the new rubberband shape
        # at the new location
    self.drawRubberShape(self.last.x, self.last.y)
    self.drawRubberShape(event.x, event.y)
        # Save the current event.x and
        # event.y as the last.
    self.last = event.point
```

`drawRubberShape()` is smart enough to erase the last shape drawn whenever it's called twice with the same point. It does this with the `setXORMode()` method of the `java.awt.Graphics` class instance, which sets the graphic mode to XOR. XOR sees to it that a line drawn more than once will be erased. Essentially, it ensures that the colors of the graphics are those specifed in `setXORMode()` for the current graphic context.

Notice that we dispose of the graphic when we're done with it, using a `finally` block. After `drawRubberShape()` sets the graphics mode, it calculates the shape's width and height and then calls the `__drawShape()` method, which actually draws the shape in the current mode.

```
def drawRubberShape(self, x, y):
    g = self.graphics

        # Set the graphics to XOR mode,
        # which allows rubberbanding.
        # Calculate the width and height.
        # Draw the outline of the shape.
```

```
    try:
        g.setXORMode(self.background)
        width = abs(self.start.x - x)
        height = abs(self.start.y - y)
        self.__drawShape(g, self.start.x, self.start.y, width, height)
    finally:
        g.dispose()
```

\_\_drawShape() checks for the shape it's supposed to draw—rectangle or oval. It then creates the specified shape and uses it to draw the corresponding shape, which in turn calls drawOval() or drawRect() accordingly. The x and y of \_\_draw Shape correspond to the starting point defined in the event handler for the mouse Press event. The width and height are the width and height as calculated from the last or current point in the mouseDrag event handler.

```
def __drawShape(self, g, x, y, width, height):
    if self.shape_type == PaintBox.RECTANGLE:
        rect=Rectangle(self.start.x,self.start.y, width,height,fill=0)
        rect.paint(g)
    if self.shape_type == PaintBox.OVAL:
        oval = Oval(self.start.x, self.start.y, width, height, fill=0)
        oval.paint()(g)
```

When the user lets go of the mouse, the mouseRelease event is fired. The handler for this event is handle_mouseRelease, which calculates the width and height of the shape and then creates a corresponding rectangle or oval.

The shape's x,y coordinates are the starting point obtained during the handling of the mousePress event. Its width and height are the distance from the starting point at which the mouseRelease event handler is invoked (that is, when the user releases the mouse button). The shape is then added to the shapes attribute. The panel's repaint() method is called with the boundary of the shape so that the shape is drawn with the paint() method.

```
def handle_mouseRelease(self, event):

        # Print the status
    self.status.setMouseRelease(event.x, event.y)

        # Calculate the width and the height
    width = abs(self.start.x - event.x)
    height = abs(self.start.y - event.y)

    shape = None #to hold the shape we are about to create

        # Create the shape based on the current shape type.
        # Then add the shape to self.shapes.
    if self.shape_type == PaintBox.RECTANGLE:

        shape = Rectangle(self.start.x, self.start.y, width, height,
            self.color, self.fill)

    elif self.shape_type == PaintBox.OVAL:
        shape = Oval(self.start.x, self.start.y, width, height,
            self.color, self.fill)
```

```
        if not shape is None:
                self.shapes.addShape(shape)
                x,y,width,height = shape.getRect()
                self.repaint(x,y,width+1, height+1)
```

The paint() method calls the shapes.paint() method, which iterates through the shapes list and calls all of the shapes' paint() methods.

```
def paint (self, graphics):
        ...
        ...
                #Draw all of the shapes.
        self.shapes.paint(graphics)
```

Since the selection of shape attributes happens in another class, PaintBox exposes the following methods so that the attributes can be set by the class that contains a PaintBox instance:

- setShapeType()—sets the current shape type
- setFill()—turns the shape fill property on or off
- setShapeColor()—sets the current color of the shape to be drawn

```
        def setShapeType(self, shape_type):
                self.status.setShapeType(shape_type)
                self.shape_type = shape_type

        def getShapeType(self):
                return shape_type

        def setFill(self, value):
                self.fill = value

        def setShapeColor(self, color):
                self.color = color
```

### DrawShapes

As the parent frame for the drawing application, DrawShapes contains StatusBox, ToolBox, and PaintBox instances. It also handles all of the options for the shapes and allows the user to pick different shapes as represented by ShapeButton in the ToolBox instance.

The DrawShapes constructor creates four panels, options (an instance of Panel), toolbar (an instance of Panel), status (an instance of StatusBox), and paint (an instance of PaintBox). The paint panel is added to the center region of the Draw Shapes frame; the status panel is added to the south region.

```
class DrawShapes(JFrame):
        def __init__(self):
                JFrame.__init__(self,title='Draw Shapes',visible=1,size=(400,400))
                self.__init__toolbar()
                self.__init__options()

                self.statusPane = StatusBox()
                self.contentPane.add(self.statusPane, BorderLayout.SOUTH)
```

```
        self.PaintPane = PaintBox(self.statusPane)
        self.contentPane.add(self.PaintPane, BorderLayout.CENTER)
...
...
```

The constructor also calls __init__toolbar and __init__option , which create the toolbar and option panels, respectively.

__init__toolbar creates two shape buttons and adds them to the toolbar pane. One of the buttons is initialized with an instance of the Rectangle class; the other, with an instance of the Oval class. The ShapeButton class represents changing the drawing mode to either rectangle or oval. Its handlers are set to the rect_pressed() and oval_pressed() methods, which change the shape to an oval or a rectangle.

__init__toolbar also adds the toolbar panel to the west region of the DrawShapes frame and is defined as follows:

```
def __init__toolbar(self):
    toolbar = ToolBox()

        # Add the rectangle button to the toolbar
    rect = ShapeButton(Rectangle(4, 4, 20, 20))
    toolbar.add(rect)
    rect.actionPerformed = self.rect_pressed

        # Add the oval button to the toolbar
    oval = ShapeButton(Oval(4, 4, 10, 20))
    toolbar.add(oval)
    oval.actionPerformed = self.oval_pressed

     self.add(toolbar, BorderLayout.WEST)
```

__init__options does the equivalent for the options pane. It creates a choice component for color and a checkbox component fill/no fill. It then adds these components to the options pane and places the pane in the north region of the DrawShapes frame.

```
def __init__options(self):
    optionsPane = Panel()

        # Set up the checkbox item for the fill option
    check = Checkbox('Fill')
    optionsPane.add(check)
    check.itemStateChanged = self.fill_clicked

        # Set up the choice for color
    colors = Choice()
    self.colors_dict = {'blue':Color.blue,
                'green':Color.green,
                'red':Color.red,
                'yellow':Color.yellow,
                'orange':Color.orange,
                'cyan':Color.cyan,
                'pink':Color.pink,
                'gray':Color.gray
                }
```

```
      for color in self.colors_dict.keys():
          colors.add(color)

      optionsPane.add(colors)
      colors.itemStateChanged = self.color_changed
      self.add(optionsPane, BorderLayout.NORTH)
```

### DrawShapes Event Handler

All of the event handlers for the components added to the `options` and `toolbar` panes correspond to setting properties in the `paint` pane (`PaintBox` instance).

- The `rect_pressed` event handler is called when the rectangle button is pressed; it sets the shape type of the `paint` pane to `PaintBox.RECTANGLE`.
- The `oval_pressed` event handler is called when the oval button is pressed; it sets the shape type of the `paint` pane to `PaintBox.OVAL`.
- The `fill_clicked` event handler is called when the user checks or unchecks the fill checkbox. If the box is unchecked, the `paint` pane fill property is set to false. If the box is checked, the `paint` pane property is set to true.
- The `color_changed` event handler is called when the user selects a new color in the choice box; it sets the color of the paint box's current paint mode to the color selected.

These event handlers are defined as follows:

```
def rect_pressed(self, event):
    self.paintPane.setShapeType(PaintBox.RECTANGLE)

def oval_pressed(self, event):
    self.paintPane.setShapeType(PaintBox.OVAL)

def fill_clicked(self, event):
    if(event.stateChange==ItemEvent.SELECTED):
        self.PaintPane.setFill(1)
    elif (event.stateChange==ItemEvent.DESELECTED):
        self.PaintPane.setFill(0)

def color_changed(self,event):
    colorname = event.item
    color = self.colors_dict[colorname]
    self.PaintPane.setShapeColor(color)
```

## The Complete Shapes and DrawShapes Modules

We've covered all of the classes. At this point, you may want to run the *Shapes* and *DrawShapes* modules to see the drawing package in action. Here's the *Shapes* module.

```
class Shape:
    def __init__(self, x, y, width=0, height=0, color=None, fill=0):
        self.x=x
        self.y=y
```

```
                self.width=width
                self.height=height
                self.color=color
                self.fill=fill

        def paint(self, graphics):

                if not self.color is None:
                        oldcolor = graphics.foregroundColor
                        graphics.color = self.color

                if self.fill:
                        self.draw_filled(graphics)
                else:
                        self.draw_outline(graphics)

                if not self.color is None:
                        graphics.color = oldcolor

        def draw_filled(self, graphics):
                pass

        def draw_outline(self, graphics):
                pass

        def getRect(self):
                return self.x, self.y, self.width, self.height

class Rectangle(Shape):
        def __init__(self, x, y, width, height, color=None, fill=0):
                Shape.__init__(self, x, y, width, height, color, fill)

        def draw_filled(self,graphics):
                graphics.fillRect(self.x, self.y, self.width, self.height)

        def draw_outline(self,graphics):
                graphics.drawRect(self.x, self.y, self.width, self.height)

class Oval(Shape):
        def __init__(self, x, y, width, height, color=None, fill=0):
                Shape.__init__(self, x, y, width, height, color, fill)

        def draw_filled(self,graphics):
                graphics.fillOval(self.x, self.y, self.width, self.height)

        def draw_outline(self,graphics):
                graphics.drawOval(self.x, self.y, self.width, self.height)

class Shapes (Shape):
        def __init__(self):
                self.__shapes=[]

        def addShape(self, shape):
                self.__shapes.append(shape)

        def paint(self, graphics):
                for shape in self.__shapes:
                        shape.paint()(graphics)
```

```python
    def getRect(self):
                # Lists to hold x,y,height and width from shape in shapes
                    xl,yl,wl,hl = [],[],[],[]
                # Iterate through the list gathering each shapes
                # bounding rectangle
            for shape in shapes:
                x,y,width, height = shape.getRect()
                xl.append(x)
                yl.append(y)
                wl.append(width)
                hl.append(height)

            return min(xl), min(yl), max(wl), max(hl)

        # This is for testing only
if __name__ == '__main__':
        from javax.swing import JFrame, JPanel
        from java.awt import Color, Font

        class TestPanel(JPanel):

            def __init__(self):
                    self.background=Color.white

            def addShape(self,shape):
                    self.shapes.addShape(shape)

            def __init__(self):
                    self.shapes = Shapes()
                    self.addShape( Rectangle( 0, 0, 100, 100,
                            Color.blue, 1))
                    self.addShape( Rectangle(100, 0, 100, 100,
                            Color.blue))
                    self.addShape( Oval( 0, 100, 100, 100, Color.blue,
                            1))
                    self.addShape( Oval(100, 100, 100, 100, Color.blue))

            def paint(self,graphics):
                    self.shapes.paint(graphics)

        frame = JFrame("Test Shapes", size=(400,440), visible=1)
        pane = TestPanel()
        frame.contentPane = pane
        frame.validate()
```

Here's the *DrawShapes* module:

```python
from Shapes import *
from java.awt import Font, Color, Dimension, BorderLayout
from javax.swing import JComboBox, JLabel, JTextField, JComponent
from javax.swing import BoxLayout, JCheckBox, JButton, JFrame, JPanel
from java.awt.event import KeyEvent, ItemEvent

class ShapeButton(JButton):
    def __init__(self, shape):
        self.shape = shape
```

```python
        def paint(self, graphics):
                JButton.paint(self, graphics)
                self.shape.paint(graphics)

        def getPreferredSize(self):
                d = Dimension(30,30)
                return d

class ToolBox (JPanel):
        def __init__(self):
                JPanel.__init__(self)

        def getPreferredSize(self):
                d = Dimension(40, 0)
                return d

class StatusBox (JPanel):
        def __init__(self):
                JPanel.__init__(self)
                self.coordinates = JTextField(15, editable=0)
                self.format = 'x = %d, y = %d'
                self.add(self.coordinates)

                self.event_type = JLabel ('MOUSE STATUS ')
                self.add(self.event_type)
                self.shape_type = JLabel ('SHAPE STATUS ')
                self.add(self.shape_type)

        def setXY(self, x,y):
                self.coordinates.text = self.format % (x,y,)

        def setMouseDrag(self, x, y):
                self.event_type.text = 'MOUSE DRAG '
                self.setXY(x,y)

        def setMouseMove(self, x, y):
                self.event_type.text = 'MOUSE MOVE '
                self.setXY(x,y)

        def setMousePress(self, x, y):
                self.event_type.text = 'MOUSE PRESS '
                self.setXY(x,y)

        def setMouseRelease(self, x, y):
                self.event_type.text = 'MOUSE RELEASE '
                self.setXY(x,y)

        def setShapeType(self, shape_type):

                        # Set the label based on the shape type
                if shape_type == PaintBox.RECTANGLE:
                        self.shape_type.text = 'RECTANGLE'

                elif shape_type == PaintBox.OVAL:
                        self.shape_type.text = 'OVAL'

class PaintBox (JComponent):
        RECTANGLE=1
        OVAL=2
```

```python
def __init__(self, status):
    JComponent.__init__(self)
     self.opaque=1
     self.background=Color.white
    self.status = status
    self.shapes = Shapes()
    self.shape_type = PaintBox.RECTANGLE
    self.mouseDragged = self.handle_mouseDragged
    self.mouseMoved = self.handle_mouseMoved
    self.mousePressed = self.handle_mousePress
    self.mouseReleased = self.handle_mouseRelease

    self.fill=0
    self.color=Color.red

def getPreferredSize(self):
    d = Dimension(400,400)
    return d

def __drawShape(self, g, x, y, width, height):

    if self.shape_type == PaintBox.RECTANGLE:
            rect = Rectangle(self.start.x, self.start.y, width,
                height,fill=0)
        rect.paint(g)
    if self.shape_type == PaintBox.OVAL:
        oval = Oval(self.start.x, self.start.y, width, height,
            fill=0)
        oval.paint()(g)

def drawRubberShape(self, x, y):
    g = self.graphics

        # Set the graphics to XOR mode, which allows rubberbanding.
        # Calculate the width and height.
        # Draw the outline of the shape.
    try:
        g.setXORMode(self.background)
        width = abs(self.start.x - x)
        height = abs(self.start.y - y)
        self.__drawShape(g, self.start.x, self.start.y, width,
            height)
    finally:
        g.dispose()

def handle_mousePress(self, event):

        # Print the status
            self.status.setMousePress(event.x, event.y)
        # Save the initial location.
        # In addition save the initial location as the last.
    self.last = self.start = event.point

def handle_mouseDragged(self,event):

        # Print the status.
    self.status.setMouseDrag(event.x, event.y)
```

```
                # Erase the old rubberband shape at the old location.
                # Create the new rubberband shape at the new location
            self.drawRubberShape(self.last.x, self.last.y)
            self.drawRubberShape(event.x, event.y)

                # Save the current event.x and event.y as the last.
            self.last = event.point

    def handle_mouseMoved(self,event):

                # Print the status.
            self.status.setMouseMove(event.x,event.y)

    def handle_mouseRelease(self, event):

                # Print the status
            self.status.setMouseRelease(event.x, event.y)

                # Calculate the width and the height
            width = abs(self.start.x - event.x)
            height = abs(self.start.y - event.y)

            shape = None #to hold the shape we are about to create

                # Create the shape based on the current shape type.
                # Then add the shape to self.shapes.
            if self.shape_type == PaintBox.RECTANGLE:
                shape = Rectangle(self.start.x, self.start.y, width,
                        height, self.color, self.fill)

            elif self.shape_type == PaintBox.OVAL:
                shape = Oval(self.start.x, self.start.y, width, height,
                        self.color, self.fill)

            if not shape is None:
                self.shapes.addShape(shape)
                x,y,width,height = shape.getRect()
                self.repaint()(x,y,width+1, height+1)

    def paint (self, graphics):
            self.fillBackground(graphics)
                #Draw all of the shapes.
            self.shapes.paint(graphics)

    def fillBackground (self, graphics):

                #Get the background color
            background=self.background
                #Get the size
            size=self.getSize()
            width, height = size.width, size.height

                # Create a rectangle that is as big
                # as the whole drawing area.
            rect = Rectangle(0,0, width, height, background, 1)
            rect.paint(graphics)

    def setShapeType(self, shape_type):
            self.status.setShapeType(shape_type)
            self.shape_type = shape_type
```

```
        def getShapeType(self):
            return shape_type

        def setFill(self, value):
            self.fill = value

        def setShapeColor(self, color):
            self.color = color

class DrawShapes(JFrame):

        def __init__(self):
            JFrame.__init__(self, title='Draw Shapes', visible=1,
                size=(400,400))
            self.__init__toolbar()
            self.__init__options()

            self.statusPane = StatusBox()
            self.contentPane.add(self.statusPane, BorderLayout.SOUTH)

            self.PaintPane = PaintBox(self.statusPane)
            self.contentPane.add(self.PaintPane, BorderLayout.CENTER)

            self.pack()
            def close(event):
                mainWindow.visible=0
                mainWindow.dispose()
                from java.lang import System
                System.exit(0)

            global mainWindow
            mainWindow = self
            self.windowClosing=close

        def __init__toolbar(self):
            toolbar = ToolBox()

                # Add the rectangle button to the toolbar
            rect = ShapeButton(Rectangle(4, 4, 20, 20))
            toolbar.add(rect)
            rect.actionPerformed = self.rect_pressed

                # Add the oval button to the toolbar
            oval = ShapeButton(Oval(4, 4, 10, 20))
            toolbar.add(oval)
            oval.actionPerformed = self.oval_pressed

            self.contentPane.add(toolbar, BorderLayout.WEST)

        def rect_pressed(self, event):
            self.PaintPane.setShapeType(PaintBox.RECTANGLE)

        def oval_pressed(self, event):
            self.PaintPane.setShapeType(PaintBox.OVAL)

        def fill_clicked(self, event):
            if(event.stateChange==ItemEvent.SELECTED):
                self.PaintPane.setFill(1)
```

```
                    elif (event.stateChange==ItemEvent.DESELECTED):
                        self.PaintPane.setFill(0)

        def color_changed(self,event):
            colorname = event.item
            color = self.colors_dict[colorname]
            self.PaintPane.setShapeColor(color)

        def __init__options(self):
            optionsPane = JPanel()

                # Set up the checkbox item for the fill option
            check = JCheckBox('Fill')
            optionsPane.add(check)
            check.itemStateChanged = self.fill_clicked

                # Set up the choice for color
            colors = JComboBox()
            self.colors_dict = {'blue':Color.blue,
                                'green':Color.green,
                                'red':Color.red,
                                'yellow':Color.yellow,
                                'orange':Color.orange,
                                'cyan':Color.cyan,
                                'pink':Color.pink,
                                'gray':Color.gray
                                }
            for color in self.colors_dict.keys():
                colors.addItem(color)

              colors.setSelectedItem('red')

            optionsPane.add(colors)
            colors.itemStateChanged = self.color_changed

            self.contentPane.add(optionsPane, BorderLayout.NORTH)

if __name__ == '__main__':
    frame = DrawShapes()
```

Notice that, for all the functionality we get, the code is relative simple.

Now let's fire up *DrawShapes* and draw some rectangles and ovals. Figure 15–3 is a screen dump of what we're going to do.

## Phase 2: DrawShapes—Adding Text

We've seen how DrawShapes handles mouse events. Now let's extend it to include a text shape that handles keyboard events. In addition to text, this second phase of our example will add squares, rounded rectangles, and circles to show the design flaw of phase 1, which we'll have to wait until phase 3 to correct.

To add a text shape, we need to do the following:

- Define a text shape in the *Shapes* module.
- Add a shape button to the toolbar that represents text.

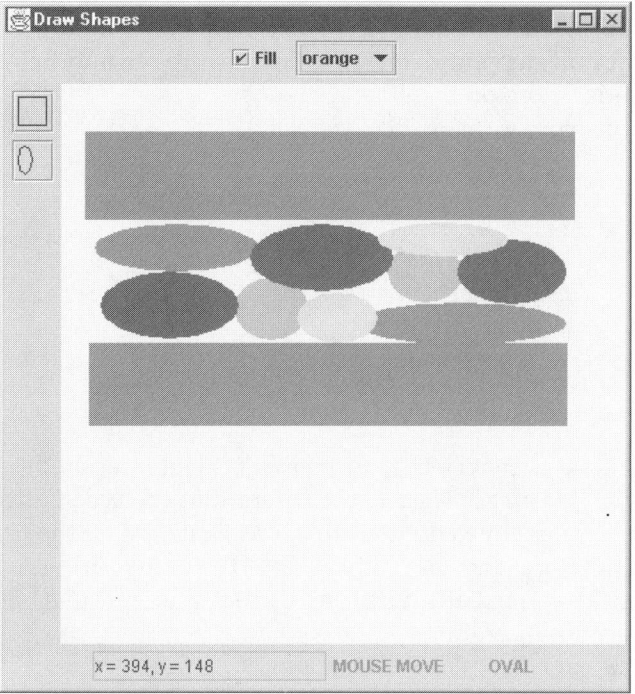

**Figure 15–3**   *Screen Dump of the* DrawShapes *Example*

- Add support for the text mode to the mousePress event handler.
- Set up event handling in the paint box for the following user actions:
  1. Clicking a point in the paint box to make it the starting position of the text
  2. Entering text
  3. Pressing the Backspace key to delete the last character entered
  4. Pressing Enter to end the text entry

  The result is that the bounding rectangle of the text is calculated and the area is repainted immediately by force.

### The Text Class

The Text class extends the Shape class and is defined in the *Shapes* module. It has font, string, and color attributes, which are passed via Shape's constructor. Text must be passed a reference to the component where it will be drawn so that it can acquire the font metrics, which it uses to calculate its ascent, descent, width, and height. (Look up java.awt.FontMetrics in the Java API documentation to learn more about fonts.) Ascent and descent determine how far above and below the baseline a character extends (more on this later).

Here's the Text class constructor (from *TwoShapes.py*).

```
Class Text(Shape):
    def __init__(self, x, y, string, font, component, color=None):
        Shape.__init__(self, x, y, color=color)
        fm = component.getFontMetrics(font)
        self.width = fm.stringWidth(string)
        self.height = fm.maxAscent + fm.maxDescent
        self.ascent = fm.maxAscent
        self.descent = fm.maxDescent
        self.font = font
        self.string = string
```

Text overrides both the draw_outline() and draw_filled() methods. Draw_filled() calls draw_outline() because Text doesn't differentiate between filled and unfilled mode. draw_outline() changes the font to Text's font, saving the original to be restored after the call to drawString(), which does the actual drawing. Saving and restoring the graphics context attributes ensure that draw_outline() doesn't adversely affect other graphics operations.

Here's the code for draw_outline() (*Two\Shapes.py*):

```
def draw_outline(self, graphics):

    if(self.font):
            #Get the original font.
        font = graphics.font
            #Set the graphics to this font.
        graphics.font = self.font

        #Draw the string.
    graphics.drawString(self.string, self.x, self.y)
    if(self.font):
            # Set the graphics back
            # to the original font.
        graphics.font = font

def draw_filled(self, graphics):
    self.draw_outline(graphics)
```

Text's final method is getRect(), which, you'll remember, is used by PaintBox to calculate the area that needs to be redrawn. Most of the other shapes simply use the inherited version of this method; however, Text needs it to calculate the bounding rectangle for the string because, unlike the other shape classes, its *x,y* coordinates don't begin in the upper left corner, as shown in Figure 15–4.

GetRect() calculates the rectangle by moving its starting point to the upper left corner. The *x,y* axis increases down and to the right, so subtracting the ascent moves the point up (if down is positive, up is negative).

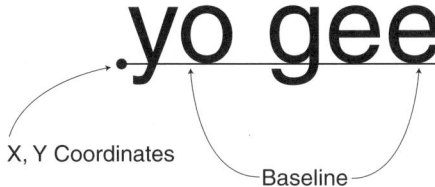

**Figure 15–4**  *Baseline, Starting Point, Width,
Ascent, and Descent*

```
def getRect(self):
        return self.x, self.y-self.ascent, self.width, self.height
```

### *The Text Class Code*

Text is the most complex shape we've seen so far, and it isn't as complex as it seems. Here it is in its entirety (from *Two\Shapes.py*):

```
class Text(Shape):
     def __init__(self, x, y, string, font, component, color=None):
          Shape.__init__(self, x, y, color=color)
          fm = component.getFontMetrics(font)
          self.width = fm.stringWidth(string)
          self.height = fm.maxAscent + fm.maxDescent
          self.ascent = fm.maxAscent
          self.descent = fm.maxDescent
          self.font = font
          self.string = string

     def draw_outline(self, graphics):

          if(self.font):
                    #Get the original font.
               font = graphics.font
                    #Set the graphics to this font.
               graphics.font = self.font
```

```
                    #Draw the string.
              graphics.drawString(self.string, self.x, self.y)

              if(self.font):
                           #Set the graphics back to the original font.
                    graphics.font = font

        def draw_filled(self, graphics):
              self.draw_outline(graphics)

        def getRect(self):
              return self.x, self.y-self.ascent, self.width, self.height
```

### Supporting the Text Class

Now let's add support for Text to our DrawShapes module—font name and point size options and keyboard event handling. Here are some typical user actions that illustrate the type of things we need:

1. Clicking the Text shape button in the DrawShapes toolbar
2. Changing the font name in the options pane
3. Clicking on the PaintBox panel
4. Typing characters
5. Pressing the Enter key

Step 1 fires the event handler for the Shape button, which sets the shape type of the PaintBox panel to TEXT. Step 2 fires the event handler for font choice, which sets PaintBox's font attribute. Step 3 fires the mousePressed event, whose handler sets the *x,y* position of the text. Then Step 4 fires the keyTyped event, whose handler draws text on the paint box. Step 5 causes a Text class to be instantiated and added to PaintBox's shapes attribute.

PaintBox also handles the Backspace key for those of us who occasionally make mistakes. (I got tired of typing "Hekko World.")

To implement Text we first need to add the text shape button to the toolbar of the DrawShapes frame. We create an instance of Text and pass it to the ShapeButton class.

```
def __init__toolbar(self):
          toolbar = ToolBox()
                   #Add the rectangle button to the toolbar
          rect = ShapeButton(Rectangle(4, 4, 20, 20))
          toolbar.add(rect)
          rect.actionPerformed = self.rect_pressed
      ...
      ...

                   # Set the current font to Arial,
                   # then get the FontMetrics
          font = Font("Arial", Font.PLAIN, 20)
          fm = self.getFontMetrics(font)
```

```
                     #Add the Text button to the toolbar.
          text=ShapeButton(Text(2, 2+fm.maxAscent, "A", font, self))
          toolbar.add(text)
          text.actionPerformed = self.text_pressed
```

As you can see, we need to get the font metrics to put the text shape in the button. The font metrics calculate where to move the start position of the text so that it's displayed in the button's upper right corner. Then we have to set the event handler for the button's action event to text_pressed.

```
def text_pressed(self, event):
     self.PaintPane.setShapeType(PaintBox.TEXT)
     self.PaintPane.requestFocus()
```

The text_pressed event handler sets the shape type of the paint box to TEXT. Calling requestFocus gives the paint box input focus, which is essential for it to receive key events. There can be no key events without input focus.

Next, the DrawShapes frame needs the font options (point size and typeface) added to its options pane. Here's the code:

```
def __init__options(self):
     optionsPane = Panel()
     optionsPane.add(Label("Font"))

             #Set up the Font point List.
     point_list = Choice()
     points = (8,9,10,12,14,16,18,20,24,32)

     for point in points:
             point_list.add(str(point))

     optionsPane.add(point_list)
     point_list.itemStateChanged = self.point_changed

             #Set up font List.
     from java.awt import GraphicsEnvironment
     ge = GraphicsEnvironment.getLocalGraphicsEnvironment()
     fonts = ge.getAvailableFontFamilyNames()
     fonts_list = Choice()
     for font in fonts:
             fonts_list.add(font)

     optionsPane.add(fonts_list)
     fonts_list.itemStateChanged = self.font_changed
```

The __init_options method creates a list of point sizes and adds it to a choice control called point_list. Next it gets a list of fonts from GraphicsEnvironment. getAvailableFontFamilyNames and adds it to a choice control called font_list. font_list and point_list are added to the options pane, and event handlers are set up for both.

The event handler for font_list sets the name property of the paint pane (an instance of PaintBox) when the user selects a font name. event.item contains the font name selected by the user and is passed to the `setFontName()` method of the `PaintBox` instance, which sets the instance's font.

The event handler for `point_list` converts `event.item` to an integer and then sets the `paint` pane's point size property.

Here are the event handlers for both `font_list` and `point_list`:

```
def font_changed(self, event):
    self.PaintPane.setFontName(event.item)

def point_changed(self, event):
    self.PaintPane.setFontPoint(int(event.item))
```

That about does it for the changes made to *DrawShapes* to support text. Now I'll describe the changes made to `PaintBox` to add text shape support. This is the interesting part.

## Test and PaintBox

`PaintBox` adds another shape type, TEXT. It adds three attributes to its class instance in its constructor: `text` (a string), which denotes the text being typed by the user but not yet entered in—that is, the transitional text; `startText` (an integer representing a Boolean value), which denotes whether or not a text operation has begun; and `text_in`, which holds the transitional instance of the text shape, that is, the text being keyed in and edited. When the shape type is TEXT and the user clicks the paint box, `startText` is set to true, and `PaintBox` begins processing key events. The key event handlers control the text operation and add characters to the `text` attribute.

Here's the definition for `PaintBox` and its constructor (from *two\DrawShapes.py*):

```
class Paint box (Panel):
    RECTANGLE=1
    OVAL=2
...
...
    TEXT=4

    def __init__(self, status):
        Panel.__init__(self)
        self.status = status
        self.shapes = Shapes()
        self.shape_type = PaintBox.RECTANGLE

        self.mouseDragged = self.handle_mouseDragged
...
...
        self.keyPressed = self.handle_keyPressed
        self.keyTyped = self.handle_keyTyped

        self.point = 20
        self.fontname = "Arial"
        self.font = Font(self.fontname, Font.PLAIN, self.point)
```

```
        self.text = ""
        self.startText = 0
        self.text_in = None

    ...
    ...
```

When the user presses the mouse button, the `mousePress` event handler is called, which sets `startText` to true and sets the text to an empty string if the shape type is TEXT. This defines the text's starting point. In the following example, code that has been added to *two\DrawShapes.py* is hightlighted in bold.

```
    def handle_mousePress(self, event):
...
...
        self.last = self.start = event.point

        if (self.shape_type == PaintBox.TEXT):
            self.text = ""
            self.startText = 1
```

`PaintBox` uses only `keyPressed` to handle control keys and `keyTyped` to handle character keys when drawing a text shape.

The `keyPressed` event handler handles the Enter and Backspace keys. When Enter is pressed, the text shape being defined is added to the paint box's shapes collection. Here's the code:

```
def handle_keyPressed(self, event):
    self.ignore = 0

            # Perfom actions for drawing text
            # if this in text draw mode.
    if self.shape_type == PaintBox.TEXT and self.startText:

            # If the user presses the Enter key,
            # We add this shape to the shape list.
        if (event.keyCode == KeyEvent.VK_ENTER):
            self.shapes.addShape(self.text_in)
            self.startText = 0
            self.text_in = None
```

When the Backspace key is pressed, the last character of the text string is removed, and the `ignore` attribute of `PaintBox` is set to true. `ignore` is needed because the Backspace key generates a character (here '\b') that we don't want to show up in our text shape (it appears as a square). A true value tells the `keyTyped` event handler to disregard any such character. Also when the Backspace key is pressed, a new text shape is created and assigned to the `text_in` attribute (whose last character was just removed), which forces a repaint of `text_in`'s bounds (before the backspace operation).

```
    def handle_keyPressed(self, event):
        self.ignore = 0
```

```
                    # Perform actions for drawing text
                    # if this in text draw mode.
          if self.shape_type == PaintBox.TEXT and self.startText:
...
...


                       # If the user presses the Backspace key,
                       # we delete the last character in the text.
             if (event.keyCode == KeyEvent.VK_BACK_SPACE):
                   x,y,width,height = self.text_in.getRect()
                   self.ignore = 1
                   self.text = self.text[:-1]
                   self.text_in=Text(self.start.x, self.start.y, \
                         self.text,self.font,self, self.color)
                   self.repaint()(x,y,width+1, height+1)
```

Unlike the keyPressed handler, the keyTyped handler works with characters the user types in, which are collected in the text string. After each character is typed, a new text shape object is created (text_in). The keyTyped event handler uses the bounds of text_in to force a repaint so that the shape is redrawn.

```
def handle_keyTyped(self,event):

             # See if this is in text draw mode,
             # and the backspace was not pressed
      if self.shape_type == PaintBox.TEXT and self.startText \
                      and not self.ignore:
             # Get the character typed, add it to the text.
          self.text = self.text + event.keyChar

             # Force the text to be shown.
             # Create the Text instance, and force repaint().
          self.text_in = Text(self.start.x, self.start.y, \
                  self.text, self.font, self, self.color)
          x,y,width,height = self.text_in.getRect()
          self.repaint()(x,y,width+1, height+1)
```

The paint()method checks to see if the text_in shape exists. If so, it draws it. Remember, the text_in attribute corresponds to the current shape, that is, the one being worked on.

```
def paint(self, graphics):

             #Draw all of the shapes.
          self.shapes.paint(graphics)

             #For showing text while we type
          if(self.text_in):
                self.text_in.paint(graphics)
```

PaintBox also creates several methods to change its font and point attributes.

```
def setFontName(self, font):
      self.fontname = font
      self.font = Font(self.fontname, Font.PLAIN, self.point)
```

```
def setFontPoint(self,point):
    self.point = point
    self.font = Font(self.fontname, Font.PLAIN, point)
```

So now we've added text shape support. Oh, yes, I said earlier that we would add squares, circles, and rounded rectangles. Well, we won't go into detail about these shapes, but we will take a look at the problem they cause.

If all you wanted out of this chapter was an introduction to graphics programming, you just got it. But if you want to learn what makes dynamic object-oriented programming tick, read on. We're going to modify *DrawShapes* and its classes and make them significantly smaller and more extensible. In other words, we're going to write tight, dynamic, object-oriented Python code.

### *DrawShapes'* Ugly, Inefficient, Nonextensible Code

Let's see what's wrong with *DrawShapes* as it stands now. We'll start with the DrawShapes class. First look at __init__toolbar (from *two\DrawShapes.py*).

```
def __init__toolbar(self):
    toolbar = ToolBox()

        #Add the Rectangle button to the toolbar
    rect = ShapeButton(Rectangle(4, 4, 20, 10))
    toolbar.add(rect)
    rect.actionPerformed = self.rect_pressed

        #Add the Circle button to the toolbar
    circle = ShapeButton(Circle(4, 4, 10))
    toolbar.add(circle)
    circle.actionPerformed = self.circle_pressed

        #Add the Oval button to the toolbar
    oval = ShapeButton(Oval(4, 4, 10, 20))
    toolbar.add(oval)
    oval.actionPerformed = self.oval_pressed

        #Add the Square button to the toolbar
    square = ShapeButton(Square(4, 4, 20))
    toolbar.add(square)
    square.actionPerformed = self.square_pressed

        #Add the RoundRectangle button to the toolbar
    rrect = ShapeButton(RoundedRectangle(4, 4, 20, 20))
    toolbar.add(rrect)
    rrect.actionPerformed = self.round_rect_pressed

        # Set the current font to Arial,
        # then get the FontMetrics
    font = Font("Arial", Font.PLAIN, 20)
    fm = self.getFontMetrics(font)

        # Add the Text button to the toolbar.
    text=ShapeButton(Text(2, 2+fm.maxAscent, "A", font, self))
```

```
toolbar.add(text)
text.actionPerformed = self.text_pressed

self.add(toolbar, BorderLayout.WEST)
```

Every time we define a new shape, we have to write three to five lines of code in __init__toolbar; then we have to write an event handler for each one. As you can see, with just six shapes it gets pretty messy.

```
def circle_pressed(self, event):
    self.PaintPane.setShapeType(PaintBox.CIRCLE)

def rect_pressed(self, event):
    self.PaintPane.setShapeType(PaintBox.RECTANGLE)

def round_rect_pressed(self, event):
    self.PaintPane.setShapeType(PaintBox.ROUND_RECTANGLE)

def square_pressed(self, event):
    self.PaintPane.setShapeType(PaintBox.SQUARE)

def oval_pressed(self, event):
    self.PaintPane.setShapeType(PaintBox.OVAL)

def text_pressed(self, event):
    self.PaintPane.setShapeType(PaintBox.TEXT)
    self.PaintPane.requestFocus()
```

They all look pretty similar, don't they? Why not replace all of the code above with this:

```
class ShapeTool:
    def __init__(self, shape_class, toolbar, PaintBox):

            # Use eval to create a shape. shape_class
            # holds a string representing the class.
        self.__shape = eval(shape_class+'()')
        button = ShapeButton(self.__shape)
        toolbar.add(button)
        button.actionPerformed = self.actionPerformed
        self.PaintBox = PaintBox

    def actionPerformed(self, event):
        self.PaintBox.requestFocus()
        self.PaintBox.setShapeType(self.__shape.__class__)
        def getShape(self):return self.__shape
```

### The ShapeTool Class

__init__toolbar uses ShapeTool to create shape buttons, add them to the toolbar, and register them with an event handler. Notice that it uses strings to denote each shape's class. The ShapeTool constructor uses the strings as arguments to the built-in eval() function.

```
class DrawShapes(Frame):
...
...
```

```
def __init__toolbar(self):
    toolbar = ToolBox()
    Shapes = ['Square', 'Rectangle', 'RoundedRectangle',
              'Oval', 'Text', 'Circle' ]

    for shape in Shapes:
        shape_tool=ShapeTool(shape,toolbar, self.PaintPane)

        if (isinstance(shape_tool.getShape(), Text)):
            shape_tool.getShape().initForToolbar('A',
                self.PaintPane)

    self.add(toolbar, BorderLayout.WEST)
```

The ShapeTool class defines the event handler for each button and adds it to the toolbar. It eliminates thirty lines of code and five function definitions. What's more, it's extensible: Any additional shapes are just added to the shapes list in __init__toolbar with no extra code. With the old way, for thirty shapes we'd need thirty event handlers and about seventy-five additional lines of code. With the new way, all we need is thirty entries in the shapes list.

Less code to write equates to less code to test and fewer bugs. In addition, we can create a text file our program can read that lists the shapes we want to display. This is extremely flexible.

Notice that the event handler for ShapeTool passes the class, not an integer representing the type. The old way passed an integer with the type as defined by constant values in the PaintBox class. This is directly from the Department of Redundancy Department (with thanks to Monty Python). A class is a type, and shapes can be uniquely identified by their class. Now PaintBox uses the class as the shape type.

### Making PaintBox Modular

There's a lot wrong with the old PaintBox. First of all, as I mentioned, every time we add a shape, we need to add a shape constant. This tightly couples shapes to PaintBox.

```
class PaintBox (JComponent):
    RECTANGLE=1
    OVAL=2
    CIRCLE=3
    TEXT=4
    ROUND_RECTANGLE=5
    SQUARE = 6
    ...
    ...
```

The shape type integer is passed to PaintBox, making it necessary to add another suite to PaintBox's if statement—drawShape()—for each new shape.

```
def setShapeType(self, shape_type):
    self.status.setShapeType(shape_type)
    self.shape_type = shape_type
```

```
def __drawShape(self, g, x, y, width, height):

    if self.shape_type == PaintBox.RECTANGLE:
        g.drawRect(self.start.x, self.start.y, width, height)

    if self.shape_type == PaintBox.ROUND_RECTANGLE:
        g.drawRoundRect(self.start.x, self.start.y, width, height, 10,10)

    if self.shape_type == PaintBox.OVAL:
        g.drawOval(self.start.x, self.start.y, width, height)

    if self.shape_type == PaintBox.CIRCLE:
        g.drawOval(self.start.x, self.start.y, width, width)

    if self.shape_type == PaintBox.SQUARE:
        g.drawRect(self.start.x, self.start.y, width, width)
```

There are a couple of things wrong with this. First, the code for drawing a shape
should be in a shape object, not in `PaintBox`. This means that the original code for
`drawShape()` isn't modular, and that's bad. If there's a problem drawing a shape,
the developer who inherits this code won't know if she should look in the *Shapes*
module or in the `PaintBox` class.

Code should be modular; that is, a class should do one set of related things.
The shape should know how to do shape things like draw itself, and this knowl-
edge should be hidden from `PaintBox`—in other words, encapsulated.

Here's our modular version (*Three\PaintBox.py*):

```
def createShape(self):
    """Create a new shape with the shape_type.
    The shape_type is a Shape class."""

    self.shape = self.shape_type()
    if (isinstance(self.shape, Text)):
        self.shape.setComponent(self)

def setShapeType(self, shape_type):
    """Set the current Shape type,
    then create an instance of the shape"""
    self.status.setShapeType(shape_type)
    self.shape_type = shape_type
    self.createShape()

def __drawShape(self, g, x, y, width, height):
    self.shape.fromBounds(self.start.x, self.start.y, width, height)
    self.shape.draw_outline()(g)
```

In the new `drawShape()`, we initialize the shape with the `fromBounds()` method,
which tells the shape to initialize itself from the given bounding rectangle. If you
look at the shape classes in the code above, you'll notice all of them either inherit
the default, `fromBound()`, from the `Shape` class or implement their own version.

The great thing about our new code is that, if we add a triangle, a hexagon, an
octagon, and so forth, it doesn't change. With the old `__DrawShapes`, each time we

add a new shape we have to add another `elif` suite to the `if` statement. Thirty shapes equal thirty `elif` branches.

This is the magic of polymorphism. All we do is tell the shape to initialize itself from the bounds we give it; we don't care if it's a triangle or a parallelogram.

Remember that there was another place where we had a long `if` statement with lots of `elif` suites—`handle_mouseRelease`, which created a shape based on the shape type defined by the integer constants. The new `handle_mouseRelease` does not need to do that, so it's not coupled to adding new shapes. Look at the differences with the few shapes we defined, and imagine what the old `mouseRelease` handler (from *Two\DrawShapes.py*) would look like if we had thirty shapes.

```
def handle_mouseRelease(self, event):

        # Print the status
    self.status.setMouseRelease(event.x, event.y)

        # Calculate the width and the height
    width = abs(self.start.x - event.x)
    height = abs(self.start.y - event.y)

    shape = None #hold the shape we are about to create

        # Create shape based on the current shape type.
        # Then add the shape to self.shapes.
    if self.shape_type == PaintBox.RECTANGLE:
        shape = Rectangle(self.start.x, self.start.y, width,
                height, self.color, self.fill)

    elif self.shape_type == PaintBox.OVAL:
        shape = Oval(self.start.x, self.start.y, width, height,
                self.color, self.fill)

    elif self.shape_type == PaintBox.CIRCLE:
        shape = Circle(self.start.x, self.start.y, width/2,
                self.color, self.fill)

    elif self.shape_type == PaintBox.SQUARE:
        shape = Square(self.start.x, self.start.y, width,
                self.color, self.fill)

    elif self.shape_type == PaintBox.ROUND_RECTANGLE:
        shape = RoundedRectangle(self.start.x, self.start.y,
                width, height, self.color, self.fill)

    if not shape is None:
        self.shapes.addShape(shape)
        x,y,width,height = shape.getRect()
        self.repaint(x,y,width+1, height+1)
```

Here's the new `mouseRelease` handler (*Three\DrawShapes.py*):

```
def handle_mouseRelease(self, event):

        # Print the status
    self.status.setMouseRelease(event.x, event.y)
```

```
                         # Calculate the width and the height
              width = abs(self.start.x - event.x)
              height = abs(self.start.y - event.y)

                         # Set the shape bounds, i.e.,
                         # the bounds the shape initializes from.
                         # Add the shape to the shape list.
                         # Calculate the shape actual bounds,
                         # and repaint().
              self.shape.fromBounds(self.start.x, self.start.y, width, height,
self.color, self.fill)
              self.shapes.addShape(self.shape)
              x,y,width,height = self.shape.getRect()
              self.repaint(x,y,width+1, height+1)

                         # Create a new shape.
              self.createShape()
```

I don't want you to confuse the fooling around with objects we're doing with defining an extensible architecture for an application. I just want to highlight those simple changes and show that dynamic object-oriented programming saves us huge headaches.

---

### A Broken Record

Remember to read *Object-Oriented Analysis and Design with Applications* (Booch, 1994) and then *Design Patterns* (Gamma et al., 1995).

---

Try these exercises, which extend the drawing package in directory 3:

- Add three new shapes: a triangle (use drawPolygon and fillPolygon), a line, and a scribble.

- Create an Undo button on the options pane that allows users to undo the last shape drawn.

- Create a button on the options pane that allows a user to change the z-order of the shapes (that is, the order in which the shapes are "stacked" in the view); this might pop up a dialog box that has a list of shapes representing the z-order.

- Add the ability to drag an already drawn shape to a new position. You'll need to do hit testing for the shape.

- Add the ability to select a shape and change its color.

- Create a composite shape, and call it TextBox. It should contain two shapes: the text to be drawn and the bounding rectangle. The user draws the textbox first and adds text to it. The text entered word-wraps; that is, it stays within the bounds of the rectangle, filling the box left to right and then top to bottom, and if the text is too long for one line, it starts a new one. If there are too many lines for the bounds, only the text that fits is shown.

If you don't do at least the first exercise, you won't get much out of this chapter. If you can handle the last one, you're well on your way to programmer stardom.

## Summary

This chapter mainly covered events and graphics using Java AWT. We learned about the different events the various graphics components publish, and we got some firsthand experience of the order in which events take place. We prototyped a FrameEvents class that allowed us to see the runtime behavior of many events. With prototyping it's much easier to see how events work.

We dealt with the basic drawing of shapes and the XOR graphics mode for rubberbanding. We were able to put together the things we learned about graphics programming and events in a very simple drawing application, which we extended to incorporate ideas in earlier chapters about object-oriented programming and the dynamic behavior of Jython.

# CHAPTER 16

*Advanced Swing*

◊ *Abstract method*
◊ *Array*
◊ *Data model*
◊ *Design pattern*
◊ *Event listening*

◊ *Functional decomposition*
◊ *Hashtable*
◊ *Helper method*
◊ *Key/value pair*

◊ *Main module*
◊ *Object wrapper*
◊ *Self-documentation*
◊ *Tree model/node*

Our coverage of Swing so far has focused on its differences from, and advantages over, AWT. But Swing is more than that. For example, it has some powerful GUI components, particularly JTable and JTree. JTable shows data in a table view, as in a spreadsheet; JTree displays data in a hierarchical view, as in Microsoft Windows Explorer.

In this chapter, we'll update the address book program, making it a JFC application that uses JTable. As we do this, we'll introduce other Swing components.

## JTable

To start out, we'll create a prototype that introduces the key features of JTable. Then we'll add JTable support to the address application. This time the application will use the MVC architecture—the AddressBook class instance will be a model for the table.

We'll begin by creating a 4-by-4 grid, but first let's learn to use the JTable component. As always, follow along in the interactive interpreter.

Import the JFrame and JTable classes from the *javax.swing* package.

```
>>> from javax.swing import JFrame, JTable
```

Create an instance of JFrame to hold the table.

```
>>> frame = JFrame('JTable example')
```

Create an instance of JTable, passing the number of rows and columns to its constructor. Then add the table to the frame.

```
>>> table = JTable(4,4)
>>> frame.contentPane.add(table)
javax.swing.JTable[,0,0,0x0,invalid,alignmentX=null,alignmentY=null,border=,flag
s=32,maximumSize=,minimumSize=,preferredSize=,autoCreateColumnsFromModel=true,
autoResizeMode=AUTO_RESIZE_SUBSEQUENT_COLUMNS,cellSelectionEnabled=false,
editing...
...
```

Pack the table in the frame, and show the frame.

```
>>> frame.pack()
>>> frame.visible = 1
```

Select a cell, and start typing if you want to. The typed text will show up in the cell, as illustrated in Figure 16–1.

### The Default Table Model

We didn't specify a model, so a default was provided in which the actual table data is kept. Here's how to access that data.

Get the first row.

```
>>> table.model.dataVector[0]
[Hello, World, Its, good]
```

Get the first row, second column.

```
>>> table.model.dataVector[0][1]
'World'
```

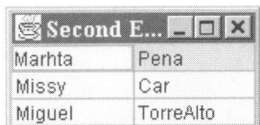

**Figure 16–1** *Cells with Text Entered*

Get the first row, first column.

```
>>> table.model.dataVector[0][0]
'Hello'
```

This method is only guaranteed to work for the default. I use it to acclimate you to the model concepts first introduced in Chapter 14, on JList.

Other forms of the JTable constructor allow you to pass in the initial values, that is, the row and column data. Here's an example.

Create the row data.

```
>>> rowData = [ ['Marhta','Pena'],['Missy','Car'], ['Miguel','TorreAlto'] ]
```

Create the column headers.

```
>>> columnNames = ['First name', 'Last name']
```

Create a table with the row data and column headers.

```
>>> table = JTable(rowData,columnNames)
>>> frame.contentPane.add(table)
javax.swing.JTable[,0,0,0x0,invalid,alignmentX=null,alignmentY=null,border=,
flags=32,maximumSize=,minimumSize=,preferredSize=,autoCreateColumnsFromModel=true,
autoResizeMode=AUTO_RESIZE_SUBSEQUENT_COLUMNS,cellSelectionEnabled=false,editing
Column=-1,editingRow=1,gridColor=javax.swing.plaf.ColorUIResource[r=153,g=153,b=1
...
```

Pack the table, and display it.

```
>>> frame.pack()
>>> frame.visible=1
```

There are other ways to set the initial data. Later we'll cover the ones that are substantially different, as well as a special method of populating a table with data using MVC.

## Getting and Setting Table Values

With the interface provided by JTable, you can get and set table values. Once the data is set, you can modify it with the setValueAt()method.

```
>>> table.setValueAt('Hightower', 0, 1)
>>> table.setValueAt('Hightower', 1, 1)
>>> table.setValueAt('Pena', 2, 1)
```

However, the more correct way of accessing data is with getValueAt().

```
>>> table.getValueAt(0,0)
'Marhta'
```

Tables can work with object wrappers of primitive types—Boolean, integer, float, and so forth. Here we set the second column's values to Boolean so that they look like Figure 16–2.

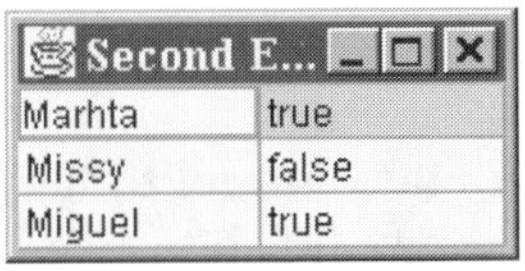

**Figure 16–2** *Example Table with the Second Column Set to Boolean Values*

```
>>> from java.lang import Boolean
>>> table.setValueAt(Boolean(1), 0, 1)
>>> table.setValueAt(Boolean(0), 1, 1)
>>> table.setValueAt(Boolean(1), 2, 1)
```

You may have noticed that our demo table doesn't show headers. I don't know why, but I suspect it's a bug in JDK v.1.2.1. As a workaround, we can put the table in a scroll pane (JScrollPane). You usually do this anyway, so there should be no problem. It wasn't necessary in earlier Swing versions.

JList makes much use of JScrollPane, which adds scrolling to a list or table via the Decorator design pattern (see *Design Patterns*, Gamma et al., 1995). Here's the last example (from *JTable2.py*) with the missing headers restored.

```
from javax.swing import JFrame, JTable, JScrollPane

frame = JFrame('JTable example')
    #Create row data.
rowData = [ ['Marhta','Pena'],['Missy','Car'], ['Miguel','TorreAlto'] ]

    #Create column headers.
columnNames = ['First name', 'Last name']

    #Create a table with the row data and the column headers.
table = JTable(rowData,columnNames)
frame.contentPane.add(JScrollPane(table))

frame.pack()
frame.visible = 1
```

Now the table should look like Figure 16–3.

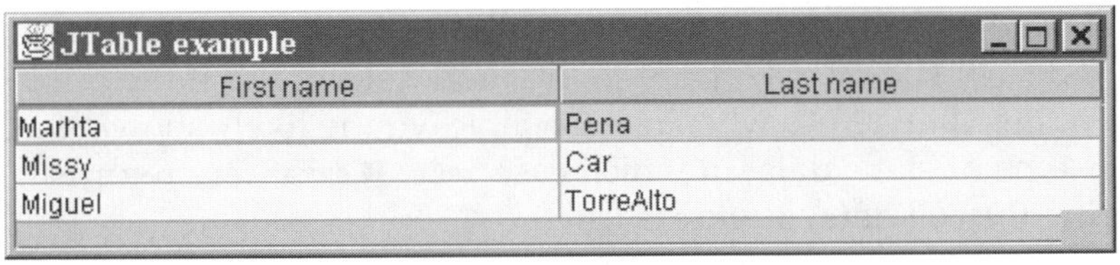

**Figure 16–3** *Table with the Column Headers Restored*

## *Working with Table Models*

The most common way to create tables is to supply the data model first. JTable works with any class instance that inherits from the TableModel interface (recall that a Java interface is like a Python class with all abstract methods). Let's first see what the TableModel methods do and then create a short example that uses our old address book application.

> #### *Data Model Review*
>
> We've covered TableModel and JList, so I won't go into the same level of detail because I'm assuming that you did your reading and your exercises and now have a basic understanding of them. If you don't, you may want to do a little review. You'll need it to understand the JTable and JTree controls, which will be covered later on.

### The TableModel Interface

The TableModel interface is contained in javax.swing.table and specifies how table model data will be treated. Any class that implements TableModel can act as a data model for JTable.

Here are TableModel's methods:

- getRowCount()
- getColumnCount()
- getColumnName(columnIndex)
- getColumnClass(columnIndex)
- isCellEditable(rowIndex, columnIndex)
- getValueAt(rowIndex, columnIndex)
- setValueAt(rowIndex, columnIndex)
- addTableModelListener(l)
- removeTableModelListener(l)

TableModel represents a tabular object just like a spreadsheet. Thus, getRowCount() and getColumnCount() return the number of rows and columns, from which the total number of cells can be calculated (row count * column count). You can access the row and column counts as the properties instance.columnCount and instance.rowCount, respectively.

setValueAt() and getValueAt() set and get cell data by specifying the cell's row and column indexes. The isCellEditable() method determines if the cell is read-only or read/write. Many times when using a table, you're likely showing a report or some other type of static data, in which case isCellEditable() returns false. If you're changing the cell data, it returns true.

getColumnName(), obviously, returns the name of a column. getColumnClass() returns the class that the column deals with, which helps in displaying and editing the column's cells, as we'll see later.

addTableModelListener() and removeTableModelListener() allow components like JTable instances to register for TableModel events.

## The AbstractDataModel Class

Firing events and tracking event listeners can be real but necessary annoyances. Wouldn't it be nice, though, if all of their functionality was in a common, extensible class? This is where object-oriented programming comes in. Our friends at JavaSoft have combined event firing and listener tracking in a class called AbstractDataModel.

AbstractDataModel is, obviously, abstract, so you have to instantiate it in a subclass (i.e., extend it). It makes no assumption about how you supply or define your data, so you don't get the getRowCount(), getColumnCount(), or getValueAt() methods with it. That's okay, because DefaultDataModel, which does have them, extends AbstractDataModel.

Remember when we initialized a JTable with no model, just data? JTable took that data and passed it to an instance of DefaultDataModel. In other words, even when we don't pass JTable a model, it still uses one, or rather it uses an instance of a class that implements the TableModel interface.

To show how AbstractDataModel works, we'll go back to our pizza topping application, but this time we'll add editable columns and Boolean values. The first column will list the toppings; the second will hold checkboxes that are set when the customer makes a selection.

Here's the complete topping code (*model.py*):

```python
from javax.swing.table import AbstractTableModel
from java.lang import Boolean, String

class PizzaTableModel(AbstractTableModel):

    def __init__(self):
        self.data = [ ['Pepperoni', Boolean(0)],
                      ['Sausage', Boolean(0)],
                      ['Onions', Boolean(0)],
                      ['Olives', Boolean(0)],
                      ['Mushrooms', Boolean(0)],
                      ['Peppers', Boolean(0)] ]
        self.columnNames = ['Topping', 'Add?']
        self.columnClasses = [String, Boolean]
        self.Add=1

    def getRowCount(self):
        return len(self.data)

    def getColumnCount(self):
        return len(self.data[0])

    def getValueAt(self, rowIndex, columnIndex):
        return self.data[rowIndex][columnIndex]

    def getColumnName(self, columnIndex):
        return self.columnNames[columnIndex]
```

```
def getColumnClass(self, columnIndex):
    return self.columnClasses[columnIndex]

def isCellEditable(self, rowIndex, columnIndex):
    return columnIndex == self.Add

def setValueAt (self, value, rowIndex, columnIndex):
    if(columnIndex == self.Add):
        value = Boolean(value)
        self.data[rowIndex][columnIndex] = value
        self.fireTableCellUpdated(rowIndex, columnIndex)
```

## A Table Model for the Pizza Topping Application—Step by Step

First we import the classes we need: AbstractTableModel and PizzaTableModel (which extends AbstractTableModel). PizzaTableModel provides the user interface. It also imports the Boolean and String classes, which it uses for the getColumnClass() method (more on this later).

```
from javax.swing.table import AbstractTableModel
from java.lang import Boolean, String

class PizzaTableModel(AbstractTableModel):
```

Next the PizzaTableModel constructor defines three variables: data, which holds the cell data in a list of lists; columnNames, which holds the column headers in a list of strings; and columnClasses, which holds the classes in a list of classes. It also defines a variable—a constant that defines the location of the Add? column. Add? consists of Boolean values that determine whether or not a customer selects a particular topping.

```
def __init__(self):
    self.data = [ ['Pepperoni', Boolean(0)],
                  ['Sausage', Boolean(0)],
                  ['Onions', Boolean(0)],
                  ['Olives', Boolean(0)],
                  ['Mushrooms', Boolean(0)],
                  ['Peppers', Boolean(0)] ]
    self.columnNames = ['Topping', 'Add?']
    self.columnClasses = [String, Boolean]
    self.Add=1
```

PizzaTableModel implements getRowCount() by returning the length of the data list.

```
def getRowCount(self):
    return len(self.data)
```

It also implements getColumnCount() by returning the length of the first list in the data variable. Recall that data is a list of lists and that all of the lists contain two items.

```
def getColumnCount(self):
    return len(self.data[0])
```

getValueAt() indexes the rows and columns of data's list of lists and returns

```
def getValueAt(self, rowIndex, columnIndex):
    return self.data[rowIndex][columnIndex]
```

getColumnNames() indexes the columnNames list with the columnIndex argument
and returns

```
def getColumnName(self, columnIndex):
    return self.columnNames[columnIndex]
```

getColumnClass() returns the value that results from indexing columnClasses.
The class it returns determines the cell editor JTable will use. Setting the second
column to Boolean values converts it to checkboxes.

```
def getColumnClass(self, columnIndex):
    return self.columnClasses[columnIndex]
```

isCellEditable() helps JTable determine if the cell can be modified. Every cell
in Add? is editable, so for that column a true value is returned. Remember, the Add
attribute is a constant that denotes the Add? column.

```
def isCellEditable(self, rowIndex, columnIndex):
    return columnIndex == self.Add
```

setValueAt() sets the value of the Add? column only. It should never be called
for the Toppings column unless the JTable instance has determined, through
isCellEditable(), that it can be modified. For this reason, setValueAt() checks if
the column index is Add? If so, it converts the set value to Boolean.

Remember that Python treats Boolean primitives as integers, so we convert
the set value to Boolean. Then we index data with the rowIndex and columnIndex
arguments, set the data's value, and notify all event listeners of the change via
fireTableCell().

AbstractTableModel implements fireTableCell() along with other helper
methods like addTableModelListener() and removeTableModelListener().

```
def setValueAt (self, value, rowIndex, columnIndex):
    if(columnIndex == self.Add):
        value = Boolean(value)
        self.data[rowIndex][columnIndex] = value
        self.fireTableCellUpdated(rowIndex, columnIndex)
```

To test the model at this point we add the following code, but only if *model.py* is
run as the main module.

```
if __name__ == '__main__':
    from javax.swing import JTable, JFrame, JScrollPane
    pizza_model = PizzaTableModel()
    table = JTable(pizza_model)
    frame = JFrame('Select your toppings')
    frame.contentPane.add(JScrollPane(table))
    frame.pack()
    frame.visible = 1
```

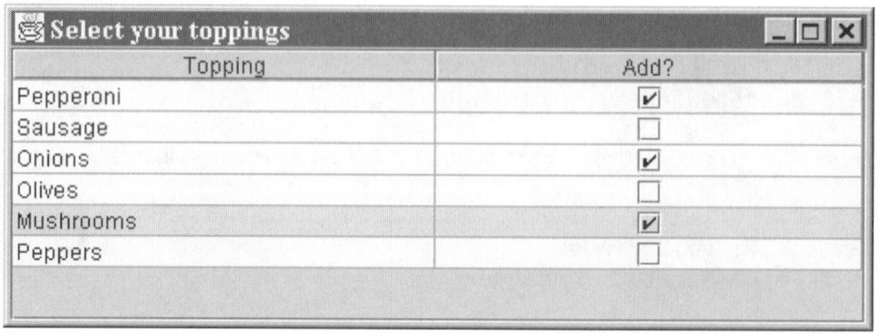

**Figure 16–4**   *The Topping Table*

The first part of the code imports JTable, JFrame, and JScrollPane. Then it creates a table and a frame and passes the table to a JScrollPane constructor, adding the JScrollPane instance to the frame's content pane. Finally it packs the frame and makes it visible.

Run *model.py*. What you get should look like Figure 16–4. Then try these exercises:

- Add five more toppings.
- Add a column called Extra for the customer to choose an extra amount of a particular topping. Make it so the cells can be edited only if the corresponding cell in the Add? column is selected.

## Putting Things Together—Adding a Table Model to the Address Book Application

In this section, we'll add a table model to the address book application and "swingify" some of the application's AWT ways.

---

**AWT to JFC**

The first time I wrote the address book application, I used all of the old AWT components (java.awt.Frame, java.awt.Panel, etc.). When I modified it, only 12 lines out of 114 had to be changed, and 9 of those dealt with JList.

The point is that the move from List to JList changed a lot, although most of the changes weren't needed. Other JFC/AWT components map nicely even though they're not closely related on the class hierarchy. Luckily, JList is the exception, not the rule.

Up to now what we've seen of JFC/Swing is pretty much the same as AWT. Most developers have migrated to Swing by now, in spite of the fact that the first few Swing versions were well short of perfect. Since then, Swing has proven its worth.

### Adding a Table and Moving the Address Data to a View

Now it's time to start tinkering with our "swingified" address book application, first adding support for a table. To do this we'll move the address data to a model, which will be a combination table and list. The purpose is to show how, with MVC, many views can be updated from a single data source.

Recall from prior examples that the address data was loaded into a dictionary (dict) from a file. We'll use this dictionary to hold the addresses, as always, but instead of making dict an aggregate member of AddressMain, we'll create a new class called AddressModel that acts as both a list model and a table model and put dict in there. Then we'll add a JFC table to the class so that both the JList and JTable instances reference the same model—that is, an AddressMain instance.

The tricky part of AddressMain is mapping the address data (stored in a dictionary) to both the list and table models. We'll accomplish this by creating a Python list to contain the sorted dictionary keys, which we'll use to sort the addresses by name into table rows. This will make it easier to get the address instance at a given row index.

For AddressModel to act as a model for both a list and a table, it needs to implement the ListModel and TableModel interfaces. As I said earlier, JFC provides AbstractListModel and AbstractTableModel classes that hold a good part of the functionality needed to implement their respective models. We want to use them, but we can't just inherit their functionality. In Java you can't extend two base classes, but you can implement many interfaces. In Jython you can't extend two Java base classes, but you can extend two Python base classes. To overcome this obstacle, what we have to do is extend from AbstractTableModel and implement AbstractListModel's interface.

### AddressModel

The following code (from *Two/AddressModel.py*) shows AddressModel's definition and constructor. Notice that AddressModel implements TableModel (through Abstract TableModel) and ListModel.

```
class AddressModel(AbstractTableModel, ListModel):
    """The AddressModel is both a ListModel and a TableModel."""
    def __init__(self):
        """Initialize the Address model.
        Read the dictionary from the file."""

        self.dict = None      # holds the dictionary of addresses.
        self.list = None      # holds the sorted list of names,
                              # which are keys
                              # into the dictionary.

        self.listeners = []  #to hold list of ListModelListeners

            # Read the addresses from the file.
        self.fname=".\\addr.dat"        # holds the file name
                                        # that holds the addresses
        self.dict = readAddresses(self.fname)
```

```
            # Store the sorted list of names.
        self.list = self.dict.keys()
        self.list.sort()

            # Define the column names and locations in the table.
        self.columnNames=['Name', 'Phone #', 'Email']
        self.NAME = 0   # To hold the location of the name column
        self.PHONE = 1 # To hold the location of the phone number column
        self.EMAIL = 2  # To hold the location of the email column
```

We can see that the list is sorted and that the rows in the table correspond to the index values of the sorted names. Thus, a given address is stored in the table based on the index of the name in the list. For the columns, we need to be more creative. The constants defined in the constructor correspond to the placement of the address instance fields in the rows relative to the columns.

## AddressModel's Helper Methods

To map the address dictionary (self.dict) in the AddressModel interface to a table, we need to define some helper methods, as shown in the following code (*Two\ AddressModel.py*). The method names are self-explanatory, and the comments should fill in any blanks. (Make sure to read the comments and document strings; think of them as integral to the concepts in this chapter.)

```
def __getAddressAtRow(self, rowIndex):
        """Get the address at the specified row.
            (Private methods begin with __)"""

                # Get the row name out of the list.
                # Use the name to index the dictionary of addresses.
                # Get the address associated with this row.
        name = self.list[rowIndex]
        address = self.dict[name]
        return address
def __getAddressAttributeAtColumn(self, address, columnIndex):
        """Get the attribute of the address at the
            specified column index. Maps column indexes to
            attributes of the address class instances."""

        value = None # Holds the value we are going to return

                # Set the value based on the column index.
        if(columnIndex == self.NAME):
                value = address.name()
```

### *Mapping to ListModel and TableModel*
The first two helper methods map the list and name attributes to ListModel and the dict and address instances to TableModel. getAddressAtRow() gets the address at the specified row. getAddressAttributeAtColumn() gets the address attribute at the specified column index; that is, it maps column indexes to attributes of the address instances. Since the name attribute is used to determine the row index,

`__changeDictKey()` and `__changeList()` keep the list and dictionary in sync with each address whose name attribute is changed.

### Comments: More Is More

Sometimes I comment the obvious in my code, but when it comes to comments I don't believe that less is more. In fact, when things aren't obvious, such as mapping a dictionary to a table model, I prefer to go overboard.

Don't be chintzy with your comments. For every minute saved by not writing them, you'll waste a hundred minutes in code maintenance.

### Stupid Methods

Most of the time you break methods into many other methods so that the same code isn't repeated in different places. This is an idea borrowed from functional decomposition. In object-oriented programming, there's another reason to do this. It's called stupid, and that's a good thing.

Keep your methods short and stupid. Long methods are hard to understand and hard to change, so you have to divide to conquer. `__setAddressAttributeAtColumn()` is a stupid method because it's called by only one other method, leaving functional decomposition out of the picture.

### Implementing the ListModel Interface

`AddressModel`'s next four methods implement the `ListModel` interface.

```
def getSize(self):
    """Returns the length of the items in the list."""
    return len(self.list)

def getElementAt(self, index):
    """ Returns the value at index. """
    return self.list[index]

def addListDataListener(self, l):
    """Add a listener that's notified when the model changes."""
    self.listeners.append(l)

def removeListDataListener(self, l):
    """Remove a listener."""
    self.listeners.remove(l)
```

`getSize()` returns the length of the `list` attribute. (Remember that `list` consists of the sorted keys of the `dict` attribute, and `name` corresponds to the address stored at the location indicated by the key.) `getElementAt()` returns the element at the index from the list. `addListDataListener()` and `removeListDataListener()` keep track of the listeners that subscribe to events from `AddressModel` instances.

### ListModel Event Notification

Every time a ListModel event occurs, AddressModel notifies the listeners that have subscribed to it using the following methods:

```
def __fireContentsChanged(self, index, index1):
    """Fire contents changed, notify viewers
       that the list changed."""
    event = ListDataEvent(self, ListDataEvent.CONTENTS_CHANGED, index,
            index1)

    for listener in self.listeners:
        listener.contentsChanged(event)

def __fireIntervalAdded(self, index, index1):
    """Fire interval added, notify viewers
       that the items were added to the list."""
    event = ListDataEvent(self, ListDataEvent.INTERVAL_ADDED, index,
            index1)

    for listener in self.listeners:
        listener.intervalAdded(event)

def __fireIntervalRemoved(self, index, index1):
    """Fire interval removed from the list,
       notify viewers."""

    event = ListDataEvent(self, ListDataEvent.INTERVAL_REMOVED, index,
            index1)
    for listener in self.listeners:
        listener.intervalRemoved(event)
```

### Implementing the TableModel Interface

The next set of methods help implement the TableModel interface, partly by extending the AbstractTableModel class and partly by mapping the addresses stored in the dictionary to the rows and columns in the table model.

```
## The following methods implement the TableModel interface. ----- ##

    def addTableModelListener(self, l):
        """Add a listener that gets notified when the data model
           changes. Since all we are doing is calling the super,
           we don't need this method."""
        AbstractTableModel.addTableModelListener(self, l)

    def removeTableModelListener(self, l):
        """Remove a listener. Since all we are doing is
           calling the super, we don't need this method.
           It's here for example."""
        AbstractTableModel.removeTableModelListener(self, l)

    def getColumnClass(self, columnIndex):
        """Returns the common base Class for the column."""
        return String
```

```
def getColumnCount(self):
    """Returns the number of columns in the data model."""
    return len(self.columnNames)

def getColumnName(self, columnIndex):
    """Returns the name of the given column by columnIndex."""
    return self.columnNames[columnIndex]

def getRowCount(self):
    """Returns the number of rows in the table model."""
    return len(self.list)

def getValueAt(self, rowIndex, columnIndex):
    """Returns the cell value at location specified
        by columnIndex and rowIndex."""

        # Get the address object corresponding to this row.
    address = self.__getAddressAtRow(rowIndex)

        # Get the address attribute corresponding
        # to this column.
    value = self.__getAddressAttributeAtColumn(address, columnIndex)

    return value

def isCellEditable(self, rowIndex, columnIndex):
    """Returns if the cell is editable at the given
        rowIndex and columnIndex."""

        #All cells are editable
    return 1

def setValueAt(self, aValue, rowIndex, columnIndex):
    """Sets the value for the cell at the given
        columnIndex and rowIndex."""

        # Get the address object corresponding to this row.
    address = self.__getAddressAtRow(rowIndex)
    self.__setAddressAttributeAtColumn(aValue, address, columnIndex)
    self.fireTableCellUpdated(rowIndex, columnIndex)
```

addTableModelListener() and removeTableModelListener() are in the code for illustration only, because AbstractTableModel already implements them. This means that the following code is unnecessary:

```
def addTableModelListener(self, l):
    ...
    ...
    AbstractTableModel.addTableModelListener(self, l)

def removeTableModelListener(self, l):
    ...
    ...
    AbstractTableModel.removeTableModelListener(self, l)
```

### Columns and Rows

AddressModel inherits functionality from AbstractTableModel, so we can leave out addTableModelListener() and removeTableModelListener() (that's what we'll do in the third iteration of this example), and it will still function.

Here are three methods that work with columns:

```
def getColumnClass(self, columnIndex):
        """Returns the common base Class for the column."""
        return String

def getColumnCount(self):
        """Returns the number of columns in the data model."""
        return len(self.columnNames)

def getColumnName(self, columnIndex):
        """Returns the name of the given column
            by columnIndex."""
        return self.columnNames[columnIndex]
```

getColumnClass() always returns a string because every attribute we expose in the AddressModel class is a string. getColumnCount() uses the length of the columnNames attribute (defined in AddressModel's constructor), which is a list of strings that contain column names for the table model. It also uses the column index (column Index) as an index into columnNames to get the name that corresponds to a given column.

Only one method deals with rows specifically, getRowCount(), which returns the length of the items in columnNames. Every item in columnNames corresponds to a key that specifies a row in the table. This means that the length of columnNames is equal to the number of rows in TableModel.

### Cell Values

The next three methods get and edit cells in the table.

```
def getValueAt(self, rowIndex, columnIndex):
        """Returns the cell value at location specified by
            columnIndex and rowIndex."""

            # Get the address object corresponding to this row.
        address = self.__getAddressAtRow(rowIndex)

            # Get the address attribute
            # corresponding to this column.
        value = self.__getAddressAttributeAtColumn(address, columnIndex)

        return value

def isCellEditable(self, rowIndex, columnIndex):
        """Returns if the cell is editable at the given
            rowIndex and columnIndex."""
            # All cells are editable
        return 1
```

```
def setValueAt(self, aValue, rowIndex, columnIndex):
        """Sets the value for the cell at the given
            columnIndex and rowIndex."""

            # Get the address object corresponding to this row.
        address = self.__getAddressAtRow(rowIndex)
        self.__setAddressAttributeAtColumn(aValue, address, columnIndex)
        self.fireTableCellUpdated(rowIndex, columnIndex)
```

getValueAt() uses __getAddressAtRow() to get the address at the current row; then it uses __getAddressAttributeAtColumn() to get the value of the attribute corresponding to the given column index, and returns the value received. (__getAddress AttributeAtColumn() is an example of a stupid method: Its name describes what it does, which makes it almost completely self-documenting.)

IsCellEditable() assumes that all cells are editable and returns true (1) no matter what the row index and column index are equal to.

Like getValueAt(), setValueAt() uses __getAddressAtRow() to retrieve the address at the given row index (making getAddressAtRow() a good example of functional decomposition). Next it uses __setAddressAttribute() to set the value of the address attribute corresponding to the column index and, finally, notifies every JTable view of the change. This way, if multiple views are listening (or using the same model), they'll all be updated.

### __setAddressAttribute()

Because it does so much, let's take a closer look at __setAddressAttribute(). Examine the code closely. If you understand it, you understand AddressModel.

```
def __setAddressAttributeAtColumn(self, value, address, columnIndex):
        """Sets the address attribute at the corresponding
            column index. Maps the Address instance attributes
            to the column in the table(s) for editing"""

            # Get the email, phone and name from the address object.
        email, phone = address.email(), address.phoneNumber()
        name = address.name()

            # Set the value based on the column
            # The columnIndex is the name so set the name
            # in the address object.
            # Since the name is used for the list and keys in the
            # dictionary, we must change both list item and the
            # dictionary key associated with name.
        if(columnIndex == self.NAME):
            address.__init__(value, phone, email)
            self.__changeList(value, name)
            self.__changeDictKey(value, name)

        elif(columnIndex == self.PHONE):
            address.__init__(name, value, email)

        elif(columnIndex == self.EMAIL):
            address.__init__(name, phone, value)
```

columnIndex maps to a particular attribute in the class instance. It's compared against three constants (name, phone, and email) to determine the attribute to set.

### *__init__ and Its Stupid Methods*

The __init__method of the address argument sets the attribute. However, if that attribute is name (i.e., columnIndex ==self.name), several things have to occur. This part of the code was tricky to write because the name of the address is a key into the dictionary and is used by the list to sort the keys. That means that if the name changes, so do the dictionary keys and list values. The best way I could think of to keep __init__ from becoming an unruly mess was to break it down into several stupid methods.

The first stupid method, __changeList(), removes the old value from the list and inserts the new value in its place.

```
def __changeList(self, newValue, oldValue):
            """Change the old value in the list to the new value.
                Keeps the JList views in sync with this
                Python list by firing an event."""

                # Get the index of the oldValue in the list.
                # Use the index to index the list,
                # and change the list location to the new value.
                # Notify the JList views subscribed to this model.
        index=self.list.index(oldValue)
        self.list[index]=newValue
        self.__fireContentsChanged(self, index, index)
```

Then it notifies the list views (JList instances) of the replacement.

The next stupid method, __changeDictKey(), removes the key/value pair in the dictionary corresponding to the name. (Recall that the name is the key into the dictionary and the value is the address instance with that name.) It's a lot like __changeList() in that it manages a collection of model data affected by a name change in an address instance.

```
def __changeDictKey(self, newKey, oldKey):
        """Change the old key in the dictionary
            to the new key."""

                # Get the address stored at the oldKey location.
                # Delete the old key value from the dictionary.
                # Use the new key to create a new location
                # for the address.
        address = self.dict[oldKey]
        del self.dict[oldKey]
        self.dict[newKey]=address
```

Using the old key (oldKey), __changeDictKey() gets the address at the old location and deletes it. Then it uses the new key (newKey) to set a new location for the address, which was extracted on the first line.

## Testing

We're not ready to put `AddressModel` in our address book application yet. Before we can integrate a fairly large piece of code like this, we have to test it with scaffolding code.

The `AddressModel` class has to fit well in the MVC architecture, so we want it to handle multiple views that work with `ListModel` and `TableModel`. To test for this we'll use `JList` and `JTable`, and we'll throw in `JTabbedPane` because it can hold several components, each in its own tab.

Here's our scaffolding code. Read the comments to get an idea of the flow.

```
if __name__ == '__main__':
    from javax.swing import JTable, JList, JFrame, JTabbedPane, JScrollPane

        # Create an instance of JFrame, JTabbedPane, AddressModel, JTable,
        # and JList. Pass the same instance of AddressModel to the table
        # and the list constructor.
    frame = JFrame('Test AddressModel')
    pane = JTabbedPane()
    model = AddressModel()

    list = JList(model)
    table = JTable(model)

        # Add the table and the list to the tabbed pane.
    pane.addTab('table 1', JScrollPane(table))
    pane.addTab('list 1', JScrollPane(list))

        # Create another table and list.
    table = JTable(model)
    list = JList(model)

        # Add the other table and list to the tabbed pane.
        # Now we have four views that share the same model.
    pane.addTab('table 2', JScrollPane(table))
    pane.addTab('list 2', JScrollPane(list))

        # Add the pane to the frame.
        # Smack it, pack it, and show it off.
    frame.contentPane.add(pane)
    frame.pack()
    frame.visible=1
```

Try these exercises:

- Run *AddressModel.py* from the command line (`jython AddressModel.py`). You should get a frame that looks like Figure 16–5.
- Change "Andy Grove" to someone else, and change his phone number and email address. What happens to the other views (`list1`, `list2`, and `table2`)?
- Use the code for `AddressModel` to create another column in the table called Cell Phone. Edit the code for `Address` and `AddressModel` to accommodate it.

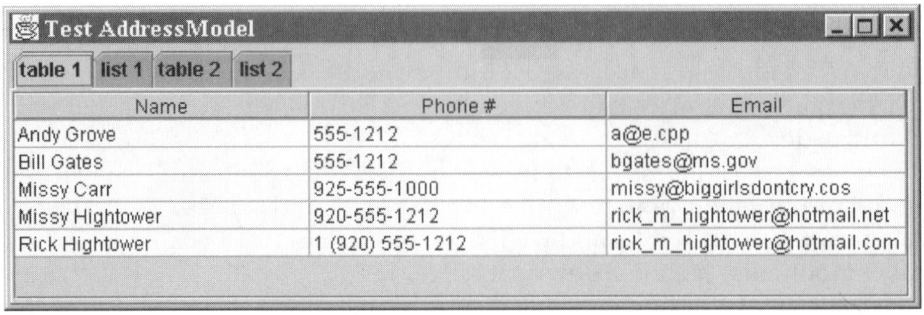

**Figure 16–5** *The Initial Test* AddressModel *Frame*

## Integrating AddressModel with AddressMain

Now that AddressModel has been defined and tested, let's put it in our address book application. To integrate it with AddressMain, we're going to need methods that will load the form with an address, add and remove an address from the model, and save an address to disk. Before this functionality was in AddressMain; now it's in the following methods in AddressModel:

- getAddressAt()—gets the address instance at a given row index
- getAddressByName()—gets the address by a given name
- addAddress()—adds an address to the model
- removeAddressByName()—removes an address from the model when given the name of the address
- writeAddress()—saves the address to disk

Here's the code for these methods:

```
def getAddressAt(self, rowIndex):
        """Get an Address by rowIndex"""
        return self.__getAddressAtRow(rowIndex)

def getAddressByName(self, name):
        """Get an Address by the name property of the address."""
        return self.dict[name]

def addAddress(self, address):
        """Add an address to the model, and notify the
           views of the change."""

                # Add the address to the dictionary,
                # and get the keys as the list.
        self.dict[address.name()] = address
        self.list = self.dict.keys()

                # Sort the addresses, and find the index of
                # the new address in the list.
                # Then notify the list and table views.
```

```
                self.list.sort()
                index = self.list.index(address.name())
                self.__fireIntervalAdded(index, index)
                self.fireTableDataChanged()
def removeAddressByName(self, name):
        """Removes the address from the model and
           notifies views of change."""

                # Remove the address from the dictionary.
        del self.dict[name]

                # Remove the name from the list.
        index = self.list.index(name)
        del self.list[index]

                # Notify the table and list views that the data changed.
        self.fireTableDataChanged()
        self.__fireIntervalRemoved(index, index)

def writeAddresses(self):
        """Write the address data to the file."""
        writeAddresses(self.fname, self.dict)
```

Whenever addresses are added or removed from the model, all table and list views—the listeners—must be notified via the __fireIntervalAdded(), __fire IntervalRemoved(), and __fireTableDataChanged() methods.

## The AddressModel Code

Now that we've covered each part of AddressModel, we can look at its complete code (from *Two\AddressModel.py*).

```
from address import *
from javax.swing import AbstractListModel, ListModel
from javax.swing.table import AbstractTableModel, TableModel
from javax.swing.event import ListDataEvent
from java.lang import String

class AddressModel(AbstractTableModel, ListModel):
        """The AddressModel is both a ListModel and a TableModel."""

        def __init__(self):
            """Initialize the Address model.
            Read the dictionary from the file."""

            self.dict = None    # holds the dictionary of addresses.
            self.list = None    # holds the sorted list of names,
                                # which are keys into the dictionary.

            self.listeners = [] #to hold list of ListModelListeners

                  # Read the addresses from the file.
            self.fname=".\\addr.dat" # holds the file name that
                                     # holds the addresses
            self.dict = readAddresses(self.fname)
```

```
        # Store the sorted list of names.
    self.list = self.dict.keys()
    self.list.sort()

        # Define the column names and locations in the table.
    self.columnNames=['Name', 'Phone #', 'Email']
    self.NAME = 0  # To hold the location of the name column
    self.PHONE = 1 # To hold the location of the phone number column
    self.EMAIL = 2    # To hold the location of the email column

def __getAddressAtRow(self, rowIndex):
    """Get the address at the specifed row. (Private method)"""

        # Get the row name out of the list.
        # Use the name to index the dictionary of addresses.
        # Get the address associated with this row.
    name = self.list[rowIndex]
    address = self.dict[name]
    return address

def __getAddressAttributeAtColumn(self, address, columnIndex):
    """Get the attribute of the address at the
       specified column index."""

    value = None # Holds the value we are going to return

        # Set the value based on the column index.
    if(columnIndex == self.NAME):
        value = address.name()

    elif(columnIndex == self.PHONE):
        value = address.phoneNumber()

    elif(columnIndex == self.EMAIL):
        value = address.email()
        return value

def __changeList(self, newValue, oldValue):
    """Change the old value in the list to the new value."""

        # Get the index of the oldValue in the list.
        # Use the index to index the list,
        # and change the list location to the new value.
        # Notify the world.
    index=self.list.index(oldValue)
    self.list[index]=newValue
    self.__fireContentsChanged(index, index)

def __changeDictKey(self, newKey, oldKey):
    """Change the old key in the dictionary to the new key."""

        # Get the address stored at the oldKey location.
        # Delete the old key value from the dictionary.
        # Use the new key to create a new location
        # for the address.
    address = self.dict[oldKey]
    del self.dict[oldKey]
    self.dict[newKey]=address
```

```
    def __setAddressAttributeAtColumn(self, value, address, columnIndex):
        """Sets the address attribute at the
            corresponding column index."""

            # Get the email, phone and name from the address object.
        email, phone = address.email(), address.phoneNumber()
        name = address.name()
            # Set the value based on the column.
            # The columnIndex is the name so set the name
            # in the address object.
            # Since the name is used for the list and keys in the
            # dictionary, we must change both list item and the
            # dictionary key associated with name.
        if(columnIndex == self.NAME):
            address.__init__(value, phone, email)
            self.__changeList(value, name)
            self.__changeDictKey(value, name)

        elif(columnIndex == self.PHONE):
            address.__init__(name, value, email)

        elif(columnIndex == self.EMAIL):
            address.__init__(name, phone, value)

## The following methods implement the ListModel interface. ----- ##

    def getSize(self):
        """Returns the length of the items in the list."""
        return len(self.list)

    def getElementAt(self, index):
        """ Returns the value at index. """
        return self.list[index]

    def addListDataListener(self, l):
        """Add a listener that's notified when the model changes."""
        self.listeners.append(l)

    def removeListDataListener(self, l):
        """Remove a listener."""
        self.listeners.remove(l)

    def __fireContentsChanged(self, index, index1):
        """Fire contents changed. Notify viewers
            that the list changed."""
        event = ListDataEvent(self, ListDataEvent.CONTENTS_CHANGED,
                index, index1)
        for listener in self.listeners:
                listener.contentsChanged(event)

    def __fireIntervalAdded(self, index, index1):
        """Fire interval added. Notify viewers that
            the items were added to the list."""
        event = ListDataEvent(self, ListDataEvent.INTERVAL_ADDED, index,
                index1)
```

```
                    for listener in self.listeners:
                            listener.intervalAdded(event)

        def __fireIntervalRemoved(self, index, index1):
            """Fire interval removed from the list. Notify viewers."""
            event = ListDataEvent(self, ListDataEvent.INTERVAL_REMOVED,
                    index, index1)
            for listener in self.listeners:
                    listener.intervalRemoved(event)

## The following methods implement the TableModel interface. ----- ##

        def addTableModelListener(self, l):
            """Add a listener that gets notified when the
            data model changes. Since all we are doing is
            calling the super, we don't need this method."""
            AbstractTableModel.addTableModelListener(self, l)

        def removeTableModelListener(self, l):
            """Remove a listener. Since all we are doing is calling the
                super, we don't need this method. It's here for example."""
            AbstractTableModel.removeTableModelListener(self, l)

        def getColumnClass(self, columnIndex):
            """Returns the common base Class for the column."""
            return String

        def getColumnCount(self):
            """Returns the number of columns in the data model."""
            return len(self.columnNames)

        def getColumnName(self, columnIndex):
            """Returns the name of the given column by columnIndex."""
            return self.columnNames[columnIndex]

        def getRowCount(self):
            """Returns the number of rows in the table model."""
            return len(self.list)

        def getValueAt(self, rowIndex, columnIndex):
            """Returns the cell value at location specified
                by columnIndex and rowIndex."""

                    # Get the address object corresponding to this row.
            address = self.__getAddressAtRow(rowIndex)

                    # Get the address attribute
                    # corresponding to this column.
            value = self.__getAddressAttributeAtColumn(address, columnIndex)

            return value

        def isCellEditable(self, rowIndex, columnIndex):
            """Returns if the cell is editable at the given
                rowIndex and columnIndex."""

                    #All cells are editable
            return 1
```

```python
    def setValueAt(self, aValue, rowIndex, columnIndex):
        """Sets the value for the cell at the given
           columnIndex and rowIndex."""

            # Get the address object corresponding to this row.
        address = self.__getAddressAtRow(rowIndex)
        self.__getAddressAttributeAtColumn(aValue, address, columnIndex)
            # Notify that we changed this value so other
            # views can adjust.
        self.fireTableCellUpdated(rowIndex, columnIndex)

    def getAddressAt(self, rowIndex):
        """Get an Address by rowIndex"""
        return self.__getAddressAtRow(rowIndex)

    def getAddressByName(self, name):
        """Get an Address by the name property of the address."""
        return self.dict[name]

    def addAddress(self, address):
        """Add an address to the model,
        and notify the views of the change."""

            # Add the address to the dictionary,
            # and get the keys as the list.
        self.dict[address.name()] = address
        self.list = self.dict.keys()

            # Sort the addresses, and find the index of
            # the new address in the list.
            # Then notify the list and table views.
        self.list.sort()
        index = self.list.index(address.name())
        self.__fireIntervalAdded(index, index)
        self.fireTableDataChanged()

    def removeAddressByName(self, name):
        """Removes the address from the model
           and notifies views of change."""

            # Remove the address from the dictionary.
        del self.dict[name]
            # Remove the name from the list.
        index = self.list.index(name)
        del self.list[index]

            # Notify the table and list views that the data changed.
        self.fireTableDataChanged()
        self.__fireIntervalRemoved(index, index)

    def writeAddresses(self):
        """Write the address data to the file."""
        writeAddresses(self.fname, self.dict)

if __name__ == '__main__':
    from javax.swing import JTable, JList, JFrame, JTabbedPane, JScrollPane
    from javax.swing.event import ListDataListener
```

```
class listenertest (ListDataListener):
        def intervalAdded(self, e):
                print 'Interval Added: ' + `e`
        def intervalRemoved(self, e):
                print 'Interval Removed: ' + `e`
        def contentsChanged(self, e):
                print 'Content Changed: ' + `e`

        # Create an instance of JFrame, JTabbedPane, AddressModel,
        # JTable, and JList.
        # Pass the same instance of AddressModel to the table
        # and the list constructor.
frame = JFrame('Test AddressModel')
pane = JTabbedPane()
model = AddressModel()
model.addListDataListener(listenertest())

list = JList(model)
table = JTable(model)

        # Add the table and the list to the tabbed pane.
pane.addTab('table 1', JScrollPane(table))
pane.addTab('list 1', JScrollPane(list))

        # Create another table and list.
table = JTable(model)
list = JList(model)

        # Add the other table and list to the tabbed pane.
        # Now we have four views that share the same model.
pane.addTab('table 2', JScrollPane(table))
pane.addTab('list 2', JScrollPane(list))

        # Add the pane to the frame.
        # Smack it, pack it, and show it off.
frame.contentPane.add(pane)
frame.pack()
frame.visible=1

addr = Address('aaaaa','aaaaaa','aaaaaa')
model.addAddress(addr)
raw_input('Hit Enter to continue')
model.removeAddressByName(addr.name())
```

The actual code for implementing AddressModel is only about 100 lines, but the file is about 280 lines. Comments, document strings, and scaffolding account for the difference. Although it takes up 28 lines, scaffolding saves a lot of time in isolating and debugging problems. In a production environment, though, you should put any testing code in its own module.

## Changes in AddressMain to Accommodate AddressModel

I had to change AddressMain to use AddressModel. In the code that follows the modifications are highlighted in bold:

```
from java.awt import BorderLayout, FlowLayout
from AddressModel import AddressModel
...
...
Frame=JFrame; List=JList; Panel=JPanel; Dialog=JDialog; Button=JButton
Menu=JMenu; MenuItem=JMenuItem; MenuBar=JMenuBar; PopupMenu=JPopupMenu;

from AddressFormPane import AddressForm
...
...

class AddressMain(Frame):
       def __init__(self):
                    # Call the base class constructor.
              Frame.__init__(self, "Main Frame")

                    # Create a list.
              self.addresses = List()

                    # Keep forward-compatible with other containers like JFrame.
              self.container = JPanel()
              self.container.layout = BorderLayout()

                    # Add the addresses list to the container, on the left side.
              scrollpane = JScrollPane(self.addresses)
              scrollpane.horizontalScrollBarPolicy =
                  JScrollPane.HORIZONTAL_SCROLLBAR_ALWAYS
              self.container.add(scrollpane, BorderLayout.WEST)

                    # Create an instance of AddressModel,
                    # and set the addresses and self model attributes.
              model = AddressModel()
              self.addresses.model = model
              self.model = model

                    # Set the event handler for the addresses.
              self.addresses.valueChanged = self.__itemSelected

                    # Create the AddressForm and add it to the east.
              self.form = AddressForm()
              self.container.add(self.form, BorderLayout.EAST)

                    # Create a tabbed pane, and add the container and table
                        in their own tabs.
                    # Add the JTabbed instance to the contentPane.
              tabbed_pane = JTabbedPane()
              table = JTable(model)
              tabbed_pane.addTab('Edit Address', self.container)
              tabbed_pane.addTab('View Address Book', JScrollPane(table))
              self.contentPane.add(tabbed_pane, BorderLayout.CENTER)

                    # Set up toolbar and menubar.
              self.__init__toolbar()
              self.__init__menu()

              self.popup = None      #to hold the popup menu
              self.__init__popup()
              self.addresses.mousePressed = self.__popupEvent
```

```
                self.windowClosing = self.__windowClosing

                    # Set the default address in the list and form.
                if self.model.getSize() > 0:
                    self.addresses.setSelectedIndex(0)
                    address = self.model.getAddressAt(0)
                    self.form.set(address)

                    # Pack the frame and make it visible.
                self.pack()
                self.setSize(600, 300)
                self.visible=1

        ...
        ...
        ...
        def __addAddress_Clicked(self,event):
                dialog = AddAddressDialog(self)
                if dialog.getState() == AddAddressDialog.OK:
                    addr = dialog.getAddress()
                    self.model.addAddress(addr)
                    ...

        def __removeAddress_Clicked(self,event):
                index = self.addresses.selectedIndex
                key = self.addresses.selectedValue
                self.model.removeAddressByName(key)

                    #Get the index of the item before this one
                    #unless the index of the item we removed is 0.
                    #Then select the index.
                if index-1 < 0: index = 0
                else: index = index -1
                self.addresses.selectedIndex = index

                    #Set the form to the current address.
                key = self.addresses.selectedValue
                address = self.model.getAddressByName(key)
                self.form.set(address)
                ...
                ...
if __name__ == "__main__":
                mainWindow = AddressMain()
```

The modifications aren't extensive, which is a good thing. An important change is the addition of JTabbedPane to include multiple tabs. Run the code. You should get the frames shown in Figures 16–6 and 16–7. Try these exercises:

- Add an address to the address book. Then check that the list and table views (JList and JTable) were updated.

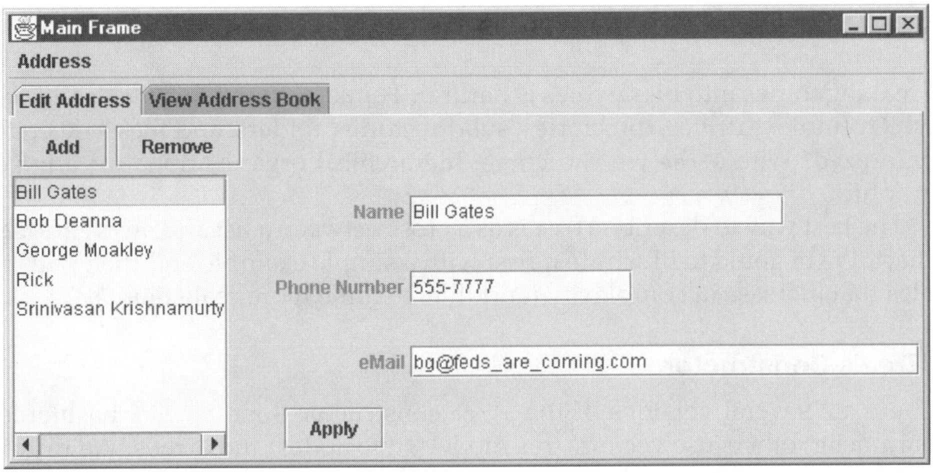

**Figure 16–6**   *Address Book Entry Form with* JTabbedPane

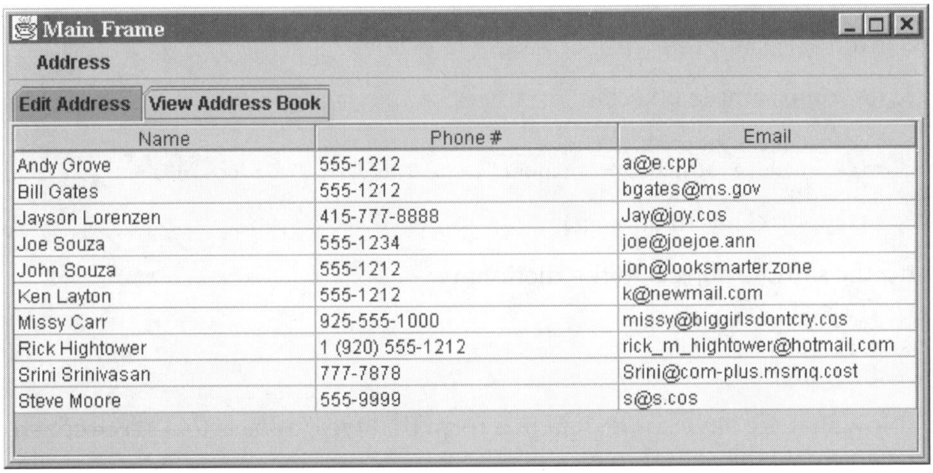

**Figure 16–7**   *Address List with* JTabbedPane

- Remove an address from the list.
- Add an optional Web site address to the address book. (That is, make it so each entry has an optional Web page URL.)

If you're feeling pretty sure of yourself, try reimplementing the complete address book application in Java.

## *JTree*

Breaking things into hierarchies is natural. Think of your computer's file system, which employs drives, directories, subdirectories, folders, and files to keep things organized. With JTree we can create hierarchical organizations for any sort of graphical display.

The best way to describe JTree is as a cross between a list and an organizational chart. We're going to illustrate it first with a simple example and then with examples that increase in complexity (and thus become more realistic).

### JTree's Constructor

There are several versions of the JTree constructor—one takes a hashtable as a parameter; others use vectors, tree models, tree nodes, and arrays. We're going to start off with the hashtable version and add some objects to it. Don't be scared. A hashtable is much like a Python built-in dictionary object—in early versions of Jython; you can use the two interchangeably.

Create the hashtable.

```
>>> from java.util import Hashtable
>>> dict = Hashtable()
```

Create some sample objects.

```
>>> from address import Address
>>> rick = Address("Rick Hightower", "555-1212", "r@r.cos")
>>> bob = "Bob DeAnna"
>>> Kiley = "Kiley Hightower"
```

Add the sample objects to the dictionary.

```
>>> dict['Rick'] = rick
>>> dict['Bob'] = bob
>>> dict['Kiley'] = Kiley
```

Now that we have some data in a form that we can pass to a JTree constructor, we can create the actual tree.

Import JTree, and create an instance of it, passing the hashtable (dict) as a parameter.

```
>>> from javax.swing import JTree
>>> tree = JTree(dict)
```

Add the tree to the frame, and show it.

```
>>> from javax.swing import JFrame
>>> frame = JFrame("Tree Test")
>>> frame.contentPane.add(tree)
javax.swing.JTree[,0,0,0x0,invalid,...
>>> frame.pack()
>>> frame.visible=1
```

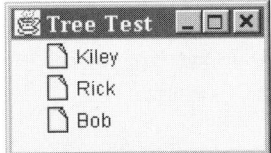

**Figure 16–8**    *A Simple*
JTree *Tree*

The frame should look like Figure 16–8. Seems more like a list than a tree, does it not? We'll fix this later when we define our own model.

## The Tree Model

Like JList and JTable, JTree uses JFC's MVC architecture, which means that every tree has a model. You don't have to specify a model because JTree does it for you with DefaultTreeModel, from *javax.swing.tree*.

```
>>> tree.model.class
<jclass javax.swing.tree.DefaultTreeModel at 9727>
```

The tree model is made up of tree nodes. The TreeNode class implements the TreeNode interface. Get the root node, and see what class it is.

```
>>> root = tree.model.getRoot()
>>> root.class
<jclass javax.swing.tree.DefaultMutableTreeNode...>
```

Check that the root implements the TreeNode interface.

```
>>> root.class.interfaces
array([<jclass java.lang.Cloneable at 95880612>,
<jclass javax.swing.tree.MutableTreeNode at -509409883>,
<jclass java.io.Serializable at 1612121508>], java.lang.Class)
```

The actual interface implemented is MutableTreeNode, which is the second element in the array. Here's how to see if MutableTreeNode implements TreeNode:

```
>>> root.class.interfaces[1].interfaces
array([<jclass javax.swing.tree.TreeNode at -277936731>], java.lang.Class)
```

A faster way to do this is with the isinstance() built-in function. As we can see, isinstance() returns a 1 (true) value, so root is indeed an instance of TreeNode.

```
>>> isinstance(root, TreeNode)
1
```

A leaf is a node that can have no children. You can check if a node is a leaf like this:

```
>>> tree.model.isLeaf(root)
0
```

The 0 (false) value tells the story.

Now we'll iterate through the root node and print out the string representation of the child nodes (we'll also find out if they're actually leaves).

```
>>> count = tree.model.getChildCount(root)
>>> for index in xrange(0,count):
...        child_node = tree.model.getChild(root, index)
...        print child_node
...        print 'isLeaf ' + `tree.model.isLeaf(child_node)`
...
Kiley
isLeaf 1
Rick
isLeaf 1
Bob
isLeaf 1
```

## The JTree Model Interface

To create our tree model we have to implement the TreeModel interface, which has the following methods:

- addTreeModelListener(listener)—allows JTree to subscribe to tree model events
- removeTreeModelListener(listener)—removes the event listener
- getChild(parent,index)—returns the child of the parent at a given index
- getChildCount(parent)—returns the child count of the specified parent node
- getIndexOfChild(parent, child)—returns the index of the child in the parent
- getRoot()—returns the root of the tree
- isLeaf(node)—checks to see if the node is a leaf
- ValueForPathChanged(path, newValue)—an abstract method

getRoot() and getChild() return instances of java.lang.Object, which are often actual tree nodes.

TreeNode defines the interface for the nodes, which is one of the reasons that JTree is so complex—it's like a model within a model. Here are its methods:

- children()—returns an enumeration of children
- getAllowsChildren()—returns if the node allows child nodes
- getChildAt()—gets the child at the specified index
- getChildCount()—returns the count of children in a specified node
- getIndex(node)—returns the index of the given child node
- getParent()—returns the parent of a specified child node
- isLeaf()—returns if a specified node is a leaf

The children() method requires that TreeNode return to it an instance of java.util. Enumeration, which must implement these methods:

- hasMoreElements()—returns true if there are more elements in the enumeration
- nextElement()—returns the next element in the collection

A short example will illustrate how tree nodes can contain other tree nodes. Our tree model contains instances of javax.swing.tree.TreeNode. It doesn't have to, but it's not a bad idea. We'll define three classes:

- ListEnumeration—implements the java.util.Enumeration interface
- SimpleNode—implements the javax.swing.tree.TreeNode interface
- SimpleModel—implements the javax.swing.tree.TreeModel interface

### ListEnumeration

The ListEnumeration class helps develop a simple tree node. In its code, you'll notice that the children() method returns an enumeration—more precisely, an instance of java.util.Enumeration—which provides a standard way to enumerate over a collection of elements while abstracting the collection type.

Here's the code (from *TreeModel1\ListEnumeration.py*):

```
from java.util import Enumeration

class ListEnumeration(Enumeration):
    def __init__(self, the_list):
        self.list = the_list[:]
        self.count = len(self.list)
        self.index = 0

    def hasMoreElements(self):
        return self.index < self.count

    def nextElement(self):
        object = self.list[self.index]
        self.index = self.index + 1
        return object
```

Let's break it down interactively. Import ListEnumeration.

```
>>> from ListEnumeration import ListEnumeration
```

Create a list containing three integers.

```
>>> mylist = [1,2,3]
```

Show that the list has been created.

```
>>> mylist.__class__
<jclass org.python.core.PyList at -992650171>
```

Create a ListEnumeration object, passing it mylist as an argument to the constructor.

```
>>> enum = ListEnumeration(mylist)
>>> enum.__class__
<class ListEnumeration.ListEnumeration at -736797627>
```

Iterate through the list.

```
>>> while(enum.hasMoreElements()):
...     print enum.nextElement()
...
1
2
3
```

### SimpleNode

SimpleNode implements TreeNode and can be used alone or with JTree. Like other classes that implement TreeNode, it's sort of a model without events. SimpleNode has a parent node, a list of child nodes (which are of type SimpleNode as well), and a property that determines whether a given node is a leaf. Its constructor optionally creates leaf nodes and adds them to its node list.

Here's the code (from *TreeModel1\SimpleNode.py*):

```
from javax.swing.tree import TreeNode
from ListEnumeration import ListEnumeration
from java.lang import Object

class SimpleNode (Object, TreeNode):
    def __init__(self, name, items=[], parent=None, leaf=0):
        self.__nodes = []

        self.__name = name
        self.__parent = parent
        self.__leaf=leaf

        for name in items:
            node = SampleNode(name, parent=self, leaf=1)
            self.__nodes.append(node)

    def getChildAt(self, index):
        "Get the child at the given index"
        return self.__nodes[index]

    def children(self):
        'get children nodes '
        return ListEnumeration(self.__nodes)

    def getAllowsChildren(self):
        'Does this node allow children node?'
        return not self.leaf

    def getChildCount(self):
        'child count of this node'
        return len (self.__nodes)

    def getIndex(self, node):
        'get index of node in nodes list'
        try:
            return self.__nodes.index(node)
        except ValueError, e:
            return None
```

```
      def getParent(self):
            'get parent node'
            return self.__parent

      def isLeaf(self):
            'is leaf node'
            return self.__leaf
```

In addition to all of `TreeNode`'s methods, `SimpleNode` implements its own:

- `__str__()`—displays the node as a Python string
- `toString()`—displays the node as a Java print string
- `__repr__()`—displays the node as a string for debugging
- `add()`—adds a `SimpleNode` child to the list of nodes
- `setParent(parent)`—sets the parent of a specified node
- `getName()`—gets the name of a specified node
- `setName()`—sets the name of a specified node

For `toString()` to function, `SimpleNode` has to extend `java.lang.Object`, which defines this method. I hope all this will take is defining `__str__` in future Jython releases.

Here's part of the `SimpleNode` class showing its helper methods:

```
def __str__(self):
      'str node'
      return self.__name

def toString(self):
      return self.__str__()

def __repr__(self):
      nodes = []

      for node in self.__nodes:
            nodes.append(str(node))

      if (self.__parent):
            tpl=(self.__name, nodes, self.__parent, self.__leaf)
            return 'SampleNode(name=%s,list=%s,parent=%s,leaf=%s)' % tpl
      else:
            tpl=(self.__name, nodes, self.__leaf)
            return 'SampleNode(name=%s,list=%s,leaf=%s)' % tpl

def add(self, node):
      self.__nodes.append(node)
      node.setParent(self)

def setParent(self, parent):
      self.__parent = parent

def setName(self, name):
      self.__name=name

def getName(self, name):
      return self.__name
```

The best way to define `SimpleNode` is to show it building a tree-like structure of nodes.

Create a parent node.

```
>>> parent = SimpleNode("Dick & Mary")
```

Create three child nodes: `child1`, `child2`, and `child3` with their spouses. Pass a list of offspring to each node.

```
>>> child1 = SimpleNode("Rick & Kiley", ["Whitney"])
>>> child2 = SimpleNode("Martha & Miguel", ["Alex", "Nicholai", "Marcus"])
>>> child3 = SimpleNode("Missy & Adam", ["Mary", "Sarah"])
```

Add the children to the parent node.

```
>>> parent.add(child1)
>>> parent.add(child2)
>>> parent.add(child3)
```

Iterate through the children in the parent node showing their names.

```
>>> child = parent.children()
>>> children = parent.children()
>>> while(children.hasMoreElements()):
...     print children.nextElement()
...
Rick & Kiley
Martha & Miguel
Missy & Adam
```

Here's an easier version of this example, using the `for loop` statement to handle the enumerators:

```
>>> child = parent.children()
>>> children = parent.children()
>>> for child in children:
...     print child
...
Rick & Kiley
Martha & Miguel
Missy & Adam
```

Now let's make the parent tree node a tree model. Import the GUI components that are needed.

```
>>> from javax.swing import JTree, JScrollPane, JFrame
```

Create a `JTree` instance, passing the parent node as the argument to the `JTree` constructor.

```
>>> tree = JTree(parent)
```

Create a frame, and add the `JTree` instance to it. Pack the frame, and make it visible.

```
>>> frame = JFrame('SimpleNode test')
>>> frame.contentPane.add(JScrollPane(tree))
>>> frame.pack()
>>> frame.show()
```

Your end result should look like Figure 16–9.

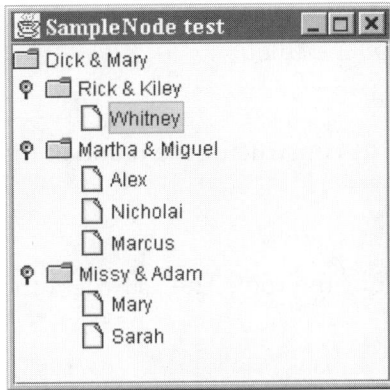

**Figure 16–9**   *A Family Tree*

### Sharing a Data Model among JTree Views

If the tree node works so well, why do we need a model? I can almost hear you asking this question. For the answer, think what will happen if `child1`, Kiley, has a second child.

```
>>> child1
SimpleNode(name=Rick & Kiley,list=['Whitney', 'Rick JR.'],parent=Dick &
Mary,leaf=0)
```

To make this clearer, we can write this:

```
>>> kiley = child1
```

Create the baby node.

```
>>> baby = SimpleNode("Rick JR.")
>>> kiley.add(baby)
```

Show Kiley's children.

```
>>> children = kiley.children()
>>> for child in children:
...      print child
...
Whitney
Rick JR.
```

If you look at Kiley's children in the `JTree` node, you'll see that it's out of sync. Worse yet, it will be out of sync with any other `Jtree` you create. That's why we need models. Unlike nodes, they keep the data and the view synchronized.

### SampleModel

Deriving your nodes from `javax.swing.tree.TreeNode` isn't mandatory if you define your own model. The `TreeModel` interface abstracts a node, which can therefore derive from `java.lang.Object` and implement no interfaces at all. `TreeModel` can have an ID of a database record as a member, so, instead of reading memory out of a Python list, you can get data out of the database via the associated tree model.

Models keep data and views in sync. The question is how. I'll show you, with a tree model I created called `SampleModel`.

Import `SampleModel` from the *SampleModel.py* module.

```
>>> from SampleModel import SampleModel
```

Create an instance of `SampleModel` by passing its constructor the name of the root node.

```
>>> tree_model = SampleModel("Dick & Mary")
```

Add the two branches (nodes) of the tree off of the root. The `addNode()` method returns the node created.

```
>>> tree_model.addNode("Martha & Miguel", ["Alex", "Nicholai", "Marcus"])
>>> tree_model.addNode("Missy & Adam", ["Mary", "Sarah"])
```

Create the last branch, and save it. `Kiley` is a handle we'll use later.

```
>>> Kiley=tree_model.addNode("Rick & Kiley", ["Whitney"])
```

Notice that we haven't called any methods on a node object. Instead, we've dealt directly with the model, which encapsulates node manipulation.

Now let's create some views for our model. Import all JFC components that are needed.

```
>>> from javax.swing import JFrame, JTree, JScrollPane
```

Create the first view.

```
>>> frame1 = JFrame("View 1--No Scroll")
>>> tree = JTree(tree_model)
>>> frame1.contentPane.add(tree)
>>> frame1.pack()
>>> frame1.show()
```

Create the second view.

```
>>> frame2 = JFrame("View 2--With Scroll")
>>> tree2 = JTree(tree_model)
>>> frame2.contentPane.add(JScrollPane(tree2))
>>> frame2.pack()
>>> frame2.show()
```

Expand the `Rick & Kiley` node in both views. Your result should be the two views in Figure 16–10.

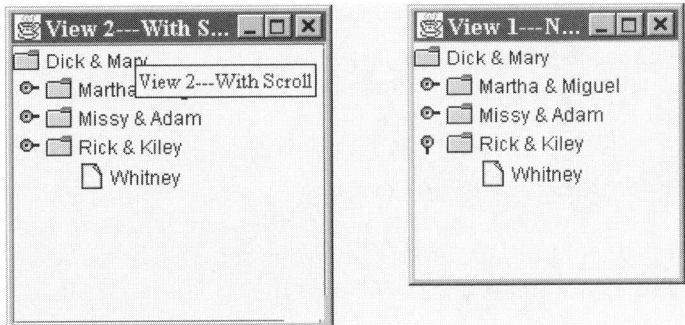

**Figure 16–10**    *Two* `SampleModel` *Views*

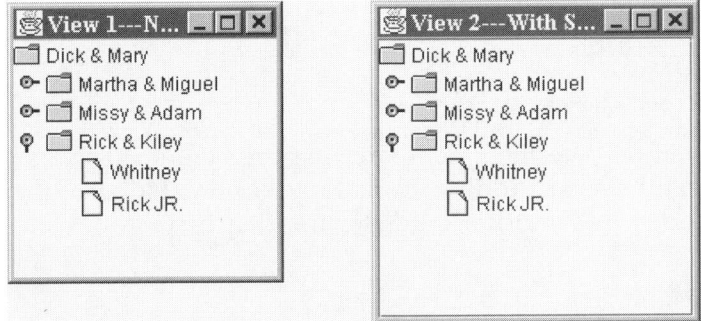

**Figure 16–11**    *A Blessed Event for Views 1 and 2*

Now for the true litmus test. Will both views be changed if the family tree changes; that is, will the views be synchronized with the data? As before, we'll say that Kiley has a second child, so we need to add a node to `Rick & Kiley`.

```
>>> tree_model.addNode('Rick JR.', parent=Kiley)
```

Figure 16–11 shows that the new node was added to both views.

### Event Notification

Just like the table model, the tree model keeps a list of listeners, all of which are notified when the model data changes. Since `TreeModel` controls access to the nodes, we can add code to it, in the `addNode()` method, to fire a notification event. Here's the `addNode()` method with its helpers:

```python
def addNode(self, name, children=[], parent=None):
        # Set the value of the leaf.
        # No children means the node is a leaf.
    leaf = len(children)==0
```

```
            # Create a SampleNode,
            # and add the node to the given parent.
     node = SampleNode(name, children, leaf=leaf)
     self.__add(node, parent)
     return node
```

addNode() creates an instance of SampleNode and passes its constructor the addNode() arguments. If the children argument is empty, the instance is set as a leaf. addNode() calls the __add() helper method and then returns the node so it can be used as a handle to other model methods. Here's the code for __add():

```
def __add(self, node, parent=None):
            # If the parent is none,
            # then set the parent to the root.
     if not parent:
          parent = self.getRoot()

            # Add the node to the parent,
            # and notify the world that the node changed.
     parent.add(node)
     self.fireStructureChanged(parent)
```

__add() adds the given node to the given parent. If the parent is None, the root node becomes the default parent. Adding the node to the parent invokes the fire-StructureChanged event, which notifies all listeners (that is, views). Here's the code:

```
def fireStructureChanged(self, node):
            # Get the path to the root node.
            # Create a TreeModelEvent class instance.
     path = self.getNodePathToRoot(node)
     event = TreeModelEvent(self, path)

            # Notify every tree model listener that
            # this tree model changed at the tree path.
     for listener in self.listeners:
          listener.treeStructureChanged(event)
```

fireStuctureChanged iterates through the listener list and calls each listener's treeStructureChanged() method, passing a TreeModelEvent instance. To create the instance, TreeModelEvent's constructor needs a path—a list of nodes—from the root to the changed node. This is how the view notification is carried out and thus how views stay in sync with the data model.

Get the path with the getNodePathToRoot() method.

```
def getNodePathToRoot(self, node):
     parent = node # Holds the current node.
     path=[]        # To hold the path to root.

                    # Get the path to the root
     while not parent is None:
                    # Add the parent to the path, and then get the
                    # parent's parent.
```

```
            path.append(parent)
            parent = parent.getParent()

        #Switch the order
    path.reverse()
    return path
```

This event does just what is says it does: it gets the node's path to the root. It should be obvious from the comments how it works.

## Additional Tree Model Methods

The rest of the tree model is somewhat boring. Two methods add and remove listeners, and several other methods delegate responsibility for specific tasks to their corresponding SimpleNode instances.

```
class SampleModel(TreeModel):
    def __init__(self, root_name):
        root = SampleNode(root_name, [])
        self._root = root
        self.listeners = [] # to hold TreeModel listeners
        #-------- The following methods implement the TreeModel interface.

    def addTreeModelListener(self, listener):
        self.listeners.append(listener)

    def removeTreeModelListener(self, listener):
        self.listeners.remove(listener)

    def getChild(self, parent, index):
        return parent.getChildAt(index)

    def getChildCount(self, parent):
        return parent.getChildCount()

    def getIndexOfChild(self, parent, child):
        return parent.getIndex(child)

    def getRoot(self):
        return self._root

    def isLeaf(self, node):
        return node.isLeaf()

    def valueForPathChanged(self, path, newValue):
        node = path.getLastPathComponent()
        node.setName(newValue)
    ...
    ...
```

You can see that most of the work is done by the underlying tree nodes and the noninterface methods.

> **DefaultMutableTreeNode and DefaultTreeModel**
>
> Another way to use `JTree` is with `DefaultMutableTreeNode` and `DefaultTreeModel`. Once you understand `TreeModel`, these classes are easy. Look them up in the Java API documentation. As an exercise, use them to implement the last interactive session.

## Handling JTree Events

`JTree` publishes the following event properties:

- `treeExpanded`—a node has expanded; associated with `javax.swing.event. TreeExpansionListener` and passed an instance of `java.swing.event.Tree ExpansionEvent`
- `treeCollapsed`—a node has collapsed; associated with `javax.swing.event. TreeExpansionListener` and passed an instance of `javax.swing.event.Tree ExpansionEvent`
- `treeWillExpand`—a node will expand (used to fetch data, as needed, into the tree model); associated with `javax.swing.event.TreeWillExpandListener` and passed an instance of `javax.swing.eventTreeExpansionEvent`
- `treeWillCollapse`—a node will collapse; associated with `javax.swing.event. TreeWillExpandListener` and passed an instance of `javax.swing.event.Tree-ExpansionEvent`
- `valueChanged`—a new node was selected; associated with `javax.swing.event. TreeSelectionListener` and passed an instance of `javax.swing.event.Tree SelectionEvent`

A little confusing? Let's look at an example that uses the event mechanism to put these properties to work. It's from *TreeModel1\TreeEvents.py*.

```
from SampleModel import SampleModel
from javax.swing import JFrame, JTree, JScrollPane
def handleTreeExpanded(event):
    global g_event
    print "Tree Expanded"
    showPath(event.path)
    g_event = event

def handleTreeCollapsed(event):
    global g_event
    print "Tree Collapsed"
    showPath(event.path)
    g_event = event

def handleTreeWillExpand(event):
    global g_event
    print "Tree Will Expand"
    showPath(event.path)
    g_event = event
```

```
def handleTreeWillCollapse(event):
    global g_event
    print "Tree Will Collapse"
    showPath(event.path)
    g_event = event

def handleValueChanged(event):
    global g_event
    print "Value Changed"
    showPath(event.path)
    g_event = event

def showPath(treePath):
    path = ""
    count = treePath.pathCount
    for index in range(0,count):
        node = treePath.getPathComponent(index)
        path = path + "-> [" + str(node) + "]"
    print path

tree_model = SampleModel("Dick & Mary")
tree_model.addNode("Martha & Miguel", ["Alex", "Nicholai", "Marcus"])
tree_model.addNode("Missy & Adam", ["Mary", "Sarah"])
Kiley=tree_model.addNode("Rick & Kiley", ["Whitney"])

frame = JFrame("Tree Events")
tree = JTree(tree_model)
frame.contentPane.add(tree)
frame.pack()
frame.show()

    # A node in the tree expanded.
tree.treeExpanded = handleTreeExpanded
    # A node in the tree collapsed.
tree.treeCollapsed = handleTreeCollapsed
    # A node in the tree will expand.
tree.treeWillExpand = handleTreeWillExpand
    # A node in the tree will collapse.
tree.treeWillCollapse = handleTreeWillCollapse
    # A new node was selected.
tree.valueChanged = handleValueChanged
```

Notice that there's an event handler for every possible event. The handler prints out the path of the event using the tree path associated with it. It also copies the last handler to a global variable, g_event.

### TreeEvents.py Example

Let's do an interactive session, first typing this at the system prompt:

```
C:\jython_book\scripts\chap16\TreeModel1>jython -i TreeEvents.py
```

Expand the first node to get the following output:

```
Tree Will Expand
-> [Dick & Mary]-> [Martha & Miguel]
Tree Expanded
->[Dick & Mary]-> [Martha & Miguel]
```

Select the first leaf in the first node to get this output:

```
Value Changed
-> [Dick & Mary]-> [Martha & Miguel]-> [Alex]
```

Collapse the first node.

```
Tree Will Collapse
-> [Dick & Mary]-> [Martha & Miguel]

Tree Collapsed
-> [Dick & Mary]-> [Martha & Miguel]
```

That was how to get the whole path, but our only interest is in the last node. We can get that by inspecting the last event, which is stored in g_event.

The event has a property called path, which is an instance of TreePath.

```
>>> g_event.path.class
<jclass javax.swing.tree.TreePath at -1128707474>
```

TreePath has a method called getLastPathComponent().

```
>>> dir (g_event.path.class)
['getParentPath', 'path', 'getPathComponent', 'pathCount',
'pathByAddingChild', 'getPath', 'isDescendant', 'getPathCount',
'lastPathComponent', 'parentPath', 'getLastPathComponent']
```

getLastPathComponent() returns the node selected.

```
    >>> g_event.path.getLastPathComponent()
  SampleNode(name=Martha & Miguel,list=['Alex', 'Nicholai', 'Marcus'],
    parent=Dick& Mary,leaf=0)
```

That about covers tree view events. To make sure you understand them, try these exercises:

- Add a JTree component to the address book example that replaces the JList component. Group the addresses by category—business, personal, and so forth. JTree will show the category and all of its addresses. Clicking on a particular category should show all of its items in the table. Clicking on a particular address should show that address in the entry form.
- Modify the tree so that categories and subcategories can be added to it.

## JToolBar and Actions

We've improved the address book application with the addition of JTabbedPane, JTable, and (if you did the exercises) JTree. Still, something's missing.

In the early days of Java there was no Swing, and AWT didn't have a toolbar. This meant that most developers used panels, which is what I did in the address book application. I had two reasons for this: to show how `JPanel` and the `Border Layout` layout manager work and to avoid introducing actions.

## Actions

We can avoid actions no longer. Any introduction to `JToolBar` has to include them. I held off until now because actions are a higher abstraction than components, and I thought you should have a good grip on components first.

Think of an action as a command. An item on a menu that says "remove address" is one example; another is a button on a toolbar that says the same thing. The main difference is that an action added to a toolbar usually becomes a button and an action added to a menu usually becomes an item.

The following code, from our third iteration of the address book application in this chapter, uses `javax.swing.JToolBar` and `javax.swing.AbstractAction` to show how actions work. Notice that the actions created are used by both a popup menu and a menubar menu, which makes the code much shorter.

First we define two classes that extend `AbstractAction`: one for adding and one for removing addresses.

```
class Add (AbstractAction):
     def __init__(self, this):
          self.this = this
          AbstractAction.__init__(self, "Add")

     def actionPerformed(self, event):
          self.this.addAddress_Clicked()

class Remove (AbstractAction):
     def __init__(self, this):
          self.this = this
          AbstractAction.__init__(self, "Remove")

     def actionPerformed(self, event):
          self.this.removeAddress_Clicked()
```

As you can see, both classes extend `AbstractAction`, and the only method they have to override is `actionPerformed()`. The `Remove` and `Add` actions respectively delegate calls to the `AddressMain` classes `removeAddress` and `addAddress`.

Next we instantiate the actions and add them to the toolbar. (Later they'll be added to the menubar and popup menus.)

```
     #Instantiate the add and remove actions.
addAction = Add(self)
removeAction = Remove(self)

     # Create the toolbar panel, and
     # add it to the North border
     # of the container.
```

```
toolbar = JToolBar()
self.contentPane.add(toolbar, BorderLayout.NORTH)

        #Add the actions to the toolbar.
toolbar.add(addAction)
toolbar.add(removeAction)
```

This code is much smaller than the code for creating menu items and buttons. Since we're using `JToolBar` instead of `JPanel`, we get the additional capability of moving the toolbar at runtime, as illustrated in Figures 16–12, 16–13, and 16–14.

### *Icons*

With `Action` in general and `AbstractAction` in particular, we can easily add support for icons. I did it with the following code:

```
class Add (AbstractAction):
      def __init__(self, this):
           self.this = this
           icon = ImageIcon("./images/add.jpg")
           AbstractAction.__init__(self, "Add", icon)

      def actionPerformed(self, event):
           self.this.addAddress_Clicked()

class Remove (AbstractAction):
      def __init__(self, this):
           self.this = this
           icon = ImageIcon("./images/remove.jpg")
           AbstractAction.__init__(self, "Remove", icon)

   def actionPerformed(self, event):
           self.this.removeAddress_Clicked()
```

The result is shown in Figure 16–15.

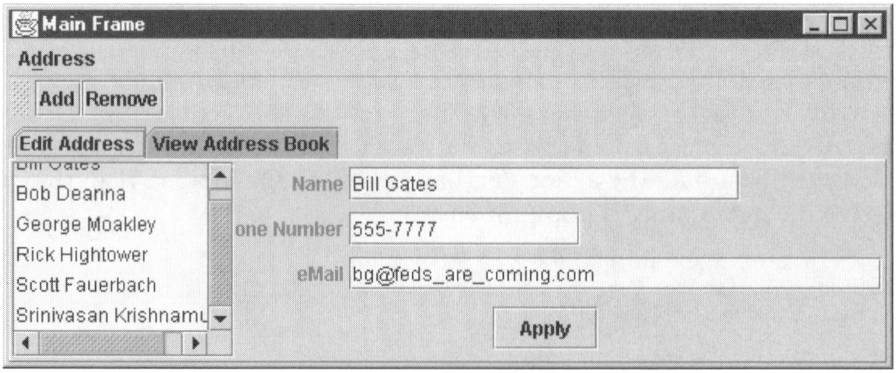

**Figure 16–12** *Main Frame with the Toolbar at the Top*

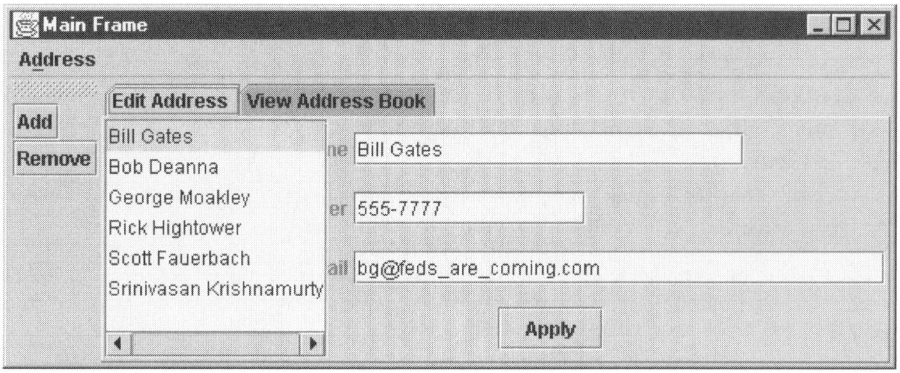

**Figure 16–13**   *Main Frame with the Toolbar at the Left*

**Figure 16–14**   *Main Frame with a Floating Toolbar*

**Figure 16–15**   *Main Frame Toolbar with Icons*

Try these exercises:

- Change the paint program from the last chapter to use JToolBar for both the shape toolbar and the color/fill panel. For extra credit, add icons for the shape buttons.
- Add mnemonics and tooltips to all of the components in the address book application.

## Summary

In this chapter, we explored advanced Swing. We showed an example that employed the JFC components JTable, JTree, JToolBar, and JTabbedPane, and we discussed JTable and JTree.

We extended the address book application to use JTable, which led to a discussion of TableModel and TreeModel. Later we changed menus and toolbars to use actions instead of buttons and menu items.

With what you learned in this and the last three chapters, you should be able to create your own Swing-based applications.

# SQL and JDBC

One of the advantages of storing data in a database is that other applications can readily access it. Another advantage is that the database takes care of indexing files and such, making data access easier and faster.

Databases are a huge topic, one that we can barely scratch the surface of. That said, let me tell you what this chapter *won't* cover: data normalization theory or any other database-specific topic. What it *will* cover is the following, which should be enough SQL for you to use JDBC with a database:

- Basic Structured Query Language (SQL)
- Rudimentary Data Definition Language (DDL)

- Connecting to a database with Java Database Connectivity (JDBC)
- Inserting, accessing, deleting, and updating data with JDBC

To get you up and running with the JDBC API, we'll do a quick interactive session. Then we'll get into SQL and DDL and finally add database support to our address book application.

---

**For More Information**

A good book on JDBC is *JDBC™ Database Access with Java™: A Tutorial and Annotated Reference* (Hamilton, Cattell, and Fisher, 1997—Addison-Wesley). Also good is the free online documentation at the Javasoft Web site, java.sun.com.

---

## A Quick and Dirty JDBC Session

Naturally I don't know what database you have access to, so on this book's Web site I'm using two standards: Microsoft Access and Java InstantDB. The exercises should work with any SQL database, as long as it has JDBC support. You may have to tweak the statements a little, but after this chapter you should feel comfortable with that.

For Microsoft Access we're going to use the JDBC–ODBC bridge, which integrates ODBC-compliant databases with Java applications. (ODBC stands for Open Database Connectivity.) Keep in mind that there are different levels of compliance. These levels range from bridges to native client support to pure Java. I picked Access because it's ODBC compliant and because you're likely to have at least one such database on your computer.

### Setting Up the ODBC Driver

If you're using Windows and ODBC, follow the instructions below. If you're using a non-Windows OS or a pure Java JDBC driver, follow its documentation.

1. Open the Windows' control panel, and double-click the ODBC icon.
2. Select the system DSN tab, and hit the Add button.
3. Select Microsoft Access from the list, or any database you want to use (see Figure 17–1), and hit the Finish button.
4. Type db_dev for the data source (see Figure 17–2).
5. Hit the Create button, and create a database as *c:\db_dev\db_dev.mdb* (see Figure 17–3).

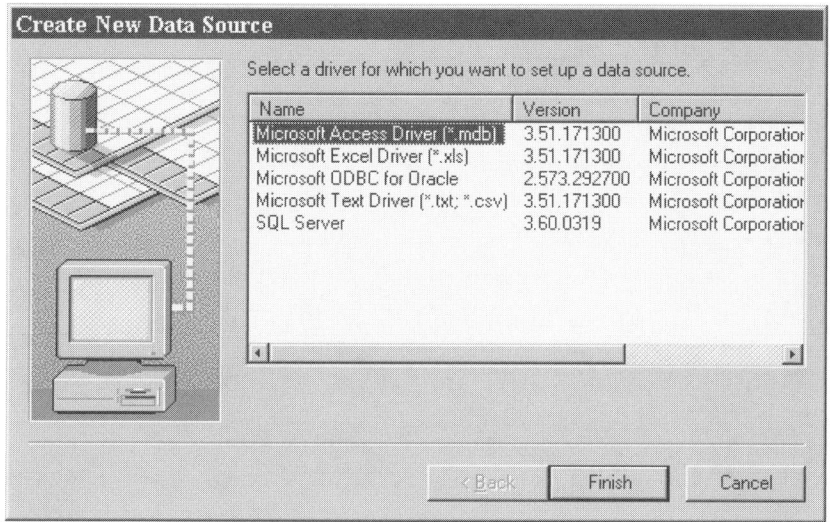

**Figure 17–1** *The Database List*

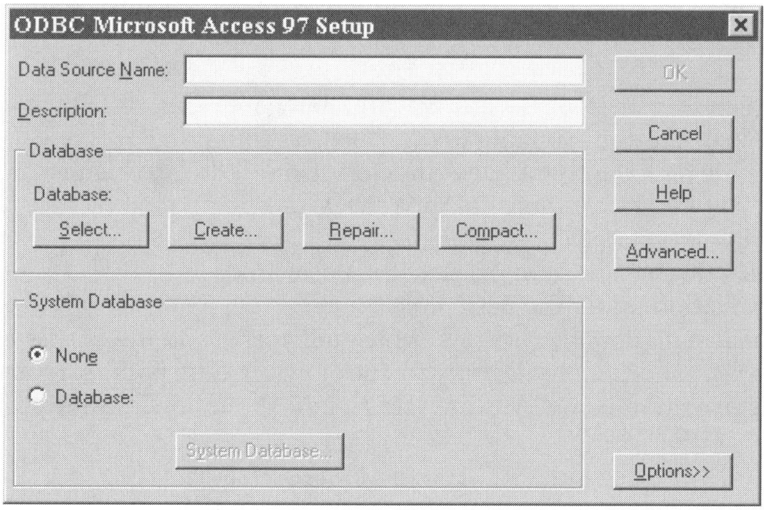

**Figure 17–2** *Microsoft Access Setup*

If you're using another database that's compliant with ODBC, the steps and the screen shots may vary, but the ideas are the same. If my instructions don't work, get some online help for the database you've chosen. Also, if you have problems with the system DSN, try creating a user DSN.

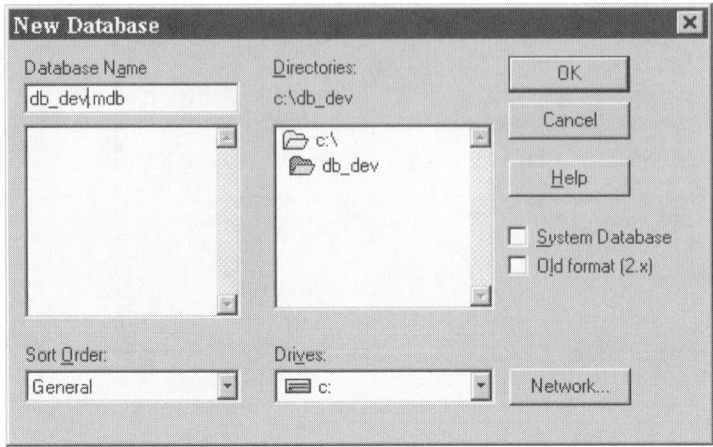

**Figure 17–3** *Creating a New Database*

## Setting up InstantDB

Whatever database you use, I recommend installing and using InstantDB, the one I use for all of the chapter examples. It's extremely easy, and it's open source (that means free). Here's how to set it up:

1. Create a directory on your hard drive, and name it *C:\InstantDB*.
2. Go to the Web site and navigate to the *Resources\InstantDB* folder.
3. Unzip the file *idb.zip* into the new directory using WinZip or an equivalent (get a copy of WinZip at the WinZip Web site).
4. Open *C:\InstantDB\DOC\index.html*.
5. On the left side (the left frame), select the Basic link.
6. Select Installation under the Basic link.
7. Follow the installation instructions, which tell you to add the *Classes/idb.jar*, *Classes/idbf.jar*, and *Classes/idbexmpl.jar* files to your class path. An easy way to do this, if you're using Windows, is to add the following lines to your autoexec.bat file:

```
SET CLASSPATH=%CLASSPATH%;C:\InstantDB\Classes\idb.jar
SET CLASSPATH=%CLASSPATH%;C:\InstantDB\Classes\idbf.jar
SET CLASSPATH=%CLASSPATH%;C:\InstantDB\Classes\idbexmpl.jar
```

8. Configure the environment variable.
9. Run the sample application by navigating to *C:\InstantDB\Examples>* and entering `javac sample.java` at the prompt and then `java sample`. The DOS prompt session may look like this:

```
C:\InstantDB\Examples>c:\autoexec.bat
C:\InstantDB\Examples>javac sample.java
C:\InstantDB\Examples>java sample
```

If you're going to use InstantDB for the first interactive session, be sure you have a copy of *db_dev.prp* in your working directory. If you don't, copy it from the *scripts\chap17\InstantDB* folder into the working directory.

## *Programming with JDBC and SQL*

To start things off, we're going to create a table, insert some values, and query them.
Import the DriverManager and Class classes to load the JDBC driver.

```
>>> from java.sql import DriverManager
>>> from java.lang import Class
```

Load the driver using Class.forName, which dynamically loads a class into the Java Virtual Machine (JVM). (See the Java API documentation for more details.) For Microsoft Access via ODBC (or any ODBC database):

```
>>> Class.forName("sun.jdbc.odbc.JdbcOdbcDriver")
<jclass sun.jdbc.odbc.JdbcOdbcDriver at -416861389>
```

For InstantDB:

```
>>> Class.forName("jdbc.idbDriver")
<jclass jdbc.idbDriver at -282805662>
```

Just as an HTML page has an HTTP URL, so a database has a JDBC URL. The last part of the URL for JdbcOdbcDriver refers to the DSN that we set up with the ODBC data source administrator in the last section. Enter this:

```
>>> url = "jdbc:odbc:db_dev"
```

The last part of the URL for InstantDB refers to the database properties file. Enter this:

```
>>> url = "jdbc:idb=db_dev.prp"
```

Now we can pass the URL to DriverManager's getConnection() method and pass the user name and password (both of which are blank, i.e., " "). Once we have a connection, we can create a table. Ours will have two columns, Name and Age, and we'll call it PERSON.
Create the JDBC connection object.

```
>>> connection = DriverManager.getConnection(url, "","")
```

Create the JDBC statement object.

```
>>> statement = connection.createStatement()
```

Create an SQL DDL statement that defines a database table.

```
>>> create_table = """CREATE TABLE PERSON (name VARCHAR(50), age INT)"""
```

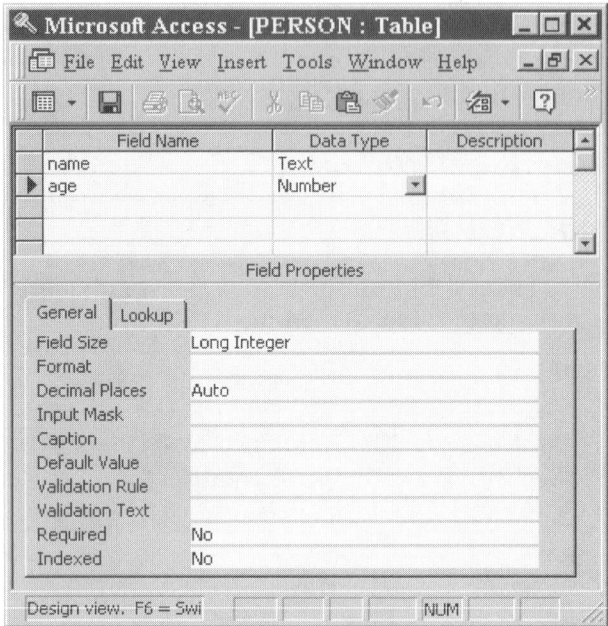

**Figure 17–4** *The PERSON Table—MS Access Version*

Execute the SQL DDL statement.

```
>>> statement.executeUpdate(create_table)
-1
```

Close the connection. (Leave it open if you're going on to the next section.)

```
>>> connection.close()
```

Go to the database tools, and see that the table was created. The Microsoft Access version is shown in Figure 17–4. (For the InstantDB version, use SQLBuilder, which comes in the InstantDB examples directory.)

### Inserting Data

Now we can start adding data to our table. If you've disconnected or restarted your JPython interactive session, you'll have to reconnect first.

**Reconnecting Your JPython Session**

Import DriverManager and Class.

```
>>> from java.sql import DriverManager
>>> from java.lang import Class
```

For ODBC:

```
>>> Class.forName('sun.jdbc.odbc.JdbcOdbcDriver')
<jclass sun.jdbc.odbc.JdbcOdbcDriver ...>
>>> url="jdbc:odbc:db_dev"
```

For InstantDB:

```
>>> Class.forName("jdbc.idbDriver")
<jclass jdbc.idbDriver at -282805662>
>>> url = "jdbc:idb=db_dev.prp"
```

Get the connection, and create the statement.

```
>>> connection=DriverManager.getConnection(url, "", "")
>>> statement = connection.createStatement()
```

Once you have a JDBC statement object, you have to create an insert format string in order to insert data. (Notice the single quotes around %s. They're important for proper SQL syntax.)

```
>>> insert = "insert into Person (name, age) values ('%s', %d)"
```

Pass a tuple containing name and age to the string format.

```
>>> insert % ("Whitney", 3)
"insert into Person (name, age) values ('Whitney', 3)"
```

Add Whitney to the database.

```
>>> statement.executeUpdate(insert % ("Whitney", 3))
1
```

Add Kiley.

```
>>> statement.executeUpdate(insert % ("Kiley", 23))
1
```

Add Scott and Nick.

```
>>> statement.executeUpdate(insert % ("Scott", 34))
1

>>> statement.executeUpdate(insert % ("Nick", 3))
1
```

Add Mary and Adam.

```
>>> statement.executeUpdate(insert % ("Mary", 2))
1

>>> statement.executeUpdate(insert % ("Adam", 23))
1
```

Notice that after each addition the executeUpdate() method returns the number of rows affected.

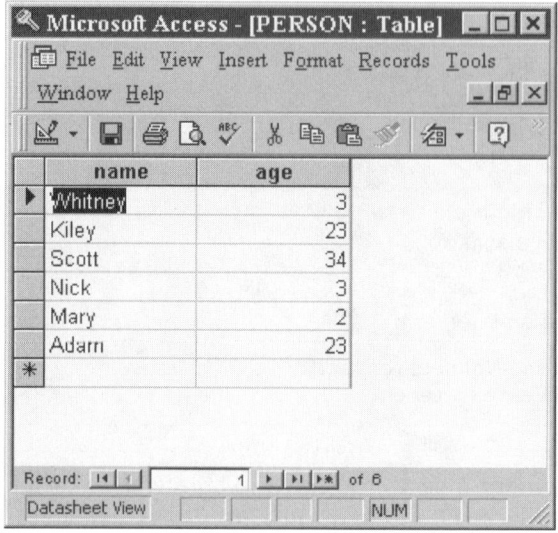

**Figure 17–5** *The PERSON Table with Data Added*

Go to your database management tools, and view PERSON. Figure 17–5 shows its Microsoft Access version; use SQLBuilder to see the InstantDB version.

By the way, keep your connection open. If you've already closed it, see the sidebar on reconnecting.

### Accessing Data

To access the names and ages in our table we query the results object (an instance of java.sql.ResultSet), which uses the following methods:

- next()—iterates through the table; returns 1 if there are more rows
- getString()—gets the name specified in the name string passed to it
- getInt()—gets the age specified in the age string passed to it

```
>>> results = statement.executeQuery("select name, age from Person")
```

Let's see how these methods work interactively.
Move to the first row.

```
>>> results.next()
1
```

Get the name.

```
>>> results.getString("name")
'Whitney'
```

Get the age.

```
>>> print results.getInt("age")
3
```

Define a function that can be used repeatedly to get the rest of the results.

```
>>> def showResults(results):
...     while(results.next()):
...             name = results.getString("name")
...             age = results.getInt("age")
...             print name + " is " + `age` + " years old."
...
```

Print the results.

```
>>> showResults(results)
Kiley is 23 years old.
Scott is 34 years old.
Nick is 3 years old.
Mary is 2 years old.
Adam is 23 years old.
```

Here's how we filter our results to get, say, only persons under the age of four:

```
>>> select = "select name, age from Person where age < 4"
>>> showResults(statement.executeQuery(select))
Whitney is 3 years old.
Nick is 3 years old.
Mary is 2 years old.
```

or persons over the age of twenty:

```
>>> select = "select name, age from Person where age > 20"
>>> showResults(statement.executeQuery(select))
Kiley is 23 years old.
Scott is 34 years old.
Adam is 23 years old.
```

Functions like count(), sum(), and stdev() allow us to get aggregate data, such as the count of persons in the table.

```
>>> results = statement.executeQuery("select count(name) as total from Person")
>>> results.next()
1
>>> print results.getString("total")
6
```

See if you can figure out what the next two interactive sessions are doing. (They won't work with InstantDB as of v.3.12.)

```
>>> r = statement.executeQuery("select stdev(age) as st from Person")
>>> r.next()
1
>>> print "Standard deviation" + r.getString("st")
```

```
Standard deviation=13.7501515143167
>>> r = statement.executeQuery("select sum(age) as [sum] from Person")
>>> r.next()
1
>>> print "Sum of ages " + r.getString("sum")
Sum of ages 88.
```

## Removing and Changing Data

The first thing you want to do is import the *JdbcTour.py* module from the InstantDB and Access directories so you can use its showResults() function in the next interactive sessions. (If you disconnected, refer to the sidebar on reconnecting.)

Let's remove everyone over twenty. (Leave out the asterisk (*) in the method arguments if you're using InstantDB.)

```
>>> statement.executeUpdate("delete * from Person where age > 20")
3
```

The executeUpdate() method returns 3, which means that three records were deleted.

Now let's do some modifying. In this next session we'll show Whitney's current age and then change it. In other words, we'll update her record. Show Whitney's current age.

```
>>> select = "select name, age from Person where name = 'Whitney'"
>>> results = statement.executeQuery(select)
>>> showResults(results)
Whitney is 3 years old.
```

Change it to four.

```
>>> statement.executeUpdate("update Person set age = 4 where name =
'Whitney'")
1
```

Show Whitney's new age.

```
>>> results = statement.executeQuery(select)
>>> showResults(results)
Whitney is 4 years old.
```

> ### SQL Subsets in InstantDB versus Microsoft Access
> InstantDB is a lightweight database that supports only a subset of the SQL syntax. Microsoft Access supports only a subset as well, but a larger one. The real problem is that the two databases don't always support the *same* subset.

## *SQL Data Definition Language*

SQL's Data Definition Language (DDL) is for working with tables and indexes. A table defines a set of columns for different fields of data and is similar to a class in Python. Columns are like class properties or variables; rows are like class instances.

DDL has five statements, which we'll look at in turn in the following sections.

### Create Table

The CREATE TABLE statement defines the table. It has the following form:

```
CREATE TABLE table
(field_name sql_type [(size)] [NOT NULL] [index1] , ...)
```

where

- field_name is the name of the field being defined
- sql_type is a valid SQL type
- size is the size of the field
- NOT NULL specifies that the column can't be empty or equal to None

The brackets in the statement denote optional parameters.

Here's how to create a table named Employee:

```
CREATE TABLE Employee (
    EmpID       INT     NOT NULL,
    Name        CHAR(20),
    DeptID      INT     NOT NULL,
```

CHAR denotes a character, so CHAR(20)denotes a 20-character field.

### Create Index

Indexing a table speeds data access. You create a table index with the CREATE INDEX statement, which has the form

```
CREATE INDEX index
ON table (field, field, ...)
```

This is how to add an index to our Employee table:

```
CREATE INDEX SalaryIndex ON Employee (Salary)
```

### Alter Table

You modify a table with the ALTER TABLE statement, which has the form

```
ALTER TABLE table
ADD COLUMN field type[(size)] [NOT NULL]
```

To add an extra column to the Employee table, do this:

```
ALTER TABLE  Employee
ADD COLUMN   Phone  CHAR(20)      NOT NULL
```

To drop a column do this:

```
ALTER TABLE table
DROP COLUMN field
```

To drop a field in the column just added do this:

```
ALTER TABLE table
DROP COLUMN field
```

## Constraint

With the CONSTRAINT clause you can mark the EmpID column as the primary key. A primary key is a unique identifier that indexes the table and defines inter-table relationships. CONSTRAINT has the form

```
CREATE TABLE Employee (
      EmpID        INT    NOT NULL,
      Name         CHAR(20),
      DeptID       INT    NOT NULL,
      Salary       INT,
      CONSTRAINT EMP_PK_KEY     PRIMARY KEY (EmpID)
)
```

Here's another, probably more common, way to define a primary key (the only method supported by InstantDB v.3.12):

```
CREATE TABLE Employee (
      EmpID        INT    PRIMARY KEY,
      Name         CHAR(20),
      DeptID       INT    NOT NULL,
      Salary       INT,
      Phone CHAR(20)      NOT NULL
)
```

To create a table that's linked to another table, you create a foreign key (the reference to another table) in one to point to a primary key in the other. As an example, we'll define a foreign key in the Employee table to point to the primary key in a table called Department.

Define the Department table.

```
CREATE TABLE Department (
      DeptID      INT    NOT NULL,
      Name        CHAR(20),
      CONSTRAINT DEPT_PK_KEY PRIMARY KEY (DeptID)
)
```

Create the Employee table with a foreign key constraint that refers to the Department table's DeptID.

```
CREATE TABLE Employee (
        EmpID       INT         NOT NULL,
        Name        CHAR(20),
        DeptID      INT         NOT NULL,
        Salary      INT,
        CONSTRAINT  EMP_PK_KEY  PRIMARY KEY (EmpID),
        CONSTRAINT  DEPT_FK_KEY FOREIGN KEY (DeptID)
                    REFERENCES Department (DeptID)
)
```

The relationship created by the linking shows that each employee must be in a department.

> **No Foreign Keys or Referential Integrity in InstantDB**
>
> InstantDB doesn't support foreign keys or referential integrity. Microsoft Access does support these concepts, as do most SQL databases you're likely to run into.

## Drop

The DROP statement has the form

```
DROP table_name
DROP index on table
```

Here's how to use it to drop the Employee table, that is, delete it from the database:

```
DROP Employee
```

Obviously, the use of DROP requires caution.

## Putting It All Together

Let's show DDL in action by running the *Access/ddl.py* module, which defines four DDL statement strings and then executes each one with the JDBC statement object's executeUpdate() method.

```
from java.sql import DriverManager
from java.lang import Class

Class.forName('sun.jdbc.odbc.JdbcOdbcDriver')
url="jdbc:odbc:db_dev"
connection=DriverManager.getConnection(url, "", "")
statement = connection.createStatement()
```

```
create_department = """
    CREATE TABLE Department (
        DeptID      INT   NOT NULL,
        Name        CHAR(20),
        CONSTRAINT DEPT_PK_KEY PRIMARY KEY (DeptID)
    )
"""
create_employee = """
    CREATE TABLE Employee (
        EmpID       INT   NOT NULL,
        Name        CHAR(20),
        DeptID      INT   NOT NULL,
        Salary      INT,
        CONSTRAINT EMP_PK_KEY   PRIMARY KEY (EmpID),
        CONSTRAINT DEPT_FK_KEY FOREIGN KEY (DeptID)
                    REFERENCES Department (DeptID)
    )
"""

alter_table = """
    ALTER TABLE      Employee
    ADD COLUMN  Phone       CHAR(20)      NOT NULL
"""

add_index = """
    CREATE INDEX SalaryIndex ON Employee (Salary)
"""

statement.executeUpdate(create_department)
raw_input("Department Table Defined - hit enter to continue")

statement.executeUpdate(create_employee)
raw_input("Employee Table Defined - hit enter to continue")

statement.executeUpdate(alter_table)
raw_input("Employee table altered by adding a Phone column.")

statement.executeUpdate(add_index)
raw_input("Adding a salary index to the Employee table.")

connection.close()
```

### InstantDB: A Little Different

InstantDB v.3.12 doesn't support the CONSTRAINT clause or foreign keys, nor can it handle the ALTER TABLE statement, even though the documentation says otherwise. Here's its version of *ddl.py* (*InstantDB/ddl.py*):

```
from java.sql import DriverManager
from java.lang import Class

Class.forName("jdbc.idbDriver")
url = "jdbc:idb=db_dev.prp"
```

```
connection=DriverManager.getConnection(url, "", "")
statement = connection.createStatement()

create_department = """
     CREATE TABLE Department (
          DeptID        INT      PRIMARY KEY,
          Name          CHAR(20),
     )
"""
create_employee = """
     CREATE TABLE Employee (
          EmpID         INT      PRIMARY KEY,
          Name          CHAR(20),
          DeptID        INT    NOT NULL,
          Salary        INT,
          Phone CHAR(20)         NOT NULL
     )
"""

#Note that InstantDB does not understand foreign keys...
# "No understanding of foreign keys or referential integrity checking "
##    REMOVED:      CONSTRAINT DEPT_FK_KEY FOREIGN KEY (DeptID)
##                         REFERENCES Department (DeptID)

add_index = """
     CREATE INDEX SalaryIndex ON Employee (Salary)
"""
statement.executeUpdate(create_department)
raw_input("Department Table Defined - hit enter to continue")

statement.executeUpdate(create_employee)
raw_input("Employee Table Defined - hit enter to continue")

#We are not able to alter the table once created log bug with InstantDB folks.
#statement.executeUpdate(alter_table)
#raw_input("Employee table altered by adding a Phone column - hit enter
     to continue")

statement.executeUpdate(add_index)
raw_input("Adding a salary index to the Employee table - hit enter to
     continue")
connection.close()
```

Try these exercises:

- Run *ddl.py* in both the Access and InstantDB directories. Note the differences.
- Run *ddl.py* with your RDBMS system and JDBC driver, and note the differences.

## SQL Data Types

We've defined a few simple tables with the *ddl.py* module. Now let's look at the different fields that can show up in a table. Until now, we've been using only two

**Table 17–1**   *JDBC, Java, and Python Types*

| JDBC | Java | Python |
|---|---|---|
| CHAR | String | String |
| VARCHAR | String | String |
| LONGVARCHAR | String | String |
| NUMERIC | java.math.BigDecimal | java.math.BigDecimal |
| DECIMAL | java.math.BigDecimal | java.math.BigDecimal |
| BIT | boolean | Integer |
| TINYINT | byte | Integer |
| SMALLINT | short | Integer |
| INTEGER | int | Integer |
| BIGINT | long | Integer |
| REAL | float | Float |
| FLOAT | double | Float |
| DOUBLE | double | Float |
| BINARY | byte[] | jarray as byte[] (sequence) |
| VARBINARY | byte[] | jarray as byte[] (sequence) |
| LONGVARBINARY | byte[] | jarray as byte[] (sequence) |
| DATE | java.sql.Date | java.sql.Date |
| TIME | java.sql.Time | java.sql.Time |
| TIMESTAMP | java.sql.Timestamp | java.sql.Timestamp |

SQL data types, CHAR and INT. Table 17–1 lists many more, most of which are similar to those in Java and Python. If you want to know what each type holds, an SQL reference can tell you.

Notice that the left column in the table is headed JDBC, not SQL. One reason for this is that SQL doesn't have a LONGVARCHAR. In fact, each database vendor seems to have its own name for this type, so there's no one-to-one mapping between JDBC and SQL (but what there is is close enough).

## Creating Fields with DDL

Let's illustrate how DDL creates fields of each type first in Microsoft Access (*Access\DDL2.py*).

```
from java.sql import DriverManager
from java.lang import Class
```

```
Class.forName('sun.jdbc.odbc.JdbcOdbcDriver')

url="jdbc:odbc:db_dev"
connection=DriverManager.getConnection(url, "", "")
statement = connection.createStatement()

create_type_table1 = """
    CREATE TABLE TypeTable1 (

            _bit            BIT,
            _int            INT,
            _smallint       SMALLINT,
            _integer        INTEGER,
            _numeric        NUMERIC,

            _char           CHAR(200),
            _varchar        VARCHAR(200),
            _real           REAL,
            _float          FLOAT,
            _double         DOUBLE,

            _binary         BINARY(200),
            _varbinary      VARBINARY(200),

            _date           DATE,
            _time           TIME,
            _timestamp      TIMESTAMP
    )
"""

statement.executeUpdate(create_type_table1)
```

The statement defined here creates every SQL type that MSAccess supports:

```
create_type_table1 = """
    CREATE TABLE TypeTable1 (

            _bit            BIT,
            _int            INT,
            _smallint       SMALLINT,
            _integer        INTEGER,
            _numeric        NUMERIC,

            _char           CHAR(200),
            _varchar        VARCHAR(200),

            _real           REAL,
            _float          FLOAT,
            _double         DOUBLE,

            _binary         BINARY(200),
            _varbinary      VARBINARY(200),

            _date           DATE,
            _time           TIME,
            _timestamp      TIMESTAMP
    )
"""
```

JDBC's LONGVARCHAR and LONGVARBINARY aren't supported by standard SQL. Again, each vendor has its own names for these types. MSAccess supports them under the names LONGCHAR and LONGBINARY and creates tables with them.

```
create_type_table2 = """
    CREATE TABLE TypeTable2 (
        _longvarbinary    LONGBINARY,
        _longvarchar LONGCHAR
    )
"""
statement.executeUpdate(create_type_table2)
raw_input("Create a type table 2")
```

There are three standard types not supported by MSAccess. In fact, if you try to run any code with them, JDBC will throw an exception. Here's an example (from *ddl2.py*):

```
create_type_table3 = """
    CREATE TABLE TypeTable2 (
        _decimal     DECIMAL,
        _tinyint             TINYINT,
        _bigint              BIGINT
    )
"""
statement.executeUpdate(create_type_table3)
```

Notice that the third table, type_table3, isn't created. Here's *Access/ddl2.py* in its entirety:

```
from java.sql import DriverManager
from java.lang import Class

Class.forName('sun.jdbc.odbc.JdbcOdbcDriver')

url="jdbc:odbc:db_dev"
connection=DriverManager.getConnection(url, "", "")
statement = connection.createStatement()

create_type_table1 = """
    CREATE TABLE TypeTable1 (

        _bit        BIT,
        _int        INT,
        _smallint   SMALLINT,
        _integer    INTEGER,
        _numeric    NUMERIC,

        _char       CHAR(200),
        _varchar    VARCHAR(200),

        _real       REAL,
        _float      FLOAT,
        _double     DOUBLE,
        _binary     BINARY(200),
        _varbinary  VARBINARY(200),
```

```
            _date           DATE,
            _time           TIME,
            _timestamp      TIMESTAMP
    )
"""

create_type_table2 = """
      CREATE TABLE TypeTable2 (
            _longvarbinary      LONGBINARY,
            _longvarchar LONGCHAR
    )
"""

create_type_table3 = """
      CREATE TABLE TypeTable2 (
            _decimal        DECIMAL,
            _tinyint        TINYINT,
            _bigint         BIGINT
    )
"""

statement.executeUpdate(create_type_table1)
raw_input("Create a type table 1")

statement.executeUpdate(create_type_table2)
raw_input("Create a type table 2")

statement.executeUpdate(create_type_table3)
raw_input("Create a type table 3")

connection.close()
```

### InstantDB Type Support

InstantDB supports fewer types than MSAccess does. In the following code (*InstantDB/ ddl2.py*), the types it does support are shown in type_table1. Those it supports but for which it has no standard SQL names are shown in type_table2.

```
from java.sql import DriverManager
from java.lang import Class

Class.forName("jdbc.idbDriver")
url = "jdbc:idb=db_dev.prp"

connection=DriverManager.getConnection(url, "", "")
statement = connection.createStatement()

create_type_table1 = """
      CREATE TABLE TypeTable1 (

            _tinyint        TINYINT,
            _smallint       SMALLINT,
            _integer        INTEGER,
            _int            INT,
```

```
            _numeric      NUMERIC,
            _decimal      DECIMAL,

            _char         CHAR(200),
            _varchar      VARCHAR(200),

            _float        FLOAT,
            _double       DOUBLE,
            _binary       BINARY(200),
            _varbinary    VARBINARY(200),

            _date         DATE,
        )
"""
create_type_table2 = """
        CREATE TABLE TypeTable2 (
            _longvarbinary      LONGVARBINARY,
        )
"""

create_type_table3 = """
        CREATE TABLE TypeTable2 (
            _real         REAL,
            _bit          BIT,
            _time         TIME,
            _timestamp    TIMESTAMP,
            _bigint       BIGINT,
            _longvarchar LONGVARCHAR
        )
"""

statement.executeUpdate(create_type_table1)
raw_input("Create a type table 1")
statement.executeUpdate(create_type_table2)
raw_input("Create a type table 2")

statement.executeUpdate(create_type_table3)
raw_input("Create a type table 3")

connection.close()
```

Strangely, the types not supported by InstantDB aren't the ones not supported by MSAccess. In other words, one unsupported list isn't a subset of another unsupported list. Fortunately, the most common SQL types *are* supported by both.

Try these exercises:

- Study and run either the MSAccess or the InstantDB version of *ddl2.py*, depending on the database type you're working with. Note the differences and similarities.

- Locate the JDBC drivers to the RDBMS system you use regularly. Create a database, run the *dml2.sql* scripts against it, and make changes as necessary. Note the differences and similarities. Let me know your results via email. I'd like a comparison for each type of database (DBw, DBASE, Paradox, Oracle, MySQL, etc.). State the version number and complete product name along with the JDBC driver information.

## SQL Data Manipulation Language

SQL's Data Manipulation Language (DML) defines the format of data by insertion, selection, updating, and deletion. The four primary DML statements are INSERT, SELECT, UPDATE, and DELETE, which we'll look at individually in the following sections.

The very first exercise in this chapter illustrated all of these statements. Here we'll see them at work in a little more advanced database structure, continuing with our Employee and Department table examples.

### Insert

If tables are like classes in Python, then rows are like instances. Since the INSERT statement inserts values into a table, we can think of it as analogous to calling a constructor, that is, creating an instance of a record.

INSERT takes the following form:

```
INSERT INTO table_name
        (field_name1, field_name2, ...)
VALUES
        (value1, value2, ...)
```

Here it's adding values to the Employee table:

```
INSERT INTO
        Employee
        (EmpID, Name, DeptID, Salary)
VALUES
        (10507, 'Bob Jones', '1', 10)
```

### Select

The SELECT statement selects rows from a table. We've already used it, so I won't belabor it at this point. Here's its form:

```
SELECT
        table.field [as alias]
FROM
        table [as alias]
[WHERE. criteria]
[GROUP BY table.field, ...] [HAVING criteria]
[ORDER BY table.field, ...]
```

The ORDER BY clause sorts the query results. The GROUP BY and HAVING clauses group items for aggregate functions, such as sum.

Here's a SELECT example:

```
SELECT
        Name, Salary
FROM Employee
WHERE
        (Salary > 10 )
        and
        (DeptID = 10)
ORDER BY Name
```

which can be rewritten as

```
SELECT Name, Salary FROM Employee WHERE (Salary > 10 ) and (DeptID == 10)
ORDER BY Name
```

With SELECT you can join tables to get columns from more than one table at a time. When you do this, you'll probably want to use an alias because the tables to be joined may have the same fields; aliasing allows such fields to be used in the WHERE clause.

The next example gets the employee's name, salary, and department. Since the department name is stored in the Department table, we have to join Department and Employee for the statement to work.

```
SELECT
        e.Name as emp_name,
        e.Salary as salary,
        d.Name as dept_name
FROM
        Employee as e,
        Department as d
WHERE
        (e.DeptID = d.DeptID) and
        (e.Salary > 10 )        and
        (e.DeptID = 10)
```

The first part of the WHERE clause specifies how the tables are to be joined. It defines our Employee and Department tables with the respective aliases e and d because both tables have DeptID and Name fields.

```
WHERE
        (e.DeptID = d.DeptID) and
```

Without the aliases, we can't differentiate a department name and an employee name. Three field aliases are also defined: emp_name, salary, and dept_name. If we were to run this query via JDBC, we'd have to use the aliases for the columns returned, not their names, in order to access the results.

Notice the as in the first line of the SELECT statement (e.Name as emp_name). It's nice to have this syntax, although many programmers don't use it. Because it's optional, the following statement is equivalent to the preceeding one:

```
SELECT
        e.Name                 emp_name,
        e.Salary     salary,
        d.Name       dept_name
FROM
        Employee     e,
        Department   d
WHERE
        (e.DeptID = d.DeptID) and
        (e.Salary > 10 )       and
        (e.DeptID = 10)
```

I like using as.

### The ANSI SQL JOIN Clause

If the database has a later version of ANSI SQL installed, you can use the JOIN clause to join tables.

```
SELECT
        e.Name as emp_name,
        e.Salary as salary,
        d.Name as dept_name
FROM
        Employee as e
JOIN
        Department as d
                on e.DeptID = d.DeptID
WHERE
        (e.Salary > 10 )   and
        (e.DeptID == 10)
```

Because it makes the syntax is more modular and easier to read (it separates the WHERE clause from the rest of the statement), I suggest you use JOIN if you have the choice.

Here's the last statement with the as syntax:

```
SELECT
        e.Name                 emp_name,
        e.Salary     salary,
        d.Name       dept_name
FROM
        Employee     e
JOIN
        Department   d
                on e.DeptID = d.DeptID
WHERE
        (e.Salary > 10 )   and
        (e.DeptID = 10)
```

*INNER Join*

Most databases assume an INNER JOIN if the JOIN clause is left by itself. However, MSAccess makes no such assumption and expects you to specify an INNER JOIN like this:

```
SELECT
        e.Name                as emp_name,
        e.Salary    as salary,
        d.Name      as dept_name
FROM
        Employee    as e
INNER JOIN
        Department  as d
            on e.DeptID = d.DeptID
WHERE
        (e.Salary > 10 )   and
       (e.DeptID = 100)
```

The four types of JOIN are INNER, OUTER, LEFT, and RIGHT. We're going to cover only INNER JOINs, which are probably the most common.

By the way, you can join more than one table at a time by adding extra JOIN clauses. You can find the exact syntax in a good SQL reference.

## Update

The UPDATE statement modifies the fields in a row. Its Python equivalent is setting an attribute of a class instance. UPDATE takes the form

```
UPDATE
        table_name
SET
        field1=value1, field2=value2, ...
[WHERE clause]
```

Here's an example of using UPDATE to give an employee a raise:

```
UPDATE
        Employee
SET
        Salary=11
WHERE
        EmpID = 10507
```

## Delete

The DELETE statement removes records from a table. Deleting a record is like setting all object references to None (forcing the garbage collector to delete the object). DELETE takes the form

```
DELETE
FROM
```

```
      table_name
[WHERE clause]
```

Deleting an employee record looks like this:

```
DELETE FROM
      Employee
WHERE
      EmpID = 10507
```

Laying off an entire department looks like this:

```
DELETE FROM
      Employee
WHERE
      DeptID = 100
```

## Using DML

To show how DML works, we'll use it to insert some departments into our Department table. Define a Python format string.

```
d_insert = """
      INSERT INTO
            Department
            (DeptID, Name)
      VALUES
            (%d, '%s')
"""
```

Define a set of tuples, departments, for sample departments.

```
departments = (
      (100, "Engineering"),
      (200, "Marketing"),
      (300, "Human Resources"),
      (400, "Manufacturing")
) #End of departments
```

Iterate through departments, and create rows in the Department table.

```
for dept in departments:
      insert = d_insert % dept
      print insert
      statement.executeUpdate(insert)
```

Now we'll add employees to the Employee table. Define an insert format string.

```
e_insert = """
      INSERT INTO
      Employee
            (EmpID, Name, DeptID, Salary, Phone)
      VALUES
            (%d, '%s', %d, %d, '%s')
"""
```

Define a tuple with some `employees` row data.

```
employees = (
        (1000, "Rick Hightower",  100,  5, "555-1212"),
        (1001, "Ricky Martin",    200, 10, "555-1213"),
        (1002, "Adam Carr",       100,  6, "555-1214"),
        (1003, "Bob Deanna",      100, 15, "555-1215"),
        (1004, "Tim Simeonov",    100, 16, "555-1216"),
        (1005, "Scott Faurbach",  100, 14, "555-1217"),
        (1006, "Mary Basset",     300,  5, "555-1218"),
        (1007, "Missy Carr",      400,  5, "555-1219"),
        (1008, "Paul Ganz",       400,  5, "555-1220"),
        (1009, "Tom Jones",       400,  5, "555-1221"),
        (1010, "Martha Pena",     200, 25, "555-1222"),
        (1011, "John Souza",      200, 15, "555-1223")
) #End of employees
```

Add the data in the `employees` tuple to the Employee table.

```
for emp in employees:
    insert = e_insert % emp
    print insert
    statement.executeUpdate(insert)
```

Try these exercises:

- Study the code in *access\dml_insert.py* and *access\connect.py*; run *access\ dml_insert.py*.
- Study the code in *instantDB\dml_insert.py* and *instantDB\connect.py*; run *InstantDB\dml_insert.py*.

The *connect.py* file varies depending on whether you connect to an ODBC database (such as MSAccess) or a pure Java database such as InstantDB. Here are both versions:

*Access\connect.py*:

```
from java.sql import DriverManager
from java.lang import Class

Class.forName("sun.jdbc.odbc.JdbcOdbcDriver")
url = "jdbc:odbc:db_dev"

connection=DriverManager.getConnection(url, "", "")
statement = connection.createStatement()
```

*InstantDB\connect.py*:

```
from java.sql import DriverManager
from java.lang import Class

Class.forName("jdbc.idbDriver")
url = "jdbc:idb=db_dev.prp"
connection=DriverManager.getConnection(url, "", "")
statement = connection.createStatement()
```

Inserting data is the same in InstantDB and MSAccess, so the following code (*dml_insert.py*) applies to both. (The JDBC-specific code is highlighted in bold.)

```python
from connect import *        # imports connection and statement object
d_insert = """

      INSERT INTO
            Department
            (DeptID, Name)
      VALUES
          (%d, '%s')
"""

e_insert = """
      INSERT INTO
            Employee
            (EmpID, Name, DeptID, Salary, Phone)
      VALUES
            (%d, '%s', %d, %d, '%s')
"""

departments = (
      (100, "Engineering"),
      (200, "Marketing"),
      (300, "Human Resources"),
      (400, "Manufacturing")
) #End of departments

employees = (
      (1000, "Rick Hightower", 100, 5, "555-1212"),
      (1001, "Ricky Martin",   200, 10, "555-1213"),
      (1002, "Adam Carr",      100, 6, "555-1214"),
      (1003, "Bob Deanna",     100, 15, "555-1215"),
      (1004, "Tim Sieonov",    100, 16, "555-1216"),
      (1005, "Scott Faurbach", 100, 14, "555-1217"),
      (1006, "Mary Basset",    300, 5, "555-1218"),
      (1007, "Missy Carr",     400, 5, "555-1219"),
      (1008, "Paul Ganz",      400, 5, "555-1220"),
      (1009, "Tom Jones",      400, 5, "555-1221"),
      (1010, "Martha Pena",    200, 25, "555-1222"),
      (1011, "John Souza",     200, 15, "555-1223")
) #End of employees

hit = " -- hit enter to continue -- "
raw_input ("testing inserts" + hit)

raw_input("Adding departments" + hit)

for dept in departments:
      insert = d_insert % dept
      print insert
      statement.executeUpdate(insert)

raw_input("Adding employees" + hit)
```

```
for emp in employees:
    insert = e_insert % emp
    print insert
    statement.executeUpdate(insert)

raw_input("testing select" + hit)

connection.close()
```

Notice that the first statement imports all of the objects from the *connect.py* module. This is so the module will hold all of the code needed for connecting. To connect to another database, just modify *connect.py* accordingly.

### Using SELECT (with Multiple JOIN Statements)

Let's use a SELECT statement to join tables. The code that follows (*Access\dml_select.py*) shows a multi-table join with MSAccess.

```
from connect import *

select = """
    SELECT
            e.Name       as emp_name,
            e.Salary     as salary,
            d.Name       as dept_name
    FROM
            Employee     as e
    INNER JOIN
            Department   as d
                on e.DeptID = d.DeptID
    WHERE
            (e.Salary > 10 )   and
            (e.DeptID = 100)
    """

results = statement.executeQuery(select)

emp_name="emp_name"
salary="salary"
dept_name="dept_name"

format = "%(emp_name)s,\t\t%(dept_name)s,\t\t%(salary)3.2f"

while results.next():
    dict = {}
    dict[emp_name]    =    results.getString(emp_name)
    dict[salary]      =    results.getInt(salary)
    dict[dept_name]   =    results.getString(dept_name)
    print format % dict

connection.close()
```

Here's the InstantDB version of a multi-table SELECT:

```
from connect import *
```

```
select = """
    SELECT
            e.Name          as emp_name,
            e.Salary        as salary,
            d.Name          as dept_name
    FROM
            Employee        as e
    JOIN
            Department      as d
                on e.DeptID = d.DeptID
    WHERE
            (e.Salary > 10 ) and
            (e.DeptID = 100)
"""

results = statement.executeQuery(select)
...
... (The rest is the same as before)
```

The two versions are nearly identical except that the JOIN's INNER modifier has been left off in the InstantDB code because it's assumed. (According to the documentation, JOIN should work when the modifier is supplied.) Also, I used the executeQuery() method of the statement object for the SELECT statement, whereas I used the executeUpdate() method for the INSERT statement. Always use the former for SELECTs and the latter for just about everything else—updates, inserts, deletes, and any DDL operations. executeQuery() returns a result set for the query, and executeUpdate() returns the number of rows affected by any table modifications.

As an exercise, run the *dml_select* module for one or both of the databases (ODBC or pure Java). Try each of the following SELECT statements. Determine which ones work as expected and which ones don't.

*No* INNER *modifer:*

```
SELECT
        e.Name          as emp_name,
        e.Salary        as salary,
        d.Name          as dept_name
FROM
        Employee        as e
JOIN
        Department      as d
            on e.DeptID = d.DeptID
WHERE
        (e.Salary > 10 ) and
        (e.DeptID = 100)
```

INNER *modifier with* as *syntax for aliases:*

```
SELECT
        e.Name          emp_name,
        e.Salary        salary,
        d.Name          dept_name
```

```
FROM
        Employee     e
INNER JOIN
        Department   d
                on e.DeptID = d.DeptID
WHERE
        (e.Salary > 10 ) and
        (e.DeptID = 100)
```

INNER *modifier without* as *syntax:*

```
SELECT
        e.Name       emp_name,
        e.Salary     salary,
        d.Name       dept_name
FROM
        Employee     e
INNER JOIN
        Department   d
                on e.DeptID = d.DeptID
WHERE
        (e.Salary > 10 ) and
(e.DeptID = 100)
```

*Old-style* JOIN *(no* JOIN *clause):*

```
SELECT
        e.Name       emp_name,
        e.Salary     salary,
        d.Name       dept_name
FROM
        Employee     e,
        Department   d
WHERE
        (e.DeptID = d.DeptID)    and
        (e.Salary > 10 )         and
        (e.DeptID = 100)
```

See if you can run these forms on both MSAccess and InstantDB. Then run them against your own database/JDBC driver pair.

### Using DELETE

The following code (*dml_delete.py*) deletes the marketing department from the Department table. It's the same for MSAccess and InstantDB.

```
from connect import *      #import statement and connection objects.
from java.lang import Exception

marketingID = 200
delete = "delete from Department where DeptID = %d" % marketingID

        # Try to delete the record.
        # Close connection no matter what!
```

```
try:

                # Try to delete the record.
                # If an exception occurs
                # print out the exception's message.
        try:
                statement.executeUpdate(delete)

        except Exception, e:
                print "Unable to delete marketing"+e.message

finally:

        connection.close()
```

Notice the `try...except` and `try...finally` blocks. `try...finally` makes sure the connection is closed if there's an exception. `try...except` prints out the exception message. It's a good idea to wrap database calls in a `try...finally` block to ensure a closed connection.

## Referential Integrity

As an exercise, see if you can run *dml_delete.py* against both InstantDB and MS-Access. You'll notice that it doesn't work with MSAccess but does work with InstantDB. MSAccess's behavior is preferred. Why?

Because the operation should *fail* to preserve referential integrity. Essentially, if you delete the department record and there are still employees in that department, your multiple JOIN SELECT statements will stop working. If that happens, you'll get this message:

**Unable to delete marketing [Microsoft][ODBC Microsoft Access 97 Driver]. The record cannot be deleted or changed because table 'Employee' includes related records.**

which means that, as long as the Employee table contains records for marketing employees, you can't delete the marketing record in the Department table. This is how MSAccess maintains its referential integrity.

If you're a little confused, the following exercises should clear things up:

- Study and run *dml_delete.py* in both the MSAccess and InstantDB directories.
- Study and run *dml_select2.py* in both. This module selects a group of employees who are in the marketing department, i.e., whose DeptID is equal to 200. What happens when you run this query against the InstantDB database? Against the MSAccess database? Which of the two exhibits the correct behavior?
- Write a query or a set of queries that will work with either MSAccess or InstantDB after *dml_delete* is run on both.

> **InstantDB/MSAccess Support for Referential Integrity**
> Because it's a lightweight, InstantDB makes no claim of supporting referential integrity.
> I don't consider MSAccess a heavyweight, but it does provide some referential integrity
> support, as we've just seen.

For the DELETE statement to work, we need to move every employee in marketing to a new department—that is, change their DeptID to one for an existing department. An alternative is to delete them from the Employee table first (that is, lay them all off).

### Achieving Referential Integrity with UPDATE and DELETE

What follows is an example that lays off some workers and moves others to a different department via the UPDATE and DELETE statements The code, *dml_delete2.py*, is the same for both MSAccess and InstantDB. (Be sure to read the comments. They tell the whole story.)

```python
from connect import *
from java.lang import Exception

marketingID = 200
mfgID = 400
engID = 100

        # Move employees whose salary is less
        # than 10 and greater than 8
        # to manufacturing.
update1 = """
        update
                Employee
        set
                DeptID=%d
        where
                salary > 8 and salary <= 10
""" % mfgID

        # Layoff employees whose salary
        # is greater than 16.
        #
delete1 = """
        delete from
                Employee
        where
                salary > 16
"""

        # Move employees whose salary is less
        # than 16 and greater than 10
        # to engineering. Also adjust their salary to 10.
update2 = """
        update
                Employee
```

```
    set
        DeptID=%d, salary=10
    where
        salary < 16 and salary > 10
""" % engID

    # Remove the Marketing department
    # from the Department table.
    # It should work this time!
delete2 = "delete from Department where DeptID = %d" % marketingID

    #Try to delete the record.
    #Close connection no matter what!

try:

        # Try to delete the record.
        # If an exception occurs
        # print out the exception's message.
    try:
        statement.executeUpdate(update1)
        statement.executeUpdate(update2)
        statement.executeUpdate(delete1)
        statement.executeUpdate(delete2)

    except Exception, e:

        print "Unable to delete marketing" + e.getMessage()
finally:

    connection.close()
```

As an exercise, run *dml_delete2.py* in both MSAccess and InstantDB. Use either the Microsoft Access GUI or the SQLBuilder GUI to look at the data. (For SQL-Builder, read the InstantDB documentation; also read the following sidebar.)

---

### *Working with SQLBuilder*

Here's how to work with SQLBuilder:

1. Compile it.
   ```
   C:\InstantDB\Examples\SQLBuilder>javac *.java
   ```
2. Run it.
   ```
   C:\InstantDB\Examples\SQLBuilder>java SQLBuilder
   ```
3. Hit the Browse button, and select the appropriate database property file—for example: *C:\JPython_book\scripts\chap17\InstantDB\db_dev.prp*.
4. Hit the Connect button.
5. Go to the Query tab.
6. Select the Employee table from the Tables dropdown list.
7. Hit the Submit button.
8. Repeat steps 6 and 7 for the Department table.

## *Putting It All Together—Adding Database Support to the Address Book Application*

Now we're ready to add database support to our address book application. First, though, let's review the application's main modules.

- *Address.py* contains the `Address` class, which represents an address entry, and the `readAddresses()`and `writeAddresses()` functions, which read and write a dictionary of `Address` class instances (the actual addresses).
- *AddressModel.py* contains the `AddressModel` class, which is both a list model and a table model for the user interface. `AddressModel` calls `readAddresses()` to read in a dictionary of `Address` class instances and maps the dictionary to the list and table models.
- *AddressFormPane.py* contains the `AddressFormPane` class, a user interface for editing address entries.
- *AddressMain.py* contains the `AddressMain` class—the main frame. `AddressMain` manages the interaction of `AddressModel`'s components and holds an instance of `JTable`, an instance of `JList`, and an instance of `JTabbedPane` (all of which are from *javax.swing*).

### Making the Application More Modular

We've done a good job of keeping the application modular, but we can do better. First, we're going to abstract out the differences between a flat-file model and a database model. Then we're going to add database support with as few changes as possible to *AddressModel.py*.

What we'll do is move the file-specific dependencies from `AddressModel`'s constructor and put `readAddresses()` and `writeAddresses()` in a module called *Address FileUtils.py*. All modified and new files will be in a directory called *AddressBook.2*. Here's the original `AddressModel` constructor:

```
class AddressModel(AbstractTableModel, ListModel):
    """The AddressModel is both a ListModel
       and a TableModel."""

    def __init__(self):
        """Initialize the Address model.
        Read the dictionary from the file."""
            # holds the dictionary of addresses.
        self.dict = None
            # holds the sorted list of names,
            # which are keys into the dictionary.
        self.list = None
            # to hold list of ListModelListeners
            self.listeners = []
            # Read the addresses from the file.
            # holds the file name that
            # holds the addresses
```

```
                self.fname=".\\addr.dat"
        self.dict = readAddresses(self.fname)

                    # Store the sorted list of names.
            self.list = self.dict.keys()
            self.list.sort()

...
...

def writeAddresses(self):
        """Write the address data to the file."""
        writeAddresses(self.fname, self.dict)
```

Here is the constructor as modified:

```
        ...

class AddressModel(AbstractTableModel, ListModel):
        """The AddressModel is both a ListModel
            and a TableModel."""

        def __init__(self):
            """Initialize the Address model.
            Read the dictionary from the file."""

                    #holds the dictionary of addresses.
            self.dict = None
                    #holds the sorted list of names,
                    # which are keys into the dictionary
            self.list = None

                    #to hold list of ListModelListeners
            self.listeners = []

                    # Read the addresses
                    # from the Address utility.
            self.dict = readAddresses()

        ...
        ...

def writeAddresses(self):
            """Write the address data to the file."""
            writeAddresses(self.dict)
```

The following are the changes we made to readAddresses() and writeAddresses(), which are now in their own module, *AddressFileUtils.py*. Notice that both functions have a default value for filename that they didn't have before.

```
...
def readAddresses(filename=".\\addr.dat"):
    ...
def writeAddresses(dict, filename=".\\addr.dat", bin=0):
    ...
```

The result, essentially, is that all file-based functionality has been encapsulated out of AddressModel. The next step is testing.

> ### How Modular Is Modular Enough?
>
> The sad fact is that we don't have all the time in the world to tinker with our address book application. In the real world, customers want a working product as quickly as possible, even if it's less than perfect. If we strive for perfection we'll never get it.
>     That said, I think our code at this point is modular enough.

As an exercise, review the changes in the address book application and then run the new version. Remember that *AddressMain.py* is the main module, so to open the application you have to type JPython AddressMain at the system prompt. As a first step, we need to create a utility module, *AddressDBUtil.py*, which will

- Allow configuration of JDBC drivers and URLs
- Create the necessary tables
- Copy data from the flat file to the database
- Hold the readAddresses() and writeAddresses() functions

As a second step, we have to modify AddressModel to work with AddressDBUtils.

## Working with Java Properties

In order to configure the necessary JDBC drivers and URLs, we have to use java.utils.Properties. This class writes properties out to a text file so that a user can manually edit text with a text editor. Here's an example.

Import the necessary classes.

```
>>> from java.util import Properties
>>> from java.io import FileOutputStream, FileInputStream
```

Create a file output stream.

```
>>> file = "addr_db.props"
>>> file = FileOutputStream(file)
```

Create an instance of Properties.

```
>>> props = Properties()
```

Set the JdbcUrl and JdbcDriver properties.

```
>>> props.setProperty("JdbcUrl", "jdbc:idb=db_dev.prp")
>>> props.setProperty("JdbcDriver", "jdbc.idbDriver")
```

Store the properties in a file (*addr_db.props*).

```
>>> props.store(file, "Database properties")
```

Look at the file.

```
#Database properties
#Tue Dec 28 14:46:27 PST 1999
```

```
JdbcUrl=jdbc\:idb\=db_dev.prp
JdbcDriver=jdbc.idbDriver
```

Notice the file format, which uses # for comments (as Python does). The properties are stored in name/value pairs, with each property occupying one line. This makes reading the properties as easy as writing them.

Now we have to neaten up the property and file objects.

```
>>> file.close()
>>> file = None
>>> props = None
```

Notice that props has been set to None to show that the properties aren't in memory anymore.

Next we read the properties from a file. Open a file input stream.

```
>>> file = "addr_db.props"
>>> file = FileInputStream(file)
```

Create a Properties instance, and load the properties with the file input stream.

```
>>> props = Properties()
>>> props.load(file)
```

Show the values of the JdbcUrl and JdbcDriver properties.

```
>>> print props.getProperty("JdbcUrl")
jdbc:idb=db_dev.prp

>>> print props.getProperty("JdbcDriver")
jdbc.idbDriver
```

## Adding Property File Support

Let's add a function to *AddressDBUtils.py* that uses java.utils.Properties to read the JDBC properties. Let's also add some error recovery and some bullet-proof functionality to check if the file exists and to create one if not.

As an exercise, try editing the property file from *AddressDBUtils.py*. Also try deleting the file and then running the module (don't forget to back up the file first). What happens?

Here's the latest version of *AddressDBUtils.py*:

```
from java.util import Properties
from java.io import FileOutputStream, FileInputStream, IOException, File

PROP_FILE = "addr_db.props"      # holds the property file for the db
                                 # connection info.
__jdbc_url = None                # holds the JDBC URL
__jdbc_driver = None             # holds the JDBC Driver

        #Set some default values.
__jdbc_url="jdbc\:idb\=db_dev.prp"
__jdbc_driver="jdbc.idbDriver"
```

```
def __loadProps():
    global PROP_FILE
    stream = None      #holds file input stream
    props = None       #holds Properties
    file = None        #Hold file associated
                       #with the PROP_FILE filename.

            #See if the file exists. If not create it.
    file = File(PROP_FILE)
    if not file.exists():
        setProps()

    props = Properties()

            #Try to load the properties.
            # Create a file input stream.
            # Load the properties with input stream.
    try:
        try:

            stream = FileInputStream(PROP_FILE)
            props.load(stream)

        except IOException, e:

            print "Problem loading db properties file=" + PROP_FILE
            print e.message
            e.printStackTrace()

    finally:
            stream.close()

    return props

def __storeProps(props):
    global PROP_FILE
    file = None #to hold the file input stream
    file = FileOutputStream(PROP_FILE)

            # Try to create a file output stream,
            # and store the properties.
    try:
        try:

            props.store(file, "Database properties")

        except IOException, e:
            print "Problem storing db properties. file=" + PROP_FILE
            print e.message
            e.printStackTrace()
    finally:
            file.close()

def getProps():
    global __jdbc_url, __jdbc_driver

            #Load the properties
    props = __loadProps()
```

```
            jdbc_url = props.getProperty("JdbcUrl", "None")
            jdbc_driver = props.getProperty("JdbcDriver")

                   # If the prop file did not have
                   # values then set some default values.
            if jdbc_url == "None":
                   setProps()
    else:

                   __jdbc_url = jdbc_url
                   __jdbc_driver = jdbc_driver

    def setProps():
           global __jdbc_url, __jdbc_driver

                   #Create properties and then store them.
           props = Properties()
           props.setProperty("JdbcUrl", __jdbc_url)
           props.setProperty("JdbcDriver", __jdbc_driver)
           __storeProps(props)

    def getJdbcDriver():
           return __jdbc_driver

    def getJdbcUrl():
           return __jdbc_url

    getProps()
```

## Adding DDL Support

We need DDL support in order to create the table for our address book application. To get it we first import class `Class` to load the driver and class `DriverManager` to create a connection object.

```
from java.lang import Class
from java.sql import DriverManager
```

Then we execute the CREATE TABLE statement, which is held in the `create_table` variable.

```
create_table = """
    CREATE TABLE Address (
           AddrID       INT      PRIMARY KEY,
           Name         VARCHAR(40),
           Phone        VARCHAR(15),
           Email        VARCHAR(50)
    )
"""
```

The `createTable()` method uses the `create_table` string to create the Address table.

```
def createTable():
    """
    Creates the Address table.
    """
```

```
        global create_table
        executeUpdate(create_table)
```

It can't load the driver or create the connection or statement object without the
assistance of helper methods.

## JDBC Helper Methods

Helper methods do common things such as execute an update, load a driver, and
create connection and statement objects. They also do error checking and cleanup.
The following code illustrates some helpers. (Pay particular attention to the document strings.)

```
def loadDriver():
    """
    Loads the driver class into the JVM.
    Checks to see if the class is already loaded.

    """
    global __loaded_driver
    jdbc = getJdbcDriver()
    try:
        if not __loaded_driver:
            Class.forName(jdbc)
            __loaded_driver=1
    except:
        error = "Unable to load the driver "+jdbc
        print error
        raise DBException(error)

def createConnection():
    """
    Creates a database connection and returns it.
    Loads the Database driver with loadDriver().

    returns a JDBC Connection object.
    """

    connection = None

    try:
        loadDriver()
        jdbc=getJdbcUrl()
        connection=DriverManager.getConnection(jdbc)

    except Exception, e:
        print e.message
        error = "Problem creating connection, exception."
        print error
        raise DBException(error)

    if connection == None:
            error = "Problem creating connection was None"
            print error
            raise DBException(error)
```

```
        return connection
def createStatement():
        """
        Creates a statement object.

        Returns a tuple containing a JDBC statement
        and connection object.
        """
        connection = createConnection()
        return connection.createStatement(), connection

def executeUpdate(str):
        """
        Executes an update statement.

        Returns the number of rows involved.
        """
        statement, connection = None, None
        num_rows=-1
        try:
                try:
                        statement,connection=createStatement()
                        num_rows = statement.executeUpdate(str)

                except Exception, e:
                        e.printStackTrace()
                        print e.message
                        print "Problem executing update\n"+str

        finally:
                if(connection):connection.close()

        return num_rows
```

Notice all of the error checking and recovery going on. Since we plan to execute more statements, it's good to have all such tasks handled in one place.

## Creating the Address Table

All the preliminaries are out of the way, leaving only the execution of the CREATE TABLE statement. This is going to be easy. All it takes is one call to executeUpdate().

```
def createTable():
        """
        Creates the Address table.
        """
        global create_table
        executeUpdate(create_table)
```

We want to run createTable() from the command line, so we need to add command-line parameter parsing in the main block (if__name__=="__main__" block), which checks to see if "c" is passed to the command line and, if so, creates the table. (Passing "p" creates the properties file.)

```
if __name__ == "__main__":
    from sys import argv

            #Process the command line arguments.
    for arg in argv:
        if arg == "c":
            getProps()
            str = "Creating the table using "
            str = str+getJdbcDriver()+" at "+ getJdbcUrl()
            print str
            createTable()

        if arg == "p":
            print "Creating the properties file: "+PROP_FILE
            getProps()
            print getJdbcDriver()
            print getJdbcUrl()
```

Now we have our *AddressDBUtils.py* module. Here's how to create it in DOS:

```
C:\JPython_book\scripts\chap17\AddressBook3>JPython AddressDBUtils.py c
```

Try creating the Address table yourself as an exercise.

### Inserting Address Records into the Address Table

To get addresses into the database, we have to transform an instance of the Address class into a record. Define the format string for the insert entries.

```
params = """AddrID, Name, Phone, Email"""
insert = """

    INSERT INTO
        Address
        (""" + params + """)

    VALUES
        (%s)

    """
```

Define functions to create an INSERT statement.

```
def insertAddress(address, statement=None):
    """
    Inserts the AddrID, Name, Phone,
    Email into a row.
    """
    id = getID()
    a = address
    tup = (
        str(id),
        formatSQLStr(a.name()),
        formatSQLStr(a.phoneNumber()),
        formatSQLStr(a.email())
    )
    values = join(tup, ",")
```

```
     if statement:
          executeUpdate(insert % values, statement)
     else:
          print insert % values
```

Invoke the helper function formatSQLStr() to transform the address information
into a string that SQL understands.

```
def formatSQLStr(str):
     """Formats a string into a SQL string"""
     str = "'%s'" % str
     return str
```

Now we'll add all of our address book data to the database (users like you to
do this for them). For this we need the loadFromFile() function, which reads the
*address.dat* file and stores a given address in the Address table.

```
def loadFromFile():
     """
     Loads the flat file of addresses into
     the Address table.
     """
     from AddressFileUtils import readAddresses
     dict = readAddresses()

          # Create a statement for the database.
          # Add all of the addresses to the table.
     try:
          statement, connection = createStatement()

          # Iterate through the collection
          # of addresses. Add each address to the
          # database.
     for address in dict.values():
          insertAddress(address, statement)

     finally:
          connection.close()
```

Next we add the following statements to the main block so we can read load
FromFile() from the command line.

```
if __name__ == "__main__":
     from sys import argv

          #Process the command line arguments.
          for arg in argv:
...
...

          if arg == "l":
               loadFromFile()
```

To load the data from the file, we run *AddressDBUtils.py* from the command line
with the "l" option. Here's the DOS prompt:

```
C:\JPython_book\scripts\chap17\AddressBook3>JPython AddressDBUtils.py l
```

## Reading Addresses from the Address Table

Now we need to implement the `readAddresses()` and `writeAddresses()` functions.
`readAddresses()` is easy—we just select all of the records and put them in a dictionary. `writeAddresses()` is more difficult. What if someone removes an address from
the dictionary—how will we know without changing `AddressModel`? We'll skip writing addresses for now and instead integrate *AddressDBUtils.py* into the application.

Here's the code for `readAddresses()` and `writeAddresses()`:

```
def readAddresses():
        """

        Read the Address data
                AddrID, Name, Phone, Email
        returns a dictionary full of addresses
        """
        dict = None

        try:

                statement, connection = createStatement()

                dict = {}
                results = statement.executeQuery(select_all)

                while results.next():
                        id = results.getString("AddrID")
                        name = results.getString("Name")
                        phone = results.getString("Phone")
                        email = results.getString("Email")
                        dict[name]=Address(name, phone, email)

        finally:
                connection.close()

        return dict

def writeAddresses(dict):
        pass
```

As you probably noticed, `writeAddresses()` isn't doing anything yet.

## Integrating AddressModel with the Database

Instead of replacing the flat file, let's see how to polymorphically add the database as an option. Via the `__import__` function, `AddressModel` imports functions
from `AddressIO` that dynamically load the I/O utility module (*AddressBook3\
AddressIO.py*).

```
from java.util import Properties
from java.io import FileInputStream, FileOutputStream, IOException

        #holds property file for the db connection info.
PROP_FILE = "addr.props"
def readAddresses():
        pass
```

```
def writeAddresses(dict):
      pass
...
...

def getModuleName():
            #Load the properties.
      props = __loadProps()
      return props.getProperty("module_name", "AddressDBUtils")
...
...
module = __import__(getModuleName())
readAddresses = module.readAddresses
writeAddresses = module.writeAddresses
```

To switch back to the flat file, all we have to do is edit *addr.props*.

```
#Database properties
#Wed Dec 29 20:24:54 PST 1999
#module_name=AddressDBUtils
module_name=AddressFileUtils
```

As an exercise, run the application in both modes, switching back and forth between them.

### A Database-Aware Dictionary

How do we know which addresses need to be written out of the database? One way is to set a dirty flag, which will tell us when one of the instance variables has changed. But what about adding new addresses—how much code will we have to modify?

In fact, we can add the functionality that will answer these questions without changing AddressModel or any of the GUI. All we need to do is define a database-aware dictionary that replaces the dictionary that AddressModel is presently using.

Recall the dictionary class that we created in Chapter 6. We can use what we learned from it to create a dictionary class that adds and removes rows in the Address table. We'll call it AddressDBDict and put it in the *AddressBook4.py* module.

```
class AddressDBDict:
...
...

    def __setitem__(self, key, value):
          statement, connection = createStatement()
          try:
                addr = AddressDB()
                addr.fromAddress(value, statement)
                self.dict[key]=addr
          finally:
                connection.close()

    def __delitem__(self, key):
          statement, connection = createStatement()
```

```
        try:
                addr = self.dict[key]
                addr.remove(statement)
                del(self.dict[key])
        finally:
                connection.close()
```

As you can see, the "overridden" __setitem__ and __delitem__ methods create a JDBC statement object and interact with AddressDBDict.

__setitem__ takes a regular address instance as an argument to create an instance of AddressDBDict. It then calls the fromAddress() method, passing it a JDBC statement object. fromAddress() is where the Address record is inserted into the Address table.

__delitem__ calls the AddressDBDict instance it retrieves from AddressModel and invokes its remove() method, passing it a JDBC statement object. remove() deletes the Address record from the Address table.

---

### How Many Connections Are Opened and Closed?

It may look like AddressDBDict creates and closes a connection every time it adds or deletes a record, but that would be awfully expensive as well as inefficient. Actually, only one connection to the database is created. Take a look at the createStatement() function and the Connect class in the *AddressBook4.py* module to see how this is done.

---

### A Database-Aware Address Class: AddressDB

AddressDB is a subclass of Address, which notifies it, via the markDirty() method, when its member variables change. Address defines markDirty() and calls it in its constructor. AddressDB overrides markDirty() and adds the ability to update the corresponding record in the Address table when changes are made.

Recall that the Address class has no setter methods for its variables but sets them through __init__. The first time __init__ is called, the dirty flag is set to 0 (false); at all subsequent calls, it's set to 1 (true).

Here's some of the code for Address and AddressDB showing the interaction between markDirty(), dirty, and isDirty():

```
class Address:
            ...
        __dirty = -1

    def __init__(self, name="", phone_number="", email="",
        address_lines=None):
                ...
                ...
                self.markDirty()
            ...
    ...
    def markDirty(self):
            ...
            self.__dirty = self.__dirty + 1
```

```
    def isDirty(self):
            ...
            return self.__dirty

    class AddressDB(Address):
    ...
    ...

            def markDirty(self):
                ...
                Address.markDirty(self)
                if(self.isDirty()):
                self.__update()

    def __update(self):
            ...
            statement, connection = createStatement()

            try:
                self.update(statement)
            finally:
                connection.close()
```

markDirty() calls the Address of the class; then it calls its isDirty() method to determine if the data is dirty. If so, AddressDB's __update() method is called by its markDirty() method in order to create a JDBC statement object and to update the record in the database.

In this way the base class and the subclass interact to determine the state of the address instance. If the data is dirty, it's written out to the database and made clean again.

AddressDB's update() method updates the record; its remove() method deletes the record; and its fromAddress() method inserts a new one. The following code shows how these methods work:

```
where = """
      WHERE
            AddrID = %(_AddressDB__id)s
      """

select = """
      UPDATE
            Address
      SET
            Name = '%(_Address__name)s',
            Phone = '%(_Address__phone_number)s',
            Email = '%(_Address__email)s'
      """ + where

delete = """
      DELETE FROM
            Address
      """ + where
```

```
insert = """
    INSERT INTO
        Address
        (AddrID, Name, Phone, Email)

    VALUES
        (
        %(_AddressDB__id)s,
        '%(_Address__name)s',
        '%(_Address__phone_number)s',
        '%(_Address__email)s'
        )
    """

class AddressDB(Address):
    ...
    ...
    def update(self, statement=None):
        ...
        if(statement):
            ...
            statement.executeUpdate(select % self.__dict__)
            self.__dict__["_Address__dirty"] = 0
...

    def remove(self, statement=None):
        ...
        if(statement):
            statement.executeUpdate(delete % self.__dict__)
...

    def fromAddress(self, addr, statement=None):
            # Copy the address.
    name = addr.name()
    phone_number=addr.phoneNumber()
    email=addr.email()
    self.__dict__["_Address__dirty"] = -1
    Address.__init__(self,name, phone_number, email, address_lines=None)

            # Insert the record into the database.
    self.__id = getID()
    str = insert % self.__dict__
    if statement:
            statement.executeUpdate(str)
    ...
```

AddressDB knows how to deal with the database, and, since it has the same interface as Address, the GUI knows how to work with either without knowing which is which. AddressDBDict, too, knows how to deal with the database. What's more, it has the same interface as a Python dictionary object, which means that, like a dictionary object, it can work with AddressModel, AddressMain, AddressFormPane, and so forth, without these classes having to be changed. This is polymorphism at its deceptive best.

To make the deception complete, AddressDBUtil's readAddresses() function has to get in on the action. Instead of a dictionary full of address instances, it now has to return AddressDBDict, which holds AddressDB instances. Here's its code (from *AddressBook4\AddressDBUtils.py*) with the interesting parts highlighted in bold:

```
def readAddresses():
        ...
        ...
        try:
                statement, connection = createStatement()
        ...

                dict = AddressDBDict()
                results = statement.executeQuery(select_all)

                while results.next():
                        id = results.getString("AddrID")
                        name = results.getString("Name")
                        phone = results.getString("Phone")
                        email = results.getString("Email")
                        addr=AddressDB(name, phone, email)
                        dict.dict[name] = addr
                        addr.setID(id)
        finally:
                #connection.close()
                pass
        return dict
```

## Using the Database-Supported Address Book Application

Now our address book application has database support. To get that support, and to keep the application backward-compatible with the flat-file format, we tapped into the power of Python and polymorphism. Try these exercises:

- Deploy the address book application in a different database than the one you've been using.
- Add the ability to track a phone conversation—that is, take notes while you're talking—and pull up a list of notes for a given address entry. To accomplish this you'll need a database table called Phone Log with a notes field, an identity field, and a foreign key field that references AddrID in the Address table. You'll also need GUI components to view, edit, and delete notes.
- Make it possible to travel with the address book application, working with a laptop and a database server.
- Add the ability to copy Address records from a database format to a flat-file format.
- Add a dialog box that allows a user to copy data to the flat-file format and work with the application in mobile mode—that is, a mode that reads from the flat file instead of from the database server.
- Enable the user to reconnect to the database.

## *Summary*

In this chapter we covered SQL/JDBC programming. We used what we learned to provide database support for our address book application. We took a brief tour of SQL fundamentals, including the SQL sublanguages, DDL and DML.

The exercises showed how to connect and use two different databases: a JDBC–ODBC bridge (Microsoft Access) and a pure JDBC connection (InstantDB). We saw some of the difficulties in porting to and running on multiple databases.

We also saw the importance of modular design when we grafted database support onto the address book application. In addition, we used `java.Utils.Properties` to make changing properties easier. We also discovered the dynamic capabilities of Python's `__import__` statement, which uses the module name in a property file to load an I/O utility module. The dynamism of Python and polymorphism was reinforced when we added database support to the `AddressModel` class by creating a database-aware subclass and a database-aware dictionary.

# CHAPTER 18

# *Applets*

- ⋄ *Applet*
- ⋄ *Batch file*
- ⋄ *Browser*
- ⋄ *Browser simulator*

- ⋄ *Code base*
- ⋄ *Context*
- ⋄ *HTTP/FTP protocol*
- ⋄ *JAR/zip file*

- ⋄ *Lifecycle management*
- ⋄ *Sandbox*
- ⋄ *Stub*
- ⋄ *Tag*

Once upon a time, there was a relatively new company named Netscape that became king of the Internet. It was Netscape's acceptance of Java applets that put Java on the map.

If you follow Java, you know that, ironically, it's had a lot more impact on the server side (J2EE, servlets, JMS, RMI, JAVA IDL, EJB, etc.) than on the client side (applets, Swing). However, change is under way. With later Java releases, Sun Microsystems has introduced a plug-in for browsers that addresses many of the shortcomings of applets by allowing them to be cached.

## What Are Applets?

Applets represent a way to deliver safe code for producing lively Internet GUIs. They execute within a browser and are associated with (i.e., embedded in) an HTML page, so they must be inherently portable to run in a variety of browsers on a variety of platforms.

Let's rewind a bit. Applets execute within a browser, which means that code that somebody else wrote is running on your computer. That may sound dangerous, but applets can run only inside a security "sandbox," which won't allow them to do things like read or write to files, read environment variables, or open network connections to any host except the one on which they originated. With current releases of Java, you can tweak the sandbox to give applets more privileges, but they'll never be allowed to do anything that would harm you. What's more, they're virus-resistant.

All applets derive from `java.applet.Applet`, and so, since Jython compiles to Java bytecode and can subclass a Java class, all we have to do is subclass `java.applet.Applet` and compile. Sounds easy enough, doesn't it? In fact, if you've worked with applets, most of this chapter will be a review, except for compiling Jython code to an applet.

## *Working with Applets*

Let's start off with an interactive session. Import `Applet` from the *java.applet* package.

```
>>> from java.applet import Applet
>>> applet = Applet()
```

An applet is a panel (`java.awt.Panel`), and, as we learned earlier, a panel is also a component.

```
>>> applet.class.superclass
<jclass java.awt.Panel at -731859681>
```

So, if an applet is a panel, and a panel is a component, an applet is also a component (and thus a component container). That means that everything you've learned about components and panels applies to applets as well.

### Surveying the Applet Landscape

`Applet` inherits all of class `java.applet.Applet`'s functionality. What's more, the `Applet` class employs the Façade design pattern, which facilitates the use of many utilities in *java.net, java.io,* and so forth, so it makes tasks such as Web image downloading as easy as possible.

To see the amount of functionality applets provide, take a look at `Applet`'s methods. Here are just the first fifteen:

```
>>> for i in range (0, 15):
...       print methods[i]
...
public void java.applet.Applet.destroy()
public java.applet.AppletContext java.applet.Applet.getAppletContext()
public java.lang.String java.applet.Applet.getAppletInfo()
public java.applet.AudioClip java.applet.Applet.getAudioClip(java.net.URL)
```

```
public java.applet.AudioClip
java.applet.Applet.getAudioClip(java.net.URL,java.lang.String)
public java.net.URL java.applet.Applet.getCodeBase()
public java.net.URL java.applet.Applet.getDocumentBase()
public java.awt.Image java.applet.Applet.getImage(java.net.URL)
public java.awt.Image
java.applet.Applet.getImage(java.net.URL,java.lang.String)
public java.util.Locale java.applet.Applet.getLocale()
public java.lang.String java.applet.Applet.getParameter(java.lang.String)
public java.lang.String[][] java.applet.Applet.getParameterInfo()
public void java.applet.Applet.init()
public boolean java.applet.Applet.isActive()
public static final java.applet.AudioClip
java.applet.Applet.newAudioClip(java.net.URL)
```

Here are the rest:

```
>>> for i in range (15, 23):
...     print methods[i]
...
public void java.applet.Applet.play(java.net.URL)
public void java.applet.Applet.play(java.net.URL,java.lang.String)
public void java.applet.Applet.resize(int,int)
public void java.applet.Applet.resize(java.awt.Dimension)
public final void java.applet.Applet.setStub(java.applet.AppletStub)
public void java.applet.Applet.showStatus(java.lang.String)
public void java.applet.Applet.start()
public void java.applet.Applet.stop()
```

That's a lot of methods to learn, and this is just the tip of the iceberg since we're not considering any methods that Applet inherits from its superclasses. (We covered those methods earlier in this book.)

## Using an Applet as a Container

Because you can use applets interchangeably with panels they're easy to test and debug. Debugging is even easier if the applet runs as a standalone application rather than within a browser. Let's run one from the interactive interpreter.

Import Applet, List, and Frame.

```
>>> from java.applet import Applet
>>> from java.awt import List, Frame
```

Create an instance of Applet and List; add the List instance to the applet instance.

```
>>> applet = Applet()
>>> list = List()
>>> applet.add(list)
java.awt.List[list0,0,0,0x0,invalid,selected=null]
```

Create an instance of Frame; add applet to it.

```
>>> frame = Frame("Frame that contains the Applet")
>>> frame.add(applet)
    java.applet.Applet[panel0,0,0,0x0,invalid,layout=java.awt.FlowLayout]
```

Pack and show `frame`.

```
>>> frame.pack()
>>> frame.visible=1
```

Add some items to `list`.

```
>>> list.add("Hello")
>>> list.add("Goodbye")
```

Figure 18–1 shows our first applet. (It may be a stretch to call it an applet since we're using it like a panel.) You can see that working with an applet is much like working with a panel, except that there's a lot more to it.

## Applet Lifecycle Management

The browser lets applets know when they're no longer active or in view. It also tells them when they're created and when they're about to be destroyed so they can create or free resources. Such notification is called lifecycle management. An applet is created and executes within a browser. The browser determines when resources should be created or restored and notifies the applet accordingly.

Here are the browser's methods for notifying an applet of a lifecycle event:

- `init()`—creates the applet
- `destroy()`—destroys the applet
- `start()`—makes the applet visible or active
- `stop()`—makes the applet invisible or inactive

To implement these methods, we have to subclass the `Applet` class.

Import the `Applet` class and the needed `java.awt` classes.

```
>>> from java.applet import Applet
>>> from java.awt import Frame, List, Button, Panel, BorderLayout
```

**Figure 18–1**  *Our First So-Called Applet*

Define a Python class that subclasses `Applet` (`java.applet.Applet`).

```
>>> class MyApplet (Applet):
...      def __init__(self):
...             self.list = List()
...             self.add(self.list)
...      def init(self):
...             self.list.add("Init called")
...      def destroy(self):
...             self.list.add("Destroy called")
...      def start(self):
...             self.list.add("Start called")
...      def stop(self):
...             self.list.add("Stop called")
...
```

We can also add a browser simulator (a "fake browser"). A simulator allows us to activate the lifecycle notifications, and thus simulate events, by hitting the corresponding buttons.

Create a frame and a `MyApplet` instance. Add the instance to the frame.

```
>>> fakeBrowser = Frame("Fake Browser")
>>> applet = MyApplet()
>>> fakeBrowser.add(applet, BorderLayout.CENTER)
```

Create four buttons, and add them to the toolbar. The buttons correspond to the individual lifecycle notifications the applet receives from the browser.

```
>>> b = Button        #Shortcut for Button class
>>> start, stop, init, destroy = b("start"), b("stop"), b("init"),
                                 b("destroy")
>>> buttons = (start, stop, init, destroy)
>>> toolbar = Panel()
>>> for button in buttons:
...      toolbar.add(button)
...
java.awt.Button[button0,0,0,0x0,invalid,label=start]
java.awt.Button[button1,0,0,0x0,invalid,label=stop]
java.awt.Button[button2,0,0,0x0,invalid,label=init]
java.awt.Button[button3,0,0,0x0,invalid,label=destroy]
```

Add the toolbar to the frame in the north region, and make the frame visible.

```
>>> fakeBrowser.add(toolbar, BorderLayout.NORTH)
>>> fakeBrowser.pack()
>>> fakeBrowser.visible=1
```

Create handlers for the buttons that call the lifecycle methods when pressed.

```
>>> def __init(event):applet.init()
...
>>> def __destroy(event):applet.destroy()
...
>>> def __start(event):applet.start()
```

**Figure 18–2** *Simulated Lifecycle Event Notification*

```
...
>>> def __stop(event):applet.stop()
...
```

Register the handlers to the buttons.

```
>>> handlers=(__start,__stop,__init,__destroy)
>>> for i in range(0,4):
...      buttons[i].actionPerformed=handlers[i]
...
```

Test the applet by hitting the buttons. Your browser simulator should look like Figure 18–2.

## Compiling an Applet

To compile a Jython class as a Java class, you have to put it in a module of the same name. Thus, *MyApplet.py* contains the MyApplet class. Here's the code:

```
from java.applet import Applet
from java.awt import List
      # Define a Python class that subclasses the Applet class.
      # (java.applet.Applet)

class MyApplet (Applet):
      def __init__(self):
            self.list = List()
            self.add(self.list)
      def init(self):
            self.list.add("Init called")
      def destroy(self):
            self.list.add("Destroy called")
      def start(self):
            self.list.add("Start called")
      def stop(self):
            self.list.add("Stop called")

if __name__ == "__main__":
      from FakeBrowser import FakeBrowser
      fakeBrowser = FakeBrowser()
      fakeBrowser.addApplet(MyApplet())
```

Notice that the main block imports the FakeBrowser class, which is based on the browser simulator we created in the last interactive session. (FakeBrowser isn't listed, but you can look it up in *FakeBrowser.py*. Running *MyApplet.py* yields the same output as before.)

To compile MyApplet, use jythonc at the command prompt.

```
jythonc -deep --package com.awl.jython_book --jar myapplet.jar MyApplet.py
```

We saw how to use Jythonc in Chapter 1. Note that the package is specified as *com.awl.Jython_book* and that the classes are put in a JAR file called *my.applet.jar*. (A Java archive file is a zip file but with a manifest denoting that MyApplet is an applet.)

Because we added FakeBrowser to the main block, we can run MyApplet as a standalone application (*com.awl.Jython_book.MyApplet*) simply by entering the following at the command line:

```
java -classpath %CLASSPATH%;myapplet.jar com.awl.jython_book.MyApplet
```

which puts *Jython.jar* and *myapplet.jar* in the classpath. MyApplet needs *Jython.jar* in order to run.

We're not done yet. We want to run this applet "embedded" in an HTML file inside a browser, so we have to configure the Applet tag for applets.

First, some exercises:

- Add a Clear button to the applet that clears the list in MyApplet.
- Recompile the applet. *Hint*: You can use a batch file called *compile.bat* for this, but be sure to open and study it first.
- Run the applet in FakeBrowser with the Java interpreter. *Hint*: Use a batch file called *run.bat*, but open and study it first.

---

### No Archive Tag

If your browser doesn't support the archive tag, or if you're having problems compiling your applet, try using the all or core arguments to jythonc. These arguments instruct jythonc to include *JythonC.jar* in the applet's jar file.

```
jythonc -core --package com.awl.Jython_book --jar myapplet.jar MyApplet.py
```

or

```
jythonc -all --package com.awl.Jython_book --jar myapplet.jar MyApplet.py
```

---

## Embedding an Applet in an HTML Page

To embed MyApplet in a Web page, we need the applet tag, which takes the following form:

```
<applet
  code="com.awl.jython_book.MyApplet"
```

```
    codebase=".\jpywork"
    archive="..\..\lib\jython.jar"
    width=400
    height=400
>
    <param name="hello" value="hello">
If you don't have a Java-enabled browser, you need to get one!
</applet>
```

Each parameter takes a name/value pair, and each has a purpose:

- Code holds the name of the applet class (in our case, `com.awl.Jython_book.MyApplet.class`).
- Codebase holds the relative path of the code base—the root directory from which the browser loads the Java classes and resources it needs. It's equivalent to the document base, from which the browser loads the document form. In other words, if an applet is loaded from *www.jython.org\demo\applet.html*, the document base is loaded from *www.jython.org\demo*. (Remember, the default operation for `jythonc` is to put the class files in the *jpywork* subdirectory of the current directory.)
- `archive` holds the name of any zip or jar files this applet uses—in our case, *\lib\jython.jar*, which holds all of the classes that Jython needs. Make sure you have the same version of *Jython.jar* as the one you compile with. You can get the right version for whatever Python version you're working with from *c:\Jython*; copy it into *c:\Jython_book\scripts\lib*.
- `width`/`height` holds the width and height of the applet in pixels.
- `<param name=value=>` specifies the applet-defined (application-specific) name/value parameters.

### *The applet Tag and Browsers*

The `applet` tag works in the applet viewer (`AppletViewer`), but to run other browsers you have to expand it to include the *myapplet.jar* file in the `archive` parameter and take out `codebase` (or set it to a period [`.`]). The following code, from *MyAppletJar.html*, works with Internet Explorer and Netscape:

```
<html>
<body>
<center>
<applet
    code="com.awl.jython_book.MyApplet"
    archive="..\lib\jython.jar,myapplet.jar"
    width=400
    height=400
>
    <param name="hello" value="hello">
If you don't have a Java-enabled browser, you need to get one!
</applet>
</center>
```

```
</body>
</html>
```

Putting the class files in a jar file speeds downloading. Unfortunately, however, `AppletViewer` doesn't recognize the `archive` parameter. This code (from *MyApplet. html*) does work with `AppletViewer` as well as Internet Explorer and Netscape, although its download time is longer than that of jar files.

```
<html>
<body>
<center>
<applet
  code="com.awl.jython_book.MyApplet"
  codebase=".\jpywork"
  archive="..\..\lib\jython.jar"
  width=400
  height=400
>
  <param name="hello" value="hello">
If you don't have a Java-enabled browser, you need to get one!
</applet>
</center>
</body>
</html>
```

### Running MyApplet with AppletViewer

The `AppletViewer` utility, which ships with the JDK, allows developers to run applets without a browser. It supports a subset of the Netscape and Internet Explorer HTML tags that are associated with a Java applet.

To run `AppletViewer` from the command line do this:

```
appletviewer MyApplet.html
```

In Netscape or Internet Explorer, open the file from the File\Open menu item. You can use the applet with either *MyApplet.html* or *MyApplet.Jar.html*.

## Configuring Applet Behavior

An applet can be customized. The following HTML, for example, defines two applet-specific parameters, "color" and "hello":

```
<html>
<body>
<center>
<applet
  code="com.awl.jython_book.MyApplet"
  codebase=".\jpywork"
  archive="..\..\lib\jython.jar"
  width=400
  height=400
>
```

```
  <param name="hello" value="hi mom">
  <param name="color" value="blue">
If you don't have a Java-enabled browser, you need to get one!
</applet>
</center>
</body>
</html>
```

Call the getParameter() method of java.applet.Applet to read the applet's parameters. This method in turn gets the parameters from the applet stub (AppletStub).

> **The Applet Stub**
>
> The applet gets the parameter information from AppletStub, which is passed to the Applet class via the setStub() method by AppletContext. Java.applet. Applet implements setStub(), so you don't have to.

## AppletBrowser

I've created a fully functioning AppletViewer-like application, called AppletBrowser (which we'll cover later in detail). AppletBrowser implements the needed stub and context. We're going to use it in our interactive sessions.

   Import JApplet, and create an instance of it.

```
>>> from javax.swing import JApplet
>>> applet = JApplet()
```

Import AppletBrowser, and create an instance of it.

```
>>> from AppletBrowser import AppletBrowser
>>> browser = AppletBrowser()
```

Add the applet instance to AppletBrowser to simulate its loading into AppletViewer or another Java-enabled browser.

```
>>> browser.addApplet(applet)
```

Get the color parameter from the applet.

```
>>> color = applet.getParameter("color")
>>> print color
"blue"
```

Get the hello parameter from the applet

```
>>> hello = applet.getParameter("hello")
>>> print hello
"hi mom"
```

The other parameters—codebase, code, archive, and so forth—which aren't defined by the param keyword, are accessible through applet.getParameter().

Get archive, code, and codebase from the applet, and print them out.

```
>>> code = applet.getParameter("code")
>>> codebase = applet.getParameter("codebase")
>>> archive = applet.getParameter("archive")
>>> print (code, codebase, archive)
('com.awl.java_book.MyApplet', './jpywork/', '..\..\lib\jython.jar')
```

Try to get a parameter that doesn't exist. getParameter() will return None.

```
>>> print applet.getParameter("my_param")
None
```

Use parameters to pass information, such as the URL and driver name of the database to which the applet connects, or the COS naming service where it looks for its stubs. Basically, the applet's parameters customize its behavior.

## An Applet Example

The following code (from *context\MyApplet.py*) shows an applet that does what the applet in the previous session does, but in a module that you can compile and use in a browser or in AppletViewer. (Pay special attention to the showParameters() method.)

```
from javax.swing import JApplet
from javax.swing import JList, DefaultListModel, JScrollPane

        # Define a Python class that subclasses the JApplet class
        # (javax.swing.JApplet)
class MyApplet (JApplet):
        def __init__(self):
                self.list = DefaultListModel()
                _list = JList(self.list)
                self.contentPane.add(JScrollPane(_list))

        def print(self, str):
                self.list.addElement(str)

        def init(self):
                self.print("Init called")
                self.showParameters()

        def destroy(self):
                self.print("Destroy called")

        def start(self):
                self.print("Start called")

        def stop(self):
                self.print("Stop called")

        def showParameters(self):
                        # Get the color parameter.
                color = "color", self.getParameter("color")
                        # Get the hello parameter.
```

```
                    hello = "hello", self.getParameter("hello")
                          # Get the myparam parameter.
                    myparam = "myparam", self.getParameter("myparam")
                    codebase = "codebase", self.getParameter("codebase")
                    params = (color, hello, myparam, codebase)
                    for param in params:
                     self.print("%s equals %s" % param)
if __name__ == "__main__":
       from AppletBrowser import AppletBrowser
       fakeBrowser = AppletBrowser()
       fakeBrowser.addApplet(MyApplet())
```

This version of AppletViewer, which derives from JApplet, uses showParameters()
to call the __init__ method. ShowParameters() shows the parameters in a listbox in
much the same way as in the interactive session.

As an exercise, compile and run *context\MyApplet.py* in the applet viewer or
Netscape Navigator. (You'll have trouble running it in Internet Explorer because
it uses Swing classes. To get it right you'll have to do some extra configuring and
download a version of Swing that's compatible with JVM v.1.1.4.)

---

> ### Assume Nothing with Browsers
>
> With applet development you can make very few assumptions about the browser. For
> example, J2ME and older browsers support only AWT.

---

## Reading Applet Files

For security reasons, you can't read files from an applet if they're on the client's
hard drive (unless you configure Java security to allow this). However, you can
read them from the Web server that serves the applet to the client. We won't cover
Java security here, but I do recommend that you read the online security documentation at the Javasoft Web site.

The way to read applet files is with a URL. We'll see how with a sample file
located on the Jython Web server. (If you have your own Web server, you can skip
this next section.)

### The Python Web Server

Python's Web server can be found in the *SimpleHTTPServer* module. Here's what
to do to get it up and running:

```
>>> from SimpleHTTPServer import test
>>> test()
Serving HTTP on port 8000 ...
```

*SimpleHTTPServer* delivers HTML pages from the current working directory, so
to run the Web server for our HTML page we have to start a DOS prompt and run
the module in the *.\scripts\chap18\context* subdirectory. Then we can access the

applet with Netscape Navigator by entering the URL *http://your_ip_address: 8000/MyAppletJar.html*, replacing "`your_ip_address`" with your server's address. On Windows NT/98, you can find that address via the `ipconfig` command.

```
C:\>ipconfig

Windows 98 IP Configuration

0 Ethernet adapter :

        IP Address. . . . . . . . . : 0.0.0.0
        Subnet Mask . . . . . . . . : 0.0.0.0
        Default Gateway . . . . . . :
```

(To use Internet Explorer you need the Java plug-in or the JFC Swing package. See the Javasoft Web site for more information.)

If you're running the Python Web server and the browser on the same machine, use the URL *http://local_host_:8000/MyAppletJar.html*. However, you'll be better off using the IP address or the domain name service (DNS) entry. On Windows NT/98, the DNS entry usually corresponds to the name of your machine, which replaces "localhost" in the URL.

If you use another Web server, you may have to adjust the port setting to match it. The default port for HTTP is 80. Also, if you don't have a network card, you can use the applet browser (`AppletBrowser`), which simulates a browser talking to a Web server. (`AppletBrowser` can do this even on a separate machine.) Lastly, you can use the File/Open menu item in Netscape Navigator to open the HTML containing the "embedded" applet.

### Working with URLs in an Interactive Session

To read a file from the server you need the `URL` class, which you can find in the *java.net* package. The `Applet` class has methods that return both the document base URL and its code base counterpart. `URL`'s `openStream()` method returns an input stream, which means that if you have a file called *data.dat* you can append it to one of `URL`'s methods.

Import `JApplet` from *javax.swing*.

```
>>> from javax.swing import JApplet
>>> applet = JApplet()
```

Use `AppletBrowser` to give the applet a context and a stub (to simulate the applet's environment).

```
>>> from AppletBrowser import AppletBrowser
>>> browser = AppletBrowser()
>>> browser.addApplet(applet)
```

Show the code base (using Java and Jython).

```
>>> applet.getCodeBase()
file:/C:/book/scripts/chap18/context/jpywork/
>>> applet.codeBase
file:/C:/book/scripts/chap18/context/jpywork/
```

Show the document base (using Java and Jython).

```
>>> applet.getDocumentBase()
file:/C:/book/scripts/chap18/context/
>>> applet.documentBase
file:/C:/book/scripts/chap18/context/
```

> ### Java.net.URL
> The Java API documentation will tell you what you want to know about `java.net.URL`. I'll just show you its form:
>
> ```
> >>> url = applet.documentBase
> >>> url.class
> <jclass java.net.URL at 960293886>
> >>> dir (url.class)
> ['ref', 'file', '__init__', 'toExternalForm',
> 'setURLStreamHandlerFactory', 'content', 'getFile', 'sameFile',
> 'getProtocol', 'openStream', 'getContent', 'protocol', 'getHost', 'port',
> 'openConnection', 'host', 'getRef', 'getPort']
> ```

There are two files in the context directory with the name *data.dat*. One is the context itself and is associated with the document base URL; the other is in the *jpywork* subdirectory and is associated with the code base URL.

Import URL from *java.net*.

```
>>> from java.net import URL
```

Get `documentBaseURL` from the applet.

```
>>> documentBaseURL = applet.documentBase
```

Create a URL instance based on `documentBaseURL`'s context.

```
>>> data_dat = URL(documentBaseURL, "data.dat")
>>> data_dat
file:/C:/book/scripts/chap18/context/data.dat
```

Get the associated input stream.

```
>>> instream = data_dat.openStream()
```

Import the classes needed to read the *data.dat* text file.

```
>>> from java.io import BufferedReader, InputStreamReader
```

Create a `BufferedReader` stream by chaining an `InputStreamReader` instance to `instream`. (See the Java API online documentation for more information about these classes.)

```
>>> data_reader = BufferedReader(InputStreamReader(instream))
```

Show the contents of the file.

```
>>> data_reader.readLine()
'Hello from the Document base!'
```

As an exercise, read *data.dat* in the code base URL.

The great thing about URL is that it works with the HTTP and FTP protocols. This means that you can download file data from anywhere on the Internet. The question is, why do this?

The answer is that an application that doesn't get data from somewhere is pretty useless. Consider the advantages of adding applet capabilities to the address book application. With them, a user could access her address book from any location on the Internet. We'll see how in the next section.

## Transforming the Address Book Application into an Applet

What we're going to do is convert AddressMain, which is currently a form, into an applet. Later we'll make changes to AddressModel so that it can deal with URLs instead of files. This means that it will be able to read and write to any files to which it refers, including any file transmitted over the HTTP protocol.

### Changes to AddressMain

First let's make it so AddressMain derives from an applet instead of a frame.

```
class AddressMain(JApplet):
```

Now let's add the __init__ and __destroy__ methods. __init__ gives us access to the database, which we need to initialize AddressModel. __destroy__ calls Address Model's writeAddress() function, which writes addresses out to a file (if the protocol supports this).

```
def init(self):

        url=None        # To hold the document base url.

        try:
            url = self.getDocumentBase()
        except:
            print "Unable to get document base URL"

def init(self):

        url=None        # To hold the document base url.

        try:
            url = self.getDocumentBase()
        except:
            print "Unable to get document base URL"
```

Now, because we have to move some of the code out of __init__, we need to create another method to initialize the GUI components based on AddressModel.

```
Def initGUI(self):
            # Move to the first address in
            # the list and table.
```

```
If self.model.getSize() > 0:
        Self.addresses.setSelectIndex(0)
        Address = self.model.getAddressAt(0)
        Self.form.set(address)
```

## Changes to AddressModel

We've made our address book application fairly modular, so it's easy to add support for reading from a URL. In fact, it takes just three lines of code. We now have a class, AddressURL (from *AddressBook\AddressModel.py*), that has its own readAddresses() and writeAddresses() methods, which means that we no longer have to import them from *AddressUtils.py*.

Here's the modified *AddressBook\AddressModel.py* module:

```
from address import Address
...
...
from AddressURL import AddressURL

class AddressModel(AbstractTableModel, ListModel):
        """The AddressModel is both a ListModel and a
        TableModel."""

        def __init__(self, url):
            """Initialize the Address model.
            Read the dictionary from the file."""

            self.dict = None      # holds the dictionary of addresses.
            self.list = None      # holds the sorted list of names,
                                  # which are keys
                                  # into the dictionary.

            self.listeners = []  # to hold list of
                                 # ListModelListeners

            self.io = AddressURL(url)
                    # Read the addresses from the AddressURL class.
            self.dict = self.io.readAddresses()

          ...
          ...
      def writeAddresses(self):
            """Write the address data to the file."""
            self.io.writeAddresses(self.dict)
```

### *AddressURL*

AddressURL uses the openStream() method to read a file from a URL. It writes to the file as well if its underlying protocol (HTTP, FTP, file, etc.) provides the necessary support. Using getOutputStream() (from java.net.URLConnection), AddressURL gets the file's associated output stream.

Take a look at *AddressBook\AddressURL.py*. Be sure to read the comments.

```
from java.io import ObjectInputStream, IOException
from java.io import ObjectOutputStream, File, FileOutputStream
from java.net import URL, UnknownServiceException
from string import split, join
class AddressURL:
        def __init__(self, url, filename="./addr.dat"):

                        # Set the url. If the url does not exist,
                        # create one based on the current
                        # directory and filename.
                if(url):
                        self.url = URL(url, filename)
                else:
                        file = File(filename)
                        self.url = file.toURL()

        def readAddresses(self):
                """
                Read in a dictionary of addresses.
                Uses URL.openStream()
                """
                file = None # to hold the file input stream

                        # Use try/finally to work with the file.
                        # If the file does not work for any
                        # reason then close it.
                try:
                                # Try to read in the addresses from the
                                # file. If you can't read the addresses
                                # then print an error message.
                        try:
                                file = self.url.openStream()
                                in_stream= ObjectInputStream(file)
                                dict = in_stream.readObject()
                                return dict
                        except IOException, error:
                                print "ERROR reading url: " + self.url
                                print error.class.name
                                print error.message
                                return {}
                finally:
                        if not (file is None): file.close()

        def writeAddresses(self, dict):
                """
                Write the addresses instances
                in the dictionary to a
                file.

                The writeAddresses method uses
                URL.openConnection().getOutputStream(), and
                attempts to write the dictionary of
                addresses to a file.
```

```
            If the writing fails because the protocol
            does not support writing, then
            writeAddresses checks to see if
            the protocol is file protocol. If it is file
            protocol, writeAddresses calls
            writeAsFile, which
            opens a file using FileOutputStream.

            """
                    # to hold the output file output stream.
            file=None
                    # Use try/finally to write the instances
                    # to a file.
                    # If all else fails then close
                    # the file object.
            try:
                            # Write the address instances in dict
                            # to a file specified by filename.
                            # If there are any errors then
                            # print an error message.
                    try:
                            urlConnection = self.url.openConnection()
                            file = urlConnection.getOutputStream()
                            out_stream = ObjectOutputStream(file)
                            out_stream.writeObject(dict)

                            # If the protocol does not support
                            # writing, do this....
                    except UnknownServiceException, noservice:
                                    # If the protocol is file,
                                    # then write it as a file.
                            if self.url.protocol=='file':
                                    filename=self.url.toString()
                                    self.writeAsFile(filename, dict)
                            else:
                                    print noservice.message + self.url

                    except IOException, error:
                            print "ERR: writing addresses"+ self.url
                            print error.class.name
                            print error.message
            finally:
                    if(file):file.close()

    def writeAsFile(self, filename, dict):
        """
        Writes out a dictionary of addresses by
        using
        FileOutputStream.
        """
                    # Extract the filename from the URL
                    # string.
            filename = filename[5:]
            filename = File(filename)
```

```
file = None #to hold the file output stream.

try:
                # Write the address instances
                # in dict to the file.
                # If there are any errors
                # then print an error message.
        try:
                file = FileOutputStream(filename)
                out_stream = ObjectOutputStream(file)
                out_stream.writeObject(dict)

        except IOException, error:
                print "ERROR writing: " + filename
                print error.class.name
                print error.message
finally:
            if(file):file.close()
```

## Running the Address Book Application

Our address book application can be run as an application or as an applet. Its main block creates an instance of JFrame and adds an instance of AddressMain to it. Here's part of the code (from *AddressBook\AddressMain.py*):

```
def __windowClosing(event):
      event.source.dispose()
      from java.lang import System
      System.exit(0)

if __name__ == "__main__":
      mainWindow = Frame("Address book application")
      applet = AddressMain()
      applet.init()
      mainWindow.contentPane.add(applet)
      mainWindow.windowClosing = __windowClosing
            # Pack the frame and make it visible.
      mainWindow.pack()
      mainWindow.setSize(600, 300)
      mainWindow.visible=1
```

Run the application with AppletBrowser so you can debug and test it as you do the exercises. (The code is from *run.py*.)

```
from AppletBrowser import AppletBrowser
from AddressMain import AddressMain

applet = AddressMain()
browser = AppletBrowser()

browser.addApplet(applet)
```

The applet browser provides AppletContext and AppletStub, which make available the getDocumentBase(), resize(), and getParameter() methods, among others.

Try these exercises:

- Add an applet parameter that specifies the address book application file name. The name should be relative to the document base, and it should correspond to a specific address book. Reviewing the section on AppletBrowser should help you here.
- Get a type-4 JDBC driver so you can get the application to work with an RDBMS system.
- Compile and run AddressBook in a browser.

## Using AppletBrowser to Develop Applets

To use AppletBrowser, configure the file *applet.props* in the current working directory. *applet.props* is a Java properties file that specifies the applet's parameters (code base, code, archive, etc.). If you want, include a toolbar for invoking the applet's __stop__, __init__, and __destroy__ methods.

AppletBrowser takes the following command-line arguments:

- -w—writes out a sample *applet.props* file
- -t—runs the browser; includes a toolbar
- -v—runs the browser in verbose mode
- -r—runs the browser
- -?—shows help text
- -prop—writes a single parameter to the property file (-propNAME:VALUE)
- -HTML—converts *applet.props* to an HTML page (-HTMLFileName)

To use the browser in a new directory, you have to execute it with the -w option. This creates an *applet.props* file with a code base that corresponds to the current working directory.

Here's the code to create an HTML file called *AddressBook.html*:

```
C:\jython_book\scripts\chap18\AddressBook>jython AppletBrowser.
    py-HTMLAddressBook
```

Here's *AddressBook.html*'s code:

```
<html>
<body>
<center>

<applet
    code=com.awl.jython_book.MyApplet
    codebase=.\jpywork
    width=400
    height=400
    archive=..\..\lib\jython.jar
>
```

```
<param name="color" value="blue">
<param name="hello" value="hi mom">
If you don't have a Java-enabled browser, you need to get one!
</applet></center>
</body>
</html>
```

Here's how to specify additional applet parameters:

```
C:\jython_book\scripts\chap18\AddressBook>jython AppletBrowser.
    py-propFileName:RicksAddrBook
```

Once you add a parameter, it will be available the next time you create an HTML file or use `AppletBrowser`.

## Advanced Topic: AppletContext and AppletStub

When an applet is created, it's given a stub via its `setStub()` method. The stub is the interface between the applet and the browser. You don't have to deal directly with the stub because the `Applet` class implements methods that use it.

Here are `AppletStub`'s methods:

- `appletResize(width, height)`—resizes the applet
- `getAppletContext()`—gets the applet's context
- `getCodeBase()`—gets the code base URL
- `getDocumentBase()`—gets the document base URL
- `getParameterName()`—gets an applet parameter
- `isActive()`—determines if the applet is active

The applet context corresponds to the applet's environment and it can be used to show status, to load other documents, and to get access to other applets. The `AppletContext`'s methods are

- `getApplet(name)`—gets the applet corresponding to a given name
- `getApplets()`—gets a collection of specific applets
- `getImage(url)`—returns an image object corresponding to the specified URL
- `showDocument(url)`—shows a Web page other than the current page and replaces the current page with it
- `showDocument(url, target)`—same as above, but specifies the frame target
- `showStatus(status)`—shows the status text in the browser

`AppletBrowser` subclasses `AppletContext` and `AppletStub` via the classes `URL` and `URL ClassLoader`.

### AppletBrowser.py

Here's some of the code for *AppletBrowser.py*:

```
from java.applet import AppletContext, AppletStub
from javax.swing import JFrame, JButton, JPanel, JLabel
from javax.swing import JTextField, ImageIcon
...
...
```

When you use the addApplet() method, AppletBrowser passes a context and calls the applet's __init__ method.

```
def addApplet(self, applet):

        ...
        ...
        # Set the applet as the applet in this instance.
        # Pass this instance as the AppletStub (stub).
        # Add this applet to the frame. Then pack this frame.
        self.applet = applet
        if debug:
                print "Set the stub, and add the applet to the container"
        applet.setStub(self)
        self.contentPane.add(self.applet, BorderLayout.CENTER)

        ...
        applet.init()
        applet.start()

        self.pack()
```

As you can see, AppletBrowser passes itself as the stub and in this way implements all of AppletStub's parameters.

```
...
...
def appletResize(self, width, height):
                self.setSize(width, height)
                self.doLayout()

def getAppletContext(self):
                return self

def isActive(self):
                return 1

def getCodeBase(self):
                codebase=self.props.getProperty("codebase")
                if not codebase:
                        return URL(self.docbase, ".")
                else:
                        return URL(self.docbase, codebase)

def getDocumentBase(self):
                return self.docbase
```

```
def getParameter(self, name):
            return self.props.getProperty(name)
```

getAppleContext() returns self, that is, the AppletBrowser instance, which means that AppletBrowser implements AppletContext's methods.

```
...
...
def getApplet(self, name):
        return self.applet #Should return an applet

def getApplets(self):
        v = Vector()
        v.add(self.applet)
        return v.elements()

def getImage(self, url):
        icon = ImageIcon(url)
        return icon.getImage()

def showDocument(self, url):
        pass

def showDocument(self, url, target):
        pass

def showStatus(self, status):
        self.status.text = status
```

To implement getImage(), AppletBrowser uses javax.swing.ImageIcon. The get Applet() and getApplets() methods return the currently loaded applet; the show Status() method shows the status in a text field called status.

AppletBrowser loads the applet specified by the code parameter, as well as all of the jar files specified in the archive tag, into the URLClassLoader class.

```
    ...
    ...
def loadApplet(self):

        # Create the class loader and get
        # the class name.
    class_loader=self.createClassLoader()
    class_name = self.props.getProperty("code")

        # Load the class, create an instance
        # of it, and add it with addApplet.
    if class_name and class_loader:
        try:
            if debug: print "Loading: "+ class_name
                clazz=class_loader.loadClass(class_name)
            if debug: print clazz

                applet = clazz.newInstance()
            self.addApplet(applet)
```

```
                    except Exception, exception:
                        global error
                        error = exception
                        print "Unable to load the class "+class_name
        def getJars(self):
            urls=[]
                #Parse the list of jarfiles in the archive tag.
            jarfiles = self.props.getProperty("archive")
            jarfiles = split(jarfiles, ",")

                # Iterate through the list of jarfiles, and add
                # each jarfile as a URL to the urls list.
            for jar in jarfiles:
            url = URL(self.docbase, jar)
            urls.append(url)
                if debug: print "Adding jar file " + `url`

            return urls

        def createClassLoader(self):
            try:
                            # Get list of URLS for each jar in the
                            # archive tag. Get the codebase URL, and
                            # add it to the list of URLS.
                            # Create a URL jarray to pass to the
                            # URLClassLoader constructor.
                            # Get the system class loader to pass to the
                            # URLClassLoader constructor.
                            # Create an instance of URLClassLoader
                            # passing the urls and the system class
                            # loader.
                urls = self.getJars()
            codebase=self.getCodeBase()
            urls.append(codebase)
            urls = array(urls, URL)
            loader = ClassLoader.getSystemClassLoader()
            url_loader = URLClassLoader(urls, loader)
            return url_loader

        except Exception, exception:
        global error
            error = exception
            print "Unable to create class loader"
```

## Summary

In this chapter, we covered applets, which are components that execute within a browser. To run Jython code as an applet, you have to compile it to a Java class. You should also put it in a jar file to make downloading easier.

We extended our address book application to work as an applet. We also covered the inner workings of AppletBrowser, which creates Jython applets through a context (AppletContext) and a stub (AppletStub).

*Installing Jython on Windows*

First we'll install J2SE v.1.4, because it's the most recent version available as I write. Then we'll install the latest version of Jython.

Before we start, let's get something straight. You might very well have trouble installing Jython because of the number of steps involved. You may need an expert computer configurator to help you with your Jython installation. This might be a computer technician or programmer, or it might even be that kid next door who's always making bootleg floppies so he can play the latest games.

If your local expert fails you, visit the newsgroups for Java and Python. They're usually willing to help new programmers. Just check out the newsgroup's FAQs (frequently asked questions) first to avoid looking stupid.

## Installing Java Runtime

Before you can use the Jython interactive interpreter, you need a Java development tool or Java runtime environment. The Java Developers Kit (J2SE) is free and, as the reference implementation for Java, is the logical choice, especially for beginners (all of the examples in the book use Jython in conjunction with the J2SE). The J2SE's latest version is available at the Javasoft Web site.

Even though I use the J2SE, I should say that Microsoft's free Java Virtual Machine (JVM) has some features that make it a good alternative with Windows. In particular, it streamlines the installation of Java packages and allows integration with ActiveX and Windows API via JDirect. Visit Microsoft's Web site for downloading instructions.

One more thing before we get started. All of the examples in the book were created on a Microsoft Windows 98 system, and the references are specific to Windows 98 users (although they should work equally well with Windows 95 and sometimes Windows NT v.4.0). I chose Windows primarily because I'm a recovering Microsoft lackey but also because it would be impossible to document J2SE and Python set up on all of the systems for which they're available. I had to choose something, and Windows was it.

I will, however, show you Jython configuration and installation on Linux systems. I figure that if you have a UNIX/Linux background, you're smart enough to translate from DOS to UNIX (or, for that matter, from DOS to Mac).

If you're not a Windows or Linux user, go to the *platform.html* page at the Python Web site (*www.jython.org*) for JVM installation instructions. Check out the links to pages specific to your platform.

## *Installing the J2SE—Step by Step*

Before you can start installation, you need to download and install J2SE v.1.4 (or the equivalent for your environment; Linux users, see Appendix B). Just follow the instructions at *http://java.sun.com/products/jdk/1.4/*. This can take a while depending on your modem's speed. Once you have the J2SE, install the software by double-clicking the file in the directory you downloaded it to.

During setup, accept all defaults. For example, the default directory is *C:\j2skd1.4.0*. The rest of the instructions assume that you've put the file there.

> ### If the J2SE Won't Start
> Be sure you saved it with an *\*.exe* file extension, which tells Windows that the file is binary executable.

### Startup

Once installation is complete, edit your *c:\autoexec.bat* file with your text editor. This file usually has Windows and DOS startup information. Make sure that the PATH environment variable contains the *J2SE1.4 bin* directory. Windows uses PATH to find executable programs. It gives you convenient access to Java, the Java interpreter, Javac, the Java compiler, and other Java tools, which will come in handy as you do the exercises.

For Windows 95, Windows 98, and Windows ME, add the CLASSPATH environment variable to *autoexec.bat* after the PATH statement. This tells Java, the interpreter, and Javac where to find Java classes.

```
REM ********* settings for J2SE ******************
SET PATH=%PATH%;C:\j2se1.3\bin;
SET CLASSPATH=.
```

Notice that CLASSPATH is set to '.', which means the current directory. If there's already a CLASSPATH statement, make sure a period is specified.

*For Windows NT4.0:*

1. Go to the Start menu and then the Settings menu. Select Control Panel.
2. In the control panel, double-click the System icon.
3. In the Systems Option dialog box, choose the Environment tab.
4. Edit the PATH environment variable by adding *C:\j2skd1.4.0\bin* to the search path.
5. Use the same technique to edit the CLASSPATH variable.

*For Windows 2000:*

1. Go to the Start menu and then the Settings menu; Select Control Panel.
2. In the control panel, double-click the System icon.
3. In the Systems Properties dialog box, choose the Advanced tab.
4. In the Advanced tab, hit the Environment Variables button.
5. Edit the PATH environmental variable by adding *C:\j2skd1.4.0\bin* to the search path.
6. Use the same technique to edit the CLASSPATH variable.

---

**A Little Tip**

Before you add the directory to the PATH statement, make sure there are no older versions of the J2SE already there. If there are, they'll be executed instead of *C:\j2se\1.3.*

---

Once you've installed the J2SE and edited the *autoexec.bat* file, reboot your PC. Then, to test that everything is okay, go to the DOS prompt, and enter java -version at the command line. You should see the following:

```
c:\java-version "1.3.0"
Java(TM) 2 Runtime Environment, Standard Edition (build 1.4.0-b92)
Java HotSpot(TM) Client VM (build 1.4.0-b92, mixed mode)
```

---

**Troubleshooting**

If you don't see the okay message, type c:\j2skd1.4.0\bin\java at the DOS prompt.

```
C:\> c:\j2sjd1.4.0\bin\java -version
java version "1.3.0"
Java(TM) 2 Runtime Environment, Standard Edition (build 1.4.0-b92)
Java HotSpot(TM) Client VM (build 1.4.0-b92, mixed mode)
```

> If this works, you have a problem with your PATH statement. Try entering PATH at the command line to see what it looks like. Probably you have a typo or you forgot to reboot (*autoexec.bat* runs only after rebooting).
>
> If you still don't see the okay message and all you're getting is "Bad command or filename," then your setup program didn't work. You may have put the J2SE in the wrong directory. Go to the Start menu and then Find Files or Folders, and look for *java.exe*. This should tell you where you installed the J2SE or if you actually installed it. If all else fails, it's time to call in an expert configurator.

## Installing Jython

Jython is free and open source. All you have to do is go to *http://www.jython.org/download.html* and do what you're told. (Jython is the latest Python release.)

Jython is backward compatible with JPython (in which all of the examples are written), so feel free to use it. Just make sure to type jython instead of jython in the interpreter and jythonc instead of jythonc in the compiler.

To install Jython, go to the directory where it's downloaded and type java jython-20 at the DOS prompt.

```
C:\temp> java jython-20
```

Note that a Java class name does *not* end with a *.class* extension, so leave it off.

While the setup program executes, read and accept the license agreement.

### Startup

Once the setup is complete, edit the *autoexec.bat* file to access the Jython interpreter. Open the file with a text editor, and add the following lines after those entered for the J2SE.

*For Jython:*

```
REM ********* settings for Jython ******************
SET PATH=%PATH%;C:\Jython
SET CLASSPATH=%CLASSPATH%;C:\Jython.jar
```

The PATH statement tells Windows to append *c:\Jython* to the PATH environment variable, which holds the file's executable search path for Windows. The CLASS PATH statement enables the Java interpreter to find the Jython class libraries.

At this point you should be able to run Jython by entering Jython at the command-line DOS prompt. More installation information is available at *www.jython.org/install html*.

Jython doesn't come with all of the standard Python modules, but you can download them from *www.jython.org/download.html* and follow the installation instructions.

***Installation Tip***

If you have any problems with installation, report them to *jython-dev@lists.source-forge.net*. (Tell them I sent you.) Make sure you've done everything you can before reporting what might turn out to be a nonproblem. You may discover that your problem is unique to your platform. To find out for sure, go to *www.jython.org/platform.html*. They'll let you know.

   To run your downloaded file, go to the directory that holds the Python library file, and run this at the command line:

```
C:\temp> jython -jar pylib152a.jar
```

Done at last. If you've come this far, you can call yourself a master configurator. Nothing can stop you from learning Python.

# APPENDIX B    *Installing Jython on Linux*

Jaysen Lorenzen

To illustrate the installation of Jython on Linux, we're using the most recent version of the SDK—1.3 glibc. Versions 1.2 and 1.3 are available only for newer distributions using the libc6 libraries (such as Red Hat v.5.x and Debian v.2.x). The libc5 versions of J2SE v.1.1x are available on the Blackdown site for those of you running older distributions.

If you're the root user of your Linux system, log in as root, or use the su command to gain "superuser" (that is, root) privileges before trying each install. If you're not the root user, you can install software only to your own user directory—*/home/<your name>*—or to directories for which you have read, write, and execute access. (If you want to install on a machine other than your own, you may have to ask your system administrator for help.)

The first step in your Linux Jython install is downloading the J2SE (v.1.3) from Blackdown (*http://www.blackdown.org*), from which you'll get a compressed tar ball, or Sun Microsystems (*http://java.sun.com*), from which you'll get a self-extracting package. The next step is unpacking the J2SE and installing it.

## Unpacking the Blackdown Package

Many, many versions of the J2SE are available from Blackdown. I chose the latest, *j2sdk1.3* (*j2sdk-1.3.0-RC1-linux-i386.tarbz2*). Only a *bziped* package is offered for this release, but earlier releases come with standard *gziped* packages.

In a shell, as the root, or using the su command, copy or move the downloaded file to a directory. This directory can be any one you want, but */usr/local/lib* is the best choice because it makes it easier for other users to find examples and documentation. (Thus, the J2SE subdirectory is */usr/local/lib/j2sdk1.x*). Then unzip and untar the file by changing the directory to its location with the command

```
bzip2 -dc j2sdk-1.3.0-RC1-linux-i386.tar.bz2 | tar -xvf-
```

If you downloaded a *gziped* package, replace `bzip2` with `gzip` in the command.

> **HotSpotClient**
>
> The default virtual machine for J2SDK v.1.3 is HotSpotClient. If it doesn't work well with Jython, change it by editing the file.
>
> /<jdk1.x>/jre/lib/jvm.cfg
>
> (where <jdk1.x> is the jdk install directory)
>     Moving "`-classic`" to the first line of the file will change the default to Linux Native Threads.

## Unpacking the Sun Package

Here we're using J2SDK v.1.3 and the self-extracting binary package (*j2sdk-1_3_0-linux.bin*). In a shell, as the root, or using the su command, copy or move the downloaded file to the directory of your choice—again we're using *user/local/lib*, so the J2SE subdirectory is */user/local/lib/jdk.1.x*.

Make the file executable with the command

```
chmod a+x j2sdk-1_3_0-linux.bin
```

Execute it with the command

```
./j2sdk-1_3_0-linux.bin
```

This launches a script and displays the license agreement from Sun (which you must read and accept). The script unpacks and installs the SDK.

## Installing the Sun and Blackdown Distributions

The installation procedures that follow are common to both Sun and Blackdown.
    First we have to set some environment variables. There are several ways to do this, all of which depend on user rights and preferences.

### Setting the Environment Variables

To set PATH and CLASSPATH, edit the *rc* file in your home directory for the shell you're using. I've chosen the bash shell, so the file to edit is *~/.bashrc*. If a PATH statement exists, add the following line just below PATH=etc/etc.

```
PATH=$PATH:/<jdk1.x>/bin
```

where `<jdk1.x>` is the J2SE directory, including the complete path created in the previous steps. If there are any references to older J2SE versions here, remove them. You should see

```
PATH=$PATH:/usr/local/lib/j2sdk1.3/bin
```

If there's no `CLASSPATH` statement, add it. If there is one, add the following line after it:

```
CLASSPATH=/<jdk1.x>/lib/tools.jar:./
```

where `<jdk1.x>` is the J2SE directory, including the complete path created during the previous steps.

Remove any references to older J2SE versions in the path. You should see

```
CLASSPATH=/usr/local/lib/j2sdk1.3/lib/tools.jar:./
```

If you don't see a `CLASSPATH` statement, add either the `PATH=$PATH` or the `CLASSPATH` line shown above. If you see an `export` statement, append a space, the word `PATH`, another space, and the word `CLASSPATH` to it. If you don't see an `export` statement, create one containing `PATH` and `CLASSPATH` at the bottom of the file.

```
export PATH CLASSPATH
```

Now you should have these `PATH`, `CLASSPATH`, and `export` lines:

```
PATH=$PATH:/usr/local/lib/j2sdk1.3/bin
CLASSPATH=/usr/local/lib/j2sdk1.3/lib/tools.jar:./
export TERM PATH CLASSPATH
```

Save and close the file. Then re-execute the shell you're working in so that the environment changes will take effect.

If the computer you're on is yours or if your system administrator is by your side, you can set the `PATH` and `CLASSPATH` variables globally as `root` (regardless of the shell used) by editing the */etc/profile* file and making the same changes as for the bash shell.

## *Installing Older Distributions*

If you're downloading a J2SE version older than 1.2, you'll have to get the JFC/Swing classes from the JavaSoft site (*http://java.sun.com/products/jfc/#download-swing*). Make sure your J2SE and JFC versions match—for example, if you have J2SE v.1.1.7, you need Swing v.1.1.1 (*swing1_1_1.tar.Z*).

> **Tar/Zip**
>
> The download page doesn't mention Linux, so choose the standard tar or zip file, not the installer.

In a shell, as root, or with the su command, copy or move the downloaded file to the directory you choose. As before, we're using */usr/local/lib* and we want the *swing-1.1.x* directory (*/usr/local/lib/jdk1.1.7/swing-1.1.x*), so we move the file to */usr/local/lib/jdk1.1.7/*. Installing the Swing classes in the J2SE directory makes it easy for all users to find the examples and the documentation.

Unzip and untar the downloaded file by changing the directory to its location (*/usr/local/lib/jdk117_vla*) with the command

```
gzip -dc swing1_1_1.tar.Z | tar -xvf-
```

which creates the Swing subdirectory.

Add the *swing.jar* file to the CLASSPATH variable by modifying the CLASSPATH line in the personal *~/.bashrc* file or the global */etc/profile* file.

```
CLASSPATH=$CLASSPATH:/<base path>/<swing path >/swing.jar
```

/<base path>/<swing path>/ is the complete path to *swing.jar*. If you installed J2SE v.1.1.7, the path should look like

```
CLASSPATH=$CLASSPATH:/jdk117_vla/swing-1.1.1fcs/swing.jar
```

Save and close the file. You'll have to restart the shell for the environment changes just made to take effect.

---

**Installation Alternatives**

There are countless ways to install the J2SE on Linux. For distributions using RPM package managers (like those here), RPM and DEB packages are available, which you can find on the Linux distribution FTP site.

---

### Testing the Installation

Test your install by starting a shell and entering java -version. You should get a message like this:

```
[jayson1@r_monkey lib]$ java -version
java version "1.3.0"
Java(TM) 2 Runtime Environment, Standard Edition (build Blackdown-1.3.0-RC1)
Classic VM (build Blackdown-1.3.0-RC1, native threads, sunwjit)
```

If you don't, there may be something wrong. Try entering the complete path to the Java executable, which in our case is

```
[jayson1@r_monkey /]$ /usr/local/lib/j2sdk1.3/bin/java -version
```

The appropriate response means that you have a problem with your environment variables. Check the *rc* file for your shell or the */etc/profile* file to make sure the paths are correct. (Remember, you have to re-execute the shell for the changes to take effect.)

If you get a "Segmentation Fault" message, chances are you installed the wrong binary release of the J2SE. If you're using an older Linux distribution (older than Red Hat v.5.x or Debian v.2.x) and chose the glibc binary, you may find you need libc5 instead. Check your Linux distribution references for the correct library type.

If the virtual machine displays "Font specified in font.properties not found," edit the file:

```
/<jdk1.x>/jre/lib/font.properties
```

where `<jdk1.x.>` is the J2SE install directory. Comment out the fonts that weren't found to stop these warning messages. Installing the fonts is an alternative solution.

If none of these quick fixes does the trick, you have a problem. Refer to the Blackdown installation FAQ page (*http://www.blackdown.org/java-linux/docs/faq /FAQ-java-linux.html#toc4*) for advice.

## Downloading the Jython and CPython Libraries

If all went well with the installation, you can download the Jython and the CPython libraries from *http://www.jython.org* or *http://www.python.org*. Then, in a shell, as root, or using the su command, change the directory to which you downloaded the class file by entering

```
java Jython1x
```

where 1x is the number of the downloaded Jython version.

In our case, the command looks like

```
java Jython11
```

This launches the java GUI version of the install shield and walks you through a series of questions. One question is which directory you want to install Python in. The default is your home directory if you've logged in as root. (Once again, although you can choose any directory I recommend */usr/local/lib.*). The result is the creation of a directory called *Jython-1.x* in the directory specified. To install Jython, replace the Jython11 install class with its Jython counterpart.

The next step is to edit your environment variables (here, in the *~/.bashrc* file) by adding the following just below the existing PATH statement:

```
PATH=$PATH:/<Jython-1x>
```

where `<Jython-1x>` is your chosen directory and the number of the Jython version you've downloaded. Here's the actual line:

```
PATH=$PATH:/usr/local/lib/Jython-1.1
```

Now add the following CLASSPATH line just below the existing one:

```
CLASSPATH=$CLASSPATH:/<Jython-1.x>/Jython.jar
```

where `<Jython` is the installation directory and `-1.x>` is the Jython version installed—in our case,

```
CLASSPATH=$CLASSPATH:/usr/local/lib/Jython-1.1/Jython.jar
```

Save and close the file, and then restart your shell so the changes take effect.

---

### If It's Your First Time

To start Jython for the first time, you need to be the root user or use the su command (to gain superuser privileges). The first run creates some new directories and searches your path to find the J2SE-installed Java classes.

---

## Running Jython

To run Jython for the first time, type Jython at the prompt, and press Enter. You should see something like this:

```
packageManager: processing new jar,"/usr/local/lib/Jython-1.1/jython.jar"
packageManager: processing new jar,"/usr/local/lib/j2sdk1.3/lib/tools.jar"
packageManager: processing new jar,"/usr/local/lib/j2sdk1.3/jre/lib/rt.jar"
packageManager: processing new jar,"/usr/local/lib/j2sdk1.3/jre/lib/i18n.jar"
packageManager: processing new jar,
"/usr/local/lib/j2sdk1.3/jre/lib/sunrsasign.jar"
Jython 1.1 on java1.3.0 (JIT: sunwjit)
Copyright (C) 1997-1999 Corporation for National Research Initiatives
```

Then press Ctrl-D to exit interactive mode.

If you want to use parts of the standard Python library that aren't included with Jython, you have two choices. You can download and install them from the Jython download page (recommended by the folks at the Jython site because the Python v.1.5.2 libs version has been modified to work better with Jython):

```
http://www.jython.org/download.html#pylib
```

or you can add a pointer in python.path to the *lib* directory of a CPython distribution (try this with your system administrator by your side).

In a shell, as root, or using su, change the directory to the one you downloaded the CPython class file to, and enter

```
jython -jar pylib152e.jar
```

There will be a flurry of activity on the screen as the CPython libraries are extracted, copied, and compiled to your directories. Your installation is now complete.

# APPENDIX C   *The Power of Scripting*

Scripting languages are dynamic, interactive environments for rapid development of Java code. Many are either object-oriented or object-based, and almost all are interpreted and use late-bound polymorphism. This makes them extremely dynamic and easy to program—essential ingredients in rapid application development (RAD), component gluing, and project prototyping.

## *Scripting Versus Programming Languages*

There's a fine line between scripting and programming languages. For example, Smalltalk is an extremely dynamic interpreted language, but it's not for scripting. A true scripting language, unlike Smalltalk, must employ late-bound polymorphism and dynamic typing.

Many UNIX programmers program in C and C++ and glue modules together with higher-level shell programming (Korn, Bourne, C, etc.). Or they use the scripting language Tcl for both programming their GUIs and gluing together their C++ classes and libraries. Another option is to use Python as the glue. It's often preinstalled with UNIX systems and is easy to extend with C.

The most prevalent object-based scripting language is Visual Basic, which is often used to glue together COM components written in different languages.

Scripting languages don't replace system languages but rather augment them in the following ways:

- Extending applications
- Debugging
- Learning and experimenting with the Java API
- Rapid prototyping

**548**

- Gluing subsystems and components
- Automating general testing and regression testing

For information about increasing productivity with scripting, read John Ousterhout's online paper *Scripting: Higher Level Programming for the 21st Century* (*http://www.home.pacbell.net/ouster/scripting.html*), which notes a sharp productivity increase with scripting languages—on the order of 5 to 10 times higher than with a strongly typed language like Java. From my own experience, I'd say they are 2 to 3 times faster depending on the application.

## Java and Scripting

I call Java a scripting language on steroids. In fact, because it uses statically typed polymorphism, it's more precisely a hybrid. This may at first seem like a disadvantage, but it turns out that Java's statically typed polymorphism, as well as its design by interface, is great for systems programming, framework definition, and component development. It would be wrong to view Java as a system programming language by classical definition. Rather, it's a virtual system programming language for a virtual system—that is, a virtual machine (the Java Virtual Machine). Like its scripting language cousins, it can be very dynamic—not as much as Python or Smalltalk but certainly more than C++.

Java's main drawback for scripting is that it can't glue components together. What you need to do is build components with Java and glue them together with a true scripting language.

Java's class reflection and bean introspection APIs make a great basis for integrating scripting languages. Essentially, the scripting language can get metadata about a Java class, which it uses to change its properties, handle its events, and invoke its methods. I have metaprogrammed with COM, CORBA, and Java, and of the three Java is my preference because of these features.

Some people think that the only language for the JVM is Java. They're wrong. Like many platforms (and the JVM is very much a platform), the virtual machine has many languages, and the list keeps growing. In particular, combining the JVM with scripting enhances rapid application development.

## Integrating Scripting with Jython

Jython is very close to Python and has been certified as 100 percent pure Java. In fact, in a recent Web poll conducted by NetBeans (the Java IDE maker bought by Sun) on integrating a scripting language with its Java IDE, Jython won by a landslide. It also won a similar poll on JDJ and the Java channel.

By the way, you can develop Java Server Pages in Jython. They're called Python Server Pages, and they run in a Java servlet. They're also open source. (Find out more about them at *http://www.ciobriefings.com.*)

## Tcl

The Java command language (Jacl) implements Tcl8.x for writing scripts for Java components and APIs. Another Tcl blend allows Java objects to be manipulated directly from Tcl. Because Tcl is the premier RAD language, many Jacl users have claimed significant reduction in development costs with its use. (Find out more about Jacl at *http://www.tcl.tk/software/java/.*)

## JavaScript (Rhino)

Rhino is an implementation of JavaScript v.1.5, a very powerful object-based language. Freely available and open source, Rhino is a natural for rapid application and prototyping in the JVM.

## Instant Basic

Halcyon's Instant Basic is a Visual Basic clone that allows quick porting of existing Visual Basic applications to the Java platform (the IDE, database components, etc.). Its iASP, a clone of JSP, works with Java so that you can use VBScript and JavaScript to access JavaBeans, CORBA, EJB, and so forth. Learn more about Instant Basic at *http://www.halcyonsoft.com.*

## Java BeanShell

BeanShell is interpreted Java with a syntax very similar to real Java's that executes Java statements and expressions. Like other scripting languages, it's dynamically typed so much of the Java syntax for type declaration and casting is optional. BeanShell is great for writing prototypes and experimenting with unfamiliar APIs. Also, it supports beans, it's very easy to use, and it's open source. To find out more about BeanShell, visit *http://www.Beanshell.org.*

## Smalltalk/Bistro

Bistro is a Smalltalk variant with extensions for Java features and integration. It offers software developers the ability to code in a readable and expressive syntax. Although it's dynamically typed, it has the option of static typing for closer Java integration, which means that you can mix and match statically and dynamically typed systems. Bistro combines Java type safeness with Smalltalk fast development.

### Scheme/Skij

Skij is a small Scheme interpreter implemented in Java. A variant of Lisp, it enables rapid prototyping in the Java environment and has many advanced features such as macros and first class continuations. There are at least 15 Scheme ports to the JVM.

You can download a copy of Skij at *http://www.alphaworks.ibm.com/tech/skij*. If it's not your favorite Java Scheme variant, let me know why.

---

**Need More?**

If I didn't mention your favorite language, or the if the ones I covered don't tickle your fancy, see Robert Tolksdorf's comprehensive list of JVM programming languages.

---

**Dynamic to Static Typing and Back**

BeanShell is essentially a Java variant with dynamic and optional static typing. Bistro is a Smalltalk variant with static and optional dynamic typing. Both languages are on the right track, given that Visual Basic, the granddaddy of all scripting languages, provides both static and dynamic typing support.

---

## Which Scripting Language to Choose

In choosing a scripting language, *ease of use* is a primary criterion. For example, a language may be easy to learn because it resembles another language that most developers know. Or it may just have an easily grasped syntax.

A particular benefit of scripting languages is that they can be embedded in a large application to make it more extensible. The question is how *embeddable* a particular language is and how well it integrates with Java.

*Resemblance to the parent language* is important because it can affect how code ports from a legacy system (i.e., non-Java). The degree of resemblance can influence how quickly developers can get up to speed.

A language's *unique features* might be those that gear it to a particular problem domain. For example, does it have a library for generating XML and HTML documents? Is it easy to integrate with JSP (making it particularly suitable for Web programming)?

Some languages excel at common tasks like *string parsing*; some don't.

A certain scripting language may be better than Java at tasks like manipulating strings and collections. Features such as extensive class libraries and useful built-in language constructs enhance programming *productivity*.

A key criterion is a language's *ease of integration* with Java classes and APIs. For example, a language that permits its classes to subclass Java classes has good integration. So does a language that allows methods to have type signatures.

Some scripting languages are better than others at code *debugging*. Some have a more pleasant *development environment*.

## Hello World—The Programming Rosetta Stone

To give you a feel for scripting, we're going to compare how it's done in three languages, Java, JavaScript, and Python. We'll make the comparison more interesting by adding a Say Hello button, which when pressed causes a window to pop up and display "Hello World" in 18-point bold type.

### The Java Version

```java
import javax.swing.*;
import java.awt.Font;
import java.awt.event.*;

class MyFrame extends JFrame{
  public MyFrame(){
      JButton sayHello;
      sayHello = new JButton("say hello");
      sayHello.setMnemonic('h');
      this.getContentPane().add(sayHello);
      this.setVisible(true);
      this.pack();

      sayHello.addActionListener(new ActionListener(){
      public void actionPerformed(ActionEvent ae){
          JButton b = (JButton)ae.getSource();
          b.setEnabled(false);
          sayHello();
      }
    });
  }
  private void sayHello(){
      JFrame helloFrame;
      JLabel helloLabel;
      Font font;
      helloFrame = new JFrame("Hello Frame");
      helloLabel= new JLabel("Hello World");
      font = new Font("Arial", Font.BOLD, 20);
      helloLabel.setFont(font);
      helloFrame.getContentPane().add(helloLabel);
      helloFrame.pack();
      helloFrame.setVisible(true);
  }
  public static void main(String [] args){
      MyFrame frame = new MyFrame();
      frame.setTitle("My Frame");
  }
}
```

Here's the JavaScript (Rhino at JavaScript 1.4) version.

```javascript
function MyFrame(){
  sayHello = new Packages.javax.swing.JButton("say hello");

  sayHello.setMnemonic('h');
  this.frame = new Packages.javax.swing.JFrame();

  this.frame.getContentPane().add(sayHello);
  this.frame.setVisible(true);
  this.frame.pack();
  sayHello.addActionListener( new Packages.java.awt.event.ActionListener() {
      __parent__ : this,
      actionPerformed : function(ae) {
ae.getSource().setEnabled(false);
         this.__parent__.sayHello();
      }
  });

  function sayHello(){
      helloFrame = new Packages.javax.swing.JFrame("Hello Frame");
      helloLabel= new Packages.javax.swing.JLabel("Hello World");
      font = new java.awt.Font("Arial", java.awt.Font.BOLD, 20);
      helloLabel.setFont(font);
      helloFrame.getContentPane().add(helloLabel);
      helloFrame.pack();
      helloFrame.setVisible(true);
  }

  this.sayHello=sayHello;
}

function main(){
  frame = new MyFrame();
  frame.frame.setTitle("My Hello");
  }
main();
```

## The Jython Version

```python
from javax.swing import JFrame, JButton, JLabel
from java.awt import Font

class MyFrame (JFrame):
  def __init__(self):
      sayHello = JButton("say hello", mnemonic='h')
      self.contentPane.add(sayHello)
      self.visible=1
      self.pack()
      sayHello.actionPerformed = self.__sayHello

  def __sayHello(self, ae):
      ae.source.enabled=0
      helloFrame = JFrame("Hello Frame")
      helloLabel= JLabel("Hello World", font=Font("Arial", Font.BOLD, 20))
      helloFrame.contentPane.add(helloLabel)
      helloFrame.pack()
      helloFrame.visible=1
```

```
if __name__=="__main__":
    frame = MyFrame(title = "My Frame")
```

Notice how well Jython integrates with the JavaBean properties and event model. Also notice how much it packs into a small package (it's about two-thirds the size of the JavaScript version).

## *What Does It All Mean?*

Basically that Python is the best scripting language for the JVM. Here's why:

- *Ease of use.* Python was designed to be easy for beginners. In Virginia, high school students are taught how to program with it.
- *Embeddability.* On a scale from 1 to 10, Python scores 10 for embeddability.
- *Resemblance to the parent language.* Jython is syntactically identical to Python.
- *Features.* Python has some of the best features of Smalltalk, Scheme, Icon, and Java.
- *String parsing.* Python has libraries for regular-expression string parsing (see Appendix E) and slice notation, as well as other features that make string parsing easy.
- *Productivity.* Python has an extensive class library as well as built-in language support for collection objects (including collection literals for defining collections). These make Python strikingly productive.
- *Working well with Java classes and APIs.* In Jython you instantiate and subclass Java classes and interfaces, invoke Java methods, set up bean events, and work with JavaBean properties. You can also compile Jython into Java classes to create JavaBeans, servlets, and applets.
- *Development environment and debugging.* Jython has a good interactive interpreter, but its development environment is its weak point. Python has some mature IDEs, but Jython has nothing. If it did, it would give Java a serious run for its money as the most popular language for the JVM.

# *Java and Python: A Comparison*

This appendix looks at the relative merits of Java and Python using the following tests as the basis for comparison: (1) a GUI application, (2) a statistics application, (3) a simple example of string parsing, and (4) an application with an embedded script.

## *Python 101*

Here's a Python class followed by its Java equivalent.

*Python:*

```python
class Employee:
    def __init__(self, fname="John", lname="Doe", id=1, manager=None, dept=1):
        self.__firstName    =    fname
        self.__lastName     =    lname
        self.__id           =    id
        self.__manager      =    manager
        self.__dept         =    dept

    def getManager(self):
        return self.__manager

    def __str__(self):
        values = self.__lastName, self.__firstName, self.__id
        return join(values,',')
```

*Java:*

```java
public class Employee{
    private String firstName, lastName;
    private int id, dept;
    private Employee manager;
```

```java
    public Employee(){
        firstName = "John";
        lastName = "Doe";
        id = 1;
        vmanager=null;
        dept=1;
    }
    public Employee(String fname, String lname, int id, Employee manager, int dept){
        firstName    =    fname;
        lastName     =    lname;
        this.id      =    id;
        this.manager =    manager;
        this.dept    =    dept;
    }

    public Employee getManager(){
        return manager;
    }

    public String toString(){
        StringBuffer buf = new StringBuffer();
        buf.append(lastName+',');
        buf.append(firstName+',');
        buf.append(""+id);
        return buf.toString();
    }
    ...
    ...
}
```

Similar to Java's `this`, Python's `self` is a reference to the class instance referred to by the first argument in each method. There's no separate declaration for member variables; they're declared when assigned a value. (You can declare class as well as instance variables.) Python's `__str__()` method is equivalent to Java's `toString()`.

In Python, to create an instance of `Employee` and print it to the screen you enter the following:

```python
print Employee()
```

The equivalent in Java is

```java
System.out.println(new Employee());
```

Here's how to create two instances of `Employee`, `joe` and `ron`, and print them to the console. Joe is Ron's manager. We get him by invoking the `ron` instance's `getManager()` method.

*Python:*

```python
joe = Employee("Joe", "Battista", 100)
ron = Employee(manager=joe, id=101, lname="Furgeson", fname="Ron")
```

```
print ron
print ron.getManager()
```

*Java:*

```
Employee joe=new Employee("Joe","Batista",100,null,1);
Employee ron=new Employee("Ron","Furgeson",101,joe,1);
System.out.println(ron);
System.out.println(ron.getManager());
```

As you can see, the syntax is similar.

Jython uses named arguments and default values. This means that when the ron instance is created the arguments are called out of order, which should be familiar to those of you who've used Visual Basic or VBScript. For those of you unfamiliar with this idea, think of it this way: You can call methods as you normally do in Java, or you can do it the Python way, passing the method name/ value pairs and saving yourself some coding, not to mention headaches. Have you ever been stuck with several versions of the same method when all you wanted was different default values? Every default value is another overloaded method, which can get messy.

A good example of the use of named arguments is Python's GridBag utility class, which manages the infamous GridBagLayout manager. I've created something similar in Java that uses overloaded methods to create GridBag constraints.

## A Simple GUI Prototype

We have our simple class. Now we'll create a simple GUI prototype. (Like the class, it's nonsensical since its only purpose is for illustration.)

Fire up the Python interactive interpreter, typing in Jython at the system prompt. Then import JFrame from *javax.swing.*

```
>>> from javax.swing import JFrame
```

Create an instance of the frame, set its size to 200,200, and make it visible.

```
>>> frame=JFrame("My Prototype",visible=1,size=(200,200))
```

This took only one line of code because in Jython any bean property of a class (by which I mean a property defined by getter and setter methods—that is, the Java-Bean design pattern for properties) can be set during the constructor call using named arguments.

Now let's add some components: labels, text fields, and a button. Import the necessary classes from *javax.swing.*

```
>>> from javax.swing import JButton,JTextField,JLabel,JPanel
```

We could have entered from javax.swing import *, as we do in Java, but that would have imported every class into our namespace, which Python considers bad style. Python's way is to let us view and manipulate a namespace.

```
>>> dir()
['JButton', 'JFrame', 'JLabel', 'JTextField', '__name__', 'frame']
```

Create a pane, using JFrame's contentPane property.

```
>>> pane = JPanel()
>>> frame.contentPane.add(pane)
javax.swing.JPanel[,0,0,0x0,invalid,layout=java.awt.FlowLayout,alignmentX=
null,alignmentY=null,border=,flags=34,maximumSize=,minimumSize=,preferredSize=
,default Layout=java.awt.FlowLayout[hgap=5,vgap=5,align=center]]
```

If this were Java, we'd have to call frame.getContentPane() to create a pane because Java does not treat bean properties like instance variables.

To lay out the pane we're going to use the infamous GridBagLayout, which is the most complex of Jython's layout managers. To tame it we'll use the GridBag utility class. Notice how few lines of code it takes up.

Import the GridBag helper class. Then create an instance of it and associate it with the pane.

```
>>> from pawt import GridBag
>>> bag = GridBag(pane)
```

Add the first component, a label, to GridBag, which will use all of GridBag Constraints's default values.

```
>>> bag.add(JLabel("Name"))
>>> frame.validate()
```

Add another label on the second row of the grid.

```
>>> bag.add(JLabel("ID"), gridy=1)
>>> frame.validate()
```

Add a text field on the first row in the second column, and pack the frame.

```
>>> name = JTextField(25)
>>> bag.add(name, gridx=1, weightx=80.0)
>>> frame.pack()
```

Add another text field for the employee ID to the right on the second row, and pack the frame.

```
>>> id = JTextField(10)
>>> bag.add(id, gridx=1, gridy=1, weightx=80.0)
>>> frame.pack()
```

Not what we want, is it? The text field components look silly because I accidentally (on purpose) aligned them centered, not at the left, in their cells. Let's fix this.

Remove the ID and name.

```
>>> pane.remove(id)
>>> pane.remove(name)
```

Put them back with the correct alignment.

```
>>> bag.add(name, gridx=1, weightx=80.00, anchor='WEST')
>>> bag.add(id, gridx=1, gridy=1, weightx=80.0, anchor='WEST')
>>> frame.pack()
```

Jython handles bean events easily because it uses introspection and reflection to create event properties. With the JavaBeans Event design pattern, event properties equate to the method name in a method's event listener interface.

To demonstrate assigning a function or method to an event property, we'll set up an Okay button that prints an employee's name and ID when clicked.

Create and add a button to the GUI.

```
>>> okay = JButton("Okay")
>>> bag.add(okay, gridx=1, gridy=2, anchor='CENTER')
>>> frame.pack()
```

Create a function that prints out the value of the name and ID text.

```
>>> def handleOkay(event):
...     print "Name " + name.text
...     print "ID " + id.text
...
>>> okay.actionPerformed=handleOkay
```

Enter some text in the name and ID fields, and hit Okay.

---

## A GUI Application

Now let's create a GUI based on our prototype in both Jython and Java. The following example shows our Python employee form; after that is its Java equivalent.

*Python:*

```
from javax.swing import JFrame, JButton, JTextField, JLabel, JPanel
from string import split
from pawt import GridBag
from Employee import Employee

class EmployeeForm(JFrame):
  def __init__(self):
      JFrame.__init__(self, "Employee Form")
      pane = JPanel()
      self.contentPane.add(pane)
      bag = GridBag(pane)

          #Create a name and id text field.
      self.__name = JTextField(25)
      self.__id = JTextField(10)
```

```python
        #Create and add a "Name" and "ID" label.
    name = JLabel("Name", labelFor=self.__name, displayedMnemonic=ord('N'))
    bag.add(name)
    id = JLabel("ID", labelFor=self.__id, displayedMnemonic=ord('I'))
    bag.add(id, gridy=1)

        # Add the name and ID text field to the form.
    bag.add(self.__name, gridx=1, weightx=80.00, anchor='WEST')
    bag.add(self.__id, gridx=1, gridy=1, anchor='WEST')

        #Create an okay button, add it, and set up its event handler.
    okay = JButton("Okay", mnemonic=ord('O'))
    bag.add(okay, gridx=1, gridy=2, anchor='EAST')
    okay.actionPerformed=self.handleOkay

    self.visible=1
    self.pack()

def handleOkay(self, event):
    fname, lname = split(self.__name.text, " ")
    id = int(self.__id.text)
    employee = Employee(fname, lname, id)
    print employee

if __name__=="__main__":EmployeeForm()
```

*Java:*

```java
import javax.swing.*;
import java.awt.GridBagLayout;
import java.awt.GridBagConstraints;
import java.awt.event.ActionListener;
import java.awt.event.ActionEvent;
import employee.Employee;

public class EmployeeForm extends JFrame{
    private JTextField name;
    private JTextField id;

public EmployeeForm(){
    super("Employee Form");
    JPanel pane = new JPanel();
    getContentPane().add(pane);

    pane.setLayout(new GridBagLayout());

        // Create a name and id text field.
    name = new JTextField(25);
    id = new JTextField(10);

        // Create and add a "Name" and "ID" label.
    JLabel nameLabel = new JLabel("Name");
    nameLabel.setLabelFor(name);
    nameLabel.setDisplayedMnemonic('N');
```

```
GridBagConstraints constraint = new GridBagConstraints();
pane.add(nameLabel, constraint);

JLabel idLabel = new JLabel("ID");
idLabel.setLabelFor(id);
idLabel.setDisplayedMnemonic('I');
constraint.gridy=1;
pane.add(idLabel, constraint);

        // Add the name and ID text field to the form.
constraint.gridy=0; constraint.gridx=1;
constraint.weightx=80.00;
constraint.anchor=GridBagConstraints.WEST;
pane.add(name, constraint);
constraint.gridy=1;
pane.add(id, constraint);

        // Create an okay button, add it, and set up its event handler.
JButton okay = new JButton("Okay");
okay.setMnemonic('O');
constraint.gridx=1; constraint.gridy=2;
constraint.anchor=GridBagConstraints.EAST;
pane.add(okay, constraint);
okay.addActionListener(new ActionListener(){
        public void actionPerformed(ActionEvent event){
                handleOkay();
        }
});

this.setVisible(true);
this.pack();
}

public void handleOkay(){

    String name, fname, lname;
    int index=0;
    int id =0;

    name = this.name.getText();
    index = name.indexOf(" ");
    fname = name.substring(0, index);
    lname = name.substring(index+1, name.length());

    id = Integer.parseInt(this.id.getText());

    Employee employee = new Employee(fname, lname, id, null, 100);
    System.out.println(""+employee);
}
    public static void main(String [] args){
            new EmployeeForm();
        }
}
```

The Jython version is 1,290 characters; the Java version is 2,139 characters.

## A Statistics Application

Remember the house price sample application we created in Chapter 4? You might want to go back and refresh your memory because we're going to be using it to continue our Python/Java comparison. I'm not going to repeat the information you'll find there, particularly the breakdown and explanation of the code, but I will highlight the important functions, as I did in Chapter 4, and show you the full code examples. A suggestion: Place a bookmark at the section on the house price example in that chapter for easy referral.

### getRange()

The getRange() function iterates through a list of numbers passed to it to calculate the minimum and maximum values in a list. It returns these values, with their range, in a tuple. Here's one way to implement it:

```
def getRange (nums):

    min = 300000000
    max = -300000000

    for item in nums:
            if (item > max): max = item
            if (item < min): min = item
    return (min, max, max-min)
```

Here's another, better, way:

```
def getRange (nums):
    return (min(nums), max(nums), max(nums)-min(nums))
```

With the first implementation, you have to be sure that the values passed to getRange() are within the minimum–maximum range. With the second implementation, you don't have to do that, thanks to the built-in min() and max() functions, which work with all numeric types.

### getMean()

The getMean() function calculates the mean of a sequence of numbers by iterating through the sequence, summing the values, and then dividing the sum by the sequence length. It also determines if the result is a sample mean or a population mean.

```
def getMean (nums, sample):
    sum = 0.0               # holds the value of sum

            # iterate through the sequence
# of numbers and sum them
    for x in nums:
            sum = sum + x
```

```
        # Check to see if this is a sample mean
    if(sample):
        average = sum / (len(nums)-1)

        # Else it is a population mean
    else:
        average = sum / len(nums)
    return average
```

As with `getRange()`, Python has a better way to find the mean. It may surprise you.

```
def getMean (nums, sample):
    sum = reduce(lambda a, b: a+b, nums)
    if sample: average = sum / (len(nums)-1)
    else: average = sum / len(nums)

    return average
```

What's new here is the `reduce()` built-in function, which takes two arguments, `function` and `sequence`. `function` is specified with the `lambda` keyword, which makes it anonymous. `reduce()` applies `function` to two items in the sequence, cumulatively from left to right, reducing it to a single value, in our case `sum`.

The result is the same as with our first implementation of `getMean()`, but it's a lot shorter.

## getMode()

The `getMode()` function finds the value that repeats most often in a sequence. First it duplicates the sequence (before modifying it); then it iterates through it, counting the occurrences of current items via the built-in `count()` method. Once an item is counted, it's removed from the duplicated sequence.

```
def getMode (nums):
        #
        # make a duplicate copy of the nums argument
    duplicate = nums[:]
    highest_count = -100
    mode = None
        #
        # calculate the highest_count and the mode
    for item in nums:

        count = duplicate.count(item)
        if (count == 0): continue
        if (count > highest_count):
            highest_count = count
            mode = item

        while(duplicate.count(item) > 0):
            duplicate.remove(item)
    return mode
```

## getMedian()

The getMedian() function finds the middlemost value once the sequence is sorted.

```
def getMedian (nums):
    "Find the Median number"

            # Create a duplicate since we are
# going to modify it.
    seq = nums[:]

            # Sort the list of numbers.
    seq.sort()

    median = None # to hold the median value

    length = len(seq) # to hold the length of the seq

            # Check to see if the length is
# an even number.
    if ( ( length % 2) == 0):
                    # Since it is an even number,
                    # add the two middle number together.
            index = length / 2
            median = (seq[index-1] + seq[index]) /2.0
    else:
                    # Since it is an odd number,
                    # just grab the middle number.
            index = (length / 2)
            median = seq[index]
    return median
```

## reportStatistics()

The reportStatistics() function calls all of the functions just described and stores their return values in two dictionaries, averages and ranges. It then places these dictionaries in another dictionary called report, which it returns.

```
def reportStatistics (nums):
            # get central tendencies
    averages = {
            "mean":getMean(nums,0),
            "median":getMedian(nums),
            "mode":getMode(nums)
            }

            # get range
    range = getRange(nums)
            # put ranges in a dictionary
    ranges = {
            "min":range[0],
            "max":range[1],
            "range":range[2]
            }
```

```
    report = {
        "averages": averages,
        "ranges": ranges
        }
    return report
```

Notice that Python, unlike Java, has a built-in syntax that allows you to specify a dictionary (which is similar to a Java hashtable) with a literal.

## runReport()

The `runReport()` function uses `reportStatistics()` to get and print the report dictionary.

```
from stat import reportStatistics
house_in_awahtukee = [100000, 120000, 150000, 200000, 65000, 100000]
report = reportStatistics(house_in_awahtukee)

range_format = """
Range:
The least expensive house is %(min)20.2f
The most expensive house is %(max)20.2f
The range of house price is %(range)20.2f
"""
average_format = """
Averages:
The mean house price is %(mean)20.2f
The mode for house price is %(mode)20.2f
The median house price is %(median)20.2f
"""

print range_format % report["ranges"]
print average_format % report["averages"]
```

The thing to notice here is the string format operator (%), which is like C's `printf()` function except that it can work with dictionaries. It's one of my favorite Python features because it makes text reporting so easy. I've even used it to generate Java code.

Here's Python's `runReport()` output:

```
Range:
The least expensive house is          65000.00
The most expensive house is          200000.00
The range of house price is          135000.00

Averages:
The mean house price is              122500.00
The mode for house price is          100000.00
The median house price is            110000.00
```

Here's the Java version.

```
package stat;
import java.util.ArrayList;
```

```java
import java.util.Iterator;
import java.util.Collections;
import java.util.HashMap;

public class Stats {

  public static double getMean (ArrayList nums,
                                        boolean sample){
      // Define mean that finds two types of mean,
      // namely:
      // population mean and sample mean
      double sum=0.0;
      double average=0.0;
      Iterator iterator = nums.iterator();

      while(iterator.hasNext())
            sum = sum +
            ((Double)iterator.next()).doubleValue();
            // Check to see if this is a sample mean.
      if(sample)
            average = sum / nums.size()-1;
      else
            average = sum / nums.size();
      return average;
  }

  public static ArrayList getRange (ArrayList nums){
            // Find the range. Returns a tuple with the
            // minimum, maximum, and range value
      double min, max;
      ArrayList ranges;

      min =
      ((Double)Collections.min(nums)).doubleValue();
      max =
      ((Double)Collections.max(nums)).doubleValue();

      ranges = new ArrayList();
      ranges.add(new Double (min));
      ranges.add(new Double (max));
      ranges.add(new Double (max-min));

      return ranges;
  }

  public static double getMedian (ArrayList nums){
            // Find the Median number.
            // Create a duplicate since we are going to
            // modify the sequence.
      ArrayList seq = new ArrayList(nums);

            // Sort the list of numbers.
      Collections.sort(seq);

      double median = 0.0; // to hold the median value

      int length = seq.size(); // to hold the length of
                                    // the sequence
```

```
          int index=0;

                  // Check to see if the length
                  // is an even number.
          if ( ( length % 2) == 0){
                      // Since it is an even number,
                      // add the two middle numbers together.
               index = length / 2;
               double m1 =
               ((Double)seq.get(index-1)).doubleValue();
               double m2 =
               ((Double)seq.get(index)).doubleValue();
               median = (m1 + m2) /2.0;
          }
          else{

                      // Since it is an odd number,
                      // just grab the middle number.
               index = (length / 2);
               median =
               ((Double)seq.get(index)).doubleValue();
          }
          return median;
    }

    private static int countMode(Object object,
                                                ArrayList list){
          int index = 0;
          int count = 0;
          do {
               index=Collections.binarySearch(list,object);
               if(index >=0)list.remove(index);
               count++;
          }
          while (index >=0);
          return count;
    }

public static double getMode (ArrayList nums){
          // Find the number that repeats the most.
                  // Make a duplicate copy of the
                  // nums argument.
          ArrayList duplicate = new ArrayList(nums);

          Collections.sort(duplicate);
          double highest_count = -100;
          double mode = -100;

          Iterator iterator = nums.iterator();
                  // Iterate through nums removing
                  // each item out of the duplicate.
                  // Calculate the highest_count and the mode.
          while(iterator.hasNext()){
               double count = 0;
               Object item = iterator.next();
               // Count the number of times the item
```

```
                    // occurs in the list.
                        // If Count is 0, go to the next
                        // iteration.
                    count = countMode(item, duplicate);
                    if (count == 0) continue;

                        // Determine the highest count. The
                        // highest counted item is the mode.
                    if (count > highest_count){
                        highest_count = count;
                        mode = ((Double)item).doubleValue();
                    }
            }
            return mode;
    }

    public static HashMap reportStatistics(
                                        ArrayList nums){
            // Get central tendencies.
        HashMap averages = new HashMap();

        averages.put("mean",
            new Double(getMean(nums,false)));
        averages.put("median",
            new Double(getMedian(nums)));
        averages.put("mode", new Double(getMode(nums)));

            // Get range.
        ArrayList range = getRange(nums);
        HashMap ranges = new HashMap();

            // Put ranges in a dictionary.
        ranges.put("min", range.get(0));
        ranges.put("max", range.get(1));
        ranges.put("range",range.get(2));

        HashMap report = new HashMap();
        report = new HashMap();
        report.put("averages", averages);
        report.put("ranges", ranges);

        return report;
    }
}

--- RunReport.java ---
package stat;

import java.util.ArrayList;
import java.text.MessageFormat;
import java.util.HashMap;

public class RunReport{
  public static String range_format = "" +
  "Range: \n"+
  "The least expensive house is {0,number,currency}\n"+
```

```
        "The most expensive house is {1,number,currency} \n"+
        "The range of house price is {2,number,currency}\n";
        public static String average_format = "" +
        "Averages: \n" +
        "The mean house price is     {0,number,currency}\n"+
        "The mode for house price is {1,number,currency}\n"+
        "The median house price is     {2,number,currency}\n";
    public static void main(String [] args){

        ArrayList houses_in_awahtukee = new ArrayList();
        houses_in_awahtukee.add(new Double(110000));
        houses_in_awahtukee.add(new Double(190000));
        houses_in_awahtukee.add(new Double(140000));
        houses_in_awahtukee.add(new Double(120000));
        houses_in_awahtukee.add(new Double(190000));
        houses_in_awahtukee.add(new Double(180000));
        houses_in_awahtukee.add(new Double(170000));
        houses_in_awahtukee.add(new Double(180000));
        houses_in_awahtukee.add(new Double(180000));
        houses_in_awahtukee.add(new Double(190000));
        houses_in_awahtukee.add(new Double(190000));
        houses_in_awahtukee.add(new Double(250000));

        HashMap report =
                Stats.reportStatistics(houses_in_awahtukee);
        HashMap ranges = (HashMap)report.get("ranges");
        HashMap averages =
                (HashMap)report.get("averages");

        Object [] m_args = new Object[]{
                averages.get("mean"),
                averages.get("mode"),
                averages.get("median")};

        Object [] r_args = new Object []{
                ranges.get("min"),
                ranges.get("max"),
                ranges.get("range")};

        System.out.println(
        MessageFormat.format(range_format,r_args));

        System.out.println(
        MessageFormat.format(average_format,m_args));
    }
}
```

Which one is shorter?

---

# A String Parsing Example

To compare Java and Python string parsing, we're going to create a readable file consisting of a comma-delimited list of house prices.

```
100000,100000,120000,150000,170000,170000,80000,50000
```

Here's the Python code broken down:
   Open the file.

```
>>> file = open("data.txt")
```

Read in the file data.

```
>>> data = file.read()
```

Import the split() function to parse the data.

```
>>> from string import split
>>> housePrices = split(data, ",")
```

For demonstration, show that split() has split the data string into a list of strings.

```
>>> housePrices
['100000', '100000', '120000', '150000', '170000', '170000', '80000', '50000']
```

Convert housePrices from strings to floating-point values.

```
>>> housePrices = map(float, housePrices)
```

Show that housePrices is now a list of floating-point values.

```
>>> housePrices
[100000.0, 100000.0, 120000.0, 150000.0, 170000.0, 170000.0, 80000.0, 50000.0]
```

   Here's the actual code (from *runReport2.py*).

```
from stat import reportStatistics
from string import split
file = open("data.txt")
data = file.read()

housePrices = split(data, ",")
housePrices = map(float, housePrices)
report = reportStatistics(housePrices)

range_format = """
Range:
The least expensive house is %(min)20.2f
The most expensive house is  %(max)20.2f
The range of house price is  %(range)20.2f
"""

average_format = """
Averages:
The mean house price is            %(mean)20.2f
The mode for house price is        %(mode)20.2f
The median house price is          %(median)20.2f
"""print range_format     % report["ranges"]
print average_format     % report["averages"]
```

Here's the Java version of the *RunReport2* module. Notice the difference in length.

```java
package stat;

import java.util.ArrayList;
import java.util.HashMap;
import java.util.StringTokenizer;

import java.text.MessageFormat;

import java.io.FileReader;
import java.io.BufferedReader;

public class RunReport2{
  public static String range_format = "" +
  "Range: \n"+
  "The least expensive house is {0,number,currency}\n" +
  "The most expensive house is {1,number,currency} \n"+
  "The range of house price is {2,number,currency} \n";

public static String average_format = "" +
  "Averages: \n" +
  "The mean house price is {0,number,currency}\n"+
  "The mode for house price is {1,number,currency}\n"+
  "The median house price is {2,number,currency}\n";

  public static void main(String [] args){

        ArrayList houses_in_awahtukee = new ArrayList();

        try {
              BufferedReader reader=new BufferedReader(
                              new FileReader("data.txt"));
              String data = reader.readLine();
              StringTokenizer tokens=
                    new StringTokenizer(data, ",\t\n\r ");
              while (tokens.hasMoreTokens()){

                    houses_in_awahtukee.add(
                    Double.valueOf(tokens.nextToken()));

              }

        }
        catch(Exception e){
              e.printStackTrace();
        }

        HashMap report =
              Stats.reportStatistics(houses_in_awahtukee);
        HashMap ranges = (HashMap)report.get("ranges");
        HashMap averages =
              (HashMap)report.get("averages");
```

```
            Object [] m_args = new Object[]{
                    averages.get("mean"),
                    averages.get("mode"),
                    averages.get("median")};

            Object [] r_args = new Object []{
                    ranges.get("min"),
                    ranges.get("max"),
                    ranges.get("range")};

            System.out.println(
            MessageFormat.format(range_format,r_args));

            System.out.println(
            MessageFormat.format(average_format,m_args));
    }
}
```

## Embedding Jython in Java

What follows is an example of embedding Jython in the Java code that ships with Jython's standard distribution. I've added comments.

```
import org.python.util.PythonInterpreter;
import org.python.core.*;

public class SimpleEmbedded {
    public static void main(String []args) throws PyException {

        // Create a Python interpreter.
        PythonInterpreter interp = new PythonInterpreter();

        System.out.println("Hello, brave new world");

        // Execute an import statement and a
        // print statement.
        interp.exec("import sys");
        interp.exec("print sys");

        // Create a variable by assigning
        // it the value 42.
        // PyInterger is a Python integer.
        interp.set("a", new PyInteger(42));

        // Execute the print statement to
        // print out the value of a.
        interp.exec("print a");

        // Assign x to equal the expression 2 + 2.
        interp.exec("x = 2+2");

        // Get the value associated with x.
        PyObject x = interp.get("x");
```

```
        // Print the value of x.
        System.out.println("x: "+x);
    }
}
```

The preceding example doesn't do justice to the true ease of Java–Jython integration.

# APPENDIX E  *Regular Expressions*

Jaysen Lorenzen

Regular expressions are patterns that match groups of characters. We can use them to find and return (or replace) characters, words, and lines. Python's standard-distribution *re* module derives from Perl's regular expressions, which, like Perl itself, combine features from UNIX utilities such as Awk, Sed, and Grep, and programs like vi and Gnu Emacs. Though the syntax and metacharacters may be slightly different, expressions in any of these tools can be written in Jython.

## *A Simple Example*

Let's say that you're looking for a job in the newspaper and you've decided to narrow your focus to ads that say, "Money is no object." This is the pattern you're searching for, and of course you're looking in the employment section, which is the group of characters you're searching in. You don't care where you find your pattern, only that it's there.

If you were writing a Python program to help you find a job, it would start out looking like this:

```
>>> from re import *
mino = compile("money is no object");

for ad in classifieds:
        if(mino.search(ad)):
        print ad;
```

Let's work through this example interactively.

Import the *re* module.

```
>>> from re import *
```

Import class re.

**574**

```
>>> classifieds = ["School Teacher; salary $20,000.","Engineer; salary money
    is no object"]
```

Make the variable `classifieds` a list of ads.

```
>>> mino = compile("money is no object")
```

Compile the search phrase, and store in it the `mino` ("money is no object") object.

```
>>> for ad in classifieds:
...        if(mino.search(ad)):
...               print ad
...
```

Compare the precompiled expression to each element in the list. If a match is found within an element, print it.

```
'Engineer; salary money is no object'
>>>
```

---

## Pattern Characteristics

A pattern can be as small as one character (as in the previous example), matching only itself, or of almost any length. It can contain wildcard and special characters, subexpressions, and so forth, depending on system resources.

Our expression "money is no object" is a string of literal characters requiring an exact match in the exact order, but regular expressions can be much more powerful. Say, for example, that you're looking for a job whose salary figure is within a certain range—that is, with a certain number of digits to the left of the decimal. To find all records with two digits before the comma and three digits after, you can write this expression:

```
>>> reStr = r'\$..,...\.'
```

Then you can compile and match it against a string.

```
>>> cre = compile(reStr)
>>> cre.search("salary: $90,000.00")
```

The figure $90,000 matches, and the statement returns a match object.

### The Raw String Construct

Notice the `r'...'` construct in the code above. This denotes a raw string—that is, one with its backslash (\) escaped characters left intact. In this case the $ and the decimal are the special characters that must be escaped to be matched with a wildcard or metacharacter.

Actually, the pattern above would work without the raw string construct, but I wanted to introduce it early on because its absence can occasionally cause problems, as you can see in the following examples.

The following expression, with r'...', returns a match:

```
>>> STR = r'(\be[ a-z][ a-z])'
>>> cre = compile(STR)
>>> cre.search("the beg the end")
```

Its matched text is end, gotten with group.

```
>>> cre.search("the beg the end").group()
'end'
```

This one, without r'...', doesn't get a match:

```
>>> STR = "(\be[ a-z][ a-z])"
>>> cre = compile(STR)
>>> cre.search("the beg the end")
>>>
```

A look at the two expressions' patterns shows why. Here's the first one:

```
>>> STR = r'(\be[ a-z][ a-z])'
>>> cre = compile(STR)
>>> cre.pattern
```

which returns

```
'(\\be[ a-z][ a-z])'
```

Here's the second one:

```
>>> STR = "(\be[ a-z][ a-z])"
>>> cre = compile(STR)
>>> cre.pattern
```

which returns

```
'(\be[ a-z][ a-z])'
```

The lesson is, use the raw string construct whenever a normal string might cause confusion. It can't hurt.

## Wildcard Metacharacters

In regular expression patterns, the period is a wildcard, that is, a special character that by default matches any character except a newline (\n). In our example, '\$..,...\' says in English, *A dollar sign followed by any two characters, except a newline, followed by a comma, then any three non-newline characters and a period.* Thus, $XX,XXX or $00,000 or even a dollar sign and six spaces makes a match. Of course, this isn't very useful, so we have to narrow our search. One way to do this is with a character class instead of a metacharacter.

## Character Classes

A character class is a group of characters enclosed in brackets, only one of which is required for the sequence to match. In our salary example, each period can be replaced with a class of numbers such as [0123456789], which gets the job done but is hard to read. Fortunately, a class can contain a range of characters expressed as [0-9], which makes for easier reading.

```
r'\$[0-9][0-9],[0-9][0-9][0-9]\.'
```

This is still a bit unwieldy. Read on.

### Escaped Special Characters

A number of escaped characters have special meaning. The \d character, for example, matches any decimal digit and is equal to [0-9], so our expression can be written as

```
r'\$\d\d,\d\d\d\.'
```

Easier still, but wait, there's more.

### Multiplier Characters

Multiplier characters modify, or multiply, the character to their immediate left. The most popular (and sometimes the most dangerous) is the asterisk (*), which requires 0 or more of the characters to its left to produce a match. In our case, all of the digit characters are mandatory, so we need another multiplier, +, which matches one or more of the characters to its right. Now our expression can be written as

```
r'\$\d+,\d+\.'
```

This is shorter and easier, but we still have a problem. The + character matches one or more of the preceding characters, which means that a salary such as $9999,99999 would be caught in its net. To avoid this, we use the sequence {min,max}, which requires at least min and no more than max repetitions of the character to the immediate left to produce a match.

Our expression can now be written precisely as

```
r'\$\d{2,2},\d{3,3}\.'
```

The only remaining problem is that we'll get salaries as low as $00,000 and as high as $99,999, but we can fix this by converting part of our pattern back to a character class containing a more sensible range. Finally, our expression can be written as

```
r'\$[5-7]\d,\d{3,3}\.'
```

which allows salaries only in the range of $50,000 to $79,000.

### Grouping and Backreferences

A very useful feature of Python regular expressions is their ability to reference (or "backreference") text previously matched and reuse it. Suppose we're looking for a salary in the range of $XX,XXX,XXX. We can extend our expression by adding another set of \d{3,3}, but, since we already have this written, we can reuse it instead. To capture the pattern we use the (...) sequence.

```
r'\$[5-7]\d(,\d{3,3})\.'
```

The piece enclosed in parentheses is called a group or a subexpression. We can use it to add another three digits to our search.

Groups are referenced within the expression by their numeric position and escaped by a backslash. The group numbers are determined by a count of the open parentheses starting from the left: (1 )(2 )(3 (4 )). Now we can extend our expression like so:

```
r'\$[5-7]\d(,\d{3,3})\1\.'
```

The \1 gives us another set of ,\d{3,3}, and our expression thus matches our chosen range.

### The Match Object—A Brief Introduction

In Python, when a match is found a match object is returned. The match object and its properties will be dealt with later, but we'll give it a brief look here.

Here's our salary example compiled and matched against the list of classifieds, now with some added records and capturing the match object for later use.

```
>>> from re import *

>>> classifieds = ["School Teacher; salary $20,000.","Engineer; salary money
is no object","Bicycle Racer; salary $75,000,000."]

>>> for ad in classifieds:
...       mo = mino.search(ad)
...       if mo:
...                   print ad
...             print mo.group(1)
...
```

The output is the ad in which the match was found on the first line and only the text matched by group 1 on the second line.

```
Bicycle Racer; salary $75,000,000.
,000
```

### Alternation

Alternation, which requires the special, or meta-, sequence ...|..., works in any type of expression in which the character class operates only with literal characters or ranges. Within a pattern, characters, classes, groups, or special characters separated by a bar (|) need only one item from either side to match.

```
a|b|c|d matches a or b or c or d
abc|xyz matches abc or xyz
123|[123] matches 123 or 1 or 2 or 3
```

Within a longer expression, the alternation sequence is used like this:

```
"(thousands|tons) of copies"
```

which matches "thousands of copies" or "tons of copies."

We can use alternation to enhance our salary pattern by allowing numbers in the range $50,000,000 to $79,999,999 or in the range $50,000,000,000 to $79,999,999,999. All we have to do is replace the \1 with (\1|\1\1).

```
r'\$[5-7]\d(,\d{3,3})(\1|\1\1)\.'
```

## Regular Expression Functions and Error and Flags Properties

The following sections describe the individual regular expression functions, including their syntax, use, arguments, and return values. Also described are the error and flag properties.

### compile()

```
compile (pattern[, flags])
```

The compile() function compiles a regular expression pattern, as a string, into a regular expression object. It enables the object to operate like the search() and match() functions and to be reused for subsequent searches. If the same expression is applied to many searches within a program and/or will never change, precompiling it and reusing it goes faster.

compile()'s arguments are

- pattern—the pattern, as a string, to search for
- flags—one or more of the following variables: I, IGNORECASE; L, LOCALE; M, MULTILINE; X, VERBOSE

It returns a regular expression.

```
>>> CompiledRE = compile("199[0-9].*")
>>> CompiledRE.search("party like it's 1999")
```

### search()

```
Search (pattern, string[, flags])
```

The search() function searches for pattern anywhere in string. It has the following arguments:

- pattern—the pattern, as a string, to search for
- string—the string to search in
- flags—one or more of the variables I, IGNORECASE; L, LOCALE; M, MULTILINE; X, VERBOSE

It returns a match object:

```
>>> search("199[0-9]$","party like it's 1999")
```

or it returns None, which means the search failed.

```
>>> search("199[0-9]$","party like it's 2009")
```

## match()

```
match (pattern, string[, flags])
```

The match() function searches for a pattern at the beginning of a string and has the following arguments:

- pattern—the pattern, as a string, to search for
- string—the string to search in
- flags—one or more of the variables I, IGNORECASE; L, LOCALE; M, MULTILINE; X, VERBOSE

It returns a match object:

```
>>> match("199[0-9]","1999 like party")
```

or it returns None.

```
>>> match("199[0-9]","party like it's 1999")
```

## split()

```
Split (pattern, string[, maxsplit = 0])
```

The split() function splits a string into a list of strings based on occurrences of the regular expression pattern. The string portions that don't match the pattern are returned as a list of strings. If flags are required with the pattern, a regular expression object, obtained with compile(), must be used in place of the pattern string, or the (?iLmsx) sequences (which will be explained later) must be used within the expression. (The compiled regular expression's split() method will achieve the same results.)
split() has the following arguments:

- pattern—the pattern, as a string, to search for
- string—the string to search in
- maxsplit—the maximum number of splits to make (the default is 0)

It returns a list of strings.

```
from re import *

alist = split(":","OS=Linux:Browser=Netscape:WM=Afterstep")

for str in alist:
...     print str
```

The output is

```
OS=Linux
Browser=Netscape
WM=Afterstep
```

## sub()

```
sub (pattern, replacement,string[, count = 0])
```

The sub() function obtains a string with the non-overlapping occurrences of the expression, starting from the left, replaced by the replacement string. If the optional third argument, count, is supplied, only the requested number of occurrences is replaced. If flags are required with the pattern, a regular expression obtained with compile() must be used in place of the pattern string. (The compiled regular expression's sub() method can achieve the same results.)

If a function is supplied in place of the replacement string, it's executed for each occurrence of the pattern, and a match object is passed as an argument.

sub()'s arguments are

- pattern—the pattern, as a string or a regular expression object, to search for
- replacement—the replacement, as a string or function
- string—the string to search in
- count—a non-negative number, the number of replacements to make (the default, 0, replaces all occurrences in the string)

It returns the modified string if a match is found, or the original argument if there are no matches.

```
From re import *
from string import *

def toUpper(matchObj):
    return capitalize(matchObj.group(0))

newStr = sub("monkey",toUpper,"monkey see monkey do, ,,")

print newStr
```

The output is

```
Monkey see Monkey do, ,,
```

## subn()

```
subn (pattern, replacement,string[, count = 0])
```

The subn() function is basically the same as sub() except that it returns a tuple containing the modified or unmodified string and the number of replacements made. Its arguments are

- pattern—the pattern, as a string or a regular expression object, to search for
- replacement—the replacement, as a string or function

- `string`—the string to search in
- `count`—a non-negative number, the number of replacements to make (the default, 0, replaces all occurrences in the string)

`subn()` returns a tuple containing the modified string if a match is found (or the original string argument if there are no matches) and containing the count of replacements made, if any.

```
from re import *
from string import *
    deftoUpper(matchObj):return capitalize(matchObj.group(0))

tup = subn("monkey",toUpper,"monkey see monkey do, ,,")

print "In \" %s \" there were %s replacements" % tup
```

The output is

```
In " Monkey see Monkey do, ,, " there were 2 replacements
```

### escape()

```
escape(string)
```

`escape()` escapes all nonalphanumeric characters before passing the expression to the compiler, and returns a string with all metacharacters escaped.

Here's an example in which the `compile()` function fails because there are unmatched parentheses:

```
>>> from re import *
>>> strVar = "((group"))
>>> cre = compile(strVar)

  Traceback (innermost last):
    File "<console>", line 1, in ?
  re.error: Unmatched parentheses.
```

In this example, the non-alphanumeric characters are escaped, so the `compile()` function works:

```
>>> cre = compile(escape(strVar))
>>> cre.search("((group 1)group 2)")

org.python.modules.MatchObject@80cceb1
```

### error

The error exception is raised when an illegal expression is passed to a function. It has the form

```
try:
...     match statement
except error,e:
...     handle the error
```

The optional argument to the except statement is a variable to catch the argument sent to the raise statement at the time of the error. This can be used in the handler statement to alert the user to a mistake.

```
>>> from re import *
>>> try:
...     search("[[[","This is a test")
... except error,e:
...     print e
...
```

The output is

```
Unmatched [] in expression.
>>>
```

### flags

The compile(), search(), and match() functions can take a number of options (or modes). These options are set via the functions' optional flags argument and are the same for all. A common example is IGNORECASE, which specifies the match as case-insensitive. Thus, if the ad list contains

```
classifieds = ["School Teacher; salary $20,000","Engineer; salary Money is NO
               OBJECT"]
```

the expression is written as

```
mino = compile("money is no object",I)
```

or

```
mino = compile("money is no object",IGNORECASE)
```

The flags available at compile time are listed and described in Table E–1 (on next page).

Note that, as of this writing, the LOCALE and VERBOSE flags aren't fully implemented; that is, their values are set to 0, which is the same as not being set at all. You can get VERBOSE functionality by setting the flags integer to 32 instead of X or VERBOSE, but check your release first, since in CPython this value is 2.

## *re Object Methods and Properties*

The sections that follow describe the syntax, use, and arguments of regular expression object methods and properties.

### search()

```
<re object>.search (string[, pos][, endpos])
```

**Table E–I**  *Optional Flags for Regular Expression Functions*

| Flag | Behavior | Example |
|------|----------|---------|
| I (IGNORECASE) | Ignore case when searching. | `search("^exam","Example",I)` returns a match object<br><br>`search("^exam","Example")` returns None |
| L (LOCALE) | The metacharacters \w, \W, \b, \B are made to fit the current locale. | |
| M (MULTILINE) | The metacharacter ^ matches at the beginning of the string and just after each newline character. The $ metacharacter matches at the end of the string and just before each newline character (by default ^ matches only at the beginning of the string and $ matches only at the end of the string). | `var = "A\nB"`<br><br>`search("^B",var,M)` returns a match object<br><br>`search("^B",var)` returns None |
| S (DOTALL) | The "." metacharacter matches any character, including the newline. (The default is for "." to match anything but a newline.) | `var = "A\nB"`<br><br>`search(".B",var,S)` returns a match object<br><br>`search(".B",var)` returns None |
| X (VERBOSE) | Allows formatting of the regular expression. Whitespace within the expression is ignored, except when it's in a character class or preceded by an unescaped backslash. If a # character is inserted, all text from the leftmost # is ignored, except when the # is within a character class or preceded by an unescaped backslash. | `exp = """`<br>`  # Start of regex`<br><br>`^t # starts with "t"`<br>`[a-z] # is a lcase char`<br>`* # any qty of`<br>`t$ # ends with "t"`<br><br>`  # end of expression`<br>`"""`<br><br>`regex = compile(exp,X)`<br>`regex.search("test")`<br>Returns a match object<br>`regex = compile(exp)`<br>`regex.search("test")`<br>Returns None |

The `search()`method looks for compiled regular expressions anywhere in a string. If the optional parameter `pos` is supplied, the search starts at position `pos`. If the optional parameter `endpos` is supplied, the search continues only until `endpos` is reached. The default is from position 0 to the end of the string. The return value is a match object.

`search()` has the following arguments:

- `string`—the string to search in
- `pos`—the position in the string to start the search
- `endpos`—the position in the string to stop the search

Here's an example:

```
cre = compile("199[0-9]$")
cre.search("party like it's 1999")
```

## match()

```
<re object>.match (string[, pos][, endpos])
```

The `match()`method searches for a regular expression at the beginning of a string. If the optional parameter `pos` is supplied, the search starts at position `pos`, which is considered the start. If the optional parameter `endpos` is supplied, the search ends when `endpos` is encountered. The default is from position 0 to the end of the string. The return is a match object.

Here's an example that doesn't match because the test isn't at the beginning of the string. Therefore, nothing is printed out.

```
>>> cre = compile("test")

>>> if (cre.match("This is a test")):
...        print "From beginning \n"
```

Here's an example in which the starting position is 10. A match is returned only if the expression is found at the beginning of the string.

```
>>> if (cre.match("This is a test",10)):
...        print "From pos 10 - \n"
```

## split()

```
<re object>.split (string[, maxsplit = 0])
```

The `split()` method splits a "string" into a list of strings based on the occurrences of the compiled regular expression to which the string is being compared. The portions of the string that don't match are returned as a list of strings.

`split()`'s arguments are

- `string`—the string to search in
- `maxsplit`—the maximum number of splits to make (the default is 0)

Here's an example:

```
>>> from re import *
>>> cre = compile(":")
>>> alist = cre.split("OS=Linux:Browser=Netscape:WM=Afterstep")
>>> for str in alist:
...     print str
```

The output is

```
OS=Linux
Browser=Netscape
WM=Afterstep
```

## sub()

```
<re object>.sub (replacement,string[, count = 0])
```

The sub() method achieves the same result as the sub() function described previously and has the same arguments (except pattern). Unlike the sub() function, however, which returns a list of strings, the sub() method returns the modified string if a match is found, or the original string argument if there are no matches.

```
>>> from re import *
>>> from string import *

>>> def toUpper(matchObj):
...     return capitalize(matchObj.group(0))

cre = compile("monkey")
newStr = cre.sub(toUpper,"monkey see monkey do, ,,")

print newStr
```

The output is

```
Monkey see Monkey do, ,,
```

## subn()

```
<re object>.subn (replacement,string[, count = 0])
```

The subn() method performs similarly to the subn() function described previously. As shown in the following example, it uses the same arguments (except for pattern) and returns a tuple.

```
from re import *
from string import *

def toUpper(matchObj):
return capitalize(matchObj.group(0))

cre = compile("monkey")
tup = cre.subn(toUpper,"monkey see monkey do, ,,")

print "In \" %s \" there were %s replacements" % tup
```

The output is

```
In " Monkey see Monkey do, ,, " there were 2 replacements
```

## flags

The flags property contains an integer that represents the sum of all flags passed to the compile() function when the object was created, or 0 if no flags were passed. It can be used to determine if a certain set of flags was passed and can take the place of flag arguments to subsequent compile(), search(), or match() function calls.

---

**Finding a Flag Value**

You can create a match object for a flag to check its property value (do this one flag at a time; if you try with more than one, the value becomes their sum). Or you can check the underlying object's flag property value, which is the only way to check VERBOSE since compile("test",VERBOSE).flags or compile("test",VERBOSE) returns 0.

To check the underlying values, import the Perl5Compiler class, and check the properties like this:

```
>>> from com.oroinc.text.regex import Perl5Compiler

>>> Perl5Compiler.CASE_INSENSITIVE_MASK
1
>>> Perl5Compiler.MULTILINE_MASK
8
>>> Perl5Compiler.SINGLELINE_MASK
16
>>> Perl5Compiler.EXTENDED_MASK
32
```

---

flags returns an integer that represents the sum of all flag values used at the time the object was created, or 0 if no flags were used.

```
>>> from re import *
>>> compile("^f",I).flags
1
>>> compile("^f",M).flags
8
>>> compile("^f",I|M).flags
9
>>> compile("^f",S).flags
16
>>> compile("^f",M|S).flags
24
>>>
>>> cre = compile("^f",M|S)
>>> compile("g$",cre.flags).flags
24
```

### groupindex

```
<re object>.groupindex
```

The groupindex property gets a dictionary of the group numbers of the expression that creates the regular expression object, with their symbolic group names as the key, if the groups were created with the (?P<key>...) construct. It returns such a dictionary or an empty dictionary.

```
>>> from re import *
>>> cre = compile(r'(?P<first>est)(?P<last>t)')
>>> dict = cre.groupindex
>>> dict["first"]
1
>>> dict["last"]
```

The output is

```
{}
```

### pattern

```
<re object>.pattern
```

The pattern property contains the expression, that is, the pattern string, with which the regular expression object was created. It returns a string containing a regular expression.

```
>>> from re import *
>>> cre = compile("^t.+t$")
>>> cre.pattern
```

The output is

```
'^t.+t$'
```

## Match Object Methods and Properties

The following sections describe the methods and properties of the match object.

### group()

```
<match object>.group([name|num][,name|num]...)
```

The group() method gets matches of each group of the expression, or all matches if no group is specified. If a single argument is passed, the return value is a string containing the group specified. If no arguments are passed, the return value is a string containing the entire match. If a group is in part of a pattern that doesn't match, the return value is None. If it's in part of the pattern that matches multiple times, the last match is returned.

```
>>> mo = search(r'(?P<first>t)(?P<last>est)',"test")
```

```
>>> mo.group()
'test'
>>> mo.group("first")
't'
>>> mo.group("last")
'est'
>>> mo.group(2)
'est'
```

The return is a tuple.

```
>>> mo.group("first","last")
('t', 'est')
>>>
```

## groups()

```
<match object>.groups()
```

The groups() method returns a tuple containing all matched text for all groups of the pattern, including those that don't match. Elements in the tuple representing groups that don't match have a value of None.

```
>>> mo = search(r'(?P<first>t)(?P<last>est)+(o)*',"test")
>>> mo.groups()
('t', 'est', None)
>>>
```

## groupdict()

```
<match object>.groupdict()
```

The groupdict() method returns a dictionary containing all matched text for all groups of the pattern, including those that don't match. Elements in the dictionary representing unmatched groups have a value of None.

```
>>> mo = search(r'(?P<first>t)(?P<last>est)+(o)*',"test")
>>> dict = mo.groupdict()
>>> print dict["first"]
```

## start() and end()

```
<match object>.start([name|num])
<match object>.end([name|num])
```

The start() and end() methods retrieve the starting and ending positions of the groups matched within the string being searched. The optional argument can be a group number (counting from the left of the expression) or a name if the group was named at the time of creation. If no arguments are passed, the start and end positions are the start and end of the entire matched text. The return value for both methods is an integer.

```
>>> mo = search(r'(?P<first>t)(?P<last>est)+(o)*',"test")
>>> mo.start(1)
0
>>> mo.start(2)
1
>>> mo.start("last")
1
>>> mo.end("last")
4
>>> mo.start(3)
-1

>>> mo.start()
0
>>> mo.end()
4
```

## span()

`<match object>.span([name|num])`

The span() method returns the starting and ending positions of a matching group as a two-element tuple. The optional argument is a group number (starting from the left of the expression). If no argument is passed, the tuple will contain the start and end positions of the entire matched text. If the group doesn't match at all, the tuple will contain -1, -1.

```
>>> mo = search(r'(?P<first>t)(?P<last>est)+(o)*',"test")
>>> mo.span(1)
(0, 1)
>>> mo.span(2)
(1, 4)
>>> mo.span(3)
(-1, -1)
```

## pos and endpos

`<match object>.pos`

`<match object>.pos`

The pos property returns the pos value, as an integer, passed to the search() or match() method. The endpos property returns the endpos value, as an integer, passed to those methods.

## string

`<match object>.string`

The string property returns the string, as a string to be searched and passed to the search() or match() method.

## re

```
<match object>.re
```

The re property gets a reference to the regular expression object from which the match was triggered. It returns a regular expression object.

```
>>> from re import *
# from a standard re object
>>> cre = compile(r'(?P<first>t)(?P<last>est)+(o)*')

>>> mo.re.groupindex
{'last': 2, 'first': 1}

# Retrieve the re object from the search function.

>>> mo = search(r'(?P<first>t)(?P<last>est)+(o)*',"test")
>>> mo.re
org.python.modules.RegexObject@80ce6f2

>>> mo.re.groupindex
{'last': 2, 'first': 1}

>>> mo.re.pattern
'(?P<first>t)(?P<last>est)+(o)*'
```

# Metacharacters

The Python metacharacters, or special characters and sequences, are listed and described in Tables E–2 and E–3.

**Table E–2**  *Python Metacharacters (Single Characters)*

| Metacharacter | Behavior | Example |
|---|---|---|
| "." | Matches any character except a newline, by default. If the DOTALL flag has been specified, this matches any character, including a newline. | search(".B","AB") returns a match object<br><br>search(".B","A\nB") returns None |
| "^" | Matches at the beginning of a string and, if the MULTILINE flag is used, also matches immediately after each newline. Used as the first character of the expression or group to match at the beginning of a string. | search("^cat","cats") returns a match object<br><br>search("^cat","a cat") returns None |

*(continued)*

**Table E–2**  *Python Metacharacters (Single Characters)*  *Continued*

| Metacharacter | Behavior | Example |
|---|---|---|
| "$" | Matches at the end of a string and, if the MULTILINE flag is used, also matches immediately before each newline. Used as the last character of the expression or group to match at the end of a line. | `search("at$","cat")` returns a match object <br><br> `search("at$","cats")` returns None |
| "*" | Matches zero or more repetitions of the preceding character, group, or character class. None of the immediately preceding characters is required to match, and any number of the immediately preceding characters will match. A greedy multiplier, "*" will match as many repetitions as possible. | `cre = compile("at*")` <br><br> `cre.search("a")` <br> `cre.search("at")` <br> `cre.search("att")` <br><br> `cre = compile("a[td]*")` <br> `cre.search("atdt")` <br><br> `cre = compile("A(BC)*")` <br> `search("ABCBC")` <br> `all return a match` <br><br> `search("e[td]*","add")` <br> `does not return a match` |
| "+" | Matches one or more repetitions of the preceding character, group, or character class. At least one of the immediately preceding characters or groups of characters is required to match, and any number of the them will match. A greedy multiplier, "+" will match as many repetitions as possible. | `cre = compile("at+")` <br> `cre.search("at")` <br> `cre.search("att")` <br><br> `cre = compile("a[td]+")` <br> `cre.search("atdt")` <br> `cre = compile("A(BC)+")` <br> `search("ABCBC")` <br><br> `all return a match` <br><br> `cre = compile("at+")` <br> `cre.search("a")` <br> `does not return a match` |
| "?" | Matches zero or one repetition of the preceding character, group, or character class. None of the immediately preceding characters or groups of characters is required to match, and only one of the them will match. A nongreedy multiplier, "?" will match as few repetitions as possible. | `var = compile("xa?bc")` <br><br> `var.search("xbc")` <br> `returns a match object` <br><br> `var.search("xaabc")` <br> `does not return a match` <br><br> `var.search("xabc")` <br> `returns a match object` |

**Table E–2** *Continued*

| Metacharacter | Behavior | Example |
|---|---|---|
| "*?" | Matches zero or more repetitions of the preceding character, group, or character class. None of the immediately preceding characters is required to match and any number of the immediately preceding characters will match. A nongreedy multiplier, "*?" will match as few repetitions as possible. | `cre = compile("(:.*:)")`<br><br>`STR = ":one:a:two:"`<br><br>`mo = cre.search(STR)`<br>`mo.group(1)`<br><br>`returns`<br>`':one:a:two:'`<br><br>`cre = compile("(:.*?:)")`<br><br>`mo = cre.search(STR)`<br>`mo.group(1)`<br>`returns`<br>`':one:'` |
| "+?" | Matches one or more repetitions of the preceding character, group, or character class. One of the immediately preceding characters is required to match, and any number of the immediately preceding characters will match. A nongreedy multiplier, "*?" will match as few repetitions as possible. | `cre = compile("(o+)")`<br><br>`STR = "Pool"`<br><br>`mo = cre.search(STR)`<br>`mo.group(1)`<br><br>`returns`<br>`'oo'`<br><br>`cre = compile("(o+?)")`<br>`mo = cre.search(STR)`<br>`mo.group(1)`<br>`returns`<br>`'o'` |
| "??" | Matches zero or one of the preceding character, group, or character class. None of the immediately preceding characters is required to match, and only one of the immediately preceding characters will match. A nongreedy multiplier, "??" will match as few characters as possible. | `cre = compile("(:.?:)")`<br>`mo = cre.search(":::")`<br>`mo.group(1)`<br><br>`returns`<br>`':::'`<br><br>`cre = compile("(:.??:)")`<br>`mo = cre.search(":::")`<br>`mo.group(1)`<br>`returns`<br>`'::'` |

**Table E–3** *Special Escaped Characters*

| Character | Behavior | Example |
|---|---|---|
| \\<No.> | Matches the same text matched previously by the group of the same number. Groups are numbered 1–99 and refer to open parentheses counting from the left. | ```STR = "y(aba)d\1"```<br>```cre = compile(STR)```<br>```mo = cre.search("yabadabadoo")```<br>```matches yabadaba```<br>```so mo.group()```<br>```returns```<br>```'yabadaba'```<br><br>```mo.group(1)```<br>```returns```<br>```'aba'``` |
| \\A | Matches at the start of the string and is equal to the ^ meta-character. | ```STR = "(\Athe [a-z])"```<br>```cre = compile(STR)```<br>```mo = cre.search("the beg the end")```<br>```mo.group()```<br><br>```returns```<br>```'the b'``` |
| \\Z | Matches at the end of the string and is equal to the $ meta-character. | ```STR = "([a-z][a-z][a-z]\Z)"```<br>```cre = compile(STR)```<br>```mo = cre.search("the beg the end")```<br>```mo.group()```<br><br>```returns```<br>```'end'``` |
| \\b | Matches an empty string at the beginning or ending of a word (that is, a sequence of characters terminated by whitespace or any non-alphanumeric character). | ```STR = r'(\be[ a-z][ a-z])'```<br>```cre = compile(STR)```<br>```mo = cre.search("the beg the end")```<br>```mo.group()```<br><br>```returns```<br>```'end'``` |
| \\B | Matches an empty string as long as it's not at the beginning or ending of a word (that is, a position within a word but not between the first or last character and a space, period, etc).<br><br>(*Note:* \\B and \\b are anchors. They do not match any literal characters, but match positions with a string.) | ```STR = r'(\Be[ a-z][ a-z])'```<br>```cre = compile(STR)```<br>```mo = cre.search("the beg the end")```<br>```mo.group()```<br><br>```returns```<br>```'e b'```<br><br><br>```STR = r'(\Be\B[ a-z][ a-z])'```<br>```cre = compile(STR)```<br>```mo = cre.search("the beg the end")```<br>```mo.group()``` |

**Table E–3**    *Continued*

| Character | Behavior | Example |
|---|---|---|
| | | returns<br>'eg ' |
| \d | Matches any decimal digit character. This is equal to [0-9]. | STR = r'(\B\d[a-z])'<br>cre = compile(STR)<br>mo = cre.search("3c59x")<br>mo.group() |
| | | returns<br>'9x' |
| \D | Matches any nondigit character. This is equal to [^0-9]. | STR = r'(\d\D\d)'<br>cre = compile(STR)<br>mo = cre.search("3c59x")<br>mo.group() |
| | | returns<br>'3c5' |
| \s | Matches any whitespace character. This is equal to [ \t\n\r\f\v] | STR = r'(\D\sat)'<br>cre = compile(STR)<br>mo = cre.search("look at that")<br>mo.group() |
| | | returns<br>'k at' |
| \S | Matches any non-whitespace character. This is equal to [^ \t\n\r\f\v] | STR = r'(\D\Sat)'<br>cre = compile(STR)<br>mo = cre.search("look at that")<br>mo.group() |
| | | returns<br>'that' |
| \w | [a-zA-Z0-9_] | STR = r'(\D\D\w\b)'<br>cre = compile(STR)<br>mo = cre.search("No. Calif")<br>mo.group() |
| | | returns<br>'lif' |
| \W | [^a-zA-Z0-9_] | STR = r'\D\D\W'<br>cre = compile(STR)<br>cre.search("No. Calif")<br>mo = cre.search("No. Calif")<br>mo.group() |
| | | returns<br>'No.' |

## Sequences of Characters

The ... | ... sequence is used for alternation and means "or." Its purpose is delimiting multiple subexpressions. The main expression matches if any of the subexpressions match. The | metacharacter has the form

```
<expression (<subexpression>|<subexpression>)>
<expression>|<expression>
```

The following expressions both return a match object:

```
>>> search("cat|dog","cat")
>>> search("a pet( cat| dog)*","I have a pet dog")
```

This expression also matches:

```
>>> search("a pet( cat| dog)*","I have a pet")
```

This expression returns dog:

```
>>> mo = search("a pet( cat| dog)*","I have a pet dog")
>>> mo.group(1)
```

This expression returns a pet dog:

```
>>> mo.group()
```

The (...) sequence has the form

```
<expression (<subexpression>)>
```

It returns a group if the subexpression with the parentheses matches. Any text matched by the group will be available through the resulting match object's group() and groups() methods.

```
>>> STR = r'(t\w\w\w) and (t\w\w\w)'
>>> cre = compile(STR)

>>> mo = cre.search("this and that")
>>> mo.group(1)
```

returns

```
'this'
>>> mo.group(2)
```

returns

```
'that'

>>> mo.groups()
```

returns

```
('this', 'that')
```

The (?iLmsx) sequence is used as a way to include flags as part of a regular expression. It has the form

```
<expression (?iLmsx)>
```

This sequence is useful if you need to use the match() or search() function but have to pass flags with the expression (instead of passing a flag argument to the compile() function and then using its search() or match() methods). The flags can be one or more of the set i, L, m, s, and x. The corresponding flags are I, L, M, S, or X for the entire expression. (Note that, even though the compile object's flags are passed as all uppercase, only the L is passed that way here.) The group containing the sequence itself matches an empty string; if it's sent as the only expression, an empty match object is returned.

Here's an example in which a match object is returned:

```
>>> search("test(?i)","THIS IS A TEST")
<re.MatchObject instance at 80c87b0>
```

Here no match object is returned because test doesn't match in the string:

```
>>> search("test(?i)","THIS IS TEXT")
>>>
```

This example returns an empty match object:

```
>>> search("(?i)","THIS IS TEST")
<re.MatchObject instance at 80ac768>
```

The (?:...) sequence has the form

```
<expression (?:<subexpression>)>
```

It treats the subexpression within the parentheses like a regular expression but doesn't return a group if matched. Any text matched by the group is unavailable through the match object returned.

```
>>> STR = r'(~\w+~)(?:\w+)(~\w+~)'
>>> cre = compile(STR)

>>> mo = cre.search("~one~two~three~")
>>> mo.group(1)
```

returns

```
'~one~'
```

```
>>> mo.group(2)
```

returns

```
'~three~'
```

The (?P<name>...) sequence has the form

```
<expression (?P<group name> subexpression)>
```

It matches the subexpression within the parentheses, saving the matched text as a group, just as in regular parentheses, but it allows the group to be given a name that can be referenced later.

This expression:

```
>>> mo = search(r'(?P<first>t)(?P<last>est)',"test")
>>> mo.group()
```

returns

```
'test'
```

This one:

```
>>> mo.group("first")
```

returns

```
't'
```

This one:

```
>>> mo.group("last")
```

returns

```
'est'
```

This one:

```
>>> mo.group(2)
```

returns

```
'est'
```

The (?P=Name...) sequence has the form

```
<expression (?P=name)>
```

It matches the text matched by the named group referenced earlier in the subexpression.

This example:

```
>>> cre = compile(r'\w(?P<first>aba)\w(?P=first)doo')
>>> mo = cre.search("yabadabadoo")
>>> mo.group(1)
```

returns this proper match:

```
'aba'
```

This one:

```
>>> mo.group(2)
```

returns an error:

```
Traceback (innermost last):
  File "<console>", line 1, in ?
IndexError: group 2 is undefined
>>> mo.group()
```

because there's actually only one group:

```
'yabadabadoo'
```

The (?#...) sequence has the form

```
<expression (?# comment text)>
```

It allows comments to be inserted in an expression with use of the VERBOSE flag. The contents of the group are ignored.

```
>>> cre = compile(r'(yaba)(?#silly example)(daba)doo')
>>> mo = cre.search("yabadabadoo")

>>> mo.group(1)
returns
'yaba'

>>> mo.group(2)
returns
'daba'
```

The (?=...) sequence has the form

```
<expression (?=<subexpression>)>
```

It acts as a conditional lookahead and matches expression only if it's followed by subexpression. Any text matched by the (?=...) group is unsaved and so is unaccessible via methods such as group() and groups().

This example doesn't return a match object:

```
>>> cre = compile(r'Jython (?=1\.1)')
>>> cre.search("Jython is stable")
```

This one does:

```
>>> cre.search("Jython 1.1 is stable")

org.python.modules.MatchObject@80ce02a

>>> mo = cre.search("Jython 1.1 is stable")
>>> mo.group()
```

and returns

```
'Jython '
```

The (?!...) sequence has the form

```
<expression (?!<subexpression>)>
```

It's a negative conditional lookahead (the opposite of (?=...)) and matches expression only if *not* followed by subexpression. Any text matched by its group isn't saved and so isn't accessible by methods such as group() and groups().

This example:

```
>>> cre = compile(r'Jython (?!1\.1)')
```

```
>>> cre.search("Jython is stable")
```

returns a match object. This one:

```
org.python.modules.MatchObject@80cdb0d
>>> cre.search("Jython 1.1 is stable")
```

doesn't return a match object:

```
>>> mo = cre.search("Jython is stable")
>>> mo.group()
```

Instead, it returns

```
'Jython '
```

The {min,max} sequence has the form

```
<expression {<min>,<max>}>
```

It requires a minimum of min and allows a maximum of max repetitions of the immediately preceding character, group, or character class. A greedy multiplier, it matches as many repetitions as possible.

This example doesn't return a match object:

```
>>> cre = compile("\$\d{2,3}(,\d\d\d){2,5}")
>>> cre.search("salary: $9,000.00")
```

Nor does this one:

```
>>> cre.search("salary: $90,000.00")
```

This one does return a match object:

```
org.python.modules.MatchObject@80ce140
```

The {min,max}? sequence has the form

```
<expression {<min>,<max>}?>
```

It's the same as {min,max}, but as a nongreedy multiplier, it matches as few repetitions as possible. Thus,

```
>>> cre = compile("(:.{3,10}:)")
```

```
>>> STR = ":one:a:two:"
```

```
>>> mo = cre.search(STR)
>>> mo.group(1)
```

returns

```
':one:a:two:'
>>> cre = compile("(:.{3,10}?:)")
>>> STR = ":one:a:two:"
>>> mo = cre.search(STR)
>>> mo.group(1)
```

returns

```
':one:'
```

The [...] sequence has the form

```
<expression [character class]>
```

It matches any one of the characters within the brackets, listed explicitly or as a range delimited by the – (hyphen) metacharacter (it understands [12345] and [1-5] as the same). Popular ranges are [0-9], [a-z], and [A-Z]. Multiple ranges, such as [a-zA-Z], can also be used.

The following examples all return a match object:

```
>>> search(r'[RTL]oad',"Toad")
>>> search(r'[RTL]oad',"Road")
>>> search(r'[RTL]oad',"Load")
>>> search(r'199[7-9a-z]',"1998")
>>> search(r'199[7-9a-z]',"1999")
>>> search(r'199[7-9a-z]',"199x")
```

The [^...] sequence has the form

```
<expression [^character class]>
```

The opposite of [...], it matches anything but the characters listed within the brackets. Possible characters can be listed explicitly or as a – (hyphen) delimited range.

This example returns a match object:

```
>>> search(r'199[^1-7]',"1998")
```

This one doesn't:

```
>>> search(r'199[^1-7]',"1997")
```

## Putting Things Together

A third-party vendor I (Rick Hightower) worked with once had a problem reading the IDL files we were trying to integrate with its product. Specifically it didn't like identifiers beginning with ::, as in ::com::mycompany::Employee, preferring com::mycompany::Employee. My job was to convert the IDL files to their liking, which I did using regular expressions. The code I wrote to do this is just four lines long (actually six but four with a little cheating).

Here's the code to read in the file and write all the replacement text:

```
f=open(filename)
fstr=re.compile(r'\s((::)(\w+))\b').sub(r' \3', f.read())
f.close(); f=open(filename, "w")
f.write(fstr); f.close()
```

Here's the complete fixIDL() function:

```
import re

def fixIDL(filename):
    f=open(filename)
    fstr=re.compile(r'\s((::)(\w+))\b').sub(r' \3', f.read())
    f.close(); f=open(filename, "w")
    f.write(fstr); f.close()
```

The key is the regular expression r'\s((::)(\w+))\b'. Let's break it down into its most basic components:

- \s—whitespace
- \w—alphanumeric
- \b—word boundary
- +—one or more

Now let's see how these components are used:

- (::)(\w+)—find a sequence of characters that begins with ::, followed by one or more alphanumeric characters
- \s(()(\w+))—find a sequence of characters that begins with whitespace, followed by ::, followed by one or more alphanumeric characters
- \s((::)(\w+))\b—find a sequence of characters that begins with whitespace, followed by ::, followed by one or more alphanumeric characters, followed by a word boundary

### re.compile

The re.compile call compiles the regular expression. It returns a regex object that has a sub() (substitute) method. The call to regex.sub(r'\3\,f.read()) means replace the matched text with a space and the third group.

A group is defined by the parentheses in regex and read from left to right. Thus,

- ((::)(\w+)) defines group 1
- (::) defines group 2
- (\w+) defines group 3

Group 0 is always the whole matched `regex`. Group 3 is important because it represents the text without the preceding `::`.

Now we'll break down the code line by line, each line followed by its explanation.

```
import re
```

imports the *re* (regular expression) module.

```
def fixIDL(filename):
```

defines the `fixIDL()` function with an argument of `filename`.

```
f=open(filename)
```

opens a file corresponding to `filename`.

```
fstr=re.compile(r'\s((::)(\w+))\b').sub(r' \3', f.read())
```

does the following:

- `re.compile(r'\s((::)(\w+))\b')`—compiles the regular expression into a `regex` object
- `.sub(r' \3', f.read())`—replaces every occurrence of the matched text with the third group in the match, returning a string with the text replaced
- `f.read()`—reads the entire file into a string:

```
f.close(); f=open(filename, "w")
```

then closes the file (`f.close()`) and reopens it in write mode:

```
f.write(fstr); f.close()
```

It then writes the entire new text into the file and closes the file.

Here's another way to write the code:

```
f=open(filename)
fstr=re.compile(r'\s((::)(\w+))\b').sub(r'\3',f.read())
f.close();
f=open(filename, "w")
f.write(fstr);
f.close()
```

But then I would have lost my bet that I could write this utility package in four lines.

*Note:* This appendix summary was written by Rick Hightower.

# Index

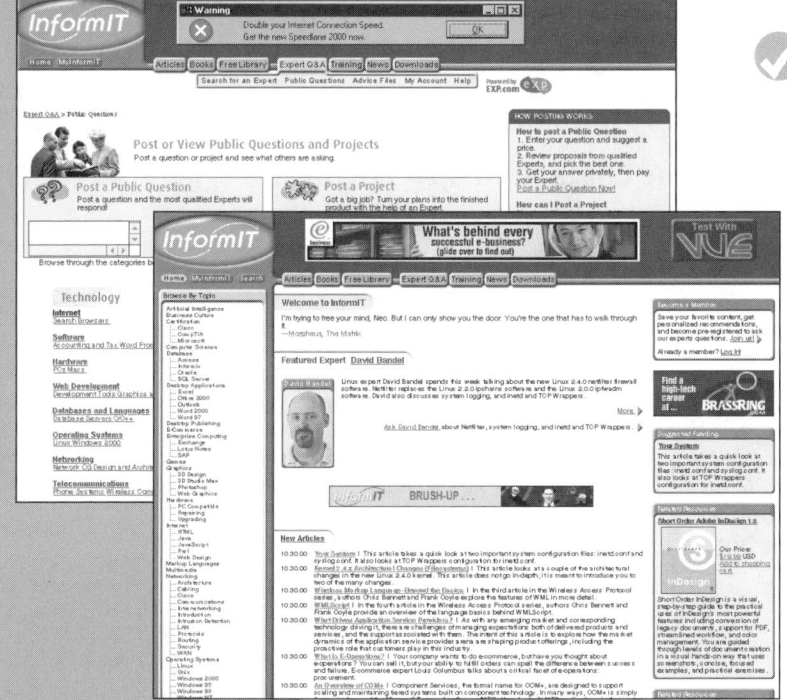